CONTEMPORARY POETS, DRAMATISTS, ESSAYISTS, AND NOVELISTS OF THE SOUTH

CONTEMPORARY POETS, DRAMATISTS, ESSAYISTS, AND NOVELISTS OF THE SOUTH

A BIO-BIBLIOGRAPHICAL SOURCEBOOK

EDITED BY
ROBERT BAIN
AND
JOSEPH M. FLORA

Greenwood Press
WESTPORT, CONNECTICUT • LONDON

Library of Congress Cataloging-in-Publication Data

Contemporary poets, dramatists, essayists, and novelists of the South:
  a bio-bibliographical sourcebook / edited by Robert Bain and
Joseph M. Flora.
      p. cm.
    Includes bibliographical references and index.
    ISBN 0-313-28765-1 (alk. paper)
    1. Authors, American—Southern States—Biography—Dictionaries.
  2. Authors, American—20th century—Biography—Dictionaries.
  3. American literature—Southern States—Bio-bibliography.
  4. American literature—20th century—Bio-bibliography. 5. American
  literature—Southern States—Dictionaries. 6. American
  literature—20th century—Dictionaries. 7. Southern States—In
  literature—Dictionaries. I. Bain, Robert (Robert A.) II. Flora,
  Joseph M.
  PS261.C568   1994
  810.9'975'09045—dc20
  [B]   93-43750

British Library Cataloguing in Publication Data is available.

Library of Congress Catalog Card Number: 93-43750
ISBN: 0-313-28765-1

First published in 1994

Greenwood Press, 88 Post Road West, Westport, CT 06881
An imprint of Greenwood Publishing Group, Inc.

Printed in the United States of America

The paper used in this book complies with the
Permanent Paper Standard issued by the National
Information Standards Organization (Z39.48-1984).

10 9 8 7 6 5 4 3 2 1

Copyright Acknowledgments

Excerpts from AND STILL I RISE by Maya Angelou. Copyright © 1978 by Maya Angelou. Reprinted by permission of Random House, Inc.

Excerpts from I SHALL NOT BE MOVED by Maya Angelou. Copyright © 1990 by Maya Angelou. Reprinted by permission of Random House, Inc.

Excerpts from the poems "When I Think About Myself" and "Just Give Me a Cool Drink of Water 'Fore I Diiie" by Maya Angelou are reprinted courtesy of Gerard Purcell Associates, Ltd., New York.

Excerpts from *Statues of the Grass* © 1975 by James Applewhite are reprinted by permission of The University of Georgia Press.

Excerpts from James Applewhite's *Following Gravity* (1980) are reprinted courtesy of the University Press of Virginia.

Excerpts from *An Audience of One* © 1980 by Gerald Barrax are reprinted by permission of The University of Georgia Press.

Excerpts from *Leaning Against the Sun* by Gerald Barrax, copyright 1992 are reprinted by permission of The University of Arkansas Press.

Excerpts from "The Old Glory," "The Dozens," "For a Black Poet," and "Filibuster, 1964" are reprinted from ANOTHER KIND OF RAIN, by Gerald W. Barrax, by permission of the University of Pittsburgh Press. © 1970 by Gerald W. Barrax.

Excerpts from *The Deaths of Animals and Lesser Gods* by Gerald Barrax (1984) reprinted by permission of the University Press of Virginia.

Excerpts from Charles Edward Eaton's *The Shadow of the Swimmer* (New York: Fine Editions Press, 1951), *New and Selected Poems, 1942–1987* (New York: Cornwall Books, 1989) and his literary papers are reprinted courtesy of Charles Edward Eaton and Associated University Presses.

Nemerov (1975) and *Those Who Blink* (1986) reprinted courtesy of Louisiana State University Press.

Excerpts from Robert Morgan, "Mountain Graveyard" from *Sigodlin* copyright 1990 by Robert Morgan and "Mockingbird" from *Green River: New and Selected Poems* copyright 1991 by Robert Morgan, published by Wesleyan University Press by permission of the University Press of New England.

Excerpts from *Sleep Watch,* second edition, copyright 1983 by Richard Tillinghast, *The Knife and Other Poems,* copyright 1980 by Richard Tillinghast, *Our Flag Was Still There,* copyright 1984 by Richard Tillinghast published by Wesleyan University Press reprinted by permission of the University Press of New England.

Excerpts from Miller Williams' *A Circle of Stone, So Long at the Fair, Living on the Surface, Halfway from Hoxie, Distractions* and *The Boys on Their Bony Mules* reprinted courtesy of Louisiana State University Press.

"try for the get-away by the light of yourself" reprinted from *Bloodlines* by Charles Wright © 1975 by Charles Wright. By permission of Wesleyan University Press.

"I write poems to untie myself, to do penance and disappear through the upper right-hand corner of things, to say grace" reprinted from CHINA TRACE by C. Wright © 1977 by Charles Wright. By permission of Wesleyan University Press.

Excerpts from "A Journal of English Days" and "December Journal" from THE WORLD OF THE TEN THOUSAND THINGS by Charles Wright. Copyright © 1990 by Charles Wright. Reprinted by permission of Farrar, Straus & Giroux, Inc.

For Blyden Jackson

Blyden Jackson has pioneered so many frontiers that he leaves his students and colleagues in awe of his fierce courage, of his commitment to students and to the study of black American literature, and of his impeccable sense of social justice. His grandparents, born into slavery, included two grandfathers who were ministers in the African Methodist Episcopal Church. Blyden Jackson spent his early years in Louisville, Kentucky, where he attended segregated schools and where he learned his passionate sense of justice and honesty from his mother, a librarian, and his father, a school principal and history teacher. He took his A.B. from Wilberforce University in Ohio in 1930 and continued his studies at Columbia University, where he met such notables of the Harlem Renaissance as Langston Hughes. Though the Depression cut short his studies at Columbia, he earned his M.A. from the University of Michigan in 1938 and his Ph.D. in 1952. After teaching at a junior high school in Louisville from 1934–45, he taught at Fisk University in Nashville, Tennessee, from 1945–54, and at Southern University in New Orleans, Louisiana, where from 1954 to 1969 he served as Professor of English, Chair of the Department, and Dean of the Graduate School. In 1969, Blyden Jackson became the first black full professor at the University of North Carolina in Chapel Hill; he also served as Associate Dean of the Graduate School from 1973–76. His retirement in 1981 meant only a redirection of his energy, intelligence, and knowledge.

In the 1940s, Blyden Jackson published about black American authors articles that critics still cite. With Louis D. Rubin, Jr., he wrote in 1974 *Black American Poetry; The Waiting Years,* an elegant autobiography of a pioneer historian and critic of black American literature, followed in 1976. In retirement, he began writing the work he had been preparing all his life—a four-volume history of African-American writing. Louisiana State University Press published the first volume of *A History of Afro-American Literature* in 1990. Reviewers wanted more.

Blyden Jackson's honors run to pages. His most recent came in 1991 when the University of North Carolina at Chapel Hill named the undergraduate admissions building for him and his beloved wife Roberta, a professor of education: Blyden and Roberta Jackson Hall. For his love of learning, truth, his students, his colleagues, black American literature, and the South, we dedicate this book to Blyden Jackson.

Contents

Contents

Contents

Preface

Contemporary Poets, Dramatists, Essayists, and Novelists of the South: A Bio-Bibliographical Sourcebook presents a preliminary report on the excellent work Southern authors have done in the last two or three decades. Doubtless, our report includes some writers whose work will merit only footnotes 25 years from now and omits worthy authors who have made their marks after we conceived of this project. Among the latter, Michael McFee, Allan Gurganus, and a dozen others come immediately to mind. For these sins of omission and commission, the editors take responsibility. Though none of the writers discussed here has yet earned the reputation of Eudora Welty or Robert Penn Warren, all have made claims for a significant place in both Southern and American literature. Only time will tell whether their fame lasts.

Fifty-one scholars and critics have contributed these reference-book entries describing and assessing the achievements of forty-nine Southern writers. Because the number of Southerners writing well exceeds that which can be treated in depth in a single book, we have edited a companion volume to this one— *Contemporary Fiction Writers of the South: A Bio-Bibliographical Sourcebook,* published by Greenwood Press in 1993. Many poets, dramatists, essayists, and novelists included here have written noteworthy fiction, and the authors featured in *Contemporary Fiction Writers of the South* have often written well in other literary forms. We have placed authors in the volume that best describes the primary thrust of their work. The table of contents for *Contemporary Fiction Writers of the South* appears as Appendix B of this book.

The forty-nine entries in this volume discuss Southerners who practice a wide range of literary forms—poetry, drama (including movies and television as well as the stage), essays by humorists and social critics, and novels. The chief events influencing contemporary Southerners are World War II, the Vietnam War, the civil-rights movement, new understandings of race and culture, changing roles of women, new sexual freedoms afforded by the age of the pill, and the horror of AIDS. These writers record their responses to such radical changes in the South as the decline of rural living; the rise of cities and the suburbs; the influence of television and shopping malls; Southerners' obsessions with sports, cars, and hunting; the preoccupation with getting rich; and the social mobility that comes with wealth.

Unlike the writers of the Southern Renascence, most of whom were white males and from the upper middle class, many contemporary poets, dramatists, essayists, and novelists come from the middling or the rising middle classes. Formidable work by women and black authors plays a much more important role in the current flowering than it did in the Renascence.

But continuities exist with the work of earlier Southern authors. These continuities include the attachments to place, the tangled web of family relationships, the importance of art, an emphasis upon the grotesque, the self-consciousness of being different from people in other regions, the pervasive influence of religion, and the impact of the past on the present. Faulkner's old verities of love and honor and courage and sacrifice continue to preoccupy Southern poets, dramatists, essayists, and novelists.

We selected writers for inclusion in this volume on three grounds: (1) each author has written at least four books or produced four plays, (2) each author has been reviewed widely, (3) each author has achieved critical recognition outside the South. With few exceptions, we have followed these guidelines.

The format of *Contemporary Poets, Dramatists, Essayists, and Novelists of the South* follows the format of its companion volume, *Contemporary Fiction Writers of the South* (1993), and its predecessors—*Fifty Southern Writers before 1900* and *Fifty Southern Writers after 1900,* both published by Greenwood Press in 1987. The entries here, written by knowledgeable scholars and critics, contain five parts: a biographical sketch, a discussion of the author's major themes and forms, an assessment of reviews and scholarship, a chronological list of the author's works, and a bibliography of selected criticism. We hope readers working their way through this volume will gain a clearer sense of what is happening in Southern letters.

We have not included in this volume any poets, dramatists, essayists, or novelists discussed in *Fifty Southern Writers after 1900,* but we have updated in Appendix A the "Works by" and "Studies of" sections for A. R. Ammons, James Dickey, and Shelby Foote, all subjects of essays in that earlier book.

We have many people to thank. The greatest debt is to our contributors for their willingness to share their knowledge and love of Southern literature. Their work constitutes an act of faith. Like all students of Southern and black American literature, we owe huge debts to Louis D. Rubin, Jr., and to Blyden Jackson, to whom this book is dedicated. Their scholarship and good sense have enlightened thousands of students and teachers. Marilyn Brownstein, Maureen Melino, Penny Sippel, and their colleagues at Greenwood Press have given us good counsel and patience in the long and complicated process of editing this book.

Laurence Avery, our department chair, has supported our work enthusiastically, and Erika Lindemann has read and criticized our pages. We thank also Frances Coombs, Charlotte McFall, Dorothy Moore, and Russ Townsley for their aid and kindnesses. Special thanks go to Christine Flora for her help, good sense, and judgment. Without the help of Mark Canada, readers would be bereft of the fine index. Finally, we thank the many teachers who have found our earlier books useful introductions for students who want to know more about Southern letters. Their enthusiasm has helped sustain us.

Robert Bain
Joseph M. Flora

CONTEMPORARY POETS, DRAMATISTS, ESSAYISTS, AND NOVELISTS OF THE SOUTH

Introduction

Contemporary Poets, Dramatists, Essayists, and Novelists of the South: A Bio-Bibliographical Sourcebook maps the literary world that Southerners have created in the last three decades. Alive with literary forms and experiments, this world has exploded with talent, energy, and vitality to rival that of the Southern Renascence after World War I. What plays the devil with mapping this literary world is that so many Southerners are writing well. Locating Eve Shelnutt, Alice Walker, Ishmael Reed, or Fred Chappell as poets, fiction writers, essayists, or critics poses problems because they have written well in so many forms. Perhaps the best label for writers discussed in this book is an old, still useful one: Women and Men of the Republic of Southern Letters.

But maps need coloring to set off boundaries and territories. To provide some boundaries for this introduction, we discuss first those writers most familiar to general readers. These authors—who work in a variety of literary forms—have earned their renown by writing best-sellers or by producing a body of work that has captured national attention. Some have gained further celebrity by appearing on television and radio or by having their work translated into film. Our second grouping includes Southerners who work principally in drama. The third group of writers we have identified as poets, though many have written fiction and other forms. The last group discussed in this introduction we have labeled novelists, though again these authors may be equally famous for other genres. Our categories will not stand close scrutiny, but they provide some boundaries to guide readers through the territory mapped here.

Writers most familiar to general readers are essayists, autobiographers, new journalists, humorists, dramatists, and social critics. Often these authors have appeared to the public in media other than the written word—television or the movies. Dramatist Beth Henley, who won the 1981 Pulitzer Prize for *Crimes of the Heart,* takes the theater as her major arena, but she also wrote the movie version of that play.

Likewise, essayist and novelist Tom Wolfe's *The Bonfire of the Vanities* (1987) and *The Right Stuff* (1979), books that sold widely, translated into successful films. Associated with the new journalists, Wolfe has examined American life ranging from race-car driver Junior Johnson to the counterculture of Ken Kesey to *Radical Chic and Mau-Mauing the Flak Catchers* (1970). Wolfe's sharp eye and pen have pierced America's social scene by recording its foibles both sympathetically and satirically. Wolfe, says Daphne H. O'Brien, has "revolutionized the world of newspaper and magazine reporting by applying techniques of fiction writing to factual reporting." He brings "to bear upon the metropolis and indeed the nation a Southern sensibility to class and mobility and writes from a traditionalist ethic."

Other writers winning approval from general readers include Maya Angelou, Wendell Berry, Roy Blount, Jr., Fred Chappell, George Garrett, Nikki Giovanni, Florence King, Willie Morris, Ishmael Reed, and Margaret Walker. All have worked in several literary forms. Many have written books appearing on bestseller lists and have captured the national limelight on book publicity tours and on television and radio talk shows. Maya Angelou probably reached a larger audience with her poem at President Bill Clinton's inauguration than she has with all her other work combined.

Although Angelou has also earned accolades for her acting and screenwriting, she is best known for her poetry and her autobiographies. *I Know Why the Caged Bird Sings* (1970), Angelou's first autobiography, won her a National Book Award nomination and wide critical acclaim. A year later Angelou published her first volume of poems, *Just Give Me a Cool Drink of Water 'Fore I Diiie* (1971). There followed six more volumes of verse and four autobiographical books—among them *Gather Together in My Name* (1974) and *All God's Children Need Traveling Shoes* (1989). The autobiographical impulse, says Lucinda MacKethan, "informs all of [Angelou's] creative work." "The African-American struggle for freedom and selfhood," argues MacKethan, "is in one sense always the poet's [and autobiographer's] singular struggle and in another the struggle of all wounded, living souls."

Roy Blount, Jr. and Florence King have delighted readers with pithy, quotable humorous books, but beneath that humor lies telling social satire and criticism. Though King and Blount confess to being Southerners who pommel their region's pretensions and peccadilloes, both take pride in their Southernness. And their canvas for social satire and criticism extends far beyond Southern boundaries to American preoccupations with trivia and trash. In the tradition of Mark Twain, both take the "Damned Human Race" for their territory.

In her books *Southern Ladies and Gentlemen* (1975), *Confessions of a Failed Southern Lady* (1985), and *With Charity Toward None: A Fond Look at Misanthropy* (1992), Florence King has zapped Southern and American icons in a prose style like H. L. Mencken's. As Kathryn VanSpanckeren points out in her essay, *Southern Ladies and Gentlemen* is "so fast-paced and funny that its astute observations may be missed on a first reading." But the astute observations are there, as they are in all of King's work. Though critics have faulted King for dealing in stereotypes, they fail to note that stereotypes are the stuff of social criticism because they ring so true. King's *Southern Ladies and Gentlemen* has become a classic little handbook on Southern sociology (she would hate that word) because readers, recognizing kinfolk and neighbors in her portraits, nod their heads in agreement.

Like King, Georgian Roy Blount scathes and delights. "The typical Roy Blount book," says Merritt W. Moseley, Jr., "is so multifarious that it does not have a theme, or even a subject; instead it has a profusion." According to Moseley, Blount's "profusion" deals with the South, the absurdities of modern life, men and women, the basic things in life, and language. In his first big book—*Crackers: This Whole Many-Angled Thing of Jimmy* [Carter], *More Carters, Ominous Little Animals, Sad-Singing Women, My Daddy and Me* (1980)—Blount takes on all of these themes in raucous fashion. He has continued his telling saga of Southern and American life in such books as *What Men Don't Tell Women* (1984) and his novel, *First Hubby* (1990).

Wendell Berry of Kentucky plays in a different key, but he, too, takes Americans to task for forgetting their physical and communal obligations. Poet, fiction writer, and essayist, Berry has written twenty-nine books since 1960, nearly all of them dealing with what Edward B. Smith describes as man's place in the natural world and the human community as well as "the division between the self and the world brought about by technological progress and economic greed." *The Unsettling of America* (1977), his best-known book, critiques "modern agricultural policy and its effect on farmers." In his poetry, fiction, and essays, ecologist Berry reminds readers of their connectedness with people and the land.

Fred Chappell, who shared the 1985 Bollingen Prize for Poetry with John Ashbery, has quietly and energetically established himself, says David Paul Ragan, as "one of the most versatile and prolific voices among contemporary writers." Publication of *The Fred Chappell Reader* by St. Martin's Press in 1987 confirmed what critics had been saying all along—that Chappell is a fine poet, story writer, novelist, essayist, critic, and literary experimenter. His verse novel, *Midquest: A Poem* (1981), and his novels *I Am One of You Forever* (1985) and *Brighten the Corner* (1989) draw upon Chappell's North Carolina mountain heritage and by themselves signal a major talent, were it not for the other fifteen books, numerous reviews and essays, and poems and stories he has written.

Like Chappell, George Garrett has earned accolades for his work in several literary forms. The author of seven volumes of poetry, eight short-story collections, seven novels, Garrett has also written plays, screenplays, an opera libretto, and critical books and articles. His three historical novels—*Death of the Fox* (1971), *The Successions: A Novel of Elizabeth and James* (1983), and *Entered from the Sun* (1990)—received critical and popular acclaim for their panoramic views of the Elizabethan period and for their insights into character. Garrett's virtuosity in other literary forms appears most clearly in his *Collected Poems* (1984) and *An Evening Performance: New and Selected Short Stories* (1985). R.H.W. Dillard notes that whatever form Garrett employs, "all of [his] characters are children of and prisoners of fortune, but his heroic characters are those who in the face of their predicament are capable of making difficult moral decisions."

Poet, essayist, and author of thirteen books, Nikki Giovanni has charmed and shocked readers with her clear perceptions of what it means to be black, a woman, and an artist. Gaining prominence as an artist and speaker during the civil-rights movement, Giovanni has continued to appeal to a large and enthusiastic audience with her poetry readings and recordings. From her first books—*Black Feeling, Black Talk* (1968) and *Black Judgement* (1969)—to the more recent *Sacred Cows . . . and Other Edibles* (1988), Giovanni has proclaimed in lively language the pride of African-Americans, jarring white audiences into an understanding of what it means to be black. Patsy B. Perry argues that Giovanni's power as artist and speaker results from consistently insisting on poetry's "universal appeal—that everyone can enter, if only for a moment, the poet's world and be soothed, entertained, inspired, challenged, enraged, or otherwise moved by language."

One of the most controversial, experimental, and talented of the new writers, Ishmael Reed in his poetry, fiction, and nonfiction has displayed his iconoclastic approach to literary forms and to American cultural traditions. An erudite student of cultural anthropology, Reed has created in such novels as *Yellow Back Radio Broke-Down* (1969), *Mumbo Jumbo* (1972), and *The Last Days of Louisiana Red* (1974) a mythic world that draws upon his "theory of Neo-Hoodoo writing" to reinterpret American history and literature. His books of poetry—*catechism of d neoamerican hoodoo church* (1970) and *Chattanooga Poems* (1973)—employ language that puzzles and delights. Jerry W. Ward, Jr. believes that Reed "uses language to stand against concepts and attitudes that are inflexible; he blends traditional literary forms and topples idols of American thought in order to show that tolerance for difference and change is necessary to achieve cultural plurality." "What is quintessentially Southern about his work," Ward argues, "is to be located in the rage to explain."

Though not as prolific as some of her contemporaries, Margaret Walker has earned critical recognition as a poet and as author of *Julilee* (1966), a historical novel translated into many languages and taught frequently in African-American, women's, and Southern literature courses. *For My People* (1942), her first collection of poems, won the Yale Award for Younger Poets in 1942, and her *Prophets for a New Day* (1970) and *October Journey* (1974) established Walker as a significant black poet writing out of the ferment of the civil rights movement. Mary Hughes Brookhart argues that Walker's "poetry and her novel restore and reaffirm for black Americans what has been denied or negated and provide hope for a new day.''

Willie Morris, editor of *Harper's* from 1967 to 1971, an essayist and social critic, and author/editor of thirteen books, takes the Deep South as his principal territory. In his novel *The Last of the Southern Girls* (1973) and such books as *Yazoo: Integration in a Deep-South Town* (1971), he scrutinizes Southern society and mores during the 1960s. *North Toward Home* (1967), his autobiography and a best-seller, won critical acclaim for his insights into Southern society of the 1950s and 1960s. Julius Rowan Raper attributes Morris's power to knowing that the best ''Southern writing dramatizes the individual heart in conflict with itself, a struggle often centered on the conflict between the challenge of change and the demands of memory—between the present and the past.'' Morris learned this lesson, says Raper, from reading William Styron, Thomas Wolfe, and William Faulkner and putting them to good use in his autobiography and his social commentaries on the South.

For the Southern dramatists discussed in this book—Alice Childress, James Duff, Lonne Elder III, Beth Henley, Preston Jones, and Marsha Norman—the roles of women and family relationships provide principal subjects. Childress, a South Carolinian, is best known for her novel *A Hero Ain't Nothin' but a Sandwich* (1976, later adapted to a screenplay), but she has written more than a dozen plays and was for eleven years associated with the American Negro Theatre of Harlem. From *Trouble in Mind* (1955) to *Moms* (1987), a play about the comedienne Jackie ''Moms'' Mably, Childress has had at the center of her work ''the truthful presentation of black women,'' according to La Vinia Delois Jennings. Jennings notes that Childress is the only African-American woman ''whose plays have been written and professionally produced over four decades.''

In *Home Front* (1985) and *A Quarrel of Sparrows* (produced 1988) James Duff explores with deft humor and skilled stagecraft what Susan Gilbert calls the ''themes of family strife and heritage, traditions of culture and religion strong in the South, and subjects controversial and timely.'' The work of Lonne Elder III, who has written for stage, television, and motion pictures, provides for John Sekora ''a sense of African-American life as 'a glorious, adventurous thing, constantly unfolding in everyday life in its beauty, speech, walk, dance, and even in its anger.' '' Elder's plays include *Ceremonies in Dark Old Men* (1965), *Charades on East Fourth Street* (1971), and *Splendid Mummer* (1988).

In *Crimes of the Heart* (1982), Beth Henley portrays in colorful language the many offbeat characters of her Mississippi background. But beneath the comic repartee, says Hilary Holladay, Henley's ''plays are serious examinations of relationships and family life,'' especially for women characters. In succeeding plays such as *The Miss Firecracker Contest: A Play* (1985) and *The Debutante Ball* (1991), Henley has continued to draw admiring audiences.

Identified with the Dallas Theatre Center repertory company, Preston Jones

(1938–1979) wrote between 1973 and his death a half dozen dramas. He is best remembered for his *Texas Trilogy: The Last Meeting of the White Magnolia* (1973), *Lu Ann Hampton Laverty Oberlander* (1974), and *The Oldest Living Graduate* (1974). In these plays and others, Jones examines gender issues and family ties, presenting what Kimball King sees as "a larger vision of a racist, sexist, materialistic society clinging to self-serving myths as it disregards religious values and a viable work ethic."

Marsha Norman, who won the 1983 Pulitzer Prize for *'night, Mother*, takes as her terrain "the walking wounded." From her first play, *Getting Out* (1979), through *The Holdup* (1987), according to Billy J. Harbin and Jill Stapleton Bergeron, Norman has taken as her major theme the "familial bonds that repress rather than nurture, that imprison rather than liberate, and the Ibsenesque imperative that the greatest individual freedom is that which comes from within." In all her plays, Norman stresses "the suffering and grace that humanizes and dignifies the ordinary."

The South boasts may important poets. But like their counterparts from other regions, they live in the shadow of fiction writers and dramatists. Southerners, like Americans generally, read more fiction and drama than poetry. In the South, the most popular poets write country-western music. They have gained the world's ear with their wonderful lyrics about "achy-breaky" and jealous hearts, wildwood flowers, D-I-V-O-R-C-E, pickup trucks and eighteen-wheelers, foolin' around, and honky tonkin'. Listening in Marakesh, Morocco, to Kenny Rogers sing about Ruby taking her love to town at first startles until one realizes that this popular poetry crossed international boundaries two decades ago. This cultural phenomenon means that "serious" poets not only attract small audiences but also take longer to achieve recognition than fiction writers, dramatists, and authors of country-western music. Few poets in the South or in America gain much national recognition before they reach the age of 50.

But the poets discussed in this book have achieved national and sometimes international acclaim for their work. The catalogue of Southern poets is long— James Applewhite, Gerald Barrax, David Bottoms, Charles Edward Eaton, Julia Fields, William Harmon, Donald Justice, Etheridge Knight, Susan Ludvigson, Jeff Daniel Marion, Jim Wayne Miller, Robert Morgan, George Addison Scarbrough, James Seay, Dave Smith, R. T. Smith, Dabney Stuart, Henry Splawn Taylor, Richard Tillinghast, Jonathan Williams, Miller Williams, and Charles Wright. If you add to this list Fred Chappell, Nikki Giovanni, Maya Angelou, George Garrett, and others mentioned above, the achievement of Southern poets is indeed impressive. The poetic worlds these authors have created range from pastoral to urban, and the forms they employ range from conventional to highly experimental. Although the topics and tones of the new Southern voices sometimes resemble those of Renascence poets, the new voices more often produce tones and topics that seem alien to the measured meters of that earlier generation.

James Applewhite's poetic world focuses, says George S. Lensing, upon a verse "world of family and experience surrounding the small-town tobacco community in North Carolina where he was born and reared." In books such as *Statues of the Grass* (1975) and *Ode to the Chinaberry Tree and Other Poems* (1986), Applewhite has created "a mythic poetry tied to the rhythms of the earth's seasons." Gerald Barrax has celebrated in *Another Kind of Rain* (1970) and *Leaning against the Sun* (1992) the African-American experience. Lucy K. Hayden identifies Barrax's major themes as human and black vulnerability and self-revelation, interspersed with the themes of "love, sex, alienation, music, existentialism and nature."

David Bottoms, who won the Walt Whitman Award of the Academy of American Poets in 1979 for *Shooting Rats at the Bibb County Dump* (1980), "draws his subjects, characters, scenes, images, events, and ideas from the woods, swamps, dumps, bars, small towns, and suburbs" of his native Georgia. Peter Stitt sees Bottoms essentially as "a realist poet who covets the epiphanic moment" and who views each of his poems as a "discrete, primarily autobiographical moment."

For Charles Edward Eaton, who published his first book of poems in 1942 and his most recent in 1991, the job of the poet is "to reaffirm the humane tradition by helping individuals to realize fully their potential, to connect and to balance the widely disparate aspects of their humanness." Glenn B. Blalock believes that Eaton throughout his career has consistently seen the poet as the "commando of consciousness" and has attempted to shape his volumes of verse around this concept. Blalock cites *New and Selected Poems, 1942–1987* (1987), for which Eaton wrote the introduction, as a "must" for first-time readers of Eaton's work.

Julia Fields, who regards poetry as "a form of will," writes poems that "have the tone of a plea for sensitivity and justice in a 'hard-boiled' world." Sara Andrews Johnston argues that Fields tempers her protest poems with "wry humor and caricature" in her portrayals "of the suffering of black people." Fields's witty "High on the Hog," a protest poem that has charmed audiences wherever Fields reads it, satirizes sentimental white notions about soul food. Johnston cites *East of Moonlight* (1973) and *Slow Coins* (1981) as collections that show Fields's lyric and thematic range; "Moonlight," says Johnston, demonstrates how Fields "can create some evocative moments, with a subtle, wistful touch."

In *Treasury Holiday* (1970), William Harmon introduces a speaker who begins: "I am the Gross National Product." With wit, learning, and "brilliant verbal inventiveness," Harmon in that long poem sings and satirizes the body politic and impolitic. For *Treasury Holiday,* he won the Lamont Award, and for later collections, Chicago's Fiske Poetry Prize, the Binyon Humanities Award, and the Elliston Poetry Fellowship. In Harmon's poetic journey from *Treasury Holiday* to his most recent book *Mutatis Mutandis* (1985), Marlene Youmans discovers "an unusual progression from the long poem and exhuberant catalogues of trifles and enormities to collections of short poems that harmonize his wit, intelligence, technical skill, and remarkable inventiveness in a range of modes and formal concerns.''

In four books of poems and in a variety of verse forms, Donald Justice has persistently examined the theme of alienation. From *The Summer Anniversaries* (1960) through *The Sunset Maker* (1987), Justice has pursued that theme—the human griefs of loss, melancholy, change, transience, disease, poverty, and indifference. But James A. Grimshaw, Jr. also notes that Justice confronts these human problems always believing that ''through writing, the poet precludes . . . total alienation, and writing becomes an act of preservation—of memory and experience.''

Since 1968 when he published *Poems from Prison,* Etheridge Knight (1931–1991), notes D. Soyini Madison, has written poetry about ''the prison experience, the African-American toast and oral tradition, and poems of love and tribute.'' Using vernacular language, Knight has described his experiences vividly and has become ''one of the most influential voices in African-American literature and art.'' Even before the appearance of *The Essential Etheridge Knight* in 1986, he had established himself as a major poet of the Black Arts Movement. Madison cites blues, jazz, and the African drum and chant as major poetic influences on Knight's voice and verse.

Susan Ludvigson, a Northerner who has identified herself with the South, has created two characteristic types of poems, argues Judy Jo Small—''openly autobiographical lyrics and dramatic renderings of other, often bizarre, personalities.'' From *Step Carefully in Night Grass* (1974) to *To Find the Gold* (1990), Ludvigson has written ''carefully crafted, informal lyrics'' that ''are streaked with dark wit and quiet passion.''

Jeff Daniel Marion locates his poetic territory in the scenes, objects, and people of the east Tennessee mountains. *Out in the Country, Back Home* (1976) ''captures the meanderings, colorful phrases, and fable-making quality of rural Southern voices,'' says Lynne P. Shackelford. Shackelford associates Marion's work with the transcendentalist nature poets and Robert Frost. But she also finds Marion's work distinctively Southern in language and diction and his poems about objects exhibiting an ''Oriental sparseness.''

Jim Wayne Miller, another Appalachian poet, also takes the mountain country and people as his subjects in such books as *Dialogue with a Dead Man* (1974) and *The Mountains Have Come Closer* (1980). Joyce Dyer cites lines from ''On Native Ground'' to capture the major theme in Miller's poetry: ''Life grows in rings around a hurt, / a tree with barbed wire running through its heart.'' Miller uses that metaphor to characterize his theme of ''growth and change.''

Author of ten volumes of poetry, Robert Morgan ''has been celebrated as one of the boldest and most engaging experimenters with verse form.'' He has located much of his work in his mountain birthplace of southwestern North Carolina. William Harmon describes Morgan as ''a poet of what Wordsworth called those 'little nameless unremembered' objects, actions, and persons.'' From *Zir-*

conia Poems (1969) to *Groundwork* (1979) to *Green River: New and Selected Poems* (1991), Morgan casts his eye on those little nameless unremembered things to remind readers of what they knew but did not know they knew. Harmon catalogues in Morgan's titles those little things: ''foxfire, watertanks, swamp, cellar, woodpile, bass, whippoorwill, stove, faucet, stump, hubcaps, flood, hogpen, rice, copse, plankroad, slop bucket, blackberries, earache, shovel, feather bed, manure pile, nail bag, odometer, rearview mirror, spirit level, uranium, overalls.''

Though George Addison Scarbrough has been a journalist and novelist, his primary interest is poetry. A native of east Tennessee, Scarbrough published in the 1940s and 1950s three volumes of poems: *Tellico Blue* (1949), *The Course Is Upward* (1951), and *Summer So-Called* (1956). Scarbrough continued to write poetry, but did not publish another book of verse until *New and Selected Poems* (1977) and *Invitation to Kim* (1989), which was nominated for a Pulitzer Prize. Robert L. Phillips believes that ''cultivation and preservation of the self'' are Scarbrough's main themes, with family and houses providing the principal metaphors for Scarbrough's exploration of these themes.

Mississippi-born James Seay has not been as prolific a writer as some of his contemporaries, but he has earned, says William Aarnes, ''the respect of fellow poets for writing accessible, resonant poems about searching for happiness in our troubled lives.'' In *Let Not Your Hart* (1970), *Water Tables* (1974), and *The Light as They Found It* (1990) Seay has crafted sonnets and free verse poems that, according to Aarnes, provide readers with a ''stay against confusion.''

Author of twelve collections of poems, several chapbooks and broadsides, Dave Smith has established himself, says Corrine Hales, as ''one of the most widely read and admired poets of his generation.'' From *Bull Island* (1970) through *Goshawk, Antelope* (1979) to *Dream Flights* (1981) and *Cuba Night* (1990), Smith's work has ranged from his early treatment of coastal Virginia people and landscapes to Wyoming and Utah and back to Virginia. Hales argues that ''Smith is also known for his narrative structure, and one of his main paradigms is a kind of mythic journey—a journey of the self—back to, through, and even away from the literal and symbolic geographies that flesh out the poem.'' Such strategies endow Smith's poetry with both regional and universal qualities.

Since 1975, R. T. (Rodney Theodore) Smith has published a dozen books and chapbooks of poetry, steadily gaining recognition for what Linda Welden calls poems that ''tend to be self-contained works of art'' and that are ''deeply religious'' in ''original and unorthodox ways.'' With an ''affection for people and things natural and close to the earth,'' Smith has created dramatic speakers ''who live his philosophy of simplicity as a crucial aspect of sophistication.'' *Birch-Light* (1986) won Smith the Brockman Award, and critics have praised his most recent volumes, *The Cardinal Heart* (1991) and *The Names of Trees* (1991).

Virginian Dabney Stuart has written nine books of verse, creating poems that "might be classified as formalist, confessional, elegaic, mythic, surrealistic, or satiric," states Gilbert Allen. Early autobiographical poems in *The Diving Bell* (1966) have yielded to the archetypal poems in *The Other Hand* (1976) and to *Narcissus Dreaming* (1990), in which Stuart "attempts to blend autobiography, myth, and surrealism." Though Stuart's poetic forms extend to several registers, Allen singles out Stuart's lyric poems for special praise.

Henry Taylor, another Virginia-born poet, won the 1986 Pulitzer Prize for poetry with *The Flying Change* (1985). Taylor wrote his first book of poems, *The Horseshow at Midnight* (1966), while he was still an undergraduate at the University of Virginia. He told Elizabeth McGeachy Mills that "a good fast hot streak for me is six poems a year." In addition to his three volumes of verse, Taylor has published broadsides, edited and written books about poetry, and has translated Euripides' *The Children of Herakles*. Taylor sets most of his poems in a Virginia pastoral landscape, and Mills argues that Taylor's principal theme is "the interplay between emotional expression and rational control, an essential ingredient of the poet's craft."

In his six books of poetry, Richard Tillinghast, born in Memphis, Tennessee, has taken the nature of consciousness as his principal subject. From *Sleep Watch* (1969) to *Our Flag Was Still There* (1984), Tillinghast has catalogued "the various nuances of consciousness," exploring the value "of memory and individual experiences." Tillinghast concludes, says Ed Ingebretsen, "that poetry is the necessary human act, a sacramental, transcendent, life-creating act. In memory you find yourself, in poetry you make yourself and construct a human place saved from time."

James Whitehead is perhaps better known for his novel *Joiner* (1971) than for his poetry, but Thomas E. Dasher finds the poems and fiction linked by Whitehead's preoccupations with the themes of "love, politics, family, friendship, community, vocation, balance, and finally, of course, death." Whitehead's *Domains* (1973) and *Local Men* (1979), republished together in 1987, present several poems about characters "trying to make sense of life and trying to communicate that struggle to us." Dasher sees the same toughness in the poems that he finds in *Joiner*, "a demanding novel" that has been called "one of the fourteen major Southern fictions after Faulkner."

In more than a dozen books of poems, Appalachian-born Jonathan Williams has established himself as "a lyrical and satirical poet whose strengths are tied to his keen sense of voice, precise observations, wit, imaginative fusion of visual and verbal arts, and sheer delight in language," according to John E. Bassett. Founder of the Jargon Society, Williams has also published the work of undiscovered writers and artists, especially photographers and visual artists. From his earliest collection, *The Empire Finals at Verona* (1959), to *An Ear in Bartram's Tree* (1969), to the revised edition of *Blues & Roots/Rue & Bluets: A Garland for the Southern Appalachians* (1985), Williams has filled his verse and visual experiments with humor and "the wordplay of acrostics, puns, and anagrams."

In his wit and wordplay, Williams is, says Bassett, "one of relatively few explicitly political Southern poets of his generation."

Trained as a biologist and zoologist and founder and director of the University of Arkansas Press, Miller Williams has won for his nine books of verse numerous national and international prizes, among them the Prix de Rome in 1976. According to Timothy Dow Adams, Williams's first book of poems, *Circle of Stone* (1964), announced the themes that have preoccupied his work: "science, doubt, form, order, religion, and chance." Other volumes include *The Only World There Is* (1971), *Halfway from Hoxie* (1973), *Why God Permits Evil* (1977), and his most recent *Living on the Surface* (1989). Adams believes that Williams has written "in a style characterized as both highly sophisticated and down home, a combination of hard philosophical debate about both practical and metaphysical worries—refined by a thinker who has been at home in both the scientific and humanistic world."

Charles Wright, born and raised in Tennessee, shared with Galway Kinnell the 1983 American Book Award for Poetry for *Country Music* (1982). His eight other books of poems—among them *The Grave at the Right Hand* (1970), *China Trace* (1977), *The Other Side of the River* (1984), and *Xionia* (1990)—received critical praise for "his linguistic and structural precision, the music of his line, and his metaphysical concerns." Wright's poetic stance, says Margaret Mills Harper, is "usually meditative: his favorite settings are rural or semi-rural landscapes; his rhythms are more painterly than musical." His poetry, argues Harper, "is preoccupied with an essentially religious, even mystical, search." In addition to his poetry, Wright has distinguished himself as a translator of Italian verse.

Given the excellence and diversity in this catalogue of poets, Southern poetry of the serious sort is probably in the best shape it's ever been. If we add to this list James Dickey and A. R. Ammons (both discussed in *Fifty Southern Writers after 1900*), the poetic achievement of Southerners in the last three decades exceeds that of all the earlier generations, with the exception of Edgar Allan Poe, who was a generation by himself.

We have labeled the remaining writers discussed in this introduction novelists, though all have worked in other forms and have often earned the right to other designations. David Madden, Heather Ross Miller, Wilma Dykeman, and Eve Shelnutt have distinguished themselves in a number of literary forms. Daphne Athas has written poetry and travel books, but is principally known for her fiction. Elizabeth Hardwick has written fiction, but she is probably better known for her literary criticism. Guy Owen wrote novels, but he was also a poet and a long-time editor of the *Southern Poetry Review*. However, prose fiction is the form that unites most authors we have located in this territory.

Daphne Athas, author of four novels, a volume of travel about Greece, and a collection of poems, sings "in a unique voice the song of the soul in quest of the experiences that define the self." In *The Weather of the Heart* (1947), *The Fourth World* (1957), *Entering Ephesus* (1971, reissued 1991), and *Cora*

(1978), Athas chronicles her characters' journeys from innocence to experience. The form of her stories, says Harriette Cuttino Buchanan, ''is dominated by the shaping metaphor of the journey, and the goal for the personal explorations and the literal and psychological journeys is self-knowledge.'' *Greece by Prejudice* (1962), argues Buchanan, reads ''very much like her novels.''

Wilma Dykeman, born in Asheville, North Carolina, has written (sometimes coauthored) twenty-two books that deal with Appalachia. In her three novels about the region—*The Tall Women* (1962), *The Far Family* (1966), and *Return the Innocent Earth* (1973)—Dykeman takes as her key themes ''woman, family, earth.'' The subjects of her fiction, according to Patricia M. Gantt and Chip Jones, ''range from nineteenth-century mountain families dealing with the divisiveness of the Civil War, to modern protagonists working to conserve the land and fight prejudice.'' Dykeman has written three biographies of Appalachian figures and has ''long been recognized as one of the best critics of her region and its literature.'' Gantt and Jones believe that Dykeman's ''early advocacy of civil rights and environmental issues, her realistic portraits of the Appalachian region and its people, and her ability to tell a winning and memorable story make her worthy of further study.''

Setting his novels and stories against the backgrounds of Louisiana and Spain, Peter Feibleman has earned critical praise, says Randal Woodland, for ''his evocation of place and compelling characterizations.'' From his first novel, *A Place without Twilight* (1958), through *Charlie Boy* (1980), Feibleman has created characters and plots tracing the ''clash of disparate cultures'' and telling ''of individuals on the boundaries of these communities.'' In addition to a half-dozen novels and collections of stories, Feibleman has also written autobiographical books about Louisiana—*American Cooking: Creole and Acadian* (1971) and *The Bayous* (1973).

Novelist, short-story writer, critic, and champion of women's writing, Elizabeth Hardwick represents ''that *rara avis,* a woman of letters,'' says Susan V. Donaldson, quoting Doris Grumbach. Born in Lexington, Kentucky, Hardwick has made New York City and its literary scene her home since 1939, but she sees Lexington as ''truly home.'' Of her three novels—*The Ghostly Lover* (1945), *The Simple Truth* (1955), and *Sleepless Nights* (1979)—the last has become, according to Donaldson, Hardwick's most important novel. It ''represents a fitting culmination for the career of a writer who has long insisted that culture and art can never be separated from politics and issues of power.'' In addition to her novels and short fiction, Hardwick helped found the *New York Review of Books* and is still a contributing editor. Her reviews there and her three collections of essays earned her the reputation of being one of America's best critics. In 1993 Hardwick received the Gold Medal for Belles Lettres and Criticism from the American Academy of Arts and Letters.

LeRoy Leatherman (1922–1984) wrote two novels, a biography of his long-time associate Martha Graham and a book about creativity. Leatherman's two novels, *The Caged Birds* (1950) and *The Other Side of the Tree* (1954), follow the odyssey of Jim Daigree, a character reminiscent of William Faulkner's Quentin Compson and Robert Penn Warren's Jim Burden. Leatherman's themes, says Alan T. Belsches, are "the importance of the past, the family, and the power of the community over the individual."

Author and editor of more than twenty-five books, David Madden is "foremost a fiction writer," though he has written in several genres: "poetry, stage drama, radio plays, screenplays, reviews, personal essays, criticism, and short and long fiction." Jeffrey H. Richards singles out for praise *Cassandra Singing* (1969), *Bijou* (1974), and *The Suicide's Wife* (1978) as "all original, engaging, and very different works." Though Madden himself discourages "theme-hunting" in his work, Richards identifies three recurring motifs in Madden's work: the problems of storytelling, the problems of "reading," and "Madden's existential use of popular culture."

Novelist, poet, short-story writer, and teacher, Heather Ross Miller has earned praise for her "exquisite style" and for creating "a rich variety of female characters who are refreshing alternatives to conventional portrayals of women." In *The Edge of the Woods* (1964), *Tenants of the House* (1966), and *Confessions of a Champeen Fire Baton Twirler* (1976), Miller has dealt with "psychological and physical violence in time-haunted existences." Miller's more recent work includes three books of poems—*Adam's First Wife* (1983), *Hard Evidence* (1990), and *Friends & Assassins* (1992). Bes Stark Spangler states that Miller has completed and handed over to agents two new novels and a collection of short stories.

Author of novels, poems, stories, and nonfiction books, William Mills takes as one of his central themes the natural world and man's relation to it through "seeing and not seeing, understanding and not understanding." Setting much of his work in the countryside and towns of Louisiana, Mills explores in his novel *Those Who Blink* (1986) the struggle of Farley Stokes to resolve his love of the land with the powers of progress and development. Similar motifs pervade Mills's three books of poems *Watch for the Fox* (1974), *Stained Glass* (1979), and *The Meaning of Coyotes* (1984). William Grimes Cherry III identifies ecology and history as principal subjects of Mills's nonfiction books, *Bears and Men: A Gathering* (1986) and *The Arkansas: An American River* (1988).

Taking mythical Cape Fear County, North Carolina, as the setting for his fiction, Guy Owen (1925–1981) charmed and fascinated readers with his novels *The Ballad of the Flim-Flam Man* (1965), *Journey for Joedel* (1970), and *The Flim-Flam Man and the Apprentice Grifter* (1972). George C. Scott starred as Mordecai Jones in that most successful movie of the first film-flam man novel. In addition to his achievement as a novelist, Owen published three volumes of poetry and from 1964 to 1977 edited the prestigious *Southern Poetry Review*. In that journal, he printed poems by such authors as A. R. Ammons, Wendell Berry, Fred Chappell, James Dickey, Josephine Jacobsen, Donald Justice, Vassar Miller, Linda Pastan, and Dave Smith. Mary C. Williams writes that Owen was intensely and self-consciously Southern because he attempted to "preserve and recreate'' a way of rural life that was rapidly passing. Williams argues that important in Owen's work ''are the cluster of characteristics he identified as Southern: the sense of place, the focus on family life, on the past, and on racial tensions; the influence of religion.''

Short-story writer and poet, Eve Shelnutt has published in the past 20 years more than fifty stories and seventy poems and has won numerous prizes for her work, among them the Pushcart Prize for short fiction. Shelnutt has also written three books on the art and teaching of writing. She has published three collections of stories—*The Love Child* (1979), *The Formal Voice* (1982), and *The Musician* (1987)—and has recently completed a fourth, *Distance*. Books of poetry include *Air and Salt* (1983) and *Recital in a Private Home* (1988). Elsa Nettels says that Shelnutt is ''best known as a writer of finely wrought short stories of family relationships.'' Shelnutt's fiction, writes Nettels, often experiments with form and ''deals with the universal themes of love and conflict, isolation and death, and with the primary feelings—desire, joy, guilt, fear.''

In the introduction to *Contemporary Fiction Writers of the South,* the companion volume to this book, we argue that the authors discussed there have discernible roots in eight sub-Souths. We also argue that gender, race, and social class play a more significant role in the present Renascence than it did in the flowering of Southern letters after World War I. Though we have not pursued those distinctions in this introduction, we believe they hold equally true for the writers discussed here. What especially emerges from the essays in both volumes is that Appalachian writers are playing a much larger role than they did in the post–World War I era. Though other sub-Souths have birthed writers alive and lively, Appalachian daughters and sons have written well and in numbers, comprising a Renascence within a Renascence.

This introduction to contemporary Southern poets, dramatists, essayists, and novelists only suggests the remarkable range and variety of their work. Henry James and Mark Twain never agreed on much, but they both believed that the first job of a writer is to be interesting. The authors discussed in the following entries are interesting because they use their Southern heritage to tell about the old verities that William Faulkner so admired and labored for. These contemporary voices might sound a little foreign to writers of the Renascence, but they would still be recognizably Southern. Perhaps the ghosts of Faulkner and his peers smile.

LUCINDA H. MACKETHAN

Maya Angelou
(1928–   )

When Maya Angelou read her poem at the January 20, 1993, inauguration of President Bill Clinton, she drew on the materials and the themes that have dominated both her poetry and her autobiographies since she began her literary career in 1970. The poem is rich in allusions to the gospel hymns and spirituals that she learned from her grandmother, whose presence and songs have provided much of the lyricism of her writings. The poem's mixture of confession and exhortation are characteristic of two of her frequently cited models, the slave narrative and the African-American sermon, while the free verse lines and the expansive view of the nation as reflective of the poet's inner landscape carry echoes of both Walt Whitman and Thomas Wolfe, whose works she read as a teenager. Angelou made the poem a blend of public and private imagery, so that it reflects her vision of the self as both uniquely individual and representative of all that is human. The inaugural poem celebrates the nurturing operations of nature; it stresses the need for careful attention to history; and it urges resilience, respect for the earth, and self-affirmation, all major themes of Angelou's work as a whole. Maya Angelou's participation in the inauguration itself illustrates the nature of her career and her sense of her role as writer: in her work her voice is that of performer and her words are performance, that is, partaking of public modes of expression while at the same time carving from private experience a way to meet and conquer the world. Angelou began her first autobiography, *I Know Why the Caged Bird Sings* (1970), with a childhood scene in which she stood before an audience, terrified to speak. From this story forward, her works record her growing recognition of and ability to capitalize upon the theatrical nature of life, which she learned perhaps best from her early enthusiastic reading of Shakespeare. As an African-American, she also adopted very early Paul Lawrence Dunbar's truth, "We wear the mask." A young black girl growing up in America learns quickly how to pose as a means of surviving racism and sexism, and Angelou turned all of these lessons, through her natural dramatic flair, into a highly successful career in musical theater and writing for stage and screen before moving on to become a nationally acclaimed autobiographer and poet.

BIOGRAPHY

Although she was born in St. Louis, Missouri, and has since 1981 made her residence in Winston-Salem, North Carolina, in the public mind Maya Angelou hails from Stamps, Arkansas, a tiny town thirty miles from the Texas border. Born on April 4, 1928, to Bailey Johnson and Vivian Baxter Johnson, Angelou (christened Marguerite Johnson) and her brother Bailey were sent, when she was three, to live in Stamps with her paternal grandmother, Annie Henderson. Her parents' divorce and seeming abandonment caused a sense of rejection and dislocation that were heightened for Angelou by the racism that she encountered in her grandmother's small Southern town. Yet Annie Henderson's dignity and courage provided a lifelong source of pride and determination. Thus the South gave Angelou, as it has many African-American writers, a mixed inheritance in which family support and strong community loyalty were constantly offset by white cruelty and bigotry. Except for a brief period when Angelou was around eight years old, Maya and Bailey lived in Stamps until 1940, when Angelou's grandmother, worried about the effect of the South's oppression and violence on her teenaged charges, sent them to their mother, who had recently remarried and lived in San Francisco. At age sixteen, Angelou gave birth to her son, Guy Bailey Johnson, and in 1945 she ended her formal education when she graduated from Mission High School in San Francisco.

Determined to support her child without help from her family, Angelou worked at a series of menial jobs before her marriage in 1952 to Tosh Angelos, a Greek-American. When the marriage ended two years later, Angelou's years of training in dance helped her to find work in several San Francisco nightclubs. In 1954 she was invited to become part of the cast of the Gershwin/Heyward musical *Porgy and Bess,* which was sent on a twenty-two-nation tour by the U.S. State Department. She returned to find her son Guy experiencing trauma that she blamed on their separation, and for the next several years she kept him with her while she traveled as a cabaret entertainer. In 1959 she moved with her son to New York, where she worked in theater and joined the Harlem Writers' Guild. She became Northern Coordinator for Martin Luther King's Southern Christian Leadership Conference after she and Godfrey Cambridge wrote and staged a fund-raising musical, *Cabaret for Freedom*, for the organization in 1960. During this period of intense political activism, Angelou appeared with a stellar cast including James Earl Jones and Cicely Tyson in Jean Genet's *The Blacks,* and she married a South African freedom fighter, Vusumzi Make. While living with Make in Cairo, Egypt, from 1961 to 1962, Angelou wrote for the *Arab Observer* and began to develop associations with many African-American writers and activists, eventually including James Baldwin and Malcolm X among her friends. After her marriage with Make dissolved, Angelou moved with her son Guy to Ghana, where Guy attended the University of Ghana in Legon-Accra and where she worked for the university and as a freelance writer. In Ghana Angelou was able for the first time to explore her dual identity as African and American in an environment where she was released from the shadow cast upon her identity by white racism. Her experiences in Africa allowed her to test her right to self-assurance and freedom of voice.

When Angelou returned to America in 1964, she was poised for success on several creative fronts. In Los Angeles she acted in Jean Anouilh's *Medea,* wrote dramas and musicals, and lectured at UCLA. In 1970, she found her most powerful artistic medium in writing *I Know Why the Caged Bird Sings,* the first of five autobiographies and a nominee for the National Book Award. The following year she published her first volume of poetry, *Just Give Me a Cool Drink of Water 'Fore I Diiie* (1971), which was nominated in 1972 for a Pulitzer Prize. In the 1970s she published two more autobiographies *(Gather Together in My Name* [1974] and *Singin' and Swingin' and Gettin' Merry Like Christmas* [1976]) and two more volumes of poetry *(Oh Pray My Wings Are Gonna Fit Me Well* [1975] and *And Still I Rise* [1978]). In 1972 her screenplay *Georgia, Georgia* was accepted by Independent-Cinema, making her the first black woman to have an original script produced for the screen. The 1970s gave Angelou phenomenal recognition in a wide variety of endeavors: two presidents, Gerald Ford and Jimmy Carter, appointed her to national commissions; she received a Tony and an Emmy nomination for her acting; and in 1975 she was awarded a Rockefeller grant for study in Italy and received a Woman of the Year in Communications Award from *Ladies Home Journal.* Her documentary series ''Afro-American in the Arts'' received a Golden Eagle award from the Public Broadcasting System in 1977. Her teleplay ''Sister, Sister,'' written in 1978 to provide a realistic picture of black women's lives, created a storm of controversy over its portrayal of the church and was not aired until 1982. Yet Angelou was honored as one of the few women named to the Directors Guild, and she has served for many years on the board of trustees of the American Film Institute.

When Wake Forest University gave Angelou a lifetime appointment as the first Reynolds Professor of American Studies, in December 1981, she made Winston-Salem, North Carolina, her permanent home and added teaching to her list of careers. By this time she was divorced from her third husband, Paul du Feu, and had become a grandmother to Colin, Guy Johnson's son. The 1980s saw her complete her last two autobiographies, *The Heart of a Woman* in 1981 and *All God's Children Need Traveling Shoes* in 1986. The song-poems that make up *Shaker, Why Don't You Sing?* appeared in 1983; a long illustrated poem *Now Sheba Sings the Song* was published in 1987; and she ended the decade with the publication of yet another poetry collection, *I Shall Not Be Moved* (1990). Angelou has received more than a dozen honorary degrees from

American colleges and universities, and her life has been chronicled in several television documentaries, including one filmed in Stamps, Arkansas, with Bill Moyers for his "Creativity" Series (January 12, 1982). In 1992 Winston-Salem witnessed the American premiere of her musical adaptation of poems from the collection *And Still I Rise,* and the year also brought her an Horatio Alger Award and an Essence Award. The year ended with the invitation from fellow Arkansan president-elect Bill Clinton to write a poem for his inauguration. About her poem she said that she was seeking to capture "the lyricism possible when one is talking about the country," and she speculated that President Clinton had asked her to write the inaugural poem "because he understood that I am the kind of person who really does bring people together" (Manegold C8).

MAJOR THEMES

Poetry

Angelou's six volumes of poetry range between the very personal, intimate poems that explore love and loneliness, and the explicitly public poems that address national problems, most often racism and the effects of America's history of oppression against blacks, from slavery times forward. The two sections of her first collection, *Just Give Me a Cool Drink of Water 'Fore I Diiie* (1971), indicate a division of themes that is common to all of the volumes. Part One is called "When Love is a Scream of Anguish," and most of these poems are first-person expressions of hopes, doubts, disappointments connected to love. Part Two, "Just Before the World Ends," turns outward to reflect on and often brood over the situation of those denied justice in America. There are meditations on political events and postures such as "Riot: 60's" and "On Working White Liberals," and several dramatic monologues like "Times-Square-Shoeshine-Composition" and "When I Think About Myself," the latter a poignant self-portrait of a black maid who remarks how "the child I works for calls me girl" (28). The poems of the first collection establish Angelou's essential moods and techniques. They are sharply imagistic, often employing the heavy rhythms of work songs or gospel hymns and the patterns of black folk speech and rituals. The personal poems are often somber, commemorating pain and loss in intimate relationships, and the public poems can be by turns raging, bitter, sarcastic, and sorrowful as they call out scenes of injustice or betrayal. "Miss Scarlet, Mr. Rhett and Other Latter Day Saints" is a good example of the caustic irony that Angelou can apply as she portrays white blindness. Another mood, one that dominates in Angelou's poetry as a whole, characterizes the first collection's last poem, "Harlem Hopscotch." Here the speaker makes a ritual game out of her own perilous situation as she sings "Cross the line, they count you out / That's what hopping's all about," and in this way she manages not only to survive but to prevail: "Both feet flat, the game is done. / They think I lost. I think I won" (52).

Although the poems of Angelou's later collections add a wider scope, the style and the concerns remain much the same. There is in *Oh Pray My Wings Are Gonna Fit Me Well* (1975) a group of intimate lyrics that look back to past happiness or address an absent lover in soft tones, similar to the earlier love poems but stressing loneliness even more, as in the poems "Alone" and the beautiful "I Almost Remember." One other set of poems uses landscapes and images of the history of both Africa and America to meet the need she names in the poem "Reverses," the challenge "to confront ourselves in our past" (64). Other poems—"For Us, Who Dare Not Dare," "America," "Elegy: For Harriet Tubman and Frederick Douglass," and "Southeast Arkansia"—blend place, history, and guilt in a search for a kind of cleansing through memory. The collection *And Still I Rise* (1978) gives this search a more encouraging tone than we encounter in *Oh Pray My Wings,* for here the title poem "Still I Rise" sounds a call to affirm black identity out of "a past that's rooted in pain" (42). The response to the call is always "I rise," whereas in companion poems with the same form, the response is "Now ain't we bad? / An' ain't we Black" (44) or "Life doesn't frighten me at all" (45). In all of these songs, the speaker turns back fear and despair through the sheer vibrations of her rising voice.

The most important image of "Still I Rise" is the speaker herself. We are greeted with a definitively womanly voice that relishes announcing to the world her own power and possibilities. This voice takes us back to "Woman Me" from *Oh Pray My Wings,* and along with other poems in *And Still I Rise,* most notably "Phenomenal Woman" and "Woman Work," shows Angelou at her most vigorous and inspiring. When she speaks of and through the African-American woman's lexicon of "sass" and "motherwit," she has found the clearest source of her own creativity. Another poem of *And Still I Rise,* "Call Letters: Mrs. V.B.," allows her mother's voice to declare "Failure? I'm not ashamed to tell it, / I never learned to spell it. / Not Failure," and this message, also resoundingly promoted by Vivian Baxter in Angelou's first two autobiographies, gives all of Angelou's woman-poems a vitality and energy that sets them apart. The voice of these poems, as Robert Stepto has noted, is "forthright about the sexual nuances of personal and social struggle," and "the woman 'rising' from these lines is largely unaccounted for in the earlier verse of men and women poets alike" (314–15). The long single poem *Now Sheba Sings the Song,* which was written to accompany a series of drawings of black women by her friend Tom Feelings, celebrates black womanhood in this manner. Likewise, the most powerful poem of her last collection *I Shall Not Be Moved* (1990), entitled "Our Grandmothers," tells of the figure of the black foremother who "sings to her loves and beloveds, / to her foes and detractors . . . I shall not be moved" (36–37).

Many of the poems of *And Still I Rise* also appear in Angelou's musical of the same title, and her next two volumes, *Shaker, Why Don't You Sing?* (1983) and *Now Sheba Sings the Song* (1987), were also composed with singing in mind, either structurally or thematically. Much of Angelou's poetry has the rhythm and simple, repetitive structure of song—both folk song and blues, which means that her poetry in its construction assumes elements of musical performance in the arrangement and the effect of the words. Her verse is often tied to nuances of voice—pitch, pronunciation, volume, pace—and to what she celebrates as the restorative power of song. The title of her first autobiography, as well as the poem "Caged Bird" in *Shaker,* indicates how for Angelou singing uniquely reflects one's ability to proclaim her identity and her place: the image of the caged bird singing of freedom presumes as well an audience learning as much through the performance of song as through the words, and Angelou works to make understanding a matter of listening in her poetry. The particular nature of the songs whose structures are recognizable in her verse is also significant; as Robert Stepto says, Angelou "is on her surest ground when she 'borrows' various folk idioms and thereby buttresses her poems by evoking aspects of a culture's written and unwritten heritage" (314–15). In all of her poems, the private ones as well as the historically referential ones, the cadences of African-American speech and song make Angelou's messages both topical and universal. The African-American struggle for freedom and selfhood is in one sense always the poet's singular struggle and in another the struggle of all wounded, living souls.

Autobiography

Angelou's poetry seems in many ways ancillary to her autobiographies, but perhaps it is more accurate to say that the autobiographical impulse informs all of her creative work. Many of her poems, for instance, speak intimately of family that we meet in *I Know Why the Caged Bird Sings* (the poem "Willie" in *And Still I Rise* and Bailey in the poem "Kin"). And the woman's voice in many poems is the voice we see struggling to come to the surface in the first two autobiographies, the voice of the black girl who sees herself as ugly and unloved and who seeks security, affection, and assurance of her worth in all of her relationships. Many of her most successful poems are dramatic monologues that merge narrative and voice, and autobiography offered her, as a writer, the form that best sustains her material and her innately performative sense of identity. She has explained that "by the time I was half finished with *Caged Bird* I knew I loved the form" and also that her reading of the slave narratives showed her how she wanted autobiography to function for her: "I love the idea of the slave narrative, using the first person singular, really meaning always the third person plural" (Neubauer 286). Autobiography has allowed Angelou to traverse the territories of private self and public, representative persona, and her autobiographical works succeed because her characters and situations, including the character of Maya herself, are embedded in richly realized personal memory at the same time that they embody universal, general types central to the racial and cultural experience of African-Americans.

Beginning with *I Know Why the Caged Bird Sings,* Angelou shapes a drama that in its entirety presents an archetypal model of the African-American woman's cultural position. Especially representative are delineations of the black girl-child's family structure and her quest for identity both within and beyond family. In her first and most famous autobiography, the child Maya moves between silence and voice, death and rebirth, isolation and recognition, innocence and experience. In tracing and resolving these oppositions, Angelou's text specifically reflects two patterns dominating African-American women's experience: Each struggle for emergence is set within crippling restrictions imposed by race and gender in American culture, and each successful escape comes not through isolated individual effort but instead through the support of other black women, mother and teacher figures. Angelou defines the situation of African-American women best in the perception that she reaches at the end of *Caged Bird:* "The Black female is assaulted in her tender years by all those common forces of nature at the same time that she is caught in the tripartite crossfire of masculine prejudice, white illogical hate and Black lack of power" (231). Yet all of the autobiographies set these assaults within a framework of maternal protection and strong women's voices: the voice of Grandmother Henderson, Vivian Baxter, and pervasively, the retrospective, introspective voice of the author herself.

Certain technical features of Angelou's writing sustain the direction and mission of the autobiographies—their portrayal of black woman's experience through the personal odyssey of the first-person female narrator. The voice of the narrator is by turns ironic, pensive, declamatory, yet always honest and also authoritative. The young Maya's insecurity and self-loathing is set before us by a narrator who speaks from the vantage point of a successful journey's completion. In each autobiography Marguerite-Maya struggles with doubts about herself, with lack of knowledge, with disappointments, and with unfamiliar, sometimes threatening experiences. The narrator, however, presents her character's evolution through language that is always assured. The combination of realistic, sometimes lavish, attention to details and lyrical rhythms of folk speech makes us always aware of the artist that the struggling child and young woman becomes. Likewise, the episodic structure of the narrative, offered in often disconnected vignettes, highlights the presence of an omniscient author projecting her finished present on the events of the past and thereby celebrating her mastery of her fate. Angelou frequently enters her own personal life story to generalize its patterns and enlarge its significance. Thus she reinforces through voice and style the idea that the individual black girl-woman's life connects with and comes to embody the rich saga of African-American women's experience of pain and triumph.

In her interview with Angelou, Dolly McPherson tells her that "you use the people who come in and out of your life as mirrors which reflect you, the growing child" (147). Each of Angelou's five autobiographies is organized according to this growing child's meetings with others, who become reflectors through which she learns about herself. Angelou's other major organizational motif is geographical; each autobiography moves through journeys to or away from places that, like the people in the books, are mirrors. *I Know Why the Caged Bird Sings* portrays Maya's early years, age three to thirteen, in Stamps, Arkansas, a town that reflects both the innocence and violence of Maya's young life. The Stamps years are interrupted by a disastrous visit to St. Louis when she is eight, a time when she gets to know her beautiful, independent mother but when she also is raped by the mother's boyfriend. The guilt and terror that Maya feels as a result of the rape, the trial of the boyfriend, and his subsequent murder, drive her into silence. Her family, helpless and impatient before her voluntary muteness, sends her back to Stamps. The small Arkansas town and the imposing, loving grandmother who lives there become twin reference points of precarious refuge. Another woman closely associated with the town, Mrs. Flowers, shows Maya a way to come out of silence through the words and world of literature. Maya can escape from her painful self-image as well as from the threatening presence of Southern bigotry through books that allow her to dream of alternative selves and situations. *I Know Why the Caged Bird Sings* ends with Maya and Bailey's journey to San Francisco. There, reunited with their mother, they are thrust unprepared into adult experiences that the large urban city represents, yet they have in Vivian Baxter a teacher whose scrapping courage provides the lessons they need for this period of growth in their lives, just as Grandmother Henderson provided the kind of nurturing dominance that they needed as children in Stamps.

Gather Together in My Name takes Maya deeper into the roughest type of urban existence in several sprawling California cities and pits her against people who represent for her a kind of dark night of the soul or necessary descent into experience. This second autobiography depicts Maya from age sixteen to nineteen, years during which she grows from acting out of an almost purely animal instinct for survival to choosing consciously, though often unwisely, modes of life that might allow her both freedom and security. Prostitutes, pimps, drug addicts, and con men show her both the depths within herself and the threat to her identity that her culture contains. Returning at the end to her mother, to be reborn into a kind of informed innocence, Maya has again in the maternal figure an answer both to her own potential dark side and the risks of the world. In *Gather Together in My Name* and all of the subsequent narratives, Maya's attachment to her son Clyde (later self-named Guy) defines the ideal of motherhood as life-giving connection to others.

In *Singin' and Swingin' and Gettin' Merry Like Christmas,* Maya's introduction to white people fittingly takes place in the artificial world of music and theater where she has her first sustained contacts with them. Her actions and her life become increasingly "staged" as she learns to meet the demands of an alien world and to navigate its challenges successfully. In this transitional work, covering roughly the years of Angelou's first marriage and her early career as singer and dancer, 1949–55, geography changes as swiftly as the private and public roles that Maya adopts in her quest for self-realization. The setting changes from San Francisco to New York to the cities of the world where Maya tours with *Porgy and Bess.* It is in this book that her "stage name" becomes her "real" name, indicating how the private, unformed child has found a way, in performance, to shape a new identity. At the end of this work, Maya returns to the United States because of her son's illness. One of her challenges at this point is to integrate the connectedness that motherhood demands with the freedom that isolates, individual identity craves. The book closes with a kind of litany to her strengths that Maya lists. It is in some ways her first poem, as well as her first self-assessment, and thus defines how her subsequent art will be shaped: I can hear / I can speak / I have a son / I have a mother / I have a brother / I can dance / I can sing / I can cook / I can read / I can write" (236).

In *The Heart of a Woman,* Angelou writes a book that is overtly a political memoir. The people who dominate the text are public figures who reflect Angelou's own growing sense of her public self: Billie Holiday, Martin Luther King, Malcolm X, James Baldwin, and a host of other well-known politicians, entertainers, and writers. Many experiences in the public realm, notably her role in Genet's *The Blacks,* cause her to explore a social, exterior self in relation to a private, internal one. Her journey to Egypt with husband Make, like Genet's play, forces her to question old assumptions about racial identity that are always also questions about herself. Angelou's last autobiography, *All God's Children Need Traveling Shoes,* continues a theme developed tentatively in *The Heart of a Woman,* the sense of Angelou's personal stake in a shared destiny that takes her, through her experience of Africa, out of the fate and identity that America prescribes for blacks. This last text, however, while organized externally around political events and geographical locations within Africa, shows Angelou developing for the first time a mystically grounded internal presence. She can recognize that she owns a self in some ways freed from place, and from racial or national identifications, through an acceptance—and, thereby, transcendance—of her past. As she prepares to leave Africa she meets a group of tribeswomen who claim her as one of their own, and she responds: "Here in my last days in Africa, descendants of a pillaged past saw their history in my face and heard their ancestors speak through my voice" (206–7). Weeping with these women, Angelou is also announcing her ability to shape history and speak her own essence: Instead of only reflecting others, she holds up a completed present self that mirrors and represents others, both African and American, with whom she shares both past and future. Her inaugural poem concentrates on this idea of shared, unique identity, a lesson learned in the life that the five autobiographies both trace and also create.

SURVEY OF CRITICISM

Individual volumes of Angelou's poetry have been widely reviewed in major publications, but there has been little scholarly attention to her poetic work as a whole. One of the best reviews is Robert Stepto's account of *And Still I Rise,* compared to Audre Lorde's *The Black Unicorn,* which provides perceptive commentary that could apply to other volumes of Angelou's poetry. Stepto has seen the poems as often "woefully thin" but has recognized that "in their celebration of a particularly defined 'phenomenal woman,' " many of her poems point to the autobiographies and contribute to both a "persona and self-portrait" that are important to literary history (315). Carol E. Neubauer has attempted to review all of Angelou's poetry in her essay in *Southern Women Writers: The New Generation* (1990). Neubauer has singled out the works that best sustain Angelou's poetic vision and has given an excellent overview of the direction her verse has taken. Erlene Stetson's collection of black women's poetry from 1746 to 1980, which includes several of Angelou's poems, provides general commentary on traditions of African-American women's voices that are very useful in assessing Angelou's work.

The 1970 publication of *I Know Why the Caged Bird Sings* coincided with a new concentration of interest in African-American studies, women's studies, and autobiography as a genre. Thus, Angelou's first autobiography very quickly generated sustained interest from many directions. Early studies such as Stephen Butterfield's placed *Caged Bird* in a tradition of black autobiography that began with the slave narratives. George Kent provided one of the first and best analyses of the work's uniqueness: "*I Know Why* creates a unique place within black autobiographical tradition," he claimed, "by its special stance toward the self, the community, and the universe, and by a form exploiting the full measure of imagination necessary to acknowledge both beauty and absurdity" (166). Liliane Arensberg in her early essay "Death as Metaphor of Self" in *Caged Bird* showed brilliantly Angelou's ability to give thematic coherence to her work by sustaining a central metaphor.

The studies of *Caged Bird* have increasingly stressed its place as a definitive exploration of African-American women's voices, and most (such as Mary Burgher's, Lucinda MacKethan's, and most recently Joanne Braxton's) have remarked especially on the tradition of black motherhood and daughterhood that the book not only reflects but has helped to shape and expand. More recently, Frances Smith Foster has taken some exception to the emphasis on women's traditions that is so often used to explain design of *Caged Bird*. She has put more emphasis on the daughter's break with motherly models and the role Maya's father played in forming her independent spirit. Françoise Lionnet's study has also read *Caged Bird* in a new light, placing it in a tradition of what Lionnet has called *metissage* (most closely translated "braiding"), which emphasizes the book's interactions within different cultural, religious, and, most important, linguistic frameworks. In her study of the shifting, multicultural naming practices and the "conning" element in the storytelling that mark all of Angelou's autobiographies, Lionnet has effectively argued for Angelou's alienation from, as well as her successful survival in, the dominant discourse of American culture.

I Know Why the Caged Bird Sings has continued to receive the greatest share of critical attention, but several studies of the late 1980s and early 1990s have

surveyed all five of the autobiographies. James Robert Saunders, Carol Neubauer, and Selwyn Cudjoe have published detailed analyses of all of the autobiographical works, and in 1990 Angelou's close friend Dolly McPherson
completed the first book-length study of them. McPherson has offered an interpretive structure for each autobiography and has assessed Angelou's use of both
specifically black and universal themes. Among the latter, McPherson has said,
are "death and rebirth, movement from innocence to experience, idealism versus
cynicism, the search for selfhood, and the importance of determining one's own
self-definitions" (129). Joanne Braxton's use of Angelou's works in her book
Black Women Writing Autobiography (1989) indicates Angelou's growing importance to scholars. Braxton has chosen *I Know Why the Caged Bird Sings* as
"representative of the autobiography of modern black women" (13). Angelou's
archetypal characters and situations, the pattern of maturation that she has traced,
the natural imagery, and the rhythmic language of her autobiographical work
have made her not only the "phenomenal woman" that so much of her work
celebrates, but also a phenomenally successful American writer whose range
and energy show no signs of diminishing.

BIBLIOGRAPHY

Works by Maya Angelou

Poetry

Just Give Me a Cool Drink of Water 'Fore I Diiie. New York: Random House, 1971.
Oh Pray My Wings Are Gonna Fit Me Well. New York: Random House, 1975.
And Still I Rise. New York: Random House, 1978.
Poems. New York: Bantam, 1981.
Shaker, Why Don't You Sing? New York: Random House, 1983.
Now Sheba Sings the Song. New York: Dutton/Dial, 1987.
I Shall Not Be Moved. New York: Random House, 1990.

Autobiographies

I Know Why the Caged Bird Sings. New York: Random House, 1970.
Gather Together in My Name. New York: Random House, 1974.
Singin' and Swingin' and Gettin' Merry Like Christmas. New York: Random House,
      1976.
The Heart of a Woman. New York: Random House, 1981.
All God's Children Need Traveling Shoes. New York: Random House, 1986.

Interviews with Maya Angelou

Elliot, Jeffrey M., ed. *Conversations with Maya Angelou.* Jackson: University Press of
      Mississippi, 1989.
McPherson, Dolly A. "An Addendum: A Conversation with Maya Angelou." In *Order*

Out of Chaos: The Autobiographical Works of Maya Angelou, 131–62. New
  York: Peter Lang, 1990.
Manegold, Catherine. "A Wordsmith at Her Inaugural Anvil." *New York Times* (January
  20, 1993): C1, C8.
Neubauer, Carol E. "An Interview with Maya Angelou." *Massachusetts Review* 28, no.2
  (1987): 286–92.

Studies of Maya Angelou

Arensberg, Liliane K. "Death as Metaphor of Self in *I Know Why the Caged Bird Sings.*"
  CLA Journal 20 (1976): 273–91.
Braxton, Joanne M. *Black Women Writing Autobiography: A Tradition within a Tradi-
  tion.* Philadelphia: Temple University Press, 1989.
Burgher, Mary. "Images of Self and Race in the Autobiographies of Black Women."
  In *Sturdy Black Bridges: Visions of Black Women in Literature,* edited by Ro-
  seann P. Bell, 108–22. Garden City, N.Y.: Doubleday Anchor, 1979.
Butterfield, Stephen. *Black Autobiography in America.* Amherst: University of Massa-
  chusetts Press, 1974.
Cudjoe, Selwyn R. "Maya Angelou: The Autobiographical Statement Updated." In
  Reading Black, Reading Feminist: A Critical Anthology, edited by Henry Louis
  Gates, Jr., 272–306. New York: Penguin, 1990.
Dandridge, Rita B., ed. *Black Women's Blues: A Literary Anthology, 1934–1988.* New
  York: Hall, 1992.
Foster, Frances Smith. "Parents and Children in Autobiography by Southern Afro-
  American Writers." In *Home Ground: Southern Autobiography,* edited by J. Bill
  Berry, 98–109. Columbia: University of Missouri Press, 1991.
Froula, Christine. "The Daughter's Seduction: Sexual Violence and Literary History."
  Signs 11 (1986): 621–44.
Kent, George E. "Maya Angelou's *I Know Why the Caged Bird Sings* and Black Au-
  tobiographical Tradition." *Kansas Quarterly* 7 (1975): 72–78. Reprinted in *Af-
  rican American Autobiography,* edited by William L. Andrews, 162–70.
  Englewood Cliffs, N.J.: Prentice-Hall, 1993.
Lionnet, Françoise. *Autobiographical Voices: Race, Gender, Self-Portraiture.* Ithaca:
  Cornell University Press, 1989.
MacKethan, Lucinda. "Mother Wit: Humor in Afro-American Women's Autobiogra-
  phy." *Studies in American Humor* 4 (1989): 51–61.
McPherson, Dolly A. *Order Out of Chaos: The Autobiographical Works of Maya An-
  gelou.* New York: Peter Lang, 1990.
Neubauer, Carol E. "Maya Angelou: Self and a Song of Freedom in the Southern Tra-
  dition." In *Southern Women Writers: The New Generation,* edited by Tonette
  Bond Inge, 114–42. Tuscaloosa: University of Alabama Press, 1990.
Olney, James. "Autobiography and the Cultural Moment: A Thematic Historical and
  Bibliographical Introduction." In *Autobiography: Essays Theoretical and Criti-
  cal,* edited by James Olney, 3–27. Princeton: Princeton University Press, 1980.
Ramsey, Priscilla R. "Transcendence: The Poetry of Maya Angelou." *A Current Bibli-
  ography on African Affairs* 17 (1984–85): 139–53.
Saunders, James Robert. "Breaking Out of the Cage: The Autobiographical Writings of
  Maya Angelou." *The Hollins Critic* 28 (1991): 1–10.

Schmidt, Jan. "The Other: A Study of the Persona in Several Contemporary Women's Autobiographies." *CEA Critic* 43 (1980): 24–31.

Shuker, Nancy. *Maya Angelou.* Englewood Cliffs, N.J.: Silver Burdett Press, 1990.

Smith, Sidonie. "Song of the Caged Bird: Maya Angelou's Quest After Self-Acceptance." *Southern Humanities Review* 7 (1973): 365–75.

Stepto, Robert. "The Phenomenal Woman and the Severed Daughter." *Parnassus* 8 (1980): 312–20.

Stetson, Erlene, ed. *Black Sister: Poetry by Black American Women, 1746–1980.* Bloomington: Indiana University Press, 1981.

Tate, Claudia, ed. *Black Women Writers at Work.* New York: Continuum, 1983.

GEORGE S. LENSING

James Applewhite
(1935–   )

James Applewhite has steadily pieced together in verse a world of family and experience surrounding the small-town tobacco community in North Carolina where he was born and reared. A mythic poetry tied to the rhythms of the earth's seasons, the nurturing of the crops, and the legends of family, Applewhite's work probes a life from which he has separated himself as a professor of English but to which he clings as the major resource of his art. A poet of scant critical attention, he came to his maturity through the decade of the 1980s. His future work seems poised between the Wilson County of his youth and the Eno River of his present life near Duke University where he teaches.

BIOGRAPHY

"When I was growing up my father ran a station and a garage in a small town of a thousand people in the eastern part of North Carolina, a town called Stantonsburg. My grandfather had a tobacco farm, which is still in the family, though at the time my father wasn't tending to that. He ran the Esso station and I worked there, too. It seems to be getting into my poems still'' (Interview with William Walsh, 1989, 67). In this small town of James Applewhite's birth (August 8, 1935) and upbringing, Applewhite was surrounded by the elements that he would later make into his poetry: strong-willed parents and a brother two years younger, religion (an uncle was a Methodist minister), tobacco farming, and, not least of all, stories.

When Applewhite was 6 years old he was diagnosed with rheumatic fever. "Forget about school," his physician said. "You may never get well." The disease frightened the future poet's family, forced him to sit out of school for a year, but also led to a self-imposed regimen of reading. An uncle who was a school teacher read him newspaper accounts of the African and Pacific campaigns of World War II. The uncle also adapted the Homeric epics into favored tales of danger and adventure. Applewhite returned to his class in the local public school, played football at Stantonsburg High School, from which he graduated in 1954 in a class of seventeen students. He also wrote a play that was produced in the school and, on occasion, was permitted to stand before his classmates and invent spontaneous fables (called "lies" by his classmates) in which his classmates were included in the action. His summers were spent working around his father's Esso station.

Choosing his father's alma mater, Applewhite enrolled at Duke University. His poetic bent pulled him toward literature and creative-writing courses, but equally attractive was the lure of philosophy, physics, and the other sciences. Among his classmates at Duke were Reynolds Price, two years older; Anne Tyler, six years younger, having enrolled at Duke at the age of sixteen; and Fred Chappell, who entered Duke the same year that Applewhite did. An undergraduate poem called "I Met Her at a Literary Party" was written about the attractive Ms. Tyler: "Her work was discussed, and I spoke in praise, / because of its grace and her loveliness. / Did not her naked face show deeply, / As if a knife had opened being?" (*Under Twenty-Five,* ed. William Blackburn, 73). William Blackburn was the teacher around whom these astonishingly gifted young writers gathered. "Blackburn," says Applewhite, "was important for my being able to see myself as a writer, and he became to me an appropriate role model for a male in the South." Blackburn loved poems for their own sake and conveyed as much to his students. He befriended undergraduates, inviting them to his apartment for cocktails or dinner. Applewhite took several courses from Blackburn. In 1956, at the age of 20, Applewhite married Janis Forrest, the daughter of the light-and-water-superintendent back home in Stantonsburg. After his graduation in 1958, Applewhite stayed on at Duke to take his M.A. in English, writing a thesis on Faulkner's *The Sound and the Fury.*

Applewhite became an instructor at Woman's College (today the University of North Carolina at Greensboro) for three years. Here he found himself in the company of another small group of distinguished writers, Robert Watson and Randall Jarrell. Jarrell in particular offered a "paradigm" of the public poet. Applewhite absorbed it all, attending Jarrell's lectures and showing him his own poems. Successful as a teacher, Applewhite won a Danforth Teaching Study Grant in 1963 and returned to Duke to earn his Ph.D.

Beginning with Poe and Faulkner, and later Emily Brontë and Hardy, Applewhite became interested in the way writers created associations with local settings and landscapes. That interest led him inevitably to the English Romantic poets and to Wordsworth in particular, on whom he would write his dissertation. Interest in landscape poetry would be long standing: In 1985, some sixteen years after completing the dissertation, Applewhite published a scholarly book of criticism, *Seas and Inland Journeys: Landscape and Consciousness from Wordsworth to Roethke.*

Returning to Woman's College in Greensboro before completing the Ph.D.,

Applewhite became an assistant professor and remained there four years. He completed his Ph.D. in 1969. His poems began appearing in *Shenandoah, Virginia Quarterly Review, Southern Poetry Review,* and *Harper's Magazine.* The poet was further encouraged when seven of his poems were selected by Paul Carroll for inclusion in *The Young American Poets* in 1968.

In 1971 Applewhite joined the faculty at Duke, where he has remained for more than twenty years. He is the father of a daughter and two sons; perhaps not surprisingly Lisa is a graduate of the University of North Carolina at Greensboro, and sons James and Jeff are graduates of Duke. In addition to being a poet and critic, Applewhite has also been a teacher of the Romantic and Modern poets, creative writing, and the standard survey courses. "I love students," he once observed, "and students have been one of the most important sources of feedback for me because our culture is not interested in poetry. . . . Randall Jarrell used to say, 'God has taken away my readers and given me students.' In some sense your students are a substitute for a wider audience" (unpublished interview). As a critic, Applewhite has found a natural cross-fertilization for the writing of poems. "Southern Voices," a poem from *Ode to the Chinaberry Tree* (1986), for example, was written while he was in the middle of writing an essay called "The Poet at Home in the South," and Wordsworth, of course, has been a major influence upon his work.

Applewhite's first volume, *Statues of the Grass,* did not appear until 1975, when he was forty. But six other volumes have appeared since, earning him a steadily widening audience and such awards as the National Endowment for the Arts Award (1970), the Borestone Mountain Poetry Award (1972, 1975), the Associated Writing Programs Contemporary Poetry Prize (1979), and the International Poetry Review Prize (1982). Applewhite has maintained his ties to the eastern part of North Carolina from which he springs and where relatives and friends still reside. The memories of that childhood world, in fact, comprise the principal source of his work. Applewhite's life has not been sensational or outwardly dramatic. Stability of family and work, including his hobbies of jogging and carpentry, define the borders of his life. "Even now," writes his wife, "he maintains his love of real objects and loves to go to hardware stores and farmers' supply stores. His love of tools is accompanied by a love of building real things" (unpublished interview). Such a life has been, like his poetry, a deliberate creation. He writes: "A lot of writers are good writers and despicable human beings. That for me won't work. If you can't have human virtues in your life that are then expressed in your life writing, I don't see what's the good. Don't give me any writers who are monsters. We've had too many of them."

MAJOR THEMES

When James Applewhite left Stantonsburg, North Carolina, in 1954 to enroll as a freshman at Duke University, he brought to an end his permanent residence in that small town of a thousand people in the tobacco heartland of the eastern part of the state. Though he had been born and had grown up in Wilson County, the freshman's journey to Durham might have been one of a thousand miles instead of merely ninety: In one sense he would never return. Although Applewhite would eventually take a Ph.D. at Duke and go on to teach at Woman's College and Duke, when he began writing his mature poetry, his imagination returned to that region of his youth where it would take up permanent residence. The powerful ties of parents, grandparents, and more distant ancestors; the ethos of Methodism and Calvinist Protestantism; the rhythms of the seasons nurturing the tobacco crop to harvest; the land of the chinaberry tree, broom sedge, pines, and oak beside the banks of the Neuse and Pamlico rivers and the Contentnea Creek; the spring time of jonquil, forsythia, spirea, and sweet william; the time of picnics and pig roasts, childhood games and part-time jobs; the world of Mary Alice Philips, L. G. Newcomb, Dee Grimes, Teaky, and Alice; the childhood memories of World War II; and the hands who work around the grease rack at his father's Esso station—this is the world of James Applewhite's poetry, seemingly inexhaustible to the poet-academician. He therefore has written as a self-conscious Southerner, independent of the fashionable trends of postmodern American poetry. A middle-aged man, he has carved out his personal world of wife and family, teaching, writing, jogging, and carpentry—a world that his poetry alludes to in passing. But the range and focus of his imagination have clung to Stantonsburg and Wilson County. "Again and again these meditations / Come, these returns. And nothing is ever clearer," he says in "Among the Old Stones" (*Lessons in Soaring,* 7).

Like many Southern writers, Applewhite has created a world out of a small acreage of memory and nostalgia. Also like other Southern writers of both fiction and poetry, his is an art whose ultimate effect is cumulative, a work that gathers strength and resonance as one reads from poem to poem and volume to volume. In his foreword to Applewhite's *Following Gravity,* the poet Donald Justice has remarked that "there is a drift or pull in Applewhite's poetry toward myth and legend, a mark of high ambition which his tact and reserve normally keep from view," (vii). With each successive volume, that "tact and reserve" have been set aside as the grounding of his poetry in myth has become stronger.

In his visit with V. S. Naipaul, reported in Naipaul's *A Turn in the South* (1989), Applewhite has spoken of the powerful effects of his return visits as a younger man to the region of his youth: "I do remember occasions of visiting back during my early years of college and once again experiencing what I have now almost forgotten—and that is a sensation of being so utterly at home in, and a part of, a place, that one feels somehow coextensive with the place" (303). At the same time, he has been aware of his separation: "I think I'm always conscious of the fact that I'm not truly of the world I've been showing you. I've not worked in tobacco" (303). It is from that vantage of being both "coextensive" with the geography of his past and, at the same time, separated from it that the first premises of Applewhite's poetry derive. In an early poem, "Revisitings," he has described a visit to his childhood surroundings, encountering among the birds, the magnolias, and mimosas, a second self, "a different self like a nobler brother":

> A wind from where shadows are generating rain tells me
> This day stands always in pools behind doors I have closed.
> How have I closed away my best self and all of his memories?
> Many of the tongues of grass are speaking to the sun,
> Obscured for a moment, in a language of vapor from underneath.
> (*Statues of the Grass,* 33)

The poems of Applewhite become mythically informed with the rhythms and seasons of the earth itself. The role of the elements is clear even from titles: "Water," "Earth Lust," "The Lumber Mill Fire," and "Following Gravity." Similarly, the seasons are measured out: "Some Words for Fall," "Snow over Soil," "Jonquils," "Summer Revival." More locally, but set within a larger agrarian myth, the poems of Applewhite and the lives of those who people them are ordered to the planting, growing, and harvesting of the tobacco crop.

Applewhite's nostalgia for his past and the transformations to be attained through that reimagining are left implicit in description itself. It is as if by re-creating the world of his boyhood with as much precision and detail as his poetic gifts will allow, the powerful and continuing efficacy of that world will become apparent by a gathering accretion. "For me there has never been any question of a need for, and a response to, the land and its culture. But there *has* been a question as to whether I could move sufficiently into a conscious perspective so as to see the local landscape with objectifying clarity" (*The Southern Review and Modern Literature,* 97). In these remarks from his essay "The Poet at Home in the South," Applewhite has described the intensity and irrationality of the Southern experience that make for vitality but also a hazard: "Perhaps that is why even major Southern writers in the past have practiced an art of musical, emotional, rhetorical intensity (from Poe to Faulkner to James Dickey) that is unable to state its premises and propositions as clearly as writing of other regions" (97). Clarity and accuracy of presentation have been set in the forefront among Applewhite's goals as a poet. Like Wallace Stevens, Applewhite has reminded himself that "imagination expands in gratitude to fact."

No one, however, would call Applewhite a minimalist, an imagist, or a disinterested reporter of his past. He is not immune to rhapsodic exclamation, however intent he may be upon a mode of realism. "Perhaps we Southerners, Oedipal intensities extended by honeysuckle to the landscape, are simply more in love with our origins than others" (102). Applewhite's own Romanticism is not just of a Southern tradition from Poe to Faulkner to Dickey. It is really part of a larger American penchant for a transcendental vision of reality, to see behind the American setting toward spirit and immortality. In this sense, Applewhite belongs to a tradition from Emerson and Whitman through Roethke to Dickey. Applewhite has sounded the Whitmanian proclamation in "The Scene":

"I wrestle the American Actual: / Legs, oysters. Huge signboards / From close up at night" (*Foreseeing the Journey*, 37). And like the meditations of Roethke, he is one with subhuman life: "Frightened at my breathing's violence, / I brooded over ants from the fence. / I felt myself continuous with everything" (*Ode to the Chinaberry Tree*, 36). There is more than a trace of Dickey in "The Presences" ("Again they come into being. / Long bark antlers / This granite forehead—thorns / The crown of seeing" [*Ode to the Chinaberry Tree*, 42].) Randall Jarrell, Applewhite's colleague and friend during his years teaching at Woman's College in Greensboro, North Carolina, perhaps offered instruction in the poetic value of childhood memories through Jarrell's "The Lost World," though Roethke is also an exemplar in this.

Finally, while Applewhite's progenitors can be linked to Southern writers and to a certain tradition of American writers, one further step outward would acknowledge his connection to the larger range of English Romanticism of the early nineteenth century and to Romanticism generally. For many years Applewhite has taught the English Romantics in various university classrooms, and in 1985 he published his treatise on the subject, *Seas and Inland Journeys, Landscape and Consciousness from Wordsworth to Roethke*. It is not surprising that what has interested Applewhite-the-critic connects with Applewhite-the-poet—namely, the alienation of the solitary Romantic figure who yearns for and attains through nature a Wordsworthian marriage between landscape and language: "A central tension of Romantic poetry derives from the interaction between the rational, subjective narrator caught in time and a fertile, sustaining, threatening, nontemporal, nonrational source-principle the narrator experiences as inspiration" (*Seas and Inland Journeys*, 26).

Applewhite's voice, however, is distinctively his own, whatever its influences. His poems typically involve a journey to a specifically defined place, often one situated in the setting of his earlier life and a stimulus to the store of memory that reanimates that earlier life. The speaker is often accompanied by another— a "we"—though the companion may be unidentified. The poet addresses us familiarly, speaking to us as to Naipaul, one who might accompany the poet on a trip to eastern North Carolina where, with the sensuous aid of actual places and people, he can make us see. Though Applewhite has said that "I sense on the part of the younger Southern poets a new capability for plain statement" ("The Poet at Home in the South," 102), plain statement is not exactly his own method. The crowd of descriptive detail imposes an inevitable kind of formality, as do the elaborations of frequent metaphor. The epigraph to one poem cites Keats: "A Man's life of any worth is a continual allegory," and the collected works of Applewhite constitute a kind of formal allegory of an idealized personal life that is past but infused by memory. Admiration has been Applewhite's noblest sentiment, and instead of plainness a necessary elevation of voice has given it utterance. On the dust jacket of *Statues of the Grass*, Stanley Kunitz noted of Applewhite, "His imagination has its roots in the tradition of the South, but his style has a special kind of modern elegance."

The recollected idealized life, however, is not totally Applewhite's own. Its fullest incarnation is seen in Applewhite's heroes, of which there are more than a few. The most important are his parents, especially his father, and his grandparents, especially his grandfather. These two generations preceding him are enriched and enobled in the poet's mind because of their steady attachment to place. For Applewhite, the worst human fate would be deprivation of access to one's origins, and it is this that troubles him in "To Alexander Solzhenitsyn, in Exile": "They have told you that your land is not your land" (*Statues of the Grass,* 27).

While many of the poems of Applewhite pursue a transcendental and noumenal reality, others, following gravity, center in the phenomenal world and the simple and almost ahistorical lives that inhabit it. The poet's connections with the milieu of Stantonsburg continue, as he returns to visit family and friends, even as it is forever associated with youth and in memory. That world constitutes what Applewhite in an interview calls a "social environment" to which he has returned as a man and a poet, a world of "shared, interpersonal values, a social placenta replacing the biological one" (Interview with George Lensing, July 11, 1990). His poems "Good as Dad" and "Back Then" remind us of the imperfections of that environment, but such realism has been subordinated to a more romantic mythos of land, family, work, continuity—the sum of which informs lives of unpretentious grandeur.

Heroes are especially appropriate from the perspective of childhood and adolescence. As Applewhite has said in a brief blurb for the jacket of his first volume: "From earliest memories a search goes outward in spreading rings for heroes through which the poet can identify his own aspirations, with which he compares, alters, completes, or forgives those figures who haunt his private imagination." And in a comment on his 1989 volume, following the first by fourteen years, he has defined the volume's "central theme" as "the struggle to come to terms with male role models widely diffused in the South, associated with command, toughness, war, tradition, religion, but also with love, with the place one has inherited" (*The News and Observer,* August 20, 1989, 5D).

In one sense, the life of Applewhite's grandfather was ordinary: a tobacco farmer, a devout Methodist, husband, and father: "He dug gray marl near the swamp, set out / Tobacco by hand, broke the suckers and tops / Before they flowered" (*Ode to the Chinaberry Tree,* 45). Here, in "For W. H. Applewhite," the grandson plays elegist to the grandfather's quiet life; at the same time, he is remade as extraordinary patriarch: "William Henry, you were the one true / Father, the Bible-carrying walker-on-water / Of a time that escapes us" (48). Applewhite has continued to write and rewrite the elegy to his grandfather: "My Grandfather's Funeral" in *Statues of the Grass* and "Grandfather Noah" in *Foreseeing the Journey.* To Naipaul, Applewhite remembered both his grandfather and father: "There was this dichotomy in my own life between my father and my grandfather. My grandfather was born in that Civil War–era farmhouse, and he was always associated in my mind with the agrarian economy. My father ran a service station and believed in progress and sold electrical appliances for a number of years. He was always in a hurry. My grandfather was never hurried'' (277). In the poems, however, the father, James William Applewhite, is not contrasted in this way with the grandfather. Instead of being remembered selling electrical appliances, the father is remembered in several poems as mowing the grass in the evening or piloting a boat in a flood. One crucial event from Applewhite's boyhood has been the rescue of the son by the father following the overturning of a boat. The poem has undergone three writings, beginning with a version published in *The Brown Bag* in 1970. Here it made up the first part of a longer poem entitled ''Steps from the Stream.'' The poem was cut by several lines and revised as ''The Capsized Boat'' in *Statues of the Grass,* his first volume; he once again rewrote and expanded it two volumes later. A more recent poem, ''A Conversation,'' addresses the father in old age, becoming a kind of proleptic elegy. Like the grandfather, he is made into the heroic: ''The unconscious still sees your face glowing like iron. / For the inalterable child of sleep, you are earth born, / One of the Titans'' (*Lessons in Soaring,* 44). The apotheosis of Applewhite's progenitors is based upon simple lives lived steadily, hard lives endured, earthbound lives tied harmoniously to a small region from which one both receives and gives.

William Blackburn, Applewhite's writing teacher at Duke, has been given a similar commemoration, but for different reasons. In ''William Blackburn, Riding Westward,'' it is the life given to the text rather to the land that is honored, a passion for Shakespeare, Conrad, and Vaughan, a life made into Lear's own in his dying. Another tribute, to the North Carolina writer Fred Chappell and the memory of Chappell and Applewhite's days as students at Duke, is offered in ''Attending Chappell.''

The association with Blackburn and Chappell reminds us that Applewhite's own adult life has been as teacher, poet, and literary critic—radically removed from the family and land of his childhood. In the poem to his father, ''A Conversation,'' he speaks to the old man on the telephone and describes himself as ''a pseudo-Yankee who has left the homeland, / I scarcely deserve a reply'' (*Lessons in Soaring,* 42). His removal from the world of Wilson County has not left the poet innocent of regret but with an inescapable sense of separation and dislocation. ''How have I closed away my best self and all of his memories?'' (33), he asks in his first volume, and the first word of the question seems to read as much a ''why'' as a ''how.''

At the same time, as a writer Applewhite seems to have recognized the necessity of separation. Even at the age of 6, he recounted to Naipaul, that isolation had already begun: ''I was put to bed when I was six with what was then said to be rheumatic fever. My mother read me the whole of *Huckleberry Finn.* I stayed in bed for a year. I was protected more than my fellow students for a few years. It set me apart. Something like that always happens to the person who is going to be a writer'' (*A Turn in the South,* 302–303). Through such men as Blackburn and Chappell, Applewhite later found his way to his vocation as a poet. Even in middle age, the poet, Applewhite has suggested, needs distance from the intensities of his Southern experience, a distancing ideally suited to the university: "The campuses (and all they represent) of schools . . . are of crucial importance in allowing the poet to be at home in the South. They offer whatever hope there is of seeing, still, past the Kudzu, used-car lots, fundamentalist congregations, and slumber of Sunday-noon dinners, that rare smoke of the soul's fire rising beyond the pines'' ("The Poet at Home in the South,'' 106). At his home under construction near Duke, the poet has sought his own kind of reconnection with the land, imposing some part of the idealized and mythic world of his youth:

> These fields toward the river are outside time.
> The horse has been grazing forever.
> That black mass of pines
> Is such as must always exist.
> (*Following Gravity,* 14)

Applewhite's *River Writing, An Eno Journal* (1988) suggests that the poet has increasingly found his own world along the Eno River of Durham County, near to where he lives and teaches. The sequence of poems chronicle the progress of the seasons unfolding along the riverbank familiar to the poet's jogging routes. It is Applewhite's most successful collection of pure lyricism. The poems create a world as natural as Audubon's, as solitary as Thoreau's, and as local as Frost's:

> The interlinked spillage
> Of phonemes, sliding, signifying
> Are made to name by things
> Like underwater dams. Rock ledge
> Roils a print, the ripple-shine of
> Current like vowel/consonant.
> I palm the oak's bark.
> Noun *tree.* Governs verb *to be.*
> Two rivers are flowing this poem.
> (*River Writing,* 13)

This collection was followed a year later with *Lessons in Soaring,* a poetry restored to the more distant and familiar county of childhood and recollection. *A History of the River* (1993) extends the poet's commitment to his original themes and settings.

Like many of the agrarian American poets of the twentieth-century, Applewhite is also aware that the very world so cherished in memory is no longer intact to be reclaimed. Tobacco, for example, has become an increasingly ostracized commodity. To Naipaul, Applewhite acknowledged as much: "I don't think the South absolutely needs to produce this poisonous substance any more." He then went on to associate the plant with a fallen world: "I think of tobacco as an Old Testamentish aspect of a past way of life, a kind of traditional, conservative, fallen world, a world marked by original sin, of which tobacco was a kind of symbol" (*A Turn in the South,* 275). In the poem "A Leaf of Tobacco" he has defined with scrupulous reverence, the shape, texture, and odor of the plant, but has concluded more ambiguously: "We die for this leaf" (*Ode to the Chinaberry Tree,* 40).

Applewhite's faith in his past and in his power to evoke it have spared his poetry from any sense of final defeat. There is something of the Emersonian transcendental optimism that he cannot shake off. In an early poem, "Poets, Now," he scorns his contemporary poets who are "closing down language" and partaking of the "great disgust" (*Statues of the Grass,* 11). In another, "Looking for a Home in the South," he pits contemporary despair against "this particular spring day," reminding us that the latter offers "unalloyed sunshine this land would learn to give us" (*Statues of the Grass,* 20). Applewhite is not unaware of the threats, seductions and falsities of modern life, nor is his optimism naive or delusory. There is a sense in which his poetry and the solitary voice who speaks it stand adamantly against a larger and harsher world of self-absorption. The lives around Stantonsburg are the principal spring from which he continues to draw that moral nourishment. Like the Southern Agrarians of the 1930s—Warren, Tate, Ransom, and so forth—Applewhite has calmly affirmed another, simpler life, one from which he is himself removed and one which itself seems in the process of change, but one which art can rescue and preserve.

SURVEY OF CRITICISM

The criticism of Applewhite remains in its preliminary stages. There are yet no book-length assessments, and even extended essays are scarce. This is partly the result of Applewhite's having only one volume published in the 1970s, followed by five in the 1980s with the most recent in 1993. Though one might say that Applewhite is now in midcareer, he seems, in another sense, to have come to his full maturity as a poet relatively late and to have arrived at the full exercise of that talent recently.

When his first volume, *Statues of the Grass,* appeared in 1975, Barbara Fialkowski (1976) shrewdly noted in *Shenandoah* "quests after transcendence" in the poems. Such quests, however, were earthbound: "Movement and detail are the stuff of Applewhite's poetry" (107), and the human figures in the poems are "of the Church of the Earth" (107). Almost anticipating the title of his next volume, *Following Gravity,* she cited three lines from a poem called "Images, Burning," adding, "The image is somewhat Jamesian; the parachute never floating out into the atmosphere while drawn to the earth itself."

As the rural, Southern world of Applewhite's childhood took on greater detail and depth in subsequent volumes, his reviewers commended him for the capaciousness and authenticity of that defined world. R. T. Smith (1981) noted, for example, that in *Following Gravity* Applewhite "seems more at home . . . when he's looking back at the men whose power or suffering he admired when he was young" (374). Richard Tillinghast agreed. The poems refuse to probe "glimpses beyond the beyond," preferring to return us "to our own world" (296). James Finn Cotter (1983–84) admired the poet's strong sense of identity: "Reading him we know who he is, where he comes from, what he wants" (713).

The empirical solidity and realism of Applewhite's world, other and later reviewers have noted, make up only a part of the poet's achievement. They have noticed that Applewhite's poems have tended to resonate with each other, building toward a whole that seems greater than its parts. An anonymous reviewer for the *Virginia Quarterly Review* (1983) has singled out the role of memory in the poems: "Reading the book forces us to live out his theory—everything we have seen and done impinges on what we see and do, and by the end of the book [*Foreseeing the Journey*] the first poems are still suggesting ways to read the last poems. It is instructive to read the book at one sitting, a demand most books cannot make" (133).

When *Ode to a Chinaberry Tree* appeared in 1986, another reviewer from the *Virginia Quarterly Review* (1987) saw evidence of modernism in the "density and fierce precision" of the poems' imagery, concluding that Applewhite was "one of the most individual and interesting of contemporary American poets" (25). Jerome Mazzaro found the influence of Wordsworth almost too evident in a few poems, but added: "His places are individual and memorable, and the volume manages a voice, pace, and rhythm distinct enough that Apple white makes necessary the very ordinariness of the past that he summons up, even as it is disappearing" (155).

Few of the reviewers have noted that change of setting in *River Writing: An Eno Journal,* where Applewhite moved the locus of his poetry from the rural North Carolina tobacco country of his youth to the poet's own immediate world along the Eno River near Duke University. The Southern world of family, religion, and farming is transformed into a private lyricism of a place that makes up the poet's daily path through a seasonal year. The forty-four poems of the sequence constitute, in Harold Blooms's estimation, "one of the few authentic and strong American poetic sequences of his generation" (Dust jacket, *River Writing,* 1989). The poet Alfred Corn noted similarities with the early work of Applewhite's fellow North Carolinian, A. R. Ammons, but he liked best the volume's steady tone of calm observation: "A consistent value in this book is the tone of—I don't know a better word for it—decency maintained throughout, so much preferable to the rant, whining, or smugness contemporary poetry is afflicted with" (231).

The publication of Naipaul's *A Turn in the South* in 1989 has helped significantly to raise Applewhite's national profile. The Indian writer's visits throughout the South described in the travelogue conclude in Applewhite's North Carolina—taking in both the world of the Eno River and of Wilson County, though Naipaul is clearly more interested in the latter. He has quoted extensively from conversations with Applewhite and has cited many poems.

The future work of Applewhite will likely continue to mine the lode that makes up the Wilson County world of earlier memory, parents, and grandparents; *Lessons in Soaring* (1989) and *A History of the River* (1993) demonstrate that world's abiding capaciousness and appeal.

BIBLIOGRAPHY

Works by James Applewhite

"Driving Home." In *Voices from Earth,* edited by James Applewhite, 24–29. Greensboro, N.C., 1971.
Statues of the Grass. Athens: University of Georgia Press, 1975.
Following Gravity. Charlottesville: University Press of Virginia, 1980.
Foreseeing the Journey. Baton Rouge: Louisiana State University Press, 1983.
Seas and Inland Journeys: Landscape and Consciousness from Wordsworth to Roethke. Athens: University of Georgia Press, 1985.
Ode to the Chinaberry Tree and Other Poems. Baton Rouge: Louisiana State University Press, 1986.
River Writing: An Eno Journal. Princeton: Princeton University Press, 1988.
"The Poet at Home in the South." In *The Southern Review and Modern Literature, 1935–1985,* ed. by Lewis P. Simpson, James Olney, and Jo Gulledge, 97–106. Baton Rouge: Louisiana State University Press, 1988.
Lessons in Soaring. Baton Rouge: Louisiana State University Press, 1989.
A History of the River. Baton Rouge: Louisiana State University Press, 1993.

Interviews with James Applewhite

Walsh, William. "James Applewhite," *Verse* 6 (Winter 1989): 66–75.

Studies of James Applewhite

Corn, Alfred. "Hindsight, Insight, Foresight." *Poetry* 153 (January 1989): 229–31.
Cotter, James Finn. "Poetry Encounters." *Hudson Review* 36 (Winter 1983–84): 711–23.
Fialkowski, Barbara. "Fields of Vision." *Shenandoah* 27 (Spring 1976): 104–11.
Mazzaro, Jerome. "Varieties of Poetic Experience." *Sewanee Review* 96 (Winter 1988): 149–58.
Naipaul, V. S. *A Turn in the South.* New York: Knopf, 1989.
"Notes on Current Books." *Virginia Quarterly Review* 59 (Autumn 1983): 133.
"Notes on Current Books." *Virginia Quarterly Review* 63 (Winter 1987): 25.

Ramsey, Paul. "The Garden of Art: What Is It to Sow?" *Chattahoochee Review* 7 (Fall
    1990): 58–63.
Smith, R. T. Untitled. *Southern Humanities Review* 15 (Fall 1981): 371–74.
Tillinghast, Richard. "Scattered Nebulae." *Sewanee Review* 90 (Spring 1982): 291–300.

HARRIETTE CUTTINO BUCHANAN

Daphne Athas
(1923–   )

An underrated writer, Daphne Athas sings in a unique voice the song of the soul in quest of the experiences that define the self. The uniqueness of her voice derives from the combination of qualities she herself has defined in Southern literature—the paradoxical juxtaposition of the plebian and the aristocratic—along with a play in language that is her own. Although her settings (with a couple of notable exceptions) are not Southern, Athas's play on the music of language reflects her sense of the music in Southern speech.

Athas's narrow reputation is probably due to a combination of the infrequency of her publication, the lack of commercial appeal of her writing, and the tendency of critics to oversimplify the intriguing complexity of her work. Although the infrequency of publication will always account for her being seen as a minor voice in the canon of contemporary Southern writers, the richness and vitality of her work deserves wider attention.

BIOGRAPHY

Daphne Athas was born on November 19, 1923 in Cambridge, Massachusetts, to Pan Constantine and Mildred Spencer Athas. One of four children, she spent her early years in Gloucester, Massachusetts, living the life of the privileged in a neighborhood of the extremely wealthy. Her father was a self-made Greek immigrant who had worked his way through Ohio University and Harvard Law School. Her mother was from a wealthy Cambridge family. The 1929 stock-market crash and the ensuing Great Depression, however, marked the end of the family's prosperity.

From the age of 7, Athas knew she wanted to be a writer. Her first ''publication'' was an essay about Bastille Day, printed in the *Gloucester Times*. Athas's early interest in writing was complemented by an interest in language fostered by her father. As an immigrant, Pan Constantine Athas was sensitive to word differences and encouraged the Athas children to play a variety of word games, developing in them a love of wordplay that indelibly marks Athas's writing.

When Daphne Athas was 13, her family moved to Chapel Hill, North Carolina, where her father went into a new business, linen supply. The events of her adolescence in Chapel Hill form the core of her admittedly autobiographical novel *Entering Ephesus* (1971). Athas entered the University of North Carolina at Chapel Hill at age 16 and, after only three years, graduated in 1943 with a B.A. in English. Athas describes the magic of growing up and going to school in the Chapel Hill of the late 1930s and early 1940s: "It was amazing to find myself in a place where there were writers who wrote, a place which made no separation between music [of language] and event, or music and being. The act and the expression of the act took on reality then as part of the same thing" ("Why There Are No Southern Writers" 297).

From the University of North Carolina, Athas returned to Massachusetts to pursue teacher certification at the Harvard School of Education. While at Harvard, she supported herself by teaching algebra at the Perkins Institute for the Blind in nearby Watertown. This experience not only provided much of the factual basis for her second published novel, *The Fourth World* (1956), but also taught her the importance of making vivid pictures with words. During this stay in Massachusetts, Athas was working on her first published novel, *The Weather of the Heart* (1947). She was encouraged in the writing of this novel by Betty Smith, her friend and mentor from Chapel Hill, author of *A Tree Grows in Brooklyn*. Without Athas's knowledge, Smith showed the manuscript of *Weather of the Heart* to University of North Carolina writing teacher Jessie Rehder, who was influential in having it published by Appleton-Century. This early success was followed by the rejection of her second novel, which she later revised as the play "Ding Dong Bell." (With coauthorship from Gurney Campbell, this play became "Sit on the Earth" and won a prize in the *London Observer* play-writing contest in 1958.)

In the mid-1950s, Athas lived in Europe, serving from 1952–58 as a service club director for the U.S. Air Force in London. After she left London, she continued her European travels, spending time in Greece, where she made the pilgrimage to her father's former home in Hora; that experience formed the basis for her work of nonfiction *Greece by Prejudice* (1963).

In 1964 Athas returned to North Carolina, working as coordinator of basic education for adults at Durham Technical Institute before joining the creative writing faculty at the University of North Carolina at Chapel Hill in 1967. She has continued as a lecturer in the English department, with the exception of the 1973–74 academic year, when she served as a Fulbright professor of American literature at Tehran University in Iran and 1980–81, spent in Greece.

Athas's career has been punctuated by the publication of her third and fourth novels, *Entering Ephesus* in 1971 and *Cora* in 1978, both of which won the Sir

Walter Raleigh Award for the year's best work of fiction published by a North Carolinian. *Entering Ephesus* was also named one of 1971's ten best novels by *Time* magazine. The excellence of *Entering Ephesus* has been recognized by its reissuance in 1991 by Second Chance Press. Athas has received several prestigious fellowships, the MacDowell Fellowship in 1962 and substantial National Endowment for the Arts awards in 1974–75 and 1979–80. In addition to her book-length works, Athas has published stories, essays, and poems in a variety of little magazines. As a teacher, Athas is admired and respected by students who respond favorably to her intensity and to her genuine concern that they discover themselves as writers. As a member of the intellectual community in Chapel Hill and the Research Triangle area, Athas regularly gives readings and participates in programs and panels about literature and the art of writing. The writer's life is for Athas not so much a list of works published as it is a sense of life explored and meaning discovered.

MAJOR THEMES

Exploration is not only Daphne Athas's chief mode of work, it is also her major theme. The characters in her stories are people in search of identity and meaning, usually on a journey of some sort that becomes the story's literal analogue to their imaginative and psychological journeys. Although the characters may not arrive at destinations that they desire, they do move through experiences that change them or bring them greater awareness. Athas's purpose is to influence the reader to follow the journey in the story and to gain an awareness of its implications for his or her own life. In "The Art of Storytelling" (1974), Athas has stated her admiration for "the novel as large, as distant but also close, full of treasures—plums, raisins, cashew nuts, olives" (260). Athas's best work achieves that kind of distance and closeness and is full of treasures, treasures that are sometimes difficult to perceive.

The journey metaphor forms only a small part of the plot of *Weather of the Heart*. Eliza Wall, the main character, and her sister Hetty are orphans supervised by their Dickensian housekeeper, Ulb Hatton. Like many other Athas characters, they are persons with an aristocratic sensibility, inherited from their intellectual but ineffectual father, plunged by circumstances into a plebeian environment. The very first sentence of the novel neatly announces the story's dual concerns: the adolescent explorations of sexuality and of personal freedom.

The sexual tension develops when Eliza becomes attracted to Claw Moreau, a one-eyed, poorly educated French Canadian. Meanwhile, the problems of personal freedom have simmered as Ulb forces the girls to work at Mrs. Harley's store. Eliza's attraction to Claw is based on both her attraction to him sexually and her sense that being with Claw, of which Ulb and everyone else in the community would disapprove, is an act of personal rebellion that asserts her personal freedom.

The crisis in the story occurs when Eliza and Claw are blamed for the death of Mrs. Harley's canary and run away together. Their journey physically takes them just south of Boston, but their failure to escape reveals the futility of their relationship. The novel ends as Eliza assumes responsibility for Hetty, Ulb's tyranny ends, Claw runs away again, and order is restored. Eliza, however, has bought peace at the cost of her carefree bird-like freedom. Eliza's journey has been from childhood to adulthood. Whereas the physical space she has explored has been small, the emotional space has ranged from the tasting of forbidden sexual fruit to an attempt to run away from societal and familial constraints to final acceptance of adult responsibility. Her aristocratic disdain for convention has capitulated to plebeian expediency.

The explorations developed in *Fourth World* involve a larger cast of central characters and move not so much through physical space as through imaginative space. There are two sets of major characters, the adults Actia Clewes and Ted Balkan and the adolescents Gobi Morgan and Rhea Thomas. The story opens as Actia journeys to Canopus Institute, a school for the blind where she has taken a position as a teacher of algebra. Of the main characters only Actia is sighted. The central conflicts of the story revolve around the issues of blindness and sight, revealing that sight can be blind and blindness seeing and that blindness is not only physical but also psychological and emotional, afflicting the sighted and sightless alike.

At Canopus, the students subvert the tyrannical system of sexual segregation by meeting in the tunnels that connect the buildings of the campus. Gobi and Rhea, in love, journey not only to the tunnels but to the Fourth World—an imaginary realm, invented by the aristocratically arrogant Gobi, in which the blind are truly equal to the sighted and where Gobi and Rhea feel omnipotent. Meanwhile in the adult's world, Actia is attracted to, and secretly marries, Ted because, despite his physical blindness, his intellectual understanding and vision are broader and deeper than those of the other characters.

The story reaches its climax when the secrets of the tunnels are revealed and when Rhea, who is pregnant, and Gobi, who has left reality for his belief in the Fourth World, are parted. In final acts of defiance, Gobi initiates a riot among the other students and, in climbing the bell tower to ring the bell, falls to his death. The journeys of Gobi and Rhea to the Fourth World have proven its fantasy and ended with the death of Gobi and the banishment of Rhea. Ted's journey on behalf of the students, because he has already learned the limitations of the blind among the sighted, is somewhat more successful. By the novel's end Gobi and Rhea have been sacrificed, but there is hope for Actia and Ted and for the other students at Canopus Institute.

Although Athas's third book *Greece by Prejudice* is classified as a nonfiction travel narrative, it reads very much like her novels. In fact, one is tempted to see all of her writing either as travel narrative that fictionalizes the experience of the travelers or as fiction that travels through realms of experience to define the limits of the characters. *Greece by Prejudice* opens as Daphne descends by train onto the plain of Athens. She has come to join her father and to return with him to Hora, the town of his birth. In the chapters that are about Athens, Daphne's travels with her father to Hora, and on a side trip she makes with a friend to Rhodes and Crete, Daphne is the typical tourist, describing streets, hotels, restaurants, and events. In the final chapters, she returns to Hora on her own and, by happenstance, stays with the family of her cousin Martha's fiancé Ioannis. Here she participates actively in the lives of peasant farmers. While her kinship with Martha enables her to share their homes, activities, and religious rituals, her sense of aristocratic distance, derived from her father's arrogance and her own education and profession as a writer, gives her the unique perspective of closeness, yet distance.

Her sense of closest kinship with Hora comes as she, Martha, Ioannis and his family huddle together to endure the force of a freak typhoon. Whereas Ioannis's family suffers partial damage to their house, many other houses in Hora have been completely destroyed, including that of Daphne's uncle Barba Ioannis who was killed in the storm.

The physical journey in this story is through the Greece described in the first half of the book. The psychological journey is into the heart of the Greek soul as it is revealed in the lives of the natives of Hora: simple and loving Martha, the more devious Ioannis, his mystical father, and the various other characters who reflect a variety of stances for which those three form the matrix. Daphne comes to recognize the ways in which she has derived from these Greek peasants and, more significantly, the ways in which she differs from them. Her descriptions of life and events in Greece are as rich and intriguing as the funeral bread, sticky with soaked grain, pomegranate seeds, almonds, currants, and cinnamon, that she helps to bake.

Greece by Prejudice achieves the combination of distance and closeness that illustrates the authorial narrative power that Athas praises in ''The Art of Storytelling.'' In addition to being the third of her five books, *Greece by Prejudice* holds a central place artistically in Athas's work, since the novels that follow display a far greater ambition and scope than the two earlier ones.

Athas's fourth book, *Entering Ephesus*, creates from the experiences of the author's adolescence a fiction that rings with factual authenticity. The story begins as Mrs. Bishop and her daughters Irene, Urania (Urie), and Sylvia (Loco Poco) move to Ephesus to join their husband/father P. Q. As the story develops Urie and Loco Poco emerge as the chief characters who, along with their friend Zebulon Vance Walley (Zebul), explore the confines of Ephesus and Haw (Chapel Hill and Carrboro). Urie and Zebul pursue explorations that take them from the top of the sawdust mountain in Haw into the depths of the university library. Urie delights in her intellect, and she and Zebul stimulate and challenge each other to abandon the cant of their plebeian environment to seek individual aristocratic truth.

The story also follows Loco Poco whose intellect is high but who lacks her sister's ambition, preferring to follow her own ''quirques'' (60)—to dance and sing and converse with ''Tootsie Morn,'' an elusive fairy. Discussing Loco

Poco's search for musical perfection in one pure note on the flute, Urie says that "Music is a pattern in time which tells a melodic story. . . . You have to have obstacles to get over, so you have to arrive at crises. You have to have crescendoes. Only that way can you arrive home. When you get back to *do,* you have the victory" (81). Urie's character is expressed in this sort of intellectual search for knowledge, for the analogies with which to express insight and understanding. For Loco Poco, on the other hand, life *is* the music. The primary crescendo of the story occurs when Loco, following the music in her head, dances into the path of a truck that fails to maintain its place in the beat of her internal music. Loco Poco's death heralds the end of a vital aspect of the family, an end reinforced when the family is evicted from its "Shack."

This outline only partially delineates the explorations of Urie, Loco Poco, and Zebul. It completely omits the characters' experiments with sex; the impact of World War II; the wild richness of the other characters—notably P. Q., Mrs. Bishop, Irene, Miss Picke, and Bostwick; and the range of Urie's and Zebul's intellectual and moral explorations.

In *Entering Ephesus* Athas achieves authorial distance by fictionalizing experience. She pursues closeness for the readers with an incredible richness of texture and detail in her characters and the scenes and events in which they participate. The literal journeys are through the streets of Ephesus and Haw. The psychological journeys are into and through the minds of the major characters. Urie and Zebul move from adolescence into early adulthood as they flex their intellectual muscle and grope for answers that will enable them to cope with reality. Loco Poco explores her sensuality and moves so deeply into the world of her private "quirques" that the real world destroys her.

A more compelling combination of distance and closeness is achieved in *Cora* (1978). The distance comes from Athas's invention of a suspense-thriller plot that follows a young male protagonist and a middle-aged female protagonist into the Greece governed by the repressive regime of the early 1970s. The closeness comes, again, from the immediacy of the vivid description of characters, scenes, and events: a richness that expresses itself in a prose so densely packed as to have a prickly texture.

Part One of *Cora* traces the journey of Sergeant Don (Adonis) Tsambalis as he embarks on a Greek odyssey and fantasizes about a pursuit of "the Goddess." He is reluctantly drawn to fellow-American tourist Cora Ellison, a vague, but self-assured, middle-aged woman. Although Don had hoped that Zoe, whom he had met earlier and from whom he carries a gift to her parents in Athens, was "the Goddess," he discovers "the Goddess" in Cora. Part One ends with Don and Cora's descent into a historic tunnel. When they emerge, they are attacked and separated.

In Part Two, Athas closes the reader's distance from the characters by shifting the point of view between a first-person account of what happens to Cora and the third person narrator who continues to follow Don. Imprisoned in an abandoned fort without food and water, Cora literally sheds her skin to emerge a new person. Don, released by the attackers, goes to Athens where he delivers Zoe's gift but is imprisoned and tortured by the authorities who assume he is engaged in an antigovernment plot engineered by Zoe and her friends. Finally he is released and reunited with Zoe. Zoe and Don then find and release a reluctant Cora.

The final chapter serves as an epilogue revealing that everything that Don and Cora learned in their explorations and journeys has had little permanent effect on their lives. When they meet again in the United States, they are remote aquaintances, nothing more. The most permanent changes have perhaps taken place within the reader as he or she explores Don's and Cora's experiences to perceive the underlying archetypal patterns.

The names of the main characters provide evidence of the mythic story in which they are engaged. Cora's name echoes that of Kore, the maiden aspect of the goddess Persephone. In Greek legend, Kore and Aphrodite (Zoe) fought over the affections of Adonis, finally settling for sharing him. This legend is reflected in Don's indecision about staying with Cora or going to Athens to complete Zoe's errand. Before the attack took place, Don had decided to go to Athens. Cora, abducted by someone named Hadjis (Hades?) whom she never sees, undergoes an underworld experience that causes her to shed her former self and to become enamored of Elias her guard. When Zoe and Don come to rescue her, Cora does not really desire to return to her former identity.

Cora is a difficult novel, but its complexity is intriguing; and the reader who persists and who participates by becoming a journeyer, on the archetypal level, with Don and Cora is rewarded not only with an emotional experience that provides the cathartic pity and terror of Greek tragedy but also with an intellectual experience that provides the recognition of the archetypal patterns in the protagonists' lives.

From her first novel to her most recent, Athas has been primarily interested in the characters' personal explorations into the realm of the self. The list of major characters in her stories is dominated by adolescents—persons who are most self-consciously exploring the limits of the self, trying to find where their personal limits are and what the possibilities are for their lives. The adults in her stories are adults who are also searching for identity and for ''home'' or roots. The form of her stories is dominated by the shaping metaphor of the journey, and the goal for the personal explorations and the literal and psychological journeys is self-knowledge.

SURVEY OF CRITICISM

The criticism of Daphne Athas's work consists almost entirely of book reviews, primarily in popular magazines and newspapers. Reviews of her early works hailed a bright new talent on the literary horizon, singling out her control of her material. The reviews of *Greece by Prejudice* underscored flaws and excesses in Athas's prose style. Although most reviewers praised *Entering Eph-*

esus, they failed to deal with the complexity of what Athas was attempting. *Cora* was less widely reviewed than *Entering Ephesus,* and again critics oversimplified the scope of the novel. If one were to believe the reviewers, Athas is a writer whose early promise has failed to materialize.

The Weather of the Heart was greeted as a remarkable achievement for such a young author, a coming-of-age novel in which the main character is presented without self-pity and without sentimentality. Diana Trilling praised "the fierce freedom of Miss Athas's imagination" (51). Nancy Lenkeith admired Athas's "expressive capacity" and "her degree of intensity" while she regretted "the basic structural weakness in the plot and . . . a complete lack of humor" (245). The evaluations of these critics have focused on qualities echoed by reviewers of subsequent books. Athas's stylistic performance is always admired, and sometimes simultaneously regretted, and her plots or structures faulted.

In reviews of *The Fourth World,* critics continued to admire Athas's ability to enter and treat the world of childhood and adolescence with unsentimental clarity and dignity. With the reviews of *Greece by Prejudice,* however, critical notes of the weaknesses in Athas's writing began to sound more stridently. In an essay that grudged that "most of her book [is] a pleasure," Sylvia Stallings took half of her column space to condemn the "broken-backed prose that Hemingway might have turned out had Hemingway written badly and been a woman instead" (13).

Critical reception of *Entering Ephesus* was more complimentary than that for *Greece by Prejudice* had been. Martha Duffy's review (in *Time,* which subsequently voted *Entering Ephesus* one of 1971's ten best novels) compared *Entering Ephesus* with Louisa May Alcott's *Little Women,* a comparison that several other reviewers picked up and turned into a touchstone for *Entering Ephesus.* The comparison with *Little Women* recognized the female consciousness of *Entering Ephesus* but oversimplified by developing the comparison in terms of which of the Bishop girls correspond to which of the March girls and by overlooking the thematic significance that Athas herself has said is the "grit of a family, the absurdity of the relation of civil lives to major war and the transcendence of death" ("The Contest Between Reality and Truth").

Athas's critical reputation peaked with *Entering Ephesus. Cora* was less widely reviewed (it is, in fact, not even listed in *Book Review Digest*), and the reviews were less comprehensive, becoming mere notes on certain aspects of the novel. The most perceptive of the reviews is Jack Raper's, who recognized, but did not develop, the archetypal mythic analogies inherent in the text. His final assessment of *Cora* is one that applies to most of Athas's works: "Exciting to read, intriguing to re-read" (93).

Reviews of the 1991 reissue of *Entering Ephesus* have generally echoed those from 1971. Once more the comparison has been made to *Little Women* and once more Athas's mastery of language usage has been noted. Awareness of the sectional difference between the Bishop's aristocratic New England roots and the plebeian Southern "red dirt" (Steinberg 52) to which they are transplanted may have been even stronger in 1991 than in 1971. Reviewer Shawn Michael Smith has gone further by comparing the reading of *Entering Ephesus* in 1971 with the reading of it in 1991 by pointing out that ''in today's steadily downturning economy, this tale of transcending Depression-era hardship is . . . likely to exorcise middle-class nightmares of personal ruin'' (15).

Critical reception of Athas's work has always been mixed, and as her work has become more complex, it has gradually become more negative. Readers must approach Athas's work prepared to participate fully in the journey of exploration on which she takes her characters in the hope of luring the readers along the paths of self-exploration that yield understanding. A patient reader will be rewarded not only with a journey of self-exploration but with a delight in the language with which Athas expresses the characters' experiences and ideas.

BIBLIOGRAPHY

Works by Daphne Athas

The Weather of the Heart. New York: Appleton-Century, 1947.

The Fourth World. New York: Putnam's, 1956.

''Sit on the Earth.'' In *The Observer Plays,* Preface by Kenneth Tynan, 77–156. London: Faber, 1958.

Greece by Prejudice. Philadelphia: Lippincott, 1963.

''The Way to Find Hestia.'' In *Chapel Hill Carousel,* edited by Jessie Rehder, 3–26. Chapel Hill: The University of North Carolina Press, 1967.

''The Hitchhiker.'' *The Carolina Quarterly* 21 (Winter 1969): 42–55.

Entering Ephesus. New York: Viking Press, 1971. Reprint. Sag Harbor, N.Y.: Second Chance Press, 1991.

''The Contest between Reality and Truth.'' *Chapel Hill Newspaper* (March 7, 1973).

''The Art of Storytelling.'' *South Atlantic Quarterly* 73 (Spring 1974): 256–60.

''Goddesses, Heroines, and Women Writers.'' *St. Andrews Review* 3 (Fall/Winter 1975): 5–13.

Cora. New York: Viking Press, 1978.

''Cyclops in Steam: A View of Russia.'' *Shenandoah* 31 (1979): 3–34.

''Why There Are No Southern Writers.'' In *Women Writers of the Contemporary South,* edited by Peggy Whitman Prenshaw, 295–306. Jackson: University Press of Mississippi, 1984.

Crumbs for the Bogeyman. Poems. Laurinburg, N.C.: St. Andrews Press, 1991.

Interviews with Daphne Athas

Brueckner, R. ''Changed South Affects Writers, Novelist Says.'' *News and Observer* (November 23, 1984).

McHugh, Cathy. ''A Childhood Desire for Writing Becomes a Prosperous Career.'' *Daily Tar Heel* (February 26, 1987).

Scandling, Mark W. ''Daphne Athas: Searching for a Cosmic Consciousness.'' ''Profiles

of Three North Carolina Writers,'' Master's thesis, University of North Carolina
at Chapel Hill, 1979.

Studies of Daphne Athas

Berkman, Sylvia. "Murmurous World of the Blind." Review of *The Fourth World. New
    York Times Book Review* (May 13, 1956): 28.
Duffy, Martha. "Little Women." Review of *Entering Ephesus. Time* 98 (September 13,
    1971): 85–86.
Haynes, Muriel. Review of *Entering Ephesus. Saturday Review* 54 (October 9, 1971):
    38–39.
Koger, Grove. Review of *Cora. Library Journal* 1 (November 1978): 2259–60.
Lenkeith, Nancy. Review of *The Weather of the Heart. Commonweal* 20 (June 1947):
    245.
Lochner, Darley. "Chapel Hill School Girl Turns Novelist at Age of 23 Years." Review
    of *The Weather of the Heart. Greensboro Daily News* (May 11, 1947). (Located
    in scrapbook file of *North Carolina Literature,* North Carolina Collection, Uni-
    versity of North Carolina at Chapel Hill, 68: 123.)
Peterson, Virgilia. "A Tale of Vision in a Sightless World." Review of *The Fourth
    World. Herald Tribune Book Review* (May 13, 1956): 3.
Raper, Jack. Review of *Cora. Carolina Quarterly* 31 (Winter 1979): 92–93.
Review of *Cora. Durham Morning Herald* (February 18, 1979). (Located in scrapbook
    file *North Carolina Literature,* North Carolina Collection, University of North
    Carolina at Chapel Hill, 69: 11.)
Review of *Entering Ephesus. Virginia Quarterly Review* 67, no. 4 (Autumn 1991): 129–
    30.
Robinson, Charles A. Review of *Greece by Prejudice. New York Times Book Review*
    (April 7, 1963): 39.
Smith, Shawn Michael. "Transcending the Great Depression." Review of *Entering Eph-
    esus. Christian Science Monitor* 83 (March 26, 1991). 15.
Stallings, Sylvia. "A True Descendant of Zeus Returns to Hellas." Review of *Greece
    by Prejudice. New York Herald Tribune,* Book section (June 9, 1962). 13.
Steinberg, Sybil. Review of *Entering Ephesus. Publishers Weekly* 237 (December 14,
    1990): 52.
Trilling, Diana. "Fiction in Review." Review of *The Weather of the Heart. Nation* 165
    (July 1947): 50–51.

LUCY K. HAYDEN

Gerald [William] Barrax
(1933–   )

Joining the chorus of other African-American poets of the 1960s and 1970s, Gerald William Barrax celebrated the African-American experience. This he has continued to do in his poetry written in the 1980s and early 1990s. Clearly his blackness inspires his poetic imagination, and each complements the other.

BIOGRAPHY

Gerald W. Barrax was born in Atalla, Alabama, near Gadsden on June 21, 1933, to Aaron Barrax and Dorthera Hedrick Barrax. In 1944 the family—now including another son, Harold—moved to Pittsburgh. From 1958 to 1967, Barrax was a clerk in the U.S. Post Office in Pittsburgh. Before moving to North Carolina in 1969, he worked at various times as a steel-mill laborer, cab driver, substitute teacher in public schools, encyclopedia salesman with zero sales, and an awning hanger.

While working in Pittsburgh, Barrax also attended Duquesne University from 1952 to 1953 as a pharmacy major. After a hiatus as an airman, he returned to Duquesne University from 1959 to 1963, where first he majored in journalism, before changing to English, in which he received a B.A. In 1967 he enrolled in the Master's program in English at the University of Pittsburgh and graduated in 1969. From 1971 to 1975, he also took graduate courses in English at the University of North Carolina at Chapel Hill.

Barrax became an English instructor at North Carolina Central University in 1969 and the next year joined the faculty at North Carolina State University, where he is currently a professor of English.

The roles of husband and father are very important to Barrax and constitute one of his poetic themes. In 1954 he married Geneva Catherine Lucy, and they became the parents of three sons: Dennis Scott (b. 1955), Gerald William, Jr.

(b. 1961), and Joshua Cameron (b. 1963). In 1971 he married Joan Dellimore from St. Vincent Island in the West Indies, and their two daughters are Shani Averyl (b. 1974) and Dara Hillary (b. 1978).

All during the time he was a student, teacher, workman, airman, husband, and father, he was writing poetry. Many of his poems chronicle and celebrate his various experiences. His first volume of poetry, *Another Kind of Rain,* was published in 1970, followed by *An Audience of One* a decade later. His *The Deaths of Animals and Lesser Gods* was issued in 1984; this volume was succeeded in 1992 by *Leaning Against the Sun.*

Barrax has received several awards and honors for his accomplishments. These include the 1991 Sam Regan Award for Contributions to the Fine Arts in North Carolina from St. Andrews Presbyterian College; a Woodrow Wilson Fellowship (Visiting Author at Lincoln University, Pennsylvania, in 1987); the 1983 *Callaloo* Creative Writing Award for Non-Fiction Prose (for an essay on Jay Wright and book reviews); a Ford Foundation graduate fellowship for black Americans, 1972 to 1977 (while at the University of North Carolina, Chapel Hill); and the Broadside Press Award for Poetry in 1973. Since 1986 he has been the editor of *Obsidian II: Black Literature in Review.*

MAJOR THEMES

In *New Black Voices* (1991) Barrax has said that he sometimes speaks as ''a vulnerable mortal and sometimes as a vulnerable Black American'' and that blackness and death ''are implicit in all my responses to people and the worlds I live in and in everything I write'' (210). Barrax could have added self-revelation as a third theme, because although related to the other two, it has dimensions all its own in his poetry. These three major themes appear in his first volume, *Another Kind of Rain,* and he has returned to them repeatedly in subsequent volumes of poetry. They are also interspersed sporadically with themes of love, sex, alienation, music, existentialism, and nature.

In his comprehensive development of the blackness theme, Barrax has traced the African-Americans from their origins in Africa to their lives in America. Their performances on various historical stages are portrayed in his poetry.

In both ''Another Fellow'' (*An Audience of One*) and ''The Death of Another Fellow'' (*The Death of Animals and Lesser Gods*), which focus on a snake, he acknowledges the belief of some Africans in ancestor worship and reincarnation. Reflecting on the cultural, symbolic, and mythical significance of the snake in ''Another Fellow,'' he recalls that his African ancestors would have welcomed it into their huts, believing it to be the reincarnation of a deceased relative:

> My ancestors, considering its immortality,
> Would've welcomed it with food and drink
> When it came as spirit of the living-dead from the forest
> To visit their huts.

In "To Waste at Trees" (*The Deaths of Animals and Lesser Gods,* 67) he contrasts the work of black men in building the United States with that of their white oppressors, and finds the former's concern for preservation of the land rooted in their African beliefs: "And unlike them, came out humanly whole / Because our fathers, being African / Saw the sun and moon as God's right and left eye" (40).

"In This Sign" (*The Deaths of Animals and Lesser Gods*) explores the black man's roles in history from Simon the Cyrenian to the Jonestown tragedy in Guyana, and Barrax avows bitterly that the God they worshiped "let them drown in their blood / And His" (26). This poem also depicts the involvement of Europeans in slave trade: the Portuguese, Spaniards, French, and English fill their coffers from their sale of black gold. He meditates extensively on the Middle Passage and in doing so evokes Robert Hayden's poem of the same name and alludes to Captain John Newton, the reformed slaver turned preacher who wrote "Amazing Grace, How Sweet the Sound." Furthermore he inveighs against slavery in the New World and its economic implications:

> We come to Jamestown.
> In time our sweat and blood bloat
> The lean vampire mistress there
> Into the Great Whore of Memphis, Charleston,
> Mobile, New Orleans, who wallows
> In her beds of cotton.

In "The Old Glory" (*Another Kind of Rain,* 24) he repeats the motif of religion used hypocritically by the "slave/traders, ships' captains, and planta-tion/owners" who found affirmation in the Bible "that God was on their side every time / they laughed away some thing pretending to be / human" (84). "Spirituals, Gospels" (*The Deaths of Animals and Lesser Gods*) asserts that the blood of the African's tribal gods was drowned by the Lord's blood in the New World. Yet these sorrow songs, as Du Bois labeled them, although sung in praise of the Christian God instead of the lesser gods of the jungle, because they are embedded in the African-American culture, enable Barrax to "know that's who I am, what I am / when the souls of Black folk sing. / While the Soul of Black folk sings" (33).

Barrax provides another perspective on plantation life in "Whose Children Are These?" (*Leaning Against the Sun*). The persona in Part One is the poet's slave ancestor who laments that he cannot provide his five children with food, fuel, and clothing and, therefore, contemplating escaping, says he will "leave now / Before dawn sets the white fields raging / And murders the North Star" (10). In Part Two the poet in an apostrophe to his grandsire con-cedes that he can provide his five children with physical comforts and can bond with them:

But we have not rescued them altogether;
we moved them through one dimension, from one killing
field to another on history's flat page,
1850s' slavery to 1980s' racism and murder. (11)

There is an existential turn to the poem at the end, as the poet perceives chance
and mysterious will at work in his life, over which he has no control. "Polar's
TV Fantasy" (*Leaning Against the Sun*) is another poem that begins with a
plantation setting, where the owner Polar has peopled it with children by his
wife and slave women; but the poet fastforwards to current TV programs where
black males are placed in families where they are "doomed never to become
men among them" (31). "Body Food" (*An Audience of One*) provides yet
another perspective on plantation life. Needing both spiritual food and physical
food, the slaves survived on what evolved into ethnic food for African Americans, which the poet catalogues as follows:

If then it is in the blood of some of us
to lust after the ears the tails the snouts
the feet the maws & even the
chitlins of the filthy beast
forgive us: with these
& the greens cornbread & molasses
that transubstantiated into the bones
brain & flesh of the black household gods
who brought us through the evil
rooted in this land,
    we honor them
in the heritage of their strength. (56–57)

The fitting imagery in this quotation speaks to certain aspects of the African-
Americans' history, sociology, and culture. The last five lines evoke Aeneas
carrying his small household gods with him as he flees burning Troy; likewise
African Americans in the twentieth century migrating from the South carried
with them ethnic foods that fed both their bodies and spirit in their new, alien
environment.

In "Uniforms" (*Leaning Against the Sun*), a poem dedicated to Martin Luther
King, Jr., Barrax chronicles the valor of African-American soldiers in the Civil
War. He alludes to Battery Wagner, South Carolina, where losses to the Fourth
Massachusetts Colored Infantry were especially severe and Colonel Robert G.
Shaw was killed; and he alludes to Fort Pillow on the Mississippi in Tennessee,
where 557 soldiers, nearly half of them black, were massacred by the Confed-
erates. The poet also alludes to historical battles in World War I, World War
II, and the Korean War. A black soldier observes: "They have never died in
our uniforms / as we have in theirs" (36). The poet also believes that Dr. King
died "in uniform, / in daily warfare, / and free, free of hate, because all he ever
wanted / was that they could be as free as we are" (37).

Moreover "Uniforms" as well as "In This Sign"—the sign being the metaphor, a burning cross—describes the cross's ironic use by the "Christian Knights," during the period of Reconstruction. In the latter poem, he says the "Knights of the Cross"

> Ride Terror and Murder, a two-horse race,
> Into the next century, out of the night,
> Out of their sheets. (25)

During the great migrations from the South during the world wars, one of the things African-Americans sought was a better education for their children. In "Narrative of Surprising Conversions" (*An Audience of One*) Barrax reports on the ironic turn to those expectations and how their dream was deferred. This poem, illustrative of Barrax's controlled and economical style of narrating, tells of a young man, attending an integrated Northern high school and aspiring to be a professional, who is told by his white guidance counselor that, according to his aptitude tests, he should learn to do something with his hands, like carpentry or auto mechanics. Paradoxically the boy later uses his hands to deal, to steal, to shoot and kill.

But Barrax can also depict the experience of an African-American male adolescent with wry humor. For example, in the following poem a little boy is initiated by an adolescent into an African-American oral tradition:

THE DOZENS (*Another Kind of Rain*)

A Small Drama in One Act, One Scene

Big Boy   (Sophisticated, worldly-wise with the knowledge learned from listening to the hip talk of other big boys):
          Yo momma yo momma yo momma
          yo mom ahhh yo maaa yo mommmmmmmmmmmUHma
          momma yo yo mommamommamomm
          ahhhhhh yo momma yoooOOOOOHHHHH MAN
          yo MOMMA!

Little Boy (The Innocent who hasn't heard the hip talk of the Big Boys. He doesn't understand why there are tears in his eyes, but he knows, vaguely, that he must reply):
          An' . . . an' . . . and you is ANOTHER one! (80)

Barrax has employed many different personae in portraying African-American experiences in his poetry. In "For a Black Poet" (*Another Kind of Rain*) the persona is that of a young black poet in the 1960s and 1970s joyously celebrating blackness:

> Beautiful as
> a Black poempoetperson should be who

knows that beauty lurks in the lives of men who
know what Shadow falls between promise and praise. (70)

Unlike his militant contemporaries at the time, Barrax tried consistently to avoid such rhetorical excesses as exhortation, "speechmaking," ranting, and raving. He parodies such excessiveness in the opening lines of "For a Black Poet":

BLAM! BLAM! BLAM! POW! BLAM! POW!
RATTTTTTTAT! BLACK IS BEAUTIFUL, WHI
TY! RAATTTTTTTAT! POW! THERE GO A HON
KIE! GIT'M, POEM! POW! BLAM! BANG!
BANG! RATATAT! BLAM! COME ON, POEM! GET
THAT WHI-TE BEAST! BLAM! BLAM! POW!
ZAP! BANG! RAAATTTTTTATAT! BLAM! BLAM! (68)

In a letter to me, Barrax defended his rhetorical stance:

I AGREED with all that my brother and sister poets were saying, but I wanted not to have to SAY it, but to make the reader FEEL it through his senses, his emotions. There was need for the rhetoric and exhortations; the TIME needed it, the PEOPLE needed it. But the poetry didn't. Too much potentially good poetry was betrayed to speechmaking. You'll notice that I can't always resist it myself, but I do it (I hope) aware of the risk I'm taking. And I always consider it a weakness in *my* poetry. There are better poets than I, of course, who can write with rhetorical sophistication, who are exhortatory, and still turn it into poetry. But there are not many, and I'm not one of them. *(Dictionary of Literary Biography,* 37–38)

Certainly "Filibuster, 1964" (*Another Kind of Rain*) typifies one of the poems in which Barrax could not resist "speechmaking." Indicating that the poem is "for a number of Senators," engaged in filibustering against civil-rights legislation, Barrax disparages eighteen Democrats ("jackasses") and "one rebel pachyderm." In the closing lines of the poem, he alludes to Klansmen, one group of the senators' constituents:

When you have done
and your last shard of eloquence falls

from

the

air
the applause you'll hear will be one hand clapping
of your hooded constituent
horribly grinning in the gallery. (25)

Vignettes of the upper–middle-class African-American today appear in "Where It Came From" (*Leaning Against the Sun*) a dramatic monologue. The speaker is the wife of a college professor who had engaged in an adulterous relationship with a married man and is talking to his sister who is returning her love letters to him now that he is dead. Because of their wealth, her lover and his wife had owned a Cadillac, possibly joined the Alpha Phi Alpha Fraternity and the Delta Sigma Theta Sorority and joined a black country club. The speaker reflects on her own participation in the civil-rights marches in the 1960s and wonders: "Was it worth my busted head freeing slaves to play golf" (42). But she implies she would have done anything for "that kinda sweet man" (43), whom she loved.

A final aspect of blackness to be considered in Barrax's poetry is his allusions to famous African-Americans. In addition to the one poem about Martin Luther King, Jr. already cited, Barrax wrote, "King: April 4, 1968." (*An Audience of One*). Barrax also provided allusions to Malcolm X ("For Malcolm: After Mecca") (*Another Kind of Rain*); W. E. B. Du Bois ("Three Meetings") (*An Audience of One*); famous female singers: Nina, Roberta, Aretha, Sarah, Ella, Carmen, Dinah, Billie, Bessie, and Ma ("The Singer") (*An Audience of One*); Duke Ellington, Ray Charles, and Sarah Vaughn ("Haunted House") (*Leaning Against the Sun*).

In numerous poems, Barrax's major theme is vulnerability to death. Although this theme is the focus of several poems in *Another Kind of Rain, An Audience of One,* and *Leaning Against the Sun,* it is in *The Deaths of Animals and Lesser Gods* that Barrax meditates most forcefully on death, speaking of it personally, historically, wittingly, and philosophically.

In "All My Live Ones" (*The Deaths of Animals and Lesser Gods*), he focuses on the death of his pets. In tones fluctuating between sincere and sarcastic, he mentions the death of his live and lively pets (two dogs and a canary) and of the two that ran away (a dog and a cat). But how much less transitory his experiences have been with human beings. He observes that since being born in 1933, "I've been the key to immortality: / All it takes is loving me" (54). Then he proceeds to list those who have loved him: his parents, his brother, two wives, five children, and lovers. They undoubtedly are the ones to whom he dedicated *Another Kind of Rain,* because it is inscribed "For All My Live Ones." Both the poem and the inscription evoke Anne Sexton's "All My Pretty Ones" as well as Macduff's *cri du coeur* when he reacts to the news that Macbeth has had his wife and children slaughtered: "All my pretty ones? / Did you say all?"

"Competitors" (*The Deaths of Animals and Lesser Gods*), abounding with concrete images, discusses the roles of death and history. Mother Earth, as portrayed in the poem, has since time immemorial competed with man in destroying life. Her devastating earthquakes, tornadoes, and tides have taken a higher toll than man's engines and devices of destruction, thus making her the victor in the competition. These lines suggest the nature of that competition:

> We die to make bodies count for something,
> to control the places of slaughter
>   that the old terror we still call Mother
>   in the earth wind and water
>   intended as fields of praise. (14)

Sometimes Barrax mixes sobriety with wit in discussing death, as in "Slow Drivers" (*The Deaths of Animals and Lesser Gods*). After defining the slow driver as smug, timid, and sometimes old, he proceeds to express the exasperation they cause when they delay his reaching his destination. He concludes the poem by saying he finally decides to take the risk of passing them:

> and pull out
> seeing death
> in their eyes
> when they smirk
> at you
> as you
> pass (32)

In "God's Button" (*The Deaths of Animals and Lesser Gods*) Barrax explains death philosophically by saying that it is one thing God is not. He concludes that "Death is eternal, absolute, animal, human," and agrees with his little daughter that "God is love"; but he adds the stipulation that this is so "as long as one of us lives" (66–67). "The Conception of Goddeath" (*The Deaths of Animals and Lesser Gods*) also discusses the mystical relation between love and death: that God was born out of man's fear and need when he realized his mortality.

The book's final and most memorable poem, "The Death of Another Fellow" (*The Deaths of Animals and Lesser Gods*), also treats death philosophically. This poem is the sequel to "Another Fellow" in *An Audience of One* in which the poet describes his reaction to finding almost the whole skin of a snake in his yard. The second poem focuses on the death of what the poet believes is the same snake, and in doing so incorporates a number of the book's other themes. The snake's death is requested by his wife because of her personal fear and her fear for their daughters. While mowing the lawn and reflecting on his experiences with love, sex, and family, he sees the "old buddy." Although systematic and methodical in planning its death, the poet is nonetheless compassionate and even ambivalent about killing it; yet he does kill it. Afterwards he and his daughter see a second sinuous snake. When his daughter later asks him if he killed it, he replies:

> No. It was gone.
> But Daddy, it was harmless anyway and wasn't
> Going to hurt anybody.
> I look at her, unbelieving. No, I said,
> It wasn't going to hurt anybody. (72)

Surprised that his daughter felt more of his compassion and none of his wife's fear, he philosophically asks himself in the two final lines of the poem: *"Then what was it I killed, what is buried / in the backyard under my window?"* (72).

Self-revelation, Barrax's third major theme, was identified by Sterling Brown (1973) as one of the chief interests of Harlem Renaissance poetry; and Stephen Henderson (1973) thought it was equally important to contemporary black poetry. Autobiographical allusions and self-revealing metaphors flourish in Barrax's poems, but he maintains sufficient distancing to preclude them from degenerating into maudlin confessionals. The autobiographical references are more numerous and more revealing in *Leaning Against the Sun* than in his other three books. Several poems from that volume illuminate this theme.

In "Eagle. Tiger. Whale" he graphically describes his appearance as a toddler standing before the long mirror of a chifforobe—"sandy hair / tightly curled, hazel eyes" (3)—with his beautiful seventeen-year-old mother somewhere behind him. In this poem he also describes seeing a homicide victim for the first time and his initiation to sex.

"Not Often Near Such Water" contains numerous autobiographical allusions. Barrax identifies his ancestry as African, Indian, and Dutch. He learned to swim immediately after several mischievous boys threw him in a pool and he almost drowned; this happened when he was ten or eleven, not long after arriving in Pittsburgh from Alabama. At the age of 12 he began taking violin lessons, and after hearing "Meditation" from *Thais* played all day on the radio the day Franklin Delano Roosevelt died, he memorized and performed it on Youth Day at the Warren Methodist Church. He recounts his crossing the Pacific in 1955 on the *USNS Sultan* on his way to Clark Air Force Base and becoming very seasick. He reveals himself as a family man with an "island-born wife who never learned to swim" (5) and two daughters. The movement in the poem is well controlled as it begins with his surfboarding in the Atlantic, while his family watches, and then periodically takes the reader back in time through the use of flashbacks.

In "Special Bus" he sees children on a school bus as it and his car stop at a light; and he remembers his five children: "Dennis, Jerry, Josh, Shani, Dara— / twenty-three years from birth to birth" (12). "Strangers Like Us: Pittsburgh, Raleigh, 1945–1985" contrasts his fun-filled youth when he could play safely on the streets of Raleigh even at night during the spring, summer, and fall with the prescriptive lifestyle of his children, who even in the daylight cannot leave their yard in Pittsburgh—"They are cycloned into our yards and hearts" (13)—because of the monsters in the street described with the anaphora, "who hunt, who hurt, who haunt" (13). Barrax's yard on Cooper Road is the setting of "Yardwork" and "What More?" where, while raking leaves or mowing, he experiences memorable moments with animals and birds.

Although references to music resonate throughout his poetry, only in *Leaning Against the Sun* does he reveal how indispensable music is to his very being. In several poems he mentions the instruments he plays. In "Haunted House" he not only mentions playing the piano; but also, in alluding to classical and popular music as well as jazz, he cites composers, performers, and song titles. "Cello Poem" provides the most comprehensive and intimate revelations of his love for music. The musical experiences are wide ranging: from hearing Gounod's *Mass for St. Cecilia* on the radio, to the importance of music during intimate moments with a woman, to listing the instruments he plays—violin, piano, guitar, and harmonica he used.

Although Barrax has increasingly used autobiography to explore themes of blackness, death, self-revelation and other topics, his poems have a significance that transcends the personal. He portrays a wide arch of human experience that encompasses his experience and ours.

SURVEY OF CRITICISM

Critical works about Gerald Barrax consist primarily of several reviews of his books and two critical essays: one essay by me and the other by Joyce Pettis, both in volumes of *Dictionary of Literary Biography* published in 1985 and 1992 respectively.

Although each book review is enlightening, two reviews of *The Deaths of Animals and Lesser Gods* are particularly perceptive. Lorenzo Thomas in *Black American Forum* (1985) has asserted that Barrax was influenced by Amiri Baraka's own militancy expressed in such poems as "Black Art" (which Barrax satirizes in "For a Black Poet"), by Lance Jeffer's erotic imagery, and by Robert Hayden's quiet reflections. Thomas perceives in *The Deaths of Animals and Lesser Gods* Barrax's continuing toward the direction of Hayden's quiet reflections. Ralph Earle in the *Carolina Quarterly* (1985) has suggested that the book's greatest strength lies in Barrax's innovative development of recurring themes. He has also provided a close reading of "The Death of Another Fellow."

Commenting of Barrax's growth in the decade between the publishing of *Another Kind of Rain* and *An Audience of One,* my essay noted not only an improvement in his poetic skills but also his stronger, more original voice—a voice far less derivative and eclectic. Joyce Pettis also noted Barrax's growth in her appreciative analysis of his four volumes of poetry. Pettis skillfully highlights several themes and topics common to poems in various volumes, emphasizing his handling of male/female relationships and various aspects of religion as well as the related concerns of life and death.

Additional evidence of Barrax's development as a poet can be discerned in his two most recent books: *The Deaths of Animals and Lesser Gods* and *Leaning Against the Sun*. In these books Barrax has written intimate and self-revealing poetry. He has more deeply mined the African-American oral tradition, endemic to his Southern roots and experiences. Historical allusions, some of them extensively developed, enrich his poetry even more than previously, as evinced in "In This Sign," textured with quotations from royalty, explorers, church officials, and politicians throughout history. There is, moreover, greater variety in his metaphors and symbols as well as in his poetic types and styles. Such innovation is apparent in the Browningesque "Where It Came From," his successful experiment with a lengthy dramatic monologue. Drawing on his narrative skills, he has conveyed through the monologist the complex personal relationships in the poem.

A poet, a teacher of poetry writing, and a critic who has passionately invoked his muse for over four decades, Barrax will undoubtedly continue to grow as he remembers lessons of the past while simultaneously pushing back the boundaries of his untraveled poetic world. As he continues to publish, he will undoubtedly attract more literary critics and a larger, more appreciative audience.

BIBLIOGRAPHY

Works by Gerald W. Barrax

Another Kind of Rain. Pittsburgh: University of Pittsburgh Press, 1970.
An Audience of One. Athens: University of Georgia Press, 1980.
"The Early Poetry of Jay Wright." *Callaloo* 6, no. 3 (1983): 85–102.
The Deaths of Animals and Lesser Gods. Charlottesville: University Press of Virginia, 1984.
Leaning Against the Sun. Fayetteville: University of Arkansas Press, 1992.

Studies of Gerald W. Barrax

Adcock, Betty. Review of *An Audience of One. News and Observer* (Raleigh, N.C.), (November 30, 1980).
Baddour, Margaret B. Review of *The Deaths of Animals and Lesser Gods. News-Argus* (Goldsboro, N.C.) (February 2, 1986).
Chapman, Abraham, ed. *New Black Voices.* New York: New American Library, 1971.
Davenport, Guy. Review of *The Deaths of Animals and Lesser Gods. Loblolly* 1, no. 2 (1985), 96–99.
Earle, Ralph. Review of *The Deaths of Animals and Lesser Gods. Carolina Quarterly* 37, no. 3 (1985), 117–18.
Hayden, Lucy K. "Gerald William Barrax." In *Afro-American Poets Since 1955,* vol.

41 of *Dictionary of Literary Biography,* edited by Trudier Harris and Thadious Davis, 36–41. Detroit: Gale Research, 1985.

Henderson, Stephen. "Introduction: The Forms of Things Unknown." In *Understanding the New Black Poetry.* Edited by Stephen Henderson, 24. New York: William Morrow & Company, Inc., 1973.

Johnston-Hale, Ellen Turlington. Review of *An Audience of One.* Newspaper (Chapel Hill, N.C.) (July 5, 1981).

Lamanna, Richard. Review of *An Audience of One. Observer* (Athens, Ga.) (September 11, 1980).

Ludvigson, Susan. Review of *An Audience of One. Observer* (Charlotte, N.C.) (April 13, 1980).

Munger, Guy. Review of *The Deaths of Animals and Lesser Gods. News and Observer* (Raleigh, N.C.) (October 21, 1984).

Pettis, Joyce. "Gerald William Barrax." In *American Poets Since World War II.* Vol. 120 of *Dictionary of Literary Biography.* Edited by R. S. Gwynn, 27–31. Detroit: Gale Research Company, 1992.

Stephenson, Shelby. Review of *An Audience of One. Pilot* (Southern Pines, N.C.) (May 21, 1980).

———. Review of *The Deaths of Animals and Lesser Gods. Pilot* (Southern Pines, N.C.) (November 7, 1984).

———. Review of *Leaning Against the Sun. Pilot* (Southern Pines, N.C.) (June 1, 1992).

Thomas, Lorenzo. Review of *The Deaths of Animals and Lesser Gods. Black American Literature Forum* 19, no. 3 (1985), 132–33.

EDWARD B. SMITH

Wendell Berry
(1934–   )

Since the publication of his first novel in 1960, Wendell Berry has written about his Kentucky homeland in poetry, prose fiction, and essays. His pragmatic advocacy for a responsible relationship between people and the land is based on a lifetime of farming. By stressing the value of connecting people to their place and community, Berry strives to heal the division between the self and the world, brought about by technological progress directed by economic greed.

BIOGRAPHY

Rarely has a writer so completely integrated his experience of place to form the basis of his writing as Wendell Berry has. Born on August 5, 1934, Wendell Erdman Berry was heir to a strong agricultural tradition of subsistence farming. His parents, John and Virgina Berry, lived fifty miles east of Louisville in Henry County, Kentucky. Both the hilly terrain of northern Henry County as well as Berry's familial tradition of farming—five generations of his father's and six generations of his mother's family had been farmers—played large roles in Berry's early years.

When Berry was 2 years old, his father moved six miles from the family home in Port Royal to the county seat at New Castle, Kentucky. Although he lived in town, John Berry still valued the country life and he "divided his interest, his life, and his mind between his profession and his land" (*Hidden Wound,* 72). A lawyer by profession, Berry's father maintained a close attachment to the land as well as a concern for farming issues, serving as president of the Burley Tobacco Growers Cooperative Association. Berry credits his father for instilling in him an early interest in farming issues, particularly those concerning small farmers.

As a child Wendell Berry was simultaneously exposed to both rural and urban lifestyles. Although he, his brother, and two sisters lived in town, Berry spent a good deal of time at his grandfather's farm in Port Royal. He was also exposed to differing styles of farming. Growing up, Berry learned traditional farming methods dependent on hand labor and horse-drawn ploughs. By the time Berry was in his teens, the rapid mechanization of agriculture that had been held in check by the Depression and World War II swept through Kentucky, quickly replacing the traditional methods. This modernization led to the migration of many people from the farm to the town since jobs that had previously required hand labor could now be done by machines. But John Berry insisted that his son stay close to the land and learn to do the work with his hands because "the ability to do such work is the source of a confidence and an independence of character" (*Hidden Wound,* 72). This division between the traditional rural culture of Berry's family and the rapid change associated with urban life would reappear later in his work.

Berry attended the Millersburg Military Institute, graduating in 1952. He then enrolled at the University of Kentucky, where he earned his B.A. in 1956 and his M.A. in 1957, both in English. At Kentucky he was influenced by the Vanderbilt Agrarians, the writings of Thomas Jefferson and Henry David Thoreau. While at University of Kentucky, he began writing, and three short stories published in the campus literary magazine *Stylus* were eventually included in his first novel, *Nathan Coulter* (1960).

In the summer of 1957 he married Tanya Amyx and took a teaching position at Georgetown College in central Kentucky. The following year, he received a Wallace Stegner fellowship in writing from Stanford University. He studied for one year at Stanford, after which he remained as the E. H. Jones Lecturer in Creative Writing. The Berry's first child, Mary, was born in the spring of 1958. Before the publication of *Nathan Coulter,* his poetry had been published in several journals—*Poetry, Prairie Schooner, Contact*—and two chapters of the novel were included in the *Carolina Quarterly.*

Awarded a Guggenheim fellowship in 1961, Berry used it to live for six months in Italy. His stay there helped him to begin to formulate his thoughts on the necessity of treating one's place with respect and love. Viewing the Italian landscape, he was struck by its timelessness, realizing that "generation after generation after generation had used it with the greatest possible care" (Wooley, 12) and that through the centuries an unbroken succession of husbandmen had developed skillful farming techniques that had, in turn, created a beautiful and productive landscape.

In 1962, after the birth of the Berry's second child, Pryor, the family moved to New York City where Berry had accepted a teaching position at New York University as an assistant professor and director of freshman English. On living in New York City, Berry stated that it was "an experience I'm glad I had. There I first understood what can happen to people who live away from their work"

(Ehrlich, 10). That same year, *Poetry* magazine awarded him the Vachel Lindsay Prize.

In 1964 Berry published his first book of poetry, *The Broken Ground,* and made two decisions that cemented his ties to the land. First, against the advice of his colleagues, he left New York to teach at the University of Kentucky. The second was to purchase the Lanes Landing farm in Port Royal to use as a "summer place." Once the work of restoring the house had begun, it quickly "became a full-scale overhaul." He, his wife, and children moved into the house on July 4, 1965. He has not moved since. His work in restoring the house and the twelve acres of land would have a profound affect on him. In restoring the farmland that had been misused, Berry began to differentiate between "knowing a place and living in it" and "cherishing a place and living responsibly in it" ("Abundant Reward," 76) and that distinction has been the guiding factor for his writing since.

His first twelve years in Kentucky were productive, both in his writing and his teaching. From 1965 to 1977 he wrote five volumes of poetry, two novels, and six volumes of essays. He was awarded a Rockefeller Foundation grant in 1967 and the Bess Hokin Prize from *Poetry* magazine. In 1971 he received a National Institute of Arts and Letters Literary award and was named the University of Kentucky College of Arts and Sciences Distinguished Professor of the Year, that institution's highest honor for a professor. In 1975 his novel *The Memory of Old Jack* (1974) won first place from the Friends of American Writers.

In 1977 Berry completed what would become his best-know book. *The Unsettling of America* is an extended critique of modern agricultural policy and its effect on farmers. That same year, Berry resigned his position at Kentucky to continue the work begun in *Unsettling* and "search out as many examples of good agriculture" as he could find (Anderson, 4). He felt that he could not teach and make that search at the same time. Through the rest of the 1970s up to the mid-1980s, Berry continued writing, publishing often in non-traditional magazines like *Organic Gardening and Farming* and serving as a contributing editor for the Rodale Press. In 1987 he returned to the University of Kentucky where he currently teaches.

The distinguishing characteristic of Berry's life has been his ability to integrate his experience of his own place into his writing. In committing himself to renewing his land, Berry has been able to develop a strong critique of contemporary culture. For over 30 years he has questioned the ways in which people are joined or separated from their work, families, and land. Just as he has integrated his place and his work, Berry has also combined his words with action. At times he has acted publicly: participating in a demonstration at the Marble Hill nuclear power plant in Indiana; speaking in Frankfort, Kentucky, at a rally opposing the Red River Dam Project; or writing letters to the editors of Kentucky's newspapers. Whether he has acted publicly or privately, Berry has demonstrated his commitment to a way of life that he fears is rapidly disappearing.

MAJOR THEMES

Developing a thematic analysis of Berry's work clarifies the similarities between his personal development and literary maturation. In his early writing Berry's attraction to his native land is clear, both from its use as a setting in his first two novels as well as from his exploration of it in his poetry and essays. After Berry settled permanently in Port Royal, the slow, careful process of restoring the neglected fields and buildings of his farm was reflected in a more specific treatment of the land in his writings. The overarching theme of Berry's writings became an exploration of a possible relationship between people and the land.

Berry has developed this relationship in terms of the connections that people make with their place. This idea of connectedness is a reflection of the integration of Berry's work as a farmer and as a writer. He is neither a farmer who also happens to write nor a writer who lives on a farm. When Berry has written about farming and the land he has done so from practical experience. His is a functional farm that provides his family not only with an income but with food as well. Moreover, the theme of integration has carried over into Berry's operation of the farm. He has operated it organically, returning all waste to the soil, eschewing the use of chemical fertilizers and tractors in favor of natural compost and horse-drawn teams.

Not surprisingly, the connectedness of Berry's personal life and writing is also reflected in the connectedness of his literary forms. Berry's poetry, fiction, and essays complement each other in defining, illustrating, or defending his advocacy of a responsible relationship between people and nature.

The choice to live in one place and write about his experiences of that place is a central concept in Berry's work. In living in and writing about his native land, Berry has often used specific aspects of his own farm in his essays, usually exploring or describing one aspect of a place as a basis for his views on American culture. For example, in his essay "The Work of Local Culture" (*What Are People For?* 1990), Berry uses an old bucket, hanging from a fence and collecting debris, to describe the activity of a culture. For Berry, the bucket does not just stand for an idea, but rather "is one of the signs by which I know my country and myself" (154). His choice to develop and write about one place is reflected in his fiction as he has gone back to the town and characters of Port William for each of his novels. In *The Wild Birds* (1986), Berry's first collection of short stories, Mat Feltner is walking across his farm when he stops to rest by a streambed and realizes that "such a little piece of the world as he has before him now would be worth a man's long life, watching and listening" (82). His poetry also benefits from an intense treatment of one place, the poet's farm. By living and working on their farms, the speakers of Berry's poetry begin to understand the nature of their specific place and, in turn, the beauty and rightness of natural order.

Another theme that permeates Berry's work is the presence of history. For Berry, any current attempt to establish a relationship with the land must acknowledge the history of the place and view the land not as a pristine Arcadia, but rather as a misused site of struggle, bearing scars left by past generations. In both his poetry and fiction he has referred to the forest of massive hardwoods that covered Kentucky before the white settlers arrived, reminding his reader that the crimes against the land began when much of the forest and, consequently, its rich topsoil were destroyed by the earliest generation of settlers. Berry has used history to remind readers that current exploitation of the land by real-estate developers or agribusiness companies is not unique, but merely the latest instance of environmental degradation.

Berry has also discussed the history of the human community as it applies to place. In his view, a human community benefits from a shared history, a memory of past uses of the land and past associations of families that comes only from successive generations nourishing and being nourished by the same land. In his prose, Berry has demonstrated that the history of Port William, which is really the history of its families, is a powerful force that enables a shared vision of land use as well as a sense of cultural identity that guides present actions. In acknowledging that current human use of the land is problematic, Berry has indicated that interaction with the land is caught up in a web of historical events that influence the present. For Berry, awareness of the past demands concern for the future, prompting the conservation of the land for following generations.

The exploration of one place as well as an awareness of the place's history are but two ways in which Berry has connected people to the land. Two other common themes in his work are marriage and farming, both of which should be based on fidelity and an awareness of the need for order. Berry has said that farming and marriage are too often based on economic principles that divide the individual from his or her land and culture. For Berry, marriage is "a state of mutual help" that mirrors his view of the relationship between the farmers and their land. In *The Country of Marriage* (1973), he contrasts his own view of marriage with that of marriage as "a prolonged and impassioned negotiation" of "rights and interests." Taking responsibility for making one's home is as integral to Berry as taking responsibility for one's land.

In his treatment of farming, Berry has repeatedly taken to task technology-based farming and its logical but destructive conclusion, agribusiness. He has opposed not only the destruction of the land but also the destruction of communities that results from farming only for economic gain. For Berry, farming of the best sort takes its mandate from the limitations and possibilities inherent in the land, not economic expedience. For Berry, farming should exemplify an intimate connection between the farmer and the land based on natural order. In advocating the use of traditional farming methods—horses instead of tractors— he has indicated that the limitations imposed on the farmer benefit the health of the land. According to Berry, simpler tools require greater skill and more complex use.

Berry has referred to his land as a marginal farm. The steepness of the land and a history of careless farming techniques have caused serious soil erosion. Over the years, he has become increasingly interested in such marginal land, arguing that its reclamation is important not only for its ecological value, but also as a corrective for the disintegrating homes and communities of America. For Berry, using horses to farm is as much a practical decision as an ethical one, since the horses are better suited to the steepness of the land. In healing the damage that has been done to the land, he states, "we have begun a restoration and a healing in ourselves" ("Abundant Reward," 80). Berry has acknowledged that the healing will be a slow process requiring generations of careful work.

SURVEY OF CRITICISM

Surprisingly, given the amount of his published material, there has been, with the exception of several dissertations, no comprehensive, book-length criticism of Berry's work by any single critic. The preponderance of critical discussion of Berry exists in the form of reviews, scholarly articles, and one collection of essays. By far, the overwhelming critical response to Berry has analyzed his treatment of nature, noting either its presence within his literature, its impact on his style, or its influence on characters.

The recurring names that critics attach to Berry are agrarian, nature poet, and pastoralist. In "Wendell Berry: A Fatal Singing" (1974), Speer Morgan compares Berry's treatment of nature to that of the Vanderbilt Agrarians, Thoreau, and the Romantic poets. Morgan indicates that Berry's acceptance of death as a natural part of the cyclical process of nature qualifies him as a new type of agrarian.

Morgan's comparison of Berry's treatment of nature with that of his agrarian predecessors is developed and, in some sense, extended by Willie Reader. In "The Concept of Nature in Twentieth-Century American Poetry" (1977–78), Reader has examined the differences between the nature poetry of Berry and the nineteenth-century concept of nature as reflected in the poetry of George Meredith. Reader states that unlike Meredith, Berry has not focused on nature as a substitute for institutional religion. Instead, Berry has been concerned with the implications of dividing the spiritual and physical worlds, one of which is the misuse of the land. Reader, in noting the differing philosophical and psychological perspectives of the two poets, ends his analysis by comparing the poets' treatments of death. Unlike Meredith, Berry sees death of the self as part of the cycle of nature that will eventually result in re-creation.

Whereas Morgan and Reader have compared Berry's work to earlier authors, David Tarbet (1972) compares Berry to Gary Snyder and A. R. Ammons, noting in all three writers' work the characteristics of the pastoral tradition. These characteristics include withdrawal, mistrust of public rather than private protest and an elegiac tone toward death. Tarbet singles Berry out as handling the elegy more deftly than the other poets.

Patrick D. Murphy provides a denser analysis of Berry's and Snyder's poetry in "Two Different Paths in the Quest for Place: Gary Snyder and Wendell Berry" (1984). Murphy states that although both are nature poets, their concepts of place are based upon divergent models. Snyder's view of nature favors a more primitive, hunter-gatherer society whereas Berry's is firmly based on the cherished ideal of the independent farmer.

Murphy continues his comparison of the two poets in "Penance or Perception: Spirituality and Land in the Poetry of Gary Snyder and Wendell Berry" (1986). In this essay, Murphy says that one reason for the difference in the two poets' perception of place is their differing religious beliefs, with Berry opting for a "fusion of Christian values, freed from religious orthodoxy and church trappings" (62). John Lang offers further discussion of religion in Berry's work in " 'Close Mystery': Wendell Berry's Poetry of Incarnation" (1983). Lang concludes that Berry's response to nature results from a religious impulse that centers on the mystery of nature and the presence of a creator. According to Lang, Berry uses "the related metaphors of song and silence" (264) to show the "presence of mystery and the appropriate human response" (264). Richard Peaver (1982) thinks that Berry's religious views have made suspect his entire treatment of nature. For Peaver, Berry's belief that the health of the world is the ultimate arbiter for human conduct "dispenses with the entire Judaeo-Christian tradition" (345) by subjugating the worth of human life for the health of nature.

Other critics have focused on the centrality of husbandry—the farmer as nurturer—as well as marriage in Berry's work. Jack Hicks (1983) analyzes Berry's novels, especially *A Place on Earth,* to see how the ideal husband gives himself "to wife, family, farm, community, and finally the cycle of great nature itself." Daniel Cornell (1983) approaches Berry's use of marriage differently from Hicks. In his analysis of *The Country of Marriage,* Cornell demonstrates how marriage informs Berry's stance toward public protest. According to Cornell, the "domestic center" that forms the basis of Berry's thought allows him to resist the typical political labels of conservative or liberal because his "decentralist" politics are based on personal responsibility.

In "Wendell Berry: Finding the Land" (1971), Robert Haas says that much of Berry's early writing has been fueled by the poet's desire to return home and remake his life there. Haas explicated several of Berry's early poems, noting that in his treatment of place Berry strives to heal the division of self and the world in order to develop a cooperative relationship between humanity and nature. Whereas Haas looks mainly to Berry's poetry in examining the desire for unity between the individual and the world, Steven Weiland (1979) approaches Berry's nonfiction. Weiland argues that Berry sees the crisis of American culture as a result of the abstraction of people from the world. Weiland discusses Berry's use of fidelity as a guiding principle that would reconnect people to the land. While discussing recent theory on cultural critique, Weiland notes that although he lacks a specific "methodology" Berry offers valuable cultural criticism from "his experience as an observer and participant" (102). Frederick Waage (1978) has also explored Berry's attempt to unite individual experience with the world. In "Wendell Berry's Personal History" Waage compares Berry to William Carlos Williams, finding Berry's use of a localized and cyclical sense of history an attempt to integrate collective and private history. Berry's ability to do this, according to Waage, results from a unity between the poet and his subject.

As Wendell Berry has repeatedly demonstrated in his own life and his writing, care for the land begins not in the government or university, but at home by people living on the land and loving it, guided by "the ancient rule of neighborliness, by the love of precious things, and by the wish to be at home" (*What Are People For?* 169).

BIBLIOGRAPHY

Works by Wendell Berry

Nathan Coulter. Boston: Houghton Mifflin, 1960.
November Twenty-Six, Nineteen Hundred Sixty-Three. New York: Braziller, 1964.
The Broken Ground. New York: Harcourt, Brace, 1964.
A Place on Earth. New York: Harcourt, Brace, and World, 1967.
Openings. New York: Harcourt, Brace, and World, 1968.
The Rise. Lexington, Ky.: Graves Press, 1968.
Findings. Omaha, Nebr.: Prairie Press, 1969.
The Long-Legged House. New York: Harcourt, Brace, and World, 1969.
Farming: A Hand Book. New York: Harcourt Brace Jovanovich, 1970.
The Hidden Wound. Boston: Houghton Mifflin, 1970.
The Unforeseen Wilderness: An Essay on Kentucky's Red River Gorge. Lexington, Ky.: University Press of Kentucky, 1971.
A Continuous Harmony: Essays Cultural and Agricultural. New York: Harcourt Brace Jovanovich, 1972.
The Country of Marriage. New York: Harcourt Brace Jovanovich, 1973.
An Eastward Look. Berkeley, Calif.: Sand Dollar, 1974.
Falling Asleep. Austin: Cold Mountain Press, 1974.
The Memory of Old Jack. New York: Harcourt Brace Jovanovich, 1974.
Horses. Monterey, Ky.: Larkspur Press, 1975.
Sayings and Doings. Lexington, Ky.: Gnomon Press, 1975.
To What Listens. Crete, Nebr.: Best Cellar Press, 1975.
The Kentucky River: Two Poems. Monterey, Ky.: Larkspur Press, 1976.
There Is Singing Around Me. Austin: Cold Mountain Press, 1976.
Clearing. New York: Harcourt Brace Jovanovich, 1977.
Three Memorial Poems. Berkeley, Calif.: Sand Dollar, 1977.

The Unsettling of America: Culture and Agriculture. San Francisco: Sierra Club Books, 1977.

The Gift of Gravity. Old Deerfield, Mass.: Deerfield Press, 1979.

"Abundant Reward of Reclaiming a Marginal Farm." *Smithsonian* 2 (August 1980): 76–83.

A Part. San Francisco: North Point, 1980.

The Salad. San Francisco: North Point, 1980.

The Gift of Good Land: Further Essays Cultural and Agricultural. San Francisco: North Point, 1981.

The Nativity. Great Barrington, Mass.: Penmaen Press, 1981.

Recollected Essays: 1965–1980. San Francisco: North Point, 1981.

Two Translations in Bliss. Columbus, Ohio: Logan Elm Press, 1982.

The Wheel. San Francisco: North Point, 1982.

A Place on Earth: Revision. San Francisco: North Point, 1983.

Standing by Words. San Francisco: North Point, 1983.

Meeting the Expectations of the Land: Essays in Sustainable Agriculture and Steward-ship. Edited by Wes Jackson, Wendell Berry, and Bruce Colman. San Francisco: North Point, 1984.

The Collected Poems: 1957–1982. San Francisco: North Point, 1985.

The Wild Birds: Six Stories of the Port William Membership. San Francisco: North Point, 1986.

Home Economics. San Francisco: North Point, 1987.

The Landscape of Harmony: Two Essays on Wildness and Community. Hereford, Eng.: Five Seasons, 1987.

Sabbaths. San Francisco: North Point, 1987.

Some Differences. Lewiston, Idaho: Confluence Press, 1987.

Remembering. San Francisco: North Point, 1988.

Traveling At Home. San Francisco: North Point, 1989.

"True Integration." *Mother Jones* 14 (June 1989): 16–18.

What Are People For? San Francisco: North Point, 1990.

Harlan Hubbard: Life and Work. Lexington, Ky.: University Press of Kentucky, 1990.

Sayings and Doings and an Eastward Look. Frankfort, Ky.: Gnomon, 1990.

The Discovery of Kentucky. Frankfort, Ky.: Gnomon, 1991.

"Out of Your Car, Off Your Horse." *Atlantic* 267 (February 1991): 61–63.

Standing on Earth: Selected Essays. Ipswich, Eng.: Golgonooza, 1991.

"What the Gulf War Taught Us." *Progressive* 55 (November 1991): 26–29.

Fidelity: Five Stories. New York: Pantheon, 1992.

"Our Tobacco Problem." *Progressive* 56 (May 1992): 17–20.

Sabbaths: 1987–1990. Ipswich, Eng.: Golgonooza, 1992.

"Decolonizing Rural America." *Audubon* 95 (March-April 1993): 100–105.

Sex, Economy, Freedom, and Community. New York: Pantheon, 1993.

Studies of Wendell Berry

Anderson, Sean. "Prize-winning Poet/Writer Wendell Berry Returns from Farm Life to Teach at UK." *The Kentucky Kernel* (September 15, 1987): 4.

Askins, Justin. "A Necessary Darkness." *Parnassus* 15 (1989): 317–30.

Basney, Lionel. "Wendell Berry: The Grace That Keeps the World." *The Other Side* 23 (January-February 1987), 46–48.

Bauer, Douglas. "We Saved Our Land." *Today's Health* 52 (October 1974): 30–34, 62.

Carruth, Hayden. "Human Authenticity in the Face of Massive Multiplying Error." *Parnassus* 13 (Spring-Summer 1986): 140–43.

Collins, Robert. "A More Mingled Music: Wendell Berry's Ambivalent View of Language." *Modern Poetry Studies* 11 (Spring-Autumn 1982): 35–56.

———. "A Secular Pilgrimage: Nature, Place and Morality in the Poetry of Wendell Berry." Ph.D. diss., Ohio State University, 1978.

Cornell, Daniel. "*The Country of Marriage:* Wendell Berry's Personal Political Vision." *Southern Literary Journal* 15 (Fall 1983): 59–70.

———. "Practicing Resurrection: Wendell Berry's Georgic Poetry, an Ecological Critique of American Culture." Ph.D. diss., Washington State University, 1985.

Crane, John Kenny. "Good Fellers." *New York Times Book Review* (November 15, 1992): 20.

Curry, David. "Wendell Berry's Natural Piety." *Pebble* 8 (1972): 1–19.

Davenport, Guy. "Masters of Time and Place." *National Review* 19 (November 14, 1967): 1282–83.

Decker, William. " 'Practice Resurrection': The Poesis of Wendell Berry." *North Dakota Quarterly* 55 (Fall 1987): 170–84.

Ditsky, John. "Wendell Berry: Homage to the Apple Tree." *Modern Poetry Studies* 2 (Spring 1971): 7–15.

Driskell, Leon V. "Wendell Berry." In *Dictionary of Literary Biography,* edited by Donald I. Greiner, 62–66. Detroit: Gale Research, 1980.

Ehrlich, A. W. "*Publishers Weekly* Interviews Wendell Berry." *Publishers Weekly* 212 (September 5, 1977): 10–11.

Fields, Kenneth. "The Hunter's Trail. Poems by Wendell Berry." *Iowa Review* 1 (Winter 1970): 90–100.

French, Robert. "From Maine to Kentucky." *Nation* 211 (November 9, 1970): 472–73.

Fussell, Edwin. "Farm Poets and Garage Critics." *Parnassus* 2 (Spring–Summer 1974): 25–32.

Haas, Robert. "Wendell Berry: Finding the Land." *Modern Poetry Studies,* 2 (Spring 1971): 16–38.

Hall, Donald. "Back to the Land." *New York Times Book Review* (September 25, 1977): 24–26.

Heinzelman, Kurt. "Indigenous Art: The Poetry of Wendell Berry." *Cencrastus* 2 (1980): 34–37.

Hicks, Jack. "Wendell Berry's Husband to the World: *A Place on Earth.*" *American Literature* 51 (May 1979): 238–54.

Hiers, John T. "Wendell Berry: Love Poet." *University of Mississippi Studies in English* 5 (1984–87): 100–109.

Kilgo, James. "Creed of Memory." *Sewanee Review* 97 (Spring 1989): lvi–lvii.

Kusma, Greg. "Wendell Berry's Natural Piety." *Pebble* 8 (1972): 1.

Lang, John. " 'Close Mystery': Wendell Berry's Poetry of Incarnation." *Renascene* 35 (Summer 1983): 258–68.

Little, Charles E. "Books for the Wilderness." *Wilderness* 52 (Summer 1989): 59–61.

McKibben, Bill. "Prophet in Kentucky." *New York Review of Books* 37 (June 14, 1990): 30–34.

Manning, Richard. "Wendell Berry and His Fight against the Red River Dam." *Louisville Courier-Journal and Times* (May 12, 1975): C1, C3.

Merchant, Paul, ed. *Wendell Berry.* Lewiston, Idaho: Confluence Press, 1991.

Morgan, Speer. "Wendell Berry: A Fatal Singing." *Southern Review* 10 (Fall 1974): 865–77.

Murphy, Patrick D. "Two Different Paths in the Quest for Place: Gary Snyder and Wendell Berry." *American Poetry* 2 (Fall 1984): 60–68.

———. "Penance or Perception: Spirituality and Land in the Poetry of Gary Snyder and Wendell Berry." *Sagetrieb* 5 (Spring 1986): 61–72.

Nibbelink, Herman. "Thoreau and Wendell Berry: Bachelor and Husband of Nature." *South Atlantic Quarterly* 84 (1985): 127–40.

Perrin, Noel. "More than One Muse." *New York Times Book Review* (December 18, 1983): 8, 16.

Pevear, Richard. "On the Prose of Wendell Berry." *The Hudson Review* 35 (Summer 1982): 341–47.

Polsgrove, Carol. "On a Scrap of Land in Henry County." *Sierra* (November–December 1990): 88–96.

Polsgrove, Carol, and Scott Sanders. "Wendell Berry: 'I'm a Person Who Is Very Badly Scared.' " *Progressive* 54 (May 1990): 34–37.

Ray, David. "Heroic, Mock-Heroic." *New York Times Book Review* (November 24, 1985): 28–29.

Reader, Willie. "A Correspondence with Wendell Berry." *Poets in the South* 1, no. 2 (1977–78): 27–31.

———. "Wendell Berry: The Concept of Nature in Twentieth-Century American Poetry." *Poets in the South* 1, no. 2 (1977–78): 32–41.

Rodale, Robert. "The Landscape of Poetry." *Organic Gardening and Farming* 23 (April 1976): 46–52.

Snell, Marilyn Berlin. "The Art of Place." *New Perspectives Quarterly* 9 (Spring 1992): 29–34.

Spikes, Michael. "The Eye of the Beholder." *Mississippi Quarterly* 44 (Spring 1991): 219–23.

Stegner, Wallace. "A Letter to Wendell Berry." *Where the Bluebeard Sings to the Lemonade Springs* (New York: Random House, 1992): 207–13.

Strawman, Thomas. " 'Futurology' and the Fruit of Industrialism in Bellamy, Schiller, and Wendell Berry: Physical Comfort, Spiritual Regression?" *Midwest Quarterly* 33 (Autumn 1990): 44–65.

Swann, Bryan. "The Restoration of Vision." *Commonweal* 113 (June 1986): 345–46.

Tarbet, David W. "Contemporary American Pastoral: A Poetic Faith." *English Record* 23 (Winter 1972): 72–83.

Tolliver, Gary Wayne. "Beyond Pastoral: Wendell Berry and a Literature of Commitment." Ph.D. diss., Ohio State University, 1978.

Triggs, Jeffery Alan. "Moving the Dark to Wholeness: The Elegies of Wendell Berry." *Literary Review* 31 (Spring 1988): 279–92.

———. "A Kinship of the Fields: Farming in the Poetry of R. S. Thomas and Wendell Berry." *North Dakota Quarterly* 57 (Spring 1989): 92–102.

Urquhart, Alexander. "Fitting in with the World." *Times Literary Supplement* (January 24, 1992): 29.

Waage, Frederick O. "Wendell Berry's History." *Contemporary Poetry* 3 (Autumn 1978): 21–46.

Weatherhead, A. Kingsley. "Poetry: The 1930s to the Present." *American Literary Scholarship* 9 (1971): 229–321.

Weiland, Steven. "Wendell Berry: Culture and Fidelity." *The Iowa Review* 10 (Winter 1979): 99–104.

Williamson, Bruce. "The Plowboy Interview: Wendell Berry." *Mother Earth News* 20 (March 1973): 6–12.

Woolley, Bryan. "An Interview with Wendell Berry." *Courier-Journal and Times Magazine,* (August 4, 1974): 8–12.

Young, Vernon. "The Death, the Lullaby, the Glory." *The Hudson Review* 30 (Winter 1977–78): 579–81.

MERRITT W. MOSELEY, JR.

Roy [Alton] Blount, Jr.
(1941–   )

One of America's most versatile writers, Roy Blount, Jr. began his career as a journalist and sportswriter. He has since published poems and songs, humorous journalism, political commentary, a book of sports reporting, and even a treatise on hair. He has appeared in a one-man show off Broadway and as a frequent guest on television and radio. Two of his one-act plays have been staged. With Nora Ephron, he has worked on a musical comedy (he has written many comic songs), and in 1990 he published his first novel. Like most of his writing, it is a work of humor with serious concerns.

BIOGRAPHY

Though born on October 4, 1941, in Indianapolis, Indiana, Roy Blount is the child of Southerners, grew up in the South, and has represented a Southern point of view in much of his prolific writing. Blount was reared in a middle-class Methodist family in Decatur, Georgia, where his father worked as a savings-and-loan executive. He has often spoken of his ambitions to be a professional athlete, a "three-sport immortal" (Ross 1990, 70), but when he realized that he didn't have the talent for an athletic career, he gradually redirected his energies into writing. His mother gets some of the credit for his writing career; as he explains (*Now, Where Were We?*), "I associate reading intimately—by no means entirely comfortably—with my mother, who couldn't breast-feed me but did infuse me with love and phonetics. She had a writerly gift herself, though she wouldn't admit it" (226). For his high-school newspaper, he wrote sports and satire in a column called "Roy's Noise," which earned him a scholarship to Vanderbilt University.

Blount graduated from Vanderbilt, magna cum laude, in 1963. While there, he wrote for the school newspaper and, in summer jobs, for the *Decatur-Dekalb*

News, the New York *Morning Telegraph,* and the New Orleans *Times-Picayune.* He was also made a member of Phi Beta Kappa, and served as an athletic mascot, Mr. Commodore. He entered graduate school at Harvard in 1963 and received an M.A. in English in 1964. Despite the folksy style he sometimes uses, Blount is an analytical and fairly bookish writer, and he has written both good literary criticism (on Mark Twain, for instance) and wicked parody of literary theory. But he decided that an academic career was not for him. In an interview with Jean Ross, he commented on his discoveries at Harvard: "To be suddenly plunged into the midst of people who read books all the time gave me a perspective on where I came from, but it also gave me a perspective on the kind of people who read books all the time" (70).

After two uneventful years in the army, Roy Blount went to work for the Atlanta *Journal* in 1966. In his two years as a *Journal* columnist, he "ridiculed cultural enemies. Wrote limericks. Boosted integration" (Shepherd 69). From Atlanta he went on to New York and seven years as a staff writer, then associate editor, for *Sports Illustrated.* In his years at *Sports Illustrated* and a later year writing a sports column for *Esquire,* he concentrated on the odd, the quirky, the funny side of sports, the unexpected approach. Examples include his treasury of great sports names ("Dedicated to Fair Hooker") and "Jock Lingerie."

Blount's first book was the result of a year he spent hanging out with the Pittsburgh Steelers. Called *About Three Bricks Shy of a Load* (one Steeler's way of expressing the craziness of the team), it focuses less on the on-field fortunes of the team—in a year when they made the play-offs, but not the Super Bowl—than on the personalities of the players, coaches, owners, wives, and others on and around the team. It was published in 1974 to generally good reviews.

Since then Blount has been a freelance writer, primarily of humor, for a bewildering array of magazines (ninety-two different titles, by his count). He published short pieces occasionally in the *New Yorker*—the magazine for which, like most American humorists, he had longed to write—but then became a regular contributor to the *Atlantic;* he has been a contributing editor since 1983, and his mainline humorous pieces now regularly appear there.

Blount's second book was published in 1980, a prolonged reflection on the South and Southernness entitled *Crackers: This Whole Many-Angled Thing of Jimmy, More Carters, Ominous Little Animals, Sad-Singing Women, My Daddy and Me.* Though this book includes previously published material from several magazines, it is far less a collection of pieces than several of his later books; instead it is a seriocomic meditation on the mind of the South and the fate of the nation.

Having moved to New York in 1968 to work for *Sports Illustrated,* Blount has lived outside the South ever since. He now lives in Mill River, a village in western Massachusetts. Though he explains in *What Men Don't Tell Women* that he doesn't belong in New England, where there is "no real pork barbecue" (183), living there has many advantages, including closeness to mulch and a small-town feeling; and living in the North permits him to continue believing there is a South, as such.

Since the mid-1980s Blount has become more of a public performer. He has made regular appearances on Garrison Keillor's "Prairie Home Companion," as well as on other television and radio shows, where he sings his own songs and tells stories. The result was "Roy Blount's Happy Hour and a Half," a one-man show that ran at the American Place Theatre off Broadway in 1986; and he has made stage appearances with Garrison Keillor since then.

After *Crackers,* the next three books were collections of published material, rather loosely linked together. *One Fell Soup, or, I'm Just a Bug on the Windshield of Life* (1982) collects pieces going back as far as 1967 and the Atlanta *Journal* and includes the largest selection of his periodical sportswriting between hard covers. *What Men Don't Tell Women* appeared in 1984. Despite the title, it includes much miscellaneous writing on such subjects as daylight savings time, the disappearance of socks, and sweating; these pieces are linked (or divided) by "blue yodels," twenty-seven monologues by men on maleness or male-female relations. *Not Exactly What I Had in Mind* (1985) is another fairly miscellaneous collection, marked by a greater self-consciousness on the part of the author about the demands of celebrity and the nature of humor.

In the following year he published *It Grows on You: A Hair-Raising Survey of Human Plumage,* with photographs. An odd book, it includes a semiserious treatment of the history of hair, chapters on shampoo, hair loss, and talking to women about their hair. The year 1987 saw the publication of a double, or joint, book, *Soupsongs/Webster's Ark,* a collection of light verse. *Soupsongs* is about food, and includes songs to butter, ham, pie, and so on. Most of these are celebratory, though there is a "Song against Broccoli." *Webster's Ark,* which is bound back to back and upside down with *Soupsongs,* is a bestiary, with poems about animals, alphabetically arranged, from *aardvark* to *zygote.* The humor in both books derives both from the observations the author makes about his subjects and from his clever technique, often involving rhymes like "excrescences" and "lessens his." Another untypical activity, compiling a monthly crossword puzzle for *Spy* magazine, began when he became a contributing editor. His introductions to his "non-British" crossword, and the sometimes lengthy explanations he incorporates in the answers, become in effect a humorous column, while the puzzle itself makes use of his fascination with language and the kind of "reading intimately" he learned from his mother.

In 1989 Blount published *Now, Where Were We? Getting Back to Basic Truths That We Have Lost Sight of through No Fault of My Own.* Though typically it collects all sorts of pieces, from a series on sodomy to a serious reflection reprinted from the "On Language" column of the *New York Times Magazine* on the use of "we" in the Constitution, this book has the most pronounced political stance of any since *Crackers.* In *Now, Where Were We?* Blount is impatient with Reagan and Reaganism, "regards the eighties as a trashy decade'' (253), and reasserts some of the ''dated white Southern liberalism'' that he has identified as his political creed (Shepherd 1990, 68).

For a number of years he had wanted to write a novel. In 1975 he reported his work in progress as a novel called *If You Can't Wave, Stop.* In 1990 he explained that ''I've always wanted—in fact, I've always been urged by publishers, and I'm responding to those urges—to write a novel. It's hard to do, but I feel that I need to write some kind of long, strange book that's not a collection'' (Ross 1990, 70). Thus, *First Hubby* appeared in spring 1990. A novel about the first woman president of the United States, narrated by her husband, it combines in a longer form Blount's interests in American politics and the media, sexual relationships, and the sounds of American voices talking.

Married twice, Blount has two grown children, with whom he is clearly determined to share the kind of strong family ties that shaped his own growth. Good friendships, to which he often pays tribute in his work, are also important to him. Though a celebrated writer, he is no ''celebrity,'' and he continues to cling to ''basic truths'' and a sensible way of life.

MAJOR THEMES

The typical Roy Blount book is so multifarious that it does not have a theme, or even a subject; instead it has a profusion. Exceptions would be *About Three Bricks Shy of a Load* (1974), a nonfiction account of one season for one team in the NFL; *It Grows on You* (1986), about hair; and *First Hubby,* the 1990 novel about the husband of the first woman president. These books at least have unity of subject. But even they are thematically diverse, and a more useful approach is to look at some of the recurrent concerns of the author's work.

1. The South: Blount often writes *about* the South, and in an important sense, whatever the subject, he always writes *as* a Southerner. *Crackers* is a book about the South and Southerners, directly and urgently. In it he explores the complex fate of being a Southerner, particularly in such chapters as ''Being from Georgia,'' ''Trash No More,'' and ''Redneck Androgyny.'' Blount is aware of all the objections to Southerners, all the stupidity and viciousness and willful wrongheadedness that they are not only capable of, but proud of. This book is full of such observations as ''Only in the South would people think polyester was *fashionable*'' (67) and ''I knew it before I ever left Georgia: there are Southern vowels that to persons of intelligence are a pain in the bowels'' (49).

But he also celebrates what is best about the South, and he does so by celebrating the extremes. He celebrates country music and wallows in it; he has praised Billy Carter. (His objection to Jimmy Carter has been that he is not Southern enough, that he should be more vulgar and tacky, more of a good old boy. He should learn to cut loose.) Some of the contents of *Crackers* are reportage and not very interesting stuff about, say, Jerry Jeff Walker; but most of the commentary is subtle and acute, and more so for being funny. Blount's later books all contain generous helpings of Southern matter: for instance, ''I Don't

Eat Dirt Personally'' in *Now, Where Were We?* (a reaction to the statement in the *New York Times* about the established Southern practice of eating dirt); ''The Lowdown on Southern Hospitality'' in *What Men Don't Tell* and the use of such touchstones as country music, Kissin' Jim Folsom, and his friend, Nashville photographer Slick Lawson. *First Hubby* is all about Southerners.

2. The absurdities of modern life: Probably this is a central theme for every humorist who is other than a fantasist; to comment, amusingly, on things is to discover and highlight their pretensions and absurdities. Some of the topics in which Blount has found absurdities are perhaps predictable, especially if we think of him as in the tradition of Benchley and Perelman: the writer's own foibles (inability to remember names, uncertainty about his status as an author, ambivalence about militant homosexuality); politics, beginning with the bathos of the Carter administration and continuing with the artificiality and dishonesty of Reagan; fads and fashions—the Filofax, ''jock lingerie,'' deconstructionism.

3. Men and women: Blount has often written about sex and about relations between the sexes. About sex, for instance, there is his striking piece called ''The Orgasm: A Reappraisal,'' originally published in *Cosmopolitan* and reprinted in *One Fell Soup.* In it he reveals that

the orgasm is not really ideal for everyone. . . . Lack of communication has generally been thought to interfere with orgasm—as when one partner cannot tell whether the other is exclaiming ''Quick, quick, quick!'' or ''Quit, quit, quit!'' . . . Fish do not have orgasms, and, so far as we can determine, neither did the late J. Edgar Hoover. . . . Almost no work was done by Americans last year in the twenty minutes following orgasm. (134)

The little things that divide men and women—like women's underwear, and the new trend for women to wear modified men's underwear—have received his wry appraisal. The interchapters, or ''blue yodels,'' of *What Men Don't Tell Women* feature men who aren't androgynous enough and men who have ''flower guilt,'' worries about ''performance anxiety'' and the proper placement of the toilet lid.

First Hubby is not only about sex roles and sex reversal but about sex as well, its theory and practice. Though some of the sexual reversals of this novel set in the near future are facetious—Marilyn Quayle has tried to bring down the government and is now a fugitive in Libya—at heart it is a feminist novel, in which Blount addresses the most serious issues about man- and womanhood.

4. The basic things in life: Roy Blount is a dedicated appreciator of food, mulch, animals, children, pretty women, simplicity. He is sophisticated, but as he explains (*What Men Don't Tell Women*), ''Then, too, I like being in a certain size of dime store in maybe Clanton, Alabama, saying 'Yes, ma'am, I bleev I do' to the saleslady, just as smooth, but privately tingling with unwonted familiarity'' (183). His humor stands up for such simplicities, stands out against unwarranted complication, obfuscation, preciousness, and indirection. Criticizing Shere Hite's compilation of men's accounts of their sexual practices, he writes

(*One Fell Soup*): "I like to read about food, but I don't want to read a lot of "I like to chew a bite of green peas three or four times and then just let it rest on the very back part of my tongue where it arches up a little and" (119).

5. Language: "You have to have an appreciation of language, whether it's instinctive or learned or both, to write a good sentence," Blount explains (Ross 1990, 72). This love for words manifests itself in the way in which he writes, the art that conceals art but that is also one of his frequent topics. A column in *One Fell Soup* is dedicated to the odd claim (on a strip joint) "ONE NUDE, THE REST TOTALLY NAKED!" In reviewing Steve Martin's book, *Cruel Shoes,* he comments expertly (*One Fell Soup*), "An item about a nationality called Turds approaches risible flatness, but why 'Turdsmania' for the country's name? Turdsey, perhaps. Turdwana" (97). He has complained that if "Edwin Meese" had been the name of anybody in the *Carter* administration, he would never have lived it down. The Ogden Nash–like rhymes in his poems and songs are another evidence of the linguistic zest, as are the puns with which much of his writing is peppered, like the complicated one in *First Hubby* about a shiftless family of criminals named White who stole collard greens: white-collard crime.

The forms that Roy Blount's writing takes are manifold. Setting aside the novel, the book about the Steelers, and the book about hair, one can see that his most congenial, most mastered form has been the short piece of funny writing, what the *New Yorker* has called the "casual," which would include "parodies, sketches, personal essays, short stories, reporting, verse." He has done so many things that it is hard to categorize them, but three genres in which he has written particularly well are the personal essay in his own voice, the comic monologue in somebody else's voice, and the parody of some other type of text.

In the personal essays he writes engagingly about his life and his own preoccupations. His accounts of why he lives where he does or how he feels about historical debunking are funny because of his treatment, and, in fact, many pieces in this first category have almost no real subject—including such delightfully nebulous essays as "How to High-Falute," "How to Sweat," "The Socks Problem," and "I Can't Play Golf." One of the funniest personal essays is his complaint about not receiving a MacArthur Grant, worrying about what this will do to his afflatus and comparing himself bitterly to actual recipients, Robert Penn Warren and Steven Jay Gould, whom he represents as an expert on pandas (*One Fell Soup*): "It has been several weeks now since the MacArthur Foundation announced it was giving tens of thousands of dollars a year, tax free, no strings attached, to a number of Americans it deemed geniuses. I have waited long enough for the apologetic phone call: "Geez, it just hit us. Are we all sitting around here feeling red-faced! Casts the whole program into doubt. Forgot you *and* Jerry Lee Lewis. It's this new computer" (25).

The best comic monologues are found in *What Men Don't Tell Women* and *Crackers.* The "blue yodels" in the former are funny and acute; but the "More Carters" in *Crackers* are even more rich and strange. Blount has invented many more relatives for Jimmy Carter, such as Freeman Carter, black fugitive; "Limber Kimber Lee'' Carter, exotic dancer; and Sartrain Lolley Carter, a writer. He is working on *A Southerner's Account,* explaining ''I think mostly what I'll write about is women out in the woods nekkid. I never have run into any out there yet, but I've got an idea what it'd be like'' (*Crackers* 78). Later books (*Not Exactly*) include ''Only Hugh,'' in which an unnamed dweller in a town where only one citizen has *not* been featured on television explains how all but Hugh Odge got to be celebrities:

Then come to find out Miz Wygrand was a folk artist, with her little figurines she makes with lard and putty and beef gristle and blow-in cards. . . . Earl and Ora Whisenant, they're the ones who had the tag sale where somebody bought as a Egyptian mummy what turned out—no, I guess it was the other way around. It was *sold* as a bundle of antique shirtwaists. . . . Terrine Pharr. She's the one—you must've seen her getting worked over by Ted Koppel—the one that adopted her father, changed his name legally, and then married him. (108)

Even in *First Hubby,* which as a first-person narrative exploits the human voice throughout, there are many overheard conversations that are strange and funny: ''In Spratt's I heard a man say, 'He does bleeve in an afterlife, now, but he runs around sinning anyway. Says he assumes that God does care about what we do, but he says he's humble enough to realize God probably has a hard time telling one of us from another.' 'That's what I thought,' another man at his table said, 'about the IRS' '' (120).

Finally there are Blount's parodies of established types of discourse. ''If You Can Read This, You're Too Close'' (*What Men Don't Tell Women*) effectively parodies modern literary theory. *One Fell Soup* contains a ''Weekly News Quiz'' making fun of the quiz in the *New York Times* and ''Wired into Now,'' a series of questions about celebrities: examples, ''All those people on 'Love Boat'—do they actually, you know, do it?'' and ''The Emperor Caligula. Was he what I think he was?'' (237–38). His piece on the orgasm parodies sexologists; ''Sitting on a Seesaw'' (*Now Where Were We?*) is a mock report on a month's worth of rejected poetry.

These do not exhaust his modes; he continues to produce funny sportswriting and travel commentary and book reviews.

The most difficult task with Roy Blount, Jr., as with any humorist, is to explain what makes him funny. Blount says (*Not Exactly*) that humor ''uses jujitsu on looming fear and shame, flirts almost pruriently yet coolly with madness and sentimentality, and fuses horse sense with dream logic'' (175). Grady Ballenger (1988) calls attention to Blount's way of mixing things together, his ''pleasure in *heterogeneity*'' (53); Deborah Mason (1989) has chosen to emphasize the ''bumpkinhood,'' the ''*faux* hayseed persona,'' the ''foxy yokelism''—surely overstated, and not themselves very funny, as a few minutes reading Josh Billings would make painfully clear. Patrick F. McManus (1985), a fellow humorist, has called attention to the "unceasing drip-drip-drip of bizarre images, intricate wordplay, droll asides and crazy asides."

All of these are suggestive. But Blount's Southernness may be a bit distracting here. It is a strength, in one way—is there any such thing as Northern humor?—but limiting, too. Blount has more in common with S. J. Perelman, in his endlessly inventive use of language, than with, say, Lewis Grizzard, for whom being called a "professional cracker" makes more sense. Like Mark Twain, Blount has spoken surprising truths in a voice extraordinarily crafted to emulate the sound of ordinary speech. And like all good humorists—like all good writers, in fact—he has, through the power and grace of his prose, taken unpromising materials and made them into something fine.

SURVEY OF CRITICISM

There has been little criticism of Roy Blount, Jr., aside from the reviews of his books. G. William Koon's essay "Roy Blount: A Redneck Heuristic" (1988) is an appreciation and analysis of Blount's significance and the basis of his humor, which Koon finds to be the "mix of intelligence and crackerism" in his persona. In his essay "Between Journalism and the Essay" (1981), an extended treatment of new books of essays, Spencer Brown dismisses *Crackers* contemptuously—and unfairly—as "a poormouth tedium devoted to hatred of Jimmy Carter." The best overview is Grady Ballenger's chapter on Blount in the *Encyclopedia of American Humorists,* which is well written, well informed, and astute in explanation. That there will be a rapid increase in scholarly writing about Blount is unlikely, given the American tendency to underrate writers of humor as long as they are alive; nor does he require exhaustive analysis, but he deserves the kind of critical awareness that is due to one of the nation's best and most versatile writers.

BIBLIOGRAPHY

Works by Roy Blount, Jr.

About Three Bricks Shy of a Load. Boston: Little, Brown, 1974.
Crackers: This Whole Many-Angled Thing of Jimmy, More Carters, Ominous Little Animals, Sad-Singing Women, My Daddy and Me. New York: Knopf, 1980.
One Fell Soup; or, I'm Just a Bug on the Windshield of Life. Boston: Little, Brown, 1982.
What Men Don't Tell Women. Boston: Atlantic and Little, Brown, 1984.
Not Exactly What I Had in Mind. Boston: Atlantic Monthly Press, 1985.
It Grows on You: A Hair-Raising Survey of Human Plumage. New York: Doubleday, 1986.
Soupsongs/Webster's Ark. Boston: Houghton Mifflin, 1987.
Now, Where Were We? Getting Back to Basic Truths That We Have Lost Sight of through No Fault of My Own. New York: Villard, 1988.

First Hubby. New York: Villard, 1990.
Camels Are Easy, Comedy's Hard. New York: Villard, 1991.

Studies of Roy Blount, Jr.

Ballenger, Grady W. "Roy Blount, Jr." In *Encyclopedia of American Humorists,* edited by Steven H. Gale, 49–53. New York: Garland, 1988.

Brown, Spencer. "Between Journalism and the Essay." *Sewanee Review* 89 (Summer 1981): 431–40.

Broyard, Anatole. "Wit's Temporary Relief." *New York Times,* April 28, 1984): 14.

Culhane, Charles. "Possum Fair." *National Review* 34 (February 19, 1982): 180–82.

Greenburg, Dan. "On Southerners, Salaries and 'Fih.' " *New York Times Book Review* (May 13, 1984): 12.

Koon, G. William. "Roy Blount: A Redneck Heuristic." *Kennesaw Review* 1 (Spring 1988): 38–44.

Lehmann-Haupt, Christopher. "Books of the Times." *New York Times,* November 1, 1982): C20.

Lyons, Gene. "Voices of Nothingness." *Nation* 231 (December 6, 1980): 616–19.

McManus, Patrick F. "The Drip-Drip-Drip of Mirth." *New York Times Book Review* (November 17, 1985): 14.

Mason, Deborah. "Blackened Red Dirt and Other Delicacies." *New York Times Book Review* (April 2, 1989): 9.

Morrison, Donald. "Fine Red Dirt." *Time* 116 (October 20, 1980): 102.

Ross, Jean W. Interview with Roy Blount. In *Contemporary Authors, New Revision Series,* vol. 28, edited by Hal May and James G. Lesniak, 69–72. Detroit: Gale, 1990.

Schine, Cathleen. "Baseball, Socks, Sex and Laughs." *Nation* 235 (November 20, 1982): 453–54.

Shepherd, Kenneth R. "Blount, Roy (Alton) Jr." In *Contemporary Authors, New Revision Series,* vol. 28, edited by Hal May and James G. Lesniak, 68–69. Detroit: Gale, 1990.

Simmons, Charles. "People from Georgia and Nearby Places." *New York Times Book Review* (September 28, 1980): 3.

Sragow, Michael. Review of *Crackers.* In *New Republic* 183 (September 27, 1980): 39–40.

Turan, Kenneth. "Curmudgeon." *Time* 123 (June 4, 1984): 72–73.

Wolcott, James. "The Laugh Pack: Is the New 'Humor' Actually Funny?" *Vanity Fair* (April 1988): 20–26.

PETER STITT

David Bottoms
(1949–   )

When he chose David Bottom's first book manuscript, *Shooting Rats at the Bibb County Dump,* for the Walt Whitman Award of the Academy of American Poets in 1979, Robert Penn Warren said: "David Bottoms is a strong poet, and much of his strength emerges from the fact that he is temperamentally a realist. In his vision the actual world is not transformed but illuminated." Bottoms has lived for most of his life in Georgia; a narrative, realistic poet who covets the epiphanic moment, he draws his subjects, characters, scenes, images, events, and ideas from the woods, swamps, dumps, bars, small towns, and suburbs of that state.

BIOGRAPHY

Following his birth there on September 11, 1949, David Bottoms was raised in Canton, Georgia. He is the only child of David H. Bottoms, a funeral director, and Louise Ashe Bottoms, a registered nurse. After earning his B.A. from Mercer University in 1971, Bottoms stayed on in Macon, Georgia, for another year, working as a guitar salesman. On February 5, 1972, he married Margaret Lynn Bensel, then moved in the fall to Carrollton, Georgia, to pursue graduate study at West Georgia College. In 1973 he wrote a thesis on the poetry and criticism of Henry Timrod, "the laureate of the Confederacy," and was awarded an M.A. in English.

From 1974 to 1978 Bottoms taught high-school English in Douglasville, Georgia, at the same time writing the poems later gathered into the volume *Shooting Rats at the Bibb County Dump* (1980). Some of these poems first appeared in the chapbook *Jamming with the Band at the VFW* in 1978. During the academic year 1978–79, Bottoms worked part-time in the Georgia Poets-in-the-Schools program, then traveled south to Tallahassee in 1979 in order to become a graduate student in creative writing at Florida State University. As he said later in an interview: "I had written *Shooting Rats* and won the Whitman Award before I had ever taken a poetry workshop" (Lott, 1983, 191). Bottoms was awarded the Ph.D. in 1982; for his dissertation he produced the collection of poems—published in 1983—*In a U-Haul North of Damascus,* which was later named Book of the Year in Poetry by the Dixie Council of Authors and Journalists.

In 1984 Bottoms collaborated with Dave Smith to produce the anthology *The Morrow Book of Younger American Poets.* In 1987 Bottoms published both his third book of poems, *Under the Vulture-Tree,* and his first novel, *Any Cold Jordan.* A group of poems from *Under the Vulture-Tree* had earlier won the Levinson Prize upon their publication in *Poetry* magazine. Bottoms has taught at Georgia State University in Atlanta since 1982; he was promoted from assistant professor to associate professor in 1987. Bottoms served as the Richard Hugo Poet-in-Residence at the University of Montana in 1986 and has read his work at such places as Kenyon College, the Library of Congress, the University of Michigan, the Guggenheim Museum, and Bennington College.

MAJOR THEMES

For David Bottoms, each poem is a discrete, primarily autobiographical moment. Although he has divided each of his major collections into five sections, there is little thematic building from one to another. Rather, the sections seem designed to allow for the gathering of poems that are vaguely similar to one another, either in theme or in method. The title poem of *In a U-Haul North of Damascus,* for example, shows the speaker waking up at a truck stop in the cab of a rented van, which he had earlier filled with all the possessions he wished to carry from one life into another. He indicates that he has left his wife because she has suffered a miscarriage. We see him begin to come to his senses in this poem, as he wonders if he is doing the right thing after all. The problem the poem raises concerning the book is that, except for one other poem alluding to the miscarriage, the powerful subject matter of the speaker's growth from self-centeredness to maturity is not so much as alluded to, much less developed thematically, anywhere else in the volume. Rather than build to this poignant moment of self-awareness—which occurs late in section five—Bottoms instead seems to have used this book primarily as a repository for individual poems that relate to one another only locally, within the individual sections.

Under the Vulture-Tree is probably Bottoms's most cohesive volume; the three poems in the final section are devoted to the speaker's dead father, and this elegiac concern lends the volume its unity. The tone of these poems is anticipated in section two, which consists entirely of elegies written in honor of Southern country artists, most of them musicians; "Homage to Lester Flatt" is an especially strong poem. In the third section, Bottoms addresses what is probably his most obsessive theme: the relationship that civilized man has to the elemental world of nature. As a creature of nature, man is of course subject to the ravages of death; however, the life that he leads within a self-created, civilized world insulates him from this fact. In section three, therefore, Bottoms has his speaker venture out into nature, to go fishing, or hunting, or just to drift down a river in a boat. What he mostly discovers is the truth of the ''Vulture-Tree,'' an unavoidable reminder of death. As Vernon Shetley (1988) has pointed out: ''Nature hints at transcendence. . . . But that promise of revelation goes always unfulfilled, the natural order is forever opaque to the human understanding, and so the only emblem of transfiguration Bottoms offers is the flock of vultures'' (100).

It is not just the fact of death that makes Bottoms's speaker feel an alien within the realm of nature that he so desires; despite his deep longing to live an authentic, natural life, he remains a creature of civilization and never feels entirely at home in the woods and on the river. This idea is the burden of the poems of section three in *Under the Vulture-Tree,* just as it is the burden of the poems in section three of *Shooting Rats in the Bibb County Dump* and section four of *In a U-Haul North of Damascus.* Bottoms's speaker is most at home in nature not when seeking mystic unity with it but when he approaches it as a typically unreflective and generally drunken cracker, a yahoo who goes ''Shooting Rats at the Bibb County Dump.'' Joel Conarroe (1983) has accurately characterized this subject matter in Bottoms's poems as reflecting a ''good-old-boys world in which true satisfaction comes from throwing knives into animals, . . . gigging frogs on the Alatoona, or drinking beer on a fishing boat'' (4).

To be sure, the ''civilized'' world of Bottoms's poems is also a rather specialized place; it has nothing to do, as I have pointed out in an earlier essay (1987), with the world of such Southern writers as ''Peter Taylor or Walker Percy,'' whose characters are likely to be found ''discussing art and philosophy in a drawing room'' (804). Instead, as Rick Lott (1983) has added, ''The South [Bottoms] writes of is that of Faulkner's Snopeses, the 'white trash' heirs of the Old South''; the poems are ''set in bars, motels, and pawnshops and [feature] truckers, waitresses, faith healers'' (186–87). David Bottoms himself plays the guitar, and the civilized world of his poems is primarily that portrayed by country-and-western music. It is this dimension of his work that Bottoms has chosen to emphasize in the titles of his books—unfortunately so, one has to feel, since the themes of death and alienation from nature are so much more profound in general and so much more seriously treated.

Bottoms has structured his individual poems as epiphanies, in which the speaker (the poems are always spoken in a first-person voice) sorts out the details of some experience in order to arrive at a moment of wisdom. The method allows for poems to be written on almost any occasion, from the time a boy fires his first rifle to the time a man hunts alligators, or from the time a trucker sees a reflection of his younger self in the fog to the time he dreams of having his rig break down in an Edenic landscape, or from the time a boy learns from his father how to bunt a baseball to the time he sits drunk on a loading dock looking at stars. The method is inherently didactic, and though Bottoms has generally handled his materials with indirection and poetic tact, there are poems that build to conclusions one cannot help but feel are too obvious and moralistic—for example ''Hiking Toward Laughing Gull Point'' in *In a U-Haul North of Damascus* and ''In the Ice-Pasture'' and ''Face Jugs: Homage to Lanier Meaders'' in *Under the Vulture-Tree*. Because—as Vernon Shetley has pointed out—''Bottoms . . . stands firmly within the strain . . . of plain-style presentation of incidents of everyday life'' (100), he is not immune from the disease of writing in an excessively literal fashion.

Bottoms's novel, *Any Cold Jordan,* chronicles what are apparently the last months in the life of its dispirited central character. Almost a cross between Camus' Mersault and Salinger's Holden Caulfield, Billy Parker has no values to base his life on more substantial than a complex of adolescent prejudices against anyone who doesn't see things his way. Though he plays guitar on weekends in a Tallahassee bar called ''The Under Thing,'' Billy has nothing but contempt for his listeners, none of whom appreciates the fine music that is in his soul. When he journeys up to Atlanta to open for a superior musician and his group, Billy goes into an existential funk and fails to appear for the second night. Billy's marriage is in at least as bad shape as his career—so bad, in fact, that we as readers are not even sure that Billy and Jean are married until far into the book. The point of view here is third person, closely limited to Billy's consciousness; so uneasy is he with his marriage that he is scarcely able to tell us he is married to the woman who shares his house.

Alienated from his music and his wife, Billy turns increasingly for support to nature—he takes great solace from the pond that lies just behind his suburban house—and to his new and exceptionally dangerous friend Jack. In fact, it is through Billy's relationship with Jack that Bottoms shows us most clearly how neurotic and dysfunctional Billy has become. As the novel opens, Billy and Jean are at Jack's lakeside cabin; Jack, a stranger in town, had called at the suggestion of a mutual friend. When the two arrive, Jack is cleaning and reassembling one of his guns—an army-issue, .45-caliber automatic pistol. Billy seems most intent on forcing Jean into Jack's arms, and at a certain point after dinner goes off into the darkness, ostensibly to fish. Later in the book, Jack proposes that he, Billy, and two other tough guys (Billy is clearly out of his league in all this) hijack the money from a drug deal about to be consummated between two biker gangs. Billy is badly shot and as the book ends it seems clear that he is about to die.

Unfortunately, there is no evidence anywhere in the book that Billy, so lost a character now, was ever anything else. In one significant flashback, he re-members his third date with Jean. They spent an afternoon making love at his apartment, then went out to eat and have a few drinks, and finally ended up at the house she was sharing with her friend Marilyn. Jean discovers that she must have left her keys at Billy's, for they are not in her purse. Luckily, Marilyn is home, so Jean and Billy say goodnight, promising to use the keys as a good excuse to meet again tomorrow. On his way home, Billy decides to return that night with the keys and surprise Jean by sneaking back in. As he tiptoes into her room, he notices that two people are making love in the bed: Marilyn and Jean. Billy tiptoes back out and later accepts from Jean the excuse that she and Marilyn were merely conducting an "experiment." Later he marries her, and the action in this book is, at least in part, the denouement to his foolishness. Marilyn remains an important presence as she visits Tallahassee as often as Jean visits her in Atlanta.

Despite a violent and action-filled ending, this novel is surprisingly static overall. Its chapters consist primarily of the internal monologues of Billy Parker, during which readers are lectured didactically on a series of adolescent prejudices. Given his conviction that nearly all country-music fans know nothing about the subject, it is natural that Billy should wish to comment endlessly on this topic; he worships Lester Flatt, but has other favorites as well. The first actual action in the novel occurs three-fifths of the way through its 256 pages, when Billy breaks a beer bottle across the face of a bar patron who has repeatedly requested the song "Cripple Creek," despite Billy's obvious reluctance to play it. When Billy says he will do the "big-tip songs" later, the man throws two quarters, one of which dents Billy's guitar. We recognize that Billy has finally gone off the deep end. It is this same lack of judgment that allows him to get involved with the hare-brained—and fatal—hijacking scheme at the end. The title of the book of course refers to the River Jordan, which consistently stands for death in all of Bottoms's works. Billy is obsessed with water throughout the novel, and has a recurrent dream about a mysterious group baptism on a river that he and his father interrupt as they are fishing; we last see Billy as he is dying in a boat on a river.

SURVEY OF CRITICISM

Because David Bottoms is still a relatively young writer—poets in this country are considered young almost until the age of sixty—nearly all of the critical attention that his work has received has come in book reviews. The one exception to this rule is also the longest piece to be devoted to Bottoms's work, though it considers only the first two books of poems. Rick Lott's entry in the *Dictionary of Literary Biography Yearbook* begins with a biographical sketch and ends with a brief interview with the author. In his critical commentary, Lott has analyzed both structure and theme in *Shooting Rats at the Bibb County Dump* and *In a U-Haul North of Damascus* concluding that, though Bottoms makes heavy use of Southern materials, his work transcends regionalism. The modern world is seen as a place of wreckage; thus the poet turns to nature and the past for sustenance and meaning. Though Bottoms is not traditionally religious, he is said to be concerned with underlying meanings. Death is an important topic for Bottoms, whose work is also said to be more introspective and domestic in the second book than in the first. Lott's most interesting biographical detail in his assertion that "James Dickey . . . taught [Bottoms] to hunt snakes with a blowgun" (191).

Among reviewers of *Shooting Rats at the Bibb County Dump,* Joseph Parisi (1980)—who, as editor of *Poetry* magazine, has published many of Bottoms's poems—argues that Bottoms is neither "a cracker or a good old boy," because his book "resonates with deeper significance, the common mortality shared by animals, ancestors, all earth's inhabitants whatever their station" (1250). David Clewell (1980) has also found broad significance in Bottoms's first book, suggesting that he is "a poet obsessed with human history, personal loss, and the frailty of systematic faith in the context of everyday life" (68). To this list, David M. Cicotello (1981) has added Bottoms's interest in characters who "reveal traits of purposelessness and ennui" (313). More negative views have been provided by Charles Berger (1982), for whom Bottoms is "yet another American vitalist, friend of truckers and hunters, who turns out to be absorbed primarily in the making of his own poems. In other words, another narcissistic poet." Kelly Claspill (1983) has seen primarily "poems filled with hunters, truckers, and dope-smokers, as well as booze drinking, bar frequenting good-old-boys and their women" (182). Claspill has been particularly hard on what she sees as Bottoms's reductive view of women.

Reviewing *In a U-Haul North of Damascus,* Joel Conarroe (1983) judges Bottoms to be a "poet who likes to discover secondary meanings in ordinary locutions. . . . Time and again the literal is translated into the figurative." Pointing out Bottoms's debt to James Dickey, Conarroe has found "in several of the poems, with their emphasis on guns and adolescent values, a sensibility that suggests the author of *Deliverance*" (4). Michael Cass (1984) agrees that "Bottoms' poems are convincing at the literal level and yet are also successful as metaphorical elevations to the level of suggested meaning" (744), while Penelope Mesic (1984) sees a commitment to "strong physical reality, upon which Bottoms relies as the one eternal verity" (296).

Though Bettina Drew (1987), reviewing *Under the Vulture-Tree,* finds that "most [of the] poems are told in a first-person narrative that becomes wearing, as the poet doesn't quite manage to be the vehicle for universality such a voice demands" (87), Bill Ott (1987) has seen the reflection of "an ever-evolving poetic consciousness, an ability to find new levels of meaning in the artifacts of the everyday" (1713). I have suggested (1987) that Bottoms is "a secular poet" whose "ritualistic, epiphanic journeys . . . seek not transcendence but naturalistic knowledge of life and death" (804). The best commentary on Bottoms's work yet published is that by Vernon Shetley (1983), who points out the tension between civilization and nature in Bottoms's poems, the centrality of death, and the evolution of Bottoms's style "toward a greater openness, with a correspondingly increased autobiographical emphasis" (100). Writing about both *Under the Vulture-Tree* and *Any Cold Jordan,* David Kirby (1988) suggests that "In flush times one of the most useful things our writers can do is to remind us how poor we are, and David Bottoms is better at that these days than almost any other young writer working in two genres'' (xxxvi). No truly useful criticism has yet been written on *Any Cold Jordan.*

BIBLIOGRAPHY

Works by David Bottoms

Jamming with the Band at the VFW. Austell, Ga.: Burnt Hickory Press, 1978.
Shooting Rats at the Bibb County Dump. New York: Morrow, 1980.
In a U-Haul North of Damascus. New York: Morrow, 1983.
Any Cold Jordan. Atlanta: Peachtree, 1987.
Under the Vulture-Tree. New York: Morrow, 1987.

Works Edited by David Bottoms

The Morrow Anthology of Younger American Poets. Edited with Dave Smith. New York: Morrow, 1985.

Studies of David Bottoms

Berger, Charles. ''Laurels.'' *Poetry* 140 (April 1982): 35–50.
Cass, Michael. ''Danger and Beauty: David Bottoms' *In a U-Haul North of Damascus.*'' *Southern Review* 20 (1984): 743–45.
Cicotello, David M. ''Loss and Ritual in the South.'' *Prairie Schooner* 55 (1981): 311–13.
Claspill, Kelly. Review of *Shooting Rats at the Bibb County Dump. Quarterly West,* no. 16 (1983): 182–87.
Clewell, David. ''Vital Assurances.'' *Chowder Review,* no. 14 (1980): 64–69.
Conarroe, Joel. Review of *In a U-Haul North of Damascus. Washington Post, Book World,* August 7, 1983. 4.
Drew, Bettina. Review of *Under the Vulture-Tree. Library Journal* 112, no. 9 (May 15, 1987): 87.
Kirby, David. ''Waking Up the Neighbors.'' *Sewanee Review* 96 (Spring 1988): xxxvi–xxxviii.
Lott, Rick. ''David Bottoms.'' In *Dictionary of Literary Biography Yearbook.* Edited by Mary Bruccoli, Jean W. Ross, Richard Ziegfield, 186–93. Detroit: Gale Research, 1983.
Mesic, Penelope. Review of *In a U-Haul North of Damascus. Poetry* 143 (February 1984): 296–97.
Ott, Bill. Review of *Under the Vulture-Tree. Booklist* 83, no. 22 (August 1987): 1712–13.
Parisi, Joseph. Review of *Shooting Rats at the Bibb County Dump. Booklist* 76 (May 1980): 1250.
Shetley, Vernon. Review of *Under the Vulture-Tree. Poetry* 152 (May 1988): 100–101.
Simpson, Louis. ''Facts and Poetry.'' *Gettysburg Review* 1 (1988): 156–65.
Stitt, Peter. ''To Enlighten, to Embody.'' *Georgia Review* 41 (1987): 800–813.

DAVID PAUL RAGAN

Fred Chappell
(1936–)

When Fred Chappell shared the 1985 Bollingen Prize in poetry with John Ashbery, readers across America began to recognize what followers of Southern literature had long known: Chappell commands one of the most versatile and prolific voices among contemporary writers. Equally adept with novels, short stories, and a dazzling range of poetic forms, Chappell is also an accomplished essayist, reviewer, and teacher of creative writing. George Garrett (1983–84) has described him as "a genuine man of letters (in the Robert Penn Warren tradition) whose work is important, indeed outstanding, in whatever form he is working in and with" (6).

BIOGRAPHY

Chappell was born on May 28, 1936 in Canton, a paper-mill town in the mountains of western North Carolina, a region which provides the setting of much of his work. His parents, J. T. and Anne Davis Chappell, both taught school when Chappell was a youth, and he practically lived with his mother's parents on their farm. Both his parents and grandparents provided models for characters in his fiction and in his four-volume "verse novel" *Midquest*. The autobiographical essay "A Pact with Faustus" describes Chappell's early interest in music and writing and suggests the isolation imposed upon the young writer by what he perceived as a largely unsympathetic environment. By his own account, he began writing seriously in 1954, first experimenting with science-fiction forms he had enjoyed as an adolescent. By high school, he had discovered more ambitious models in Thomas Mann, Tolstoy, and the French symbolist poets.

Chappell earned his undergraduate degree at Duke University in 1961 and continued to work there toward his M.A.; his thesis was a hand-assembled concordance to the English poetry of Samuel Johnson, a monumental project he recalled having undertaken because he "needed the discipline." While at Duke, Chappell studied under the celebrated creative-writing teacher William Blackburn, who became an important older friend and mentor and whose students included William Styron, Anne Tyler, and Reynolds Price. In his essay "Welcome to High Culture," Chappell acknowledges Price's impact as an honest critic with whom he was free to argue as he could not with Blackburn; Price also encouraged the young Chappell to write poetry. At a Duke literary festival, Chappell met Hiram Hayden, the founding editor of *Atheneum,* who was impressed by the young writer's work and invited him to submit a novel. Initially hesitant—Chappell considered himself primarily a poet—he accepted Hayden's offer since his National Defense Education Act fellowship did not cover summer expenses. Expanding a short sketch entitled "January," Chappell composed his first novel, *It Is Time, Lord,* in five weeks. The story of James Christopher, a man whose obsessions with the past destroy his capacity to function in the present, the novel is structurally demanding, juxtaposing fanciful constructions and evocative memories of the protagonist's childhood. It appeared in 1963. The following year Chappell took his M.A. and moved with his wife, Susan, and son, Heath, to begin teaching at the University of North Carolina at Greensboro, where he is currently Writer in Residence.

A series of grants allowed Chappell to devote serious attention to his writing as well as to travel during the following years. His second novel, *The Inkling,* also written in a five-week period, appeared in 1965. It examines the dissolution of the Anderson family, motivated largely by the opposition of the two children, Jan, whose compulsive attempts to assert his will contrast the unbridled destructive appetites of his retarded sister, Timmie. The following year Chappell received a Rockefeller Foundation grant and took his family to Florence, where he completed his third novel, *Dagon* (1968), the composition of which had occupied an arduous three years. A modern version of the Sampson and Delilah story, *Dagon* projects the concerns of the first two novels into a surreal world dominated by the sadistic Mina, who virtually cannibalizes Peter Leland, the puritanical minister who willingly sacrifices himself to her. With the financial assistance of an award from the National Institute of Arts and Letters, Chappell completed while in Italy the first draft of his fourth novel, *The Gaudy Place,* on the backs of the galley proofs of *Dagon.*

Reviewers of Chappell's first three novels praised his command of language and his evocation of place. His violent plots, interest in aberrant psychology, and structural experimentation were conveniently labeled "Southern Gothic" and linked with such predecessors as William Faulkner, Carson McCullers, and Flannery O'Connor. The attention that Chappell's early work sparked was not limited to the United States. Maurice-Edgar Coindreau's accomplished translations of *It Is Time, Lord* (as *L'Hameçon D'Or* [1965]) and *Dagon* (*Le Dieu-Poisson* [1970]) added Chappell's name to the list of American writers such as Poe and Faulkner for whom recognition in France preceded attention in the

United States. *The Inkling,* translated by Claude Levy as *Prémonitions,* appeared in 1969. In 1972 the Academie Française awarded Chappell the prestigious Prix de Meilleur des Livres Étrangers for *Le Dieu-Poisson,* an award that Chappell typically disclaimed as intended to honor Coindreau, the translator, rather than the author. *It Is Time, Lord* also attracted critical respect in an English edition.

At the Hollins Writing Conference in 1970, Leslie Phillabaum, an editor at Louisiana State University Press, approached Chappell about submitting a collection for a fledgling poetry series. He assembled his first volume, *The World Between the Eyes* (1971), a combination of previously published selections and a good deal of newly written material. It was an attempt to create a "full volume poem," one with narrative selections broken into individual units. Though Chappell has referred to the book as "simply and frankly weak in conception and execution" ("Fred Chappell," 1986, 122), it earned reviewers' praise in 1972. The idea of a full-volume poem relying heavily upon narrative materials was one to which Chappell would later return.

When Chappell turned to revising *The Gaudy Place* (1973), composing multiple drafts, his work had undergone a conscious change: "I set myself very deliberately the challenge . . . of writing a novel about the same length as the others, but having scope in it, and trying to draw a larger social picture . . . [and] more variety of character" (personal interview). It was a decision that would have a far-reaching impact upon Chappell's subsequent career both as novelist and poet. In "A Pact with Faustus" (1983–84) he explains the impulse that led him away from the highly philosophical designs of his first three novels: "In my case adventurous experimentation with form seems to lead to over-intellectualization, to desiccation, of content. I have got to where I should like for my work to be humane, and I do not much care if it even becomes sentimental" (16). If he perhaps overstated the case—the poet himself has censured some of the selections in *Midquest* as bordering too heavily upon sentimentality—*The Gaudy Place* clearly signals a watershed in approach as well as in theme. Its tone is essentially comic; its violent conclusion is not fatal, more revelatory than tragic.

Chappell's next, most ambitious project, "the four-volume poetic autobiography" ("Fred Chappell," 1986, 122) *Midquest,* is a comic work in the tradition of his model, Dante. He recalls its inception: "The hardest decision was about whether to undertake it or not. The amount of concentrated labor it would require was staggering and the technical command still beyond my grasp. But I determined to go ahead with this fictional tetralogy which was to be organized around the four elements of earth, air, fire, and water and to take place during one twenty-four hour period, the speaker's birthday, May 28, 1971" ("Fred Chappell," 1986, 122). He assembled a rough outline and fleshed out the role of the persona, Ole Fred, whose musings would "include [his] whole past life in one sense or another." The titles of the individual volumes signal the organizational image patterns: *River* (1975), *Bloodfire* (1978), *Wind Mountain* (1979), and *Earthsleep* (1980). *Midquest* occupies a special place in Chappell's career, in part because of the pleasure he found in writing it: "I have never experienced such unalloyed joy in the act of writing, and rarely in life itself, as when working on this poem" ("Fred Chappell," 1986, 122).

The completed *Midquest* (1981) was greeted with near universal praise. Though the approach was unique and the outlook more affirmative, the materials that provided the basis for much of the poetry harkened back to Chappell's first novel. The reuse of familiar material was quite deliberate, growing out of Chappell's opinion that *It Is Time, Lord* had suggested many undeveloped issues. The poem's sensibilities and evolving moral concerns can in fact be traced through practically all of the author's previous work. Indeed, Robert Morgan (1982) has asserted that Chappell's writing exhibits a "wholeness," that "whatever he does fits with all the rest" (45).

Poetry did not occupy Chappell's exclusive attention during the composition of *Midquest.* He contributed essays and reviews to a wide array of books, journals, and newspapers. He also continued to place short stories, which he has found the most "difficult" of literary forms. From over forty published stories, eleven were collected in *Moments of Light* (1980), which Chappell has admitted "may well be my favorite child among my books of fiction" (1986, 123). The selections trace their genesis back to the beginning of Chappell's career. Included are "January," the sketch that had been expanded into the first chapter of *It Is Time, Lord,* and other pieces that were arranged into general thematic groupings. Three stories set in the eighteenth century are followed by contemporary explorations of despair and loss of innocence. Though the settings range from a mythical world before the advent of civilized man to the London Haydn visits in the title piece, many are set in the locale Chappell had long claimed as his own—the mountains and piedmont of North Carolina. A perceptive preface by Annie Dillard began to draw serious attention to Chappell's achievement in this genre.

The directions that Chappell's career have taken in the past decade have been as various as those he pursued before the appearance of *Midquest,* though he has largely maintained his resolve to avoid overly intellectual ideas as underpinnings for his works. This is hardly to suggest, however, that he has contented himself with the humorous or folksy "lyric narratives" that many reviewers singled out for praise in *Midquest. Castle Tzingal* (1984), a series of interior and dramatic monologues that create "a sort of chamber opera" ("Fred Chappell," 1986, 124) in a corrupt medieval castle, shares more in common with *Dagon* than with *Midquest.* The mysterious disappearance of a traveling minstrel is investigated by an ambassador from a neighboring kingdom. He discovers a horrifying world haunted by the disembodied voice of the murdered poet, who continues to sing from the dungeon. The darkness is intensified by the murders and suicides providing the book's resolution.

The lyrics in Chappell's two most recent collections return to familiar territory. Both *Source* (1985) and *First and Last Words* (1989) are more varied, less tightly organized than the volumes of *Midquest,* yet in each collection, Chappell has attempted to emphasize unifying themes and images linking poems together into larger units. The thirty-six lyrics in *Source* appear in four sections, each bearing the title of the selection providing a thematic or symbolic center. Many lyrics are brief, and most are collected (and occasionally revised) from periodical publications. The organizing principle of *First and Last Words* is more loose: selections allude to earlier masterpieces of literature, art, or music; the first group provides "Prologues" to such works, the third, "Epilogues." Between is a series appropriately entitled "Entr'acte," which, though less closely connected to other materials, explores similar subject matter. As always, the selections demonstrate a multiplicity of poetic forms and styles.

Chappell's most recent novels, *I Am One of You Forever* (1985) and *Brighten the Corner Where You Are* (1989), are likewise freer, more episodic in structure, resulting from his intention to incorporate material which "never quite fit into the design" ("Fred Chappell," 1986, 124) of *Midquest*. In fact, he has projected "a quartet of novels which would balance the *Midquest* tetralogy, surrounding that poem with a solid fictional universe" ("Fred Chappell," 1986, 124). In outlook the books blend nostalgia with humor, and though the darkness that informed the author's early fiction is hardly absent, death and cultural disintegration are attenuated through the perceptions of the adult narrator Jess. *I Am One of You Forever* concerns Jess's coming of age during World War II. He lives with his parents in his grandmother's rambling brick house—the structure familiar from *It Is Time, Lord, Dagon,* and *Midquest.* But the house, like the characters who inhabit it, has largely lost the gloomy, inimical qualities it had acquired in the earlier works. The daily routine of farm life is interrupted by family visitors whose stories are firmly in the American literary tradition of the tall tale. Like *Midquest,* the novel has remained among Chappell's most popular works.

In the sequel, *Brighten the Corner Where You Are,* Jess remains as omniscient narrator, though the episodes review a day in the life of his father, Joe Robert, whose job is threatened for teaching Darwin in his rural mountain school. Though the point of view is not entirely convincing and the atmosphere is considerably darkened, the novel continues in the rustic tradition of *I Am One of You Forever*—warmly evocative and humorous without glossing over the hard realities with which earlier Chappell protagonists had wrestled and by which they had sometimes been defeated.

Chappell's energies show no signs of abating, and interest in his work continues to grow, spurred by the appearance of *The Fred Chappell Reader* in 1987, the paperback reissue of *Dagon* and *The Gaudy Place,* and the increasing appearances of Chappell's poetry and short fiction in anthologies. He publishes poems, stories, essays, and reviews at an astonishing rate, considering his teaching responsibilities. An accomplished reader of his work, he is in growing demand at schools and colleges, and he frequently conducts seminars and workshops. He has outlined ideas for poetry and novels that promise his continued presence as a major voice in Southern letters for years to come.

MAJOR THEMES

Despite a great diversity of subject matter and literary forms, Chappell's entire body of work has explored a group of essentially related ideas. Perhaps the most pervasive is both a theme and an attitude that he takes toward all his writing: the moral responsibility of literature, a topic, that Chappell has called "the only reality an artist is interested in" ("Two Modes," 338). The characters in his fiction and the voices in his poetry are preoccupied with moral or ethical dilemmas, which often arise from their inability to fathom their responsibilities, either to themselves or to those around them. From this basic tenet, Chappell has woven an elaborate fabric of connected themes, including the effects of time and of imagination on the individual's perception of reality; the burden of original sin, defined by Chappell as "a condition of things that exist before a character shows up" (personal interview) and thus closely linked to his emphasis upon family relationships; the corruption of innocence; the opposition of will and appetite, flesh and spirit, doubt and faith; and, perhaps most important, the attempts of individuals to assert themselves anew, to cultivate rebirth. Of vital significance in this renewal is the rejuvenative and empowering capacities of the arts, especially music and poetry, prominent as subjects in Chappell's lyric poetry.

Virtually all these ideas make their debut in *It Is Time, Lord,* the foundation upon which so much of Chappell's work rests. James Christopher has come to his dark wood in early middle life, and he finds his will paralyzed by inability to reconcile past and present. He attempts to resurrect his energies through constructing a fictional account of his life, in which he fashions himself a Methodist minister whose sermon, addressing Christopher's own psychological crises, ends with the injunction, "Take yourself up." Having yielded almost totally to his spiritual malaise, he quits his job, alienates himself from his faithful wife, and enters the tawdry world of Preacher, a small-town rake who introduces Christopher to Judy. When his brief affair with her leads to Preacher's murder by Judy's irate husband, Christopher is obliged to examine his own culpability, a process that takes the form of three recurring dreams concluding the novel. Through these dreams, Chappell hints that Christopher has embarked on a genuine quest for renewal, a process of self-discovery in which he will overcome his obsessions and embrace the sustaining love of his wife.

James Christopher's problems provide the paradigm for many later characters. His need to assert his will becomes the primary motivation of Jan Anderson in *The Inkling,* and Peter Leland in *Dagon* shares many of Christopher's traits, including a fascination with his family's past. Ole Fred, the persona of *Midquest,* is as closely related to Christopher, his literary antecedent, as to Chappell himself, who asserts in the preface that "the 'I' of the poem is no more myself than any character in any novel I might choose to write" (x). The moral ambiguities that have so mesmerized Christopher are similarly puzzling to the young Linn Harper and to his father, Professor Andrew Harper, in *The Gaudy Place,* and they are echoed in such stories as "The Thousand Ways," "The Weather," and "Broken Blossoms," in *Moments of Light.*

Chappell's stories and poetry are full of characters who refuse the call to moral engagement with their worlds or who fail to discover satisfying answers to the questions that engagement elicits. "The World Between the Eyes" and "The Father" present such figures in the poet's first collection. Ole Fred in *Midquest* constantly wrestles with discontent, doubt, and isolation. *Castle Tzingal* is peopled entirely by figures who have either abandoned their struggles against corruption and apathy or who have been completely destroyed by their efforts. The ultimate consequences of such human failures on both personal and societal levels provide the terrifying visions in *Source* such as "The Evening of the Second Day" and "The Capacity for Pain." In *First and Last Words,* "An Old Mountain Woman Reading the Book of Job" memorably considers these puzzling and pervasive issues.

Chappell's methods of presenting his themes often rely heavily upon allusions or upon construction of philosophical foundations upon which the story is developed. He explains this approach in "A Pact with Faustus": "I decided that the intellectual structure of a novel, its larger themes and purposes, could be drawn up outside the literal narrative, could be determined in the preliminary working stages and then abandoned except as a large system of reference" (19). The technique is most obvious in *The Inkling,* which according to Chappell, is "an allegorical novel of Desire and Will, distantly based upon the unhappy story of the French symbolist poets, Rimbaud and Verlaine" ("Fred Chappell," 1986, 118). The superstructure of *Dagon* emerges within Peter's sermon drawing upon William Bradford's *History of Plymouth Plantation.* The destruction of Thomas Morton's Dagon colony is the "literal event" Chappell seized upon as "metaphorically true of our own times" (1970, 517). Though the structural experimentation of both books owes a good deal to these motivating ideas, the narrative development exists apart from the philosophical underpinning, particularly in *The Inkling.* Certainly both novels create impressions of vitality deriving more from the author's powers of description and character development than from the underlying patterns of ideas.

Annie Dillard has recognized thematic connections similar to those among Chappell's novels in *Moments of Light.* The first story, "Three Boxes," introduces "the notions of justice and destiny" (x), ideas that are then extended in "Judas" and through three stories set in the eighteenth century, completing what Dillard sees as "the first half of man's moral history" (xi). The second half of the volume makes use of contemporary settings and subject matter: "Here ... is a world thick with materials, emotions, and a thousand ambiguities" (xii). In each, as Dillard has explained, "innocence is lost" (xii). But hopeful prospects endure. The young narrator of "Broken Blossoms," for instance, emerges a sadder but a more perceptive youth. And Stovebolt Johnson may have lost out to the reversed discrimination of the bar's owner in "Blue Dive," but he departs with his guitar, symbol of the sustaining strength of his art, intact, hopeful of finding people who will appreciate his talents. All the stories in *Moments of Light* address similar issues; read as a whole, they provide glosses of each other as well as of concerns familiar in Chappell's other work.

The use of an underlying structural plan to link themes and to develop them is most successfully employed in *Midquest.* Chappell's preface provides clues to the grand framework: Classical elements unify each volume, and each reflects the structures of the others, except *Wind Mountain,* which ignores the stricter patterns "to suggest the fluid and disordered nature of air" (x). Though some readers have criticized the poem for failing to adhere to Chappell's somewhat disingenuously stated intentions, the larger thematic patterns, drawing extensively upon the quest motif in Dante, become obvious as the reader progresses. The poet's rebirth, addressed most directly in the first and last poems of each section, is won only through sometimes difficult engagements with issues in Chappell's earlier works: the reconciliation of past and present; the influence of inherited family values; the opposition of matter and spirit, desire and hope; the potency of creative effort; and the reconciling power of love. That the poem is autobiographical links it most closely with *It Is Time, Lord,* underlining the thematic connections and essentially sanguine outlooks at the end of each. Both Christopher and Ole Fred turn toward their wives for comfort and consolation, but even more, for confirmation of identity through shared attitudes and goals. As Chappell has asserted in the preface, *Midquest* is "in its largest design a love poem" (xi).

Despite its thematic unity, *Midquest* leaves the reader with the impression of tremendous variety, in part because of the richness of styles; the poet has aimed at the effect of the sampler, "that elder American art form" (ix). Toward that end he announces the desire "to restore to my work . . . qualities sometimes lacking in the larger body of contemporary poetry: detachment, social scope, humor, portrayal of character and background, discursiveness, wide range of subject matter" (x).

Imagistic and structural connections highlight shared themes in Chappell's most recent collections of lyric verse, *Source* and *First and Last Words.* In both books he has emphasized the artist's imagination as a means of transcending the commonplace and of embracing reality. Both also contain disturbing nightmares of man's destructive capacities—of the world "drifting toward the place where Mozart / goes unheard forever" (*First and Last Words* 44). Chappell uses the freedom offered by a loosely connected format to experiment even more than in *Midquest* with verse forms and with subject matter, though several themes recur, such as music, poetry, doubt, lost innocence, and affirmation. Settings and characters reminiscent of *Midquest* occasionally appear, and the variety of tones, ranging from despairing and surreal to bright, witty, and whimsical, confirms the poet's commitment to extending the ranges of contemporary poetry. Many lyrics examine means of perceiving the world, of pursuing truth— either realistically or imaginatively. Following the pattern of *Midquest,* the figures who creatively engage experience emerge as largely hopeful.

A similar hopefulness informs Chappell's two most recent novels. *I Am One of You Forever* extends the lyrics' emphasis upon imagination as a key to perception of reality. Jess explores the world through a wildly chaotic group of relatives who visit the farm. Uncle Luden, for instance, reveals the delights (and excesses) of drink and of women; Uncle Runkin acquaints him with death, Uncle Zeno with the way narrative can inform and even transform experience, Cousin Sam with the restorative value of music and the nurturing ties of family and community. From them and others, Jess discovers nothing less than his humanity, so that he may respond to the novel's closing question, "Well, Jess, are you one of us or not?" (184) with its trumpeted title.

The graver concerns of *Brighten the Corner Where You Are* largely force family issues into the background as Jess's father struggles to unravel nothing less than the nature of truth. The episodes follow Joe Robert through a day of confrontation with the school board, before whom he has been summoned to defend his teaching of Darwin. During the day (which like Ole Fred's birthday telescopes practically an entire lifetime), Joe Robert's quest acquires heroic, even mythic proportions. He confronts death in the underworld created by the recent world war, and he embraces life through his favorite student's prospects of marriage and pregnancy. He often must reevaluate his role within the school and the larger community. As in Chappell's first book, the resolution takes the form of a dream; Joe Robert finds himself defending the great Charles Darwin against the forces of ignorance and violence that have stained human history. Although powerless to ignore the pain of much of that history, Joe Robert's personal assertion of truth—all that any of Chappell's characters can realistically hope to achieve—undercuts the pessimism of the final pages. Like Ole Fred, Joe Robert is comforted by the presence of his wife sleeping beside him, a scene familiar from the close of *It Is Time, Lord,* the novel to which so many of Chappell's characters and themes owe their origins.

SURVEY OF CRITICISM

For a decade after the publication of *It Is Time, Lord,* criticism of Fred Chappell's work was limited to reviews of his first four novels. In most cases, the reviewers praised the writer's stylistic and descriptive abilities while expressing reservations about structure, character motivations, and thematic obscurity. For the most part, however, the reviews were favorable and encouraging. The first more substantial notice was R. H. W. Dillard's assessment in *The Hollins Critic* (1973), an essay that explored the philosophical bases of the novels and unravelled their structural complexities.

Apart from reviews, Chappell's writing has drawn most serious attention in essays evaluating individual works, with *Midquest* receiving the lion's share. Commentators have united in their praise of the poem, signaling out the technical dexterity, the rich evocation of landscape and character, and the honesty of the persona's voice for special praise. Some of the longer meditative lyrics have been censured for becoming tiresome or self-indulgent, but carping voices have been few.

The most substantial contributions to Chappell studies have been journals that have devoted entire issues to his work. Though some of these (*ABATIS* and *Iron Mountain Review*) have limited circulations, the *Mississippi Quarterly* issue (1983–84) devoted to Chappell is both useful and widely available. In addition to the initial appearance of "A Pact with Faustus," an assessment by George Garrett, and five essays examining both novels and poetry, a valuable primary bibliography by James E. Kibler, Jr. is included. That bibliography is being updated and extended by Stuart Wright for inclusion in the first book-length treatment of Chappell's poetry, currently being assembled by Patrick Bizzaro.

Chappell has granted frequent interviews, though many are difficult to locate, and he has written several autobiographical or critical essays that illuminate his artistic intentions. The most comprehensive and revealing of these is his contribution to the *Contemporary Authors Autobiography Series*. A collection of essays and his more important reviews is badly needed, as are more inclusive gatherings of his short fiction. Scant attention has been paid to Chappell's most recent collections of poetry and his latest novels. Clearly, much remains to be done in interpreting and evaluating Fred Chappell for his growing audience.

BIBLIOGRAPHY

Works by Fred Chappell

It Is Time, Lord. New York: Atheneum, 1963.

The Inkling. New York: Harcourt, Brace, and World, 1965.

Dagon. New York: Harcourt, Brace, and World, 1968. Reprint. New York: St. Martin's Press, 1987.

"Six Propositions about Literature and History." *New Literary History* 1 (Spring 1970): 513–22.

The World Between the Eyes. Baton Rouge: Louisiana State University Press, 1971.

The Gaudy Place. New York: Harcourt Brace Jovanovich, 1973. Reprint. New York: Manor Books, 1976.

River: A Poem. Baton Rouge: Louisiana State University Press, 1975.

Bloodfire: A Poem. Baton Rouge: Louisiana State University Press, 1978.

"Two Modes: A Plea for Tolerance." *Appalachian Journal* 5 (Spring 1978): 335–39.

Wind Mountain: A Poem. Baton Rouge: Louisiana State University Press, 1979.

Earthsleep: A Poem. Baton Rouge: Louisiana State University Press, 1980.

Moments of Light. Los Angeles: New South, 1980.

Midquest: A Poem. Baton Rouge: Louisiana State University Press, 1981.

"A Pact with Faustus." *Mississippi Quarterly* 37 (Winter 1983–84): 9–20. Reprint in *The Fred Chappell Reader*, 479–90. New York: St. Martin's Press, 1987.

Castle Tzingal: A Poem. Baton Rouge: Louisiana State University Press, 1984.

I Am One of You Forever. Baton Rouge: Louisiana State University Press, 1985.

Source. Baton Rouge: Louisiana State University Press, 1985.

"Fred Chappell." In *Contemporary Authors Autobiography Series,* vol. 4, edited by Adele Sarkissian, 113–26. Detroit: Gale Research, 1986.

The Fred Chappell Reader. New York: St. Martin's Press, 1987.

First and Last Words. Baton Rouge: Louisiana State University Press, 1989.

Brighten the Corner Where You Are. New York: St. Martin's Press, 1989.

More Shapes than One. New York: St. Martin's Press, 1991.

C: Poems. Baton Rouge: Louisiana State University Press, 1993.

Plow Naked: Selected Writings on Poetry. Ann Arbor: University of Michigan Press, 1993.

Interviews with Fred Chappell

Broughton, Irv. "Fred Chappell." In *The Writer's Mind: Interviews with American Authors,* vol. 3, edited by Irv Broughton, 91–122. Fayetteville: University of Arkansas Press, 1990.

Carr, John. "Dealing with the Grotesque: Fred Chappell." In *Kite-Flying and Other Irrational Acts: Conversations with Twelve Southern Writers,* edited by John Carr, 216–35. Baton Rouge: Louisiana State University Press, 1972.

Garrett, George. "Fred Chappell." In *Craft So Hard to Learn: Conversations with Poets and Novelists about the Teaching of Writing,* edited by George Garrett, 36–40. New York: Morrow, 1972.

———. "Fred Chappell." In *The Writer's Voice: Conversations with Contemporary Writers,* edited by George Garrett, 31–50. New York: Morrow, 1973.

Jackson, Richard. "Fred Chappell, 1980, on the Margins of Dreams." In *Acts of Mind: Conversations with Contemporary Poets,* edited by Richard Jackson, 153–57. Tuscaloosa: University of Alabama Press, 1983.

Rubin, Louis D., Jr. "Welcome to High Culture." In *An Apple for My Teacher: Twelve Authors Tell about Teachers Who Made the Difference,* edited by Louis D. Rubin, Jr., 14–28. Chapel Hill, N.C.: Algonquin Books, 1987.

West, James L., III, and August J. Nigro. "William Blackburn and His Pupils: A Conversation. *Mississippi Quarterly* 31 (Fall 1978): 605–14.

Studies of Fred Chappell

"Fred Chappell." In *Contemporary Literary Criticism,* vol. 40, edited by Daniel G. Marowski, 136–49. Detroit: Gale Research, 1986.

Campbell, Hilbert. "Fred Chappell's Urn of Memory: *I Am One of You Forever.*" *Southern Literary Journal* 25 (Spring 1993): 103–11.

Cherry, Kelly. "Watersmeet: Thinking about Southern Poets." *Book Forum* 3 (1977): 264–74.

———. "A Writer's Harmonious World." *Parnassus* 9 (Fall-Winter 1981): 115–29.

Coindreau, Maurice-Edgar. Preface to *Le Dieu-Poisson.* Translated by Coindreau. Paris: Bourgois, 1970.

Cooper, Kate M. "Reading between the Lines: Fred Chappell's *Castle Tzingal.*" In *Southern Literature and Literary Theory,* edited by Jefferson Humphries, 88–108. Athens: University of Georgia Press, 1990.

Dillard, Annie. Foreword. *Moments of Light.* Newport Beach, Calif.: New South, 1980.

Dillard, R.H.W. "Letters from a Distant Lover: The Novels of Fred Chappell." *The Hollins Critic* 10 (April 1973): 1–15.

Edgerton, Clyde, et al. "Tributes to Fred Chappell." *Pembroke Magazine* 23 (1991): 77–92.

Flynt, Candace. "Fred Chappell as Teacher." *Iron Mountain Review* 2 (Spring 1985): 27.

Garrett, George. "A Few Things about Fred Chappell." *Mississippi Quarterly* 37 (Winter 1983–84): 3–8.

Gray, Amy Tipton. "R'lyeh in Appalachia: Lovecraft's Influence on Fred Chappell's *Dagon*." In *Remembrance, Reunion, and Revival: Celebrating A Decade of Appalachian Studies,* edited by Helen Roseberry, 73–79. Boone, N.C.: Appalachian Consortium Press, 1988.

———. "Fred Chappell's *I Am One of You Forever:* The Oneiros of Childhood Transformed." In *The Poetics of Appalachian Space,* edited by Parks Lanier, Jr., 28–39. Knoxville: University of Tennessee Press, 1991.

Hobson, Fred. *The Southern Writer in the Postmodern World.* Athens: University of Georgia Press, 1991.

Jones, Rodney. "The Large Vision: Fred Chappell's *Midquest*." *Appalachian Journal* 9 (Fall 1981): 59–65.

Kibler, James E., Jr. "A Fred Chappell Bibliography, 1963–1983." *Mississippi Quarterly* 37 (Winter 1983–84): 63–88.

Lang, John. "Illuminating the Stricken World: Fred Chappell's *Moments of Light*." *South Central Review* 4 (Winter 1986): 95–103.

Morgan, Robert. "*Midquest*." *American Poetry Review* 11 (July–August 1982): 45–47.

Morrison, Gail M. " 'The Sign of the Arms': Chappell's *It Is Time, Lord*." *Mississippi Quarterly* 37 (Winter 1983–84): 45–54.

Mosby, Charmaine Allmon. "*The Gaudy Place:* Six Characters in Search of an Illusion." *Mississippi Quarterly* 37 (Winter 1983–84): 55–62.

Nadel, Alan. "Quest and Midquest: Fred Chappell and the First-Person Personal Epic." *New England Review and Breadloaf Quarterly* 6 (Winter 1983): 323–31.

Ragan, David Paul. "Fred Chappell." In *Dictionary of Literary Biography,* vol. 6, edited by James E. Kibler, Jr., 36–48. Detroit: Gale Research, 1980.

———. "At the Grave of Sut Lovingood: Virgil Campbell in the Work of Fred Chappell." *Mississippi Quarterly* 37 (Winter 1983–84): 323–31.

Root, William Pitt. " 'The Earth Is Shoving Us to Sea': *River: A Poem*." *ABATIS ONE* (1983): 46–48.

Seacreast, Donald. "Images of Impure Water in Chappell's *River*." *Mississippi Quarterly* 37 (Winter 1983–84): 39–44.

Smith, Barbara. "Chappell at Midquest." *ABATIS ONE* (1983): 49–51.

Stephenson, Shelby. "Fred Chappell's Four-Part Autobiographical Epic." *Pembroke Magazine* 14 (1982): 11–13.

———. "Vision in Fred Chappell's Poetry and Fiction." *ABATIS ONE* (1983): 33–45.

———. "*Midquest:* Fred Chappell's Mythical Kingdom." *Iron Mountain Review* 2 (Spring 1985): 22–26.

Stuart, Dabney. " 'Blue Pee': Fred Chappell's Short Fiction." *Iron Mountain Review* 2 (Spring 1985): 13–21.

———. " 'What's Artichokes?': An Introduction to the Work of Fred Chappell." In *The Fred Chappell Reader,* xi–xx. New York: St. Martin's Press, 1987.

————. ''Spiritual Matter in Fred Chappell's Poetry: A Prologue.'' *Southern Review* 27 (January 1991): 200–220.

Tucker, Ellen. ''Fred Chappell: His Life in Mid-Course.'' *Chicago Review* 33 (Summer 1981): 85–91.

Wiloch, Thomas. ''Fred Chappell.'' *Contemporary Authors: New Revision Series,* vol. 8, edited by Ann Evory and Linda Metzger, 94–95. Detroit: Gale Research, 1983.

LA VINIA DELOIS JENNINGS

Alice Childress
(1920–   )

Alice Childress's contributions to the American stage and literature seem to be well-kept secrets. She is the first black woman to write a play that was professionally produced on the New York stage, and she holds the distinction of being the only African-American woman whose plays have been written and professionally produced over four decades. She is also the first female playwright to win the Obie Award for the best original off-Broadway play *Trouble in Mind* (1955). Although her favorite creative genre is the play, Childress is best known for her first novel, *A Hero Ain't Nothin' but a Sandwich,* first published in 1973 and later adapted into a screenplay in 1978. Like much of her work, it is ahead of its time in terms of its social awareness. Being African-American, female, and a literary forerunner in examining and exposing inequities dictated by race, class, and gender at a time when integrationist fiction was in vogue did not enhance Childress's chances of receiving critical acclaim. Seldom recognized by scholars, critics, and theatre historians, she refers to herself as ''one of the best known of unknown persons'' (Harris 1985, 68). With the surge of interest in women's literature and Beacon Press's 1986 reprinting of her 1956 book of sketches, *Like One of the Family—Conversations from a Domestic's Life,* Childress's skill as a playwright and a dramatic novelist is slowly receiving the critical attention that is long overdue.

BIOGRAPHY

The great-granddaughter of a slave who was abandoned by her master when he could no longer violate the decree of emancipation, Alice Childress was born October 12, 1920 in Charleston, South Carolina. When she was five, her mother and father separated, and she was taken to New York where she grew up in Harlem under the supervision of her maternal grandmother Eliza Campbell

White. Childress attended Public School 81, The Julia Ward Howe Junior High School, and Wadleigh High School but did not complete her secondary education. Her maternal grandmother Eliza, who urged her to write, activated her imagination and exposed her to art, community, and other cultures. Miss Thomas, her third-grade teacher during a year she spent in Baltimore, inspired her to read incessantly. The Wednesday-night testimonials of women who revealed their troubles of a son in jail, a sick daughter, or a suicide in the family to the congregation of Salem Church in Harlem, which she and her grandmother attended, taught her to master the art of dramatic storytelling. Her literary influences include Paul Laurence Dunbar, Shakespeare, and the Bible.

Childress married twice. During her first marriage she gave birth to her only child, Jean. On July 17, 1957, Childress married her second husband, Nathan Woodard, a musician.

As an original member of the American Negro Theatre, Childress devoted the 1940s to learning every aspect of the theatre. Her various assignments included erecting sets, coaching new actors, attending to props and make-up, designing costumes, directing shows, and serving for one year as personnel director. During her eleven-year association with the American Negro Theatre, she appeared in John Silvera and Abram Hill's *On Striver's Row* (1940), Theodore Browne's *Natural Man* (1941), and as Blanche in the adapted American version of Philip Yordan's *Anna Lucasta* (1944), which later provided background for *Trouble in Mind.* She repeated the role of Blanche in the Broadway production of Yordan's play and was nominated for a Tony Award.

The American Negro Theatre's need for good writing motivated Childress to try her hand at playwriting. In 1949, the theatre group produced *Florence,* a one-act play that Childress wrote overnight at the American Negro Theatre. The play examines whites stereotyping of blacks. Set in a small Southern town, *Florence* opens with the encounter of two women in a Jim Crow railway-station waiting room. Mama, a proud, poor, black woman, sits on one side, and Mrs. Carter, a seemingly liberal-minded white woman who at one time aspired to the stage, sits opposite of her. Mama, using her rent money to finance her trip, is on her way to New York to retrieve her daughter Florence, a struggling and starving actress. After Mrs. Carter wins Mama's confidence by convincing her that she views blacks as her equals, Mama petitions her to assist Florence through her New York connections. Although Mrs. Carter understands that Mama is asking for stage connections for her daughter, she offers to refer Florence to a director for employment as a maid. Quietly angered by the white woman's obvious racial condescension, Mama decides not to go to New York but rather to send her travel money to her daughter to keep her dream of becoming an actress alive. The character of Mama serves as a prototype for Childress's later depictions of the ''genteel'' poor who choose personal sacrifice and exhibit grace under social and economic pressure.

The following year, Childress adapted Langston Hughes's recently published *Simple Speaks His Mind* (1950) into *Just a Little Simple* (1950), for the Committee for the Negro in the Arts. Opening that September at the Club Baron Theatre in Harlem, the play featured Kenneth Mannigault as Jesse B. Semple—the master-of-ceremonies in a Harlem variety show. *Florence* also appeared on the program. Despite the show's success, its producers would not allow it to be moved to Broadway. They stated that the uptown production was intended to build a Negro theatre, not to hold Broadway tryouts.

Between 1952 and 1956, Childress attained several "firsts" in her career and established her importance as an American dramatist. In 1952 *Gold Through the Trees,* which ran from April 7 to May 19 at the Club Baron, became the first play by a black woman to be professionally produced on the American stage. The play deals with Africans who ultimately become slaves, then progresses to the present and the struggle against apartheid in South Africa. Its success, along with *Just a Little Simple* three years earlier, led to the first off-Broadway union contracts that recognized the Actors Equity Association and the Harlem Stage Hand Local. Both she and Lorraine Hansberry worked at Paul Robeson's newspaper *Freedom,* and Hansberry, who wrote reviews for the publication, covered the show.

It was the off-Broadway, professional production of *Trouble in Mind* (1955) that was the first play by Childress to be seen outside of Harlem and to receive media attention. *Trouble in Mind,* a play within a play, portrays the frustration that black actors and actresses experience because only demeaning parts and limited roles are available to them within mainstream white theatre. The plot centers on a racially mixed group of actors rehearsing "Chaos in Belleville," a white playwright's account of racial conflict in the South. The script, which promises to be a serious antilynching protest, reinforces stereotypes of Southern blacks as ignorant, "darky" figures. Al Manners, the white director of the production, is determined to present the stilted view of blacks because of his own racism and the belief that the white American public does not want to see blacks in any other light. Wiletta Mayer—the veteran actress who has been cast as the mother of the young black man who is lynched for attempting to vote—initially advocates racial complacency as a way of dealing with Manners and the other whites in charge of the production. Ultimately, her integrity will not allow her to turn her back on the truth. She courageously defies Manners and the script's directions, which call for her character to deny her maternal instinct and turn her son over to whites whom she knows will lynch him. She attempts to rally the other black cast members to protest the racist script, but their desire for stage work, fame, and fortune, even at the expense of their dignity, is too seductive.

Trouble in Mind opened November 4, 1955 at the Greenwich Mews Theatre and ran for ninety-one performances. Childress and Clarice Taylor, who played the role of Wiletta, directed the production. It won the *Village Voice* Obie Award for the best off-Broadway play of the 1955–56 season. Edward Eliscu optioned it for Broadway for two years, but a production never materialized. Disputes over theme, interpretation, and demands for changes eventually led Childress to withdraw it from consideration. The play itself, which anticipated the black naturalistic drama of the late 1960s, seems divided in its alternate endings. The Greenwich Mews performance included a third act ending in the cast members' solidarity. The published version in *Black Theatre* (1971), edited by Lindsay Patterson, ends after the second act with the audience's anticipation that Wiletta will be dismissed from the cast for challenging the authority of the director. The play was revived years later when the British Broadcasting Company (BBC) aired two performances in October and November of 1964.

Childress followed *Trouble in Mind* with the publication of *Like One of the Family—Conversations from a Domestic's Life* (1956). Similar to the conversations of Hughes's Semple, the sixty-two dramatic monologues of Mildred, a sassy, defiant, 30-something, black maid in New York, combines satire and humor as a political weapon to combat prejudice and hypocrisy. Relating her day work experiences in the homes of whites to Marge, her friend and confidante whom the reader never hears speaking directly, Mildred portrays herself as a black woman who is unafraid to speak her mind to her white employers and who refuses "to exchange dignity for pay" (xxxii). She often shames her white employers into a sobering recognition of their true lack of humanity. Mildred's art form of storytelling draws heavily from the black oral tradition, especially that of signification. Sketches of Mildred appeared in Paul Robeson's *Freedom* and continued in *The Baltimore Afro-American* as a column entitled "Here's Mildred" prior to the publication of *Like One of the Family*. In her depiction of Mildred, Childress drew upon the real-life experiences of her Aunt Lorraine and some of her own experiences as a domestic in New York. During her early years with the American Negro Theatre, Childress did day work to support herself and her young daughter, Jean, whom she often took with her on assignments.

Over the next two decades, Childress's playwriting and interactions with other artists intensified. During the 1960s she wrote *Wedding Band* (1966), *Wine in the Wilderness* (1969), *String* (1969), and *The Freedom Drum* (1969), which she later retitled *Young Martin Luther King, Jr.* She eventually wrote telescripts for these first three plays, and the fourth became a touring production of the Performing Arts Repertory Theatre from 1969 to 1972. In the mid-1960s Childress served on a number of discussion panels with other well-known literary figures. In 1965 she participated in a BBC panel entitled "The Negro in the American Theatre" with James Baldwin, LeRoi Jones, and Langston Hughes. Later, on a panel entitled "What Negro Playwrights are Saying," she appeared with William Branch, Lonne Elder, LeRoi Jones, Loften Mitchell, and Douglas Turner Ward. A high point in Childress's career came when Tillie Olsen recommended her for a Harvard appointment as playwright and scholar to the Radcliffe Institute (now the Mary Ingraham Bunting Institute) for independent study from 1966 to 1968. The program, which consisted mostly of appointees with doctorates, awarded her a graduate medal for her writing.

At the Radcliffe Institute, Childress revised *Wedding Band,* a two-act play subtitled *A Love/Hate Story in Black and White,* that tackled the controversial subject of miscegenation. In summer 1918, Julia Augustine, a black seamstress, and Herman, a white baker, have secretly conducted a ten-year, common-law marriage. Because South Carolina state law prohibits interracial marriage and cohabitation, the two plan to move North, but repaying a loan from his mother prevents Herman from selling his bakery. The play begins with Julia's move to yet another community in search of acceptance. Although her new working-class black neighbors are more tolerant than the whites of the interracial relationship, they express their condemnation of her choice of a poor white for her lover. The legally illicit relationship ends tragically with the volatile confrontation of Julia and Herman's mother and the death of Herman from influenza. In addition to her indictment of racist laws preventing intermarriage, Childress, through a supporting character, addresses the manner in which law prohibiting divorce oppresses women. When first performed at the University of Michigan in December 1966, Ruby Dee, Abbey Lincoln, Clarice Taylor, and Moses Gunn were among the cast. On November 26, 1972, Joseph Papp produced the play at the New York Shakespeare Public Theatre. Ruby Dee and James Broderick were cast in the leading roles. The following year, ABC television aired the Public Theatre production during prime time. Because of its interracial theme, 8 local stations out of 168 in the New York area refused to broadcast the drama. Others aired it only after midnight.

Both *Wine in the Wilderness* and *String* comment on the way in which education, success, and status brainwash bourgeois blacks into rejecting underclass blacks. Bill, the black artist in *Wine in the Wilderness* who is painting a triptych portraying three aspects of "black womanhood," has allowed his white assimilation and white stereotypes of black women to control and separate him from members of his own race. *String,* a loose adaptation of Guy de Maupassant's "The Piece of String," tells of the encounter of Joe—an impoverished, inarticulate black man who collects useless objects—with a group of middle-class black picnickers who view themselves as his superiors. When Joe stoops to pick up a piece of string, members of the picnic accuse him of picking up the missing wallet of L. V. Craig, a wealthy businessman. Childress wrote *Wine in the Wilderness* for WGBH in Boston, which aired it on March 4, 1969, as the first production in the "On Being Black" series. *String,* first performed by New York's Negro Ensemble Company, appeared on PBS in 1979.

Although her adult play *Mojo: A Black Love Story,* performed at the New Heritage Theatre in Harlem in November 1970 ushered in her next decade of writing, Childress's creative efforts centered primarily upon writing stories and plays for and about children and adolescents. *Black Scenes,* an anthology she edited containing fifteen short dramatic sketches, included a scene from her short, unproduced, play *The African Garden.* In it Simon Brown, a young schoolboy, meets Maytag Diamond Ashley when he comes to rent a room from Simon's mother. The lures of the street appeal to Simon, but Ashley warns him against their dangers and espouses the belief that the poor must ban together to overcome their common social plights. Childress followed this short play with an adolescent novel, its screenplay, and two other plays for children. She concluded the 1970s with a musical about the Gullah people and a novel for adults.

The adolescent novel *A Hero Ain't Nothin' but a Sandwich* (1973), depicts 13-year-old Benjie Johnson's addiction to heroin from his and ten other viewpoints. Comparable in structure to Faulkner's *As I Lay Dying* (1930), *A Hero* contains twenty-three monologues that narrate the impressions and attitudes of Benjie's teachers, principal, parents, peers, and self-justified pusher. Childress presents a realistic portrait of how Benjie, as an outgrowth of his loneliness and ghetto environment, views himself as capable of taking care of himself and how his drug habit leads to crimes against his family and community. Childress also directly addresses how the forces of the street overwhelm a fragmented family. Benjie starts his experimentation with drugs at a friend's house, while his mother, Rose, struggling to support her family without a husband, is at work. Other individuals in positions to intercede in Benjie's downward spiral fail to act because of personal or political reasons. For example, Benjie, whose drug usage is revealed at school, is an embarrassment to his principal, who sees the drug bust as a blight on his career. By the novel's end, however, Butler Craig, Benjie's common-law stepfather who saves his life and demonstrates to him that he is an important human being, promises to be a positive force in Benjie's recovery.

A Hero and its screenplay garnered much public censure and praise. It was the first book to be banned from a Savannah, Georgia, school library since J. D. Salinger's *The Catcher in the Rye* in the early 1950s and one of nine books banned by the school board of Island Trees, Long Island, New York. In 1974 *A Hero* received the Jane Addams Honor Award for one of the best young adult novels. The following year it won The Achievement Award from the New York Club of The National Association of Negro Business and Professional Women's Clubs in addition to The Lewis Carroll Shelf Award from the University of Wisconsin. Childress's screenplay of the same title received two awards in 1978: the Virgin Islands Film Festival Award and the Paul Robeson Award for Outstanding Contributions to the Performing Arts. The movie, which New World Pictures produced, starred Cicely Tyson, Paul Winfield, Glynn Turman, and Larry Scott.

Appealing to a much younger audience, Childress published *When the Rattlesnake Sounds* (1975) and *Let's Hear It for the Queen* (1976), two short children's plays. *When the Rattlesnake Sounds,* a one-act drama with a static setting and compressed action, focuses on the summer Harriet Tubman worked as a laundress in Cape May, New Jersey, to raise money for the abolitionist cause. Tension rises between Lennie and Celia, two other washers, but Harriet reminds them of the meaning of commitment. They end singing a hymn together as they scrub. Many critics praised the play as tightly crafted. To commemorate the eighth birthday of her granddaughter, Marilyn Alice Lee, Childress wrote *Let's*

Hear It for the Queen. Easy for children to perform, the play is based on the nursery rhyme about the Queen of Hearts who made some tarts. The play's intent was to disrupt sexist typecasting and to address in a simplified manner the theme of crime and punishment.

In 1977 Columbia and Charleston, South Carolina, officially observed Alice Childress Week for the opening of *Sea Island Song,* a play about the Gullah-speaking people of the islands off the South Carolina coast. The South Carolina Arts Commission funded the project, and Childress's husband collaborated with her on the music for the production. Five years later at a production at the University of Massachusetts at Amherst, Childress restored the play's original title, *Gullah.* The Commission of the South Carolina production had thought that the word "Gullah" conjured up negative images of backward country folk. Two years later, *A Short Walk* appeared. The plot follows Cora James, the heroine, from her birth in South Carolina during the early 1900s to Harlem, where she dies in the mid-1940s. Like Janie Crawford's search in Zora Neale Hurston's *Their Eyes Were Watching God* (1937), Cora James's search during her short walk from the cradle to the grave is a search for selfhood and freedom from social strictures and persons that attempt to define and limit her. Racism, husbands who plot to break her spirit and put their personal fulfillment before hers, and genderized social restrictions threaten to stifle her personal, professional, and artistic growth. Presented in first- and third-person vignettes that are written in the present tense, the novel resonates with the stylistic intonations of dramatic stage direction and calls to mind *A Hero* and *Like One of the Family.*

Two adolescent novels, *Rainbow Jordan* (1981) and *Those Other People* (1989), and a play, *Moms* (1987), about the comedienne Jackie "Moms" Mabley (Loretta Mary Aiken), compose Childress's leading accomplishments during the 1980s. Similar in structure to *A Hero,* Childress's *Rainbow Jordan* portrays—in seventeen sections which Rainbow, her young mother Kathie, and her foster parent Josephine Lamont narrate—Rainbow's refusal, despite her lack of a responsible full-time mother, to allow the menace of the street and peer pressure to dominate her. *Those Other People* bears the same dramatic first-person construction as the two aforementioned works. Narrated by ten characters in nineteen chapters, the novel explores the homophobia and bigotry that young people must confront in their journey toward adult- and selfhood in small-town America. A closet homosexual, Jonathan Barnett, the protagonist, runs from his parents, his childhood friend Fern, and his ex-lover Harp to a job as a high-school computer instructor in Minitown in order to grapple with his sexual identity and feelings of suicide. When he and Tyrone Tate, a black student, become the only witnesses to a well-respected teacher's attempted rape of a fifteen-year-old female student, the tension turns on whether Jonathan will remain silent or testify to what he has seen at the personal expense of having to affirm his homosexuality to the school and the community. In both *Rainbow*

Jordan and *Those Other People* Childress considers for her young readers the taboo subjects of heterosexuality and homosexuality with sensitivity and insight.

Childress's play *Moms.* subtitled *A Praise Play for a Black Comedienne,* appeared at the Hudson Guild Theater for a month's run in February 1987. Tickets for the production sold out in two days. Actress Clarice Taylor, who commissioned Childress to write the stage play from research that Taylor had conducted, starred in the title role; Childress's husband interpolated songs for the production. Childress's treatment, according to a *New York Times* reviewer, lets Mabley's "comic sensibility speak for itself. The excerpts from her routines are unquestionably the choicest parts of the evening, and in her attacks on racism and sexism, we can see the soul of a social commentator" (Mel Gussow 1987, 16). Childress later brought suit against Taylor for infringement of copyright and unfair competition when Taylor produced a similar version of *Moms* in August of the same year at the Astor Place Theatre. The second production not only failed to credit authorship to Childress, but attributed the play to Ben Caldwell, whom Taylor had enlisted to write a revised version from her original research of the comedienne's life.

Alice Childress is writing the life's story of her maternal great-grandmother Annie Campbell as a prelude to her own autobiography. In a 1987 interview, Childress spoke candidly about her status as the "first" African-American female playwright to tread both literary and theatrical grounds that have been traditionally male and primarily white:

I never was ever interested in being the first woman to do anything. I always felt that I should be the 50th or the 100th. Women were kept out of everything. It almost made it sound like other women were not quite right enough or accomplished enough, especially when I hear "the first Black woman." When people are shut out of something for so long, it seems ironic when there's so much going on about "the first." (quoted in Brown-Guillory 1988, 68)

MAJOR THEMES

Rejecting stereotyped roles of blacks, Childress has sought to depict realistic, accurate, and more universal portraits of black life and characters in her plays and novels. In her youth, according to Childress in "A Candle in a Gale Wind," teachers urged her to follow the trend of writing "about Blacks who were 'accomplishers'" but she "turned against the tide . . . to write about those who come in second, or not at all" (112). Hence, throughout her career Childress has continually portrayed what she has called the "genteel poor," the "have-nots in a *have* society, those seldom singled out by mass media, except as source material for derogatory humor and/or condescending clinical, social analysis" (112). Accordingly, her settings are simple and unglamorous—backyards, backrooms, train stations and the like—and the occupations of her characters reflect those of poor working-class blacks, such as domestics, seamstresses, dancers, washerwomen, artists, and the unemployed.

At the heart of Childress's dedication to creative realism lies the truthful presentation of black women. She has asserted in a 1966 essay, "A Woman Playwright Speaks Her Mind," that "the Negro woman has almost been omitted as important subject matter in the general popular American drama, television, motion pictures and radio" (75). When depicted, the black woman is either "the constant but empty and decharacterized faithful servant" or the strong matriarchal figure, the black wife or mother who dominates and emasculates her husband and son (75). Childress, too, has created matriarchs, but she has also extended her female characterizations into more positive areas. In doing so, she has demonstrated how racism, sexist and racist laws, and oppressive intraracial structures have forced black women to develop strength to survive. Childress has negated the myth that all black women are emasculators. Tomorrow-Marie in *Wine in the Wilderness* resists the charge that she has stripped the black male of his manhood. She, along with her fictional sisters Mildred Johnson, Wiletta Mayer, Cora James, and Rainbow Jordan resist conformity, struggle for independence, search for selfhood, and affirm their blackness and femaleness.

Focusing on the "genteel poor" and strong black women, Childress has refused to compromise her creative principles and to conform her artistic pursuits to please the aesthetic and social tastes of whites and blacks. Presenting the theme of miscegenation has jeopardized her acceptance by white audiences and critics, yet she has chosen to treat it. The popularity of black militant and integrationist fiction has not deterred her from examining negative issues in black life such as drug addiction among its youth, intraracial prejudice, and the detrimental impact white assimilation has had on African Americans.

SURVEY OF CRITICISM

When one compares the volume of work Childress has produced with the amount of criticism it has generated, one quickly realizes that in proportion to the former the latter has been scattered and sparse. The production of *Trouble in Mind* in 1955 drew the first critical attention for Childress outside of Harlem, yet more than ten years elapsed before extended commentaries on her works appeared with some frequency in scholarly publications and popular journals. Between 1965 and 1972, critical essays focusing on Childress were published in black publications such as *Black World, Crisis, Freedomways, CLA Journal, Negro Digest,* and *Black Creation.* The *New York Times, New York Theatre Critics' Review,* and *New Yorker* occasionally made note of her theatre endeavors. Three theatre studies of the mid- to late 1960s—Doris E. Abramson's *Negro Playwrights in the American Theatre, 1925–1959* (1969), Loften Mitchell's *Black Drama: The Story of the American Negro in the Theatre* (1967), and Fannie Ella Frazier Hicklin's dissertation "The American Negro Playwright,

1920–1964'' (1965)—provided historical background and artistic assessments of Childress's literary contributions.

For the most part, critics and scholars have responded favorably to Childress's work. Some, however, have maintained that she has been more interested in character than plot and that she has packed her plays with too much racial assault by putting her own words into the mouths of too many of her characters. In the last fifteen years, critical discussions have leaned more toward analyses of Childress's work with respect to the presentation of black women (Mary Louise Anderson's "Black Matriarchy: Portrayal of Women in Three Plays" [1976] and Jeanne-Marie A. Miller's "Images of Black Women in Plays by Black Playwrights" [1977]), feminist issues (Janet Brown's *Feminist Drama: Definitions and Critical Analysis* [1979], Gayle Austin's "Alice Childress: Black Woman Playwright as Feminist Critic" [1987], and Catherine Wiley's "Whose Name, Whose Protection: Reading Alice Childress's *Wedding Band*" [1990]), and the black literary tradition (Sandra Y. Govan's "Alice Childress's *Rainbow Jordan:* The Black Aesthetic Returns Dressed in Adolescent Fiction" [1988] and Denise Troutman-Robinson's "The Elements of Call and Response in Alice Childress' *Like One of the Family*" [1989]). La Vinia D. Jennings's book-length study of Childress's plays and novels is slated for fall 1994 publication with G. K. Hall/Twayne.

BIBLIOGRAPHY

Works by Alice Childress

Published Works

Florence: A One Act Drama. Masses and Mainstream 3 (October 1950): 34–37.

Like One of the Family—Conversations from a Domestic's Life. Brooklyn, N.Y.: Independence Publishers, 1956. Boston: Beacon Press, 1986.

"The Negro Woman in American Literature." *Freedom Ways* 6 (Winter 1966): 14–19. Reprinted as "A Woman Playwright Speaks Her Mind." In *Anthology of the American Negro in the Theatre: A Critical Approach,* edited by Lindsay Patterson, 75–79. New York: Publishers Co., 1968.

String. New York: Dramatists Play Service, 1969.

The World on a Hill. Plays to Remember, edited by Henry B. Maloney, 103–25. New York: Macmillan, 1970.

The African Garden. In *Black Scenes,* edited by Alice Childress, 137–45. Garden City, N.Y.: Doubleday, 1971.

Mojo: A Black Love Story. Black World 20 (April 1971): 54–82.

Trouble in Mind: A Comedy-Drama in Two Acts. In *Black Theatre: A 20th Century Collection of the Work of Its Best Playwrights,* edited by Lindsay Patterson, 135–74. New York: Dodd, Mead. 1971.

A Hero Ain't Nothin' but a Sandwich. New York: Coward, McCann, and Geoghegan, 1973.

Wedding Band: A Love/Hate Story in Black and White. New York: Samuel French, 1973.

Wine in the Wilderness: A Comedy-Drama. Plays By and About Women, edited by Victoria Sullivan and James Hatch, 379–421. New York: Vintage, 1973.
When the Rattlesnake Sounds. New York: Coward, McCann, and Geoghegan, 1975.
Let's Hear It for the Queen. New York: Coward, McCann, and Geoghegan, 1976.
A Short Walk. New York: Coward, McCann, and Geoghegan, 1979.
Rainbow Jordan. New York: Coward, McCann, and Geoghegan, 1981.
Those Other People. New York: Putnam's, 1989.

Unpublished Works

Just a Little Simple. New York. Club Baron Theatre, September 1950.
Gold Through the Trees. New York, Club Baron Theatre, 1952.
Hell's Alley.
A Man Bearing a Pitcher. c. 1955.
The Freedom Drum. (Retitled *Young Martin Luther King, Jr.*). Performing Arts Repertory Theatre, on tour 1969–72.
Sea Island Song. Charleston, S.C., Stage South, 1977. (Retitled *Gullah.* University of Massachusetts, Amherst, 1984.)
Moms: A Praise Play for a Black Comedienne. New York, Hudson Guild Theater, February 1987.

Articles and Essays by Alice Childress

"Alice Childress." *Speaking for Ourselves: Autobiographical Sketches by Notable Authors of Books for Young Adults,* edited by Donald R. Gallo, 39–40. Urbana: NCTE, 1990.
"The Black Experience: Why Talk About That? *Negro Digest* 16 (April 1967): 17–21.
"Black Writers' Views on Literary Lions and Values." *Negro Digest* 17 (January 1968): 36, 85–87.
"But I Do My Thing": "Can Black and White Artists Still Work Together?" *New York Times* 2 February 1969, sec. 2: 9.
"A Candle in a Gale Wind." *Black Women Writers (1950–1980): A Critical Evaluation,* edited by Mari Evans, 111–16. New York: Anchor, 1984.
"For a Negro Theatre." *Masses and Mainsteam* 4 (February 1951): 61–64.
"Knowing the Human Condition." *Black Literature and Humanism,* edited by R. Baxter Miller, 8–10. Louisville: University Press of Kentucky, 1981.
"The Negro Woman in American Literature." *Freedomways* 6 (Winter 1966): 14–19. Reprint as "A Woman Playwright Speaks Her Mind," in *Anthology of the American Negro in the Theatre: A Critical Approach,* edited by Lindsay Patterson, 75–79. New York: Publishers Co., 1968.
"The Soul Man." *Essence* (May 1971): 68–69, 94.
"Tribute—to Paul Robeson." *Freedomways* 2 (First Quarter 1971): 14–15.

Interviews with Alice Childress

Betsko, Kathleen, and Rachel Koenig. "Alice Childress." In *Interviews with Contemporary Women Playwrights,* edited by Kathleen Betsko and Rachel Koenig, 62–74. New York: Morrow, 1987.

Brown-Guillory, Elizabeth. "Alice Childress: A Pioneering Spirit." *Sage* 4 (Spring 1987): 66–68.

"Conversation with Alice Childress and Toni Morrison." *Black Creation Annual* 6 (1974–75): 90–92.

Studies of Alice Childress

Abramson, Doris E. *The Negro Playwrights in the American Theatre, 1925–1959.* New York: Columbia University Press, 1969.

Anderson, Mary Louise. "Black Matriarchy: Portrayal of Women in Three Plays. *Negro American Literature Forum* 10 (1976): 93–95.

Austin, Gayle. "Alice Childress: Black Woman Playwright as Feminist Critic." *The Southern Quarterly* 25 (Spring 1987): 53–62.

Brown, Elizabeth. "Six Female Black Playwrights: Images of Blacks in Plays by Lorraine Hansberry, Alice Childress, Sonia Sanchez, Barbara Molette, Martie Charles, and Ntozake Shange." Ph.D. diss., Florida State University, 1980.

Brown, Janet. *Feminist Drama: Definitions and Critical Analysis.* Metuchen, N.J.: Scarecrow, 1979.

Brown-Guillory, Elizabeth. "Black Women Playwrights: Exorcising Myths." *Phylon* 48 (Fall 1987): 229–39.

———. "Images of Blacks in Plays by Black Women." *Phylon* 47 (September 1986): 230–37.

———. *Their Place on the Stage: Black Women Playwrights in America.* Westport Conn.: Greenwood, 1988.

Curb, Rosemary. "An Unfashionable Tragedy of American Racism: Alice Childress's *Wedding Band.*" *MELUS* 7 (Winter 1980): 57–68.

———. "Alice Childress." In *Twentieth-Century American Dramatists,* vol. 7 of *Dictionary of Literary Biography,* edited by John MacNicholas, 118–24. Detroit: Gale Research, 1981.

Govan, Sandra Y. "Alice Childress's *Rainbow Jordan:* The Black Aesthetic Returns Dressed in Adolescent Fiction." *Children's Literature Association Quarterly* 13 (Summer 1988): 70–74.

Gussow, Mel. "The Stage: 'Moms.' " *New York Times,* February 10, 1987, Sec. 3:16.

Harris, Trudier. " 'I Wish I Was a Poet': The Character as Artist in Alice Childress's *Like One of the Family.*" *Black American Literature Forum* 14 (Spring 1980): 24–30.

———. *From Mammies to Militants: Domestics in Black American Literature.* Philadelphia: Temple University Press, 1982.

———. "Alice Childress." In *Afro-American Writers After 1955: Dramatists and Prose Writers,* vol. 38 of *Dictionary of Literary Biography,* edited by Thadious M. Davis and Trudier Harris, 66–79. Detroit: Gale Research, 1985.

Hay, Samuel A. "Alice Childress's Dramatic Structure." In *Black Women Writers (1950–1980): A Critical Evaluation,* edited by Mari Evans, 117–28. Garden City, N.Y.: Anchor-Doubleday, 1984.

Hicklin, Fannie Ella Frazier. "The American Negro Playwright 1920–1964." Ph.D. diss., University of Wisconsin, 1965.

Hill, Elbert R. "A Hero for the Movies." In *Children's Novels and the Movies,* edited by Douglas Street, 236–43. New York: Ungar, 1983.

Holliday, Polly. "I Remember Alice Childress." *The Southern Quarterly* 25 (Spring 1987): 63–65.

Killens. John O. "The Literary Genius of Alice Childress." In *Black Women Writers (1950–1980): A Critical Evaluation,* edited by Mari Evans, 129–33. Garden City, N.Y.: Anchor-Doubleday, 1984.

Miller, Jeanne-Marie A. "Images of Black Women in Plays by Black Playwrights." *College Language Association Journal* 20 (June 1977): 494–507.

Mitchell, Loften. "Three Writers and a Dream." *Crisis* 72 (April 1965): 219–23.

———. *Black Drama: The Story of the American Negro in the Theatre.* New York: Hawthorn Books, 1967.

Newberry, Lynn. "A Hero Still Ain't Nothin' But a Sandwich." *Virginia English Bulletin* 36 (Winter 1986): 27–29.

Ortiz, Miguel A. "The Politics of Poverty in Young Adult Literature." *The Lion and the Unicorn* 2 (Fall 1978): 6–15.

Troutman-Robinson, Denise. "The Elements of Call and Response in Alice Childress' *Like One of the Family.*" *MAWA Review* 4 (June 1989): 18–21.

Walker, Alice. "A Walk Through 20th Century Black America." *MS* 8 (December 1979): 46–47.

Walker, Melissa. *Down from the Mountaintop: Black Women's Novels in the Wake of the Civil Rights Movement, 1966–1989.* New Haven: Yale University Press, 1991.

Wiley, Catherine. "Whose Name, Whose Protection: Reading Alice Childress's *Wedding Band.*" In *Modern American Drama: The Female Canon,* edited by June Schlueter, 184–97. Rutherford, N.J.: Fairleigh Dickinson University Press, 1990.

SUSAN GILBERT

James Duff
(1955–   )

James Duff with his first play, *Home Front,* was recognized as a playwright deft in humor, skilled in stage craft, possessed of a dramatist's native ability to reveal character through dialogue, sure in traditional modes of theatrical construction, and capable of terrifying power. His second play, *A Quarrel of Sparrows,* showed a more controlled satire of contemporary issues, and his film for television, *Doing Time on Maple Drive*, was noted for its depths of psychological probing. His work to date suggests that he will continue to explore themes of family strife and heritage, traditions of culture and religion strong in the South, and subjects controversial and timely.

BIOGRAPHY

James Duff was born September 3, 1955, in New Orleans and taken in infancy to Texas, the adopted son of James Henry Duff and Blanche Ainsworth Duff. Then he traveled a great deal in Texas. His father moved from town to town, working for Sears, Roebuck, and Co. Duff attended eleven different schools in Beaumont, San Angelo, Dallas, Wichita Falls, Arlington, and Lubbock.

If there was a good deal of moving in place in his childhood, there was also much of a conservative Southern family, one son, one daughter, his parents' lasting marriage, his father's steady career in merchandising, his rearing in the Southern Baptist Church.

His last year in high school, resisting another move and resentful, he said, of being "jerked around" (Nemy, H5), he left his family to return to high school in Lubbock. For a year and a half after high school he was enrolled at Texas Tech University in Lubbock and for a year and a half after that at Tarrant County Junior College, the northeast campus.

At the time of the opening of *Home Front,* originally titled *The War at Home,* he said in an interview that he had been a wretched student, majoring in "parties and social affairs" (Nemy, H12). But from the two colleges he did find his life's work, writing for the theater. At Texas Tech he was often in plays though his father opposed his majoring in theater on the grounds that he'd "never make a living at it" (Nemy, H12). For all his desultory ways as a student, Duff has expressed affection for his teachers, among them especially an English teacher who urged him to try creative writing.

Dropping out of college he lived in or near Dallas from 1976 to 1981, working as bartender and actor and learning the theater. He acted in numerous productions and, with Theater Three of Dallas, began his career as a playwright with three plays for children produced by the Grimm Magician Players.

In 1981 Duff moved to New York City and lived there until December 1989, surviving, he enumerated in a letter to me, as "an actor, a waiter, a bartender, a restaurant manager, and a writer." In theaters as well as bars and restaurants he made friends and contacts and pursued his ambition. A year after he arrived in New York, *The War at Home* was staged at the Hotel Carter on a slim budget his friends provided. After several disappointments and delays from problems with financing and the death of the director Alan Schneider, *The War at Home* was finally performed in England at the Hampstead Theater Club in June 1984 and, retitled *Home Front,* at the Royale Theater in New York in January 1985. Duff's second play, *A Quarrel of Sparrows,* premiered in Dallas in 1988, was produced by the Cleveland Play House in 1992, and ran off-Broadway in 1993. Duff lived in the early 1990s in Los Angeles, writing TV movies and screen plays, arranging for productions of *A Quarrel of Sparrows,* and adapting *Home Front* for a film version. *Doing Time on Maple Drive,* a Fox film for television appeared in March 1992. *Without a Kiss Goodby,* a CBS tele-play was screened in March 1993. Duff was content in California to be living as a writer only, but expressed plans eventually to return to New York, the center still of American theater.

Duff is not one of the South's bitter exiles. *Home Front* presents a never-to-be reconciled Southern family. Some critics have found in it Oedipal rage and anti-American fury. But, interviewed then in 1985, Duff expressed regret for his family's suffering caused by his leaving home in high school and said that he and his family were once again very close. He described his father with affection: "My father is a most wonderful man but he was very strict" (Nemy, H12). Far from being "anti-American," he said, "I come from Texas and they breed patriotism into us there.... I'm so American I couldn't live anywhere else" (Nemy, H12). For all his affection for his family, for Texas, and for the Dallas theater, he said in 1990 that he never expects to live again in the South.

If the pattern of *Home Front* and *A Quarrel of Sparrows* continues, he will be one more Southern playwright living elsewhere, writing about Southern families, attitudes, and traditions. But Duff is not easily pushed to assume the label of Southern writer. Responses to *Home Front* from around the world have convinced him of the universality of the familial tensions that he has portrayed; everywhere he has heard, "that was my family." The historical issue of the play was global, not provincial. Duff says that his father would not be pleased to hear the family called Southerners, as they are Texans; the difference, Duff explains, is that Texans are less prejudiced than Southerners. But he also describes *A Quarrel of Sparrows* as a conflict between Southerners and Yankees; the elder hero and his niece are from Georgia; their family name, Ainsworth, is Duff's mother's family name; the niece's Christian fundamentalism is native to Duff's Texas.

MAJOR THEMES

Home Front is aptly named for the arena of conflict, for the themes of war and of home, and for that of appearance, "putting up a front." Set in Dallas, on the eve and day of Thanksgiving 1973, it is a play with four people: the mother, a caricature of middle class cheer and officiousness; the father, withdrawn but initially sympathetic; the sister, absorbed in her teenage world and her boyfriend; and, the central character, the son Jeremy, a Vietnam veteran too scarred by what he has seen and done in the war to resume his life.

It is a well-made play after the fashion of drawing-room comedy, two scenes one evening, two the next day. It shows the preparation for the intended celebration, the rituals, the recipes, the notes of music as they have always been and as the family would have them go on, to affirm the worth and permanence of the American bourgeois way. The son will not be drawn in, nor will he dress for dinner. His refusal is adequate, however small the sign. As if a Moslem refused to remove his shoes at the door to the mosque and the Arab woman uncovered her head in the market place, the simple gesture refuses the faith and defiles the sacred tradition. The American son, refusing to don a tie for Thanksgiving dinner, refuses the whole of the culture's self-satisfaction and announces his *non serviam.*

It is a culture that sent him to the horrors of war for purposes that were a sham. The father had refused him the money to escape the draft, had refused to be dishonored by a defector. The family members refuse now to acknowledge the horror they have perpetrated, on the Vietnamese, on the American sons who conveyed the injuries and suffered them. They would have the past be past and look to a booming America, without self-doubt or recrimination.

They want their son back as he was; they want to go on as they were; they want to forget. In Vietnam he lost innocence and faith and his very soul. The holiday for which his mother feverishly prepares is a mockery; their shows of caring for him cannot redeem him. They have nothing to tell him to justify the horrors he has seen, his agony of terror and violence. They do not want to hear what he has seen or become. They want normality, placidity, respectability; they want to forget and go on. He is too soul-seared to be again the American boy, looking for a job, planning for his future. He cannot formulate his pain as desire, only as unspeakable regret that erupts into violence and vituperative abuse. The play moves from comic bickering to a terrific outburst of anguish and Jeremy's being cast out of the home by his father.

Home Front is a play about destruction, about the disintegration of values, of the family unit, and of the hero's psyche. It proceeds inexorably from estrangement and misunderstanding to violence and to utter dissolution of the family.

A Quarrel of Sparrows is also about disputes and families, about the values of familial tradition, about communication within families, and about tolerance. Here the central characters are godfather and godson, not father and son. The godfather is pithy, wise, and gentle. The older Southern woman, his niece, is comic in her old-fashioned ways and relentless piety. They are sympathetic in their enduring affection. This time Duff's focus is the world of theater and entertainment, not the international politics of the war in Vietnam.

The young hero Paul Palmer is a promising playwright on his way to sign a contract for a film production of his work when he has a vision from God, not on the road to Damascus, but on Fifth Avenue, "between Gucci's and the Park." He is lifted into the air, shown the city below, and endued with a message like the Old Testament prophets' of God's imminent wrath on an iniquitous city. He flees to his godfather's Long Island retreat. His wife, his friend, his agent are in terror that he will let go their long anticipated chance for success and wealth.

A Quarrel of Sparrows moves from conflict and threatened dissolution to understanding and affirmation of the bonds within families: the "sibling" pair who are here uncle and niece, with long memories of shared experience and tolerated differences; the husband and wife. It shows symbols of tradition passed along: a child to be born and a tree to be planted in a garden where future generations of sparrows may mate. And the hero is reconciled to his work. However crass and inimicable to the spirit the commercialism of contemporary American theater, he comes to see it as a place where he can carry on "God's work," the divine work of spirit's inspiration, albeit in a modern guise.

He learns this from the wonderful figure of his godfather August Ainsworth, who has spent his life in service of a passing art, the study of the harp. The harps are dying, like him. He hates their successors, electronic gimmickry, but will go in resignation, not defeat, knowing that the larger cause he served, the spirit of music, will endure in another form.

Duff's plays employ rituals, preparing for holiday meals, setting tables, receiving guests, dressing for holiday meals, singing hymns, saying grace. Memory, he shows in both his plays is a moral force, transcending the trinkets that stand for the heritage of the past, and necessary for the old and the young.

A Quarrel of Sparrows, for all its genial humor, is a topical play as much as *Home Front.* In Dallas its satire of fundamentalist Christian complacency seemed the main point. As a play of New York, its chief conflict concerns a commercial contract for a play; its antagonists are the playwright and his producer with whom the wife, intent on her own acting career, sides.

The playwright may be mad, claiming his vision of God; the agent, wife, and friend are undeniably sane, seeking profit. Mad or inspired, the playwright is a purist and as unlikely as Jeremiah to be bought off from his pronouncement of truth by a concern for the realities of the market. In the alignment, the wife wants her career, the friend wants his piece of the pie, the agent needs to make his payment on his boat. All would live, parasites, off an art grossly debased.

Only Uncle August understands Paul's devotion to his vision and can show him that a modern artist can remain true to his beloved medium and to the truth of his message in a callous world.

If critics read the young protagonist's as the author's voice, the play may appear self-righteous, as some have called *Home Front.* A young, misunderstood man in a crass, self-serving culture that will not hear him, Paul is unyielding, like his predecessor, Jeremy. What are different are the older men, father and godfather. Jeremy's father was unbending and blind to any values or perceptions but his own. August, Paul's godfather, as avatar of an older civilization has more than false fronts to pass along with his hospitality, his wine and water and bread and bed, his cornucopias of fruit, and his garden. Undergirding these important stage props of home and shelter is his sense of self-worth. He has been true to his art in an indifferent world. He can see through manners to their informing principles, through ritual to the sacraments they typify. So, with slight adjustment to the lingo of the times, he is able to guide Paul to work in a modern way that is true to the essence of his vision. And August is able, with some adjustment of terms, to pray with Rosanna.

If as craft *A Quarrel of Sparrows* shares a defect with *Home Front,* it is in its overpreachy close. Duff is more skillful than he perhaps knows. Both plays point with economy and precision to their ends. But Duff has hammered a bit with explanations at the close of both plays. Those of August will go down better with their humor and wit than the lesson of Jeremy with its bitterness. With observation of productions Duff may become more confident in closing his plays.

In *Doing Time on Maple Drive,* a 1992 Fox film for television, Duff again presents American home life as a prison of pretense and hypocrisy. Set anywhere in middle America, this play of the picture-perfect American family seems headed for the same destructive fury that seared *Home Front.*

It too begins at a homecoming meal, this one a celebration of the engagement of son Matt, the focus of the parents' pride and all-driving ambition. A model student at Yale, he is engaged to Alicen, an all-American beauty from the wealthier, more sophisticated Northeast. Matt seems prepared to sacrifice truth, love, even his life to perpetuate his parents' illusion. The secret that comes out is his homosexuality, a truth his mother had seen but denied, his fiancée only suspected.

Like *A Quarrel of Sparrows* and unlike *Home Front, Maple Drive* ends happily. It is a play not of Oedipal rage but of every son's longing for his father's approval and for being loved for himself alone. The boy's attempted suicide fails; his father says, ''whatever you are, you're my son.''

The happy ending seems more sudden and less likely than either the rage at the end of *Home Front* or the reconciliation of *A Quarrel of Sparrows,* for there is little in the character of the father to show him capable of being suddenly hit by truth, even by a jolt like Matt's attempted suicide. Alicen's naiveté would be more believable in an earlier time, but she is a minor player.

Principals here are again the family, and the central issue is that of children struggling within the imprisoning facade of their parents' middle-class conventions.

Duff works here with a slightly larger cast. The family on Maple Drive has two sons, a daughter, and a son-in-law. Son Tim is a dead-beat and a drunk who flunked out of school. He is bitter and sad, unable to live up to his father's expectations or, it appears, to live without his approval. A dark brooding presence, he is seen last sweeping up the wreckage of the pictures his mother has thrown about in her fury of disappointment at the shame her imperfect children have inflicted on her. The film holds some hope even for him in that the father kneels with him, sweeping up the remains of their pasts, the pictures of what they were not. The two sons, drop-out and homosexual, have both disappointed their father. Their very lives depend on the father's ability to abandon his false hopes for their real needs.

The daughter, Karen, is prepared to abort her child to live by her father's prescriptions that nothing interfere with their relentless march to prosperity. Her husband, Tim, is one of the outsiders who, with Matt's lover Kyle, intervene to keep this family from imploding, preferring death for themselves and their children to abandoning the facade. Tim's art photos are a foil to the posed pictures that punctuate the theme of pretense.

The mother, Lisa, is a villainess who would require her children to "be something" to redeem the sacrifice of her own life. Having walked in on Matt and Kyle years before, she is not innocently but willfully blind, insisting, "I don't know and I don't want to know."

Doing Time on Maple Drive is set deliberately in a generic middle America. It shares with the specifically Southern settings of Duff's plays the sense of provinciality. Like the family of *Home Front,* they are ordinary people, but their ordinariness is stultifying, and none are truthful. The father cheats in business and would hide Tim's drinking and failures from his wife. She is only too glad to pretend. Karen hides her pregnancy as Matt hides his homosexuality. Their attempts at middle-class respectability nearly destroy the family they profess to love above all.

Strong echoes of Tennessee Williams's Southern families appear in Duff's giddy women, in the imprisoned sons, the sacrificed sister, the hopelessly blind mother, and in the homosexuality denied behind the facade, the Belle Reve, of idyllic families.

The constraints of religion and the strengths of family ties, if not exclusively Southern themes, have a Southern emphasis in Duff's work. Alicen, the fiancée from the Northeast in *Doing Time on Maple Drive,* remarks that her family gathers only when lawyers are present. Duff's families have force to draw and keep siblings and relatives in life-long arguments and quests for each other's approval.

SURVEY OF CRITICISM

Critics have hailed *Home Front* as a work of great power. In London in the *Sunday Times* John Peter (1984) wrote, "The final 15 minutes are among the most fearless and harrowing pieces of dramatic writing I've seen for a long time: when I call this play stunning I use the word advisedly, and with a terrible admiration" (A39). In New York, Clive Barnes (1985) called it a "searingly memorable play. . . . I cannot overpraise the adroitness with which Duff has planned his attack on our emotions" (23). In Australia, Bob Evans (1988) has declared it "as funny and familiar in its moments of domestic stress as it is terrifying in its climax" (16).

Home Front, in addition to London, New York, and Sydney, played for ten months in Israel, played in South Africa and won the Vita Award, played in Sweden, and was translated into several languages. But in New York it ran only two weeks because the subject matter wouldn't go down.

Critics, even notoriously harsh or erratic ones, praised its technical facility. Brendan Gill in the *New Yorker* (1985) declared, "One is in no doubt whatever of his talent" (110). Frank Rich in the *New York Times* (1985) noted "slick, professionally polished scenes and jokes" (1). Mel Gussow also in the *New York Times* (1985) admitted "a certain theatrical facility" (1). John Simon of *New York* (1985) found "throughout most of the play a low-level proficiency" (60). But these faulted it on several counts: a fatal disunity between its comic, "sit-com" early scenes and the late violence; a self-pitying and "anti-American" attitude of the hero, which some identified with the author's; a shop-worn theme of another Vietnam homecoming.

All critics have acknowledged, with varying degrees of praise, Duff's gift for domestic humor. They have been sharply divided on how well the humor and despair have been meshed. Barnes greatly admired "The way we are lulled with the clever familiarity of near atavistic family phrases of . . . family bickering" (23). But Richard Corliss (1985) found the late "didacticism" destructive of the "season's finest new play" (79); Gill said the play "falters" in construction (110); and Gussow complained that it "splits in two," that its first half given all to "frivolity" is "overly concerned with domestic trivialities," leaving the audience unprepared for the violence to come (1).

It is, however, on moral, not technical grounds that the objectors have heaped scorn or failed to acknowledge Duff's skill in presenting the hero as a deliberate construct. Although Barnes noted that in Jeremy's "self-satisfied self-pity and self-hatred . . . [he is] deeply wounded, perhaps irreversibly disturbed" (23), the plays' New York detractors attributed Jeremy's attitudes directly to Duff. Gussow charged that the attitude of the play is cynical and self-righteous with a protagonist who "shoulders no responsibility for his actions," "wallows in his own contempt" and blames his parents, a father well-intentioned, a mother who is "at worst, harmless" (1). Rich complained of the hero, "sulky sneering," "an unsympathetic lout . . . alternately vicious and self-pitying" and dismissed Duff with the cut that the "author's anger, however genuine, is juvenile, not righteous" (1). Simon carped, "The only thing that elevates it above TV is that it turns nasty in the end: anti-family, anti-received wisdom, anti-American" (60).

The extreme divergence in critical responses to the New York production provoked comment at the time. A commentator for *Variety* attributed it to the weight New York criticism gives to performance and to the sharply divided view of Carroll O'Connor's performance as the father. There was division, if not as widespread, over Frances Sternhagen's performance as mother. To some degree the different temper of the reception of the play in New York from the rest of the world was unquestionably due to the emphasis on performers on New York stages.

In London critics praised the Hampstead production actors and directors, and the mother and the director were the same in the later production in New York. But on the opening of the play in New York Holly Hill reported in London that the productions differed and that in New York the balance had shifted to comedy. In Australia the production, performers, and director received overwhelmingly favorable reviews.

That the play fared so much better throughout the world than it did in New York is probably attributable more to the political mood of America in the mid-1980s than to differences in production. Everywhere critics noted that its theme wasn't new, but "old hat" (Fender, 728) and "shopworn" (Rich, 1). Some questioned: "Do we need to see another play about Vietnam?" (Evans, 16); "New York had its Vietnam homecoming plays 10 years ago . . . who needs them now?" (Wardle, 8). The different answers depended on whether critics saw an intrinsic connection between bourgeois family values and American participation in and reaction to the aftermath of Vietnam. In London, Stephen Fender (1984) judged "that it is unfair to blame the war on American bourgeois family values" (C728).

In New York, Barnes insisted that the war was cause enough for the hero to be so scarred. Peter, in London, best identified the theme of *Home Front* as not the "rights and wrongs" of the war in Vietnam but "the solid American concepts of honour and virtuous paternalistic legality that went into its making, and the terrible spiritual destruction of its aftermath." He praised Duff for "asking to whom America belongs now: the uncomprehending, aging parents who want to live and forget or the maimed children who can't forget and don't know how to survive" (A39).

Glibly, the American dismissers sided with "forgetting." Rich closed his review with the father's line that closes the play; all should "forget about it and go on'' (1). In Australia Evans argued that the play is ''principally concerned with memory'' and noted its likeness to the Australian veterans' organization, the RSL, and its motto ''Lest We Forget'' (16).

It is probably not coincidence, but a sign of the mood of the era, that two powerful American works about Vietnam and about memory appearing in 1984–85, Joan Didion's novel *Democracy* and Duff's *Home Front,* were reviewed with heavy scorn in the *New York Times.* Both linked the moral disintegration of family and of the nation, in war and its aftermath, to the refusal to remember. Both coupled the disintegration of private honesty and families' acknowledgment of guilt to the larger political issues of public morality. Both were scorned as hackneyed repetitions of well-worn themes that U.S. audiences would do better to put behind them.

When *A Quarrel of Sparrows* premiered in Dallas, Gary MacDonald called it deft and hilarious, ''an extraordinarily refreshing comedy'' (McDonald 1988, 14). He praised Duff for the intellectual force of the work as well as for its easy humor. The play and its subject, identified as ''the varieties of religious faith'' (Garrett, 1988, 28), were found not only amusing but thought-provoking. And playwright and director were called ''brave'' for poking fun at fundamentalist Christianity in Dallas (McDonald 1988, 14).

In Cleveland the play received similar commendation for earnestly treating the theme of religion, but the production was faulted as *Home Front* had been in New York for an imperfect blend of comedy and ''awkward moralizing'' (Jones 1992, 174). Similarly one New York reviewer faulted it for a ''collision'' between the serious religious theme and the old-fashioned genre of ''commercial comedy'' (Feingold 1993, 119). Another, Ben Brantley for the *New York Times* (1993) found it pure comedy and, in a judgment strikingly at odds with many reactions to *Home Front,* a ''perfectly pleasant refuge from the Sturm und Drang of real life and more challenging forms of theater'' (C20). Both New York reviews called its neat form old-fashioned.

Most reviewers of *A Quarrel of Sparrows* have had praise for Duff's creation of the elder characters, Ainsworth and niece Rosanna, and their ''delicately rendered'' relationship (Brantley 1993, C20). The younger characters—wife, manager, and agent—have been accused of being stock types (Jones 1992, 174), and ''broadly drawn'' (Brantley 1993, C20). Paul, the young hero, in Cleveland was called ''whining'' and selfish (Jones 1992, 174), a judgment which echoed some of the harsh reviews of the young Jeremy of *Home Front.*

Doing Time on Maple Drive received favorable notice for dealing earnestly with ''gritty family problems in a forthright, realistic way'' (Gardella 1992, A4) and, from its director, Ken Olin, for the subtlety and psychological complexity of the characters (Lundin 1992, F10).

BIBLIOGRAPHY

Works by James Duff

Home Front. New York: Dramatists Play Service, 1985.
A Quarrel of Sparrows. Unpublished play, 1988.
Doing Time on Maple Drive. 20th Century Fox TV, 1992.

Studies of James Duff

Barnes, Clive. "Carroll O'Connor and Company Give a Royale Performance." Review of *Home Front. New York Post* (January 3, 1985): 23, 24.

Brantley, Ben. "Lo, It's Armageddon in an Old-Fashioned Comedy." Review of *A Quarrel of Sparrows. New York Times* (November 10, 1993): C:19, 20.

Carbo, Rosie. " 'Sparrows' Comedy Shows Success Not Always Enough." Review of *A Quarrel of Sparrows. Star Courier* (Plano, Texas) (October 20, 1988): A6, 7.

Corliss, Richard. "A Ghost Sonata in Sitcom Land." Review of *Home Front. Time* 125 (January 14, 1985): 79.

"Crix Disagree on 'Home Front': Is That Archie Bunker or Not?" *Variety* 317 (January 9, 1985): 189.

Evans, Bob. "No Quiet on the Home Front." Review of *Home Front. Sydney Morning Herald* (September 15, 1988): 16.

Feingold, Michael, "Clarity Ward." Review of *Careless Love, Timon of Athens,* and *A Quarrel of Sparrows. Village Voice* 38 (November 16, 1993): 117, 119.

Fender, Stephen. "Panic at Thanksgiving." Review of *The War at Home. Times Literary Supplement* (June 29, 1984): C728.

Gardella, Kay. "All in the Fractured Family." Review of *Doing Time on Maple Drive. Daily News* (New York) (March 16, 1992): A4.

Garrett, Jerry. "Local Theater Offers World Premiere of Duff's Opus: *A Quarrel of Sparrows* Onstage at Dallas' Theatre Three." Review of *A Quarrel of Sparrows. Dallas Voice* (October 26, 1988): 28.

Gill, Brendan. Review of *Home Front. New Yorker* 60 (January 14, 1985): 110.

Gussow, Mel. "Protagonists Who Substitute Self-Pity for Courage." Review of *Home Front. New York Times* (January 13, 1985): II, 3: 1, 24.

Hill, Holly. "Joyful Hymn to National Game." Review of *Diamonds, Messiah, Home Front,* and *Dancing in the End Zone. Times of London* (January 17, 1985): C9.

Holt, Jo Ann. "Cross over the Bridge." Review of *A Quarrel of Sparrows. Oak Cliff Tribune* (October 27, 1988): C7.

Jones, Chris. Review of *A Quarrel of Sparrows. Variety* 346 (April 6, 1992): 174.

Kerr, Walter. "Taking Comedy Seriously." Review of *Home Front, Madwoman of Chaillot,* and *Noises Off. New York Times* (January 27, 1985): II, 3:1.

Lundin, Diana E. "Direct Approach Beats Acting." Review of *Doing Time on Maple Drive. Daily News* (Los Angeles) (March 16, 1992): F9, 10.

McDonald, Gary. "No Fear of Flying." Review of *A Quarrel of Sparrows. Dallas Observer* (November 10, 1988): 14.

Nemy, Enid. "It's How We Got Where We Are." Interview with James Duff. *New York Times* (December 30, 1984): H5, 12.

Peter, John. ''Causes for Thanksgiving.'' Review of *The War at Home. Sunday Times* (June 17, 1984): A39.

Rich, Frank. ''Stage: Family Strife in 'Home Front.' '' Review of *Home Front. New York Times* (January 3, 1985): III, 13:1.

Simon, John. ''End Games.'' Review of *Home Front. New York* 18 (January 14, 1985): 60, 61.

Tighe, Mary Ann. ''Bringing Home 'The War at Home.' '' Review of *The War at Home. Vogue* 174 (December 1984): 86.

Wardle, Irving. Review of *The War at Home. Times of London* (June 14, 1984): D8.

PATRICIA M. GANTT AND CHIP JONES

Wilma Dykeman
(1920–)

Wilma Dykeman has made her mark as a chronicler of life in Appalachia and throughout the South. The subjects of her fiction range from nineteenth-century mountain families dealing with the divisiveness of the Civil War, to modern protagonists working to conserve the land and fight prejudice. In addition to fiction, she has written three biographies, several studies of history and civil rights, and numerous magazine and newspaper articles.

BIOGRAPHY

Wilma Dykeman was born May 23, 1920, in Asheville, North Carolina, the only child of Willard J. and Bonnie Cole Dykeman. Her mother's family had lived in the area since the eighteenth century, while her father was from New York. She attended local public schools, and went first to Biltmore Junior College (now the University of North Carolina at Asheville) and then to Northwestern University, where she majored in speech, graduating Phi Beta Kappa in 1940.

Upon graduation, she had planned to move to New York City to teach at Miss Finch's School, but during her summer at home, she met James Rorex Stokely, Jr., a young poet and essayist. They were introduced by Julia Wolfe, mother of Thomas Wolfe, and her daughter, Mabel Wolfe Wheaton. Stokely, a protégé of the late author, had adapted *Look Homeward, Angel* for the stage and befriended Wolfe by offering him a remote mountain cabin in which to escape the crowds. Dykeman changed her New York plans.

Dykeman and Stokely were married on October 12, 1940, and divided much of their time for the next fifteen years between apple orchard operations in Stokely's hometown of Newport, Tennessee, and Asheville. In the 1950s they moved permanently to Newport, where they lived with their two sons, Dykeman, born September 5, 1949, and James R., III, born August 6, 1951.

Dykeman began her writing career in 1948 with short stories published in *Southwest Review* and *Prairie Schooner.* She was soon in demand for book reviews and essays for newspapers and other periodicals, often cowritten with Stokely.

Her first book, *The French Broad* (1955), part of the Rivers of America series, explores the history and geography of the French Broad River, which begins in western North Carolina and flows into eastern Tennessee. It does much more than trace the path of a body of water, delineating the mountain region and its people with dignity, affection, and frequent lyricism—as well as establishing themes that would recur in Dykeman's work. The book won the Thomas Wolfe Memorial Trophy as the year's best treatment of North Carolina and a Colonial Dames award for originality in research. It also helped Dykeman secure a Guggenheim Fellowship the next year, when she planned to study the Civil War history of the North Carolina mountains.

In 1956 she and Stokely began a project to determine the mood of Southerners regarding the Brown v. Board of Education integration decision. They spent nearly a year conducting interviews with a variety of people, including farmers, politicians, segregationists, and civil-rights activists. The result was *Neither Black nor White* (1957), which won the Hillman Award as the year's best book on world peace, civil liberties, or human relations.

In 1962 Dykeman published her first novel, *The Tall Woman.* Set in the North Carolina mountains between the Civil War and the turn of the century, this book emphasizes a strong sense of place and family without acceding to traditional local color motifs. It shows a mountain middle class ignored by Mary Noailles Murfree and her counterparts. The mountains are important to the action, and the lessening isolation of the characters is crucial to the plot, but it is characterization that drives the novel and provides its vigor. Particularly significant is Dykeman's portrayal of the heroine, Lydia McQueen. This character, a selfless community leader of strength and high principle, is the first of such women for whom the author is noted. Here, too, Dykeman reinforces a theme—conservation of the land—that appears in her work, early and late.

Dykeman wrote a sequel, *The Far Family* (1966), tracing the McQueen family's transition to the twentieth century. The tensions inherent in such a chronological move—''progress'' versus tradition and prejudice versus understanding—mirror major concerns of the region and nation during this period. As its title might suggest, it also examines traditional family ties. The book is structurally interesting for its use of the interchapter technique.

Her third novel, *Return the Innocent Earth* (1973), explores a subject she knows intimately: the story of a mountain family that starts its own canning company. Based loosely on the Stokelys' own enterprise, this work continues her questioning of Southern ''progress,'' in which land is often used up for the sake of today's company profits and relationships are deemed useful only for business purposes. The protagonist is, for the first time in Dykeman's work, male—although several "tall women" are present, including a survivor of Auschwitz.

In addition to novels, Dykeman has written three biographies of subjects who worked in the Appalachian region. These subjects share her convictions on such topics as education and civil rights, so the books are more laudatory than critical. Dykeman and her husband continued their focus on civil rights with *Seeds of Southern Change* (1962), a biography of Will Alexander, founder of the Appalachian Regional Commission. In 1966 she wrote *Prophet of Plenty: The First Ninety Years of W. D. Weatherford,* exploring the career of the long-time trustee of Berea College and promoter of positive self-image for three generations of Appalachian people. Her third biography, *Too Many People, Too Little Love* (1974), traces the life and career of Edna Rankin McKinnon, champion of birth control throughout the South and especially in Third World countries.

Dykeman has also written extensively on the history of the Southern Appalachians. Building on the popularity of *The French Broad* and her delight in research, she wrote *Tennessee: A Bicentennial History* (1975) as part of the Norton "States of the Nation" series; in 1978, she added *With Fire and Sword: The Battle of King's Mountain.* She has written one other Tennessee history (1984), and in 1980 was named State Historian for Tennessee. She is currently working on a book about the Native American genius, Sequoyah, who created the Cherokee alphabet.

Travel has always been a prime interest of Dykeman. She and her husband traveled extensively both around North America and in Europe when their children were young; her observations during these travels have resulted in dozens of articles for the *New York Times* and other periodicals. In 1968 she and Stokely wrote *The Border States: Kentucky, North Carolina, Tennessee, Virginia, and West Virginia.* This book looks at the history, geography, culture, and future of the region she knows best.

Since the early 1950s, she has been writing a column for the Knoxville *News-Sentinel.* She has collected her best columns and essays into two books: *Look to This Day* (1968) and *Explorations* (1984). She has also written books with each of her sons: *Highland Homeland: The People of the Great Smokies* (1978, with Dykeman Stokely) and *Appalachian Mountains* (1980, with Jim Stokely).

Dykeman has long been recognized as one of the best critics of her region and its literature. In 1973 she wrote *Southern Appalachian Books: An Annotated, Selected Bibliography,* one of the earliest critical bibliographies of Appalachian writing. Since 1975, she has taught a course in Appalachian literature at the University of Tennessee, where she is a full professor. She has for years been interested in Berea College in Kentucky, and was named its first female trustee. She has also received many awards, including a senior fellowship from the National Endowment for the Humanities. In 1985 the North Carolina General Assembly gave her its highest distinction, the North Carolina Award. The Appalachian Writers' Association recognized her in 1988 for "Outstanding Contributions to Appalachian Literature,'' and she was honored at the 1989 Southern Festival of Books with the Distinguished Southern Writers Award.

Dykeman divides her time between Newport and Asheville, but is frequently on the road, speaking or giving seminars. She is writing a fourth novel and a critical volume on Appalachian literature.

MAJOR THEMES

The major themes of Dykeman's fiction are the key words in her titles: *woman, family, earth*. Determined to depict the mountain mother without condescension or stereotype, Dykeman partially based Lydia McQueen in *Tall Woman* on the actual matriarchs she had interviewed for *French Broad*. She drew her title from a mountain saying: ''A tall woman casts a long shadow.'' As the narrator says of Dykeman's heroine: ''If strength was what was called for, then she could be strong. She would be stout enough to carry every day as it came'' (35). The author has often expressed her dismay at presentations of mountaineers that treat them as ''a strange little body of people'' (Larson 1983, 39). Lydia McQueen is her literary rejoinder to these innumerable distortions, as she struggles to attain a school for her Thickety Creek community, torn apart by wounds left over from the Civil War and sometimes by the community's own greed. The author continued to foreground female characters in her subsequent novels, preferring to add to her confrontation of Appalachian stereotypes an investigation of the double burdens of gender and class.

From her earliest works, she has insisted on a more inclusive definition of the Appalachian family than the reading public was used to seeing, giving balanced portrayals of blacks as well as whites. An enduring focus from the first has been civil-rights issues. Her scope has included civil rights in its broadest sense—the idea that all people should have the right to be different, yet treated as equals.

In *Neither Black nor White* and other books, she exposes long-standing myths and stereotypes about blacks and black/white relationships. These myths include the concept of a solid, or monolithic, South; the belief that blacks did not really want civil rights; and the perception that the civil-rights movement was a communist plot. Dykeman has shown the damage such myths have done the entire South, affecting the national image of all Southerners.

Her fiction reflects many civil-rights themes through characters who at times exemplify—and at other times, refute—the stereotypes discussed in the nonfiction. Her white characters have attitudes toward blacks that range from blatantly racist to idealistic, and her black characters are neither saints nor savages, but realistic and representative.

Far Family, which deals most directly with civil rights, boldly centers upon relationships between blacks and whites and white attitudes toward blacks at the height of the civil-rights movement. Dykeman sets the stage in the first few pages: ''Everything that happened now between a white person and a black

person became more than an encounter of individuals—it became a confrontation of groups, two races, two histories'' (16). In this novel, set in the mountains
of North Carolina, a white man is accused of killing a black man. The plot is
complicated when the accused, Clay Thurston, cannot remember whether he
killed the man; further, no one in the entire community is really sorry the victim,
Hawk Williams, is dead. In addition to presenting these nonstereotypical characters in a realistic setting, Dykeman has honestly explored the state of black
life in Appalachia and much of the South.

Dykeman's forceful yet unforced exploration of race relations indicates a genuine concern for social change, while avoiding the temptation to sermonize. This
theme has been largely overlooked by most Dykeman critics, who have focused
instead on her fiction as it relates primarily to Appalachia. Dykeman herself
considers her early advocacy of equal rights to be one of her major literary
contributions. She views the South's racial problems as a tragic waste; in fact,
in *Neither Black nor White,* she sees a definite link between the squandering of
its human and natural resources: ''As we have misused our richest land, we
have misused ourselves; as we have wasted our beautiful water, we have wasted
ourselves; as we have diminished the lives of one segment of our people, we
have diminished ourselves'' (5).

Another thread that unites Dykeman's work is her concern for Appalachia's
very real struggle for survival. She has called environmental conservation the
South's second greatest problem, eclipsed only by the related need for self-
government. Her early interest in environmental conservation came at a time
when most people had never heard of water pollution and considered strip mining progressive. She made her position known in her first book, *French Broad.*
As she explores the geography and history of the region around the French
Broad River, she also traces a pattern of abuse affecting both land and water.
She castigates even the earliest settlers for their lack of foresight in clearing the
forests: ''The bitterest irony of all the years of settlement is in the process by
which a people so frugal they utilized every element in nature . . . could waste,
with prodigal abandon, the vast harvest of centuries as if it were not only useless
but also an enemy'' (51). In *Border States,* she and Stokely complain that ''the
region as a whole has allowed its trees to be demolished, its waters to be poi-
soned and its air to be polluted with only the faintest of protests'' (162). Their
voices have added some much-needed legitimacy to current protests.

Dykeman became an early and active opponent of strip mining. Used extensively in the coal-mining areas of Appalachia, this practice is both cheaper and
safer than underground mining, but can leave permanent scars on the land.
Dykeman understands that most abuses have occurred in the name of progress,
but she also sees the irony of being drawn to a place for its natural beauty, yet
wasting the land's resources until it becomes ugly.

Instead of simply complaining about environmental pollution, Dykeman has
offered constructive criticism and suggestions for immediate improvements. In
French Broad, she calls on her readers to assume personal responsibility for

both reclamation and prevention—to be "not poetic but practical"—and proposes laws calling for each town or factory to be held responsible for its own wastes (285). Seven years before Rachel Carson's *Silent Spring* chastised a heedless public and formally ushered in the environmentalist movement, Dykeman warned: "Filth is the price we pay for apathy" (291). In each of her novels, she has advocated a sense of obligation to nature. Lydia McQueen in *Tall Woman* dies of typhoid contracted from a polluted stream; a main character in *Far Family* is a senator who tries to enact legislation assuring proper land use; Jonathan Clayburn in *Return the Innocent Earth* is a corporate CEO whose combination of stock holdings and vision empower him to work for "a few of us idealists who may not want to come in last" (424). Throughout her writing, fiction and nonfiction, Dykeman has asked her audience to respond to the hard questions: What do we owe the land? How can we utilize its resources without destroying them? How can we reconcile our very real responsibilities to ourselves and those we love and not jeopardize our common future? Dykeman underscores repeatedly her convictions about the need for proper care of the natural world.

SURVEY OF CRITICISM

Aside from reviews of her seventeen books, Dykeman has received little in the way of critical study. Two master's theses have concentrated on her mountain writings and social activism. One chapter in a doctoral dissertation explores her contribution to a more realistic interpretation of the mountaineer and assesses her work favorably. In 1989 Emory and Henry College honored Dykeman with a symposium on her works; the papers presented there are collected in a special issue of the *Iron Mountain Review*.

Dykeman's greatest literary strength lies in her depiction of character, done with respect and sure knowledge of her subjects, their contexts, and their idioms. Her most important contribution through characterization is her refusal to perpetuate stereotypes, whether based on region, race, or gender. The Bludsoes in *Tall Woman* and *Far Family,* Burl McHone in *Far Family,* and Janus Rathbone in *Return the Innocent Earth* come closest to the traditional mountaineer: poor, uneducated, living in tumble-down shacks—what Thomas Wolfe would call "mountain grills"—yet they are clearly more than one-dimensional, and indeed compose only a segment of their communities. Likewise, while both Hawk Williams and Lonas Rankin are troublemakers who end up murdered, character—not race—is the basis for the disdain all segments of their communities feel for them. The mountain "granny," Lydia McQueen's Aunt Tildy, is quickly shown to be wise both in the lore of the woods and in common sense. Dykeman does not even allow the reader to see her dip snuff or hear her snort with laughter until after she has constructed a solid base of respect for her. Depictions like these deconstruct stock images.

Wilma Dykeman has been treated as a talented author, but not an important one, perhaps because her novels are set in Appalachia, an area that has suffered doubly under pejorative definitions of ''regionalism.'' Thus, she is considered more of an ''Appalachian'' writer than a ''Southern'' writer, and is less likely to be studied in Southern literature classes. But her early advocacy of civil rights and environmental issues, her realistic portraits of the Appalachian region and its people, and her ability to tell a winning and memorable story surely make her worthy of further study.

BIBLIOGRAPHY

Works by Wilma Dykeman

''The Breakdown.'' *Southwest Review* 33 (1948): 260–65.

''The Prison.'' *Prairie Schooner* 22 (1948): 203–9.

''Summer Affair.'' *American Magazine* 152, no. 3 (1951): 42–45, 130–33.

The French Broad. New York: Rinehart, 1955.

Neither Black nor White. With James Stokely. New York: Rinehart, 1957.

Seeds of Southern Change: The Life of Will Alexander. With James Stokely. Chicago: University of Chicago Press, 1962.

The Tall Woman. New York: Holt, Rinehart, and Winston, 1962.

The Far Family. New York: Holt, Rinehart, and Winston, 1966.

Prophet of Plenty: The First Ninety Years of W. D. Weatherford. Knoxville: University of Tennessee Press, 1966.

The Border States: Kentucky, North Carolina, Tennessee, Virginia, West Virginia. With James Stokely. New York: Time-Life Books, 1968, 1970.

Look to This Day. New York: Holt, Rinehart, and Winston, 1968.

Return the Innocent Earth. New York: Holt, Rinehart, and Winston, 1973.

Southern Appalachian Books: An Annotated, Selected Bibliography. Knoxville: Appalachian Resources Project, University of Tennessee, 1973.

Too Many People, Too Little Love. Edna Rankin McKinnon: Pioneer for Birth Control. New York: Holt, Rinehart, and Winston, 1974.

Tennessee: A Bicentennial History. States of the Nation Series. New York: Norton; Nashville: American Association for State and Local History, 1975.

Tennessee Women, Past and Present. With Carol Lynn Yellin. Memphis: Tennessee Committee for the Humanities and Tennessee International Women's Decade Coordinating Committee, 1977.

Highland Homeland: The People of the Great Smokies. With Jim Stokely. Washington, D.C.: Division of Publications, National Park Service, U.S. Department of the Interior, 1978.

With Fire and Sword: The Battle of King's Mountain, 1780. Washington, D.C.: Office of Publications, National Park Service, U.S. Department of the Interior, 1978.

Nashville: The Faces of Two Centuries, 1780–1980. With John Edgerton, Robert Penn Warren, David Wright, and Louis Littleton Davis. Nashville: PlusMedia, 1979.

Tennessee. Portland, Oreg.: Graphic Arts Center Publishing, 1979.

Appalachian Mountains. With Dykeman Stokely. Portland, Oreg.: Graphic Arts Center Publishing, 1980.

At Home in the Smokies: A History Handbook for Great Smoky Mountains National Park, North Carolina and Tennessee. With Jim Stokely. Washington, D.C.: Division of Publications, National Park Service, U.S. Department of the Interior, 1984.

Explorations. Newport, Tenn.: Wakestone Books, 1984.

Tennessee: A History. New York: Norton; Nashville: American Association for State and Local History, 1984.

Tennessee: A Homecoming. With John Netherton, Peter Taylor, and John Edgerton. Nashville: Third National 1985.

Studies of Wilma Dykeman

Aston-Wash, Barbara. "Lady of Letters: At Home with Wilma Dykeman." *Knoxville News-Sentinel* (April 6, 1986): E1.

Banner, Laura Leslie. *The North Carolina Mountaineer in Native Fiction.* Ph.D. diss., University of North Carolina-Chapel Hill, 1984.

"Dykeman Resents Regional Label." *Courier-Journal and Times* (29, April 1973).

Gage, Jim. "Place in the Fiction of Wilma Dykeman." *Iron Mountain Review* 5, no. 1 (1989): 3–7.

———. "The 'Poetics of Space' in Wilma Dykeman's *The Tall Woman.*" In *The Poetics of Appalachian Space,* edited by Parks Hanier, Jr., 67–80. Knoxville: University of Tennessee Press, 1991.

Gantt, Patricia M. "Wilma Dykeman's Tall Women: Challenging the Stereotypes." *Iron Mountain Review* 5, no. 1 (1989): 14–16, 21–25.

Hodges, Betty. "Book Nook." Review of *The Tall Woman,* by Wilma Dykeman. *Durham Morning Herald* (September 2, 1962): 5D.

Hoyle, Bernadette. "An Asheville Author Talks Shop." *News and Observer* (August 15, 1954): sec. 4, 5.

———. *Tar Heel Writers I Know.* Winston-Salem, N.C.: John F. Blair, 1956.

Jones, Chip. "Social Criticism in the Works of Wilma Dykeman." *Iron Mountain Review* 5, no. 1 (1989): 26–32.

———. "A Wilma Dykeman Bibliography." *Iron Mountain Review* 5, no. 1 (1989): 33–36.

Larson, Ron. "The Appalachian Personality: Beginning a Series of Five Interviews with Prominent Appalachians." *Appalachian Heritage* 11, no. 1 (1983): 30–40.

Miller, Danny. "A MELUS Interview: Wilma Dykeman." *MELUS* 9, no. 3 (1982): 45–59.

Moore, Martha Kiser. "The Appalachia of Wilma Dykeman's Fiction." Master's thesis, East Tennessee State University, 1975.

Marius, Richard, and Wilma Dykeman. "The Rooted Heart and the Ranging Intellect: A Conversation." *Iron Mountain Review* 5, no. 1 (1989): 8–13.

Smith, Sam B. "Wilma Dykeman—Tennessee: A Bicentennial History: An Essay Review and an Appreciation." *Tennessee Historical Quarterly* 35 (1976): 95–103.

"Wilma Dykeman—She Casts a Tall Shadow." *Southern Living* 1, no. 5 (June 1966): 74.

GLENN B. BLALOCK

Charles Edward Eaton
(1916–   )

Not one year has passed since 1940 during which Charles Edward Eaton's work has not appeared in a wide range of respected literary magazines and numerous anthologies; and not a decade has passed without the publication of one or more volumes of his poetry, his fiction, or both. Writing and publishing during the first and the second Renascence, Eaton is an important member of the second because he so consistently supports and articulates the values associated with the first, values that shaped him and his work. Eaton has taken his stand for more than five decades, and he offers readers an opportunity to examine how one committed artist has adapted and applied a particular constellation of values and principles to a changing world.

BIOGRAPHY

Born on June 25, 1916, in Winston-Salem, North Carolina, the youngest of eight children, Charles Edward Eaton was the fifth son of Oscar Benjamin Eaton (1859–1945) and Mary Gaston Hough Eaton (1875–1933). Descended from several generations of Southerners, the Eaton family had attained a respected position in Winston-Salem by 1916, and Charles reaped the benefits of a familial and social environment that encouraged and enabled his subsequent development as a writer. His father, a former school teacher and a successful tobacco businessman, served ten terms as mayor of Winston (and later Winston-Salem), and his mother was a college graduate. Eaton, in his introduction to *New and Selected Poems, 1942–1987* (1987), remembers that his "father, a businessman, knew more poetry by heart than any professor I have ever known, [and] my mother and sister were painters" (22).

In an interview in 1976, Eaton recalls being encouraged to begin writing at an early age: "I began to write poetry in grammar school, and I cannot think of any time after I became conscious of language that I did not intend to become a poet'' (9). While attending R. J. Reynolds High School in Winston-Salem, 1928–32, Eaton edited the school's literary magazine and contributed verse; in 1931 he won a state essay contest award. In 1932 Eaton earned a scholarship to Duke University, which he attended for one year, transferring to the University of North Carolina at Chapel Hill where he was a Phi Beta Kappa and an active member of the theater group, the Carolina Playmakers.

Finishing at the University of North Carolina in 1936, he went on to graduate school, spending a year at Princeton as a philosophy major. He left Princeton to teach high school in Ponce, Puerto Rico, where he worked from 1937–38, returning North in 1938 to begin work on his M.A. in English at Harvard University. At Harvard, Eaton studied with Robert Hillyer and Robert Frost, beginning a personal friendship with Frost that lasted until Frost's death in 1962. After earning his M.A. at Harvard in 1940, Eaton accepted an appointment at the University of Missouri at Columbia, where he taught from 1940 to 1942.

Eaton had been writing and publishing poetry at Harvard, and his poems began to earn national attention. In 1941 ''Cold Spring'' appeared in the anthology *Best Poems of 1940.* In the same year, he earned a Robert Frost Fellowship to attend the Breadloaf Writers Conference. In 1942 Eaton published his first volume of poetry, *The Bright Plain,* comprising poems that he had written during his years at Harvard and his first year at Missouri. This volume received favorable reviews in respected journals, including *New Republic, Poetry,* and *Yale Review.*

In 1942 Eaton accepted a State Department appointment as a vice-consul in Brazil, serving as a cultural liaison officer and working in the American Embassy in Rio de Janeiro. Eaton's years in Brazil, 1942 to 1946, provided for him the life experiences that paralleled the war experiences of so many of his contemporaries. Eaton's poor eyesight had made him ineligible for the draft; as a result, his service in Brazil became his tour of duty during the war. Eaton's experiences in Brazil served as the stimulus for and subject of much of the poetry and all of the fiction he wrote and published through the 1950s, the 1960s, and into the early 1970s. In his introduction to *New and Selected Poems,* he acknowledges Brazil as ''a landscape that was essential and inevitable for my particular disposition,'' allowing him ''to explore the 'tropical side' '' of his nature (''Introduction'' 19).

In 1946 Eaton returned to North Carolina to teach creative writing at the University of North Carolina at Chapel Hill, a position he held until 1952. At the University of North Carolina, Eaton developed and taught the first course in writing original poetry. Meanwhile, Eaton wrote and published regularly. Allen Tate included several of Eaton's poems in his anthology *A Southern Vanguard* (1947), which included stories and poems by Southern writers. In 1951 Eaton published his second collection of poems, *The Shadow of the Swimmer* (1951), which won the Poetry Society of America's 1952 Ridgely Torrence Memorial Award for the most distinguished book of lyric poetry published in

1951. In the same year, one of his early short stories about Brazil, "Death is Sometimes a Lover," was published in *Best American Short Stories of 1951.*

While teaching at Chapel Hill, Eaton considered returning to Harvard to continue his graduate work. By 1950, however, he had made other choices: On August 16, 1950, Eaton married Isabel Patterson, a woman who had enrolled as a graduate student in one of his classes in fall 1947. Their relationship thrives to this day. When he received a leave of absence from the University of North Carolina for 1952 to 1953, Eaton and his wife moved to Woodbury, Connecticut, where they had purchased a home. There he devoted himself full-time to writing. He did not return to regular classroom teaching, although he did continue to accept correspondence students.

For the next three decades, the Eatons split their time between New England and North Carolina, visiting Chapel Hill several times during the year and spending part of the summer on Cape Cod. When he settled in Connecticut, Eaton established what would become a lifelong routine for work, devoting part of his day to writing and part of his day to other interests such as gardening, swimming, or reading. During these initial years as a full-time writer, he established his practice of writing poetry, generally but not exclusively, in the spring and summer, and writing prose and revising in the winter. Eaton lived purposefully, conscious of his need to achieve and maintain a balance between the active and the reflective aspects of his life.

During the 1950s, Eaton's poetry and fiction won numerous awards, and anthologies included his work regularly. By 1955, Eaton had assembled his third book, selecting poems from among those he had published previously. *The Greenhouse in the Garden* (1955) was a finalist for the National Book Award in 1957. In 1958 the Library of Congress invited Eaton to record his work for its taped collection. In 1959 he published *Write Me from Rio,* his first volume of short stories, all based on his experiences in Brazil. By the end of the decade, Eaton was working on his longer, philosophical poem, "Robert E. Lee: An Ode" (1961), a poem that continues to be a central statement of Eaton's philosophy.

In 1961 the Eatons purchased a home in Chapel Hill. The following year Eaton published his fourth volume of poetry, *Countermoves.* Though the late 1950s and early 1960s saw the beginning of more than a decade of social ferment and radical change, Eaton resisted what he saw as the faddish reactions of the beatnik poets and the protests of many of his contemporaries, establishing himself firmly as a modern traditionalist, but not as a reactionary. At a 1962 writer's symposium, he defined himself as a "democrat in politics" and "an aristocrat in the arts."

By 1970, Eaton had arrived as a writer. In fact, in an unpublished letter to his brother Ben (September 10, 1968), Eaton wrote, "The magazines take anything I write these days, and that is a nice reward for having written as long as I have." He was writing and publishing scores of poems and several short stories every year in respected magazines such as *Poetry, The Sewanee Review,*

Harper's, Saturday Review, Arizona Quarterly, and *Yale Review.* From his growing store of work, he assembled his fifth volume of poetry, *On the Edge of the Knife* (1970), winning the Oscar Arnold Young Memorial Award from the Poetry Council of North Carolina as well as the Roanoke-Chowan Award from the North Carolina Literary and Historical Association in 1971. A novella, *A Lady of Pleasure,* and his second volume of short stories, *The Girl from Ipanema,* appeared in 1972, the same year that the New England Poetry Association honored Eaton with their Golden Rose Award.

The Eatons had become avid collectors of American artwork during the 1960s, particularly the works of Karl Knaths, Maurice Sterne, Milton Avery, George Ault, Robert Broderson, and Philip Evergood. This avocation blossomed in the early 1970s: The Eatons were invited to exhibit their paintings at Michigan State University and at the University of North Carolina in 1971; in 1973 they organized with the International Exhibition Foundation of Washington, D.C., a retrospective of Karl Knaths that opened at the University of North Carolina's Ackland Art Museum and circulated nationally. Eaton wrote a masterful critical introduction for the exhibition catalogue that was published in hardcover by Museum Publications of America in 1974. In 1971 he had published a critical biography of Knaths, and in 1975 he wrote a critical study of painter and family friend Robert Broderson.

As the number of his published poems and stories grew in the late 1960s and through the 1970s, Eaton was able to assemble volumes of his poetry and of his short stories more frequently. His sixth collection of poetry, *The Man in the Green Chair* (1977), had won the 1976 Alice Fay di Castagnola award for work-in-progress, at $3500 the largest competitive award given to an American poet. In 1978 he published his third volume of short stories, *The Case of the Missing Photographs,* a collection that included only stories that grew from his experiences in Connecticut.

In 1980 the Eatons moved permanently to Chapel Hill. In the same year, Eaton's poem ''Sentimental Education'' was a prize winner in the 1980 Arvon Foundation Poetry Competition, selected for the honor from among more than 35,000 entries from the English-speaking world. In the next five years three collections of Eaton's poetry were published: *Colophon of the Rover* (1980), *The Thing King* (1983), and *The Work of the Wrench* (1985), the two later works earning numerous awards. Eaton devoted the last half of the decade to compiling a volume of poetry and a volume of short stories that gathered together work from his entire career, including works not published in earlier collections. *New and Selected Poems, 1942–1987* made available again ''Robert E. Lee: An Ode''; and Eaton composed an illuminating introduction to this collection, surveying his career and offering a valuable assessment of and critical commentary on his work. His *New and Selected Stories, 1959–1989* (1989) includes a group of stories based on his experiences in Chapel Hill, stories that he began writing in the mid-1970s.

Even though the two retrospective volumes might have seemed to signal in some way the conclusion of Eaton's active composing and publishing career, that has not been the case. He continued to publish poems and stories; and in 1991 he brought forth his eleventh collection of poetry, *A Guest on Mild Evenings,* which won for him the third time the Roanoke-Chowan Award. In 1993 he published his first novel, *A Lady of Pleasure,* expanding substantially the shorter 1972 work by the same name.

Eaton's continued productivity points to perhaps his most significant achievement. In an unpublished letter to his brother Ben in 1976, Eaton reflected on his life: "I remember Henry James's famous exhortation; 'Live, Live all you can, for at least you will have had your life,' and though I am still committed to my work, I try to devote some part of the day to pleasure. Still, in the deepest sense, my work is my pleasure—So the pen moves on." Charles Edward Eaton has synthesized fully his life and his work, attaining a balance rarely achieved, by artists or by others, wedding life and work into life's work, with each composition and each successful publication affirming his success, his life once again. And that is an accomplishment we too often fail to recognize and to celebrate.

MAJOR THEMES

During the five decades that Charles Eaton has been publishing successfully, the cultural landscape of America has been changing dramatically. But with his work—the poetry, the fiction, the critical essays, the lectures and interviews— Eaton has been resisting these changes, developing and presenting consistently one major theme in all aspects of his life and his work. When he recorded his poetry for the Library of Congress in 1958, Eaton observed that "renascence or spiritual rejuvenation [is] a primary concern in our time." He knew then that art could effect that rejuvenation: "The poet is basically a seeker for truth[,] which by giving significance creates union—a complete person in a complete world" (unpublished transcript). In a published 1972 symposium, he sounded the same theme, arguing that poetry "clarifies the mind and ministers to the spirit," that poetry "can literally save a man's spiritual life" (856). Spiritual salvation on an individual scale is a prerequisite for spiritual salvation on a larger, cultural scale, and art is one means to those ends. Charles Eaton believes that art can effect significant change, one human at a time.

Even though Eaton has resisted labels, his beliefs resemble those of the Agrarians, as his 1974 critical review of an edition of correspondence between Donald Davidson and Allen Tate attests. In that essay, Eaton argues that the Agrarians' principles continue to be relevant: "[T]heir position warned us prophetically, long before the riots and air pollution, against the dangers of our industrial-scientific world" (698). Eaton agrees with the Agrarian position that the "mind can, and should, feed itself . . . on . . . concepts . . . [that] suggest man's idealistic possibilities." To state most clearly the legacy of the Agrarians, Eaton turns to Allen Tate, arguing that Tate "said it best when he said . . . the movement . . .

was 'a reaffirmation of the humane tradition, and to reaffirm that is an end in itself' '' (698).

With his writing, Charles Eaton has sought to reaffirm the humane tradition by helping individuals to realize fully their potential, to connect and to balance the widely disparate aspects of their humanness, to be ''civilized at the same time that . . . [they] stay warmly in touch with the Noble Savage within'' (unpublished notes, reading for the North Carolina Poetry Society, November 18, 1978). The fully integrated individual is both the fundamental ingredient and microcosm of a humane society. Ideally, as more humans achieve wholeness on an individual level, they will begin to enact that ideal on a communal level. For Eaton, art enables individuals to discover, to connect, to balance the opposing realms of idea and feeling, achieving an individual wholeness that provides for humans, and ultimately humanity, the sense of structure, order, and unity that modern society lacks.

Achieving this ideal of connection and balance—a fully integrated individual—demands of poetry and fiction that it enact a dialectical process. In his introduction to *New and Selected Poems,* Eaton acknowledges that ''the predilection for full process—thesis, antithesis, and the hope of some prospect of synthesis—is in all of my work'' (21). In his commentary for the Library of Congress recording in 1958, Eaton described this process in more concrete terms: ''Poems must move from idea to feeling to value, or from feeling to idea to value.'' If idea and feeling—the rational and the emotional, the civilized and the natural—are thesis and antithesis, Eaton's hoped-for synthesis is value, and value signifies an ideal realm where a ''complete person'' enables and enacts a ''complete world.''

Eaton addresses the dilemma of disjunction and imbalance in many of his poems. In ''The Tree-Frog'' (*On the Edge of the Knife*) Eaton proclaims,

> I have a powerful nature in pursuit of pleasure,
> Peace, good will, and I do not share
> My time's contempt for passion balanced by strict
> measure. (14)

In a more recent poem, ''The Lynx'' (*Guest on Mild Evenings*), Eaton asks his reader, ''Who told you beauty and the beast could never share the selfsame paradise?'' (17). In ''The Cane,'' from the same collection, as he does in other poems, Eaton wants individuals to realize ''How incurably physical we are, / And how incorrigibly of the mind'' so they will reconcile and fully integrate the realms of feeling and idea, so they will recognize the widest range of possibilities that constitute their individual and cultural potential (74).

For Eaton, art is the primary vehicle for transporting individuals to this higher realm of consciousness. He traces this connection in ''A Peony for Apollo'' (*Countermoves*) where the poet bemoans the modern dilemma, the ''riot of images'' that mark civilization's penchant for self-delusion and self-destruction, announcing that he would not be a

dissolute, divided man:
Such a one as wastes the world
By thinking it too closed or too unfurled. (27)

Arguing instead for connection and balance, for a view that mediates between "too closed" and "too unfurled," he advocates individuals' taking advantage of their fullest capabilities and having the "courage . . . [t]o make the unimagined world more real" (27), calling for an individual response that entails an active imagination, a faculty exercised most successfully by art and by artists.

To argue that Eaton has consistently developed and presented one major theme throughout his career does not mean that his works are didactic or indistinguishable from each other. Eaton has been richly imaginative with his writing, seeking always to explore as many different ways to achieve his ends as his rich imagination and ample talent will permit him. Examining how his poems express the dialectical process—moving from idea to feeling or from feeling to idea—reveals the rich variety of Eaton's work. In Eaton's poetry, the categories of feeling and idea manifest themselves in various ways, most obviously in terms of nature and civilization or society. Each poem foregrounds a distinctive territory, sometimes one that is associated with the natural realm and at other times one that is associated with the civilized or the social realm. But no matter what Eaton has chosen to foreground, he has always attempted to connect feeling with idea by enacting that connection with the poem itself.

When Eaton foregrounds nature as setting, scene, or subject for his poetry, he focuses on landscapes, seascapes, flora, or fauna. When asked about his creative process, Eaton said in a 1976 interview, "I get my material and my ideas from the life around me, filtered through my own consciousness and personality" (11). In a 1978 interview he said, "Wherever I am, that is the soil out of which blooms my deepest experience. Each poem comes out of my life." Though he was for years a resident of both New England and North Carolina, he recognizes the influence of his birthplace: "The landscape of the South is important to me. . . . I am very influenced by its flora and fauna, but there is more to it. My Southern nature is throughout my work. Southerners seem to have a sensuous nature, an opulence of human nature that they love."

More recently, Eaton has acknowledged further how his work may partake of a "Southern nature." Citing a story about Brazil, "Boat with an Eye of Glass" (*Write Me from Rio*), from his first collection of short fiction, Eaton in his introduction to *New and Selected Poems,* has quoted a passage that describes Rio de Janeiro as "the visionary South of all my snow-bound Northern yearning, the fructive center of the earth's body, the pith of appetite, the climate of blessed mornings and benign evenings, the luxuriant frontier of Adventure that blooms at the edge of Order" (19). Eaton's poetry has consistently evoked the sensuous, the opulent, the "frontier of Adventure," the "luxuriant" realm of feeling that "blooms at the edge of" the realm of ideas.

But sensuality, opulence, and "Adventure" are only part of the equation that

Eaton's poetry attempts to solve; his poems are not simply "nature poems." To accomplish his objective of connecting the realms of feeling and idea, his poems address the natural, the emotional, the sensual, and the civilized, the rational, the intellectual. By probing and questioning the significance of the natural scene, he always introduces the rational element, seeking ultimately to connect the two, challenging readers to reconsider the relations between the two.

For example, the final poem of *Greenhouse in the Garden,* "Sense in the Darkness the Purple Jet," relies on natural, sensual imagery to conduct from start to finish a rigorous analysis of how individuals might perceive anew by reconsidering fully with all of their senses and faculties a natural phenomenon. The poem opens by commanding the reader to "sense in the darkness the purple jet, / The iris in the garden. . . "; the first line of the second stanza commands further, "Be the darkness, be it. . . "; and the final stanza tells the reader to "conceive the spring." The poet argues throughout that a more creative act of perceiving, a more active use of imagination, will awaken individuals to "the morning-birth of dreams you thought you had forgotten" (64). The content and the performance of the poem establish a reciprocal relation between feeling and idea, demonstrating for readers what is possible when they attempt to know more fully the natural element—they will better know themselves.

When Eaton turns from the natural to the social, foregrounding the realm of ideas, he explores the individual psyche contemplating an individual's relation to self, to others, to society, or to nature. The figure of the swimmer appears in a number of Eaton's poems over the years, and "O Swimmer," the closing poem of his second collection, *The Shadow of the Swimmer* (1951), illustrates explicitly how Eaton uses this figure to foreground the realm of ideas. Though the poem opens by pointing to a landscape, the poet is clearly introspective: "The mind [is] ardent / In the arduous ascension" (85). Reflecting on "harmony," and defining "wholeness" as "appetite and ease, / Wisdom and good will: balance, felt and thought," the poet describes the complete individual:

> Divided life that wishes to be whole
> Must apprehend and will the man who strains
> Toward union of reason in the blood, muscle in his thought:
> The whole and glorious swimmer. (86)

The swimmer is "the man of symmetry" who "stands risk, alone, in order to be free" (87). The swimmer signifies in this poem and others the possibility of an individual in whom "thought and dream [are] blent smooth," one who is "in deepest sense humane" (86).

Other examples of how Eaton foregrounds the social realm are found in the poems in which Eaton focuses on or evokes associations with misfits or characters who might occupy a territory on the margins of society, those whom Thomas Mann has called "life's delicate children." For example, *Man in the Green Chair* contains poems titled "Madame Midget," "The Eunuch," "The

Hypochondriac,'' ''The Gigolo,'' ''The Centaur,'' and ''The Woman with the Scar.'' Poems in *Colophon of the Rover* include ''The Pigmy,'' ''The Amazon,'' ''The Deaf-Mute,'' and ''The Blind Man.'' And ''The Amputee'' and ''The Cannibal'' are companion poems in *Thing King*. With these poems and the others like them, Eaton evokes and explores the unfamiliar, attempting both to demystify and to complicate readers' understandings of ''normal'' and ''natural'' so they might understand more fully themselves and their relations to others.

Eaton's use of painting and paintings as the subject of many poems illustrates further how he has attempted to connect idea and feeling: Works of art such as paintings partake of both realms, integrating intellect and emotion, understanding and imagination. Beginning in the 1960s, examples of these poems include ''Rooms by the Sea'' (*Countermoves*), ''The Lepidopterist'' and ''The Gallery'' (*On the Edge of the Knife*), ''Sofa by Matisse'' (*Colophon of the Rover*), ''After Degas'' (*Work of the Wrench*), and ''Stylebook'' (*Guest on Mild Evenings*); all exemplify the influence that painting has on Eaton's writing. In fact, Eaton has always attempted to construct word portraits, and the titles of so many of his poems encourage associations with painting, titles that one could label still-life paintings as well as poems. Titles such as ''The Parrot,'' ''The Clown,'' ''The Enfabled Nude,'' ''Purple Dwarf, White Lilacs,'' ''Bodies of Water,'' ''The Wrench,'' ''Life Preserver,'' all evoke a strong visual sense that enhances further the poems' attempts to connect for readers the realms of idea and feeling.

One of the more powerful examples of Eaton's dialectical process is ''Robert E. Lee: An Ode,'' a poem in which Eaton gathers together many of the thematic threads that run through all of his work: realization of self, of one's personal and cultural past, of one's relation to society and to a future as a contributing member of that society. Adopting Lee as a spiritual model, evoking the tradition, humanity, and elegance long associated with Lee, borrowing Lee's ''mask of soul'' as the ''temperament'' through which he will see the world, the poet crowns Lee as ''pater familias'' (153, 155). Modeling Lee's response to life, the poet opens the poem with this self-realization:

> I who love grace in life and morals
> Still serve the Pythoness,
> A buried goddess of magnificent coils
> Who undulates in my caress. (151)

The poet recognizes the opposing aspects of his humanity, his civilized ''grace'' and ''morals'' and the primitive, natural ''Pythoness.'' He returns to those images in his concluding statement, reaffirming the necessity to connect the rational and the emotional:

> How lucid it would make the sky
> If we should love all caution

Somewhat less, proportionate
To the stirrings at our feet! (159)

Eaton advocates a return to or a renewal of a way of being that integrates past
and present, tradition and change, instinct and intellect. As with all of his poetry,
but here more fully, Eaton seeks to elevate readers to a level of awareness that
will renew them by making of them more complete individuals.

Although Eaton's work is thematically consistent, his poetry and fiction has
changed over the years. He alluded to this development in 1958, after he had
published three volumes: "The earlier poems were lived by the poet in communion with himself and nature as though he were preparing himself to submit
his values to skeptical resistance" (unpublished transcript, Library of Congress).
With his fourth volume, *Countermoves,* Eaton began to confront more regularly
and more explicitly that "skeptical resistance" with poems that developed and
emphasized more the realm of ideas, of philosophical questioning and analysis.
His use of nature, the realm of feeling, became more sophisticated, more complex, and less often the foreground or focus of a poem, though always an important element of the poem. Eaton has suggested that his poems developed
over the years from "the ingenuous," such as his first volume, *The Bright Plain,*
to "the more sophisticated," which would characterize *Countermoves, Man in
the Green Chair,* and his more recent publications such as *Work of the Wrench*
or *Guest on Mild Evenings.* But he has suggested, too, an organic connection
among his works, "as if the original seed is never quite disclaimed by the
branching tree" ("Introduction" 17). Readers of works early and late will agree
with his assessments.

Even formally and technically, Eaton enacts his central theme, his attempt at
synthesis. Calling himself a modern formalist, Eaton has said that he finds "freedom more exciting when, at some point, it recognizes a formal limit" (unpublished notes, reading tour 1963). An apt line from "Life among the Natives"
(*Colophon*) vividly characterizes this relationship as "juicy freedom within stric-
ture" ("Life among the Natives" 21). By insisting on the essentiality of form,
Eaton enacts again the dialectic of feeling and idea, with the poem comprising
an idea and a form that shapes the feeling and the substance. The reciprocal
interaction between the form and substance, the idea and the feeling, transforms
both aspects, ultimately producing a performance in which form and feeling are
unified.

Eaton has employed a variety of forms, turning most often to rhymed stanzas
of three or four lines and to longer blank-verse paragraphs. He uses both a long,
free-flowing line and short, terse, concise lines. His mastery of form and line
signals a writer who attends to the nuances of language, to the rhythm of speech
and sound. His ear is as sensitive to the sound of his poetry as his eye is sensitive
to the portraits he paints with words. His command of language marks him
immediately as a poet of distinction. He seeks to create for readers sensual
images and thought-provoking propositions, and he brings to the task an im-

mense and immensely learned language store as well as an artist's eye for color and form and a musician's ear for sound. Coupled with those abilities are the intellectual rigor of a serious philosopher and, perhaps most important, the background and broad experience of a literary scholar and serious student of writing. The result is a writer and writing that is difficult to classify, poetry that resists being part of a school, poetry that is not aimed at every reader, poetry that demands of its readers an ability to engage the intellectual and the emotional faculties fully when reading Eaton's work.

What can be said of Eaton's poetry applies to his four volumes of short stories. His fiction focuses primarily on an individual's relation to himself and to others—in many instances, a woman. More than the poetry, the sequence of stories, from the early to the more recent ones, charts a clear progression, a change, a maturation of the protaganists, the narrators, and the author. His first two volumes of stories, *Write Me from Rio* and *Girl from Ipanema,* and a novel, *Lady of Pleasure,* developed from Eaton's experiences in Brazil. They are set there, and as Eaton has acknowledged, they partake of the sensuous, independent, natural environment embodied by Brazil, an extreme example of what the South might mean for Eaton. Because Eaton was in Brazil when he was young, single, and unfettered, and because for the most part the stories are composed by him years after the experiences, they offer a retrospective view of what it might have meant to experience that environment, those situations, those feelings, from the point of view of the young man in Brazil, tempered or mediated by the older writer, who is attempting to understand the experiences.

The third volume of stories, *Case of the Missing Photographs,* comprises stories about Connecticut, about Eaton's experiences as a more mature member of society, but also a less independent member, one more fully enmeshed in social structures and relations, one less innocent, one more experienced in the advantages and disadvantages of being fully civilized. In contrast to the Brazil stories, the later fiction explores social and psychic territory that would be more familiar to readers: local scenes, personal situations, characters struggling to attain or maintain some sense of individual identity in a society that does not necessarily support or reward the attempts. In his recent *New and Selected Stories, 1959–1989,* Eaton gathers for the first time "The Carrolton Stories," six pieces set in a university town in the South, not unlike Chapel Hill. As in the Connecticut stories, these six explore individuals in relation to one another in a social setting where formality and rationality seem to govern actions, but where disjunction and irrationality rule as often as not.

Over the years, Eaton has also used critical review essays to explore his central theme. His review essays are scholarly, insightful, and helpful in understanding where Charles Eaton stands on the issues he is discussing. For instance, in his review of Donald Davidson's poetry, "Donald Davidson and the Dynamics of Nostalgia" (1966), Eaton not only illuminates Davidson's poetry and Davidson's place in our literary history, but he uses the essay as a forum in which to define his own position as a poet, as an artist, by asserting: "In the future, our strategy as poets must be to heal . . . [the] split, . . . [the] gap in man's soul'' (267). And by celebrating especially ''one of Davidson's finest poetic conceptions, . . . his notion of 'wilderness'—the basic stuff of life underlying all manmade theories and prejudices and to which even the most high-minded humanist must return continually to test the validity of his ideas and for refreshment of the spirit'' (265), Eaton further illuminates his own thematic concerns.

As one might expect from a former student and long-time friend of Robert Frost, Eaton's review of a 1974 critical work on Frost shares with readers several insights that illuminate Frost and that delineate clearly the relation between Frost and Eaton. Eaton's critical biography of Karl Knaths (1971), written as the introduction to the catalogue of the 1973–74 retrospective, illustrates how influential painting and painters have been for Eaton's poetry. Eaton demonstrates that he has a firm understanding of the artist's work, his methods, his creative processes. In his biography he writes as an insider: He was a close friend of Knaths, he collected his work, and he shared with Knaths a fundamental belief in art as a passionate endeavor, as a process and product that was meaningful, for artist and for audience. One of Eaton's most accomplished critical essays serves as the introduction to his *New and Selected Poems, 1942–1987.* Here Eaton has cogently assembled a rigorous self-examination and a remarkably objective review of his career and his works. For first-time readers of Eaton, this piece is a must.

Though he has consistently prosecuted the same thematic argument over the years, pursued the same artistic ends, held finally to the same set of values, Eaton has been especially successful in presenting his message in refreshingly different and provocative ways. His virtues may well be his disciplined versatility, his rigorous flexibility, his willingness to take risks without discarding or undermining his firmly held principles—aesthetic, moral, or intellectual. Eaton has observed of Donald Davidson: ''I take pleasure in the knowledge of this man who has remained so faithful to person, place, and principle'' (263), and readers who come to know Eaton's work will experience similar pleasure. The two authors, however, should not be too closely aligned, for Eaton's and Davidson's works are very different in style, tone, and content. If comparisons with the Agrarians must be made, Eaton is perhaps more compatible in temperament and aspiration with Tate and Warren; but in the end, he evades any attempts at classification.

SURVEY OF CRITICISM

In spite of Eaton's consistent production for more than 50 years, surprisingly little has been published about his work beyond reviews of his books as they appeared. In fact, except for Eaton's own assessments of his works, only Dave Smith (1974) has devoted a full journal article to Eaton's work, although extended reviews by John T. Irwin (1973) and Thomas Swiss (1986) offer readers significant critical insights.

Over the years, reviewers have offered remarkably consistent assessments of Eaton's work. Observations of May Swenson (1957), of Wallace Fowlie (1963), and of John Engels (1963), for instance, could easily apply to his most recent volume. May Swenson has recognized how Eaton's "energy gathers to express some strong, balanced, exquisitely textured poems, their frenetic content mastered by the form" (374). Most reviewers have echoed Fowlie's assessment of Eaton as "an able craftsman," one who avoids successfully "decorative syntax," one who "knows that if the right word is found, it will be able to resuscitate the world" (36). And critics have confirmed Engels's analysis of Eaton's use of process, his attempt at synthesis. In his 1963 review of *Countermoves,* Engels observes: "Most of the poems begin descriptively, with a composition of place, an attempt to see something in the most physical aspect of its being, and to focus the mind on it. And there follows analysis and colloquy, the whole characterized and animated by an imagination always in evidence, freely and expansively at work. Sometimes, . . . this pattern is reversed" (404–5).

In his 1973 essay John T. Irwin has placed Eaton in the debate taking place during the 1970s about the function of poetry and the role of traditional forms. Irwin opposes the contemporary poets who have advocated an aesthetic of "immediate experience" and the movement "away from regular surface forms" to the "creation of a unique form," an "open" form, for each new poem (158–60). Irwin celebrates Eaton's "highly crafted poems" because they "affirm that freedom is gained by seeking a discipline rather than by avoiding one—no easy affirmation to make nowadays" (161). Irwin helps readers to understand Eaton's role in the ongoing debate about the function of poetry: "If we moderns believe that external reality is chaos, is our poetry to embody that reality or man's counterstatement to that reality?" (171); obviously, Irwin and Eaton value the traditions that enable and enact a counterstatement.

Dave Smith analyzes Eaton's production through 1972, recognizing Eaton's "consistent attempt to envision a balanced, rational, and passionate man" and focusing on the "psychic struggles" that Eaton explores in his poetry and fiction (420). Smith celebrates Eaton's work, its "energy, depth, [and] multiplicity"; and he compares Eaton favorably to William Faulkner. Eaton "has consistently refused to pander to contemporary popular taste by providing easy answers." Instead, to counter the desperation of the modern condition, "Eaton posits a seeking, embracing man of energy. Like Faulkner, he believes that a man is capable of being better than he is, and that life is essentially potential if we only have the courage and the intelligence to see it" (424). Smith argues that Eaton deserves attention: "He speaks to all men of sense and sensibility with what is the only convincing argument, the argument of art and imagination which says that there is a condition of joy to which we must not only aspire, but also actively and at any cost struggle" (424).

Thomas Swiss has been helpful in offering a retrospective commentary that places Eaton's most recent works in the context of his earlier achievements. In his 1988 review of Eaton's *New and Selected Poems,* Swiss briefly reviews

Eaton's career, outlining for readers Eaton's development from the early "influence of Robert Frost" to the later influence of Wallace Stevens. Swiss acknowledges "how little change Eaton's work exhibits in general aim, voice, or manner" over the years, arguing that Eaton's "growth is primarily stylistic: his recent poems are less ornate, his diction less strained" (x). But Swiss concludes that Eaton "has mined for himself a particular niche in the landscape of contemporary poetry" (xi).

With his insightful introduction to *New and Selected Poems,* Charles Eaton has done for himself what no critic has done; offered an extended commentary on his work and on his career, a retrospective that achieves and maintains a remarkably consistent level of critical objectivity. In fact, by examining Eaton's papers in the Southern Historical Collection at the University of North Carolina, by tracing Eaton's development and assembling the numerous self-conscious evaluations of his work that Eaton has offered over the years, readers will discover that Eaton has been remarkably consistent when he has turned his critical gaze on himself, as consistent as he has been at developing and presenting his central thematic argument in his poetry and fiction. In his introduction to *New and Selected Poems,* Eaton has said of poets—and, thus, of himself: "I think of the poet as a commando of consciousness with all that means as to courage and provisional conviction—an adventurer indeed with a respect for home base and an enduring devotion to civilization" (23). Eaton's work and life have exemplified his "courage," his "respect" for self and others, and his "enduring devotion" to humanity.

BIBLIOGRAPHY

Works by Charles Edward Eaton

The Bright Plain. Chapel Hill: University of North Carolina Press, 1942.
The Shadow of the Swimmer. New York: Fine Editions Press, 1951.
The Greenhouse in the Garden. New York: Twayne, 1955.
"Sea Psalm." *North Carolina Drama.* Richmond: Garrett and Massie, 1956.
Write Me from Rio. Winston-Salem, N.C.: Blair, 1959.
Countermoves. New York: Abelard-Schuman, 1962.
"Donald Davidson and the Dynamics of Nostalgia." *Georgia Review* 20 (1966): 261–
    69.
On the Edge of the Knife. New York: Abelard-Schuman, 1970.
"Preface." *Charles and Isabel Eaton Collection of American Paintings.* William Hays
    Ackland Memorial Art Center, University of North Carolina, Chapel Hill, 1970.
Karl Knaths. Washington, Conn.: Shiver Mountain Press, 1971.
The Girl from Ipanema. Lunenburg, Vt.: North Country Publishing, 1972.
"Why Poems, and Why in College English? A Symposium." *College English* 33 (1972):
    851–57.
Karl Knaths: Five Decades of Painting. Washington, D.C.: International Exhibitions
    Foundation, 1973.

"A Friendship of Poets: The Statesman and the Soldier." Review of *The Literary Correspondence of Donald Davidson and Allen Tate. Georgia Review* 28 (1974): 688–99.

Robert Broderson: Paintings and Graphics. Washington, Conn.: Shiver Mountain Press, 1975.

"Personality or Pariah: The Fate of the Poet in America." Review of *Robert Frost: A Living Voice* and *Letters of Hart Crane and His Family. Georgia Review* 30 (1976): 447–60.

The Man in the Green Chair. New York: Barnes, 1977.

The Case of the Missing Photographs. New York: Barnes, 1978.

Colophon of the Rover. New York: Barnes, 1980.

The Thing King. New York: Cornwall Books, 1983.

The Work of the Wrench. New York: Cornwall Books, 1985.

New and Selected Poems, 1942–1987. New York: Cornwall Books, 1987.

New and Selected Stories, 1959–1989. New York: Cornwall Books, 1989.

A Guest on Mild Evenings. New York: Cornwall Books, 1991.

A Lady of Pleasure. New York: Cornwall Books, 1993.

The Charles Eaton Papers (comprising personal papers and poetry manuscripts). Southern Historical Collection, Library of the University of North Carolina, Chapel Hill. (For this essay, Mr. Eaton has graciously given his permission to quote from the unpublished letters, notes, and transcripts that are available in this collection.) (Eaton's fiction manuscripts are collected at Mugar Memorial Library, Boston University.)

Interviews with Charles Edward Eaton

Interview. *Delta of Sigma Nu Fraternity* 92 (1976): 8–11.

Interview. *Raleigh News and Observer* (November 18, 1978).

Studies of Charles Edward Eaton

Bauer, William A. Review of *Case of the Missing Photographs. International Fiction Review* 8 (1981): 66–68.

Davidson, W. W. "The Poetry of Charles Edward Eaton." *Georgia Review* 7 (1953): 84–85.

"Eaton, Charles Edward." *World Authors, 1975–1980.* Edited by Vineta Colby, 200–203. New York: Wilson, 1985.

Engels, John. Review of *Countermoves. Poetry* 102 (1963): 404–5.

Fowlie, Wallace. "Not Bards So Much As Catalyzers." *New York Times Book Review* 112 (May 12, 1963): 36.

Francis, M. E. Review of *The Girl from Ipanema. Georgia Review* 26 (Winter 1972): 524–26.

Hester, M. L. Review of *The Man in the Green Chair. Southern Humanities Review* 13 (1979): 363–64.

———. Review of *Colophon of the Rover. Southern Humanities Review* 15 (1981): 374–75.

Hillyer, Robert. Review of *Shadow of the Swimmer*. *New York Times Book Review* 100 (July 22, 1951): 12.

Hollander, John. "Poetry in Review." *Yale Review* 73 (1983): xxi.

Irwin, John T. "The Crisis of Regular Forms." *Sewanee Review* 81 (1973): 158–71.

Meier, T. K. Review of *New and Selected Stories, 1959–1989*. *Studies in Short Fiction* 26 (1989): 569.

Meyer, Gerard P. "Lyrics in the Garden." *Saturday Review* 39 (March 31, 1956): 33.

Miller, Jim Wayne. Review of *The Work of the Wrench*. *Chattahoochee Review* 8 (1987): 70–74.

Miola, Robert. Review of *The Man in the Green Chair*. *Commonweal* 105 (August 18, 1978): 540–41.

———. "Eaton, Charles Edward." *Contemporary Poets*. 5th ed. Edited by James Vinson and D. L. Kirkpatrick, 256–58. Detroit: St. James Press, 1991.

Morrow, Mark. *Images of the Southern Writer*. Athens: University of Georgia Press, 1985.

Ramsey, Paul. "Going Beyond Tink and Tank." Review of *New and Selected Poems, 1942–1987*. *Chronicles* (May 1989): 32–33.

Shear, Walter. Review of *Colophon of the Rover*. *Midwest Quarterly* 22 (Spring 1981): 304–6.

———. Review of *The Thing King*. *Midwest Quarterly* 25 (Autumn 1983): 350–54.

———. Review of *New and Selected Poems, 1942–1987*. *Midwest Quarterly* 30 (Summer 1989): 529–31.

Smith, Dave. "The Shining Figure: Poetry and Prose of Charles Edward Eaton." *Meanjin Quarterly* (Australia) 20 (1974): 420–24.

Spector, Robert D. "Betwixt Tradition and Innovation." *Saturday Review* (December 26, 1970): xx.

Swenson, May. Review of *The Greenhouse in the Garden*. *Poetry* 89 (1957): 373–74.

Swiss, Thomas. "Current Books in Review." Review of *The Work of the Wrench*. *Sewanee Review* 94 (1986): xxviii–xix.

———. Review of *New and Selected Poems, 1942–1987*. *Sewanee Review* 96 (1988): x–xi.

Untermeyer, Louis. *Yale Review* 33 (Winter 1944): 350–51.

Williams, William Carlos. Review of *The Greenhouse in the Garden*. *Arizona Quarterly* 13 (1957): 89.

Witt, Harold. "Possibilities of Light." Review of *New and Selected Poems, 1942–1987*. *Chariton Review* (Fall 1988): 117–23.

JOHN SEKORA

Lonne Elder III
(1931–   )

A man of letters for the latter twentieth century—working for the stage, television, and motion pictures—Lonne Elder III is the link in performance writing between Lorraine Hansberry in the 1950s and August Wilson in the 1980s and 1990s. Celebrated for powerful examples of family drama, he provides a sense of African-American life as "a glorious, adventurous thing, constantly unfolding in everyday life in its beauty, speech, walk, dance, and even in its anger."

BIOGRAPHY

The watershed event in modern black American drama began to unfold March 11, 1959, with the first of 530 Broadway performances of *A Raisin in the Sun.* The first play by a black woman to be produced on Broadway and the first to be directed by a black director in more than half a century, it brought to Lorraine Hansberry the first New York Drama Critics Circle Award ever to go to a black playwright. While the production alone was sufficient to rejuvenate African-American theater, virtually everyone concerned with it became creative forces in their own right. Directed by Lloyd Richards, its actors included Claudia McNeil, Ruby Dee, Sidney Poitier, Diana Sands, Ivan Dixon, Louis Gossett, Douglas Turner Ward—and Lonne Elder III. For Elder the experience was galvanizing. Besides revealing what talented people could achieve working together, it provided extraordinary lessons in personal opportunity. Richards would soon become a major figure in Broadway directing and in theater education. Dee, Sands, and Dixon would be familiar on stage and screen for the next two decades. Gossett and Poitier would earn Academy Awards for their acting in films, Poitier turning successfully also to directing and producing. Turner Ward would become a founder and driving spirit of yet another landmark institution, the Negro Ensemble Company, America's longest standing black repertory group. As each of the others learned from this portentous period, so Elder discovered that his earlier work in poetry and fiction was not nearly so satisfying as the collective enterprise of performance work.

When *Raisin* opened, Elder, in his late 20s, was still unsure of his future. Born December 26, 1931, in Americus, Georgia, to Quincy Elder and Lonne Elder II, he encountered disappointment, uncertainty, and loss quite early. While he was yet a baby, his family—including two brothers and twin sisters—moved to New Jersey. There, when he was ten, his father died, and his mother was killed shortly thereafter in an auto accident. Several unhappy months on a relative's farm ended when he was sent to live with an aunt and uncle in Jersey City. Such was the opening of his informal education and the source of much of the urban texture of his plays. For the uncle was a numbers runner who quickly saw the value of his bright and eager nephew. Elder recalled: "I used to go with him when he made his rounds, walking about 50 feet behind him. He used to get frisked, he was well known, but I had the slips. He paid me well. I was making $40 or $50 a week when I was 12. He was never busted by the police but once." Although the uncle used Elder for protection, he also treated him as a capable partner, taught him the ways of the city, and demonstrated the positive side of hustling—the hard work required to survive on the streets. All would become familiar elements of his plays.

Formal and informal, his education was sporadic. He attended college, first in New Jersey, then in New York City, for parts of three years, and was drafted into the army in 1952 during the Korean War. Throughout, he cultivated writing as a form of therapy and self-education: "I just liked the idea of writing to myself; it was a way of expressing feelings that I didn't know how to express in other ways, like talking." But if writing held the soul together, he kept the body intact any way he could: as waiter, gambler, phone clerk, dock worker. Although he often had no place regularly to live, he still volunteered his energies to several civil rights organizations.

Interested in writing and, after 1953, living in Harlem, Elder gravitated toward the Harlem Writers Guild. He had been encouraged by two prominent figures, Robert Hayden and John Oliver Killens. Yet it was not until meeting Turner Ward (who then called himself Douglas Turner) that he became convinced he might earn a living by writing. While the two were sharing an apartment, he watched Ward finish his first play and marveled that one of *his* friends could accomplish such a prodigious feat. They meanwhile attended every play they could afford, Elder gradually realizing that he could do better than most of the scripts being produced. He and Ward collaborated on several projects during the decade, especially the establishment of the Negro Ensemble Company, for which he became director of the playwright's division. They of course acted together; after *Raisin,* Elder had the role of Clem when Ward's *Day of Absence* was staged in 1965, and Ward had the central role of Russell Parker in *Ceremonies in Dark Old Men* in 1969. After Ward, his most influential friends were Alice Childress and Lorraine Hansberry. A writer, director, and member of the

Guild, Childress strongly encouraged him to take up acting. Hansberry in turn admired that acting and in 1958 offered him the role of Bobo in *Raisin.* From that role came his first regular and substantial income and the first chance to concentrate on his own writing.

By 1963 his writing had progressed sufficiently to earn a position as staff writer for the CBS television series *Camera Three,* an ambitious omnibus program relegated to the Sunday morning "arts slot." In the same year he did the script for an NBC drama, *The Terrible Veil.* His initial play of note, "A Hysterical Turtle in a Rabbit Race," was completed in 1961 but has never been published or produced (a fate shared by his other one-act dramas).

An early version of *Ceremonies* was performed at Wagner College in New York in 1965. Armed with such credits, Elder won a John Hay Whitney Fellowship to study drama and filmmaking at Yale from 1965 to 1967; it is significant that at this early period he already saw himself moving back and forth between stage and motion pictures. While he was at Yale, the New York City Mobilization for Youth commissioned *Charades on East Fourth Street* about a gang of black youths staging a kangaroo court trial of a white policeman. It was originally performed at Expo '67 in Montreal and published in *Black Drama Anthology* edited by Woodie King and Ron Milner (1971). From the Whitney Fellowship followed a series of other grants, the most substantial being the ABC Television Writing Fellowship which itself led to a position as staff writer on the series *N.Y.P.D.* in 1967–1968. Because this realistic police drama was one of the few series then being filmed in New York, Elder was able to do the assignment and still remain near the theater district. It allowed him to polish his skill with dialogue and to write for one of the first black characters in a continuing series, Detective Jeff Ward, played by Robert Hooks. The association with Hooks eventually brought the latter into the Negro Ensemble Company, the cast of *Ceremonies,* and partnership with Elder in Banneker Productions, a short-lived film company committed to more positive portrayals of blacks.

In 1969, with the production of the revised version of *Ceremonies in Dark Old Men* by the Negro Ensemble Company, Elder's apprenticeship was officially at an end. Like "Hysterical Turtle," this play involves a family in crisis, deciding individually and collectively how best to carry on. Until her recent death, the materfamilias has held the Russell family together in Harlem with her strength and her earnings. Now father, daughter, and two sons are thrown back upon their own devices; as a family they face reunion or disintegration, for the status quo will hold no longer. For better *and* worse, each has at least one solution; each can correct the plans of the others, but not himself. Because they care deeply for one another, they haggle and debate. A death at the eleventh hour—recalling a similar situation and resolution in James Baldwin's novel *Go Tell It on the Mountain*—brings final affirmation qualified by irony and tragedy. To audiences perplexed by Ed Bullins and Amiri Baraka, to Broadway regulars indifferent to confrontational plots and exotic characters, *Ceremonies* was a revelation. It portrayed a recognizable family, wounded and struggling, yet coherent and intact; a family who had not only a story, but also a logic and an ethic. Although a few critics found the play formulaic, the overwhelming majority saw it as rich and powerful. The awards it received included the Los Angeles Drama Critics Award and the Outer Circle and Drama Desk awards; it was second in balloting for the Pulitzer Prize. It has been revived many times, and in 1975 was produced on ABC television; for the teleplay Elder received the Christopher's Television Award. After completing the initial version of the play, he also completed two as-yet unpublished and unproduced one-act scripts: "Kissing Rattlesnakes Can Be Fun" (1966) and its comic companion piece "Seven Comes Up and Seven Comes Down" (1966).

With the success of *Ceremonies,* Elder received several offers and (citing the need for a better place to rear a family) made a not-entirely-fortunate move to California to write for another detective series, *McCloud* (1970–1971). His continuing intention to reach as large an audience as possible led in 1972 to credits on two quite diverse films. *Melinda* is a violent mystery that, without disavowing, he calls a commercial attempt to take advantage of the large market for such exploitative films as *Sweet Sweetback* (1971), *Shaft* (1971), and *Superfly* (1972). (It has the distinction of featuring Elder in his sole screen role, as police Lieutenant Daniels.)

Sounder, on the other hand, is a film of which he is justly proud. This, his most important screenplay, was adapted from the Newbery Award–winning novel for young adults by William H. Armstrong and represents his mature efforts to investigate the effects of deprivation and racism on black personality. In what he found to be a happy collaboration with producer Robert Radnitz and director Martin Ritt, he depicted hardship and dignity in a family of sharecroppers during a year in rural Louisiana in the 1930s. As the Parker family in *Ceremonies* must cope after the mother's death, so the Morgan family must survive after the father Nathan Morgan (Paul Winfield) is jailed and unjustly sentenced to a year of hard labor. During her husband's absence, Rebecca Morgan (Cicely Tyson) sustains her family with love and determination. Eldest son David (Kevin Hooks, son of Robert) seeks his father at a distant prison farm. It is a symbolic journey of growth leading in fact not to a prison but to a school: deprivation is a spur to knowledge and culture. Sounder is the hound who accompanies David, an emblem of the family's dauntless loyalty and its struggle to grow and thrive despite great loss. The film was among the most critically acclaimed of the year, earning Academy Award nominations for best picture, best actress, best actor, and best screenplay. In 1976 Radnitz and Elder reunited on *Sounder, Part 2,* but this continuation of the story did not enjoy so sensitive a cast or director; it does underscore the writer's commitment to parables of self-help and self-realization.

Most of his work since the mid-1970s has been for television, with occasional forays into film and back to the theater. His script on the life of Harriet Tubman, *A Woman Called Moses,* was done as a mini-series by NBC in 1978. It is testimony to the regard with which Elder is held that Cicely Tyson, one of the very finest actors of her generation, sought to work with him on the project. She returned yet again in 1981 for the film *Busting Loose,* his lone screen credit for the 1980s. He is listed as adapting the screenplay from a story by Richard Pryor, who conceived, produced, and starred in the film. He was the natural choice for a profile of the Negro Ensemble Company done for the American Masters series on Public Broadcasting in 1987. He brought a revival of *Ceremonies* to New York City in 1985 and returned in 1988 with a monodrama on the life of the nineteenth-century black Shakespearean actor Ira Aldridge entitled *Splendid Mummer.* Besides his early one-act plays, his unpublished and unproduced scripts include some of what he terms his best work: a play, ''After the Band Goes Home;'' a screenplay on the record business, ''Number One with a Bullet;'' and a screen version of Richard Wright's novel *Native Son.* As the laurel for a long and varied career, he wishes to become an influential producer dedicated to sensitive and responsible portrayals of African-American life.

MAJOR THEMES

''There is nothing enigmatic about being black,'' Elder once said. No enigmas? Perhaps not. But for his work, paradoxes aplenty! The boy who begins watching people and listening to their speech as a twelve-year-old running numbers in Jersey City grows up to be a celebrated writer for Hollywood cop shows. Yet, whenever he has the chance to choose his own subjects, as often as not he writes about robbers. This cops/robbers split touches practically everything he has written. In an earlier century he would have been hailed as a man of letters of arresting scope. So distrustful is he of titles and positions, however, that he uses every opportunity to deflate any applause.

When he was acting in *Raisin in the Sun,* he formed the plan to use his time and income to become a first-rate playwright. The plan ended when *Raisin* closed because he could find no other acting jobs. There were almost no roles for black actors because no writers were creating them. He couldn't write such scripts himself because he first needed a job acting. He often describes the dread circularity of much of American life because it has been the paradigm of his career. If he wishes to do something important, he must first do two or three preliminary chores. *Ad infinitum.* In the early 1970s he conceived several goals. Although plays were his first love, they reached but a small audience and that mostly in the Northeast. Motion pictures, on the other hand, would touch many more people, of all social classes and in all parts of the country. He wanted to write for the movies, too, because he was appalled by the violent, reductive images of blacks, especially young black males, in the usual Hollywood portrayal. And California held out the promise of a better, happier place for his growing family. Flooded with such aspirations, he is given at arrival the task of writing a violent, reductive film about blacks for the exploitation market. *Sounder* helped to reduce that bad taste but not remove it. Writers in Hollywood, he notes, enjoy wealth and celebrity, but little control. For many people, from the stars to the producer's chauffeur, may take a hand in the script. Writers are often regarded as whores, to be kicked out of a job/bed at the earliest failure to give full satisfaction. For good reason, he has sought to gain greater influence over his films as an independent producer.

For good reason, the tensions in the lives of Elder's characters mirror the stresses in his own career. No one writes more vividly about the kinds and nature of work: How it ennobles, when it degrades. When Theo Parker in Act I of *Ceremonies* discovers that his father has been "downtown, seeing about some jobs," his quick response is, "You sure don't care much about yourself." To which his father replies, "I can agree with you on that because lookin' for a job can really hurt a man." An electrifying moment comes to the play when Blue Haven reflects upon how he came to be the villain he is. Every member of the Parker family, like the Morgans in *Sounder,* must consider what work means for personality, when it supports, how it stunts. The situation is equally vivid in *Melinda, Woman Called Moses,* and the one-act plays. All show Elder as a master of family drama—a genre he admires in Hansberry and Sean O'Casey—for they have only one another to try, test, and win. The larger white society does not directly, immediately intrude, as in Baraka. Yet it is there, represented by the local sheriff in *Sounder,* waiting to exploit weakness or failure.

Elder's treatment of the family—strong without sentimentality—links his work with Hansberry in the 1950s and a dozen writers in the 1970s and 1980s: the most important period of African-American performance writing ever. To produce their work, more than 600 community and university black theater groups were started. And in this renaissance many playwrights paid tribute to Elder. To cite but a few: Douglas Turner Ward, Leslie Lee, Charles Gordone, Adrienne Kennedy, Samm-Art Williams, Charles Fuller, George Wolfe, Vy Higginsen, and August Wilson.

Beyond influence, he is known as the epitome of expansive imagination. At each stage of his successes, he remained so dissatisfied that he could not relinquish previous deprivations. While an honored writer for Broadway and Hollywood, he was still very much the 12-year-old numbers runner who must hustle to make ends meet and avoid the police. His writing reveals that he cannot turn his imagination off to suit present circumstances; he cannot separate himself from the struggling, the streetpeople, the sharecroppers simply because they are not physically present. It is not so simple as that he does not forget his origins. Rather, his scripts can be both liberating and diagnostic because those origins are still very much with him. They are not past history. They are not even past.

SURVEY OF CRITICISM

In time and volume, most of Elder's work has been for television. And since this writing has hardly been evaluated at all, it can be said that his work has not yet been properly assessed. Still, much has been written about him. The best place to begin and probably the best guide to his work would be the candid interviews he has given. Under Studies below, they are listed under Bigsby (1969), Gant (1973), Reed (1973), Sheperd (1969), and Sullivan (1975). They contain important biographical information, frank assessments of his goals, and valuable advice to young writers. They represent, in fact, a version of "What Every Young Writer Should Know" about performance writing. Reviews of the original production of *Ceremonies in Dark Old Men* can be found in the 1969 volumes of *The New York Times Theater Reviews* and *New York Theatre Critics' Reviews*. Commentary on the films he has worked on can be found in the similar compendia of reviews by Los Angeles and New York critics. The best overall discussion of contemporary black drama is by Fabre (1983). Bibliographical studies are listed below under Arata (1979), Arata and Rotoli (1976), and Peterson (1988). Valuable overviews of his theatrical writing are provided by Cherry (1985) and Turner (1973); Millichap (1986) essays the same task for the screenplays. Jeffers (1972) provides a valuable study in context.

Transcripts of Elder's one-act plays are housed in the Hatch-Billops Collection, 491 Broadway, in New York City. A collection of his manuscripts is maintained by Boston University.

BIBLIOGRAPHY

Works by Lonne Elder III

Plays

Ceremonies in Dark Old Men (two-act). Wagner College, New York, July 1965; revised Saint Mark's Playhouse. February 4, 1969; transferred to Pocket Theatre. April 28, 1969; revived Theatre 4, May 10, 1985. Published by Farrar, Straus, 1969. Reprint *Black Theater*. Edited by Patterson, 1971; and in *Drama: Principles and Plays*. Edited by Hatten, 1975.
Charades on East Fourth Street (one-act). Expo '67, Montreal, 1967. Published in *Black Drama Anthology*. Edited by Woodie King and Ron Milner, New American Library, 1971.
Splendid Mummer (mono-drama). American Place Theater, April 24, 1988.

Motion Pictures

Melinda (MGM, 1972), screenplay.
Sounder (20th-Century Fox, 1972), adaptation.
Sounder, Part 2 (Gamma III, 1976), screenplay.
Bustin' Loose (Universal, 1981), adaptation.

Television

Camera Three (CBS, 1963), scripts.
The Terrible Veil (NBC, 1963), scripts.
N.Y.P.D. (ABC, 1967–1968), scripts.

McCloud (NBC, 1970–1971), scripts.
Ceremonies in Dark Old Men (ABC, January 6, 1975), teleplay.
A Woman Called Moses (NBC, 1978), teleplay.
The Negro Ensemble Company (PBS for American Masters series, 1987), script.

Essays

"Comment: Rambled Thoughts." *Black Creation* 4 (Summer 1973): 48.
"Lorraine Hansberry: Social Consciousness and the Will." *Freedomways* 19 (Fourth
    Quarter 1979): 213–18.

Studies of Lonne Elder III

Arata, Ester Spring. *More Black American Playwrights: A Bibliography.* Metuchen, N.J.:
    Scarecrow, 1979.
Arata, Esther Spring, and Nicholas John Rotoli. *Black American Playwrights: 1800 to
    the Present: A Bibliography.* Metuchen, N.J.: Scarecrow, 1976.
Bigsby, C.W.E. "Lonne Elder III: An Interview." *The Black American Writer: Vol. II:
    Poetry and Drama.* Leland, Fla.: Everett/Edwards, 1969.
Bosworth, Patricia. "Life Is Dangerous but Beautiful, Too." *New York Times,* February
    16, 1969, II:3.
Cherry, Wilsonia E.D. "Lonne Elder III." *Dictionary of Literary Biography: Vol. 38:
    Afro-American Writers after 1955: Dramatists and Prose Writers.* Edited by Tha-
    dious M. Davis and Trudier Harris. Detroit: Gale, 1985.
Duberman, Martin. "Theatre 69: Black Theatre." *Partisan Review* 36 (1969): 488–89.
Eckstein, George. "The New Black Theatre." *Dissent* 20 (Winter 1973): 112.
———. "Softened Voices in the Black Theatre." *Dissent* 23 (Summer 1976): 306–08.
Fabre, Genevieve. *Drumbeats, Masks, and Metaphor: Contemporary Afro-American The-
    atre.* Cambridge, Mass.: Harvard University Press, 1983.
Fenderson, Lewis H. "The New Breed of Black Writers and Their Jaundiced View of
    Tradition." *CLA Journal* 15 (September 1971): 18–24.
Fontenot, Chester. "Mythic Patterns in *River Niger* and *Ceremonies in Dark Old Men.*"
    MELUS 7 (Spring 1980): 41–49.
Gant, Liz. "An Interview with Lonne Elder." *Black World* 22 (April 1973): 38–48.
Harrison, Paul Carter. *The Drama of Nommo.* New York: Grove, 1972.
Hart, William B. "Lonne Elder III." *Dictionary of Literary Biography: Vol. 7: Twen-
    tieth-Century American Dramatists.* Edited by John MacNicholas. Detroit: Gale,
    1981.
Hay, Samuel A. "African-American Drama, 1950–1970." *Negro History Bulletin* 36
    (January 1973): 5–8.
Jeffers, Lance. "Bullins, Baraka, and Elder: The Dawn of Grandeur in Black Drama."
    CLA Journal 16 (September 1972): 32–48.
Mattox, Michael. "The Day Black Movie Stars Got Militant." *Black Creation* 4 (Winter
    1973): 40–42.
Millichap, Joseph. "Lonne Elder III." *Dictionary of Literary Biography: Vol. 44: Amer-
    ican Screenwriters.* Edited by Randall Clark. Detroit: Gale, 1986.
Peterson, Bernard L., Jr. *Contemporary Black American Playwrights and Their Plays: A
    Biographical Directory and Dramatic Index.* Westport, Conn.: Greenwood, 1988.

Potter, Vilma R. "New Politics, New Mothers." *CLA Journal* 16 (December 1972): 147–155.

Reed, Rochelle. "Lonne Elder on *Sounder*." *Dialog on Film* 2 (May 1973): 2–12.

Rosenberg, Harold. "The Artist as Perceiver of Social Realities: The Post-Art Artist." *Arts in Society* 8 (Summer 1971): 509–10.

Sheperd, Richard F. "Lonne Elder Talks of Theatre in Black and White." *New York Times* (February 8, 1969): I: 22.

Sullivan, Dan. "What's a Nice Black Playwright Doing in a Place Like This?" *New York Times* (January 5, 1975): II: 23.

Turner, Darwin T. "Lonne Elder III." *Contemporary Dramatists.* Edited by James Vinson. New York: St. Martin's Press, 1973.

Peter Steinam Feibleman
(1930–   )

The distinctiveness of Peter S. Feibleman's fiction lies in his evocation of place and compelling characterizations. His novels are rich with the detail of culture and landscape, and his several nonfiction books share this attention to sensory experience. His plots trace the clash of disparate cultures and tell of individuals on the boundaries of these communities. From this marginal perspective, these individuals confront the roots of their identities and struggle with knowledge that moves them from innocence to maturity.

BIOGRAPHY

Born in New York City on August 1, 1930, Peter Steinam Feibleman was raised in New Orleans. His father, James Kern Feibleman, a professor of philosophy at Tulane University for 29 years, published over forty philosophical works for academic and popular audiences and six volumes of poetry. The elder Feibleman met Dorothy Steinam on a passenger liner en route to Europe when she was 16 and he 23. Secretly engaged, they were married in December 1928.

In Peter Feibleman's early years, the family lived in an old house on St. Peter Street in the French Quarter between, his father remembered, a bootlegger and a "house of assignation." A few years later, his parents built a modernistic house of steel, concrete, and glass brick in Metairie, a suburb of New Orleans. While the new house was under construction, they lived with Peter's paternal grandparents in uptown New Orleans. His later writings recall a childhood spent very much at ease in the city, with the independence to move freely in different neighborhoods and make friends readily.

In the Feibleman household writing and writers were held in high esteem; by the time he was 10, Peter Feibleman had met Sherwood Anderson, William Faulkner, and Henry Miller. Thus he was not overly enthusiastic about being summoned in pajamas and bathrobe to meet a successful playwright from New York. He recalled being struck first by the strength of her back, and when Lillian Hellman asked how old he was, he responded "only ten." "I don't know what you mean by 'only' " was her response. "Ten isn't so young."

Feibleman's first professional success came as a child actor. Winning a New Orleans audition for CBS Radio, he worked from 1940 to 1942 in the serial *Hans Brinker and the Silver Skates.* After his parents divorced in 1944, he moved with his mother to New York. (His father married novelist Shirley Ann Grau in 1955.) Though his father's work interested him in writing, Feibleman felt that acting offered a quicker route to success. A self-described bad actor who relied on technique, he studied acting at Carnegie Institute of Technology and Columbia University and with Constance Collier and Stella Adler.

Feibleman lived in Spain from 1951 to 1958, acting in French, Spanish, and Italian films. Though he initially planned a one-month visit, he was so enamored with the country that he found work with film companies in order to stay and later managed a Spanish ballet company touring Europe and North Africa. With his dark looks, Feibleman could pass for Spanish as long as his accent didn't give him away. To avoid labor laws he feigned laryngitis until his Spanish could stand close scrutiny. Speaking little or no English for more than seven years helped "clarify" and "crystallize" his own sense of language. Living in Madrid for five of these years and in Seville, he developed an abiding knowledge and love of Spanish language and culture.

The public acclaim that greeted his first novel, *A Place without Twilight,* in 1958 was so unexpected that Feibleman remained in Spain until after its publication. Focusing on a New Orleans African-American family, the novel traces the destructive influence of a mother upon her three children. Because of their light skin color, the children are not readily accepted: "It was a not-quite color in a place where you had to be something." Cille Morris tries to help her two brothers escape their mother's fearful religiosity and distrust of the world but succeeds only in gaining her own independence. Her elder brother Clarence works secretly as a hustler to support the family, and her younger brother Dan slips into an obsessive search for acceptance that ultimately turns violent. In 1959 the promise of the first novel won Feibleman a Guggenheim award.

When a New York friend, writer Sama Rama Rau, offered to throw a party to celebrate the publication of *A Place without Twilight* and asked Feibleman whom he would like to invite, he named Lillian Hellman and Greta Garbo. Both attended. This second meeting with Hellman proved more fruitful than their first; as friends, lovers, and companions, Feibleman and Hellman were part of each other's lives for the next 25 years, linked in part by their common childhood experience as the only child of a Jewish family in New Orleans. Until Hellman's death in 1984, Feibleman regularly spent summers writing at her house on Martha's Vineyard, and the two traveled together widely.

Feibleman's second novel, *The Daughters of Necessity* (1959), was published only a year after his first. Set in an unnamed Southern town, the novel focuses on Edmund Choate and the tragic fate embodied in his two daughters. Raised in the finest house on Melpomene Drive (the finest street in town), Choate commands the respect and love of the community, though this esteem is tested when he returns to the family mansion with his Italian wife and her illegitimate daughter, Loris Licia, whom he has adopted. After his wife dies of diphtheria, Choate sends his daughter off to Europe, and marries childhood sweetheart Anne Legrange, a neighbor on Melpomene whom he had abandoned years before. She dies giving birth to his second daughter, Adrianne. When Loris Licia returns to live in the Legrange mansion (haunted by one of Choate's wives), Choate is forced to confront the consequences of his youthful choices.

In 1962 Feibleman turned his attention to the stage, reworking some of the characters in his first novel for *Tiger Tiger Burning Bright* (1963). This play centers on Clarence, whose crafty grace has earned him the nickname "Tiger," and on his struggle to escape the domination of Mama's obsessive love. Directed by Joshua Logan, the production starred Claudia McNeil and Alvin Ailey and featured Roscoe Lee Browne, Cicely Tyson, and Diana Sands. The play had the misfortune to open on December 22, only two weeks after New York newspaper workers went on strike; it closed after thirty-three performances.

Feibleman's interest in drama and the need to make money drew him to Hollywood, where he worked with director-producer Josh Logan on the screenplay for *Ensign Plover,* the 1964 Warner Brothers sequel to *Mister Roberts.* Feibleman settled in a house in the Hollywood hills in 1973. He has written for both film and television, developing a reputation as a consultant and "script doctor" on such films as *Heaven Can Wait* and *Reds.* With Joan Didion, John Gregory Dunne, and Elaine May, he formed a screenplay consulting agency in 1980 and was awarded the Golden Pen Award in 1983 for his screenwriting.

Feibleman returned to Spain in the early 1960s to research what was to become *The Columbus Tree,* the novel he published in 1973. He stayed at the palace of the Duchess of Medina Sedonia in the village of Sanlúcar de Barrameda, on the southern coast near Cadiz. The Duchess was a political opponent of Franco, and Feibleman became involved in the underground resistance, collating the archives in the palace attic to keep them out of Franco's hands. He recalled wryly, "The difference between Louisiana under the Long administration and Spain under the Franco regime was not as noticeable as you would think."

Feibleman's next book, *Strangers and Graves* (1966), comprises four thematically related short novels, two set in New Orleans, two in Spain. The first novella, "Death of Danaüs," is a revision of the last section of *The Daughters of Necessity.* "Fever" traces the coming of age of a New Orleans boy befriended by a French Quarter madam named Ladybird. In the last two novellas Feibleman attempts to capture the rhythms of the Spanish language in an idiomatic English that one critic described as "Hemingway translated into and out of Spanish." In "Along the Coast" an elderly Andalusian fish peddler compromises her honest reputation to get medical care for her dying grandson. Her futile quest is mirrored in "Eyes": A son watches his blind father capitulate to necessity and abandon his pride. These stories reveal a familiarity with Spanish culture equal to Feibleman's earlier use of Louisiana settings.

Feibleman's knowledge of Iberian culture led to the first of three nonfiction works for Time-Life Books. Though he had written about New Orleans and Spain in articles for magazines, these books gave him room to explore the deep bonds of culture underlying these distinctive communities. More than literary hack work, these books reveal Feibleman's skill in evoking the details of a particular place and his understanding of the historical forces that shape the lives of its people. Interspersed with photo essays and recipes, Feibleman's text reveals a deep engagement with culture and landscape. As in his fiction, he reads distinctive cultural artifacts as a record of the history and beliefs of a people.

In *The Cooking of Spain and Portugal* (1969), Feibleman attempted, in his words, to "trace back the history of Spain and Portugal in terms of their food" (Dorgan, 177). He mixes memories of his earlier sojourn in Spain with an account of more recent travels, explaining distinctive foods and customs of particular regions, evoking a late afternoon in Valencia, riotous Holy Week festivities in Seville, and an epic banquet at a Basque gastronomic society. Reflecting his flair for narrative, he tells stories of the coming of the electric blender to Seville and of an encounter with a ghostly Catalan woman in Barcelona.

In the two books on Louisiana, *American Cooking: Creole and Acadian* (1971) and *The Bayous* (1973), Feibleman frames his recent travels in the area with own childhood memories, introducing south Louisiana cuisine through the remembered excitement of childhood rambles through New Orleans. Not bound to a particular neighborhood, he is equally at home crabbing in Lake Pontchartrain with his friend Richard, observing an elegant meal at a friend's home in the Garden District, and exploring the forbidden pleasures of the Vieux Carré: "The cold shadowy alleys rang with the echoes of jazz from Bourbon Street; elegant restaurants and cheap jive joints flung their sounds and smells at each other; and all this cacophony was, for me, like an end to childhood and a prelude to the music of the adult world" (45). A comic highlight is a grand battle between the family cook Thelma and her sister-in-law Ruby over the merits of gumbo made with okra and that made with filé powder.

The Bayous is cast even more completely as remembrance. Four of its six chapters recall youthful encounters: a canoe trip with Richard Breax and his father on Bayou Dorcheat in north Louisiana, a visit with his own father to Bayou Teche, and a week of fishing in the Atchafalaya Basin when he and a friend are trapped in the path of a hurricane. Feibleman's text balances a keen descriptive eye and a wealth of knowledge about animal and plant life with a deep sense of awe at the mystery and potential destructiveness of the natural world. His contributions to these three books testify to the strong pull these places exert on his consciousness; they also served as testing grounds for trying out ideas that he would exploit more fully in his next two books.

The southern coast of Spain provides the setting for *The Columbus Tree*. The novel's central locales are the Hotel Malage, a luxury resort recently built in the seaside village of Suelo, and the palace of Count Guzmán in Sanlúcar. Twelve-year-old Will Locke is the novel's central figure; the summer marks his passage from childhood to maturity. Will's mother Helen is the hotel's unofficial social director, trying to parlay her connections into economic reward. Detached and silent, Will observes these attempts and the activities of the hotel's wealthy tourists. Another silent observer is Eugenia, a Suelo native and housekeeper at the hotel whose son is rescued by the Count from the reprisals of a corrupt police captain. Will's only soulmate is his half-sister Littlejohn, who becomes involved with Guzmán and is the unwitting agent of his downfall. On the Guzmán palace grounds is the eponymous tree, planted, tradition has it, by Columbus on his return from the New World and revered for its purported mystical powers. When the vengeful peasantry hacks it to pieces, its rotten center is laid bare, as decadent as the descendants of Columbus who loll away the season at the Hotel Malage.

Charlie Boy (1980) marks a return to the New Orleans setting of Feibleman's first novel. Again he writes about tourists and other strangers. Josiah Moment, a conventioneering Boston physician, explores the city under the guidance of E. L. Sitwell, an African-American boy on the cusp of manhood. Their lives become entangled with the misfit ''Charlie Boy'' Breaux, the target of a massive manhunt to track down a serial killer terrifying the city. Though Breaux is indeed responsible for some of the murders, Moment believes him innocent, and works to keep him from roving vigilante squads. The flight of the three takes them to the Atchafalaya basin and into the path of a fierce hurricane. Trapped for several days by floodwaters, each comes to an uncomfortable new knowledge of himself and his companions. Breaux claims E. L. as the brother he never had, E. L. confronts the limits of his self-imposed isolation; and Moment, looking into the heart of Breaux's dark evil, finds something that commands his belief: he kills Charlie with his own knife.

Feibleman's most recent books, *Eating Together: Recipes and Recollections* (1984) and *Lilly: Reminiscences of Lillian Hellman* (1988), arose from his life-long relationship with Hellman. As collaborative autobiographies, they extend concerns that Feibleman explores in other work. *Eating Together,* as its subtitle suggests, blends specific recipes with reminiscences of particular occasions; this interweaving is particularly rewarding in Feibleman's section. Understanding the cooking and eating of food as essential forms of human interaction, he discusses meals as almost sacramental expressions of human love and community.

Although *Lilly* seems initially to follow the more traditional form of the literary memoir, much of the book is given over to letters from Hellman to Feibleman and transcripts of their conversations. These bring Hellman's own voice into the narrative to compete with Feibleman's for prominence and control. The book is as much a mutual account of their relationship as a memoir by the surviving partner. Upon her death, Hellman left Feibleman the Martha's Vineyard house, and he took up residence there in 1984.

MAJOR THEMES

Peter Feibleman has drawn on a core of important themes. He explores natural landscapes, tracing their influence on those who inhabit them. These characters, carefully drawn products of their culture, reveal the social dynamics of the community. The most illuminating characters live "in between," caught in conflicting models of what they might become. In portraying their struggles for identity, Feibleman has limned the boundaries of fate and volition, of social construction and individual will. His natural landscapes provide an Edenic locus where these characters wrestle with the knowledge of good and evil.

The most striking thematic unity of Feibleman's work has been a continuing attention to the influence of place. Highly detailed landscapes frame his narratives, and his people are most content when they are at ease in the natural world. Feibleman shares with his father a fascination with the bayou country of southern Louisiana, a region described by Feibleman *père* as "that fantastic land of strange and ill-assorted people, and of the salt marsh with its animals, its monotony and its decayed and foetid air which is timeless and so beautiful that to get it in one's blood means to be drawn back more than once" (Feibleman, 156). The younger Feibleman's descriptions in *The Bayous* carry the same sense of awe. When the three refugees in *Charlie Boy* are driven into the Atchafalaya swamp to escape their pursuers, their fight for survival against the natural forces unleashed by the hurricane prefigures Moment's own moral struggle to understand the evil that Breaux constitutes. A similarly significant landscape supports *The Columbus Tree.* The land and the people who inhabit it are shaped by the painful memory of a tidal wave that once destroyed the village of Suelo. Against the broad sweep of the Andalusian coastline and the timeless rhythms of its people, the scurrying and frantic activity of the hotel guests seem impotent.

Climate shares with landscape this powerful, even deterministic, role for Feibleman. In *Charlie Boy,* Moment's disaffection from his former life comes not so much from the exotic culture of New Orleans as from its subtropical miasma. There is a sense of plague about, recalling the nineteenth-century yellow fever epidemics attributed by civic authorities to stagnant air. As one critic points out, "The oppressive heat and cloying humidity of Louisiana become the chief catalysts in Feibleman's laboratory" (Atchity, 1); the figure of Charlie that takes hold of the city's imagination seems as much a product of the dizzying heat as of Breaux's own twisted psyche. This atmospheric naturalism is evident even in the unspecified setting of *The Daughters of Necessity.* The same humid conditions that breed a serial killer give rise in this novel to the ghostly daughters that force Edmund Choate to his final bout of self-knowledge. The canal that laps the Choate mansion seems as sentient as the ocean beyond Suelo: "There is an understanding in the feel of it" (9). The lives of the Morris family are similarly constrained by the natural world, a constraint expressed most clearly in *Tiger Tiger Burning Bright* when Mama contrasts the flat swampland of New

Orleans with her native Georgia, whose hills cradle the setting sun and create twilight, "the color of dreams" (53), a phenomenon that doesn't exist in Louisiana. Caressing Clarence's tawny skin, she cries, "What can you do in a place without no twilight?" (53). In such a world, her children are better off dead. The stage setting for Feibleman's play makes this point even more clearly, situating the Morris home next to the Riverview cemetery; the bleak sky above offers little solace.

Yet even the most barren of Feibleman's landscapes are peopled, and his novels make extensive use of ethnographic detail. The inhabitants of Suelo organize their lives by ritual: Eugenia fixes breakfast, greets her neighbors on the way to work, and curses the *foreño*, the evil wind. She once made a pilgrimage to the Virgin of Pilar in thanksgiving for her son's recovery from paralysis; in the novel she begs the Columbus tree to deliver her son from prison and torture. Eugenia and her neighbors are as at home in their world as are Ulysses and Alcibiade, the Cajun fishermen Feibleman visits in his books about Louisiana. His attention to surface detail has also extended to the languages people speak. He has employed several techniques to give the reader a sense of the linguistic patterns of his Spanish speakers, translating idioms into English and sprinkling dialogue with Spanish words and phrases. The effect of these linguistic techniques varies; at times they create additional distance between character and reader, but at others they help to reveal a state of mind or a way of perceiving the world.

Many of the rich characterizations for which Feibleman has been praised take their strength from the cultural roles his characters embody. Feibleman has granted them an authenticity of language, action, and motivation that give them an immediacy and believability. Even relatively minor characters are so compellingly drawn that the novels form a rich procession of people from the various communities inhabiting a place. By grounding even his minor characters within a social community, Feibleman has enriched their presence in the novel and has elaborated the complex field within which the major characters act. The old woman in "On the Coast" lives entirely within the boundaries her community has set. She pursues no passionate love affair, betrays no family member, protests no oppressive government: she seeks only to serve her family. Yet she demonstrates Feibleman's sense of culture's limits, for as she moves along the well-worn paths of her life, trading on the community's knowledge of her integrity, she cannot comprehend that she has betrayed that trust. Although her social role has served her well, it has not equipped her to deal with change. Eugenia faces a similar conflict, yet her quiet persistent ways seem likely to endure against the encroachment of the tourist industry.

The central characters in the novels face these conflicts forcefully, and their resolution of the conflict is neither so easy nor so uncomplicated. Cille Morris, Robert Whiteacre (the boy in "Fever"), Will Locke, and E. L. Sitwell are all adolescents searching for an identity in a world that has no room for them.

Feibleman's treatment of these characters may reflect his own troubled adolescence (he was molested by a family employee when he was 10, and his parents divorced when he was 14.)

Cille's racial ambiguity outlines the limitations of her mother's stark view of the world's dangers. Her work as a domestic in two very different upper-class white households has given Feibleman the chance to contrast race relations in the Old and New South. Cille's first job, at a modern plantation home north of Lake Pontchartrain, places her among a family that insists on maintaining a respectful distance from their servants. Her role in the household is carefully delimited, and when she transgresses those bounds, she is disciplined. Almost equally bewildering to Cille, however, is the forced liberalism of the second family, whose modern glass brick and concrete suburban home seems clearly modeled on the Feibleman's Metairie residence. (While settling a household dispute, Mrs. Jenkins assures Cille of her own good intentions: "We don't want you to feel *awful* simply because you are a *Negro*" [285]). Robert, perhaps the most autobiographical of Feibleman's characters, escapes an unsatisfying home life by exploring the French Quarter's adult mysteries. Abandoned by those he loves, he seeks not familiarity but dissonance; the family cook Thelma analyzes him this way: "Strangers and that cemetery is all you ever did care about. Only doom you got on you is you will never love anything in your whole life but strangers and graves" (142). Befriended by the outcasts in Ladybird's house, he learns to accept death and change and moves forward confidently into the changes of his own life.

Of all Feibleman's marginalized characters, Will Locke articulates his situation most clearly, describing himself as "an inbetween man." The summer is a time of strange new experiences for Will, and Littlejohn's death at summer's end closes a chapter of his life. Though he still has many questions about his identity, he can more readily resist the competing claims that beset him. E. L. is similarly situated outside the many communities that surround him. Physically small for his age, but mentally superior to his family and friends, he spends his days outside the Royal Creole Hotel watching the tourists come and go. The first person to take him seriously is Moment, himself learning to live as an outsider: outside his marriage (his wife and oldest friend are having an affair), outside his job (the practice gets along fine without him), and outside the familiar confines of Massachusetts. E.L., Moment, and Breaux form an unholy trinity of complementary personalities. Rejecting the roles society has designed for them, they turn to their fellow outcasts for solace and, more important, for knowledge about themselves.

Often classed with Eudora Welty, Truman Capote, and Tennessee Williams as a purveyor of local color charm and Southern Gothic excess, Feibleman has cited as his major influences Joseph Conrad and Dostoevski. Among American writers, he has claimed as models Carson McCullers, Flannery O'Connor, and Mark Twain. Although he lacks the distinctive humor of Twain or O'Connor, he shares with them an interest in the darker side of human nature and the channels by which encounters with such darkness foster growth. Feibleman's understanding of the presence of evil has shifted through the course of his work. In the first two novels, the strong will of a parent exercises a fateful determinism on the lives of parent and children; in the later work, no single person wields such influence. Characters struggle against a Fate equally powerful, but capricious and untraceable to the actions of anyone. Feibleman has highlighted the random pettiness of evil in *The Columbus Tree*. When Pepe Luis, Eugenia's son, comes in conflict with the authorities, it is not because of a principled stand against fascism, but by crossing a police captain who married his old girlfriend. He is brought in by the authorities and subjected to the cruelties of the police state, yet the casual malevolence of the captain has a banal neglectfulness about it. The captain's actions flourish in the corrupt atmosphere of the Franco regime, but the blame cannot be laid explicitly at the Generalissimo's door.

In "Charlie Boy" Breaux, Feibleman has posed the question of evil more sharply. Charlie is a complex figure: He claims to be the psychotic killer created by the news media, then acts out that role. He is a peculiarly disturbing personification of evil: In him we see none of the crafts and deceits of the devil, but an impersonal expertise in killing, a motivation both casual (he kills only to cover a botched mugging) and unconsciously erotic (his arousal after a killing seems more a side effect than a motive), and a sense of powerlessness (he attributes a string of profitless murders to bad luck).

The almost Manichean opposition of the early work gives way to an embrace of ambiguity in the last two novels. The early landscapes are harsh and unforgiving; New Orleans is a place without twilight, a place with no time to dream, no room for the ambiguous. The New Orleans of *Charlie Boy* is a different place, a city rich with the possibility of life on the boundary. Suelo's encompassing coastline can take in the sweep of Will's daydreams and nightmares. Those who survive the tumultuous events that transpire in those landscapes have been stretched by the extremes of human experience they have witnessed. Will Locke feels the ambivalence of his identity strongly, yet he struggles not against a deterministic world but within it. Through his in-betweenness he comes to a sense of himself that is influenced by the cultures in which he lives, but which he can claim as his own. Josiah Moment is remembered as a man who would "accept nothing," that is, accept no one else's version of reality; yet he is also a man who does not reject anything, save that which is banal and superficial. By refusing to view E.L. or Breaux through the distorted view of the community, he comes to a deeper knowledge of himself, and helps E.L. to reach a place from which he can move into a confident adulthood.

SURVEY OF CRITICISM

The critical response to Feibleman's work has generally been mixed. Although reviewers have tended to discuss similar features of his work, such as his striking characterization, detailed plot, and distinctive language, their evaluation of these features has varied widely.

Critics have greeted *A Place without Twilight* as a promising first novel and have been almost uniform in their praise of Feibleman's realistic portrayal of the lives of African-Americans in the South. Some have criticized the pacing of the novel, calling it long on incident and short on coherent plot. Although *A Woman of Necessity* has met with a more subdued reception, reviewers have acknowledged its more complex claims on the reader. It is a less realistic novel than *A Place without Twilight,* and its characters seem less sympathetic. Some reviewers found the more fantastic and symbolic narrative of this novel rewarding; others thought it pretentious and long-winded. R.G. Davis (1959) captures the latter view: "The conversation of these beautiful worldly creatures is often coarse and banal. Nor do they have the quality of mind that can give their contradictory experiences meaning—and hence reality" (5).

The critics have been kinder to *Tiger Tiger Burning Bright,* praising its energetic portrayal of life and its imaginative characters. Howard Taubman called it "an honest, compassionate drama." Others judged the play skillful in parts, but lacking in dramatic integrity; Walter Kerr found it "essentially directionless," the outcome "altogether arbitrary." (During the strike, the reviews of newspaper drama critics were published in *Firstnite;* they are collected in *New York Theatre Critic's Reviews.*)

Strangers and Graves has generally been thought an ambitious failure. Drawing particular attention have been Feibleman's attempts to capture the flavor and feel of the Spanish dialects spoken by his characters. Critics have found the two New Orleans novellas the more successful part of the book. Rollene W. Saal (1966) found that the stories are overly governed by abstraction and "start with an idea and only later are fleshed out with human qualities." Josephine Jacobsen (1966) found them more compelling: "The force, the conviction, the passion of these novellas bite their image into the mind, so that one knows that years later they will still be there. Mr Feibleman has the pure gift for fiction."

Despite the complexity and maturity of *The Columbus Tree,* the novel has received less critical attention than his earlier work, though its selection by the Book-of-the-Month Club helped assure it a certain popular success. Critics have been drawn to its rich evocation of Spain, but have found fault with the elaborate plot and heavy-handed symbolism. Reviewers have been more enthusiastic about *Charlie Boy,* praising its convincing atmosphere and complex characters. Larry McMurtry (1980) called Feibleman's ability to keep the reader interested in the boring Josiah Moment "a minor miracle" (14), while Kenneth John Atchity (1980) approved of the congruence of character and setting.

The two Hellman books have garnered little critical response. *Lilly* has played into the public squabbles about Hellman that continued after her death. As a defense of Hellman's life, critics have found it inadequate and disingenuous. Only one critic, David Miller (1989), has given attention to the literary form of the book, deeming it "carefully crafted and poetic" (1287).

Given the thematic unity of Feibleman's work, and his concern with the cultural construction of race, gender, and class, his novels offer unexplored territory for critical inquiry. Readers may find that territory as rich and compelling as the peopled landscapes of Louisiana and Spain that Feibleman has created.

BIBLIOGRAPHY

Works by Peter S. Feibleman

A Place Without Twilight. Cleveland: World, 1958.
The Daughters of Necessity. Cleveland: World, 1959.
Tiger Tiger Burning Bright. Cleveland: World, 1963.
Strangers and Graves: Four Short Novels (includes "Death of Danaüs," "Fever," "Along the Coast," and "Eyes"). New York: Atheneum, 1966.
The Cooking of Spain and Portugal. New York: Time-Life, 1969.
American Cooking: Creole and Acadian. New York: Time-Life, 1971.
The Bayous. New York: Time-Life, 1973.
The Columbus Tree. New York: Atheneum, 1973.
Charlie Boy. Boston: Little, Brown, 1980.
Eating Together: Recollections and Recipes. With Lillian Hellman. Boston: Little, Brown, 1984.
Lilly: Reminiscences of Lillian Hellman. New York: Morrow, 1988.

Interviews with Peter S. Feibleman

Interview with Jean W. Ross. In *Contemporary Authors,* vol. 110, edited by Hal May, 175–78. Detroit: Gale Research, 1984.

Studies of Peter S. Feibleman

Abrahams, William. "Eden on the Rocks." Review of *The Columbus Tree. Saturday Review of the Arts* 1 (February 1973) 63–64.
Atchity, Kenneth John. "Masterful Touches in a Delta of Dusty Swamps and Death." Review of *Charlie Boy. Los Angeles Times Book World* 90 (August 3, 1980): 1.
Boles, Paul Darcy. "Slow Journey Into Murder." Review of *The Daughters of Necessity. Saturday Review* 42 (August 1, 1959): 17.
Curley, Thomas F. "A Mind Alert to the Motions of Necessity." Review of *The Daughters of Necessity. Commonweal* 70 (September 18, 1959): 522–23.
Davis, R. G. "Five Beautiful Women and the Life of Edmund Choate." Review of *The Daughters of Necessity. New York Times Book Review* 108 (August 2, 1959): 4–5.
Dorgan, Charity Anne. "Feibleman, Peter S(teinam) 1930–" In *Contemporary Authors,* Vol. 110, edited by Hal May, 174–178. Detroit: Gale Research, 1984.
Feibleman, James K. *The Way of a Man: An Autobiography of James K. Feibleman.* New York: Horizon Press, 1969.

Gutwillig, Robert. "Ambitious Attempt." Review of *A Place without Twilight*. *Commonweal* 68 (April 4, 1958): 21–22.

Jacobsen, Josephine. Review of *Strangers and Graves*. *Commonweal* 85 (December 9, 1966): 299–300.

McMurtry, Larry. "Of Hurricanes and Homicide." Review of *Charlie Boy*. *New York Times Book Review* 129 (June 17, 1980): 14, 24.

Mano, D. K. Review of *The Columbus Tree*. *New York Times Book Review* 122 (February 25, 1973): 3.

Miller, David. "Literary Lives." Review of *Lilly*. *Sewanee Review* 97 (Spring 1989): 283–88.

Saal, Rollene W. "Spokesmen for a Theme." Review of *Strangers and Graves*. *New York Times Book Review* 116 (October 9, 1966): 54–55.

SARA ANDREWS JOHNSTON

Julia Fields
(1938–   )

The vitality of Julia Fields's poetry, its sympathetic portrayal both of suffering and of rejoicing in the simple delight of existence, along with its usually gentle satiric undertone, form a unique contribution in literature both of blacks and whites. It does not call attention to itself through harshness, stridency, or flashiness, but rather through sensitivity, warmth, and delight. Fields's comment at the close of her 1973 collection of poems, *East of Moonlight,* sums up a philosophy behind her particular achievements: "Poetry is a form of will. It is determination to be in the world and free from the world while giving to it and loving it. It's also wishing after some kinds of beauty to be born" (51).

BIOGRAPHY

Julia Fields was born in Perry County, Alabama, on January 21, 1938. Throughout her childhood and adolescence, she lived and worked on a farm. Mary Williams Burger (1985) has supplied pertinent biographical details. Among them is her love of the outdoors, her childhood being spent as a "shepherdess" and among "streams and wildflowers." She grew up in a large family; her father was variously called "a preacher, farmer, and storekeeper" (124). Fields herself remembers alternating manual-labor tasks like chopping wood with memorizing poetry; and two early passions, for botany and poetry, have been lifelong. She recited her own poems at school and at church, which apparently played a significant part in her life. Not allowed to listen to radio jazz, she remembers church music instead. In her Baptist upbringing, she was often made aware of poetry as a teaching instrument in the Bible and has noted that poetry simply seemed a natural part of life, as she grew up listening to poems and to the Bible being read aloud. Fields remembers being encouraged when one of her high-school poems, "The Horizon" (about six nearby hills, one containing the cemetery where her ancestors had been buried), was published by a national high-school poetry association and then by a Montgomery, Alabama, newspaper. Her high-school studying was mingled with work in a factory, restaurant waitressing, and selling vegetables. And she still, in her own teaching, likes to have students mix practicality with a life of the mind—for instance, encouraging them to submit for an art exhibit both the products of practical craftsmanship and their own poems.

At Knoxville College in Tennessee, a Presbyterian school from which she graduated in 1961, Fields studied literature and also acted in plays. Her own play *All Day Tomorrow* was produced by the Knoxville College Drama Workshop in 1966 to benefit the alumni fund. Her training in drama has contributed to her engaging way of reading her own poetry. Two of her early poems ("I Heard a Young Man Saying" and "Madness One Monday Evening") were published in a black literature anthology, *Beyond the Blues,* edited by Dr. Rosey Pool, in 1962. She then received encouragement from Langston Hughes, who republished these poems in his anthology *New Negro Poets, USA* (1964), giving her national recognition. After graduation she taught high school in Alabama for several years. Though she later lived for a time in New York City, she returned to the South and has been poet-in-residence or instructor at various Southern colleges, including Miles College, Hampton Institute, St. Augustine's College, East Carolina University, Howard University, North Carolina State University, and the University of the District of Columbia. Despite some bitter satirical gibes at teachers in her poetry, she has an enthusiastic interest in teaching and a desire to involve students in writing. She has told them what any writer would wish for himself or herself: "Write and write until you write yourself into happiness and discovery."

Interviewed for the *Negro Digest* in 1968, she commented that " 'The black experience' seems the most intense experience in the modern world. It is better that black people write it ourselves rather than have it written for us Exploitatively" (25). (According to the *Digest,* the "Exploitatively" refers to three white writers she selected as 'most important': William Styron, Robert Penn Warren, and Allen Tate.) She believes that black students are not urged to fulfill their potential, but that they are searching and need more encouragement to read all types of literature. She herself is an avid reader, crossing racial and cultural lines. She has studied briefly at the University of Edinburgh in 1963, traveling then through England and Scotland. She also earned an M.A. at the Bread Loaf School of English in 1972 and was awarded a National Endowment for the Arts grant in 1967 and the Seventh Conrad Kent Rivers Memorial Fund Award in 1973. She has two daughters, now grown, and currently lives in Washington, D.C., where she has been absorbed by watching the workings of congress firsthand.

MAJOR THEMES

Julia Fields's poems have the tone of a plea for sensitivity and justice in a "hard-boiled" world. Without being self-righteous or shrill, her poems have an undercurrent of moral insight, probably originating with her religious upbring-ing. At the same time, many are funny, lighthearted, or folksy. There is wry humor and caricature even in their atmosphere of racial consciousness and their sensitive portrayal of the sufferings of black people. Fields's first book, simply entitled *Poems,* was published in 1968 by Kriya Press in New York. It was followed in 1973 by *East of Moonlight,* from Red Clay Books in Charlotte, North Carolina. In 1976 *A Summoning, A Shining* was printed with the help of Hampton Institute in Virginia; the place of publication is given as Scotland Neck, North Carolina, where she was then living. *Slow Coins,* considered her finest collection of poetry and prose poems, was published by Three Continents Press in Washington, D.C., in 1981. Her short stories have appeared in *Negro Digest, Black World,* and *Callaloo.* Her children's book, *The Green Lion of Zion Street,* was published in 1988 by Macmillan.

There are poems of protest, but they are usually made delightful by a twist of wit or sensitivity. "High on the Hog," a poem that she read on national television and that elicits enthusiasm wherever it is read, is an excellent example. Apparently written in response to a *Wall Street Journal* article on soul food and in light of a romanticizing of it, the poem wittily overturns what Fields sees as a bit of sentimentality in a laudable raising of black consciousness:

> Take my share of Soul Food—
> I do not wish
> To taste of pig
> > Of either gut
> > or Grunt
> > from bowel
> > Or jowl
>
> I want caviar
> Shrimp souffle
> Sherry
> > Champagne
> > > And not because
> > > These are the
> > > Whites' domain
> > > But just because
> > > I'm entitled—
>
> For I've been
> > > V.d.'d enough
> > > > T.b.'d enough
> > and
> > > Hoe-cake fed Knock-Knee'd enough

> Spindly led-bloodhound tree'd enough
> To eat
> High on the Hog (41)

But several poems provide an interesting countercurrent through their anti-materialist flavor, critical of the pervasive "greed is good" mentality. "American Gluttony," in *Slow Coins,* is trenchantly condemning, but humor rescues it from a too intense bitterness—as in the notion of after-Christmas diets for those who think that for them it is "Christmas all year long." In order to maintain some reasonable shape, even they too must face a January purge:

> . . . The
> Diets by those who
> Are too evil to keep
> Their mouths shut or
> To feed the truly hungry. (51–52)

Fields can be eloquent and also funny while praising technology, as in "A Toaster Still Is Not a Sexual Beast" (*Slow Coins*). In such forms as telephones and typewriters, technology seems to play a subordinate and supportive role to man, much as nature, in her more benign moments, was once thought to do. But in an earlier poem with skyscraper imagery, technology is simply an overpowering element in a greedy American landscape. But that poem escapes bitterness by its imposition of a touching refrain. Though a typically American movement is among "cool skyscraper rows" of things

> . . . shepherded by bells which toll
> Our bill of sales and chide us back into the
> Fold with music and ¼ off signs . . . (*Poems*)

there is a slightly redemptive touch in the repeated lines

> In the marketplace my love
> and I together
> In the marketplace
> In foul and fair weather. (*Poems*)

Still the marketplace seems to be the only American place for love.

Both *East of Moonlight* and *Slow Coins* end with a lyrical climax in a group of four "Benediction" poems. In *Slow Coins* the order has been changed so that the concluding poem is both a condemnation of materialism and a hope for rescue from it. The speaker, who has seen "tinsel where / . . . souls should be," warns "Brothers, Sisters,"

> You would see them, lost, dangle
> From their dreams, more piteous even than greed.
> Pass quietly by them in the street.
> Do not bother even to smile.
> The dead would stone you. (205)

They are exhorted to take their "selfhood" and "beauty of being" and "rise up" "to weather this doom. / Nothing which you have known would lead you to believe" (206).

Among Fields's other poems that present a similarly fruitful mix of lyricism and social criticism are those that portray the stultification and lack of vitality in American culture. In *East of Moonlight* this criticism is directed toward suburbia; in *Slow Coins* teachers and academics are targeted. "Arcadia" (*East of Moonlight*) depicts suburbia as a place both of elegance—summarily excluding any "taste not of the grain"—and of boredom:

> no puddles in the street
> no branch or leaf unordered
> no noise not lined with music
> no color not obtuse as death. (11)

And in "Settled" (*East of Moonlight*) the speaker renounces an earlier suburban dream to

> be the nomad that I am—
> carry my babies papoose style
> and reach for personhood
> brick be damned. (19)

One means of Fields's reaching for "personhood" has been teaching; hence, her criticism of the profession seems a little odd. She has satirically captured the foibles of the teaching profession in the prose poem "What Donne Meant" (*Slow Coins*). The teacher's dramatic monologue rambles on, revealing her at once laudable and ludicrous aspirations to enlighten her students with

> what Donne was "attempting" to say, as he cannot say it
> and as I myself will speak for him, and as I am not
> ashamed to sit here and attempt it, I will tell you
> what all the "qualified" scholars said that he said
> which they have read that someone else said that he
> meant which someone said that he meant to have said to
> have meant. (177)

Academics are seen as "make-believe humanists," eagerly awaiting the deaths of poets—to which they come with "mute ears" and "notebooks"—pouncing and ransacking them

for materials for "papers"
To deliver at their make-believe
Conferences on Art and Humanity,
Neither of which interests them
More than their comfort or coffee. (17)

A section of *Slow Coins* is entitled "Indians." One of its poems is actually about Jewish people, who are considered "other indians," indicating Fields's interest in oppressed peoples of a variety of cultures. And it is possibly the oppressed, the outsiders, who are the best critics of any culture. In "Inertia," however, they come back to renew ours, for

one of these exhausted days
Everybody in America is going
To sit down in the middle of
Life and wait for the return
Of the Indians, or the return
Of some old tribe that even
Impotent old library-mongers
Do not remember . . . (153)

A number of Fields's poems deal with the suffering of black people; some depict the trials of specific black workers traditionally forced into menial jobs (such as the ironic "Heir" and "Lily Black Blonde from Wig Haven among the Urinals"); and some sympathetically portray black women in these and other trying circumstances ("Muriel Just Quit," "Saturday City," and "Anita's Swinging Weekend Father"). Both "Heir" and "Anita's Swinging Weekend Father" use classical allusions ironically, much as T. S. Eliot does in the "Sweeney" poems; but in "Heir" (*East of Moonlight*), the caricature that emerges is reverent, almost tender:

The Aga Memnon's dust mop
is dark as his face
He pushes the trash can nearer the dust.
                    so many kings have died.
. . . .
The dust, emblem of a power eclipsed, he thrusts into
a bin brighter than the tinkle of fresh gold.
And when he shatters the quiet of the embalmed day
his face is anonymous as the full prophetic moon.
                    so many kings have died. (12)

The tragedy of a lost heritage is deftly portrayed. A similar irony depicts Anita's "week-end [sic] father," who seems to have been "spawned by the / Cold

conjurings of abstract, deathly Zeus'' (90–91), in what is a reference to the
''Leda and the Swan'' myth retold in Yeats's poem. Raising ''his hard / Thighs''
above a motorcycle, her father creates metaphoric plagues compared with those
engendered by Leda's supposedly giving birth to Helen after her contact with
Zeus the swan (hence, according to legend, starting the Trojan War, the conflict
said to be fought over Helen). Anita's father spends the weekend with sunglasses
shading ''away his sight,'' tearing around the countryside with his daughter
hanging on, all the while cursing ''his wife's / Womb,'' though possibly filling
it again—and no doubt leaving as swiftly as Zeus dropped Leda from his ''indifferent beak.'' But the characters are not distanced by either the irony or the
allusions; there is sympathy in the caricature.

Displaying a range of styles, Fields can be lyrical in condemning the treatment
of blacks, as in her poem ''in memory of niggers,'' or humorous through the
use of dialect, but in a manner that is no less serious, as in ''A Xmas Poem for
Brother Jack.'' Dudley Randall (1973) has noted that Fields gives dignity to the
term ''nigger'' (4). In ''in memory of niggers'' she uses repetition and an or-
atorical style to make a moral point; she tells us not to

> forget one buck nigger
>   hanging.
> don't forget one blood hound track
> of one nigger dying, one nigger
>   burning.
> let the shopping centers cover the
> traces of their wasted blood, let the
> furniture factories carve the memories of their
> lynching into suburban dreams.
> . . . .
> . . . but don't forget (14)

''A Xmas Poem for Brother Jack'' demonstrates the ''seriousness in humor''
that, Mary Williams Burger has noted, Fields admired in the work of Langston
Hughes. Burger has also shown how Fields drew on Hughes's penchant for both
celebrating and satirizing the black experience in the Jesse B. Semple stories
(126); and the ''Xmas Poem'' (*East of Moonlight*) is another example of that
fruitful mix of tones. In witty dialect, the poem questions whether Jesus will
actually return, implying that blacks have been too ready to believe in a ''pie
in the sky'' to assuage an immediate misery. But their faith is treated with
reverence as well as humor.

> Brother, you are high in the sky.
> Way up there—like a bird.
> Wave your arms to us.
> Say howdy do.

Hi, Jack.
When you be back, man? . . . (31)

Among Julia Fields's poems from a feminine point of view, there is a range
of moods, from the long endurance of suffering (as in "Saturday City" [*Slow
Coins*]: "The women who have know pain so long / That they seek it from
habit" [82]), to a delight in eroticism (as in "Benediction I"), to criticism of a
male proclivity for brutality and war (in "I Heard a Young Man Saying" and
to a lesser extent in "Man My Mate"), to the assertion of a newly won independence from an entangling relationship (in "Benediction II"). "I Heard a
Young Man Saying" (*Poems*), one of Fields's first published poems, expresses
an antiwar sentiment that predates the political activism of the 1960s. The female
speaker is somewhat tentative about her position, which is ironically juxtaposed
with the firm male voice (" 'War' / There's talk of war"), and the irony is part
of the point. The woman wonders what is the matter with her, but cannot escape
an intuitive, inescapable position:

I, a woman, listened by the door,
By the broken-hinged door,
"I somehow planned on living." (n.p.)

In "Benediction II" (*Slow Coins*) the voice is more assertive. In contrast to
"Man, My Mate" (*East of Moonlight*), in which the female speaker expresses
an attitude of forebearance and even worship ("I pay / My homage to your
power, your brass / Sinews, iron, steel, gaunt astoundings, / Brutalities. . . "
[39]), for the sake of an erotic bond the speaker in "Benediction II" disentangles
herself from a relationship in which she realizes she has been chasing an illusion.
And she expresses her desire for independence with confidence:

. . . Do you think that I
Will tuck you inside a trunk like some
Wistful widow where you may rise and
Ride my mid-nights, cold as stone?
That time will be my own.
To do with as I choose.
And I choose to put your love down.
Carelessly. As one does a book, too highly
Recommended, or old maps from childhood
Plotted to dreams, or shapes of snowflakes. (203)

In her poems Fields has created some evocative moments, with a subtle,
wistful touch, as she has done in "Moonlight"—one poetic symbol for the
imagination. This poem, which opens *East of Moonlight* and gives it its name,
is actually about Moonlight, North Carolina, a miniscule town in the eastern
part of the state. But like Coleridge's "Frost at Midnight," it is also about the

imagination. As readers approach this town in the hinterlands with its anonymity and poverty, they find that the poem has become myth making and storytelling, suggesting a range of African-American experiences in the South: war and working the land, poverty and the poetry that can result from the retelling of these experiences. And the movement is made lyrical, like a moonlight sonata:

> moving eastward, passing the soil, the only holiness,
> moved from the cities sitting on their tails
> bound solidly to asphalt and steel and stone, moving
> to wide visions, serenity and modest kinds of
> joys . . . (9)

Fields's children's book *The Green Lion of Zion Street* is also about the power of the imagination, the fear and awe it can evoke. Children waiting in the cold and fog for a late school bus stroll into a nearby park, where they are both frightened and impressed by what they think is a real lion, ruling the park like a czar. When the fog clears, they realize that the "lion" is simply a stone statue, "A stone cat / perched up snooty like that." But the experience has delighted, even as it has frightened; it has been an addition to waiting at the bus stop in early morning light. Hence, it sums up the effect of Fields's poetry—that fairly ordinary experiences (like viewing a statue in daylight, watching someone sweeping, cruising through the suburbs, or approaching a small poverty-ridden town) can become tinged with awe.

SURVEY OF CRITICISM

Julia Fields's poetry has been favorably mentioned in several studies of black authors, usually written by poets themselves. Among the studies are Don L. Lee's *Dynamite Voices: Black Poets of the 1960s* (1971) and Eugene Redmond's *Drumvoices: The Mission of Afro-American Poetry* (1976). Fields has been recognized as a distinctive poet, but her work has been given little detailed attention, except by Mary Williams Burger in the *Dictionary of Literary Biography*. Treating all of her collections of poetry and some short stories, Burger is relatively exhaustive, providing the most complete picture (among the works mentioned) of the range of Fields's themes.

Don L. Lee, comparing Fields with Margaret Walker "in her eloquence and dignity and warmth," has discussed several specific poems in Fields's first published collection (*Poems*), especially "Black Students." His attention has helped to elucidate that fine poem's satirical criticism of an absence then of the teaching of African traditions and a false hope being placed in what could actually be seen as a "brainwashing" of students with white culture, creating automatic thinking patterns that obscured their own anger or puzzlement.

Eugene Redmond praises Julia Fields's *East of Moonlight* (1973), especially pointing out "High on the Hog," asserting that her "subtle dart, but direct power'' could suggest ''a healthy future for black poetry,'' in its movement away from the romanticism of pain (380). Dudley Randall (1973), another poet and a publisher, whose Broadside Press in Detroit has made many black authors available, including Gwendolyn Brooks, has written a short appreciative review of *East of Moonlight,* introducing Julia Fields as ''a spirited, warm and sensitive poet'' whom Kenneth Rexroth has considered to be ''one of the leading young black poets.''

Both Mary Williams Burger and Mercedese Broussard (1976) have discussed *A Summoning, A Shining* with some specific detail and appreciation, though they have noted an unevenness. Mary Williams Burger has considered *Slow Coins* to be Fields's best book, finding in most of its narrative poems the rhythm of ''oral black language,'' usually without the dialect, which was a prominent feature in black poetry of the 1960s and 1970s, and without the unusual spellings or typographical changes that caricature the language, often missing its ''force and beauty'' (130). This opinion has been countered by Rochelle Ratner, poetry editor of the *Soho Weekly News,* who finds an attempt to re-create black dialect—and, occasionally, unconventional spacing—gimmicky. She asserts that Fields's most successful poems are character portraits.

Fields's children's book *The Green Lion of Zion Street,* with Jerry Pinkney's boldly attractive pencil and watercolor illustrations, has been favorably noticed in numerous journals. Some reviewers describe a confusing movement from black vernacular to abstract, multisyllabic words; but Gloria Jacobs, in the *New York Times Book Review* (1988), concludes that ''the challenge . . . is part of the pleasure'' and that in its complex and vivid imagery, Fields's children's story is ''worthy, like the epics, of many retellings'' (30). In *Reading Teacher,* Susan Cox and Lee Galda (1990) chose *The Green Lion of Zion Street* along with other multicultural books as aesthetically valuable for children and as mirroring and validating ethnic experiences and providing a window for those of different backgrounds to look through and learn (582). Through both her children's stories and poetry, Julia Fields has provided many windows and mirrors.

BIBLIOGRAPHY

Works by Julia Fields

Poems. Millbrook, N.Y.: Kriya Press, 1968. (unpaged)
East of Moonlight. Charlotte, N.C.: Red Clay Books, 1973.
A Summoning, A Shining. Scotland Neck, N.C., 1976.
Slow Coins. Washington, D.C.: Three Continents Press, 1981.
The Green Lion of Zion Street. New York; Macmillan, 1988. (unpaged)

Studies of Julia Fields

Anderson, Lois F. Review of *The Green Lion of Zion Street. The Horn Book* 64 (1988): 478.

Bailey, Leaonead Pack, ed. *Broadside Authors and Artists.* Detroit: Broadside Press, 1974.

Behrmann, Christine. Review of *The Green Lion of Zion Street. School Library Journal* 35 (May 1988): 96.

"Black Writers' Views on Literary Lions and Values." *Negro Digest* 17 (January 1968): 25.

Broussard, Mercedese. "Blake's Bard." Review of *A Summoning, A Shining. Callaloo* 1 (December 1976): 60–62.

Burger, Mary Williams. "Julia Fields." In *Dictionary of Literary Biography,* vol. 41, *Afro-American Poets since 1955,* edited by Trudier Harris and Thadious M. Davis, 123–31. Detroit: Gale Research, 1985.

Contemporary Authors. New Revision Series, no. 26. Detroit: Gale Research, 1989.

Cox, Susan, and Lee Galda. "Multicultural Literature: Mirrors and Windows on a Global Community." *Reading Teacher* 43 (1990): 582–89.

Interracial Books for Children Bulletin 19, no. 5 (1989): 11–12.

Jacobs, Gloria. Review of *The Green Lion of Zion Street. New York Times Book Review* 137 (July 17, 1988): 30.

Lee, Don L. *Dynamite Voices: Black Poets of the 1960s.* Detroit: Broadside Press, 1971.

Major, Clarence. *The Dark and Feeling: Black American Writers and Their Work.* New York: The Third Press, 1974.

Randall, Dudley. "Poet Shines in 'Moonlight.' " *Charlotte Observer* (December 16, 1973): D4.

Redmond, Eugene. *Drumvoices. The Mission of Afro-American Poetry: A Critical History.* Garden City, N.Y.: Anchor/Doubleday, 1976.

R. H. W. DILLARD

George Garrett
(1929–   )

Of all the American writers of his generation, none has more thoroughly fulfilled the traditional definition of *man of letters* than George Garrett. The author of seven books of poetry, eight collections of short fiction, and seven novels, he has also written plays, screenplays, an opera libretto, scholarly and critical articles and books, and many essays on a wide variety of literary, political, and personal topics. In addition, he has edited eighteen books, and he has taught and mentored hundreds of younger writers (many of whom are included in this volume). But the main reason that he deserves close and detailed reading and study is not the quantity and range of his writing but rather the coherence and high quality of that work. It is also of considerable importance that, in his Elizabethan trilogy of novels, he has, in the words of Kelly Cherry (1989), "redefined the historical novel," or, as Thomas Flanagan has put it, he "has shaped the historical novel into an unchallengeable model of literary power and energy." His recently being granted the T. S. Eliot Award for Creative Writing by the Ingersoll Foundation and the PEN/Faulkner Bernard Malamud Award for Short Fiction offers evidence that his special contribution to modern American letters is finally beginning to receive the attention it deserves.

BIOGRAPHY

George Palmer Garrett, Jr., was born (in Orlando, Florida, on Tuesday, June 11, 1929) into a Southern family of English, Dutch, French, Welsh, Scottish and Irish descent. In his autobiographical writing, he has referred to the great influence this large and often eccentric family had upon him, particularly his maternal grandfather, Colonel William Morrison Toomer, a lawyer who "made two fortunes and spent three," and his father, George P. Garrett, also a lawyer, but one who successfully battled the Ku Klux Klan, fought the big railroads that were so powerful in Florida, and consistently took the side of the poor, both black and white. The high style and extravagance of the one and the embattled generosity of the other have marked both Garrett's life and his work, especially in his complete commitment to the integrity of his craft and art despite current literary fashion and in his almost equally complete determination to go against the grain of received opinion in matters of literary pecking orders and politics.

There were also in his family writers who influenced him by their example: Harry Stillwell Edwards, who was Colonel Toomer's cousin and author of the prize-winning novel *Sons and Fathers* (1896) and whose novella of the Reconstruction *Eneas Africanus* (1920) is surely one of the most widely read pieces of Southern fiction ever; Garrett's aunt, Helen Garrett, who wrote many popular children's books; and his uncle Oliver H. P. Garrett, a screenwriter and one of the founders of the Screenwriters Guild, among whose films are *Street of Chance* (1930), *Gone With the Wind* (1939), *Duel in the Sun* (1946), *Sealed Cargo* (1947), and *Manhattan Melodrama* (1934) (the gangster movie John Dillinger saw on the night he was killed as he left the movie theatre).

Garrett grew up in Orlando, where he attended public schools through junior high school. He was graduated from the Sewanee Military Academy in 1946 and from the Hill School in 1947. A boxer and football player, Garrett has written compellingly of the great influence sports and his coaches had on his life and his writing in the essay "My Two One-Eyed Coaches" (1987). He went on to Princeton, where he took his B.A. (magna cum laude, Phi Beta Kappa) in 1952. Garrett entered the U.S. Army Active Reserves in 1950 and spent two years on active duty (1953–55) as a sergeant in the Field Artillery in Trieste and Linz, Austria, the scenes of many of his army short stories and his second novel, *Which Ones Are the Enemy?* (1961). After his military service, Garrett returned to Princeton for graduate study, where he took his M.A. in English in 1958 and completed all of the work for his doctorate, with the exception of his proposed dissertation on Sir Walter Ralegh. He finally received his Ph.D. in 1985 when, at the urging of his major professors, Princeton accepted his first two Elizabethan novels, *Death of the Fox* (1971) and *The Succession* (1983), as his dissertation. A lively account of his final public oral examination may be found in his mysterious, hilarious and completely original satirical novel *Poison Pen* (1986).

In 1952 George Garrett and Susan Parrish Jackson were married in Philadelphia; they are the parents of three children—William, George, and Alice—and have one grandchild. They have traveled and lived around the country (and in Rome, when Garrett was a fellow at the American Academy in 1959) as Garrett's academic career has carried him from Wesleyan to Rice, the University of Virginia, Hollins College, the University of South Carolina, Florida International University, Princeton, Columbia, the University of Michigan, Bennington, the University of Charleston, VMI, and back to the University of Virginia, where he is now the Henry Hoyns Professor of Creative Writing. His home for many of these years was in York Harbor, Maine, in an eighteenth-century house by the York River, which his wife inherited and which the Garretts still visit regularly. Along the way, Garrett also worked as a writer for CBS television and as a screenwriter at Goldwyn Studios in Hollywood. He has also worked at more writers conferences and visited more schools and universities as a visiting writer than it is even possible to list—and, probably, even to discover.

Rooted as he undeniably is in his Southern heritage and in the northern Florida of his childhood, Garrett is nevertheless a genuinely cosmopolitan writer. The development and progress of his work has traced a steady movement away from directly personal experience into explorations of the very ground of identity and experience itself, and that growth has doubtless been strongly influenced by Garrett's travels and his peripatetic academic career (although it is difficult to imagine the restless intellect and imagination of George Garrett ever allowing him to become provincial even if he had been a Florida Cracker who never wandered more than ten miles from home).

Garrett's literary career could be said to have begun at Princeton in the spring of 1951 with the publishing by the *Nassau Literary Magazine* of a dozen of his poems, or possibly with his winning of the Kathryn Irene Glascock Intercollegiate Poetry Contest at Mount Holyoke College, also while he was a Princeton undergraduate. Garrett met Marianne Moore at Mount Holyoke, and some years later she chose him to give a reading at the Museum of Modern Art in New York and introduced him at that event as a promising young poet. (Garrett dedicated his first book of poems, *The Reverend Ghost,* to Moore.)

He began to publish poems and stories regularly in 1957, and by 1962 he had published three collections of poems, two collections of stories, two novels, and one play for children. Three of these books—a novel, *Which Ones are the Enemy?;* a collection of poems, *Abraham's Knife;* and a collection of stories, *In the Briar Patch*—were published on the same day in 1961. His poetry gained the strong support of such established literary figures as Marianne Moore, Babette Deutsch, and John Hall Wheelock; and I remember Katherine Anne Porter's telling me in the spring of 1959 that the one young American writer from whose work I could learn the most about the craft and art of fiction was George Garrett.

Garrett fulfilled the promise of his early success with the major novels that followed, although he did not abandon poems and short stories: His *Collected Poems* was published in 1984, and *An Evening Performance: New and Selected Short Stories,* in 1985. His trilogy of Elizabethan historical novels (*Death of the Fox* [1971], *The Succession: A Novel of Elizabeth and James* [1983], *Entered From the Sun* [1990]) mark the pinnacle of his critical and popular success. And yet, for all his productivity and the critical attention he has gained, Garrett's path has never really been an easy one, for he was never taken up by the American literary establishment. As his interest and major work in the unfashionable form of the historical novel evidence, his literary integrity and determination to follow his own interests and intuitions have made him an unpredictable writer—and, therefore, not one who has been easily categorized or placed. ''When I was young and proud and poor and feisty,'' Garrett wrote in 1985, ''and such things seemed to matter, I was vain about my independence, eager to be, if I could, like Mr. Faulkner, *the cat who walks alone. . . .* And so, from time to time, I paid a price for the privilege of my freedom.''

Despite his independence and his eagerness to ''walk alone,'' Garrett has not been an outsider or a loner. He is, on the contrary, known widely as a generous mentor and booster of the careers of not only his many students but large numbers of other writers whom he has met along the way. Writers as varied in manner and style as Richard Bausch, Madison Smartt Bell, Fred Chappell, Alan Cheuse, Brendan Galvin, Alyson Hagy, Cathryn Hankla, Jill McCorkle, James Seay, Mary Lee Settle, David R. Slavitt, Darcey Steinke, Henry Taylor, Richard Tillinghast, and Allen Wier are among the many who have expressed their indebtedness to Garrett for his enthusiastic support over the years. He was one of the founding editors of the revival of the *Transatlantic Review,* a literary magazine known for its openness to new and innovative writers; and a number of the eighteen books Garrett has edited have been anthologies dedicated in great part to the task of introducing younger and lesser known writers to a wider audience: especially *New Writing From Virginia* (1963), *The Girl in the Black Raincoat* (1966), the four volumes (1974–78) of the Associated Writing Programs' *Intro* series that he edited, and *''Eric Clapton's Lover''* (1990). No biography of Garrett will ever be able to ignore the positive impact his support of other writers has had on the American literature of his time.

George and Susan Garrett live today in Charlottesville, Virginia, where Garrett is working on an eighth novel and a number of other projects.

MAJOR THEMES

A close examination of the poems, stories, novels, plays, and essays that George Garrett has produced over the last 40 years reveals that, for all the variety of manner and matter, his writings form a remarkably coherent body of work. Whether Garrett is writing a poem about his habit of having his shoe soles repaired one at a time (''Luck's Shining Child,'' in *The Collected Poems of George Garrett* [1984]), a story about an archetypal army sergeant (''The Old Army Game,'' in *An Evening Performance: New and Selected Stories* [1985]), a comic screenplay about death (*The Playground,* [1965]), or a novel about the aftershocks following the violent death of Christopher Marlowe (*Entered from the Sun* [1990]), the work is the product of a stable and consistent vision that has remained constant even as his technical resources have increased and his testing of the limits of literary form has grown increasingly more radical.

The stability of his vision comes in great part from Garrett's suspicion—and even rejection—of the modern idea of progress, especially the idea of social and moral progress as it has developed from the time of the French Encyclopedists through the nineteenth-century historicists and into our own time. His researches into Elizabethan history have led him to believe that our idea of progress in human history is in many ways just a myth, that for all our modern advances in, for example, navigation or medicine, we have also lost vast amounts of sailing and medical knowledge that were known to the Elizabethans. In his repeated comments about the great contrast between the bland faces of our modern political leaders and the faces in Brady's photographs, or in a poem like "Main Currents of American Political Thought" in *The Collected Poems of George Garrett,* or the satirical novel *Poison Pen* (1986), he has shown himself to believe that an actual devolution in human character has been occurring over the last century.

As a fully committed Christian and artist, he has held to a view of history and of life in which substantial change can only occur suddenly and radically by supernatural intervention or by an equally radical act of the human imagination. Meaning, to Garrett, is not inherent in particular experience, but neither does it accrue progressively with the linear accumulation of experience in time. It is rather the fluid product of a vital intercourse across time of past, present, and future experience, each giving meaning to and drawing meaning from the other in a transformative, nonlinear exchange. To a Christian, the presence of Christ in the world draws its meaning from the rich historical, poetic, and prophetic text of the Old Testament; but, at the same time, the meaning of that text is radically deconstructed by the presence of Christ. Garrett's structurally complex novel *The Succession* (1983) is his most direct exploration of the creation of meaning in human experience; but all of his work constitutes a much larger exploration of those moments when meaning explodes into the world, either from beyond ordinary human experience in what might be called "angelic visitations"—as in the stories "An Evening Experience" and "The Victim" in *An Evening Performance,* the poems "Caedmon" and "Angels" in *The Collected Poems of George Garrett,* and the novel *Do, Lord, Remember Me* (1965)—or directly from ordinary experience in those intensely imaginative moments when moral struggles are resolved by almost blinding bursts of insight.

"Garrett's favorite story," according to one of his most perceptive critics, W. R. Robinson (1965, 16), "is an account of moral change, a fall from innocence into knowledge, begotten by a violence without evoking a violence within, of involvement in a power struggle from which there is no intellectual or moral escape." In his early fiction, the work prior to *Do, Lord, Remember Me,* this story is most often initiatory, an account of a coming of age, or of the rupturing of the comfortable illusion of a sheltered life by hard experience. But at the same time, Garrett began to examine moments of moral change in the enigmatic and difficult relations between men and women in a group of sensitive stories, often told from the woman's point of view, which have disappointingly been overlooked even by the most serious of feminist critics.

Although the novel *The Finished Man* (1959) tells the story of a young man's downward path to wisdom in the context of a Florida senatorial campaign, it was not until the novella "Cold Ground Was My Bed Last Night" (later retitled

"Noise of Strangers" in *An Evening Performance*) and *Do, Lord, Remember Me* that Garrett effectively broadened the scope of his "favorite story" to include not only individuals in the grip of moral change but also the conglomerate experiential field of entire communities. This expansion of his moral vision opened the way to his Elizabethan trilogy, in which the complexity of an entire society in another place and time becomes the center and subject of the fictional construct. And, too, it allowed Garrett to point out the moral failings of his own time in the group of satirical poems and stories that culminate in the novel *Poison Pen*.

In Garrett's poetry and his fiction as in the work of one of his literary heroes, Henry Fielding, scorn and even cruel satire have been directed only at those characters (or actual public figures) who have been inflated by vanity, hypocrisy, and self-regard into grotesques, whereas the characters who have engaged Garrett's fullest sympathy are those capable of moral change, the ones who have tried to learn the hard, deep lessons of survival. The latter are inherently flawed dwellers in a fallen world, sinner-saints who are capable at any moment of a conscious act of good or evil. As Monroe K. Spears (1985) has pointed out, insofar as *The Succession* has a hero, "the hero has to be James, the villain of [*Death of the*] *Fox*''; and the Sir Walter Ralegh who appears in *Entered From the Sun* as a very dangerous man whose hands may have been soiled with the blood of Christopher Marlowe is the same Ralegh whose thoughts and behavior during his last days in *Death of the Fox* have such positive moral force. All of Garrett's characters are children—and prisoners—of fortune, but his heroic characters are those who in the face of their predicament are capable of making difficult moral decisions. And yet their author's sympathy (to call it "charity" would not be wrong) has not failed his characters who struggle with, but fail to make, the moral choice. Although the title character of his poem "Salome" in *The Collected Poems of George Garrett,* certainly failed at the moment of her most severe testing, Garrett has nevertheless allowed her to speak pointedly to her own and to the human condition. The poem concludes in this way:

> A bad marriage from the beginning,
> you say, a complete mismatch.
> Flesh and spirit wrestle
> and we call it love.
>
> We couple like dogs in heat.
> We shudder and are sundered.
> We pursue ourselves,
> sniffing, nose to tail
> a comic parade of appetites.
>
> Do me a little justice.
> I had a dream of purity
> And I have lived in the desert ever since. (7)

SURVEY OF CRITICISM

George Garrett's early poetry and fiction were very well received by reviewers in both the mass media and in literary journals. The simultaneous publication in 1961 of *Abraham's Knife, In the Briar Patch,* and *Which Ones Are the Enemy?* was given a two-page spread in *Newsweek.* His third novel, *Do, Lord, Remember Me,* fared less well and was often misrepresented as a latter-day version of *Elmer Gantry.* The popular and critical success of *Death of the Fox* restored Garrett to critical good graces, where he has remained for the most part ever since. But, of course, few of these reviews offer much in the way of serious critical insight into his work.

Garrett is consistently mentioned in surveys of contemporary American fiction as an important writer, although he is mentioned less consistently in similar surveys of contemporary poetry, quite possibly because, in an era of specialization, he has become catalogued in the academic mind as a fiction writer. There have been a number of serious critical considerations of his work, however, which are certainly valuable and even central to further examinations of the body of that work.

There have been two books on Garrett's work: my monograph, *Understanding George Garrett* (1988) and a *Festschrift* titled *To Come Up Grinning: A Tribute to George Garrett* (1989), edited by Paul Ruffin and Stuart Wright and presented to Garrett on the occasion of his sixtieth birthday. Although it is somewhat difficult to come by, a special issue of the *Mill Mountain Review,* edited by Irv Broughton with my assistance in 1971, contains a number of important pieces about Garrett and his work.

I am certainly no fair judge of the quality of *Understanding George Garrett,* a volume in the "Understanding Contemporary Literature Series" edited by Matthew J. Bruccoli. In the book, I have focused primarily on Garrett's novels, although I have attempted to demonstrate by analyses of short stories and poems as well as the novels that his work is consistent in its vision and has "genuine coherence and stability." It was my hope in writing the book that it would not only introduce new readers to Garrett's work, but would also stimulate further critical study and assessment of that work.

The bulk of the other serious critical work on George Garrett concerns the fiction. The earliest to examine the fiction as a whole and still among the best of the essays on the novels are W. R. Robinson's "The Fiction of George Garrett" (1965) and "Imagining the Individual: George Garrett's *Death of the Fox*" (1971). In the earlier essay, which dealt with short stories as well as novels, Robinson isolated what he identified as Garrett's "favorite story" and examined the body of his fiction in that light. Grounded theoretically in the radical empiricism of William James, Robinson found the work to be a series of explorations of change through the lives of individuals who are simultaneously free and responsible, empowered but moral. In the later essay, Robinson focused on *Death of the Fox* and its relationship to the other novels, concluding that they are all celebrations of the imagination that acts to incarnate what it values.

The most important essay on the novels since Robinson's is Monroe K. Spears's "George Garrett and the Historical Novel," which first appeared in 1985. In the essay, Spears assesses *Death of the Fox* and *The Succession* as products of historical research and as novels, finding them to be "historical in every sense compatible with remaining novels." He considers the complex nature of Garrett's "imaginary past" and examines the place of these novels in the tradition of the historical novel, concluding that they are so remarkable that "they may be considered either fulfillments of the genre or repudiations of it" (262).

Among the many other essays on Garrett's historical novels, Tom Whalen's stands out as particularly important because of his study of Garrett's formal innovations. In "The Reader Becomes Text: Methods of Experimentation in George Garrett's *The Succession: A Novel of Elizabeth and James*" (1983), Whalen views that novel as a mannerist work which uses a full range of experimental techniques to make the past palpable to its readers. In "Eavesdropping in the Dark: The Opening(s) of George Garrett's *Entered from the Sun*" (1989) Whalen continues his study of Garrett's experimental techniques and has begun a fruitful examination of the relationships between the three novels in the trilogy. This essay is also of interest because it was based on a manuscript of the novel and reveals some differences between that earlier version and the published text. Kelly Cherry's "Meaning and Music in George Garrett's Fiction" (1989) is also important as the first real study of the way in which Garrett's distinctive syntax and prose rhythms are integral to the meaning of his work.

Another significant essay on Garrett's novels is "Madison Smartt Bell on George Garrett's *Do, Lord, Remember Me*" (1988), in which Bell argues that the "inheritance of religious tradition still does its work, albeit unconsciously, in the wilful darkness of the blind and shattered self" (28).

Garrett's short stories, perhaps because of their range and variety, have not received the close study that his novels have, but a student of Garrett should not overlook Fred Chappell's "The Lion Tamer: George Garrett's Short Stories" (1971), which is especially interesting for its comments on Garrett's use of formal parable; William Peden's "The Short Fiction of George Garrett" (1978), a study of the experimental and innovative techniques in the stories; David Madden's "Continually Astonished by Everything: The Army Stories of George Garrett" (1989), which uses Garrett's *Contemporary Authors* autobiographical essay as a mode of ingress to the content and "different aesthetic means" of the army stories; and David R. Slavitt's "The Huge Footprint: The Short Stories of George Garrett" (1989), which uses Garrett's poems as an approach to the method of his fiction.

Garrett's poetry is the least discussed body of his work. John Hall Wheelock's introduction to Garrett's first book, *The Reverend Ghost* (1957), is still interesting for its description of the strangely musical but almost tormented approaches to the essence of things in the early poems; but the fullest study of the poetry so far is Henry Taylor's "The Brutal Rush of Grace: George Garrett's Poetry'' (1989), an overview of the work that emphasizes Garrett's willingness to go against the grain and in which Taylor argues that Garrett's "poetry is among the treasures of contemporary literature" (73).

No critical examination has yet been made of George Garrett's plays or screenplays, the novels are far from exhausted, and the ground has just begun to be broken on his short fiction and poetry. Certainly it is too fertile a ground to lie fallow much longer, and I predict that the rising critical interest in his work will soon bring forth a rich harvest of thorough critical studies.

BIBLIOGRAPHY

Works by George Garrett

The Reverend Ghost. In *Poets of Today IV,* edited by John Hall Wheelock, pp. 21–72. New York: Scribner's, 1957.

King of the Mountain. New York: Scribner's, 1958; London: Eyre and Spottiswoode, 1959.

The Sleeping Gypsy and Other Poems. Austin: University of Texas Press, 1958.

The Finished Man. New York: Scribner's, 1959; London: Eyre and Spottiswoode, 1960.

Abraham's Knife and Other Poems. Chapel Hill: University of North Carolina Press, 1961.

In the Briar Patch. Austin: University of Texas Press, 1961.

Which Ones Are the Enemy? Boston: Little, Brown, 1961; London: Allen, 1962.

Sir Slob and the Princess: A Play for Children. New York: French, 1962.

Cold Ground Was My Bed Last Night. Columbia: University of Missouri Press, 1964.

Do, Lord, Remember Me. London: Chapman and Hall, 1965; Garden City, N.Y.: Doubleday, 1965.

For a Bitter Season: New and Selected Poems. Columbia: University of Missouri Press, 1967.

A Wreath for Garibaldi and Other Stories. London: Hart-Davis, 1969.

Death of the Fox. Garden City, N.Y.: Doubleday, 1971; London: Barrie and Jenkins, 1972.

The Magic Striptease. Garden City, N.Y.: Doubleday, 1973.

Welcome to the Medicine Show: Flashcards/Postcards/Snapshots. Winston-Salem, N.C.: Palaemon Press, 1978.

To Recollect a Cloud of Ghosts: Christmas in England 1602–1603. Winston-Salem, N.C.: Palaemon Press, 1980.

Enchanted Ground: A Play for Readers' Theater. York, Maine: Old Gaol Museum Press, 1981.

Luck's Shining Child: A Miscellany of Poems and Verses. Winston-Salem, N.C.: Palaemon Press, 1981.

The Succession: A Novel of Elizabeth and James. Garden City, N.Y.: Doubleday, 1983.

The Collected Poems of George Garrett. Fayetteville: University of Arkansas Press, 1984.

James Jones. New York: Harcourt Brace Jovanovich, 1984.

An Evening Performance: New and Selected Short Stories. Garden City, N.Y.: Doubleday, 1985.

Poison Pen; or, Live Now and Pay Later. Winston-Salem, N.C.: Wright, 1986.

Understanding Mary Lee Settle. Columbia: University of South Carolina Press, 1988.

Entered from the Sun. Garden City, N.Y.: Doubleday, 1990.

The Sorrows of Fat City: A Selection of Literary Essays and Reviews. Columbia: University of South Carolina Press, 1992.

Whistling in the Dark: True Stories and Other Fables. New York: Harcourt Brace Jovanovich, 1992.

Produced Screenplays by George Garrett

Frankenstein Meets the Space Monster. Original screenplay by Garrett, R. H. W. Dillard,
and John Rodenbeck. A Vernon production, directed by Robert Gaffney. Allied
Artists, 1965.

The Playground. Screenplay based on *My Brother, Death,* by Cyrus Sulzberger. Produced
and directed by Richard Hilliard. Jerand, 1965.

The Young Lovers. Screenplay based on the novel by Julian Halevy. Produced and directed by Samuel Goldwyn, Jr. MGM, 1965.

Books Edited by George Garrett

New Writing From Virginia. Charlottesville, Va.: New Writing Associates, 1963.

The Girl in the Black Raincoat: Variations on a Theme. New York: Duell, Sloan, and
Pearce, 1966.

Man and the Movies. Edited by W. R. Robinson, with assistance by George Garrett.
Baton Rouge: Louisiana State University Press, 1967.

Film Scripts One. Edited with Jane Gelfman and O.B. Hardison, Jr. New York: Appleton-
Century-Crofts, 1971.

Film Scripts Two. Edited with Jane Gelfman and O. B. Hardison, Jr. New York: Apple-
ton-Century-Crofts, 1971.

New Writing in South Carolina. Edited with William Peden. Columbia: University of
South Carolina Press, 1971.

The Sounder Few: Essays From the Hollins Critic. Edited with R. H. W. Dillard and
John Rees Moore. Athens: University of Georgia Press, 1971.

*Craft So Hard to Learn: Conversations With Poets and Novelists About the Teaching of
Writing.* Edited with John Graham. New York: Morrow, 1972.

Film Scripts Three. Edited with Jane Gelfman and O. B. Hardison, Jr. New York: Ap-
pleton-Century-Crofts, 1972.

Film Scripts Four. Edited with Jane Gelfman and O. B. Hardison, Jr. New York: Ap-
pleton-Century-Crofts, 1972.

The Writer's Voice: Conversations with Contemporary Writers. Edited with John Graham. New York: Morrow, 1973.

Botteghe Oscure Reader. Middletown, Conn.: Wesleyan University Press, 1974.

Intro 6: Life As We Know It. Garden City, N.Y.: Anchor/Doubleday, 1974.

Intro 7: All of Us and None of You. Garden City, N.Y.: Anchor/Doubleday, 1975.

Intro 8: The Liar's Craft. Garden City, N.Y.: Anchor/Doubleday, 1977.
Intro 9: Close to Home. Edited with Michael Mewshaw. Austin, Texas: Hendel and
    Reinke, 1978.
Festival 88. Charlottesville, Va.: Virginia Festival of Film, 1988.
"Eric Clapton's Lover" and Other Stories from the Virginia Quarterly Review. Edited
    with Sheila McMillen. Charlottesville, Va: University Press of Virginia, 1990.
Contemporary Southern Short Fiction: A Sampler. Edited with Paul Ruffin. Huntsville,
    Texas: The Texas Review, 1991.
The Wedding Cake in the Middle of the Road: 23 Variations on a Theme. Edited with
    Susan Stamberg. New York: Norton, 1992.
Elvis in Oz: New Stories and Poems from the Hollins Creative Writing Program. Edited
    with Mary Flinn. Charlottesville: University Press of Virginia, 1992.

Autobiographical Essays by George Garrett

"George Palmer Garrett, Jr." In *Contemporary Authors Autobiography Series,* vol. 5,
    edited by Adele Sarkissian, 71–90. Detroit: Gale Research, 1987.
"My Two One-Eyed Coaches." In *An Apple for My Teacher: Twelve Authors Tell about
    Teachers Who Made the Difference,* edited by Louis D. Rubin, Jr., 77–114.
    Chapel Hill, N.C.: Algonquin Books, 1987.
"Uncles and Others." *The Missouri Review* 13 (1990): 28–44.

Interviews with George Garrett

Broughton, Irv. "George Garrett." In *The Writer's Mind: Interviews with American
    Authors,* vol. 2, edited by Irv Broughton, 275–308. Fayetteville: University of
    Arkansas Press, 1990.
Carr, John. "Kite-Flying and Other Irrational Acts: George Garrett." In *Kite-Flying and
    Other Irrational Acts: Conversations with Twelve Southern Writers,* edited by
    John Carr, 174–98. Baton Rouge: Louisiana State University Press, 1972.
Graham, John. "Fiction and Film: An Interview with George Garrett." *Film Journal* 1
    (1971): 22–25.
Graham, John, and W. R. Robinson. "George Garrett Discusses Writing and His Work."
    Mill Mountain Review 1 (1971): 79–102.
Huber, J. Argus. "The Balanced Shelf: Understanding Beyond George Garrett." *Albany
    Review* 2 (August 1988): 44–47.
"An Interview with George Garrett." In *Dictionary of Literary Biography Yearbook,
    1983,* edited by Mary Bruccoli and Jean W. Ross, 157–61. Detroit: Gale Research,
    1984.
Israel, Charles. "Interview: George Garrett." *South Carolina Review* 4 (1973): 43–48.
Wier, Allen. "An Interview with George Garrett." *Penny Dreadful* 4 (1975): 13–18.
———. "George Garrett." *Transatlantic Review* Nos. 58/59 (1977): 58–61.

Studies of George Garrett

Bausch, Robert. "George Garrett's Military/Army Fiction." In *To Come Up Grinning:
    A Tribute to George Garrett,* edited by Paul Ruffin and Stuart Wright, 8–11.
    Huntsville, Tex.: Texas Review Press, 1989.

Bell, Madison Smartt. "Madison Smartt Bell on George Garrett's *Do, Lord, Remember Me.*" In *Rediscoveries II: Important Writers Select Their Favorite Works of Neglected Fiction,* edited by David Madden and Peggy Bach, 23–29. New York: Carroll and Graf, 1988.

———. "George Garrett: In the South and Out of It." In *To Come Up Grinning: A Tribute to George Garrett,* edited by Paul Ruffin and Stuart Wright, 12–15. Huntsville, Texas: Texas Review Press, 1989.

Carr, John. "In Contention With Time: George Garrett's *Death of the Fox.*" *Mill Mountain Review* 1 (1971): 19–26.

Chappell, Fred. "The Lion-Tamer: George Garrett's Short Stories." *Mill Mountain Review* 1 (1971): 42–46.

Cherry, Kelly. "Meaning and Music in George Garrett's Fiction." In *To Come Up Grinning: A Tribute to George Garrett,* edited by Paul Ruffin and Stuart Wright, 16–20. Huntsville, Tex.: Texas Review Press, 1989.

Davis, Paxton. "Breadth, Depth, and Elevation: George Garrett's *Death of the Fox.*" *Mill Mountain Review* 1 (1971): 12–13.

Dillard, R. H. W. *Understanding George Garrett.* Columbia: University of South Carolina Press, 1988.

Fleming, Thomas. "Free Adaptations." *National Review* 38 (November 7, 1986): 52–54.

———. "Realms of Lead." In *To Come Up Grinning: A Tribute to George Garrett,* edited by Paul Ruffin and Stuart Wright, 21–30. Huntsville, Tex.: Texas Review Press, 1989.

Galvin, Brendan. "Class Inside and Out: The Testimony of George Garrett's Students." In *To Come Up Grinning: A Tribute to George Garrett,* edited by Paul Ruffin and Stuart Wright, 31–46. Huntsville, Tex.: Texas Review Press, 1989.

Israel, Charles. "George Garrett." In *American Poets Since World War II,* vol. 5 of *Dictionary of Literary Biography,* edited by Donald J. Greiner, 264–69. Detroit: Bruccoli Clark/Gale Research, 1980.

McCullough, Frank. "George Garrett's Ralegh." *Mill Mountain Review* 1 (1971): 15–18.

Madden, David. "Continually Astonished by Everything: The Army Stories of George Garrett." In *To Come Up Grinning: A Tribute to George Garrett,* edited by Paul Ruffin and Stuart Wright, 47–54. Huntsville, Tex.: Texas Review Press, 1989.

Moore, Richard. "The Poetry of George Garrett." *Mill Mountain Review* 1 (1971): 47–50.

Peden, William. "The Short Fiction of George Garrett." *Ploughshares* 4 (1978): 83–90.

Rhodes, Jack Wright. "George Garrett." In *American Novelists Since World War II,* vol. 2 of *Dictionary of Literary Biography,* edited by Jeffrey Helterman and Richard Layman, 185–90. Detroit: Bruccoli Clark/Gale Research, 1978.

Robinson, W. R. "The Fiction of George Garrett." *Red Clay Reader* 2 (1965): 15–16. Reprinted in *Mill Mountain Review* 1 (1971): 39–41.

———. "Imagining the Individual: George Garrett's *Death of the Fox.*" *Hollins Critic* 8 (1971): 1–12.

Ruffin, Paul and Stuart Wright, eds. *To Come Up Grinning: A Tribute to George Garrett.* Huntsville, Tex.: Texas Review Press, 1989.

Slavitt, David R. "History—Fate and Freedom: A Look at George Garrett's New Novel." *Southern Review* 7 (1971): 276–94.

————. "George Garrett, Professional." *Michigan Quarterly Review* (1986): 218–25.

————. "The Huge Footprint: The Short Stories of George Garrett." In *To Come Up Grinning: A Tribute to George Garrett,* edited by Paul Ruffin and Stuart Wright, 55–60. Huntsville, Tex.: Texas Review Press, 1989.

Spears, Monroe K. "George Garrett and the Historical Novel." *Virginia Quarterly Review* 61 (1985): 262–76. Reprinted in *American Ambitions: Selected Essays on Literary and Cultural Things.* Baltimore: Johns Hopkins University Press, 1987, and in *To Come Up Grinning: A Tribute to George Garrett,* edited by Paul Ruffin and Stuart Wright, 61–72. Huntsville, Tex.: Texas Review Press, 1989.

Taylor, Henry. "The Poetry of George Garrett." *Latitudes* 2 (1968): 30–31.

————. "The Brutal Rush of Grace: George Garrett's Poetry." In *To Come Up Grinning: A Tribute to George Garrett,* ed. Paul Ruffin and Stuart Wright, 73–89. Huntsville, Tex.: Texas Review Press, 1989.

Whalen, Tom. "The Reader Becomes Text: Methods of Experimentation in George Garrett's *The Succession: A Novel of Elizabeth and James.*" *Texas Review* 4 (1983): 14–21.

————. "Eavesdropping in the Dark: The Opening(s) of George Garrett's *Entered From the Sun.*" In *To Come Up Grinning: A Tribute to George Garrett,* edited by Paul Ruffin and Stuart Wright, 90–99. Huntsville, Tex.: Texas Review Press, 1989.

Wheelock, John Hall. "Introductory Essay: To Recapture Delight." In *Poets of Today IV.* 3–17. New York: Scribner's 1957.

PATSY B. PERRY

Nikki Giovanni
(1943–   )

Author of thirteen books of poems and essays, recorder of her times in two dialogues (with James Baldwin and with Margaret Walker), and editor of an anthology of poems by black women, Nikki Giovanni represents a respectable library of ideas. Her achievement lies, however, not just in her creative and literary success but also in her powerful demonstration that poetry has universal appeal—that everyone can enter, if only for a moment, the poet's world and be soothed, entertained, inspired, challenged, enraged, or otherwise moved by language. In the tradition of the African griot and the medieval poet-singer, Giovanni brings poetry to the people. Generally acclaimed as the most widely read living black American poet, Giovanni rose to fame during the civil rights movement, and has maintained an enthusiastic following through her published poetry, poetry readings, and recordings.

True to her contradictory nature, Giovanni is warm, sensitive, quick to smile, and thoroughly charming; but she is also uncompromising and fiercely courageous in her social and political activism. Having come of age during the turbulent 1960s, she is a freedom fighter who has used her poems to advocate revolutionary change and, since the early 1970s, to express personal and universal truths. She accepts her role as the messenger; in fact, the title essay of her latest work, *Sacred Cows . . . and Other Edibles* (1988), begins: ''Well, OK, it seems to always fall on me to tell the truth'' (123). Giovanni's significant truths place her among those writers important to modern American poetry and its subgenres, including black poetry, feminist poetry, and Southern poetry.

BIOGRAPHY

Yolande Cornelia Giovanni, Jr., the younger of two daughters of Jones ''Gus'' and Yolande Cornelia (Watson) Giovanni, was born in Knoxville, Tennessee, on June 7, 1943. According to her own account, she enjoyed "groovy" childhood years with her sister Gary, her parents, maternal grandmother, aunts, and cousins. These loving relatives provided a secure middle-class environment in which Giovanni's naturally independent spirit found expression.

When Giovanni was still quite young, the family moved to Wyoming, Ohio, a suburb of Cincinnati, and later to the black community Lincoln Heights. Both her parents worked in Cincinnati, Yolande as a Department of Welfare supervisor and Jones as a social worker. Giovanni attended public and parochial schools in Cincinnati. As a kindergartner, she easily won rock-throwing, braid-pulling contests against Gary's opponents and earned a reputation as her elder sister's fierce protector. Indeed, a key to understanding Giovanni's nature is the vivid description she gives of herself at age four, in her autobiography *Gemini* (1971), hurling rocks from her porch and successfully keeping the neighborhood bullies at bay (13). She has extended the love and responsibility she then felt for her sister to other family members, to her race, and eventually to those outside her race. Although her weapons changed from rocks to militant race poems to love poems, her goal remained constant—protection of those worth saving. As Giovanni explains in *Gemini,* fighting was "in [her] blood" (29). Her grandmother Louvenia Terrell Watson—who was militant, outspoken, and intolerant, especially of white people—and her grandfather John Brown "Book" Watson were whisked out of Albany, Georgia, one night for fear of Louvenia's being lynched. Giovanni deeply loved and was profoundly influenced by her grandmother, with whom she lived while completing her tenth and eleventh grades in high school.

In September 1960 Giovanni arrived as an early entrant at Fisk University, John Brown "Book" Watson's alma mater. By Thanksgiving, however, she had already decided that she "could not . . . adjust to the Fisk social life" and, without permission from the dean of women, left school for her grandmother's home in Knoxville. Upon her return following the holiday, Giovanni was duly informed of her probationary status at Fisk; nonetheless, by February 1, she was "released" because her "attitudes did not fit those of a Fisk woman" (7, 8). In 1964 she returned to school, enrolled in the Fisk Writers Workshop directed by acclaimed novelist John Oliver Killens, and contributed to the literary journal *Élan.* She established a solid academic record, and in February 1967 graduated magna cum laude with a B.A. in history.

During the 1960s, coincident with Giovanni's intellectual, emotional, and spiritual awakening, there was violent upheaval throughout America as black people engaged in a mass movement toward the long-deferred dream of justice under the law. The civil rights movement, ignited by Rosa Parks and led by Martin Luther King, Jr., produced voter registration campaigns, sit-ins, freedom rides, and marches to state capitals and to the nation's capital. Although these demonstrations involved many white participants and sympathizers, there were numerous other whites supported by local governments committed to maintaining racial inequality. The inevitable confrontations, despite King's passive-resistance philosophy, often ended in mass arrests, property destruction, and death. In this environment, surely Louvenia Watson's legacy would become real in her granddaughter's life. Giovanni shifted from her position of a Barry Goldwater/Ayn Rand Conservative to that of a black-power revolutionary, adopted the Afro hairstyle, and joined demonstrations and conferences dedicated to nation building. In 1964 she was the leading force in reorganizing the Fisk Chapter of the Student Nonviolent Coordinating Committee. Always self-determined, however, she maintained her independence of spirit even as she valued the movement for its liberating effects.

Following graduation from Fisk, Giovanni returned to Cincinnati where she continued working for black liberation. In June 1967 she organized the first Cincinnati Black Arts Festival, helping to give a heightened sense of pride to the black community and providing the nucleus from which the New Theatre emerged. Speaking, organizing, encouraging youth, she was a catalyst for change. Her mother felt, Giovanni says in *Gemini,* that too little positive change was occurring for Giovanni and insisted that she "get a job or . . . go to school" (38). Resisting, but finally bowing to commonsense arguments from both of her parents, Giovanni enrolled in 1967 at the University of Pennsylvania School of Social Work on a Ford Foundation grant. She did not complete the program, however. In 1968 she studied at the School of Fine Arts at Columbia University on a National Foundation for the Arts grant and taught at Queens College of the City University of New York and at Livingston College of Rutgers University. Again, she completed neither the master's degree nor the novel she had proposed as her thesis.

During 1967 and 1968, creative energies, in evidence since her early childhood, now spilled over into poems that captured the tumultuous times. Giovanni wrote about the black revolution, its leaders, her place in the revolution, her dreams, and many other subjects in an auspicious publishing debut: *Black Feeling, Black Talk* (1968) and *Black Judgement* (1969). By the time these titles were combined and issued as *Black Feeling, Black Talk/Black Judgement* (1970), Giovanni had attracted a large audience of readers and listeners who considered her chief among the "new" school of revolutionary black poets.

Mercurial and action driven, Giovanni made important decisions affecting both her personal life and creative activities during 1969, 1970, and 1971. She decided that she wanted a child, knew that she could afford to have one, and so became a mother in August 1969. Thomas Watson Giovanni, born in Cincinnati during Giovanni's visit home for Labor Day, has deepened her sense of family pride and unity; nevertheless, she has remained unmarried, observing in an essay entitled "An Answer to Some Questions on How I Write," in *Black Women Writers,* that "traditional married life is for traditional people" (Evans 1984, 209). In 1970 Giovanni established NikTom, Limited, a publishing cooperative; participated in collecting and editing poems for *Night Comes Softly: An Anthology of Black Female Voices;* and issued her third book of poetry, *Re: Creation.* Between 1969 and 1971, she traveled in Haiti and Barbados with son

Tommy, and in 1971 she published *Gemini: An Extended Autobiographical Statement on My First Twenty-Five Years of Being a Black Poet,* dedicating it, in part, to her son and to his father, whose name she declines to reveal. In 1971 she also dedicated to Tommy her first collection for young readers, *Spin a Soft Black Song: Poems for Children.* In both her children's book and in *Gemini,* Giovanni explores attitudes and reforms needed to effect a moral revolution. Still angry but subdued, Giovanni explains in *Gemini,* ''Nobody's trying to make the system Black; we're trying to make a system that's human so Black folk can live in it'' (50). In *Spin a Soft Black Song,* Giovanni continues this focus on positive human values, connecting dreams for her own child with dreams for children everywhere. Her softening attitudes, certainly influenced by motherhood, travel, maturity, and reflection, are clear in these 1971 volumes, both of which received mixed critical reviews.

Even so, Giovanni has been wholeheartedly embraced as a poet of the people. She enjoys celebrity status as the ''Princess of Black Poetry'' and continues to be in great demand for poetry readings and lectures in numerous cities, on college campuses, on television, and in prisons. In 1971 she attracted an audience of even greater diversity with *Truth Is on Its Way,* a recording on which she reads her poetry against a background of gospel music sung by the New York Community Choir. Played repeatedly on radio stations around the country, *Truth* became a top-selling album. Giovanni later recorded *Like a Ripple on a Pond* (1973), *The Way I Feel* (1975), *Legacies* (1976), and *The Reason I Like Chocolate* (1976).

For her excellent performances, both recorded and live, Giovanni has received numerous awards, including the *Mademoiselle* Magazine Award for Outstanding Achievement (1971); a plaque for Meritorious Service from the Cook County Jail (1971); the Omega Psi Phi Fraternity Award for Outstanding Contributions to Arts and Letters (1971); a Life Membership and Scroll from the National Council of Negro Women (1972); the *Ladies Home Journal* Woman of the Year—Youth Leadership Award (1972), keys to the cities of Dallas (Texas), Gary (Indiana), and Lincoln Heights (Ohio) (1972); and the National Association of Television and Radio Announcers Award (N.A.T.R.A.), Best Spoken Word Album for *Truth Is On Its Way* (1972).

Another media event, a PBS program featuring James Baldwin and Giovanni, occurred on December 15 and 22, 1971. These conversations between writers of different generations, both of whom were actively involved in the civil-rights movement, created such widespread interest that Baldwin and Giovanni revised and edited the transcribed tape, publishing it in 1972 under the title *A Dialogue: James Baldwin and Nikki Giovanni.* Following the positive reception of this book and the successful joint appearance in October 1972 of Giovanni and Margaret Walker on the Paul Laurence Dunbar Centennial Program, a participant in the program suggested that Giovanni and Walker record a dialogue. The result was *A Poetic Equation: Conversations Between Nikki Giovanni and Margaret Walker* (1974), in which Giovanni and Walker present vastly different views on child rearing, racial conflict, violence, Vietnam, black writers, black music, and many other topics. Although they agree on some issues, it remains clear throughout that these are views of two excellent minds shaped by different periods in American history.

In 1972 Giovanni published *My House,* her fourth volume of poetry in which she emphasizes love, home, and family, and in her poem "We" characterizes political activity as generally futile, specifically describing the revolution as "screeeeeeeeeeching / to a halt." Although her shift from political to personal themes disappointed some readers and critics such as Kalamu Ya Salaam (Val Ferdinand) who "moved into Blackness aided by Nikki's poems" (64), her new focus helped to maintain and solidify her growing popularity. Already a favorite among general readers, she was initiated into membership in the academy between 1972 and 1975 when five educational institutions awarded her honorary doctorates—Wilberforce University (1972); Worcester University (1972); The University of Maryland, Princess Anne Campus, (1974); Ripon University (1974); and Smith College (1975).

In 1973 Giovanni collected and published a second volume of poems especially for adolescents, *Ego-Tripping and Other Poems for Young People.* Though most of the selections had been published previously, *Ego-Tripping* proved to be very popular, attracting a new generation of readers. In 1980 she appealed to preadolescents with such titles as "Paula the Cat" and "Tommy's Mommy" in *Vacation Time: Poems for Children.* Between the publication of these volumes for young readers, Giovanni produced two collections for adults, *The Women and the Men* (1975) and *Cotton Candy on a Rainy Day* (1978). She dedicated *Cotton Candy* to her father, who suffered a serious stroke in 1978, the same year in which the book was published. During this family crisis, although she maintained an apartment in New York City, she and Tommy moved back home to Lincoln Heights, Ohio. There she renovated the basement of her parents' house, creating her own territory so as "to feel at home in order to write" (Tate 1983, 75). Her dramatic changes in subject and technique between 1978 and 1983 were likely influenced by the changes in her family relationships and physical environment.

As Giovanni has broadened her vision to embrace the individual in modern society, especially the "leader," she has reinforced her commitment to freedom in moving both as a single spirit and as a member of a group. She dedicates *Those Who Ride the Night Winds* (1983) to the risk takers who "are determined to push us into the next century, galaxy—possibility" (5). The subjects of poems in this volume—Lorraine Hansberry, John Lennon, cancers, wildflowers, Giovanni herself—transcend race, gender, and specific time and place. Similarly, Giovanni's most recent volume, *Sacred Cows ... and Other Edibles* (1988), takes an eclectic approach in deflating modern hypocrises, including some disappointing developments in the black community.

The production of *Sacred Cows* is a milestone, marking the twentieth anniversary of the publication of Giovanni's first book. It is worth noting, too, that

Giovanni was one of the first poets of the 1960s to be published by major commercial firms. William Morrow has issued seven of her sixteen volumes; Bobbs-Merrill, Hill and Wang, and Lippincott are other large publishers responsible for her titles.

Giovanni's appeal to both general and academic audiences has continued to bring her recognition in the 1980s. She was named to the Ohio Woman's Hall of Fame (1985); she was named Outstanding Woman of Tennessee (1985), Co-Chairperson of the Literary Arts Festival for Homecoming '86 in Tennessee, the Duncanson Artist-in-Residence of the Taft Museum in Cincinnati (1986); and she was made a member of the Ohio Humanities Council (1987). She has also maintained a following on college campuses, receiving an honorary doctorate from The College of Mount St. Joseph on-the-Ohio (1983). In addition, subsequent to her early teaching assignments at Queens and at Livingston colleges, she has held positions at Ohio State University; at the College of Mount St. Joseph; and, since 1988, at Virginia Polytechnic and State University, where she is currently one of only three female tenured full professors.

Seated at her neatly organized desk, Giovanni is a model of efficiency. Somehow she is able, simultaneously, to answer telephone inquiries from an aspiring poet, sort mail, outline one of her creative-writing assignments, and characterize this period in fiction as the Age of Toni Morrison. Aside from writing, teaching, and building a home in Blacksburg, Virginia, Giovanni is busy with poetry readings and volunteer work at nursing homes and public schools. She has returned to the South that she knows and loves. Giving every appearance of feeling very much at home and exhibiting boundless energy, she will likely continue to write poems that entertain and inspire.

MAJOR THEMES

Nikki Giovanni has enjoyed a symbiotic relationship with the black community; and beyond race as part of a larger society, she has drawn upon common experiences and attitudes and contributed to readers' understanding of them. Chief among the shared experiences examined in her poems are public and private rebellions, racial pride, family, the need for love and security, dreams, the past, and physical and spiritual places.

As early as her college days, Giovanni demonstrated an interest in and a commitment to people, organizations, and institutions dedicated to individual and group freedom and integrity. In fact, she herself has commented, ''I find I'm being influenced not by other writers, but by people. I'm responding to the community'' (Weller 1969, 127). It is not surprising, therefore, that she gained a national audience through her involvement in civil-rights activities during the 1960s. Her militant, race-related poems explore self-determination, black unity, violence, and desired changes in American society. Several poems in her first two volumes challenge black youths to free their minds and their communities of white control. Such is the message in her most volatile poem ''The True

Import of Present Dialogue, Black vs. Negro'' (*Black Feeling, Black Talk*), in which she asks two revolutionary questions:

> Nigger
> . . .
> Can you kill a white man (11)

and

> can you kill the nigger
> in you. (12)

Relentless in its repeated variations on these questions and unsettling in its ironic review of blacks' involvement in the nation's wars ''everywhere for all alphabet but BLACK'' (12), the true impact is felt in the closing lines that encourage violence not for the sake of violence but for selfhood and nation building:

> Can we learn to kill WHITE for BLACK
> Learn to kill niggers
> Learn to be Black men. (12)

This message is reinforced in ''Of Liberation,'' a long poem in *Black Judgement* in which Giovanni calls for ''ammunition for gun and mind,'' (48). Again, however, the real purpose is not destructive but constructive, as demonstrated in lines that present rebellion in patriotic, esteem-building tropes:

> Support your local bookstore
> . . .
> Support your local rebellion—
> . . .
> It is time for the Resurrection of Blackness. (48)

Though strikingly similar to her first two volumes in exploring the anger and frustration of blacks in America, *Re:Creation* includes poems on numerous general subjects. From 1970 onward, in fact, her themes can be identified as chiefly personal rather than political. For example, the poems in *My House*, all dated between 1970 and 1972, make extensive use of dialogue as a technique for introducing, advancing, and opposing ideas about mothers, grandmothers, children, lovers, Negro leaders, and Africa. Divided into two sections, ''The Rooms Inside'' (twenty-three poems) and ''The Rooms Outside'' (thirteen poems), *My House* opens onto scenes of intimacy and warmth that are keenly etched through actual conversation. A grandmother says to her granddaughter in ''Legacies,'' ''i want chu to learn how to make rolls'' (5), and in ''Mothers,'' a daughter is lovingly invited to ''Come here . . . I'll teach you / a poem'' (7). In direct contrast to these comforting interior scenes, the second section concerns people and struggles outside the home. More significant, however, is the contrast between Giovanni's earlier revolutionary poems and those in *My House* that present her ideas about living free of labels and proscription. Indeed, she ends her poem "Categories" with the revelation, "I just realized that / I'm bored with categories," (30). Similarly, the speaker in "When I Die" admits wanting "to be a new person," recalls a "stifled" rebirth, and hopes that any life she has touched knows "that i know that touching was and still is and will always / be the true / revolution" (37). Here, and elsewhere in the volume, Giovanni establishes her changed view of what constitutes a revolution.

Ego Tripping and Other Poems for Young People is memorable for its title poem written in the style of the "boast" and developing through hyperbole all the attributes of the omnipotent goddess-speaker. Ending in exhilaration, "I mean . . . I . . . can fly / like a bird in the sky" (5), "Ego Tripping" develops an important theme found throughout Giovanni's canon: the generating and sharing of love and racial pride. In fact, on this theme her life and art become one. Having declared in "Nikki-Rosa"—her signature poem, according to Margaret Walker—that "Black Love is Black Wealth" (17), Giovanni is impatient with strife and violence that seem too frequently to characterize American life. From the 1960s onward she has mourned the riots, the senseless bombings, and the assassinations of civil-rights advocates. In "Word Poem" (*Black Feeling, Black Talk*), she encourages, instead, dreaming and building "what we become/when we dream" (26).

"Poem—for BMC NO. 2" (*Black Feeling, Black Talk*) contains a recurring dream in Giovanni's poetry—her beloved childhood home, the Southland, "where once we walked / Among the clover and crabgrass and those / Funny little things that look like cotton candy" (10). Her home, lovingly characterized in "Knoxville, Tennessee" (*Black Judgement*), was also that place where there was fresh corn, okra, greens, and cabbage from her daddy's garden, and where she was warm "all the time" (65). Although this poem was written during the civil-rights struggles of the 1960s, there is no doubt about the warmth and security felt among the people and places of her Southern childhood.

On the other hand, Giovanni's racial past, or memories of Africa, are not so reassuring. In three poems on Africa—"Africa I," "Africa II," and "They Clapped" (*My House*)—Giovanni demonstrates that the dream of Africa and the reality of Africa are quite different. For example, when the poet-persona in "Africa I" announces "a lion waving," she is reminded that "there are no lions / in this part of Africa" (47). And in "They Clapped," black American tourists applaud as they land in Mother Africa, but they soon realize that "they are strangers all over" (52). These tourists learn, in effect, that they have no home except that which they establish in the present. Thus, they clap again as they depart, for "despite the dead / dream they saw a free future" (52).

Concurrent with advances in the feminist movement during the 1970s, Giovanni focused attention on sex roles and manifestations of sex discrimination. Her 1975 publication *The Women and the Men* is divided into three sections— "The Women," "The Men," "And Some Places"; in addition to poems on these topics, Giovanni develops excellent stanzas on writing poetry, and on self-realization, human understanding, and love. Continuing these interests in *Cotton Candy on a Rainy Day* (1978), she completes what Paula Giddings calls "the circle . . . of dealing with society, others and finally oneself" (16).

Giovanni's *Those Who Ride the Night Winds* evoked what has been one of the most spirited debates concerning her poetry since the 1972 discussion of *My House*. Martha Cook (1990) calls *Night Winds* an "impressive volume," but Rochelle Ratner (1983) and James Finn Cotter (1984) find the poems "superficial"; Ratner further charges Giovanni with forsaking the "individual self" in "striving for a collective black voice" (400). With twenty-four of the twenty-eight poems written in verse paragraphs set off by ellipses, *Night Winds* is certainly Giovanni's most innovative volume to date. Giovanni writes about both famous and ordinary people who walk in advance, who are molders of change. Specifically, she describes inner, spiritual places—for example, in "This Is Not for John Lennon"—reached only by those who are willing to travel to "the edge of this universe," to face and rise above the "Blackness" (19–21). Further, Giovanni explores the ultimate freedom from physical place in "Flying Underground," written for the children murdered in Atlanta during the early 1980s. Free of all physical restraints, even the grave, these children are described as "flying underground" while enjoying themselves and their new opportunities for playing, working, and reading books. On the significance of physical and spiritual places in Giovanni's poetry, Martha Cook asserts that "the need to belong to a place or in a place and the necessity of moving beyond physical places to spiritual or metaphysical ones" are greatest in thematic importance (299).

As if her powerful voice, registered in varying poetic themes and forms, were not enough to convince most readers of her versatility, Giovanni's most recent work, *Sacred Cows . . . and Other Edibles,* is a reminder of her skills as a prose stylist. Nineteen essays cover politics, sports, seat-belt laws, parenthood, her life as a poet, and her introductions to other writers in humorous and persuasive details. Though previously published in anthologies, magazines, or newspapers, these essays are described by *Publishers Weekly* (December 18, 1987) as "addicting . . . fresh and funny—and enjoyable out-loud reading" (48). Both Giovanni's poetry and prose benefit from oral presentation, and Giovanni is an excellent reader of her own works. Inspired by stylistic features of black idioms and musical forms—including blues, jazz, popular songs, and gospel—she combines many of these elements with edited American English to form varied speech patterns. As a popular poet of the people, Giovanni is indeed a messenger whose importance lies in her development of significant themes in forms accessible to a vast public.

SURVEY OF CRITICISM

In a 1982 interview with Arlene Elder (1982), Nikki Giovanni spoke passionately about certain hallmarks that serious writers must demonstrate, including trust, integrity, honesty, and separation of "what they do from who they are" (71–75). Ironically, many critics have failed to consider these very qualities in evaluating Giovanni's poetry. Pointing up this fact in a perceptive critique of Giovanni scholarship, Margaret B. McDowell (1986) asserts that "critics have allowed personal and political attitudes not merely to affect their judgment but to dominate it" (136). Similarly, William J. Harris, in *Black Women Writers* notes "a curious tendency of normally perceptive critics to undervalue [Giovanni], to condescend to her rather than to criticize her," citing Michele Wallace who calls Giovanni "a kind of nationalistic Rod McKuen," Eugene Redmond who claims that her poetry "lacks lyricism and imagery," Haki Madhubuti (Don L. Lee) who finds Giovanni lacking in "the sophistication of thought demanded of one with pretensions of a 'political seer,' " and finally Amiri Baraka and Saunders Redding, who see her as "simply an opportunist." Harris concludes that Giovanni has not gained the critics' respect (218).

Generally listed as reasons for these uneven, subjective assessments are the one-dimensional, inflexible classifications of Giovanni as either a revolutionary civil-rights firebrand who deserted the cause, or as a popular versifier undeserving of serious attention by academic critics, or as a poet of great potential who is unwilling to master her art. In answer to all of her critics, Giovanni has asked that they understand her work. In fact, she has amended her once narrow view— which she expressed, for example, in "Nikki-Rosa," when she wrote "I really hope no white person has cause to write about me' "—to the broad acceptance of white or black critics who read and understand her poetry (Tate 1983, 64).

At least four studies published during the 1980s have discussed Giovanni's evolving reputation. Alex Batman (1980) concludes that while Giovanni "has not yet realized her full promise . . . careful reading of her verse . . . shows that talent is indeed there" (289). Mozella G. Mitchell (1985) notes Giovanni's tremendous creative, intellectual, ethical, and political growth "and expects much . . . in the future, as each publication in the past has proven to be a progressive manifestation of her true genius" (151). Other assessments, however, are not as positive. For example, Paula Giddings, in *Black Women Writers,* comments favorably on Giovanni's "evolvement away from the political poems" of the 1960s but charges that the poet's books, "particularly those published after 1975, [demonstrate] that as her persona matured, her language, craft, and perceptions did not" (215). Similarly, William J. Harris sees Giovanni's writing career in three distinct stages but he calls her a "frustrating poet" who "clearly has talent which she refuses to discipline" (228).

Several critics have discussed the first stage in Giovanni's career, noting the purpose, themes, and techniques of her revolutionary poems. Two of the earliest critiques, "The Poetry of Three Revolutionists: Don L. Lee, Sonia Sanchez, and Nikki Giovanni," by R. Roderick Palmer, and "The Motif of Dynamic Change in Black Revolutionary Poetry," by A. Russell Brooks, both published in September 1971, characterize Giovanni as impatient for change. Palmer, in fact, labels her the "most polemic, the most incendiary" of his three subjects. By

1971, however, Giovanni was already beginning to broaden her focus to include private as well as public revolutions.

Assessing Giovanni's work from 1968 to 1972, Suzanne Juhasz (1976) outlines an evolving feminist consciousness in an essay entitled " 'A Sweet Inspiration . . . of My People': The Poetry of Gwendolyn Brooks and Nikki Giovanni.'' Juhasz notes that Giovanni moves from separate expressions of personal love in her private life and public love in her political life to a blending of her private and public lives. Juhasz sees this achievement as Giovanni's validation of herself as a black woman poet acting through the interrelation of love and power to effect a revolution. Erlene Stetson has also noted Giovanni's special prominence among black women poets of this century whose lines draw upon both black women's tones and expressions in the blues and other musical forms and their political activity. Giovanni's explorations into these new expressions and relationships have given her poetry a distinctive stamp.

Focusing on a large number of Giovanni's poems in a study entitled "Nikki Giovanni: Place and Sense of Place in Her Poetry,'' Martha Cook emphasizes the point that neither the personal nor the political view is essential to their success. Instead, she analyzes poems in the context of Southern literature in which the sense of place functions both as a vehicle and as a theme. She identifies these poems as the works that will determine Giovanni's reputation in American poetry. That reputation extends far beyond the United States, as Giovanni's poems have been translated into several languages.

In "Groundwork for a More Comprehensive Criticism of Nikki Giovanni,'' Margaret McDowell establishes the need for a carefully selected collection of Giovanni's poetry and for a comprehensive study of the entire body of her work, giving attention to the 1971 shift in critical responses that it generated, to its relationship to Afro-American poetry in the post-1960s, and to developments in modern poetry. In this useful essay, McDowell also summarizes, and provides some explanations for, the contradictory critical responses to Giovanni from 1969 to 1974, the period that marked her meteoric rise to prominence.

Guides to a comprehensive evaluation of Giovanni's work include her own essays and prefaces; published interviews, notably those with Arlene Elder and Claudia Tate; several book chapters and evaluative essays; entries in bio-critical reference books; Ph.D. dissertations; and numerous reviews of her books and record albums. Two volumes by Virginia C. Fowler make major contributions. The first, *Nikki Giovanni* (Twayne Publishers), is a critical introduction to Giovanni's life and work. The second, *Conversations with Nikki Giovanni*, is a collection of interviews covering the last twenty-five years, including a 1992 interview with Fowler herself.

All who write about Giovanni do well to heed the consistency of her inconsistency throughout her career, a point on which she has given fair warning. In a 1969 article in the *Negro Digest* entitled "Black Poems, Poseurs and Power," she opposes the tendency of black revolutionaries "to look at the Black experience too narrowly'' (30). In her afterword for *A Singer in the Dawn: Reinter-*

pretations of Paul Laurence Dunbar (1975), she expands her argument against narrowness of view, asserting that "Every artist, should he create long enough, will come full cycle again and again" (244). And in her preface to *Those Who Ride the Night Winds,* she reminds the audience that "Art . . . and by necessity . . . artists . . . are on the cutting edge . . . of change" (7). Giovanni also speaks of growth and change in her 1983 interview with Claudia Tate: "If I've grown, and I have, if I share that growth, and I do, then my readers are allowed to grow. I expect growth." Moreover, she expects recognition for her productivity, summarizing her 1983 record as follows: "In twelve years I produced fifteen books. That's not bad. I would like to have a little more attention" (75, 76). Explaining further in her 1984 essay "An Answer to Some Questions on How I Write," in *Black Women Writers,* she hopes that her work will not be "just a consistency of unformed and untested ideas . . . acquired somewhere in [her] late teens or early twenties" (210). Clearly, Giovanni invites an objective evaluation of the entire body of her work.

BIBLIOGRAPHY

Works by Nikki Giovanni

Books

Black Feeling, Black Talk. New York: Black Dialogue Press, 1968.
Black Judgement. Detroit: Broadside Press, 1969.
Black Feeling, Black Talk/Black Judgement. New York: Morrow, 1970.
Re:Creation. Detroit: Broadside Press, 1970.
Gemini: An Extended Autobiographical Statement on My First Twenty-five Years of Being a Black Poet. Indianapolis: Bobbs-Merrill, 1971.
Spin a Soft Black Song: Poems for Children. New York: Hill and Wang, 1971.
My House: Poems. New York: Morrow, 1972.
A Dialogue: James Baldwin and Nikki Giovanni. Philadelphia: Lippincott, 1973; London: Joseph, 1975.
Ego-Tripping and Other Poems for Young People. New York: Hill, 1973.
A Poetic Equation: Conversations between Nikki Giovanni and Margaret Walker. Washington, D.C.: Howard University Press, 1974.
The Women and the Men. New York: Morrow, 1975.
Cotton Candy on a Rainy Day. New York: Morrow, 1980.
Vacation Time: Poems for Children. New York: Morrow, 1980.
Those Who Ride the Night Winds. New York: Morrow, 1983.
Sacred Cows . . . and Other Edibles. New York: Morrow, 1988.
Knoxville, Tennessee. New York: Scholastic, 1994.
Racism 101. New York: Morrow, 1994.

Recordings

Truth Is on Its Way. Right-on Records, 1971.
Like a Ripple on a Pond. Nik Tom, 1973.

The Way I Feel. Atlantic Records, 1974.
Legacies. Folkways Records, 1976.
The Reason I Like Chocolate. Folkways Records, 1976.

Other

"Black Poems, Poseurs and Power." *Negro Digest* 18 (June 1969): 30–34.
Night Comes Softly: An Anthology of Black Female Voices. Edited by Nikki Giovanni.
    Newark, N.J.: Medic Press, 1970.
"Afterword." In *A Singer in the Dawn,* edited by Jay Martin, 243–46. New York: Dodd,
    Mead, and Company, 1975.

Studies of Nikki Giovanni

Bailey, Peter. "Nikki Giovanni: I Am Black, Female, Polite." *Ebony* 27 (February 1972):
    48–50, 52, 54, 56.
Barksdale, Richard K. "Humanistic Protest in Black Poetry." In *Modern Black Poets:
    A Collection of Critical Essays,* edited by Donald B. Gibson, 157–64. Englewood
    Cliffs, N.J.: Prentice-Hall, 1973.
Batman, Alex. "Nikki Giovanni." In *Dictionary of Literary Biography,* vol. 5, edited
    by Donald J. Greiner, 286–89. Detroit: Gale Research, 1980.
Bell, Bernard W. "New Black Poetry: A Double-Edged Sword." *CLA Journal* 15 (Sep-
    tember 1971): 37–43.
Brooks, A. Russell. "The Motif of Dynamic Change in Black Revolutionary Poetry."
    CLA Journal 15 (September 1971): 7–17.
Cook, Martha. "Nikki Giovanni: Place and Sense of Place in Her Poetry." In *Southern
    Women Writers,* edited by Tonette Bond Inge, 279–300, 367–68 (Notes). Tus-
    caloosa: University of Alabama Press, 1990.
Cotter, James Finn. "Poetry Marathon." *Hudson Review* 37 (Autumn 1984): 499–500.
Duffy, Martha. "Hustler and Fabulist." Review of *Gemini. Time* 99 (January 17, 1972):
    63–64.
Elder, Arlene. "A *Melus* Interview: Nikki Giovanni." *The Journal of the Society for the
    Study of the Multi-Ethnic Literature of the United States* 9 (Winter 1982): 61–
    75.
Evans, Mari, ed. *Black Women Writers (1950–1980).* New York: Anchor Press, 1984.
Fowler, Virginia C. *Conversations with Nikki Giovanni.* Jackson: University Press of
    Mississippi, 1992.
Georgoudaki, Ekaterini. "Contemporary Women's Autobiography: Maya Angelou,
    Gwendolyn Brooks, Nikki Giovanni, Lillian Hellman, and Audre Lorde." *Dia-
    vazo* 237 (April 1990): 62–69.
Giovanni, Nikki. Papers. Mugar Memorial Library, Boston University.
Howard, Lillie P. "Nikki Giovanni." In *Black Women Writers: A Critical Reference
    Guide from Colonial Times to the Present,* edited by Lina Mainiers and Langdon
    Lynne Faust, 135–37. New York: Ungar, 1980.
Juhasz, Suzanne. "A Sweet Inspiration . . . of My People": The Poetry of Gwendolyn
    Brooks and Nikki Giovanni." In *Naked and Fiery Forms: Modern American
    Poetry by Women A New Tradition.* 144–76. New York: Harper and Row,
    1976.

Lee, Don L. *Dynamite Voices I: Black Poets of the 1960s.* Detroit: Broadside Press, 1971.

McClain, Ruth Rambo. "Re:Creation." *Black World* 20 (February 1971): 62–64.

McDowell, Margaret B. "Groundwork for a More Comprehensive Criticism of Nikki Giovanni." In *Belief vs. Theory in Black American Literary Criticism,* edited by Joe Weixlmann and Chester J. Fontenot, 135–60. Greenwood, Fla.: Penkeville, 1986.

Mitchell, Mozella. "Nikki Giovanni." In *Dictionary of Literary Biography,* vol. 41, edited by Trudier Harris and Thadious M. Davis, 135–51. Detroit: Gale Research, 1985.

Noble, Jeanne. *Beautiful, Also, Are the Souls of My Black Sisters: A History of the Black Woman in America.* Englewood Cliffs, N.J.: Prentice-Hall, 1978.

Palmer, R. Roderick. "The Poetry of Three Revolutionists: Don L. Lee, Sonia Sanchez, and Nikki Giovanni." *CLA Journal* 15 (September 1971): 25–35.

Ratner, Rochelle. Review of *Those Who Ride the Night Winds. Library Journal* 108 (February 15, 1983): 400.

Salaam, Kalamu Ya (Val Ferdinand). Review of *My House* and *Like a Ripple on a Pond. Black World* 23 (July 1974): 64–70.

Shouse, Elaine Marie. "An Analysis of the Poetry of Three Revolutionary Poets: Don L. Lee, Nikki Giovanni, and Sonia Sanchez." Ph.D. diss., University of Illinois at Urbana-Champaign, 1976.

Stetson, Erlene. *Black Sister: Poetry by Black American Women, 1746–1980.* Bloomington: Indiana University Press, 1981.

Stokes, Stephanie J. " 'My House': Nikki Giovanni." *Essence* 12 (August 1981): 84–88.

Tate, Claudia, ed. *Black Women Writers at Work.* New York: Continuum, 1983.

Thompson, M. Cordell. "Nikki Giovanni: Black Rebel with Power in Poetry." *Jet* 42 (May 25, 1972): 18–24

Torrence, Juanita Marie. "A Literary Equation: A Comparison of Representative Works of Margaret Walker and Nikki Giovanni." Ph.D. diss., Texas Woman's University, 1979.

Weller, Sheila. "To Be a Poet." *Mademoiselle* 70 (December 1969): 126–77, 159–60.

Yamada, Hiroyasu. "Sensational Hummingbird: Nikki Giovanni." *Eigo-Seinen, Chiyoda-Ku* 133 (1987): 19–20.

SUSAN V. DONALDSON

Elizabeth Hardwick
(1916–)

A distinguished literary critic as well as a novelist and short-story writer, Kentucky-born Elizabeth Hardwick represents, in Doris Grumbach's apt phrase, "that *rara avis,* a woman of letters" (1). Since 1945 her fiction has attracted critical praise and awards, and her reviews and essays for numerous journals, including the *New York Review of Books,* which she helped establish, have earned her a reputation as a formidable critic of contemporary culture and literature. In the 1970s feminism emerged as a major force in both her nonfiction and her fiction. Also figuring large in Hardwick's work is New York City itself, long her intellectual and emotional touchstone. Her Kentucky background, though, as the autobiographical narrator of Hardwick's third novel, *Sleepless Nights,* observes, continues to make its stubborn claim on her sensibility: "Fading, it is sad; remaining, it is a needle" (11).

BIOGRAPHY

Born on July 7, 1916, Elizabeth Hardwick spent the first 23 years of her life in Lexington, Kentucky, and has continued, despite her long residence in the Northeast, to see her native city as "truly home." In a 1969 *Harper's* article, "Going Home Is America," describing her roots in Lexington, Hardwick observed that she is often asked about the supposed incongruity between her liberal political beliefs and her Kentucky background. "What can I answer," she noted, "except to say that I have been, according to my limits, always skeptical, and that I have, always, since my first breath, 'been from Kentucky' " (78). Hardwick grew up in a family of nine children headed by Eugene Hardwick, a small businessman, and Mary Ramsey Hardwick in Lexington's North End, a hodge-podge of different races and classes. "The most interesting thing," Hardwick recalled in this Lexington essay, "was to be witness day in and day out to the mystery of behavior in your own neighborhood, to the side-by-side psychodramas of the decent and wage-earning, and the anarchic and bill-owing, to the drunken husband and the prayer-meeting couple'' (80).

An eager reader from childhood, Hardwick attended Henry Clay High School and then went on to study literature at the University of Kentucky, where she earned a B.A. in 1938 and a M.A. in 1939. Even then, she recalled in a 1985 *Paris Review* interview, she was an enthusiastic follower of the *Partisan Review,* a New York journal founded in 1933 by Philip Rahv and William Phillips and dedicated to combining literary modernism with radical politics. As a Kentucky student, Hardwick had flirted first with Communist and then with ex-Communist politics, and her dream then, she once joked later, was to be a New York Jewish intellectual. "I say 'Jewish,' " she explained in a *New York Times* interview (Locke 1979), "because of their tradition of radical skepticism; and also a certain deracination appeals to me—and their openness to European culture . . . the questioning of the arrangements of society, sometimes called radicalism" (68).

For Hardwick "a critical, defining moment" in her life came in the summer in 1939, when she turned down a fellowship at Louisiana State University, "a magical place, then," she recalled, "with the *Southern Review* and all sorts of brilliant writers around" (Pinckney, 33). Instead, she abruptly decided to pursue a Ph.D. at Columbia University without the benefit of a fellowship. Moving to New York City that fall, Hardwick brought with her, in the words of Barbara Probst Solomon (1974), "a certain Southerner's baggage, a love of language and an ease of expression" (4). Hardwick remained in Columbia's graduate program for the next two years and initially found herself drawn to seventeenth-century English literature.

Writing fiction, though, proved to be a stronger attraction. By 1945 Hardwick had already published her first novel, *The Ghostly Lover,* the story of a young Southern woman who slowly extricates herself from suffocating family ties and who eventually rejects the seemingly inevitable destiny of marriage and dependence awaiting her. The novel's critical reception was uneven at best, in part because reviewers were puzzled by the absence of a conventional plot, but even the most negative reviews acknowledged the compelling power of the novel's dreamlike style and passages of emotional intensity. Less qualified was the success of Hardwick's early venture into short fiction. By 1947 her short stories had already been included in two O. Henry Prize collections and two Best American Short Stories anthologies. A year later Hardwick's reputation was strong enough to win her a Guggenheim fellowship for fiction.

It was in the late 1940s that Hardwick also began to make a name for herself as an exacting literary critic and book reviewer for the *Partisan Review.* Shortly after the publication of *The Ghostly Lover,* she received a call from Philip Rahv, one of the editors of the *Partisan Review.* "I was terrified of the great pasha, usually described as gruff or grumpy—he was also curious, sly and prying," Hardwick recalled in the 1979 *New York Times* interview. "During our conversation the name of a respected critic came up and I said something like, 'I think he's terrible.' Nothing pleased Rahv so much as a vehement negative, and so he pronounced me 'not as stupid' as he had expected. Thus was the lowly reviewer born'' (62). Those who read her reviews, though, were unlikely to underestimate Hardwick as ''lowly.'' Short-story writer Peter Taylor complained vehemently about Hardwick's hard-hitting criticism of his work, as Ian Hamilton noted in his biography of Robert Lowell (1982). Hamilton added that Hardwick's stay at the Yaddo writers' colony in late 1948 elicited a half-serious warning from poet Elizabeth Bishop, who wrote her good friend Lowell, ''I forgot to comment on Elizabeth Hardwick's arrival—*take care*'' (140).

Already acknowledged as perhaps the outstanding poet of his generation, Lowell was to emerge as one of the most important influences on Hardwick's life. The two writers did indeed meet at Yaddo, despite Bishop's humorous admonition, and in the summer of 1949 they were married in the home of Lowell's parents. The union was to be rich, long, and tumultuous, producing a daughter, Harriet Winslow Lowell, in 1957, and several books by both writers. In the early years the Lowells' lives were filled with extensive travels in Europe, Lowell's teaching stints in Iowa, Ohio, and Massachusetts, his tragic periodic bouts with manic-depression, and important writing projects undertaken by both writers. During the 1950s Lowell produced his pathbreaking *Life Studies,* a volume bearing ''extensive evidence,'' Hamilton observed, of Hardwick's editorial presence (238). Lowell, in turn, played a special role in Hardwick's own development as a writer. As Hardwick herself observed in a *Paris Review* interview (Pinckney, 1985), ''In literary matters, his immense learning and love of literature were a constant magic for me. As an influence on my own writing,'' she added, ''that is more difficult to figure out. . . . Let me shift the subject a little. Maybe I was led to this by Cal's library, led by the prose written by poets. The poet's prose is one of my passions'' (49).

By the 1950s Hardwick's own prose, particularly her work in fiction, had taken on a sly satirical edge reflecting her continuing concern with social and political issues and her dislike of intellectual pretensions and falsehoods. Her second novel, *The Simple Truth* (1955), delivered a few well-aimed digs at cloistered intellectuals defined, in the words of one reviewer, by ''the snobbery of insight'' and by unacknowledged assumptions of class superiority. Similarly, ''The Classless Society'' and ''The Purchase'' (1960), two short stories originally published in the *New Yorker* and selected for later anthologies, skewered the backbiting and maneuvering of academic and artistic circles.

Perhaps this sort of skepticism and clear-eyed perspective of social follies had a good deal to do with her appreciation of William James, a selection of whose letters Hardwick edited and published in a separate volume in 1961. What drew her in particular to James, Hardwick noted in the introduction to *The Selected Letters of William James,* was his intellectual curiosity coupled with ''a recurring hesitation to commit himself.'' He was, she concluded, very much a part of the twentieth century and its own hosts of hesitations.

One of Hardwick's greatest concerns in this period, though, was maintaining the integrity of the book review and the essay form. In 1959 in an article in Harper's titled "The Decline of Book Reviewing" she delivered a blistering attack on the state of book reviewing. The book-review sections of the *New York Times* and the *Herald Tribune,* she charged, were "in a state of baneful depression insofar as liveliness and interest are concerned." More and more, she noted, book reviews tended toward the congenial and the benevolent: "Sweet bland commendations fall everywhere upon the scene; a universal, if somewhat lobotomized, accommodation reigns. A book is born into a puddle of treacle; the brine of hostile criticism is only a memory" (138).

At the very least, Hardwick observed, a good review should show some indication of the way "an unusual mind, capable of presenting fresh ideas in a vivid and original and interesting manner, thinks of books as they appear (141)." This sort of exchange between an individual, inquiring mind and books under review was precisely what was most notable about Hardwick's 1962 volume *A View of My Own: Essays in Literature and Society,* a collection of reviews and essays previously published in the *Partisan Review, Harper's Magazine,* the *New Republic,* and the *New York Times Book Review.* The volume contains literary essays, including reviews of (1) letters of Sherwood Anderson, Hart Crane, and Edna St. Vincent Millay; (2) Mary McCarthy's fiction; (3) Graham Greene and Catholicism; (4) Eugene O'Neill; (5) David Riesman's sociological studies; and (6) incisive commentaries on contemporary culture, ranging from the celebrated Caryl Chessman case to America's infatuation with Dylan Thomas.

By the time *A View of My Own* was published, Hardwick had become firmly established in New York City. She and Lowell had moved to the West Side of Manhattan in 1960, and the next year they bought a spacious apartment in a building built for artists in the early 1900s. In 1964 Hardwick began teaching as an adjunct professor of English at Barnard College; but it was the previous year that turned out, in Ian Hamilton's words, to be "a turning point" in her life. During a 114-day newspaper printers' strike in early 1963, Hardwick helped found the *New York Review of Books.* Hardwick's contribution to the periodical was significant from its inception: She served as advisory editor, working with the publication's two editors, Barbara Epstein and Robert Silvers; and according to Philip Nobile's popular history of the periodical, *Intellectual Skywriting* (1974), the first issue was pasted up on the Lowells' dining-room table.

As conceived by Hardwick, Silvers, and Epstein, the *New York Review of Books* mirrored in part the *Times Literary Supplement* and other British publications offering rigorously high standards in book reviewing. A notice in the first issue of the *New York Review* declared that the periodical was founded not just to fill the void left by the absent *New York Times Book Review* during the printers' strike but, in the editors' words, "to take this opportunity which the strike has presented to publish the sort of literary journal which the editors and contributors feel is needed in America." Asserting a combative tone from the very beginning, the editors added that no time or space was to be devoted to "books which are trivial in their intentions or venal in their effects, except occasionally to reduce a temporarily inflated reputation or to call attention to a fraud."

The *New York Review of Books* has played a major role in Hardwick's life since its founding. Lively, belligerent, and frequently subjected to hard-hitting criticism from leftist allies and rightist foes, the *Review* provided Hardwick with a friendly forum for her no-nonsense reviews, a refuge of sorts during her 1972 divorce from Robert Lowell, and a sounding board for essays reflecting her growing feminist concerns. In addition, Hardwick wrote a good many essays on the theater for the *Review,* and as a result in 1967 she became the first woman to win the George Jean Nathan award for drama criticism. Today she continues to serve as the periodical's advisory editor and to contribute both nonfiction and fiction to its pages.

In 1974 Hardwick's interest in feminist issues resulted in the publication of the widely praised collection of essays titled *Seduction and Betrayal: Women and Literature.* Drawn largely from pieces published in the *New York Review of Books,* the essays in the volume offer a witty, mordant, and sometimes angry view of women as fictional characters, as helpmates of male writers, and as writers in their own right. One critic in particular described the volume as "a critical odyssey of the female consciousness in our literature of the past two hundred years" (Richardson, 1974, 87). By and large the collection established Hardwick as a pioneer in feminist criticism and earned her a growing audience beyond the pages of the *New York Review of Books.*

The next several years turned out to be particularly important for Hardwick, her work, and her critical reputation. In 1977 she served as advisory editor for Arno Press's 18-volume series "Rediscovered Fiction by American Women." Selected by Hardwick, the volumes concentrate on fiction by American women between the 1870s and 1930s and include works by Louisa May Alcott, Mary E. Wilkins Freeman, Josephine Herbst, Ellen Glasgow, Elizabeth Stuart Phelps Ward, Constance C. Harrison, Ruth Suckow, Elizabeth Madox Roberts, Frances Newman, and Evelyn Scott. That same year Hardwick was elected to the American Academy and Institute of Arts and Letters for her contribution to literature. It was also in 1977, finally, that Robert Lowell returned to Hardwick after a seven-year absence. Shortly after their reconciliation, Lowell died of a heart attack.

Two years after Lowell's death Hardwick's third and most important novel, *Sleepless Nights* (1979), was published to great critical acclaim. Narrated by a writer named Elizabeth, the novel discards conventional plot, character development, and closure and offers in their place a fragmentary collage of memories ranging from Kentucky to New York City and evoking figures as disparate as Billie Holiday, Elizabeth's mother, disaffected intellectuals, and cleaning women. "The result," Joan Didion reported in the *New York Times Book Review* (1979), "is less a 'story about' or 'of' a life than a shattered meditation on it, a work as evocative and difficult to place as Claude Levi-Strauss's *Tristes Tro-piques,* which it oddly recalls'' (1).

Since the publication of *Sleepless Nights,* Hardwick has continued to publish short stories, most of them set in New York City, and to write essays and reviews for the *New York Review of Books.* Many of her recent stories, like ''The Bookseller'' (1980) and ''Back Issues'' (1981), come close to blurring generic boundaries between the short story and the essay. In 1983, her third collection of literary and cultural criticism, *Bartleby in Manhattan and Other Essays,* was issued. Included in this volume were essays on literature, film, and drama and a number of pieces probing popular culture in the 1960s and 1970s, from the assassination of Martin Luther King, Jr. to television evangelists. Hard-wick's ongoing interest in the essay form also resulted in the 1986 publication of *The Best American Essays 1986,* coedited with Robert Atwan. Acknowledg-ing the generic differences between fiction and the essay, Hardwick noted in the volume's introduction, ''Yet the most interesting essays will have the self-propelled interior life of imaginative literature, and this is true even when they are responses to an occasion'' (44).

MAJOR THEMES

As Barbara Probst Solomon noted perceptively in her 1974 review of *Seduc-tion and Betrayal,* Hardwick ''was molded by the world of the *Partisan Re-view.*'' This world, she added, ''had a high belief in the perfectly written essay, nonconformist left-wing politics, serious attention to literature, and curiosity about mass culture'' (4). Above all, the *Partisan Review* refused to separate issues of politics and power from those of culture and art, and Hardwick herself continues to insist on the conjunction of the realms of art and power. ''As always,'' she noted in the *Paris Review* interview, ''cultural and political atti-tudes swim along in the same bloodstream'' (35).

Hardwick's long association with the *Partisan Review* and with the *New York Review of Books* has also fostered a keen skepticism coolly unreceptive to the clichéd, the expected, and the superficial in her fiction and her nonfiction. How-ever much memories of Kentucky continue to weave in and out of her fiction, Hardwick has particularly resisted the label Southern writer and has even de-clared in her 1983 essay ''Southern Literature'' that ''Southernness is more a decision than a fate, since fine talents are not necessarily under the command of place of feeling'' (18). Southern writers that she especially values—William Faulkner, Walker Percy, and Flannery O'Connor—are praised for their sensitiv-ity to ''the follies of literary Southernness'' and their willingness to question and probe.

Those writers and intellectuals disinclined to question their own assumptions and those of their culture are usually targeted for Hardwick's satirical wit and are scrutinized by her merciless eye for falsehoods and self-serving justifications. In Hardwick's second novel, *The Simple Truth,* two self-designated intellectuals at the University of Iowa, a graduate student and a faculty wife, are pilloried for their close-minded obsession with a murder trial and the supposed innocence of the defendant. The graduate student is convinced that the defendant is a victim of class tensions and struggles, while the faculty wife turns to psychological explanations and unconscious motivations for her own notion of the case. Both figures are outraged in the end when a jury of "ordinary" Iowa citizens returns a verdict of not guilty. Surely, the two "intellectuals" argue, the jury has reached the right verdict for the wrong reasons.

Similarly, Hardwick takes careful aim in "Evenings at Home," a 1948 *Partisan Review* story, at the self-dramatizing anxieties of a young woman from New York visiting her Kentucky family. In a like vein, a 1956 *New Yorker* story called "A Season's Romance" exposes the emptiness beneath assertions of class superiority made by a shabbily genteel mother and her daughter. And in "The Oak and the Axe," another 1956 *New Yorker* story, Hardwick probes the failing marriage of a young businesswoman and a world-weary, would-be writer infatuated with his own melancholy and mementoes of a more successful time.

More recently in her short fiction Hardwick has turned her sights on lonely and lost figures of the periphery cast adrift in the bewildering cityscape of New York. In the *Paris Review* interview, she observed, "I guess I'm very much drawn, in thought, to drifters, to frauds, to working-class people, waitresses, 10-cent clerks, bus stations. Maybe it comes from living so long in a fairly small town." The desultory daily routine of a New York bookshop owner, for instance, is the focus of "The Bookseller," and "Back Issues" relates a brief encounter in the New York Public Library between the nameless narrator and a Greek waiter down on his luck.

Similarly concerned with issues of power and powerlessness, centers and margins, insiders and outsiders, are many of Hardwick's essays in *A View of My Own, Seduction and Betrayal,* and *Bartleby in Manhattan.* More often than not Hardwick usually takes the occasion of reviewing a book or discussing an event to examine larger cultural and political issues. Hence, in an essay on Selma, Alabama, in 1965, she explores the class tensions underlying Southern white bigotry; in her essays "The Oswald Family" and "Svetlana" (Stalin's daughter), she ponders the compulsions of publicity; and in "Seduction and Betrayal," she examines the impact of birth control technology on traditional narratives of illicit sex and guilt.

Above all, Hardwick's nonfiction and fiction from the beginning of her career have been largely concerned, as Joan Didion points out in her sensitive review of *Sleepless Nights,* with "the mysterious and somnambulistic 'difference' of being a woman." This has been the topic, Didion argues, that has repeatedly drawn Hardwick—"the undertow of family life, the awesome torment of being a daughter—an observer in the household, a constant reader of the domestic text" (60). Even her first novel, *The Ghostly Lover,* adumbrated Hardwick's feminist concerns of the 1970s to a striking degree. Elusive in its style and occasionally impassioned, *The Ghostly Lover* follows the journey of Marian

Coleman, a young woman who leaves her claustrophobic Southern family for graduate study in New York and there discovers that a "phantom" lies behind nearly every woman she meets: "a man or a family who was, or had been, or might be waiting" (118). In the end, however, Marian herself rejects the refuge of "a ghostly lover" and the easy closure of marriage and strikes out to find her own identity.

In ensuing years Hardwick continued to examine women's perspectives and consciousness in her short fiction, as in "The Mysteries of Eleusis," a brief 1946 story about a young woman's preparations for her marriage day, and in such essays as her half-admiring, half-resistant review of Simone de Beauvoir's *Second Sex,* included in *A View of My Own.* But it was in her collection *Seduction and Betrayal* and her novel *Sleepless Nights* that Hardwick's fascination with women writers and women's issues took on strongly feminist configurations. As Hardwick herself noted in the 1979 *New York Times Book Review* interview, "I call myself a feminist in that I believe there are cultural, social and economic boundaries set for women which are immoral and unnecessary and which should be resisted publicly and privately" (62). In both works she sets out to breach those boundaries. The collection of essays entitled *Seduction and Betrayal* contains an examination of women fictional characters, women writers, and women companions of male artists largely within the context of nineteenth-century Anglo-American bourgeois society and its imposed limits on women. Among the figures and topics discussed are the Brontës, Ibsen's women characters, Zelda Fitzgerald, Sylvia Plath, Virginia Woolf and Bloomsbury, and diarists Dorothy Wordsworth and Jane Carlyle. In this collection Hardwick's strategy is primarily one of exposure. She seeks to uncover what she calls "the other side of the question"—the often untold stories of women—and to reveal in particular the underlying complicity between nineteenth-century narrative traditions of sexual intrigue and hierarchies of gender (89). "The novel—deterministic, bourgeois in spirit for all its questioning of the hard terms of life," she tartly concludes in the title essay, "always understands that the men must get on." Only for women, seduced and betrayed in novel after novel, she adds, is biology "destiny" (192).

Perhaps even more daring is Hardwick's novel *Sleepless Nights,* an experimental work that purposefully or not seems to fulfill Hardwick's description of a feminist theory of fiction in *Seduction and Betrayal*—that is, "a way of testing and confronting the very structure of the novel itself." Hardwick's third novel resists the tidiness of plot and closure, even the reassuring centrality of a protagonist. Instead, *Sleepless Nights* allies itself with the narrator's fragmentary glimpses of outsiders, outcasts, and figures on the margin. It is, as Daphne Merkin noted in a review for the *New Republic* (1979), "a novel that is constantly belying itself, caught in the act of its own reconsiderations. In this sense, at least," Merkin added, "Hardwick can be said to be a 'feminine' writer, if what one means by the term is a proclivity to *suspend* oneself *in* rather than *impose* oneself upon the flow of the narrative" (36). Indeed, the novel's resistance to centrality and its attraction to marginality recall to a remarkable extent the sensitivity to otherness counseled by Hélène Cixous and other French feminist critics. In this respect, *Sleeping Nights* represents a fitting culmination to the career of a writer who has long insisted that culture and art can never be separated from politics and issues of power.

SURVEY OF CRITICISM

The scholarship available on Hardwick's fiction and nonfiction is limited to contemporary reviews in periodicals; but from the beginning her work has attracted respectful, if somewhat puzzled, attention. Her first book, *The Ghostly Lover,* was reviewed in the *New Republic,* the *Nation,* and the *New York Times Book Review;* and although reviewers Diana Trilling and Gertrude Buckman took Hardwick to task for seemingly eschewing conventional structure and narrative unity, they invariably took notice of the novel's haunting, nearly hallucinatory, style. At times, Trilling (1945) noted, the novel comes "close to the slashing courage of D. H. Lawrence" (523).

It is, in fact, Hardwick's style that has continued to draw the most notice from critics down through the years. Commentary on Hardwick's second novel, *The Simple Truth,* has been relatively sparse; but reviewers of her three volumes of essays have been particularly struck by her condensed, aphoristic mode of writing, influenced in part by the prose of poets whom Hardwick so highly values. Her style is marked, Ruth Bernard Yeazell observed in a 1975 review of *Seduction and Betrayal* for *Nineteenth-Century Fiction Studies,* by "the elliptical and allusive phrase, the elegantly compressed apercu, rather than the carefully documented argument" (227). Indeed, David Lodge suggested that Hardwick's nonfiction and fiction are of a piece, revealing "the unity of a sensibility wedded to a style, the one inseparable from the other." In his 1983 review of *Bartleby in Manhattan,* Lodge described Hardwick as a writer who is both "a distinguished exponent of the lyrical novel" and "a 'lyrical' critic—the nearest equivalent we have to the Virginia Woolf of *The Common Reader*" (1237).

Also drawing commentary is Hardwick's growing feminism over the years. Barbara Probst Solomon, in her review of *Seduction and Betrayal*—one of the best pieces on Hardwick's work in general—compared Hardwick with Simone de Beauvoir. "Like Beauvoir," Solomon noted, "Hardwick directly addresses herself to female vulnerability, to women's relations to men, to their own work, their options and lack of options" (4). Rosemary Dinnage, in a review in the *Times Literary Supplement* (1974) of *Seduction and Betrayal,* noted that the subject of the book is "seduction and betrayal itself, in literary contexts; the implicit axiom being that arrangements made between men and women are never satisfactory" (1333).

Some of the best responses to Hardwick's work, though, have been reviews of *Sleepless Nights,* especially those appearing in 1979 by Margaret Peters for the *Chicago Review,* Joan Didion for the *New York Times Book Review,* and Diane Johnson for the *New York Review of Books.* Didion used the occasion of the review to make a far-ranging assessment of Hardwick's work as a whole, and Johnson commented perceptively on the experimental nature of the novel and its feminist implications. Its style, Johnson concluded, "is literary, learned, manly—how many women have such courage of their aphorisms?—and womanly, bounded by images of windows, mantelpieces, the behavior of people indoors" (7). Such initial assessments have established solid groundwork for future scholarly commentary examining Hardwick's use of narrative, her feminism, and the conjunction between her fiction and nonfiction.

BIBLIOGRAPHY

Works by Elizabeth Hardwick

Fiction—Novels

The Ghostly Lover. New York: Harcourt, Brace, 1945. Reprint. New York: Ecco, 1982.
The Simple Truth. New York: Harcourt, Brace, 1955. Reprint. New York: Ecco, 1982.
Sleepless Nights. New York: Random House, 1979.

Fiction—Selected Short Stories

"The People on the Roller Coaster." *New Mexico Quarterly Review* 14 (1944): 444–54. Reprinted in *O. Henry Memorial Award Prize Stories of 1945,* edited by Herschel Brickell and Muriel Fuller, 125–36. Garden City, N.Y.: Doubleday, 1946.
"The Mysteries of Eleusis." *Partisan Review* 12 (1945): 207–13; Reprinted in *The Best American Short Stories, 1946,* edited by Martha Foley, 203–13. Boston: Houghton Mifflin, 1947.
"Saint Ursula and Her Eleven Thousand Virgins." *Yale Review,* n.s., 34 (1945): 524–31.
"The Golden Stallion." *Sewanee Review* 54 (1946): 34–65. Reprinted in *Best American Short Stories, 1947,* edited by Martha Foley, 141–70. Boston: Houghton Mifflin, 1948.
"The Temptations of Dr. Hoffman." *Partisan Review* 13 (1946): 405–19.
"What We Have Missed." In *O. Henry Memorial Prize Stories of 1946,* Ed. Herschell Brickell and Muriel Fuller, 123–32. Garden City, N.Y.: Doubleday, 1946.
"The Classless Society." *New Yorker* 22 (January 19, 1947): 30–48. Reprinted in *Stories from the New Yorker, 1950–1960,* edited by *The New Yorker.* 728–47. New York: Simon and Schuster, 1960.
"Evenings at Home." *Partisan Review* 15 (1948): 439–48; Reprinted in *The Best American Short Stories, 1949,* edited by Martha Foley, 117–26. Boston: Houghton Mifflin Company, 1950.
"The Friendly Witness." *Partisan Review* 17 (1950): 340–51.
"Two Recent Travelers." *Kenyon Review* 15 (1953): 436–54.
"A Season's Romance." *New Yorker* 32 (March 10, 1956): 36–44.
"The Oak and the Axe." *New Yorker* 32 (May 12, 1956): 49–72.

"The Purchase." *New Yorker* 35 (May 30, 1959): 28–62. Reprinted in *The Best American Short Stories, 1960,* edited by Martha Foley, 143–64. Boston: Houghton Mifflin, 1961.

"Scene from an Autobiography." *Prose* 4 (1972): 51–63.

"The Faithful." *New Yorker* 55 (February 19, 1979): 36–42. Reprinted in *The Best American Short Stories, 1980,* edited by Stanley Elkin and Shannon Ravenel, 196–209. Boston: Houghton Mifflin, 1981.

"The Bookseller." *New Yorker* 56 (December 15, 1980): 38–45; Reprinted in *The Best American Short Stories, 1981,* edited by Hortense Calisher and Shannon Ravenel, 158–70. Boston: Houghton Mifflin, 1982.

"Back Issues." *New York Review of Books* 28 (December 17, 1981): 6, 8, 10, 12.

"On the Eve: A Story." *New York Review of Books* 30 (December 20, 1983): 14, 16, 18, 20.

Nonfiction—Editions and Collections

CONTRIBUTIONS AS EDITOR

The Selected Letters of William James. Ed. Elizabeth Hardwick. New York: Farrar, Straus, and Cudahy, 1961.

The Best American Essays, 1986. Edited with Robert Atwan. New York: Ticknor and Fields, 1986; Houghton Mifflin, 1987.

CONTRIBUTIONS AS ADVISORY EDITOR AND WRITER OF INTRODUCTION

Alcott, Louisa May. *Work: A Story of Experience.* 1873. Reprint. New York: Arno, 1977.

Austin, Mary. *A Woman of Genius.* 1912. Reprint. New York: Arno, 1977.

Freeman, Mary E. Wilkins. *The Shoulders of Atlas.* 1908. Reprint. New York: Arno, 1977.

French, Alice. *The Man of the Hour.* 1905. Reprint. New York: Arno, 1977.

Glasgow, Ellen. *The Descendant.* 1926. Reprint. New York: Arno, 1977.

———. *The Romantic Comedians.* 1926. Reprint. New York: Arno, 1977.

Harrison, Constance C. *The Anglomaniacs.* 1890. Reprint. New York: Arno, 1977.

Herbst, Josephine. *Nothing Is Sacred.* 1928. Reprint. New York: Arno, 1977.

———. *Money for Love.* 1929. Reprint. New York: Arno, 1977.

Newman, Frances. *The Hard-Boiled Virgin.* 1926. Reprint. New York: Arno, 1977.

———. *All Dead Lovers Are Faithful Lovers.* 1928. Reprint. New York: Arno, 1977.

Rediscovered Fiction by American Women: A Personal Selection. 18 vols. New York: Arno, 1977.

Roberts, Elizabeth Madox. *Black Is My True Love's Hair.* 1938. Reprint. New York: Arno, 1977.

Scott, Evelyn. *The Narrow House.* 1921. Reprint. New York: Arno, 1977.

———. *Narcissus.* 1922. Reprint. New York: Arno, 1977.

Suckow, Ruth. *Country People.* 1924. Reprint. New York: Arno, 1977.

———. *Iowa Interiors.* 1926. Reprint. New York: Arno, 1977.

Ward, Elizabeth Stuart Phelps. *The Story of Avis.* 1879. Reprint. New York: Arno, 1977.

Woolson, Constance Fenimore. *Anne.* 1882. Reprint. New York: Arno, 1977.

Nonfiction—Collections, Selected Essays, and Reviews

A View of My Own: Essays in Literature and Society. New York: Farrar, Straus, and
    Cudahy, 1962.
Seduction and Betrayal: Women and Literature. New York: Random House, 1974.
Bartleby in Manhattan and Other Essays. New York: Random House, 1983.
"Faulkner and the South Today." *Partisan Review* 15 (1948): 1130–35.
"Elizabeth Bowen's Fiction." *Partisan Review* 16 (1949): 1114–21.
"America and Dylan Thomas." *Partisan Review* 23 (1956): 258–64.
"The Decline of Book Reviewing." *Harper's* 219 (November 1959): 138–43.
"Going Home Is America: Lexington, Kentucky." *Harper's* 239 (July 1969): 78–82.
"Reflections on Fiction." *New York Review of Books* 12 (February 13, 1969): 12–17.
"Reflections on Simone Weil." *Signs* 1 (1975): 83–91.
"Reading." In *Reading in the 1980s,* edited by Stephen Graubard, 13–18. New York:
    R. R. Bowker, 1983.
"Southern Literature: The Cultural Assumptions of Regionalism." In *Southern Literature
    in Transition: Heritage and Promise,* edited by Philip Castille and William Os-
    borne, 17–28. Memphis: Memphis State University Press, 1983.
"The Genius of Margaret Fuller." *New York Review of Books* 33 (April 10, 1986): 14–
    22.
"Its Only Defense: Intelligence and Sparkle." *New York Times Book Review* (September
    14, 1986): 1, 44–45.
"Gertrude Stein." *Threepenny Review* 31 (1987): 3–5.
"The Fictions of America." *New York Review of Books* 34 (June 25, 1987): 12, 14, 16–
    18.
"Mrs. Wharton in New York." *New York Review of Books* 34 (January 21, 1988): 28–
    34.
"Church Going." *New York Review of Books* 35 (August 18, 1988): 15–16, 18, 20–21.
"On Washington Square." *New York Review of Books* 37 (November 22, 1990): 25–28.
"Wind from the Prairie." *New York Review of Books* 38 (September 26, 1991): 9–12,
    14–16.
"Mary McCarthy in New York." *New York Review of Books* 39 (March 26, 1992): 3–
    4, 6.
"The Eternal Heartbreak." *Opera News* (March 28, 1992): 8–11.

Interviews with Elizabeth Hardwick

Gray, Francine Du Plessix. "Elizabeth Hardwick: A Fresh Way of Looking at Litera-
    ture—and at Life." *Vogue* 169 (June 1979): 202–3, 250.
Locke, Richard. "Conversation on a Book." *New York Times Book Review* (April 29,
    1979): 1, 61.
Pinckney, Darryl. "The Art of Fiction, LXXXVI." *Paris Review* 96 (1985): 20–51.

Studies of Elizabeth Hardwick

Biographical and Critical Studies

"Elizabeth Hardwick." *Current Biography Yearbook, 1981,* edited by Charles Moritz,
    188–91. New York: Wilson, 1982.

"Elizabeth Hardwick." In *World Authors, 1950–1970,* edited by John Wakeman, 615–16. New York: Wilson, 1975.

Goreau, Angeline. "Elizabeth Hardwick." In *Modern American Women Writers,* edited by Elaine Showalter, Lea Baechler, and A. Walton Litz, 189–96. New York: Scribner's, 1991.

Hamilton, Ian. *Robert Lowell: A Biography.* New York: Random House, 1982.

Johnson, Diane. "The Female as I: Elizabeth Hardwick." In *Terrorists and Novelists,* 24–29. New York: Alfred A. Knopf, 1982.

MacPike, Loralee. "Elizabeth Hardwick." In *American Woman Writers: A Critical Guide from Colonial Times to the Present,* vol. 2, edited by Lina Mainiero, 241–44. New York: Ungar, 1980.

Nobile, Philip. *Intellectual Skywriting: Literary Politics and the New York Review of Books.* New York: Charterhouse, 1974.

Selected Reviews

Bell, Pearl K. "Elizabeth Hardwick and Mary McCarthy." Review of *Sleepless Nights. Commentary* 68, no. 4 (1979): 65–67.

Buckman, Gertrude. "Wandering Parents." Review of *The Ghostly Lover. New York Times Book Review* (April 29, 1945): 6.

Caplan, Brina. "The Teller as the Tale." Review of *Sleepless Nights. Georgia Review* 33 (1979): 933–40.

Carey, John. "The Subjugation of Women." Review of *Seduction and Betrayal. New Statesman* 88 (November 29, 1974): 779–80.

Chernaik, Judith. Review of *Seduction and Betrayal. London Magazine,* n.s., 15, no. 2 (1975): 102–4.

Chisolm, Lawrence W. "Reflections on American Situations." Review of *A View of My Own. Yale Review,* n.s., 52 (1962–63): 270–77.

Didion, Joan. "Meditation on a Life." Review of *Sleepless Nights. New York Times Book Review* (April 29, 1979): 1, 60.

Dinnage, Rosemary. "Men, Women and Books: The Rule of Heroism." Review of *Seduction and Betrayal. Times Literary Supplement* 73 (November 29, 1974): 1333.

Donoghue, Denis. "Big Effects and Hard-Worked Perceptions." Review of *Bartleby in Manhattan. New York Times Book Review* (June 12, 1983): 7, 40.

Fitzsimmons, Thomas. Review of *The Simple Truth. Sewanee Review* 63 (1955): 325–27.

Gilbert, Sandra M. "Abandoned Women, in All Senses." Review of *Seduction and Betrayal. Nation* 220 (June 14, 1975): 728–31.

Grumbach, Doris. "The Eternal Feminine." Review of *Seduction and Betrayal. Washington Post Book World* 12 (May 1974): 1–2.

Halio, Jay L. "Fiction about Fiction." Review of *Sleepless Nights. Southern Review,* n.s., 17 (1981): 225–34.

Hampshire, Stuart. "Real Women." Review of *Seduction and Betrayal. New York Review of Books* 21 (June 27, 1974): 21–22.

Hardy, Barbara. "Gilded Cage." Review of *Bartleby in Manhattan. New Statesman* 106 (October 28, 1983): 28–29.

Hay, Sara Henderson. Review of *The Ghostly Lover. Saturday Review of Literature* 27 (May 5, 1945): 20.

Johnson, Diane. "Beyond the Evidence." Review of *Sleepless Nights*. *New York Review of Books* 26 (June 14, 1979): 7.

Leonard, John. "Books of the Times." Review of *Sleepless Nights*. *New York Times* (May 4, 1979): C29.

Lodge, David. "Sensible Sympathies." Review of *Bartleby in Manhattan*. *Times Literary Supplement* 82 (November 11, 1983): 1237.

Merkin, Daphne. Review of *Sleepless Nights*. *New Republic* 180 (June 9, 1979): 36–37.

Parks, Clara Claiborne. "Fictional Chronicle—Reviews." Review of *Sleepless Nights*. *Hudson Review* 32 (1979–80): 572–84.

Peters, Margaret. "Fiction under a True Name." Review of *Sleepless Nights*. *Chicago Review* 31, no. 2 (1979): 129–36.

Pritchett, V.S. "One of Them Can Write." Review of *A View of My Own*. *New Statesman* 67 (April 3, 1964): 529–30.

Rainer, Dachine. "The Truth and the Vacuum." Review of *The Simple Truth*. *New Republic* 132 (February 14, 1955): 17–18.

Richardson, Jack. "The Death of Venus." Review of *Seduction and Betrayal*. *Harper's* 249 (July 1974): 87.

Rogers, Katherine M. Review of *Seduction and Betrayal*. *Victorian Studies* 18 (1975): 362–64.

Solomon, Barbara Probst. "Seduction and Betrayal." Review of *Seduction and Betrayal*. *New York Review of Books* 21 (May 2, 1974): 4, 13.

Sullivan, Walter. "The Feckless Present, the Unredeemed Past: Some Recent Novels." Review of *Sleepless Nights*. *Sewanee Review* 88 (1980): 432–41.

Tanner, Tony. "The Great Symbol Hunt." Review of *A View of My Own*. *Spectator* 212 (April 10, 1964): 492.

Trilling, Diana. "Fiction in Review." Review of *The Ghostly Lover*. *Nation* 160 (May 5, 1945): 522–24.

White, Edmund. "Portraits Etched on Glass." Review of *Sleepless Nights*. *Washington Post Book World* (May 6, 1979): F1, F4.

Yeazell, Ruth Bernard. Review of *Seduction and Betrayal*. *Nineteenth-Century Fiction Studies* 30 (1975): 225–29.

MARLENE YOUMANS

William Harmon
(1938–   )

A poet of brilliant verbal inventiveness, William Harmon has mastered the highest level of technical skill. In addition, he has drawn from a treasury of knowledge—general, literary, and scientific—and in his most recent books has added a radiant new warmth and insight to his achievements. Yet, despite numerous awards for his poetry and notable accomplishments as critic and anthologist, he has not received the critical attention that he deserves.

BIOGRAPHY

William Ruth Harmon once humorously described himself as the son of a traveling salesman and a farmer's daughter, types not fond of the "whole truth." This child of fiction was born on June 10, 1938, in Concord, North Carolina, to textile executive William Richard Harmon and Virginia Pickerel Harmon. After the death of his father, Harmon was raised as the only child of a single parent. Sally Frances and William Richard II are the children of his December 1965 marriage to Lynn Chadwell. The marriage ended in divorce, and in May 1988 Harmon married for a second time. He and Anne Margretta Wilson became parents of Caroline Ruth in May 1989.

A graduate of the University of Chicago (A.B. 1958, A.M. 1968), the University of North Carolina at Chapel Hill (M.A. 1968), and the University of Cincinnati (Ph.D. 1970), Harmon is a professor of English at the University of North Carolina at Chapel Hill and was, for a time, chairman of the English Department (1972–77).

Harmon's achievements are not confined to literary and academic areas. His active duty service as a naval officer (1960–67) earned him the Navy Commendation Medal with Combat "V"; the Vietnamese Staff Service Honor Medal, first class; and the Cross of Gallantry.

In the years since graduate school, he has held a series of important editorial, consulting, and executive posts while publishing an extensive body of poetry and criticism. He has received many awards for scholarship and writing, including Chicago's Fiske Poetry Prize, the Binyon Humanities Award, and the Elliston Poetry Fellowship; the Lamont Award for a first book of poems; a Rockefeller Humanities Fellowship; the William Carlos Williams Award for the year's best volume of poetry, *Mutatis Mutandis* (1985), published by a small, nonprofit, or university press; and a Pulitzer Prize nomination, also for *Mutatis Mutandis.*

He continues to live in Chapel Hill, North Carolina, where he is currently at work on new essays and two collections of poetry, tentatively titled *To a Friend* and *Prose Songs.*

MAJOR THEMES

In the journey from Harmon's first book of poetry, *Treasury Holiday* (1970), to his most recent, *Mutatis Mutandis,* the figure of the poet in an American landscape of language evolves and matures. His writing is an unusual progression from the long poem and exuberant catalogues of trifles and enormities to collections of short poems that harmonize his wit, intelligence, technical skill, and remarkable inventiveness in a range of modes and formal concerns.

The speaker of *Treasury Holiday* is a multifaceted figure whose attempt to encompass America is reflected in his multiple selves. He allies himself with Whitman and Ginsberg in form and scope: "I am the Gross National Product" (i), and he is indeed gross in goods, embracing "Borax / Kleenex Clorox Kotex Kodak & Ex-Lax" (i). He loafs to examine not a spear of grass but a pretty girl's tongue (vi). Like Whitman he will absorb all, refusing to discriminate. In doing so, he resembles the "melting pot mulligan mulligatawny & huge buildings" of the United States (i). He invokes the land and its creatures like Whitman, claiming to "participate" in the "organization" of plants and animals, but he is measured out in trillions of dollars. The land he surveys is a "loom graph" of interstate highways shuttling athwart a warp of east-west roads. The speaker becomes the "dance" of warp and woof, a dance of earth and cash (xxxi).

Early on, he refers to the poet William Carlos Williams, the "good doc" who diagnosed the craziness of America's "pure products." As GNP, he himself is clearly at risk. He proves a splintered creature, alive with selves. His unlived lives—as a circus runaway, a "Redskin," a Red Skelton, a Muslim (William Ruth X, a priest (William Cardinal Harmon)—are wildly varied and colorful (ix). So too is his self-created myth. Raised by "a pack of jackals in Cabarrus County, N.C.," he is sold to the local paper, christened Jackal Girl (hence Harmon's middle name), washed and renamed *William* Ruth, but even so, still manages brief forays into "the chaste forest," where he is greeted by "friendly familiar cries of Auurhnga! Auurhnga!" (vii). Digging into the word hoard, the poet adds a further dimension to this "Harmon." He cites "Harmon from

Herrmannus oldest name in Europe carried in the Book of Doom'' (vii) and defines his mixed name and nature: Harmon or Herman, ''Army-Man & Warrior''; Ruth, beauty and pity; William or Wilhelm, ''Old High German Resolute-Helmet & Defender & Protector'' (viii). (This same etymologist in ''in A Helmet Made of Boar's Teeth,'' in *One Long Poem* [1982], tells us: ''If in the beginning they name you William / You have a helmet with you all the time'' [11].) Etymology leads to personal history, for Harmon-the-speaker or ''William the Teller'' (of dollars and decay) is indeed a wounded warrior who claims the company of ''Angles & Swaefs,'' claims skirmishes in Prague and South Vietnam, Italy, and Louisiana (x). Instead of heroic songs, our warrior poet has written operating manuals in Saigon. As national war ''product'' he has served as Ishmaelean witness, a gross national figure who has heard the ''hallelujah of hogs & warships,'' seen nuclear explosions in the Pacific, visited Hiroshima (xvii).

What survives of this persona in the less personal ''choruses'' of Harmon's second book of poetry, *Legion: Civic Choruses,* is his sense of the ''empire going out of biz,'' as Harmon says in ''Taps & Coda'' (29), and his identity as wounded world-warrior who has ''crossed Poland & the Trojan plain & gone on our stomachs southeast many smoking miles & hit the beach & monkey jungle mercy,'' as he says in ''The Legion'' (17). In Harmon's third book of poetry, *The Intussusception of Miss Mary America,* the reader meets a female double of the all-devouring National Product. She, like the William-Ruth of *Treasury,* has a private and particular history; a purified teenage virgin, she is ritually deflowered in the Ceremonial Intussusception, then remade as ''Mary,'' an artificial virgin and ''healer'' of faith. Like Harmon-the-GNP, this public self hugs all places, things, and flaws in her enormous grip. Diabetic with the ''sugar'' of war, rusty with nineteenth-century industrialism, Mary is a contemporary dark lady and mistress, haloed with voltages of ''Black wires [that] grow on Her head'' (24). Belied by no ''false compare,'' Mary's corrosive features may yet be ''fair,'' for ''it is a paradox of supernatural measure that She is a force for virtue in the universe'' (25). The ''America'' that was ''O holy poetry the only Mary the only money'' in *Treasury* (iii) emerges here as gross and great.

Although William-in-the-helmet and William the warrior reappear in *One Long Poem,* the poet-persona in this collection is warmer, more particular, and more engaging than those of previous volumes. He is vulnerable but open, unlike the original William of concealing masks and fantastic unlived lives. No longer self-absorbed, no longer thinking to absorb the continent, he assumes strong attachments to children, friends, and fellow poets, to the extended family and the human family. He moves in the mundane precincts of house, window, park, the ''larval lar'' (tutelary television) of home, the haunts of domestic cat and dog. In these square suburbs he finds remnants of the gods, mysterious closets and corners, elegiac hours. In *Mutatis Mutandis,* Harmon returns the reader again to the banal checkerboard of suburbs; though we recognize favorite themes and concerns in this muser on mortality and verse, the poet is buried further in the landscape than in *One Long Poem.*

The vision of America as an artifact of merchandising and mortgages, an immense suburb scarred by war, lingers on in the "humbug" world of *One Long Poem* and *Mutatis Mutandis.* Against what is false stand Poe, destroyed by humbug, and James Wright, of the big, corny, and very American heart. Harmon still proffers a litany of the American ugly, but he takes a new stance toward this landscape. The "what-the-hell" attitude of *Legion* surfaces only to admit impediment; in *Mutatis Mutandis* Harmon confesses that he cares and assumes that we care too.

Always, poetry itself is one of the major matters for his care. In Harmon's first three volumes of poetry, the American landscape is, as it was for Whitman, a mighty poem. Examination of America equals transcription of that poem. This equation leads the poet to pay homage to poets. Rhythms, internal forms, and puns suggest a pride of poets. Parallelism suggests Whitman, Ginsberg, and even Christopher Smart in lines such as "no for there is salt. / there is the gold flow. / there is shooting pool" (*Legion,* 21). Harmon's pun-perversions embrace Moore, Yeats, Marlowe, and others, as in these lines from *Legion:* "imaginary gardens with real turds" (39), "constant gore booth" (47), and "see see where my blood streams in the fundament" (48). By the time Harmon reaches *One Long Poem* and *Mutatis Mutandis,* he has leaped from literary pun to swash-buckling parodies. Other changes in stance occur in the former collection: The act of naming or bringing a phrase to perfection involves the energies of the universe and is a redemptive act. In both volumes poetry regains its miraculous footing: the poet sets his feet in matters of earth and grave, and our odds-opposed existence becomes confirmation of some blessedness.

The nature of truth, imagination, and the artist becomes an absorbing interest of the poet. Truth and fiction jostle. Harmon's warriors are now beautiful be-cause fictive. Products and poems of imagination teach us the fallacy of expe-rience. A saving love for fictive truth remains. The artist—that rare blossom in American lawns—gropes his way not toward truth or beauty but toward the next phoneme, as in "The Missionary Position" (*Mutatis Mutandis*). Or, as Harmon puts it in "Robert Morgan's Pelagian Georgics": "The next word comes from a lexicon tipped over on its side and opened to the magnetic field of acoustic connections that matter almost as much as semantic connections" (11). In our suburbs a poet falters at describing Grecian urns. Thus, against a stage setting of "ugly glass and glass again," the Harmon of *Mutatis Mutandis* rejects the Rilke of "Archaïscher Torso Apollos" and the lure of the stone torso's superior reality, its completion and power in romantic incompletion that challenge the viewer to change (see "A Poet in a Landscape of Language" and "Inking In" in *Mutatis Mutandis*). Harmon pays lovely homage to another of Rilke's sensual and inward figures, the father in "Jugend-Bildnis Meines Vaters" (*Neue Ged-ichte*), a poem in which the daguerrotype of Rilke's father and Rilke himself fade together—an appropriate choice for a poet who writes of fathers and sings with one foot in the grave.

Just as Harmon's early preoccupation with the corrosive and entrancing poem of the United States evolves into such concerns as the poet's place in the American landscape and the nature of poetry, so his interest in book-length structures, form in shorter poems, and poetic devices evolves. Even the most cursory of examinations reveals a sea change between the early long poems and the collections of *One Long Poem* and *Mutatis Mutandis.*

Harmon orginally planned his first volumes as portions of a nine-part long poem, *Looms. Treasury Holiday,* where the poet is dancer and dance of the loom of highways, is the first book of *Looms. Legion* is the middle third of *William Tecumseh Sherman,* planned as the third book of the proposed *Looms.* Harmon's first three volumes reveal a straightforward organization: Treasury relies on thirty-four segments or "Fits"; *Legion* depends on "choruses" and a weighty series of partitions and subtitles; and *Intussusception* presents a sequence of hymns to 'virgin' Mary. For obvious reasons poetic form and style in these volumes are frequently compared with those of Whitman and Ginsberg. The books are rife with catalogues and lists, and each utilizes parallelism as a way to organize both related and random items. Notable too in *Looms* are the vitality of the speaking voice, the verbal play (a blend of the vernacular with the more outré), the ambitious scope, and the subject matter that covers the continent.

Though it may be unexpected that Harmon turns from *Looms* and the long poem to lyric and meditation in—of course—*One Long Poem,* his books remain tightly unified sequences. The books, like a dynastic line, persist in family resemblance. *One Long Poem*—a collection of short poems named for the web of family, people, and "flamboyant animals and hapless plants" that sleep "in the dormitory of the dead," as Harmon says in "Scars" (37)—displays as much concern for shapeliness as the three earlier poems. Alice-like, the reader must begin at the beginning—even before beginnings, before the time-notching sun. The opening, "A Dawn Horse," emerges as if from one of Harmon's prehistorical echochambers—and the reader does not see the slow, heightening steps of dawn but only glimpses the shadowy horse as he "starts to step" (2). The second poem, "The Dragon-Fire-Priest," shifts fluently from an imagined mythic past and the universal family to the present and the poet's own family. The speaker is he who utters the "immemorial word" and whose wise girl-child of Dragoncraft knows that a poem opens and shuts the world; he is also the tribal teller who inherits the priest-king's powerful synaesthesia that spins the world in cosmic dance. The alighting of the speaker within a space-time continuum; the cosmic family; the mysterious lair of one's own family; the pursuit of word, name, and memory: these concerns inform the entire book. *One Long Poem* closes as strongly as it opens: Poems about endings and final words shut up its world. The last half-dozen poems meditate on "the roll / of poets and fathers down the hatch,'' linking Berryman and his ''felo de se of a father'' with Harmon and his father (46). Musings on father and child, the autumnal decay of Harmon's maternal grandfather, and his census of other dead point toward closure. Despite all hoverings of Marvellean chariots, the poet promises his children a special space and instant to be filled by ''every totemic syllable'' of their true names (54). The magical naming in ''There'' and the praise of things ''that have the grace to end'' in ''When It Comes'' bring the reader to a final ''immemorial'' word expressive of cycles and transformation: *butterflies* (56).

The structure of Harmon's second collection of short poems, *Mutatis Mutandis,* sets such moments of grace and realization against secular arenas. One of the organizing elements of the book is the poem as ''invoice,'' form appropriate to a banal ''civilization founded on . . . retail merchandising'' (31). These consignments to the world, these accounts of values and charges are also a ''Chamber Piece'' for ''Reader (Unseen)'' and a dancer whose steps deny the mood and rhythm of the poems, as in a ''dance . . . discontinuous'' (2). The idea of invoice as music and dance may appear surprising, but it is not so far from the GNP-Harmon who becomes a dancer and dance in *Treasury Holiday.* All of these terms—*invoice, music, dance,* and *poem*—postulate a reader, listener, or spectator. When the speaker of *Mutatis Mutandis* creates a synaesthesia by sleight of pen, transforming invoices into chambered music, he also creates a reader who, like himself, lives in a discontinuous world where mystery must commute to a ''square suburban square'' (3). The poet gives his reader music in voices, voices in chambers, a chamber piece in pieces, a chamber piece in invoices.

Although both collections of short poems display unities of theme and an overarching structure, there are elements in the design of *Mutatis Mutandis* that suggest a repetition of items or musical phrases. Certain figures recur: Poe, Dickinson, and Rilke. Certain figures of speech recur: for example, in this book Harmon plays with and distorts cliché more than in any other. Phrases and lines reappear in various ''invoices'' like popular items or musical motifs. Thus, the speaker writes, sings, and walks with the iambic pulse of a man with ''one foot in the grave''—a reference to Bach noted first in *One Long Poem* and a foretaste of the poet's manipulation of cliché. Other lines that recur as refrain throughout the book deal with persistence. Flecks of ''everlasting light'' ''persist'' and drop eternally through the one realm, the one poem, the ''Universe.'' In a universe where meter offers only ''facsimiles of continuity,'' particles of light maintain their endless plummet in the one long poem. Human beings run to corpses, then bone and royal air; the knottiest navel dissolves into particles of dust. Light persists. Music, also composed of particles, needs and makes ''covenant with shapely silence'' in order to repeat itself and persist (see ''Pantomimesis''). So poems make covenant with the poet's disjunctive world, bringing discontinuous elements into unstable harmony in order to become continuous, whether for ''Millisecond or the Ming'' (see ''Eldorado''). Repetition within *Mutatis Mu-*

tandis establishes a continuity of pattern and form and helps to make a Universe of the book.

Harmon's shorter poems in *One Long Poem* and *Mutatis Mutandis* revel in a variety of forms—some old, some new, some borrowed. Clearly his "Stevens," "Auden," and "Berryman" pay homage in form and content to those masters. Likewise in "Thunder Stuns Stutterers Mum Among Jumbo Doombooms" Harmon calls the reader back to Stevens's *Harmonium*. The two-line, end-stopped stanzas, sound play, and link between star and cock suggest Stevens and, more specifically, his heroic bantams, sunny turkey-cocks, and the Crispin who echoes back "quavers" of thunder. "Zubby Sutra" is teasingly akin to Ginsberg in form and references while demonstrating Harmon's fluid, free-wheeling imagination. The shape of a small, intricately plotted circle in "To Suffer" shares kinship with some of A. R. Ammons's clever miniatures, such as "Reflective." Harmon's fluent handling of line and stanza is evident in selections from *One Long Poem,* where he moves easily from clipped and end-stopped phrases to long enjambed lines and stanzas. At times he unites these seeming polarities in a single poem, as in "Danang—Spring MCMLXXV." The emphatic refrain of "No" serves to correct the speaker's vision:

> Our archers are combing out their long hair in the moon's light.
> No.
> Our fusiliers are combing out their long hair in the moon's light.
> No.

Denial widens as the poet rejects romantic visions of his fellow warriors, dream warriors and their "historical battle," and the ancient white-lit weaponry of museums. "No," a curt and dramatic counterpoint to long and often enjambed lines, is a signpost toward a closure of black and white oppositions; the speaker recalls a white-sheeted war against bedbugs, notes the defeat of "our army," and sets rows of black "news" against white strands of hair that shine "dead center" in the denied kingdom of moonlight and dream.

Another curious example of Harmon's ingenuity is "Totem-Motet," a poem whose form reinforces its study of metaphor (*One Long Poem*). Vehicle, a wristwatch "with its crystal shattered / complicatedly," appears before tenor—the Atlantic Ocean. Delicate complexity of ocean and crystal yields to a second vehicle as the glass splits into bitter (briny?) children who are churches or "religions / Progressively subdividing." A seaborne beaker of salt water resolves this three-in-one when its "tipping impromptu" illustrates "The timing mechanism / Of a complicated schism." The poem is the metaphor, and its form extends metaphor. It, too, is "vehicle," its fractured lines further mimicking the dissolution of crystal and church. Like the glass beaker of water, its broken lines tip "first one way, then another" across the page. The poem as vehicle thus concerns itself with "timing," division of language, and the containing of bits of its own unruly forces (21).

The happy exploration of form that enlivens *One Long Poem* spills over into *Mutatis Mutandis.* In the later book, however, ideas of fidelity and persistence shape form. Lack of things that "remain" may equal breakage in meaning and form, as in "Digits, Syllables": "There is no con- / tinuity. / Sextus Empiricus." Meter makes only an ambiguous fidelity, for "Given a regular meter, anything goes." Thus we have "Saxifrage marmalade: kerosene sherbet; / Laser taco: a world of names means zero" (27). The poet himself is discontinuous, as in "The Third Sunday After Epiphany": "So say I write with one foot in the grave" (3). Reeling between ground and grave, time and eternity, he creates a dotted metrical line, as in "Alexander and Caesar":

> Walking, that is, with one foot in the grave
> Produces the iambic pulse, more leap
> Than limp (limping now and then, even so)
> The fixed foot like a lighthouse for the other,
> Which tacks all ways but adds up to a circle
> When all the parallelograms are balanced. (26)

The uneasy marriage between fidelity and mortality implied in *Mutatis Mutandis* leads Harmon to a fresh interest in the "pulse" of iambic pentameter, the metrical line that marks much of the volume. Short blank-verse poems (recalling Stevens), villanelles, and sonnets offer their "facsimiles" of the continuous. His unrhymed iambic pentameter is an extremely flexible medium that can veer back and forth from the light to the weighty. The villanelles fuse serious ideas of 'what remains' with playful treatment; they are circular forms in which elements both persist and renew themselves. In Harmon's "Eldorado," the traditional closed chamber of an Elizabethan sonnet rejects its identity as "pretty room." Although resisting neat rhyme, tidy end-line breakage, and pat closure, the poem catalogues elements that persist—time, rain or shine, proverbial expression, the ubiquitous "They"—and at last circles back to identify persisting time ("the Ming") as "shine." The struggle to compose continuity in "Pictures of a Dark Girl Working on a Petrarchan Sonnet," written in free verse, is resolved with the poet's Petrarchan sonnet, an address to his dark opposite. With elaborate decorum in this *tornata*-like close, the poem becomes its own subject. In addition, the sonnet presents a further circle, one in which cycles of error will run "on and on." Subject, idea, and form establish repetition and "facsimiles of continuity."

Pleasure in rhetorical figures and tropes, in sound and rhyme informs all of Harmon's writing. This play achieves a new flowering with the wildly varied poems of *One Long Poem,* a volume that shows off the poet's verbal conquest of "charismatic archaisms, musical tools," as he says in "Auden" (45). Figures of speech riot through his "madly formal gardens" (45): the synaesthesia of "barkings, preSocratic aloha shirts of basic racket" (40) or "among deep empty drums of sound unreeling hungrily" (1); the complex metaphor of "Totem-

Motet''; the epitrope of "Redounding"; the epizeuxis of ticks and "That's it" in "There" (55); the hyperbole of "Zubby Sutra." The list continues. A notable addition to these random examples is Harmon's beloved pun, clothed in a variety of guises: repetition with a shift in meaning, as in "square suburban square" (3), "bay tree by the bay" (20), or "Last things last" (41) in *Mutatis Mutandis;* paronomasia, as in the shift from "middleman" to "middlebeast" in *One Long Poem* (33); substitution for the expected word, as in "a pan of midnight ink" (3), "sea to whining sea" (13), or "one day they'll put your money where your eyes are" (5) in *Mutatis Mutandis;* hysteron proteron, as in "mouth-to-hand" in *Mutatis Mutandis* (11); coined words, as in the use of "hooving" to express the action of a (Hoover) vacuum cleaner in *Mutatis Mutandis* (4). Many of the above examples are drawn from *Mutatis Mutandis,* where two of the elements that "persist" are the cliché and proverb, with Harmon's shocking them new through punning distortions. His puns extend to form as well: the "Dawn Horse" of *One Long Poem* (the first poem or "dawn" of the book) is an aubade stripped of love and the human; "Totem-Motet" shatters its form in *One Long Poem;* "con- / tinuity" is broken in *Mutatis Mutandis* (27). The latter book gives us "Jackson, exhaling like a Samurai / His seventeen classic syllables, died" (8), a clause of seventeen syllables and Dickinson's rhopalic "necklace" of (p)earl, (o)nyx, and (e)merald, seen as an acrostic (27).

In *One Long Poem,* Harmon's use of sound play includes parallelism ("Scars"), repetition ("Danang"), the juggling dance of sound and meaning, and outrageous rhyme: Stevens-like "rightnesses," the found satisfaction of sound. Sound produces meaning, so that *necromancy* leads to *necking* (36), *coronets* to *nets* and *cornet* (40), *fuse* to *fusses* (53). The pleasures of sound. The poet—who in his first book, *Treasury Holiday,* tallies up American 'poems' with the beginning "When in," "We the," and "Four score" (ii)—orchestrates a complex, subtle music in *One Long Poem.* Take a modest lyric ("By Myself in a Public Park in the Early Morning") as an example:

> I came across a horseshoe among weeds at a big field's edge,
> a real one, with holes for nails and slots for countersinking
>   the nails' heads.
> I heaved it underhand a hundred feet
> to where there was a wooden croquet stake.
>
> With wet rust red on my humming fingers, I was alone;
> there was nobody to witness my magnificent ringer,
> snugly at rest against the stake's foot, iron to wood,
> just as the sun's lower limb lifted from the horizon
> as though seized, gripped, filled, taken, inspired
>   mouth-to-mouth.
>
> Noble Achilles of the world-historical shield:
> royal Arjuna, peerless archer of the Eighteen Days:
> greatest *Kshatriya* princes of antiquity: be with me.

> Nothing like that will ever happen to me again
> at daybreak or any other hour of the day or night. (20)

Both the title and first stanza of this mock-heroic, sonnet-length poem are un-assuming. Focused on the "I" and his actions, they are heavy with prepositional phrases. The prosaic lines move slowly, and a deliberate awkwardness marks the heaving of a "shoe" for so many "feet." In the regular iambic pentameter of lines three and four, the awkwardness continues in "to where there was" and the lumbering repetition of sound in "underhand a hundred." Sound becomes a more striking element with the interesting fifth line, in which distortion of expected word order (wet-red-rust) is matched by distortion of sound. The assonance rhyme between the almost proximal "wet" and "red" combined with the alliteration of "rust red" generates a tongue-twister that forces the reader into deliberate, heavily stressed syllables. A tactile focus is immediately renewed in "humming," and the sound of "-ing" vibrates on in "fingers" and "ringer." The sonority of "alone" finds in "nobody" its aural mate—and its mate in meaning. In a generous epic simile the "ringer" is allied with the sunrise, its importance affirmed by rhythm and sound. Heavy stresses increase: "stake's foot, iron to wood," "lower limb lifted," and "seized, gripped, filled, taken." Simultaneously the density of sound increases: the assonance of *foot-wood* and *sun's-from-horizon;* the mingled consonance and assonance of "lower limb lifted"; the repetition in "mouth-to-mouth" (a rhythmic echo of "iron to wood," as well.) As horseshoe joins stake, sun and horizon disengage in images of life, resuscitation, breath, kiss. Shoe and foot, sun's limb and sky: emphatic stress and sound help to "lift" the original event into the heroic realm, even though the acts portrayed are polar—one an image of small union and the other an image of the sundering of huge elements. The little hero invokes powers mysterious in sound and identity: Arjuna and *kshatriya* princes. Notable in the last stanza is the ear-pleasing parallelism in syntax, so different from the poem's initial parallelism, and the bold stresses that open all but the modest final line. After the grand invocation of wide and heroic space and time, the speaker's request is simple and direct in its monosyllables, its perfect rhyme: *Be with me.* In his closure, a two-line summation reminiscent of the Elizabethan sonnet's couplet, the speaker denies himself heroic identity and links his life not with the "world-historical" but with the round of hours.

Harmon is a poet alive to what he calls the "articulatory artery" of related sounds. His essay "Rhyme in English Verse" establishes a revised nomenclature for a range of "acoustic-articulatory phenomena." A glance through several short poems reveals a variety of redundant, perfect, and deficient rhyme: *blinks* (v.)-*blinks* (n.), plenary redundant; *dawn-yawn,* plenary perfect; *typhoon-simoon,* compound perfect; *Geckoes'-echoes* or *luminous-numinous,* augmented perfect; *eidolon-on and on,* heteromerous deficient; *grandiose-caboose,* heterobaric deficient; *tears-cloud-unbuilders,* puny deficient; and the peculiar and deficient *hai karate-cardigan party.*

The range of rhyme and figures of speech and the variety of forms governing individual volumes and single poems suggest something of Harmon's deft and intelligent handling of language. In "A Poet in a Landscape of Language" (*Mutatis Mutandis*) "The one universe" celebrated from *Treasury Holiday* to *Mutatis Mutandis* is a place and a long poem in which, despite GNP and mercantile crookery, one may stumble upon "those miracles we do manage to get— / Flourishing orchards of outlandish eloquence" (31).

SURVEY OF CRITICISM

Despite its excellence, very little has been written about Harmon's poetry. His receiving the Lamont Award garnered some attention, and most of the reviewers of *Treasury Holiday* have praised its felicitous phrases, vitality, originality, and expansiveness. This high praise is tempered, however, by Robert Shaw's wholesale condemnation of the book as a boring assault on the corporate state. Although *Legion* won some accolades for the author's ingenuity and intelligence, it appeared to small notice. Once again *Poetry* provided a harsh review, finding the book clotted with devices, heavy with humor, burdened with structure, and thick with meaningless surface. Even if it is acknowledged that *Legion* suffers from an overdensity of ornate language and devices and does not provide the warmth of later volumes, the attack was excessive. *Intussusception of Miss Mary America* received less attention than the previous book, although noted as one of Kayak's most interesting books of 1976. The neglect continued with the appearance of Harmon's very fine book *One Long Poem* after a six-year hiatus from book publication. Brief reviews pointed to Harmon as an underappreciated poet, noting the linguistic fireworks, lively persona, and human insight in *One Long Poem*. In a discerning essay in *Georgia Review* (1983), Peter Stitt reviewed works by several poets and wrote that "Harmon is surely one of the most neglected contemporary American writers, a poet of astonishing intellect and verbal range, who does not neglect the warmer virtues of poetry" (433). In a perceptive essay (1986), Cary Wolfe has lauded Harmon's award-winning *Mutatis Mutandis;* it is one of the few reviews of Harmon's work to take note of the growth and change in his poetry.

The lack of critical attention to Harmon's poetry is difficult to understand. Perhaps interest in his work was slowed because of the poor reception of *Legion* and the publication of his third book by a small press. Perhaps some of the neglect is due to the perceived difficulty of his poems, since many of Harmon's supreme virtues—wit, keen attention to sound, stores of knowledge, joyful play with moods and modes—are only too rare in contemporary poetry.

BIBLIOGRAPHY

Works by William Harmon

Poetry

Treasury Holiday. Middletown, Conn.: Wesleyan University Press, 1970.
Legion: Civic Choruses. Middletown, Conn.: Wesleyan University Press, 1973.
The Intussusception of Miss Mary America. Santa Cruz, Calif.: Kayak Books, 1976.
One Long Poem. Baton Rouge: Louisiana State University Press, 1982.
Mutatis Mutandis. Middletown, Conn.: Wesleyan University Press, 1985.

Critical Books

Time in Ezra Pound's Work. Chapel Hill, N.C.: University of North Carolina, 1977.
What Rhymes. In press.

Edited Books

The Oxford Book of American Light Verse. New York: Oxford University Press, 1979.
The Uneeda Review. New York: Lyons Books, 1984.
A Handbook to Literature. New York: Macmillan, 1985 (5th ed.), 1992 (6th ed.).
The Concise Columbia Book of Poetry. Columbia University Press, 1990. Reprinted in
    paperback in 1993 as *The Classic Hundred: All-Time Favorite Poems.*
The Top 500 Poems. Columbia University Press, 1992.

Essays

''Robert Morgan's Pelagian Georgics: Twelve Essays.'' *Parnassus* 9, no. 2 (1981): 5–
    30.
''Rhyme in English Verse.'' *Studies in Philology* 84, no. 4 (1987): 365–93.
''Is Southern Poetry Southerner Than Southern Fiction?'' *Mississippi Quarterly* 46
    (Spring 1993): 273–78.

Studies of William Harmon

Cunningham, William. Review of *Treasury Holiday. Carolina Quarterly* 23, no. 1
    (1971): 68–70.
Ostriker, Alicia. ''Weapons and Words.'' *Partisan Review* 39, no. 3 (1972): 464–68.
Pritchard, William H. Review of *One Long Poem. Poetry* 143, no. 4 (1984): 232–33.
Ramsey, Paul. Review of *Legion: Civic Choruses. Sewanee Review* 82, no. 2 (1974):
    402–3.
Review of *Treasury Holiday. Antioch Review* 30, nos. 3–4 (1970–71): 465.
Review of *Treasury Holiday. Virginia Quarterly Review* 47, no. 3 (1971): cvi.
Review of *One Long Poem. Kirkus Reviews* 50, no. 18 (1982): 1099.
Shaw, Robert B. ''The Long and the Short of It.'' *Poetry* 119, no. 6 (1972): 342–55.
Smyth, Paul. ''Less Tit than Tat.'' *Poetry* 123, no. 3 (1973): 165–73.

Stitt, Peter. "Words, Book Words, What Are You?" *Georgia Review* 37, no. 2 (1983), 428–38.

Wolfe, Cary. "The Dancer in the Chamber." *Carolina Quarterly* 38, no. 3 (1986): 86–93.

HILARY HOLLADAY

Beth Henley
(1952–   )

Beth Henley is best known for her first play, *Crimes of the Heart,* winner of
the 1981 Pulitzer Prize for drama. In that play and subsequent works, Henley
has mined her Mississippi heritage for colorful language and memorably offbeat
characters. Even the most serious scenes are punctuated by amusing dialogue.
But beneath the surface of comic repartee and outlandish situations, her plays
are serious examinations of relationships and family life. Henley shows a special
empathy for women characters struggling to find their niche in the world. Her
plays typically end on a conciliatory note, with everyone at least momentarily
achieving harmony.

BIOGRAPHY

When Beth Henley won the Pulitzer Prize in 1981, shortly before her 29th
birthday, she exclaimed with the comic self-effacement typical of her own creations, ''Winning the Pulitzer Prize means I'll never have to work in a dog-
food factory again'' (quoted in Haller 1981, 44). If not exactly the rags-to-riches
story that remark suggests, Henley's life does divide neatly into two parts: before
Crimes of the Heart and after its enormous success.

Born on May 8, 1952, in Jackson, Mississippi, to Charles Boyce Henley, an
attorney and state legislator, and Elizabeth Josephine Becker Henley, an amateur
actress, Elizabeth Becker Henley was the second of four daughters. Both sides
of her family were Mississippi-born and bred. Beth Henley's father was from
Hazelhurst; her mother, from Brookhaven. While growing up, Beth Henley frequently visited relatives in those small towns, and her family vacationed nearly
every summer in Biloxi, Mississippi.

A shy, sickly child, Beth Henley spent much of her time recuperating from
asthma attacks. By her own account, she did not distinguish herself as a student

in the local public schools. Drama captured her imagination early on, thanks to her mother's involvement in Jackson's New Stage Theater. Henley grew up reading scripts and attending plays. By the time she reached high school, she was (perhaps unwittingly) preparing for an acting career by spraying her hair orange and causing disturbances in movie theaters (Corliss 1982, 80).

But even such innocent-sounding acts of rebellion appear to have been the exception, not the rule. In a 1987 interview Henley said that she spent much of her adolescence "reading, writing, listening to records, just biding my time. My parents were breaking up then," and, as a result, "I wanted to please them; I didn't want to be more of a burden" (quoted in Rochlin 1987, 12). A summer working with the New Stage Theater seems to have released her from "the boredom, the pain of having nothing to care about" that she felt as a teen-ager (quoted in Rochlin 1987, 12). The apprenticeship convinced Henley that she should study acting in college.

Although acting was her main interest, there were hints during Henley's years at Southern Methodist University (SMU) in Dallas that she would succeed as a playwright. *Am I Blue,* a one-act play she wrote as a sophomore, was staged by SMU in her senior year. According to an interview published in 1987 (Betsko and Koenig), she hid behind a pseudonym ("Amy Peach") when *Am I Blue* premiered and perceived only much later what the play was really about:

When I wrote *Am I Blue* I was so emotionally covered up that I didn't even realize what I was saying about myself or about life or loneliness, family situations. I just thought it was a kind of funny piece that I wrote to pass playwriting class. When I went back to it, I was so glad I'd written it down because I'll never be that innocent again . . . with that point of view, knowing nothing about life. At eighteen, I was simply terrified of being a failure. (213)

Despite her fears of failure, Henley seems to have thoroughly enjoyed her college years. She read classical and modern drama and reveled in the excitement of bringing literature to life on stage. "This was alive theater, someone bringing you in touch with a world you hadn't understood before," she said of her college experience; for her, "the veils of the mind lifted" at SMU (quoted in Corliss 1982, 80). She graduated with a BFA in acting in 1974.

Henley's apprentice effort, *Am I Blue,* attracted the interest of a friend who wanted to stage an original musical. The year after Henley's graduation, Henley wrote the script for *Parade,* a musical set in the 1940s that was produced at SMU. *Parade* was the only play Henley's father lived to read, and Henley's memories of his reaction are revealing: "He hated it because he'd been in World War II. He thought the work was completely abysmal and historically inaccurate. He didn't see me as a writer" (quoted in Betsko and Koenig 1987, 214). If Henley saw herself as a writer at this point in her life, she did not force the issue. She was more intent on her acting. During the time she was writing

Parade, she was also performing with the Dallas Minority Repertory Theatre and holding down a series of odd jobs.

Henley left Dallas for graduate study in acting at the University of Illinois. After a year of classes and a summer of acting in an outdoor historical drama at New Salem State Park, she left graduate school and moved to California. In Los Angeles, she joined Stephen Tobolowsky (her boyfriend at SMU) and other college friends trying to break into the movie industry. Thus began a humbling time for Henley: She rarely heard from her agent; she was unable to make a living as an actress; and, like just about everybody else in Hollywood, she was writing a screenplay that would go nowhere without a literary agent to represent it.

Under these depressing circumstances, Henley decided to write a play that she could either stage with friends or peddle to regional theaters. She was committed to keeping the production inexpensive. The play would have only one set—a family kitchen—and she would figure out a way to eliminate the large birthday cake from the last scene because she considered the prop an extravagant expense (Haller 1981, 44). The result of these musings in 1978 was *Crimes of the Heart,* her first full-length play.

In the end, Henley did not have to produce the play herself, nor did she have to eliminate the cake. Although regional theaters initially rejected the manuscript, the Fates smiled on her the day director Frederick Bailey (another SMU friend) entered *Crimes* in the Great American Play contest sponsored by the Actors Theater of Louisville, Kentucky. Since Bailey had not told her he had submitted her play, the telephone call informing her that she was cowinner of the 1979 competition was as startling as it was gratifying.

The Louisville premiere of *Crimes* was a hit, as were the regional productions that quickly sprang up across the country. The Manhattan Theater Club launched an off-Broadway run in late 1980, and suddenly Beth Henley and her brainchild were coasting toward fame. In the *New Yorker* (1981), Edith Oliver declared: ''This kind of play (loose-knit, precise, and free) and this kind of acting (first-rate by any standard) are what Off Broadway is all about'' (81).

The accolades heaped on *Crimes* in 1981 marked a stunning debut for a young playwright who still thought of herself as an actress. In April, even before the play arrived on Broadway, Henley won the Pulitzer Prize (and became the first woman playwright to receive that honor in 23 years). In June, the New York Drama Critics Circle named *Crimes* the best American play of the season. In August, Henley won the George Oppenheimer/*Newsday* Playwriting Award. In November, the play began a triumphant 535-performance run on Broadway.

Henley's big year had its share of ironies. Her role as a bag lady in a Los Angeles play excited critics who were impressed by the playwright's diverse talents. More significantly, the Hollywood studios that had once spurned Henley the actress now yearned for Henley the writer. She sold the screen rights to *Crimes* for a million dollars (Haller 1981, 40).

The success of *Crimes* meant that Henley's subsequent efforts would meet intense scrutiny. In October 1982 her streak of good luck ended when *The Wake of Jamey Foster* received poor reviews and folded after less than two weeks on Broadway. Maybe Henley had just committed the sin of creating a play less lovable than *Crimes.* In the presence of Jamey Foster's corpse for much of the play, his querulous survivors have little of the Magrath sisters' winsome charm and seem much less likely to overcome their problems. In any event, Henley took her play's failure in stride and even expressed a perverse exhilaration: ''I was stunned after *The Wake,* but as a woman from the South, I was ready for it. . . . I thought, 'You can overcome this! You can live with this! . . . ' When people praised *Crimes,* I felt like I had to be so self-effacing it wasn't any fun. I felt I had to say, 'Ah . . . it's really nothing. I didn't mean to write that . . . I was really writing a grocery list.' When you have a flop you can fight. I must say I did love *The Wake*'' (quoted in Betsko and Koenig 1987, 221).

The respectable off-Broadway run of *The Miss Firecracker Contest* in 1984 helped blunt memories of the dismal reception of *Wake.* Although the play has its share of the strange (Popeye, a young seamstress who believes she hears voices through her bulging eyes) and the grotesque (recollections of an aunt whose body grew long black hair, thanks to a pituitary gland transplanted from a monkey), the focus of *Miss Firecracker* on a small-town beauty pageant was more palatable to audiences than the grimly plotted *Wake* had been. Holly Hunter played Carnelle Scott, the earnest contestant who believes that winning the contest will restore her reputation and turn her life around. Hunter would go on to star in *Miss Firecracker,* the 1988 movie adaptation that Henley wrote, and to become the actor most closely associated with Henley's productions.

Although Henley has lived in Los Angeles since 1976, her plays have retained a Southern flavor. Like *Crimes, The Wake* and *Miss Firecracker* are set in Mississippi. *The Lucky Spot,* moderately successful in an off-Broadway run in 1987, moves over to Pigeon, Louisiana, and back in time to the Great Depression. The desperation of the era infiltrates the lives of Reed Hooker, a rough-talking gambler; Sue Jack, his ex-convict wife; and Cassidy, the teen-aged girl he won in a card game. *The Debutante Ball,* which finally made it to off-Broadway in 1988 after a series of rewrites, returns to present-day Mississippi with a vengeance: The play, set in a Hattiesburg mansion, is filled with sadness, rage, and miscommunication among family members.

Abundance, which opened off-Broadway in 1990, marks a change in setting: It chronicles the long friendship between two mail-order brides living in the Wyoming Territory during the nineteenth century. Still, the colorful frontier setting afforded Henley ''poetic license in the use of language,'' she explained in 1988. ''You can be more poetic, use stranger twists of phrase, which is what I always liked about the South'' (quoted in Hoffman 1989, 5).

Of her recent plays, *Debutante Ball* seems to have been especially important to Henley. She has called the tale of Teddy, a self-destructive young woman, her crazed, social-climbing mother, and an assortment of other, equally unhappy characters ''the most psychically autobiographical play I've written'' (quoted in

Betsko and Koenig 1987, 218). It is probably no coincidence that Henley began working on this violently emotional play (which features an on-stage miscarriage) not long after the embarrassing failure of *Wake*. She worked on *Debutante Ball* sporadically for several years; and after numerous rejections by regional theaters, California's South Coast Repertory Theater finally agreed to produce it in 1986. Despite good casting, the play did not come together on stage: "The first preview was so painful that I left the auditorium at intermission and threw up in a jade bush behind the theater," Henley confesses with characteristic candor in her preface to an illustrated edition of the play (xii).

No longer the wunderkind of Broadway, Henley has established herself as a mature playwright whose growing body of work interests scholars of contemporary drama and of women's writing as well as theatergoers. She has written for television and film as well as the stage. Her screen credits include *Nobody's Fool* (1986) and the adaptations of *Crimes of the Heart* (1986) and *Miss Firecracker* (1989). She and Tobowlosky collaborated with rock musician David Byrne on *True Stories* (1985).

Beth Henley is five feet and three inches tall, with long brown hair and brown eyes. As a Mississippian who has opted for voluntary captivity in Los Angeles, she exudes an aura of eccentricity; and observers have looked for, and found, connections between the playwright and her creations. The actresses who played the Magrath sisters on screen, for instance, said they watched Henley closely for idiosyncrasies they could build into their characters. (Jessica Lange picked up Henley's habit of opening an aspirin bottle with her teeth, and Sissy Spacek copied the playwright's preference for pajama tops) (Rochlin 1987, 12). In interviews, however, Henley does not sound especially eccentric. She comes across as articulate about her own work, by turns deeply depressed and greatly amused by her own life, and matter-of-fact about her early success. Although she periodically visits her hometown, Jackson, she has expressed no desire to return permanently to the region that lives so vividly in her plays.

MAJOR THEMES

Beth Henley's plays are more concerned with human relationships than with any particular chain of events. Like the creations of William Faulkner, Flannery O'Connor, and Eudora Welty, her small-town Southern characters (many of them women) engage in running dialogues about their past, present, and future lives. In their reasoning, they are intuitive; in their conversation, emotional. They fuss and fight and often hurt each other's feelings. Dissatisfied with themselves, they sometimes resort to physical violence to get the attention they crave. They would be insufferable if they were not so often funny and easy to forgive.

Reunions of one kind or another provide the people in Henley's fictional world with forums for rehashing old problems or discovering new ones. These reunions are caused—or at least preceded by—startling, sometimes shocking, events. In *Crimes,* Babe's shooting of her husband is the reason the Magrath sisters reunite in their family home, and Jamey Foster's death at age 35 is the catalyst for the contentious gathering in *Wake*. Likewise, Sue Jack's release from prison provokes the Christmas Eve combat in *Lucky Spot*. The emotional stakes are already high before the confrontations begin.

Henley's characters are almost always looking for catharsis, even if they do not realize it. Given the opportunity to talk about themselves, trade stories, or just take potshots at each other, they always do so. The conversations build on each other, gradually revealing individual and familial pasts and showing how entwined the lives of these people are. Conversation is especially vital when siblings are discussing their parents. When the Magrath sisters discuss their mother's suicide, for instance, or when Elain and Delmount in *Miss Firecracker* recollect their late mother's small cruelties, these exchanges are filled with longing and bafflement as well as flashes of self-preserving humor. Conversations such as these may temporarily open old wounds, but ultimately they allow the grown children to take comfort in their shared past.

The husbands and wives in Henley's plays have crucial talks as well. Sue Jack and Hooker in *Lucky Spot* have an ''all-out, lowdown and rutty brawl'' (35–36), during which they vent the anger and accusations they have held inside since Sue Jack went to prison for throwing Hooker's mistress over a balcony. Their argument quickly degenerates into wrestling, name-calling, and finally ''a double knockout'' (37). In Henley's oeuvre, a tussle of this magnitude can mean only one thing: true love. No matter how vicious the exchanges, the lesson seems to be that talk is the sustaining force in any relationship.

Dead mothers and fathers haunt Henley's characters, and lost parents are the subject of many of their cathartic conversations. The Magrath sisters as well as Carnelle Scott (*Miss Firecracker*) lost their mothers when they were children, and their fathers deserted long ago. Similarly, in *Lucky Spot,* the mother of 15-year-old Cassidy is dead, and she never mentions her father. In *Wake* Pixrose is an orphan; in *Debutante Ball,* Bliss has never known her father, and Teddy has killed hers. Even in *Am I Blue,* Henley's apprentice effort, teen-aged Ashbe lives apart from her mother and has an unstable father. The absence of one or both parents leaves all of these female characters insecure and desperate for affection.

This need for affection sometimes takes the form of promiscuous—or at least precocious—sexual behavior. Because of her sexual exploits, Carnelle has had a venereal disease and has acquired the nickname ''Miss Hot Tamale.'' Bliss has admitted to sleeping with all of her husband's friends. Cassidy has become pregnant at 15, and Babe has slept with a 15-year-old boy. But by the end of their respective plays, none of these women is promiscuous anymore. Carnelle has learned to cope with being on her own; Bliss has found an unlikely but affectionate companion in Frances; Cassidy has recognized real love in the relationship that Sue Jack has with Hooker; and Babe has taken solace in her sisters.

Henley's penchant for upbeat endings suggests that her vision of society is essentially hopeful. The use of music and dancing in her plays, especially in the conclusions, adds to this sense of hope. *Am I Blue* ends with Ashbe and John Polk dancing to the title song on the radio; *Lucky Spot* ends on Christmas morning with everybody dancing to ''Sunny Side of the Street.'' That Henley's endings are also poignant can be easily argued. After all, the joyous cake-eating scene in *Crimes* comes right after Babe's suicide attempts, and Teddy's peace-making scene with her mother in *Debutante Ball* shows her mother covered with psoriasis, vulnerably crouching in a bathtub. Even so, the pervasive feeling at the end of a Henley play is that companionship, especially among family members, is good and necessary. The only villains are the people who die unexpectedly or vanish without explanation.

The comic dimensions of Henley's plays are largely responsible for their popular success. Even the most serious-minded critics of *Crimes* seem to delight in quoting Babe's initial explanation for shooting Zachary: ''I just didn't like his looks'' (13). That play, more than any of Henley's others, abounds in funny exchanges. But even this often hilarious play is no frothy comedy. Henley's wit is as dark as it is zany, and her characters' actions are often painfully misguided. All three of the Magrath sisters hover on the edge of tragedy: Pretty young Babe has shot her abusive husband; talented Meg has failed in her Hollywood singing career and has spent time in a mental institution; and sweet-natured Lenny, who is unable to have children, has spurned her only suitor. Significantly, all of these events (along with several other devastations) happen before the action begins. It is the dialogue that puts the comic lining in every tragic cloud. The following exchange between Lenny and Doc Porter early in *Crimes,* during which Doc informs Lenny that her childhood pony has died, shows how Henley wrests comedy from pathos:

Lenny: Struck by lightning? In that storm yesterday?

Doc: That's what we think.

Lenny: Gosh, struck by lightning. I've had Billy Boy so long. You know. Ever since I was ten years old.

Doc: Yeah. He was a mighty old horse.

Lenny: (Stung.) Mighty old.

Doc: Almost twenty years old.

Lenny: That's right, twenty years. 'Cause; ah; I'm thirty years old today. Did you know that?

Doc: No, Lenny, I didn't know. Happy Birthday. (10)

The recognizably ''Southern'' qualities of Henley's work fall into two main categories: domestic life and grotesque death. Most of her plays take place in family homes where people talk easily about pets, children, and food even as they confront major crises. Her characters' self-indulgent fondness for sweets adds to the feeling of domesticity: Consider the prominence of lemonade, candy and cake in *Crimes;* brownies in *Miss Firecracker;* Easter candy in *Wake;* candy canes and oranges in *Lucky Spot.* Henley's hungry characters may need these treats to help them temporarily forget the macabre events looming in their past: a mother who hanged herself and her cat; another whose corpse was covered with long, black hair; a husband fatally kicked in the head by a cow. For the living, memories of these startling deaths resonate with private pain as well as public horror.

In recent plays, Henley has lost neither her gallows humor nor her faith in the resilient human spirit. But she seems to be moving toward a harsher view of familial and romantic relationships. In *Debutante Ball* and *Abundance,* the characters do not seem to enjoy each other's company nearly as much as do the crisis-prone Magrath sisters in *Crimes* or the quarreling cousins in *Miss Firecracker.* Even so, the continuing desire of Henley's characters to communicate with each other—and to do so in a vivid vernacular—infuses Henley's plays with an undeniable glimmer of hope.

SURVEY OF CRITICISM

Beth Henley's plays have been widely reviewed by the popular press, and she has been the subject of profiles and two long interviews; but *Crimes* is her only play thus far receiving significant scholarly attention. There are as yet no books or dissertations on her work alone, possibly because most of her plays— with the exception of the two made into movies, *Crimes* and *Miss Firecracker—* are not well-known outside New York and Los Angeles theater circles.

Positive reviews of *Crimes* in *The New Yorker, Time, Newsweek,* and an especially ebullient notice in *New York Magazine* quickly established Henley as a promising playwright whose arrival on Broadway was cause for celebration. But not everybody was charmed by *Crimes.* Michael Feingold (1981) of the *Village Voice,* the play's most outspoken detractor, declared: "The play gives the impression of gossiping about its characters rather than presenting them, and the playwright's voice, though both individual and skillful, is the voice of a small-town southern spinster yattering away on the phone, oozing pretended sympathy and real malice for her unfortunate subjects" (106). All of the negative reviews of *Crimes* have tended to slip into ad hominem (or more precisely, ad feminem) vitriol. It may be that the writers of these reviews have felt threatened by an undercurrent of feminism that most of the other reviewers, in their positive evaluations, have missed or just decided to ignore.

Feminist scholars are now beginning to recognize Henley's contribution to literature about women. In "Criminality, Desire, and Community: A Feminist Approach to Beth Henley's *Crimes of the Heart*" (1986), Karen Laughlin concludes that the play "offers striking and significant images of the oppressive though unseen presence of patriarchal forces, of their impact on women's desires, and of their ultimate rejection in favor of a vision of female bonding and community" (49). In their respective studies, Jean Gagen (1989) and Joanne B.

Karpinski (1990) note the revisionist echoes of Chekhov's *Three Sisters* in *Crimes,* with Gagen finding *Crimes* an amusing, if flimsy, update and Karpinski celebrating its optimistic portrayal of women. In *Feminist Theatre* (1984), however, Helene Keyssar argues that *Crimes* fails to address women's issues in a sustained or serious way. Dismayed by the Broadway cast's exaggerated Southern mannerisms, she observes, "Laughing at these women is boring and allows a particularly dangerous condescension when the audience's frame is a play by and about women" (158).

Other essays have paired Henley's *Crimes* with fellow Southerner Marsha Norman's *'night, Mother,* winner of the 1983 Pulitzer Prize. In her useful study Laura Morrow (1988) shows how eating and drinking help define female identities in the two plays. In "Diverse Similitude: Beth Henley and Marsha Norman," Lisa J. McDonnell (1987) establishes the playwrights' common ground—storytelling, focus on family, use of Southern vernacular—and has pointed out their differences within these areas. She concludes that "Norman tends to view family ties more suspiciously" than Henley does (102) and that Norman, a former teacher, is the more literary playwright while Henley, the former actress, is more attuned to performance.

In *Beyond Naturalism* (1988), William W. Demastes devotes a chapter to the "new realism" found in Charles Fuller's *A Soldier's Play* (the Pulitzer winner of 1982), Henley's *Crimes,* and Norman's *'night, Mother.* According to Demastes, "Henley has taken the conventional realistic format and has infused it with the esoteric reflections of absurdist thinkers and writers" (143).

Helpful analyses that consider plays in addition to *Crimes* are starting to appear. In "The Tragicomic Vision of Beth Henley's Drama" (1984), Nancy D. Hargrove examines structure and symbolism in *Crimes, Miss Firecracker,* and *Wake.* She finds Henley's vision of humanity "realistic, painfully honest, and yet consistently compassionate" (69). By contrast, in "Familial Bonds in the Plays of Beth Henley" (1987), Billy J. Harbin looks at the same three plays and concludes that "Henley's modern South is a world of estrangement, spiritual longing and grotesquerie, made all the more remarkable by the calm acceptance of the bizarre as perfectly ordinary" (93).

The emerging differences of opinion on Henley's work suggest room for further critical inquiry. Essays analyzing more recent full-length plays, such as *Debutante Ball* and *Abundance,* will help fill a gap in the criticism, as will inclusive studies examining all of Henley's plays to date.

BIBLIOGRAPHY

Works by Beth Henley

Am I Blue. New York: Dramatists Play Service, 1982.
Crimes of the Heart. New York: Dramatists Play Service, 1982.
The Wake of Jamey Foster. New York: Dramatists Play Service, 1983.

Hymn in the Attic. In *24 HOURS—PM,* 49–53. Edited by Oliver Hailey, New York: Dramatists Play Service, 1983.

The Miss Firecracker Contest: A Play. New York: Dramatists Play Service, 1985.

The Lucky Spot. New York: Dramatists Play Service, 1987.

The Debutante Ball. Jackson: University Press of Mississippi, 1991.

Abundance. New York: Dramatists Play Service, 1991.

Interviews with Beth Henley

Betsko, Kathleen, and Rachel Koenig. "Beth Henley." *Interviews with Contemporary Women Playwrights,* edited by Kathleen Betsko and Rachel Koenig, 211–22. New York: Morrow, 1987.

Jones, John Griffin. "Beth Henley." In *Mississippi Writers Talking,* edited by John Griffin Jones, 169–90. Jackson: University Press of Mississippi, 1982.

Studies of Beth Henley

Berkvist, Robert. "Act I: the Pulitzer, Act II: Broadway." *New York Times* (October 25, 1981): D4, D22.

Brustein, Robert. "Broadway Inches Forward." Review of *Crimes of the Heart. New Republic* 194 (December 23, 1981): 25–27.

———. "She-Plays, American Style." Review of *Abundance. New Republic* 203, no. 25 (December 17, 1990): 27–29.

Corliss, Richard. " 'I Go with What I'm Feeling.' " *Time* 119 (February 8, 1982): 80.

Demastes, William W. "New Voices Using New Realism: Fuller, Henley, and Norman." In *Beyond Naturalism,* 125–54. New York: Greenwood, 1988.

Feingold, Michael. "Dry Roll." Review of *Crimes of the Heart. Village Voice* (November 18, 1981): 104, 106.

———. "Israel in Greece." Review of *Am I Blue. Village Voice* (January 13, 1982): 101, 103.

Gagen, Jean. " 'Most Resembling Unlikeness, and Most Unlike Resemblance': Beth Henley's *Crimes of the Heart* and Chekhov's *Three Sisters.*" *Studies in American Drama, 1945–Present* 4 (1989): 119–28.

Gill, Brendan. "The Theatre: Backstage." Review of *Crimes of the Heart. New Yorker* 57 (November 16, 1981): 182–83.

———. Review of *The Wake of Jamey Foster. New Yorker* 58 (October 25, 1982): 161.

Gussow, Mel. "Women Playwrights: New Voices in the Theatre." *New York Times Magazine* (May 1, 1983): 22.

Haller, Scott. "Her First Play, Her First Pulitzer Prize." *Saturday Review* 8, no. 11 (November 1981): 40, 42, 44.

Harbin, Billy J. "Familial Bonds in the Plays of Beth Henley." *Southern Quarterly* 25, no. 3 (1987): 81–94.

Hargrove, Nancy D. "The Tragicomic Vision of Beth Henley's Drama." *Southern Quarterly* 22, no. 4 (1984): 54–70.

Hoffman, Roy. "Brash New South Is Still a Stranger to Its Dramatists." *New York Times* (July 2, 1989): 5, 24.

Jaehne, Karen. "Beth's Beauties." *Film Comment* 25 (May–June 1989): 9–12, 14–15.

Kalem, T. E. "Southern Sibs." Review of *Crimes of the Heart*. *Time* (November 16, 1981): 122.

Karpinski, Joanne B. "The Ghosts of Chekhov's Three Sisters Haunt Beth Henley's *Crimes of the Heart*." In *Modern American Drama: The Female Canon*, edited by June Schlueter, 229–45. Rutherford, N.J.: Fairleigh Dickinson University Press, 1990.

Kauffmann, Stanley. "Two Cheers for Two Plays." Review of *Crimes of the Heart*. *Saturday Review* 9, no. 1 (January 1982): 54–55.

Kerr, Walter. "Offbeat—But a Beat Too Far." Review of *Crimes of the Heart*. *New York Times* (November 15, 1981): 3, 31.

———. "Two Parts Gimmickry, One Part Discretion." Review of *Am I Blue*. *New York Times* (January 24, 1982): 3, 10.

Keyssar, Helene. "Success and Its Limits: Mary O'Malley, Wendy Wasserstein, Nell Dunn, Beth Henley, Catherine Hayes, Marsha Norman." In *Feminist Theatre: An Introduction to Plays of Contemporary British and American Women*, 148–66. London: Macmillan, 1984.

Kramer, Mimi. "The Theatre." Review of *Abundance*. *New Yorker* (November 12, 1990): 105–6.

Kroll, Jack. "Birthday in Manhattan." Review of *Crimes of the Heart*. *Newsweek* 98 (November 16, 1981): 123.

Laughlin, Karen L. "Criminality, Desire, and Community: A Feminist Approach to Beth Henley's *Crimes of the Heart*. *Women and Performance: A Journal of Feminist Theory* 3, no. 1 (1986): 35–51.

McDonnell, Lisa J. "Diverse Similitude: Beth Henley and Marsha Norman." *Southern Quarterly* 25, no. 3 (1987): 95–104.

Morrow, Laura. "Orality and Identity in '*Night, Mother* and *Crimes of the Heart*." *Studies in American Drama, 1945–Present* 3 (1988): 23–39.

Oliver, Edith. "The Theatre." Review of *Crimes of the Heart*. *New Yorker* 57 (January 12, 1981): 81.

———. "The Theatre." Review of *The Lucky Spot*. *New Yorker* 63, no. 12 (May 11, 1987): 80–81.

Rochlin, Margy. "The Eccentric Genius of *Crimes of the Heart*." *Ms.* 15 (February 1987): 12–14.

Sauvage, Leo. "Reaching for Laughter." Review of *Crimes of the Heart*. *New Leader* (November 30, 1981): 19–20.

Simon, John. "Living Beings, Cardboard Symbols." Review of *Crimes of the Heart*. *New York Magazine* 14 (November 16, 1981): 125–26.

———. Review of *The Wake of Jamey Foster*. *New York Magazine* 15 (October 25, 1982): 78+.

———. Review of *Abundance*. *New York Magazine* 23 (November 12, 1990): 92–93.

Torrens, James. Review of *Abundance*. *America* (December 8, 1990): 453–54.

Walker, Beverly. "Close-Up: Beth Henley." *American Film* 12 (December 1986): 30–31.

KIMBALL KING

Preston Jones
(1936–1979)

Preston Jones, a theatre professional identified primarily with the Dallas Theatre Center Repertory Company, became a playwright so that he could re-create everyday life in the rural Southwest on the stage. By design a regional writer, Jones at his best transcended his Texas and New Mexico settings to reveal a larger vision of a racist, sexist, materialistic society clinging to self-serving myths as it disregards religious values and a viable work ethic.

BIOGRAPHY

Preston St. Vrain Jones was born in Albuquerque, New Mexico, on April 7, 1936. He was the youngest of five children and was probably unexpected: His mother was 42 and his father 50. His precocity, his sense of being a rare, "special" person as well as certain infantile tendencies (boasting, fabricating, drinking too much) may be partly attributed to his birth order and his parents' advanced ages during his childhood. His father was very proud of his progeny and even took baby Preston to the local pool hall to show him off. Both Jones's mother, Maud St. Vrain Jones, and his father, James Brooks ("Jawbone") Jones were middle-class people with certain pretensions of gentility. While James Jones's primary career was as a salesman at Proctor and Gamble, he did serve two terms as the Democratic lieutenant governor of New Mexico. He also had literary aspirations and at one time deserted his family to become a novelist; he soon returned to them—without a manuscript. Preston Jones was 11 when his father died, and he continued to live with his mother. Eventually, she had a stroke and had to be cared for by her family for many years.

Baptized a Roman Catholic, Jones attended parochial schools. When his family lived in the country, Jones's friends were largely Chicanos. Disturbed that he was speaking English with a Spanish accent, his parents transferred him to a more prestigious Catholic boys' school; but he retained both admiration and sympathy for Hispanic Americans and often got into fights over ethnic slurs. His performance as a student was uneven; but he read voraciously, as is witnessed by the many quotations and other literary allusions tucked into his own plays. He began to perceive himself as an artist, although at first he imagined he might become a sculptor; later he joined the acting profession. Jones worked his way through the University of New Mexico and graduated in 1958, a semester after he married his first wife, Gaye. His first job was teaching English at a high school, which he forsook after a single semester. He wanted to return to New Mexico as a graduate student in drama, but the university had no graduate drama program at the time. He therefore matriculated as a "special" graduate student, took classes, and performed in school plays. During the next two summers he would return to his wife who lived in Colorado City, Texas, where his two children, Sam and Mary Alice, were born. The marriage failed—not surprisingly, considering his long absences for continued schooling; and he was permanently alienated from his ex-wife and two children.

Beginning formal graduate studies at Baylor, Jones switched to Trinity College in San Antonio, where he graduated in 1966. His M.A. thesis was an adaptation of Davis Grubb's novel *The Night of the Hunter,* although Jones was probably more influenced by a 1955 film version of the book. The thesis provided Jones with his first opportunity to "construct" a drama out of narrative materials and to work through a play from an authorial point of view. Most of Jones's plays have a cinematic quality—they can nearly always be visualized in the context of movie theatre reality.

Trinity College had an affiliation with the Dallas Theatre Center, the only public theatre designed by the late Frank Lloyd Wright. Jones began as an actor with the company and later directed plays as well. In 1964 he married his second wife, Mary Sue Fridge, who was also an actor, director, and general factotum for the company. Unlike most actors, the Joneses had a steady, comfortable income and were valued permanent members of a reputable theatre ensemble. Both were frustrated with the absence of the talented new American dramatists and bored with plays set against urban backdrops. Jones decided in the early 1970s to try his own hand at writing plays since he had a professional's knowledge of the theatre and a personal gift of storytelling. In fact, he often regaled people with tall tales and fantasies at local bars where an assortment of drifters and Texas "good ole boys" appreciated his talents. He began a draft of *Lu Hampton Laverty Oberlander,* the first of the three plays on which his reputation largely depends; but the second play of the trilogy, *The Last Meeting of the Knights of the White Magnolia,* was actually performed first, in the Down Center Stage at the Theatre Center on December 4, 1973. A few months later, in February 1974, *Lu Ann* was also performed in the same theatre. Finally, in November 1974, *The Oldest Living Graduate* opened in the upstairs Kalita Humphreys Theatre. The first two plays of the trilogy were revised and alternated in the repertory, referred to collectively as the *Bradleyville Trilogy.* In the final week of the trilogy's production, it was possible for audiences to see all these plays during a six-and-a-half-hour period each night. The project was so successful that it established Jones as the most popular playwright at the theatre center and spawned regional productions of his works in Chicago, Washington, and Seattle. New York, however, was not so receptive. Although the scheduling of the *Trilogy* was generously heralded by the popular press, some critics of the actual production were skeptical. The drama reviewers in the *New Yorker* and the *New Republic* found Jones's work derivative, sentimental, and insignificant. Stunned by the negative publicity, Jones retreated to the Theatre Center with which he had been associated for nineteen years and where he remained a celebrity. Ultimately his heavy drinking and the late-night schedule of constant theatre productions caught up with him, and he began to experience continuing difficulties with a stomach ulcer. Following an attack of bleeding ulcers, he underwent surgery and died in the intensive care unit on September 19, 1979, in Dallas, Texas.

MAJOR THEMES

Although Jones has been primarily admired for his naturalistic portrayals of regional culture, he provided a troubling analysis of the social attitudes that have led to the dissolution of wholesome American values and the establishment of crass materialism. Sexist attitudes, racism, the loss of religious conviction, and the ravages of time are major themes in all of his works; but in the *Trilogy,* Jones appears to have placed consecutive emphasis on the separate themes in each play. *Lu Ann Hampton Laverty Oberlander,* the first play of Jones's famous trilogy (though produced several months after the second of the series) covers 20 years in the life of a sad but appealing Texas woman, whose experiences from 1953 to 1973 in many ways reflect the victimization of women in American society. The play's title indicates that the protagonist is known by her own name only in Act One, where her immature personality has already been shaped by destructive social conventions. She fails to see that her dream of upward mobility is inconsistent with her scornful rejection of a work ethic. Unquestioningly, she divides her neighbors into two social classes: those who go to the high-school prom in pickup trucks and those who arrive in step-down Hudson Hornets. She makes no connection between an education and professional success, and is contemptuous of her mother's wish that she attend nursing school as her mother had done. Furthermore, attractive men are football players, hard-drinking and sexually promiscuous; ''nice girls'' are cheerleaders whose worth depends on a youthful, attractive appearance and the possibility of marriage to a well-to-do man. The moral and somewhat self-righteous Billy Bob Wortman is too unathletic and studious to appeal to Lu Ann, and she develops an interest in an ex-football player, Dale Laverty, who served in Korea with her shiftless older brother.

In Act Two ten years have passed; Lu Ann has been married and abandoned by Laverty and is a single parent with a little girl. She supports herself as a beautician and scandalizes the community by spending her free time at a local bar. Here she meets Corky Oberlander, who has recently been divorced.

In Act Three, set in 1973, our protagonist is finally Lu Ann Hampton Laverty Oberlander, a recent widow still supporting herself, now as a hostess for the Howdy Wagon, raising a tough-talking, increasingly rebellious daughter and caring for her invalid mother. Her first beau, Billy Bob Wortman, visits the town one day and encounters Lu Ann. A successful preacher in Kansas City, he is appalled by her circumstances but can only suggest that she put her mother in a nursing home. Lu Ann responds that her "mama ain't no vegetable, she's a flower, a great old big pretty flower."

At 40 Lu Ann has become the person her mother was at the play's opening. Her attempts to define herself through marriage have destroyed her dreams and brought new burdens. Her own daughter despises her, and the future would seem to hold no pleasant surprises. Lu Ann's loyalty to her mother, however, indicates a warmth and growth that the audience did not anticipate in the first act. Her attempts to escape from home to seek a new identity through marriage have failed, and she appears to be neither more happy nor more prosperous than her mother had been; yet she seems to have found peace in a life that has been determined by her acceptance of traditional gender roles and a kind of martyrdom synonymous with feminine courage in a west Texas community. Jones condemns the sexism of such a society but shows that Lu Ann ironically assumes personhood when she trusts her own feelings—and, in that sense, rises above her limited milieu.

The burden of gender is a central issue in *Last Meeting of the Knights of the White Magnolia,* too, but Jones more emphatically explores racism and the failures of organized religion when he depicts Lu Ann's brother, Skip, fighting for identity as a white male in an anachronistic and somewhat sinister fraternal order. It is 1962 and Lu Ann is by now the divorced Mrs. Laverty.

A culture that nurtures rigid stereotypes of masculine and feminine behavior takes its toll on individuals of both sexes. Skip, when he is introduced in *Lu Ann,* already embellishes his record in the Korean war and escapes from reality by boasting, drinking, and shirking responsibility. Social success to him implies induction into a formerly prestigious secret society that has Klan-like origins and that now caters to rednecks rather than aristocrats. All that has been preserved from the past is its racism. The current generation of Knights is a motley group; with little education and no tangible achievements or religious beliefs, they are especially vulnerable to bigotry and mindless conformity. Skip Hampton's world consists of part-time jobs, dart games, and binges. He and the other Knights his age make vain attempts at ceremony in their meetings but cannot find the order's original charter or recall its liturgy. All formal activity is a prelude to drinking cheap whiskey. When the order's oldest member, Colonel Kincaid, attends a meeting, he is strangely out of place. Once a leading citizen of the community, he is uncomfortable with the oafs who now inhabit his lodge.

Ramsey-Eyes, a black custodian of the club is nearly as old as the Colonel. He disregards the insults and racial slurs of the younger members; clearly, Colonel Kincaid has more in common with Ramsey-Eyes than the lodge's new recruits. The two old men, white and black, possess a dignity and a sense of history alien to later generations. The Colonel still recites the Magnolia rituals from memory, but later he develops paranoid fantasies and appears to have a seizure of some sort. After the other Knights phone the Colonel's son Floyd, Skip Hampton can only stagger down the steps in search of a bar still open to serve him.

Colonel Kincaid becomes the protagonist of the trilogy's third play, *The Oldest Living Graduate,* because its actions focus on the Colonel's being honored as the oldest alumnus of the Mirabeau B. Lamar Military Academy. Texas audiences considered Kincaid an authentic west Texas gentleman of a certain vintage (he was born in 1887) and a sentimental portrayal by the late Henry Fonda on television made him Jones's best-known character. The play begins in the Colonel's home when he lives with his son and his daughter-in-law Maureen. It progresses to include the moment when Floyd is telephoned by the Knights of Magnolia to inform him of his father's confusion and illness, an event witnessed in the trilogy's second play. The nurse called in to help the Colonel is Claudine, the mother of Lu Ann Laverty and Skip Hampton. She emphasizes the importance of treating a patient at home, which provides a dramatic irony, for any audience familiar with the first play knows Claudine will be wheelchairbound herself ten years later. The most significant of the 20 years spanned by the trilogy is 1962, the setting of the second act of the first play and of all the acts in the middle and final plays.

Colonel Kincaid abhors contemporary western films because they foolishly contrast with his fondest memories of Texas. He is unable to communicate his feelings or wishes to his son, just as Claudine Hampton is misunderstood by Lu Ann. Yet these older characters appear to be more valued by their author than their younger counterparts. Each new generation seems more shallow and greedy than its predecessor. Floyd's business partner, Clarence Sickenger, his name suggesting disease, represents the new Texan who has no respect for tradition and dreams, only of developing for profit the last unspoiled wilderness in his hometown. The Colonel opposes such a plan because he once loved Suzanne Genet, whose father owned the land. But Floyd and Clarence prevail and sell the property; they cannot afford sentimental gestures. The dream of a small rural paradise recalls to a degree Lady Torrence's recollection of her father's winegarden restaurant in Tennessee Williams's *Orpheus Descending,* which was burned down by local racists because her Italian father had sold whiskey to blacks. It was also the setting of her first love affair. Jones lacks Williams's lyrical gifts, however, and neither the romance of the past nor the evil of the present are wholly convincing. Sexism and racism are present in the final play of the trilogy, but are less blatant. The Colonel rails that Floyd will sell off tiny parcels of land that would be of interest to Chinese farmers, leading him to embark on an insane anti-Asian digression. The inferior position of women, totally subordinate to their husbands' whims, is illustrated in the characteristics of Maureen Kincaid and Martha Ann Sickenger, although the former is at least unafraid to utter satirical protests against the establishment.

Nothing is resolved in the *Texas Trilogy,* and the forces of sexism, racism, and greed tend to prevail over nonwhite and female inhabitants of the region. Younger men relinquish even the pretense of heroic behavior and bolster their self-esteem by crudely dominating others or by escaping in alcoholic reveries. The failure of generations to communicate and the individual's inevitable compromise with his or her childhood dreams is conventional naturalism and effectively rendered. Jones's artistic strength, nevertheless, depends more upon his recognition that the feudal hierarchy of white male dominance celebrated in the tales of a glorious western past are the roots of contemporary dissatisfaction and decay.

Juneteenth was the last of Jones's dramas to have a specific Texas locale. The Actor's Theatre in Louisville, Kentucky, had organized a special holiday program, composed of several short plays that commemorated a particular holiday. Jones submitted a brief piece about a once-a-year celebration by Texas African-Americans of emancipation, known as *Juneteenth.* It reads like a "local color" story and includes the time-worn device of a naive outsider who is tricked into believing that the holiday is a genuine state-wide celebration instead of a patronizing recognition by Texas writers of an unofficial black "time out." Nevertheless, Jones is able to offer penetrating insights into Texas sociology as he creates a passably entertaining dramatic anecdote with disturbing currents of continuing racism.

Mayor Furd, of Furd, Texas, in 1976 (the year of the bicentennial anniversary of the United States) is a bigot running for reelection. As he chats at dinner with Betty the waitress, a recent Highway Department employee, George Lewis, who has moved to Furd from out of state, asks about the significance of "Juneteenth" as a holiday. The answer is provided by George's boss, a black highway supervisor, who explains it is a day "when all my people celebrate the freeing of the slaves." George, embarrassed, realizes that white men are not included in the celebration. Both his college-educated black employer—living proof of a partly changed social order—and the racist mayor and waitress enjoy ridiculing someone ignorant of their mutual Texas heritage. The bureaucracy has changed enough to permit educated blacks to work as supervisors of whites, but social equality between the races is considered a possibility only by "lowly" and slightly absurd outsiders.

Perhaps to demonstrate his versatility or to avoid being stereotyped, Jones's next two plays were set in his native New Mexico. They are less ambitious works than *Texas Trilogy,* with its large cast of characters and complex use of time. *A Place on the Magdalena Flats* (1976) has a deterministic quality. The dry heat and perpetual windstorms of the desert contribute to the sense of entrapment and desperation experienced by Carl and Charlene Grey on their forlorn ranch. The severe drought of 1956 is as relentless as the enveloping fog of

O'Neill's *Long Day's Journey Into Night,* confining psychologically damaged characters in an environmental prison. *Magdalena Flats* contains elements of unresolved sibling conflicts, which unleash potentially dangerous rivalries in the male protagonists, as well as grotesque twists of fate in the plotting and a sense of impending future doom. The theme of potential incest (Carl Grey's brother, Frank, is drawn to his older sister-in-law/surrogate mother Charlene) has parallels in O'Neill's plays (*Desire Under the Elms, Mourning Becomes Electra*) and Sam Shepard's plays (*True West, Buried Child*). The sense that a harsh life has molded a personality, which partially accounts for the elderly father's inability to love his wife and children in *Desire Under the Elms,* makes an apt parallel to Carl Grey's embittered bullying of his sensitive younger brother and frail wife, who have difficulties sustaining the vicissitudes of the New Mexico wilderness. The young stepmother Abbie murders her healthy baby in the O'Neill tragedy in a misguided attempt to retain Eben's (her lover's/stepson's) love. Charlene Grey gives birth to a stillborn child, which is symbolic of her precarious mental and physical health, and Frank is banished by his brother— a harsh personal judgment but ultimately in the best interests of the family.

Unlike *Magdalena Flats,* which is as yet an unpublished play, *Santa Fe Sunshine* was printed by the Dramatist's service in 1977. It was written between the first version of *Magdalena Flats* in 1975 and its revision in 1979. Again Jones chooses a New Mexico setting, but he appears to be trying his hands at comedy. *Sunshine* is a satire of semitalented American artists whose work primarily interests well-to-do philistines of a liberal persuasion. The "art" patrons congratulate themselves in discovering and purchasing what appear to be hideous examples of regional paintings, pottery, sculpture, and poetry. They resemble the "benefactors" of the Chicago Art Institute in the second act of *Sunday in the Park with George,* by Stephen Sondheim and James Lapine. Jones had doubtless encountered dedicated but untutored collectors in Dallas and elsewhere and part of the fun of his play is his presentation of the artist as a con man to a "mark" who deserves to be "gulled." The spirit of the devilish trickster of Mark Twain in *Innocents Abroad* haunts the Santa Fe bazaars where quasi artisans are perceived to be authentic new American talent. A possibly self-deprecating element, heretofore missing from the playwright's works, reflects his awareness that the security of his Theatre Center home base is partially the result of the newly affluent community's provincial origins. Claude's hideous black and red self-portrait, called *Hate,* Lyman's maudlin poem, "Death of a Wino," and Gino's ugly green plaster frog are revealed onstage to the amusement of the playwright and his audience. He offers proof of his own aesthetic sophistication by his graphic depictions of bad taste. *Sunshine* is not a major play, but it does illustrate Jones's potential for good-natured satire. His worst dramatic error was doubtless his shockingly homophobic caricature of Thurman Vogel as a flamboyant gay poet. Perhaps he was pandering to the prejudices of audiences accustomed to rigid gender stereotypes. Then again, he may have been "deconstructing" such a stereotype by deliberately resorting to tasteless excess.

In either case the inclusion of the gay poet strikes a sour note in an otherwise lighthearted and potentially fertile spoof of contemporary cultural values.

In his last and most autobiographical play, *Remember* (1979), produced in the Dallas Theatre Center a few months before his death, Preston Jones created the part of an actor named Adrian, whose life paralleled Jones's. Adrian identifies with the fate of Ishmael, his favorite literary character, in what Adrian calls "two pretty good novels," the Old Testament and Melville's *Moby-Dick.* The Ishmael of Melville's tale, *The Pequod's* sole survivor, fares rather better than his biblical prototype, the illegitimate son of Abraham and his servant Hagar, who is banished to the wilderness and becomes a wild man: "And his hand will be against every man and every man's hand against him." Significantly Adrian/Jones takes pride in his role as an unappreciated iconoclast, forever restless, angry, and misunderstood: a victim. Like Melville, however, Jones in writing *A Texas Trilogy* was attempting an epic drama, similar to Melville's most famous novel, in that the trilogy attempts to present a romantic appraisal of a dark, paradoxical universe, rooted in specific American experiences. As an artist, Jones's life does not resemble Melville's since Melville was a great popular success in his youth but forgotten by his readers by the end of his life. Jones, like Walt Whitman, made his first major contribution when he was 37, and he also gloried in his association with low-life characters and his frank discussions of sex and the details of everyday life; but unlike Whitman, Jones retained the public's respect, especially in Texas, until his early death. He wrote seven plays in about as many years. Nevertheless, it is hard to believe that even if Jones had lived to old age he would have received the admiration of future generations accorded to both Melville and Whitman. Jones captured the imaginations of theatre professionals in the 1970s who were eager to find native talent to compete with the major British playwrights whose transported productions filled Broadway and off-Broadway theatres during the same era.

Following Tennessee Williams, Arthur Miller, and somewhat later, Edward Albee, there seemed to be a dearth of original American voices on the stage. It was a propitious moment for an "authentic" American provincial—backed by the considerable resources of a then-prosperous Dallas Center Stage—to gain recognition. Famous theatrical directors and producers flew to opening-night performances of Jones's plays, among them the late Alan Schneider, director of Beckett's plays, and the late Richmond Crinkley, producer of *Elephant Man.*

In the 1950s Larry McMurtry, Larry King, William Owens, and other novelists had begun to employ a Texas backdrop for new fictional purposes. A tawdry, mainly impoverished Southwestern state was reexamined in an ironic contrast to its mythic past. Jones, 20 years later, continued the tradition on stage for audiences now sufficiently reflective to perceive the inadequacies of contemporary Texas life. To an extent he is a precursor of Sam Shepard and David Mamet, who, although they began writing earlier, became theatrical celebrities in the 1980s. Shepard in *True West* and Mamet in *American Buffalo* dramatize the powerful tensions engendered by a sense of lost purpose and glory. Certainly the impact of western film with its generally heroic presentation of macho males, adventurous vigilantes, and populist politicians had intensified even the average Texan's awareness of contemporary mediocrity. Jones often draws on Texas history, and his admirers praise his authentic setting and dialogue. Bette Brady Sewell (1984), however, has pointed out that Jones's dialogue, in particular, is closer to cinematic stereotypes than to actual western Texas speech patterns. Jones sometimes compared himself to Flannery O'Connor. Both artists were Roman Catholics who explored a shallow, fundamentalist Protestant culture and hoped to find in commonplace people and events emblems of God's grace. Yet Jones concerns himself with the unseemly rather than the grotesque and lacks O'Connor's powerful narrative skills. His plays either lack a compelling plot or suffer from obvious contrivances. He is often depressing without being "affecting." The reappearance of characters and allusions to mythic or historical events in his seven plays may recall William Faulkner's or Thomas Wolfe's pageantry but does not create a metaphorical universe similar to theirs.

If one compares Jones to other American writers, the influence of Tennessee Williams is apparent, especially in Jones's sympathy toward exploited, neurotic women and his revulsion at male chauvinists. Yet his male characters generally lack the electrifying meanness that makes Williams's so predatory, and the women are incapable of delivering the lyrical, memorable soliloquies of a Blanche Du Bois or Maggie the Cat. The father who abandons his responsibilities, the ineffectual mother, and Jones's contentious siblings also lack the vitality and offbeat humor associated with Shepard's best work. Finally, there are overtones of O'Neill. Jones often surpasses O'Neill in creating believable dialogue, but he seldom evokes the deep emotional audience responses that the latter's skillful adaptation of classical myths and exposé of raw feelings can stimulate.

Perhaps Jones is most plausible as a 20th-century "local colorist," propitiously writing in an era when promoting regional theatre was an American obsession. His is a lonely but insistent voice, decrying the spiritual emptiness of the late 20th century and recording futile attempts to recapture a more vital past or to create a more meaningful future. The growing popularity of the Appalachian novel and other literature at the end of this century about average Southerners, who believe that their religious beliefs and traditional values are endangered, but who nevertheless find themselves economically dependent on the new technologies and attracted to the materialistic values of Madison Avenue and Hollywood, testifies to the veracity and power of Jones's vision.

SURVEY OF CRITICISM

Early criticism of the works of Preston Jones primarily consisted of reviews of particular theatre productions, but in 1981 Andrew Bruegge wrote a succinct biography of the late playwright and an analysis of his works in *Dictionary of Literary Biography*. This was updated by Mark Busby's Western Writers monograph in 1983. Brugge and Busby have assessed Jones's contribution and have provided a groundwork for further critical examination. By far the most complete treatment of Jones's works is Bette Brady Sewell's dissertation, completed at the University of California in Los Angeles in 1984. A former West Texas native, Sewell embarked on her project with the author's full support. She has uncovered new biographical information and has offered her own textural readings. The limitations of a dissertation format, requiring her to quote lengthy passages from the plays, sometimes repetitiously, in order to document several approaches, results in a compendious (more than 500 pages) volume. Nevertheless, Sewell has established herself as a major scholarly resource on Jones. A short autobiographical essay in the *Dramatist's Guild Quarterly,* "Tales of a Pilgrim's Progress from Bradleyville to Broadway" in 1977, was followed a year later by Annemarie Marek's *Preston Jones: An Interview,* published by the New London Press. Jones had a self-deprecating sense of humor and liked to project a slightly macho, pragmatic image; he seldom acknowledged emotional pain or his disappointment at being labeled a regional playwright.

Jones's artistry was recognized in a major periodical, the *Smithsonian,* in 1976, when Tom Prideaux wrote "The Classic Family Drama is revised in *A Texas Trilogy.*" Prideaux's specific inspiration was a Washington, D.C., production of *Trilogy,* but his five-page article is not so much a review as an acknowledgment of Jones's place in an established American theatrical tradition. Ten years later the *Southern Quarterly* featured a thematic discussion of *Trilogy,* "Humor, Dreams, and the Human Condition in Preston Jones's *A Texas Trilogy,*" by R. C. Reynolds. Reynolds praised the playwright's sense of timing, his professionalism, and his careful balancing of sentiment with satire. Reviewers have alternated between considering Jones an authentic American voice or derivative, self-indulgent regionalist. Jack Kroll of *Newsweek* has noted many of Jones's strengths while Martin Gottfried has sarcastically emphasized the playwright's maudlin and inchoate vision.

BIBLIOGRAPHY

Works by Preston Jones

Dramatic Productions

The Last Meeting of the Knights of the White Magnolia. December 4, 1973, Dallas Theatre Center; Spring 1976, Arena Stage, Washington, D.C.; Spring 1976, Eisenhower Theatre, Washington, D.C.; September 22, 1976, Broadhurst Theatre, New York.

Lu Ann Hampton Laverty Oberlander. February 5, 1974, Dallas Theatre Center; Spring 1976, Arena Stage, Washington, D.C.; Spring 1976, Eisenhower Theatre, Washington, D.C.; September 21, 1976, Broadhurst Theatre, New York.

The Oldest Living Graduate. November 19, 1974, Dallas Theatre Center; Spring 1976, Arena Stage, Washington, D.C.; Spring 1976, Eisenhower Theatre, Washington, D.C.; September 23, 1976, Broadhurst Theatre, New York.

A Place on the Magdalena Flats. January 14, 1976, Dallas Theatre Center.
Santa Fe Sunshine. April 19, 1977, Dallas Theatre Center.
Juneteenth. February 3, 1979, Actors' Theatre of Louisville.
Remember. March 20, 1979, Dallas Theatre Center.

Published Plays

A Texas Trilogy. (comprising *The Last Meeting of the White Magnolia, Lu Ann Hampton Laverty Oberlander,* and *The Oldest Living Graduate*). New York: Hill and Wang, 1976.
Santa Fe Sunshine. New York: Dramatists Play Service, 1977.

Studies of Preston Jones

Bruegge, Andrew V. "Preston Jones." In *Twentieth-Century American Dramatists.* Pt. 1, vol. 7 of *Dictionary of Literary Biography.* Edited by John MacNicholas, 337–44. Detroit: Gale Research, 1981.

Busby, Mark. *Preston Jones.* Boise: Boise State University, 1983.

Coe, Richard L. Review of *A Texas Trilogy. Washington Post* (May 9, 1976): K1–3.

Cook, Bruce. "Preston Jones: Playwright on the Range." *Saturday Review* (May 15, 1976): 40–42.

Gottfried, Martin. "A Weak Graduate." *New York Post* (September 24, 1976): 11.

Jones, Preston. "Tales of a Pilgrim's Progress from Bradleyville to Broadway." *Dramatist's Guild Quarterly* 13, no. 4 (Winter 1977): 7–18.

Kroll, Jack. "Texas Marksmanship." *Newsweek,* 87 (May 17, 1976): 95–96.

Marek, Annemarie. *Preston Jones: An Interview.* Dallas: New London Press, 1987.

Prideaux, Tom. "The Classic Family Drama Is Revived in *A Texas Trilogy,*" *Smithsonian* 7 (October 1976): 49–54.

Reynolds, R. C. "Humor, Dreams, and the Human Condition in Preston Jones' *A Texas Trilogy.*" *Southern Journal of Arts in the South* (Spring 1986): 33–41.

Schlatter, James F. "Some Kind of a Future: The War for Inheritance in the Work of Three American Playwrights of the 1970s." [Jones, Shepard, Wilson] *South Carolina Review* 7, no. 11 (1990): 59–75.

Sewell, Bette Brady. "The Plays of Preston Jones: Background and Analysis." Ph.D. diss., University of California in Los Angeles, 1984.

Shirley, Don. "Preston Jones, Regional Hero." *Washington Post* (April 25, 1976): G1–3.

Taitte, W. L. "Keeping Up with Jones." *Texas Monthly* 3 (December 1975): 50–51.

Wilson, Edwin. "Significant Drama, but Not Instant O'Neill." *Wall Street Journal* (September 28, 1976): 12.

JAMES A. GRIMSHAW, JR.

Donald Justice
(1925–   )

With his roots set deeply in the poetic tradition of Ralph Waldo Emerson, Emily Dickinson, Trumbull Stickney, Frederick Tuckerman, Walt Whitman, E. A. Robinson, Hart Crane, Ezra Pound, William Carlos Williams, Wallace Stevens, T. S. Eliot, Robert Frost, and John Crowe Ransom, Donald Justice's appeal creates a longing to return to a tradition in which rhythm and truth are not forgotten. His accomplished poetry in so many different forms and his relatively small canon have perhaps discouraged the more critical investigation his work inherently deserves.

BIOGRAPHY

The Walker Evans photograph "Mule Team and Poster," Justice reported in a 1980 interview with David Hamilton and Lowell Edwin Folsom, "made a connection with [his] own life and the life of [his] relatives in the South in the thirties. . . . It was like a photograph made of a long-ago part of [his] life" (100). It provides a link to Justice's Southern heritage, his father's birth and kin in southern Alabama where the Justice family visited relatives, "poor farmers and store clerks," in the mid-1930s. Beyond that, he says, family recollections on paternal and maternal sides do not go back beyond what would be his great-grandparents (101). Mr. Justice, a carpenter, married Mary Ethel Cook (1897–1974), who bore him a son, Donald Rodney Justice, on August 12, 1925, in Miami, Florida. Reared a Southern Baptist, Donald Justice said in a 1975 interview (Dodd and Plumly) that his upbringing may be the reason that he lost his faith and does not believe in the spiritual (48). At age 6, while on a shopping trip with his parents, Justice became enthralled with a rhythm band he heard in a downtown Miami department store. The leader of that band, Mrs. Snow, became his first piano teacher and mentor, about whom he has written tenderly and tellingly in an autobiographical essay, "Piano Lessons: Notes on a Provincial Culture." Through the influence of his piano teachers, he developed an interest in composing and even met the composer Carl Ruggles, who took him on as a "free pupil." Justice speculates that had he "met Ruggles at thirteen or fourteen," he might "now be writing music." That, however, was not to be. His early desire to become a musician was thwarted by two events during those years: the loss of a close friend to rheumatic fever and his own illness osteomyelitis-anesthesias, or "Mickey Mantle's disease," as he later described it. His imagined—yet real?—illusions about music may have prepared the way for other inspired imaginings, for "secret subjects" he has chosen not to announce (Dodd and Plumly 1975, 58).

Justice received his B.A. from the University of Miami in 1945 and his M.A. from the University of North Carolina at Chapel Hill in 1947. That same year he married Jean Ross; they have one son, Nathaniel. Justice continued his education at Stanford University from 1948 to 1949 and subsequently attended the Writers Workshop at the University of Iowa, where he earned a Ph.D. in 1954. Among his instructors who exerted more than average influence on his development as a teacher and as a writer were Yvor Winters, Paul Engle, Karl Shapiro, Robert Lowell, and John Berryman. Considered by his students as an excellent writing teacher, Justice has taught for varying periods of time at Syracuse University, the University of California at Irvine, Princeton University, the University of Virginia, the University of Iowa, and most recently the University of Florida until his retirement to Iowa City in 1992.

Justice began by writing stories and showed some promise in that genre. One of those stories was selected for an O. Henry Award, but Justice says he "had always wanted to write poems" (*Platonic Scripts* 15). In 1959 his first volume of poetry, *The Summer Anniversaries,* was the Lamont Poetry Selection. Other ventures emerged along the way. His translation of contemporary French poets, such as Eugene Guillevic, has been an attempt to translate Guillevic's style into American verse; his librettos have continued his musical interests; and his dreams have revealed an unrequited passion for trying something new. In a 1980 interview Justice reported that he was working on four plays: one would deal with Lorca, another would be an update of *The Tempest, Faust: A Skit* would be a farce, and *The Whistler* would probe the issue of anti-Semitism (*Platonic Scripts* 96–97).

Each of his three books of poetry after *The Summer Anniversaries* reflects shifts in his poetic development, a loosening of syllabics, and a less formal style. *Night Light* (1967) consists of variations of his more formal poems, especially the sestinas and villanelles; *Departures* (1973) displays further departures from the poems in his first volume; and *The Sunset Maker* (1987) begins to mirror a return to some of the more traditional forms, though Justice has never strayed too far afield. In self-assessment, Justice feels he has turned from his Southern heritage. As early as 1977, he stated: "So I began—while respecting the writing of Ransom, Tate, and Warren—less and less to believe that the

dreams of past glory meant a damned thing anymore. Certainly not to me"
(*Platonic Scripts* 62). And by 1983, he was bold enough to say, "It is true that
there was a brief period, three or four years perhaps, when I thought of myself
as a Southern writer" (*Platonic Scripts* 218). Although that label is more for
academic convenience than for accurate description of a poet's work, Justice's
poetry still reflects his heritage, disclaimers notwithstanding. But his confession
is meaningful in a biographical statement about a man who is otherwise quite
private about his life. More meaningful is his self-acknowledgment: "I write or
try to write," he has noted, "as if convinced that, prior to my attempt, there
existed a true text, a sort of Platonic script, which I had been elected to transcribe
or record" (*Platonic Scripts* 138).

That attempt at perfection may explain, in part, why his writing has received
relatively minor attention to this point. Nonetheless, Justice has received other
awards and recognitions: two Ford fellowships, one for poetry in 1954 and the
other for theater in 1964; two grants from the National Council on the Arts in
1967 and 1973; A Guggenheim Fellowship in 1976; the University of Michigan
Hopwood Lecture in 1988; the Pulitzer Prize in 1980 for *Selected Poems,* which
includes a section of sixteen previously uncollected poems; and the Bolingen
Prize for poems in 1991. Even with the recognition in 1980, Donald Justice's
books have been neglected, a fact sadly demonstrated by the current nonavail-
ability of those published before 1987.

MAJOR THEMES

Justice's poetic strength resides in his ability to harmonize sound and sense.
His strength draws from the Platonic ideal of a true text, from his education and
studies of traditional form, and from his unrelenting devotion to metrics. Encompassing the various targeted themes identified by various critics, Justice's
poems in general can be discussed in terms of one major theme, a theme predominantly associated with Southern writers: the theme of alienation. Alienation
is felt as a result of sundry kinds of relationships, of loss, of melancholy (Hirsch
1987), of change (De Jong 1985), of the transience of being (Swiss 1980), of
imprisonment within self (Howard 1980), of disease, of poverty, of indifference
(Kazin 1984); and that alienation gives Justice sufficient space for the subject
of his poetry and simultaneously allows him adequate diversity for the poetic
forms in which he carefully, painstakingly contemplates the ramifications of
alienation. Through writing, the poet precludes that total alienation, and writing
becomes an act of preservation—of memory and experience. To this understanding, Justice's essays, notes, and interviews about his poetry are significant.

In a 1980 interview, Justice commented: "Poetry at its best is fulfilling its
nature most entirely when it has a great mastery of form, or technique, and
shows considerable, though perhaps a hidden or disguised, interest in its own
formal or technical character" (*Platonic Scripts* 103). The development of his
poetry demonstrates that principle to which he ascribes. *Summer Anniversaries*

contains Justice's most formally structured poems (thirty-two of them) including sestinas, villanelles, odes, Italian sonnets, and variations on most of those forms. Clearly a defiant act contrary to the trend in the 1960s, Justice's insistence on form possibly reduced his output and increased his quality. He quickly establishes a self-effacing voice, borrowing here and there from other writers and constructing variations on their themes and thoughts—for example, Weldon Kees (whose collected poetry Justice edited in 1960), Henry James, E. A. Robinson, Wallace Stevens, and William Carlos Williams.

The principle of uncertainty sets up a basis for the alienated self in the first poem, ''Anniversaries,'' as the expectations at birth are eroded by childhood disease that separates the narrator from life and aggravates adolescent fears until, at age 30, he realizes the uncertainty of it all. By the last poem in the volume, ''To Satan in Heaven,'' that uncertainty has become despair, the emptiness of a Prufrock reflected in the morning mirror. The mirror is but one recurring image within Justice's canon, but the focus on childhood memories and maladies of the aged predominates. Grouped in a rather loose fashion, the first four poems preserve the memories of a child's relationship to the natural world of a glorious morning (''Song''), to a somewhat artificial world of strangers (''To a Ten-Months' Child''), and to the indifference of adults and the consequence of loneliness (''The Poet at Seven''). The next five poems pursue the loss of a child's innocence through the death of a friend, through change in a neighborhood and the fact that things cannot be as they were (''Landscape with Little Figures''), and perhaps through acquired knowledge of original sin (''Sonnet''). The mood shifts to life's promises and enigmas in the following eight poems, and the narrator seems to be trying to break with his Southern heritage (''Southern Gothic'' and ''Beyond the Hunting Woods''). The poem ''Here in Katmandu'' (Katmandu being the starting point of the expedition that first conquered Mt. Everest) moralizes on the notion of failure and success, explains Justice (*Platonic Scripts* 23). Justice displays a pleasing conceit in the vein of Shakespeare and Donne in a potentially sentimental poem ''Sonnet to My Father.'' His skillful use of the Italian sonnet meter with a variation of the sestina rhyme helps maintain the necessary aesthetic distance. The opening poem of the second part of *Summer Anniversaries* is a sonatina titled ''Thus.'' The remaining poems explore relationships of love. Borrowings abound in several poems, such as ''Variations on a Theme from James'' and ''Ladies by Their Windows,'' containing John Crowe Ransom images—a poem that Vernon Young (1979) has praised for its musical and evocative qualities (237). Love, however, remains unfulfilled, estranged in most of these relationships that time and human foibles alter. One can almost hear the Ecclesiastical preacher saying, ''Vanity of vanities! All is vanity'' (1:2), or the madness couched within the ''This Little Piggy'' parody in ''Counting the Mad.''

Night Light followed in 1967 with thirty-eight poems about decay, loss—particularly the loss of loved ones—the facade of society, and man's insensitivity to man. The title of the volume gives a clue to keep a night-light burning;

and the poems are steeped with light-dark imagery, shadows that obscure reality for the persona. In his *Ohio Review* interview, Justice states that some poems in *Night Light* "are probably more objective transcriptions of what would appear to be reality" (1984, 42–43). The difficulty in obtaining self-knowledge—and, by implication, the ability to recognize reality—is distinguishing mere reflection from the actual, as in "Men at Forty," "The Evening of the Mind," and "Poem for a Survivor." Vestiges of Fugitive influence are evident in the poem "To the Uncommon Lady Who Wrote the Letters Found in the Hatbox," (a title worthy of Robert Penn Warren) or in "But That Is Another Story." Although the reason for such influences is obvious given Justice's background and his master's thesis on Ransom, Tate, and Warren, this collection seems to make more use of the subjects that those fugitives explored in such poems as "The Grandfathers," "Dreams of Water" with its son-father-grandfather relationship, "Party" with the facade of society (also in the Eliot mode), "The Suicides," "Narcissus at Home," and "To Waken a Small Person" with its stream-of-consciousness thought. Justice seems to be making other explorations in forms less formal than used previously by him. These later poems use a predominant number of three- and four-line stanzas. "Anonymous Drawing" reminds one of Flannery O'Connor's short story "The Artificial Nigger"; and "American Sketches" takes the free verse form of the imagistic poetry of William Carlos Williams, to whom the two-poem sequence is dedicated. "After a Phrase Abandoned by Wallace Stevens" and "The Evening of the Mind" follow syntactical and metrical patterns of Stevens. And "The Man Closing Up" has near Haiku imagery. One poem that stands as an aberation in this gathering is "To the Hawks," a "quiet poem about violence" just prior to the escalation of U.S. involvement in Vietnam; it again points to Justice's search for the challenge. In "Meters and Memory" (1978) Justice says that "meters serve as a neutral and impersonal check of self-indulgence and whimsy; a subjective event gets made over into something more like an object" (319).

The title of his third volume, *Departures,* also suggests the thrust of his collection: In form, these twenty-nine poems represent his farthest departure from the formal style of the first volume. The opening poem, "ABC," speaks to the purity of art (poetry, sculpture, and music) and seems with its freeness of form to announce that departure. Moreover, the subjects have much to do with the departed—deceased people, broken relationships, lost talents—most frequently the loss of something or someone and self-effacement on the part of the persona. "Variations on a Text by Vallejo" exemplifies the self-effacing image, and the narrator even refers to himself as "Donald Justice." In an interview with Wayne Dodd and Stanley Plumly (reprinted in *Platonic Scripts*) Justice explained: "Because that is a case, I think, of a borrowed voice. And borrowing the voice allows me, it seems, to speak of myself more directly, more objectively, because the voice is not mine" (29). The "other voice" then allows an interrogation in a poem with the descriptive title "Twenty Questions" and allows a confession by an aging poet who has lost the calling in "The Telephone

Number of the Muse.'' Two other points in *Departures* are evident. One is the achieved balance of "wildness and the formal" elements in "The Assassination," a poem on the death of Robert Kennedy. An obvious way for countering the dullness in an openly formal poem "is to put into it material with a certain strangeness, unexpectedness, even—if you like—wildness" (*Platonic Scripts* 59). The other point is the more pronounced emotion associated with the people and events in "Absences," because it represents yet another departure in Justice's poetic style, a style that strives ardently to be objective, to maintain aesthetic distance.

The book that brought Justice's poetry national attention is *Selected Poems*, which contains selections from the first three volumes and one section of sixteen "uncollected poems." For this collection Justice received the Pulitzer Prize for poetry in 1980. Among the uncollected poems are an English sonnet written in the summer of 1948, "Sonnet: An Old-Fashioned Devil," in which the persona places the blame for all life's ills on the Devil, and "from *Bad Dreams* | Epilogue: To the Morning Light," which draws on well-established Justice images of an old house, dreams, mirrors, and a sundial. In a note to this poem, Justice writes that it "was to have been composed mostly of the dreams dreamed by the kinspeople gathered together in the house of the head of the family during the night on which he lay dying" (137). He attributes some debt to James Agee, Peter Taylor, and Dylan Thomas. And dreams are, we see, one form of alienation. The poem "Summer Anniversaries" is apparently an earlier version of "Anniversaries," which appears in the first volume of poems. Two Tremayne poems are also included in this volume; they are republished with very minor alterations (a word division and italics added in one line) and with two additional Tremayne poems—thereby completing the seasonal cycle—in Justice's fifth volume, *The Sunset Maker*.

Justice's poetry continues with the same variations on the theme of alienation. That theme is perhaps best illustrated in the story "Artificial Moonlight," a tale reminiscent of F. Scott Fitzgerald. The collection also contains two memoirs that provide background for the last poems in the volume. Overall, the poems represent a return to the more formal restraints, with variations on the strict traditional forms of Italian and English sonnets; with couplets; with three- and four-line stanzas in tetrameter, pentameter, and other meters; and with a villanelle. Again, Justice's poetry contains borrowings—from Dickinson ("Lines at the New Year"), Warren (the three-poem sequence entitled "My South"), Henry James ("Epilogue: Coronado Beach, California"), Baudelaire ("Nineteenth-Century Portrait"), Kafka ("Young Girls Growing Up"), Rilke ("Seaward: A Song" and "Last Evening"), and Eliot ("In Memory of the Unknown Poet, Robert Boardman Vaughn"). The persona experiences loss of time, promises unrealized, failure, loss of the past, death of a loved one, and the social lines between the rich and the poor. The title piece "The Sunset Maker" and the companion piece "Little Elegy for Cello and Piano" mix musical allusions and color and blend nicely Justice's motive "for much if not all art, . . . to keep memorable what deserves to be remembered,'' as Justice says in ''Meters and Memory'' (315).

SURVEY OF CRITICISM

Perhaps because Donald Justice has been writing against the grain these past 30 years, his poetry has not received the attention it deserves. Or, because he does not mass-produce poems, critics have perhaps assumed he is not serious about his craft. Or, possibly because he fails to seek the spotlight, the camera focuses on others. Whatever the reason, the appearance is painfully real: How fleeting is the recognition gained after receiving a Pulitzer Prize. During the 1980s, Justice was subject for three articles in the *New York Times:* in 1980, when the Pulitzer recipients were announced and *Selected Poems* was reviewed, and in 1987, when *The Sunset Maker* was reviewed. In her praise of Justice's work, Cathrael Kazin (1984) may have fingered the most valid reason for the critical neglect: He is a ''poet's poet. The precision of his language, his fascination with poetic technique, and the meticulous and supple quality of his diction'' make him a superb craftsman (267).

Even Justice's fault-finding critics give him credit for his early work *Summer Anniversaries*. In Vernon Young's judgment, ''Justice has lacked the gift for renewing himself poetically; however, the initial gift remains sufficiently impressive to inhibit critical reproaches'' (234). In contrast, however, Edward Hirsch has concluded that ''in his fifth collection of poems, *The Sunset Maker,* Donald Justice establishes himself as an elegiac poet of the first order'' (20). The recognition is confirmed in one way by references, albeit brief, to Justice in the *Harvard Guide to Contemporary American Writing* (1979), *The History of Southern Literature* (1985), and *A History of Modern Poetry: Modernism and After* (1987). In another way, Justice seems conspicuously absent in recent anthologies—that gateway to the coveted canonization.

At this time, his following seems few but firm. Thomas Swiss's 1980 article, one of the first substantive criticisms, focuses on Justice's use of language, ''the particular idiom and pattern of the poems'' (44); and Swiss has noted that Justice's ''substantial talent is simply in balance with the poetic tradition evoked, implicitly or explicitly, by the individual poem'' (45). That same year, Richard Howard wrote a glowing essay on Justice in his book *Alone with America* (292–303). Howard has attributed Justice's artistry to his ability to achieve ''a special accommodation of the poem's shape and body to its impulse or 'message' until nothing remains outside the form, left over to be said in any way *except by the poem itself*'' (294). But then, Howard is a poet writing about a poet. Michael Sheridan (1981), another admirer has declared that ''to meet Donald Justice in a poem is to meet . . . a gentleman'' (114); and Michael Ryan (1984) has praised Justice's style, ''its unusual lucidity and perfect decorum'' (220). Mary Gosselink De Jong's essay (1985) grapples with musical possibilities and memory in Justice's poetry. Some of the critics even identify ''the finest'' poem in Justice's canon: Swiss (1980) picks "A Dancer's Life"; David Perkins (1987), "Ladies by Their Windows." The choosers, however, are merely selecting the best of the best.

The most revealing and probably most accurate insights into Justice's poetry come from Justice himself in his several interviews, many of which are included in *Platonic Scripts*. He seems quite willing to talk about his verse, his philosophy, his poetic roots in the tradition, though he is most modest in his claims. Dana Gioia reviewed *Selected Poems* in 1981. Her observation may help readers understand more clearly the problems that critics have had in assessing Justice's work: "Justice's work presents a uniquely difficult job in seeing as a whole because the poet has self-consciously tried to write in as many new and different ways as possible. There is not a poet in America who has mastered as many styles as Justice" (672). To that statement one might add James Justus's words (1985): "Preferring understatement to energy, Justice writes a poetry of measure, boundaries, control. . . . It is the most civilized poetry of his Southern contemporaries" (537).

BIBLIOGRAPHY

Works by Donald Justice

Poetry

The Summer Anniversaries. Middletown, Conn.: Wesleyan University Press, 1960. Revised 1981.
A Local Storm. Private edition, 1963.
Night Light. Middletown, Conn.: Wesleyan University Press, 1967. Revised 1981.
From a Notebook. Iowa City: Seamark Press, 1972.
Departures. New York: Atheneum, 1973.
Selected Poems. New York: Atheneum, 1979.
The Sunset Maker: Poems/Stories/A Memoir. New York: Atheneum, 1987.
A Donald Justice Reader: Selected Poetry and Prose. Edited by Robert Pack and Jay Parini. Hanover, N.H.: University Press of New England, 1991.

Essays

"Meters and Memory." *Antaeus* 30–31 (1978): 314–20.
"Appreciation [for R. V. Cassill]." *December* 23 (1981): 45–47.
"The Invention of Free Verse." *Iowa Review* 15, no. 2 (1985): 8–11.
"The Prose Sublime." *Michigan Quarterly Review* 27 (1988): 577–85.

Works Edited by Donald Justice

The Collected Works of Weldon Kees. Iowa City: Stone Wall Press, 1960. Reprint. Lincoln: University of Nebraska Press, 1975.
Contemporary French Poetry. Edited with Alexander Aspel. Ann Arbor: University of Michigan Press, 1965.

Platonic Scripts. Ann Arbor: University of Michigan Press, 1984.

The Collected Poems of Henri Coulette. Edited with Robert Mezey. Fayetteville: University of Arkansas Press, 1990.

The Collected Poems of Weldon Kees. Rev. ed. Lincoln: University of Nebraska Press, 1992.

Interviews with Donald Justice

Gerber, Philip L., and Robert J. Gemmett, eds. "Falling into Place: A Conversation with Donald Justice." *Prairie Schooner* 47 (1973): 317–24.

Studies of Donald Justice

Beacham, Walton, Erica Dickson, and Charles J. Moseley, eds. *Research Guide to Biography and Criticism.* Vols. 5 and 6. Washington, D.C.: Research Publications, 1991.

Bruns, Gerald L. "Anapostrophe: Rhetorical Meditations upon Donald Justice's 'Poems.' " *Missouri Review* 4, no. 1 (1980): 71–76.

De Jong, Mary Gosselink. " 'Musical Possibilities': Music, Memory, and Composition in the Poetry of Donald Justice." *Concerning Poetry* 18, nos. 1–2 (1985): 57–66.

Gioia, Dana. "Three Poets in Mid Career." *Southern Review* 17 (1981): 667–74.

Hirsch, Edward. Review of *The Sunset Maker. New York Times Book Review* (August 23, 1987): 20.

Hoffman, Daniel. "Poetry: Dissidents from Schools." In *Harvard Guide to Contemporary American Writing,* edited by Daniel Hoffman, 564–606. Cambridge: Harvard University Press, Belknap Press, 1979.

Howard, Richard. *Alone with America.* Enl. ed. New York: Atheneum, 1980.

Jarman, Mark. "Ironic Elegies: The Poetry of Donald Justice." *Pequod: A Journal of Contemporary Literature and Literary Criticism* 16–17 (1984): 104–9.

Justus, James H. "Poets after Midcentury." In *The History of Southern Literature,* edited by Louis D. Rubin, Jr., Blyden Jackson, Rayburn S. Moore, Lewis P. Simpson, and Thomas Daniel Young, 535–55. Baton Rouge: Louisiana State University Press, 1985.

Kazin, Cathrael. "Donald Justice." In *Dictionary of Literary Biography Yearbook,* edited by Mary Bruccoli and Jean W. Ross, 266–71. Detroit: Gale Research, 1984.

Molesworth, Charles. Review of *Selected Poems. New York Times Book Review* (March 9, 1980): 8.

Perkins, David. *A History of Modern Poetry: Modernism and After.* Cambridge: Harvard University Press, Belknap Press, 1987.

Ryan, Michael. "Flaubert in Florida." *New England Review and Bread Loaf Quarterly* 7 (1984): 218–32.

St. John, David. "Scripts and Water, Rules and Riches." *Antioch Review* 43 (1985): 309–19.

Sheridan, Michael. "The Poetry of Donald Justice, Gentleman." *New Letters: A Magazine of Fine Writing* 48, no. 1 (1981): 114–16.

Swiss, Thomas. ''The Principle of Apprenticeship: Donald Justice's Poetry.'' *Modern Poetry Studies* 10, no. 1 (1980): 44–58.

Young, Alan. Review of *Selected Poems. Times Literary Supplement* (May 30, 1980): 620.

Young, Vernon. ''Two Hedgehogs and a Fox.'' *Parnassus* 8 (1979): 227–37.

KATHRYN VANSPANCKEREN

Florence King
(1936–   )

A humorist and social satirist, Florence King is best known for outspoken, witty, and idiosyncratic nonfiction. Her humorous perspective on the South has earned her a reputation as a regional writer. Her bold treatment of relations between the sexes is well known, but she has also satirized white Anglo-Saxon Protestants, men, and feminists—and most recently she has lampooned national foibles. Some of her best work contains lively passages of engaging autobiography. Critical opinion on King is just beginning to take shape; while a few reviewers have found her work ephemeral, most have found it hilarious and on the mark.

BIOGRAPHY

Born on January 5, 1936, in Washington, D.C., King was the only child of a tomboy and a bookish English dance-band musician. King's mother, Louise Ruding King, was a chain-smoking, baseball fan; King's indomitable Southern grandmother, Mrs. Ruding, ran the house. The precocious King thrived on the adult attention she received as an only child. Her devoted father, Herbert King, took her to the library, discussed recondite ideas with her, and taught her to write in script. She learned to read before entering school, devouring her "first adult book," *Gone with the Wind,* at the age of eight. A pretty girl, King was expected to be sweet and reticent in school; luckily, her unconventional parents always supported her outspoken independence.

King's formative years brought the misadventures encountered by those of slender means. For years, her father slept on a cot in a corner of the kitchen; as soon as King was out of a crib, she slept with her grandmother on a fold-out couch. Perhaps as a result, King developed an underlying affection for odd people managing in unusual arrangements. Her father's dry English wit taught her to view her family and Southern female experience with the eyes of a sympathetic but amused outsider. Many of the Southern traits King later lampooned were embodied in her droll grandmother, a Daughter of the Revolution and tenth-generation Virginian. The Dickensian Mrs. Ruding aspired to raise Florence as a Southern lady. Instead, King took after her father, becoming a bookworm, skipping a grade, and earning top marks. In high school she was known as a "brain," relishing French and the works of Dostoevsky and Ayn Rand. She did not date by preference; though curious about sex, she remained inexperienced until she graduated from college.

Mindful of her family's limited finances, King commuted to American University, from which she graduated in 1957. Since American had offered her full scholarship, she did not apply elsewhere. King intended to study French in order to be a translator and was bitterly disappointed to learn that American did not offer a Fench major; she received her B.A. in history. In college King met female professors who preferred to be addressed as "Mrs." rather than "Doctor" and sorority sisters who were working for their "Mrs. degree," but she herself shunned marriage. In the summer of her sophomore year, King worked for a State Department annex, where she met a young man who courted her and at length proposed. Pressured to marry, she found strength to decline and began to think of herself as an unmarried intellectual.

King became convinced that "dating chipped away tiny pieces of a woman's self-confidence; piece by piece, date by date, she was diminished by some form of unnatural behavior forced on her by social usage." As a college junior she enlisted in the Marines' Woman Officer Candidate School at Quantico and attended a twelve-week summer course that could have enabled her to graduate from school commissioned as a second lieutenant. Though King decided against the Marines, she completed eleven weeks of the course and respected the female colonel, who thought King would make a good Marine and called her "a lady to [her] fingertips."

Returning to American University for her senior year, King went inactive from her sorority and considered her options after graduation, aware that there were few good jobs for young women. She was not consciously a feminist; discrimination for her—as for most Americans in the 1950s—was based not on gender, but race. Unwilling to work as a secretary and enjoying the intellectual challenge and equality of college, King applied for the master's degree program in history at the University of Mississippi and was offered a full scholarship. Elated at the prospect of an independent life, she found a female doctor who fitted her with a diaphragm; and during the summer after graduation she enjoyed her first affair, with a young married professor.

King's scholarship at "Ole Miss" provided for tuition and one hundred dollars a month, which she supplemented by working as a dormitory proctor for room and board. This arrangement gave her a private room for the first time. King had wanted to compare the upper and deep South, and the glamour of the campus and the Southern mannerisms of the people appealed to and amused her. Most of all, she appreciated her own library carrel, where she met a languid, bohemian, older female graduate student in classics who initiated her into the Deep South, graduate school, and romantic love.

King's intense love for Bres ended suddenly and traumatically. When King began publishing stories in true-confessions magazines instead of pursuing grants in order to continue her graduate study, Bres broke off the relationship with no explanation. Shortly thereafter, Bres and her new lover were killed in an automobile accident. King was left uncertain whether her affair signified a lesbian orientation or simply love for an individual. She was protected from the stigma of lesbianism—seen as a "nigger-loving Jewish Communist threat" in Mississippi—by a wealthy, strong-willed Southern belle whom King had assisted in French.

King returned to her family that summer, lacking her master's degree (she never finished her thesis, on Bérénice), but flush with checks from true-confessions magazines. Finding writing difficult while sharing a room with her grandmother, King rented a studio apartment until the family moved to a larger house in Ballston, Virginia. Since then, King has lived in Bayonne, New Jersey; Boston; Mattapoisett, Massachusetts; Phoenix, and Seattle, where she spent ten years before returning to Virginia. Since 1982, she has lived in an apartment in Fredericksburg, Virginia. She has never married, considering her work her first love.

Fiercely independent, King has lived by her wits and pen for many years. According to her humorous autobiography *Confessions of a Failed Southern Lady* (1985), she was trying to write a grant application in order to continue work on her M.A. when she came across *Writer's Market* in the stacks. Writing for *True Confessions* looked like a surer bet than writing the grant, so she read a copy of the magazine in order to "study the market" and dashed off 3,500 words in three hours. This opus was auspiciously entitled "I Committed Adultery in a Diabetic Coma." Its deadpan title, salacious content, and presentation of the first person narrator as a "blundering female Dagwood" forecast King's later satires.

King has written journalism throughout her career. She authored true confessions from 1958 to 1964; during this period she first worked for American Can in New York City, and then taught tenth-grade history from 1959 to 1960 in Suitland, Maryland. From 1964 to 1967 she was the woman's-page reporter for the Raleigh *News and Observer,* winning two North Carolina Press Women awards for reporting and interviewing. From 1967 to 1968 King worked as assistant editor of *Uncensored Confessions* magazine and began to write pornographic novels with titles like *Moby's Dick* under such pseudonyms as Cynthia, Veronica King, Emmett X. Reed, Niko Stavros, and Mike Winston, penning thirty-seven "erotic adventures" before she stopped in 1973. Each paid about $1,600; to write one took about a month. Since 1968 she has worked as a freelance writer.

King has published in *Cosmopolitan, Harper's, Ms., Penthouse, Playgirl, Redbook, Southern,* and *Viva.* She worked briefly for *Playgirl* and wrote an

"Advice to the Lovelorn" column for *Viva,* but her mocking treatment of sex offended some. Essays for magazines often formed chapters of her humorous books; occasionally writing books has, in turn, provided King with material for articles. For example, "Ripping Clio's Bodice—the Chronicles of a Sweet Savage Hack," a humorous essay about writing romance novels, at first appeared in the *New York Times Book Review* and reappeared, revised, as the chapter "Sex and the Saxon Churl" in *Reflections in a Jaundiced Eye* (1989). The chapter recounts her writing of *The Barbarian Princess* (1978), an historical romance set in fifth-century Britain published under the pseudonym Laura Buchanan. King has also written reviews for *Newsday,* the *Philadelphia Inquirer,* the *Baltimore Sun,* and the *New York Times Book Review.* Since 1975, she has published eight books under her own name. They are all deft, witty, and provocative. She serves on the Usage Panel of *The American Heritage Dictionary* and is a member of the National Book Critics Circle.

MAJOR THEMES

French and history play important roles in King's writing; her vigorous, cutting style and social criticism show her debt to the incisive seventeenth-century French satirists. King's usual approach is a taxonomy of "types" (of WASPS, of American Men, of Southerners, etc.), reminiscent of the French encyclopedists. Her categories also recall structuralist, anthropological, and literary studies by Vladimir Propp, Lord Raglan, and Claude Lévi-Strauss; and she has been termed a "pop anthropologist."

King's books show a gain in control and emotional depth as she has outgrown a format based on formula writing. Her earliest book, *Southern Ladies and Gentlemen* (1975), established King's brisk tone, psychological viewpoint, and jokey delivery in its opening sallies. The Author's Note reads, "I am neither living nor dead, and being purely coincidental runs in my family." In her Acknowledgments, or "Belles vs. Lettres" she neatly skewers her editor at Stein and Day, who "knows 435 ways to get 'because' out of a sentence, and . . . shared every one of them with her author." The book's theme appears on page one: "I was not sane, I was a Southerner."

This book, like her next two, is organized by categories, one per chapter. In Chapter 2, "Thou Shalt be Kings No Matter Who Begat Thee, or I Dreamt I Dwelt in Marble Halls," King inspects the Southern interest in "genealogy, or Tombstone Twitch." Chapter 3 is entitled "Would Youall Be Good Enough to Excuse Me While I Have an Identity Crisis, or The Cult of Southern Womanhood." "The Good Ole Boy" of Chapter 6 is afflicted with gyneolatry and bouts of the "Deliverance Syndrome, otherwise known as the hunting weekend." King humorously explains Southern regionalism and its effects on sex roles in the chapters "Old and Young Maids," "Gay Confederation," and "Dear Old Things, Rocks, and Dowagers."

Southern Ladies and Gentlemen is so fast-paced and funny that its astute observations might be missed on a first reading. The book presents a rich collection of regional stereotypes or folk ideas about the South, seen from a Southern viewpoint. Critics loved the humor, but some, like Margo Jefferson in *Newsweek* (1975), complained that "time and again she settles for entertainment."

King's second book, *WASP, Where Is Thy Sting?* (1977), dissects white Anglo-Saxon Protestants; like its predecessor, it is organized as a parodic treatise. King's "Author's Note" defends the literary tradition of stereotyping, listing female humorists as models:

Stereotyping, better known as "perceptive pointing up," is an ancient and honorable ingredient of the humorous literary genre. Betty MacDonald pointed up rural people in *The Egg and I*. Margaret Halsey pointed up the British in *With Malice Toward Some*. Cornelia Otis Skinner and Emily Kimbrough pointed up both the French and the innocent Americans abroad in *Our Hearts Were Young and Gay*. Gail Parent points up Jews in *Sheila Levine is Dead and Living in New York*.

He: An Irreverent Look at the American Male (1978) employs a catalogue to explore masculinity and male sexuality. King's categories include "The Confirmed Bachelor," "The Misogynist," "The Liberated Man," and "The Forty-Niner" (middlebrow, middle-aged convention-goer on the make) whose line is "I guarantee you the best time in bed you've ever had, Scout's Honor." As Lynn Felder observes in the *Dictionary of Literary Biography Yearbook* for 1985, most critics find the book hilarious except when King deprecates the group "with which the critic aligns him—or herself."

King's next book, *When Sisterhood Was in Flower* (1982), is a bawdy, open-ended, picaresque novel reminiscent of Henry Fielding that recounts the offbeat friendship between the humorless, far-left Bostonian reformer Polly Bradshaw and the reactionary Virginian Isabel Fairfax. Literally thrown together when a Weatherman bomb explodes in their apartment house basement, Bradshaw and Fairfax travel from Boston to California, gathering other archetypal or stereotypical women en route: the far-out hippie medievalist Gloria Hammond; the battered housewife Agnes Mulligan; and Aunt Edna, a middle-aged, moonstruck housewife. In California, Bradshaw founds a feminist commune, while Fairfax writes pornography. Though the end seems a bit forced, the book offers salutary digs at numerous sacred cows. Critical reception was uneven; a reviewer for *Atlantic* called it "just plain shamelessly, roaringly, outrageously funny," whereas a critic for *Library Journal* scolded that King's manner "becomes offensive when it means to be witty."

Confessions of a Failed Southern Lady (1985) is a hilarious autobiography whose characters delight with their originality and authenticity, from the overbearing Granny, who undertakes to turn King into a Southern Belle against all odds, to the emphatic, pious African American maid Jensy, who becomes a part of the extended family. The two old ladies are counterparts, each a pillar of her social set: religious, given to fanatical acts of charity, so willfully conventional as to be extreme and eccentric. Both of them observe racial barriers in public, but plot like inseparable cronies in private. A matriarch, Granny dominates the book, as she does the household; but King's rebellious, athletic mother and meditative father provide alternative visions of the South.

Confessions avoids stereotyping, offering rounded characters and a richly realized milieu. King vividly re-creates "shabby genteel" Virginia family life during World War II and college in the early 1950s: coupons, rationing, stylish big bands, streetcars, the armed services, the double standard. Coeds lusted for the "Mrs. degree"; King's university campus resembled "a swamp wafting deadly vapors of marriage fever." King's headstrong intellectuality and amorous adventures were, in retrospect, a bid for selfhood against the suffocating sexism of 1950s America. From a feminist perspective, King's passionate, finely evoked lesbian love affair validates King as a human being and vindicates her rejection of woman's role as wife/mother.

The book's title is ironic, because King's persona clearly is becoming a lady (as King defines "lady") by searching for inner strength and ethical values. The book's closure underscores the need for new terms denoting woman's experience. Only one word describes Granny, who dies at the end, unable to continue in life without her friend Jensy (and this theme of female bonding between Granny and Jensy resonates with King's affair with Bres). The right word is *virago,* "a woman of great stature, strength and courage who is not feminine in the conventional ways." The quest for articulation of strong, unconventional womanhood echoes the persona's search for an authentic way of being a woman. Given the direction King's work has taken, she seems gradually to be affirming central feminist positions—the needs for a positive self-image, for words to describe it, for supportive relations with other women as companions and models. Critical reception of this humorous novel about education has been remarkably positive. Both male and female reviewers have praised the accurate evocation of the 1950s and the poignant autobiographical passages.

Reflections in a Jaundiced Eye (1989), the first of three collections, tackles American foibles of all regions and both sexes. King's targets include anti-intellectualism, worship of children, "Nice-Guyism," and "Helpism and its handmaidens," "Education 'n' Awareness." Claiming that hype and ignorance have triumphed over common sense, King instances compulsive hugging, hypocritical mouthings of truisms, silliness in publishing, and egregious euphemisms masking unpleasant facts that need changing. King theorizes that "people are so busy dreaming the American Dream, fantasizing about what they could be or have a right to be, that they're all asleep at the switch." Through humorous anecdote and observation, King commends logic, high standards, hard work, and self-respect, addressing issues serious enough to content her most humorless critics.

In *Lump It or Leave It* (1990) King continues her humorous critique of contemporary American culture, satirizing excesses in academe, best-sellers, the movies, gender politics, and language (e.g., the pejorative newspeak suffixes "ist" and "phobe"). Everywhere she looks, King discerns rampant illusion, delusion, and hypocrisy. Considering corrupt politicians and financiers, she muses that "the more immoral we become in big ways, the more puritanical we become in little ways," as seen in personals ads that run, "handsome masochist, 28, seeks disciplinarian to tie me up, beat me with cat o' nine tails, dunk me in ice water, ram me with baseball bat, and stick arrows in me for St. Sebastian fantasy. Non-smokers only." On Hollywood movies: "There is more sexism in a year's worth of movies than actually exists in a woman's entire lifetime."

King's third book of essays, *With Charity Toward None: A Fond Look At Misanthropy* (1992), is another sortie on American idiocies, this time in the guise of a treatise on misanthropes. The book's gallery of real and fictional exemplars range from Ambrose Bierce, Ring Lardner, G. Gordon Liddy, and Richard Nixon to Timon of Athens, Coriolanus, and Molière's original misanthrope Alceste. They hilariously illustrate King's thesis that misanthropy is "a realistic attitude toward human nature" that may correct contemporary American "compulsory gregariousness, fevered friendliness [and] we-never-close compassion." King drives her points home with eminently quotable quotations: From Ambrose Bierce we learn the art of the one-sentence book review ("The covers of this book are too far apart") and higher philosophy ("Death is not the end, there remains litigation over the estate"). In this, as in her earlier books of essays, through humorous anecdote and observation King plumbs quintessentially Southern depths, evoking the grotesque, the family, race relations, and the sense of history. Alienation permeates her work. King transposes these themes into an audacious storytelling that has antecedents in Old Southwestern writers such as Augustus Baldwin Longstreet and Thomas Bangs Thorpe, who explored grotesque characters in regional settings, depicting unusual events, often in salty dialect. King's amoral persona and bawdy wit make her literary kinswoman of George Washington Harris as well. Like the Old Southwest humorists described in Kenneth Lynn's *Mark Twain and Southwestern Humor* (1959), King is a well educated but not "genteel" Southern patriot with a large popular following.

Walter Blair in *Native American Humor* (1937) has noted that folk humor is often told by a persona that Lynn has called a "Self-controlled Gentleman." King's early books use literary paraphernalia such as mock dedications, author's notes and introductory essays to cast a mantle of respectability based on notions of literary and sociological value over the rest. In *Confessions* the figure of King as a self-controlled girl seeking release from her respectable family mediates King's comical sexual adventures. The effect is not to sanitize the sex but to humanize it: For the protagonist to become authentically self-controlled and self-directed, she must turn respectable Southern traditions on their heads. Presenting respectability and wild excess together and subtly undermining respectability are traits of Southwestern humor: King makes overt what was hidden and merges what was heretofore kept distinct. King uses her wit to carry forward Southern traditions in new directions. Her work is original and profoundly funny—and increasingly speaks to issues of lasting concern.

SURVEY OF CRITICISM

Such critical attention as King has received has been in the form of book reviews and occasional interviews. Unfortunately, the first interview was done in 1974, before she had published a book. This breezy piece by Tim Menees appeared in the *Seattle Post-Intelligencer,* provoked by the mixed response to King's article "The Good Ole Boy" in *Harper's* and the fact that King was then living in Seattle. Menees' gossipy article stressing King's pornography was reprinted and given wide national circulation by the reference work *Authors in the News* (1976) and has provided the basis for influential later appraisals. For example, the article on King in *Contemporary Authors* (1982) is based on the Menees piece, despite the fact that King had published five entire books—had, in fact, launched and brought to maturity her serious writing career—since Menees wrote. Lynn Felder's thoughtful entry in the *Dictionary of Literary Biography* is more current; it briefly discusses all of King's books through *Confessions* and includes an informative interview with King centering on important literary issues. Since then short interviews have been conducted during King's book tours or at her apartment. Though some errors have crept in— Robert Merritt (1985) writes "black" for "quack"—the interviews are the best sources of information.

Reviews of King's individual books have appeared since 1975. Generally speaking, her reputation has increased over time, and successive books have received increasing numbers of reviews. Reviews have appeared in England in the *London Observer, London Review of Books,* and *Times Literary Supplement,* as well as in all regions of the United States, particularly the South. Her recent work has been reviewed by major organs, including the *New York Times* and *New York Times Book Review.* Although most reviews consist of plot summary, Rosemary Daniell in her 1985 review of *Confessions* compares King to Rita Mae Brown, Lisa Alther, and Blanche McCrary Boyd, calling them all "ironists" who have unwrapped their Southern roots from around their necks. Reviewers increasingly mention King alongside such authors as Willie Morris and Walker Percy as writers that offer non-Southerners an authentic feeling of the South. King's work has also drawn notices in *Publisher's Weekly, Library Journal, Booklist, Book World,* and the *Kirkus Review.*

There are no critical essays on King, with the exception of one by me in the *Kennesaw Review.* King's humor, her place in contemporary humorous writing, and her contribution to women's writing and Southern literature are a few of many worthwhile topics. Clearly King's works deserve more critical attention.

BIBLIOGRAPHY

Works by Florence King

"The Good Ole Boy." *Harper's* 248 (April 1974): 78–82.
"Is It True What They Say About Southern Women?" *Redbook* 145 (June 1975): 38–49.
Southern Ladies and Gentlemen. New York: Stein and Day, 1975.
WASP, Where Is Thy Sting? New York: Stein and Day, 1977.
He: An Irreverent Look at the American Male. New York: Stein and Day, 1978.
(as Laura Buchanan). *The Barbarian Princess.* New York: Berkley, 1978.
When Sisterhood Was in Flower. New York: Viking Press, 1982.
Confessions of a Failed Southern Lady. New York: St. Martin's Press, Marek, 1985.
"Ripping Clio's Bodice: The Chronicles of a Sweet Savage Hack." *New York Times Book Review* (May 3, 1987): 27.
Reflections in a Jaundiced Eye. New York: St. Martin's Press, 1989.
Lump It or Leave It. New York: St. Martin's Press, 1990.
With Charity toward None: A Fond Look at Misanthropy. New York: St. Martin's Press, 1992.

Interviews with Florence King

Menees, Tim. "Good Ol' Florence King." *Seattle Post-Intelligencer* (May 12, 1974). Reprinted in *Authors in the News,* vol. 1, edited by Barbara Nykoruk, 279–80. Detroit: Gale Research, 1976.
Merritt, Robert. *Richmond Times-Dispatch* (January 20, 1985).
O'Briant, Don. *Atlanta Journal* (January 29, 1985).
Felder, Lynn. "Florence King." In *Dictionary of Literary Biography Yearbook, 1985,* 395–401, edited by Jean W. Ross. Detroit: Gale Research, 1986.
Moose, Debbie. "Shooting from the Lip: Florence King on the Firing Line." *News and Observer* (Raleigh, N.C.), (May 24, 1989): D1.
Zitz, Michael. "Guns and Roses." *Free Lance-Star* (Fredericksburg, VA.), (May 27, 1989); Lifestyle 1.

Studies of Florence King

Braaten, David. Review of *With Charity Toward None.* *Washington Times* (April 19, 1992).
Cantwell, Mary. Review of *When Sisterhood Was in Flower.* *New York Times* (October 29, 1982): B2.
Creaturo, Barbara. Review of *Confessions of a Failed Southern Lady.* *New York Times Book Review* (February 10, 1985): 27.
Daniell, Rosemary. Review of *Confessions of a Failed Southern Lady.* *Philadelphia Inquirer* (May 5, 1985).
Felder, Lynn. "Florence King." In *Contemporary Authors,* edited by Ann Evory, 57–60, 285–86. Detroit: Gale Research, 1982.

Gannon, Frank. Review of *Reflections in a Jaundiced Eye. New York Times Book Review* (April 9, 1989): 11.

Hays, Charlotte. Review of *Reflections in a Jaundiced Eye. Washington Times* (April 25, 1989).

Irwin, Edward E. "Freedoms as Value in Three Popular Southern Novels." *Proteus* 6, no. 1 (Spring 1989): 37–41.

Jefferson, Margo. Review of *Southern Ladies and Gentlemen. Newsweek,* 85 (June 30, 1975): 66–67.

Lingeman, Richard R. Review of *WASP, Where Is Thy Sting? New York Times* (June 30, 1977): B2.

Morrison, Ellen Rossler. Review of *Confessions of a Failed Southern Lady. Birmingham News* (Jan. 30, 1985).

Pal, Pratapaditya. Review of *Reflections in a Jaundiced Eye. Los Angeles Times Book Review* (April 30, 1989): 2.

Reed, John Shelton. Review of *Lump It or Leave It. Raleigh News and Observer* (July 8, 1990).

Slater, Joyce. Review of *Lump It or Leave It. Atlanta Journal and Atlanta Constitution* (July 1, 1990): N10.

Stumpf, Edna. Review of *Reflections in a Jaundiced Eye. Philadelphia Inquirer* (April 2, 1989).

VanSpanckeren, Kathryn. "Pop Anthropology as Humor: The Works of Florence King." *Kennesaw Review* 1–2 (Spring 1988): 50–58.

Yardley, Jonathan. Review of *Reflections in a Jaundiced Eye. Washington Post* (March 29, 1989): C2.

D. SOYINI MADISON

Etheridge Knight
(1933–1991)

Recognized as one of the major American poets of his time, Etheridge Knight survived war, prison, and a narcotics habit to publish five books of poetry and to be one of the most influential voices in African-American literature and art.

BIOGRAPHY

Etheridge Knight was born to Bushie and Belzora Knight on April 19, 1933, in Corinth, Mississippi. Like many African-American families who migrated North during the early 1900s to seek their future in Northern cities, the young Etheridge was also introduced to this new landscape; his home became Indiana. Although he spent many formative years in Indianapolis, it was the culture of the South that most influenced his views toward community, self, and expression. It was the ''blues'' country of his Mississippi birthplace that was, according to Knight, his frame of reference. The blues, along with country-and-western music, were part of the collective voices that informed his identity. Etheridge was surrounded by storytellers who taught him the realities and truths of the everyday world. It was this pervasiveness of song and story, as well as the spirit of the men and women who were the celebrants of this oral tradition, that contributed to Knight's love for the spoken, performed word. Knight once asked, What is a word ''other than something that represents sound?'' He continued, ''It's all oral, the short story—the novel is an extension of the story teller. Nothing stands up on the page as well as it does out loud . . . that's all it is . . . and it's not ended until it's said aloud. A poem isn't finished unless the reader reads it aloud. That's where that's at'' (Tracy 1985, 10). In keeping with his blues and country-music roots, he discussed music and poetry:

My reference to lots of blues singers and musicians in my poetry, to me, is pretty simple because poetry itself, of all the art disciplines, it seems that poetry is more intertwined with music, but you think even the vernacular is different than prose. There are no sentences in poetry, there are lines. There are no paragraphs, there are stanzas and rhyme . . . and rhythm and meter, are all musical terms and it follows. And poets are primarily sayers and chanters, so the relationship between poetry and music is closer than the relationship of say, poetry to sculpture or painting. (Tracy 1985, 10)

It was this rural Southern beginning of word, song, and story that kept the everyday and the sacred alive, laying the foundation for Knight's artistry. It was perhaps this same foundation that was his source of survival in the hard years ahead.

Etheridge Knight's formal education extended as far as 2 years of high school. Later he trained as a medical technician in the army and served active duty in the Korean War. During his years in the army, narcotics became the threatening force in his life. He left the army with a narcotics habit that later led to his imprisonment. In 1960 Knight was sentenced on robbery charges to a 10- to 20-year term at Indiana State Prison in Michigan City: "I died in Korea from a shrapnel wound and narcotics resurrected me. I died in 1960 from a prison sentence and poetry brought me back to life" (quoted in Bremen 1973, 305). He was released on parole at the end of 1968.

Like Malcolm X before him, and long before the establishment of prison education programs, Knight educated himself behind prison walls. He taught himself by working on the prison newspaper and by reading and studying the *New York Times* and every book, article, and pamphlet available. Through his studies, his love for music, words, and capturing the sounds and meanings of the African-American oral tradition, he was rejoined with the poetics of his roots. The other inmates would call upon him to write letters to lovers, friends, and family; he would perform in the African-American tradition of the toast, the boasts, and signifyin'. His way with words and rhythm gained him the respect of his fellow inmates and "saved" him from the "death" of a world without freedom. For Knight, freedom was based upon two fundamental abilities—to communicate and to be mobile.

With poetry came the liberation of his voice; it was both his weapon and armor. And as a result Knight wrote prolifically. Dudley Randall and Gwendolyn Brooks believed Knight to be one of the most important American poets of his era. Brooks's visits to the prison were inspiring. Recognizing the value of his work, Brooks advised Knight on technique. In 1968 Dudley Randall published Knight's first book, *Poems from Prison*. Gwendolyn Brooks describes Knight in the preface: "The warmth of this poet is abruptly robust. The music that seems effortless is exquisitely carved." She adds, "And there is blackness, inclusive, possessed and given; freed and terrible and beautiful" (9).

Knight's first book of poems, as Brooks described, was a "major announcement." Knight had not only begun to make his mark as an outstanding American poet but as one of the most powerful and influential voices of the Black Arts Movement of the 1960s. In his first volume of poetry, Knight shared the sounds

and music of words that were so much a part of his Southern roots. He shared
the ill-fated and agonizing pieces of his life, the pain of addiction, oppression,
and war. And he brought us face to face with the realities of prison life: "Prison
is a very oppressive, painful, alienating world. You've been, not exiled, you've
been in-ziled" (Tracy 1985, 21). Knight experienced the horrors of prison where
solitary confinement meant lying naked on a cold dirty floor, seeing nothing but
darkness, and where the tight, surrounding walls in this small black box most
resemble a "grave." For Knight, the nature of prison disallowed the freedom
of movement, it disallowed communication, and it disallowed feeling:

See, when you go in prison, the first thing most guys do in jail is to somehow build a
still kind of protection around their bellies. They try not to feel, 'cause it's painful to
feel in that joint, you know what I mean? And sometimes they build such a deep shield
they become cut off from their feelings almost. I mean this is the situation. You walk
out of your cell and you see a guy stabbing another guy in the cell. You got to keep on
walking. You got to act like you don't see it. You know what I mean? And that's
inhuman. It's not the human way. We naturally don't do that. (21)

Knight was committed to making us understand the prison system as a denial
of humanity by cutting off the individual's natural need for community, feelings,
mobility, and communication. Knight found in poetry a way of reclaiming mobility and movement, and he also found the path that rejoined and extended him
to a community beyond prison walls. Poetry brought him back to life, and he
found comfort in feeling again. Knight did not view his poetry as a solipsistic
rebirth; the damaging effects of the penal system upon other incarcerated men
and women concerned him. When Knight was paroled in 1968, he continued to
work with the incarcerated through poetry readings and writing workshops. In
1970 he published his second book, *Black Voices from Prison,* an anthology of
poetry, prose, and fiction by Knight and inmates of the Indiana State Prison.
Knight saw the Black Power Movement of the 1960s as a powerful and positive
source in promoting pride, dignity, unity, and values for black men and women
in the prisons. He saw this movement as a movement of courage and principal
that defied the spiritless and defeated existence prisons impose.

Describing the men whose writings are included in *Black Voices from Prison,*
Knight writes in the preface:

Prisons usually break men, but not these cats; they are a new breed of convict. Unlike
the old convicts who sink lead-like into a sea of inertia, these young men *think* and
feel—regardless of the accompanying pain. They are restless; they emit a great energy
wherever they gather, on the yard or in the cellhouses . . . in the meantime, what is going
to happen to these young men here who might have been hewers of wood or climbers
of high mountains? Well, they will wait, milling about with sparks dancing in their eyes,
until the storm breaks, until the built-in contradictions of this racist, exploitive system
burst through its already cracking seams. (10)

Knight's comments reflect his passion for freedom and justice, and although Knight was critical of the inhumanity that pervades the penal system, he never condoned the criminal acts that put men and women behind prison cells. Knight believed that to hurt another human being deliberately and willfully was against human nature; for Knight it was unnatural to kill, harm, and destroy. He felt that all of us by natural instinct are more loving than violent. Knight believed there are circumstances and external forces that impede the purity of the human spirit when one man or woman violates another. His life and work addressed the issues of social reality, freedom, justice, and love, as well as the relationships we struggle through to find peace with ourselves and others. He saw himself as a political poet: "You find that poets as a group are more involved in the forefront of political activity than any other artists" (quoted in McCullough 1982, 8).

When he was able to move beyond prison walls, this activist poet shared his message and artistry with a variety of listeners and readers. In 1973 his third book, *Belly Songs and Other Poems,* was nominated for the National Book Award and the Pulitzer Prize; his fourth book, *Born of a Woman,* including new and selected poems, was published in 1981; and in 1986 *The Essential Etheridge Knight* provided the most complete collection of his work. Guiding every poem in each of these volumes is Knight's philosophy of the "trinity" of poetry, that is, the three inextricable elements—the poem, the poet, and the people. For Knight, if one of these elements is taken away, the poem cannot live; it is dysfunctional because it is neither art nor communication. Knight's work is motivated by the belief that if there is no technique, no poetics, no discipline, then there is propaganda; however, if you take away the poet, leaving only the poem and the people, then you have commercialism; and if you take away the people where the concern is only between the poet and her or his poetics, then you have the art-for-art's-sake school.

As a result of Knight's belief and praxis in the unity between poet, poem, and people, his poetry is appreciated by diverse audiences and readers. Called the "bar-room poet," he read in bars and taverns throughout various communities, as well as in artistic and intellectual settings, at political rallies, on college campuses, and at the Library of Congress. Along with the nomination for the National Book Award and the Pulitzer Prize in 1973, other honors included: A National Endowment for The Arts Grant (1972), A Guggenheim Fellowship (1974), and The Shelly Memorial Award by the Poetry Society of America (1986). But for Etheridge Knight, recognition by these institutions was not as important as recognition by those who shared a common history and understanding of the world through common symbols and images. In an interview Knight stated, "Art exists within a context, a political, economic, and social context and the only real critics of any artists is that artist's audience" (Tracy 1985, 17).

Knight's audiences not only include the various communities where he performed his poetry, but students whom he influenced as an editor, poet-in-residence, and teacher. Knight served as poet-in-residence at the University of Pittsburgh (1968); at Hartford University in West Hartford, Connecticut (1970); at Lincoln University in Jefferson City, Missouri (1970–71); and at Temple University, Philadelphia (1985). He was poetry editor for *Motive* in Jefferson City and was coeditor of *Black Box* in Washington, D.C.

Knight died of lung cancer on March 10, 1991, at his home in Indianapolis. He was 57 years old.

MAJOR THEMES

Etheridge Knight's poetry can be examined through various themes: the prison experience; the African-American toast and oral tradition; the poems of love and tribute.

In his prison poetry, the poetry that kept him "alive," we observe powerful refections of the prison culture and his personal insights into the men, the system, and the outside world. These poems do not just touch on simple oppositions of justice versus injustice or freedom versus confinement but on the more complex issues in between that hold them in tension. One of Knight's best known poems "Hard Rock Returns to Prison from the Hospital for the Criminal Insane" (*Born of a Woman,* 3) speaks to the impenetrable "bad dude," the fearless hero, the undefeated one with whom the other men live a vicarious existence of resistance and empowerment. But a greater power, through its oppressive forces to control, overcomes Hard Rock, who is defeated through the American penal system that can only restrict him by boring a hole through his head and cutting out a portion of his brain. Hard rock is now "tamed" into submission, no longer "the doer of things" but an impotent mass of flesh who can hardly speak his own name. The demise of Hard Rock was also the demise of the dreams and aspirations of the men who revered him. Knight illustrates that we must have our heroes; they help keep the spirits of the dispossessed hopeful and alive.

In contrast to the fallen hero theme in "Hard Rock" is the poem "He Sees through Stone" (*Born of a Woman,* 6). Here the protagonist is not described as a verbose, wild, and fearless character, but as a man of immense experience, gentle dignity, and wisdom. This man who sees through stone typifies the traditional African-American elder/shaman/griot. He has persevered the years and triumphs as counselor and guide enlightening the other prisoners through his teachings. "He Sees through Stone" is a testimony not only to the endurance and courage of the survivors of the penal system whose penetrating visions see beyond prison walls but to the isolation, persecution, and bitterness in the stone feelings of the younger, and less wise.

In another prison theme Knight addressed the deprivation of innocence. "Freckle Face Gerald" (*Born of a Woman,* 15) describes a 16-year-old boy who has been sent to prison and whose youth, innocence, and inexperience prevent him from combating the violence against him. As a result, his "precise speech and an innocent grin'' (15) make him ''pigmeat / for the buzzards to eat'' (15). The buzzards are the inmates who exploit Gerald sexually and at every other level of his personhood. Knight's tone is both sad and indignant, for he puts Gerald's tragedy in a larger context. For Knight, the buzzards are part of the unjust and encompassing system that ''plotted'' Gerald's dehumanization and emasculation long before he entered a jail cell.

Gerald's alienation and loss of innocence is in juxtaposition to Knight's other well-known poem ''The Idea of Ancestry'' (*Born of a Woman,* 8). Here Knight explores ancestry as an extension of self ''I am all of them, they are all of me'' (8). It is the family bond that makes him less vulnerable and sustains him. He reminisces the scenes of family life and his personal struggles as he gazes upon the forty-seven pictures of his family taped to the cell wall. The first section of the poem resembles the narrative quality of autobiography. Knight reminisces about family scenes with love and regret. He is part of them, and they are part of him; but he also realizes he is separate because of his criminal deed and isolation: ''They are farmers, I am a thief, I am me, they are thee'' (8). In the second section, the pictures of his relatives on the cell wall transform his thoughts to personal suffering. We are brought full circle, from the prison cell of bars and family faces looking across his confined space, to the scene of family rituals in a storied past, and then back to the prison cell where this continuum of family and memory takes on a more profound significance. Knight laments having no children to continue his ancestry. Patricia Liggins Hill (1983) has described Knight's painful resolution, ''The poem involves the galvanization of the poet's genes—his sense of ancestry. He has no sons to hold his ritualistic space within the family'' (118).

Knight's prison poetry speaks to us on many levels of brutality, hope, and survival. He is steadfast in presenting an uncensored picture of the reality and the dreams of incarcerated existence.

A second major theme in Knight's work, which brings us outside the realm of prison themes, are poems reflective of the African-American *toasts and oral traditions.* In his toast poems, Knight is in keeping with the persona of the boaster, the unbridled machismo, the jive talker, and confident hipster. The black man with money, big cars, and women, who knows the game of the streets and always wins. Knight presents the black man who speaks in trope and hyperbole of his exploits, equating this with power while the concrete reality of his powerlessness is the ironic impetus that keeps the boast alive. In ''Words by Slick'' (*The Essential Etheridge Knight*), the hero, even in death, must be grand and flamboyant. He orders his listeners not to stand around in sadness and tears, but to bury him in fine clothes, a pink cadillac, and reefer/weed, while Dizzy blows his golden trumpet. Slick's dictates are ostentatious and commanding, because this is a requirement for the ''slick life,'' the life of the streets where black men must have unrelenting control and ''cool'' in order to be men—even in their last good-bye.

Just as tough as the colorful Slick, is the character Shine, in ''Dark Prophecy:

I Sing of Shine'' (*Born of a Woman*). In the toast tradition, Shine is victorious. Knight depicts the sinking of the Titanic as a representation of American luxury and the white bourgeoisie in order to illustrate the white bourgeoisie's "poverty" of tenacity and survival in comparison to the lone black hero. Neither the banker's million-dollar check nor the young white women's promise of sex could convince Shine to save them. Knight ridicules the myth that the two commonly held aspirations for all black men are to be as rich as white men and to procreate with white women. The man and the woman drown; neither money nor sex could save them. But more important, Knight not only rejects the myth, but also shows that these values are an obstacle to Shine's surviving. The refrain in the poem, "And Shine swam on——Shine swam on——" speaks to Knight's theme that the essence of freedom and courage is shaped by the dynamics of all that it means to be black in America, thus giving black people the inner resources to stay alive. For Knight the toast provides an unveiling of willfulness, of creative modes of resistance, and of self-determination under the cloud of dispossession. It also reveals the power of imagination and language in creating illusions that can be empowering.

One of the masters of the toast, Knight was also a "singer" of African and African-American music and chant. His poetry is that of the blues and jazz musician, yet still echoing the roots of the African drum and chant. He shows us that the spoken words of black people cannot be divorced from the rhythms that embellish them. In "Ilu, The Talking Drum" (*Born of a Woman*), we are participants in a ritual interwoven in African-American song and story by the sound and pulsations of an African talking drum. The poem carries us through the beats of an African presence, an African American presence, and then back to Africa. Knight re-creates the drum calling to action a consciousness of the black diaspora. The voice is the drum, and the drum is the voice creating a ritual of unity:

> Kah doom / kah doom-doom / kah doom / kah doom-doom-doom
> Kah doom / kah doom-doom / kah doom / kah doom-doom-doom
> Kah doom / kah doom-doom / kah doom / kah doom-doom-doom
> Kah doom / kah doom-doom / kah doom / kah doom-doom-doom
>
> the heart, the heart beats, the heart, the heart beats slow
> the heart beats slowly, the heart beats
> the blood flows slowly, the blood flows
> the blood, the blood flows, the blood, the blood flows slow
> kah doom / kah doom-doom / kah doom / kah doom-doom-doom
> and the day opened to the sound
>
> kah doom / kah doom-doom / kah doom / kah doom-doom-doom
> and our feet moved to the sound of life
> kah doom / kah doom-doom / kah doom / kah doom-doom-doom
> and we rode to the rhythms as one
> from Nigeria to Mississippi

and back
Kah doom / kah doom-doom / kah doom / kah doom-doom-doom (55, 56)

When the Nigerian rises and begins to play the drum, we are transformed. The meditative, trancelike rhythm of the African diaspora drumbeat repels individual consciousness and awakens the beat of a collective heart. Now in harmony, the hearts and drum are the powerful force linking kinship and blood ties across continents. Howard Nelson (1981) has stated: "If one follows habits learned from reading newspapers and most other prose, and skims over this as if it were so much filler, the point of the poem is missed. But if one reads the words carefully, actually sensing the reverberations, one is pulled inside a rhythmic flow that stands for life itself" (10).

We move from a celebration of the collective in "Ilu, The Talking Drum" to the singular, personal, autobiographical experience of Knight's life in "A Poem For Myself (or Blues for a Mississippi Black Boy)" (*Born of a Woman* 59). Knight tells his story through the blues ballad. The poem recounts leaving the South for the Northern cities, only to realize that the perils and oppression of being a black boy from Mississippi is not obliterated by geographic location: "I'm still the same old black boy with the same old blues" (59). His resolve is to go back to Mississippi, rejoined with his history and roots, whether it means freedom or death. As in "Ilu, The Talking Drum," the poem's form, as well as meaning, is dependent upon the musicality of sound, rhythm, and voice. Those themes in Knight's work based upon the oral traditions of African-American toasts, chant, blues, and jazz reflect his affinity for the word as an entity that is first and above all sound. Knight tells us that we cannot know these poems unless we breathe the life of our voices into them, voices that are inherently musical.

In the final theme, described here as love and tribute, Knight's voice is gentle, sensual, compassionate, and admiring—but no less striking in its forcefulness. A poem that typifies this voice is "Circling the Daughter" (*The Essential Etheridge Knight*), a poem of affection and dedication, as well as fatherly advice. Tandiwe has come of age; she is a young woman and her fourteen years "have brought the moon-blood, the roundness." We observe Tandiwe's growth into womanhood as we observe the fears of Knight as he experiences her blossoming, "Now I sit, trembling in your presence." The man who is the poet of "bad dudes" like Hard Rock and Shine and who mesmerized us with the power of the talking drum and the life/death existence of the blues, is soft, lyrical, and vulnerable as he experiences his daughter becoming a woman. And being a poet he must give words to his fears for Tandiwe to hold close:

O Tandiwe, my Beloved of this land,
Your spring will come early and
When the earth begins it humming,
Begin your dance with men

With a Grin and a Grace of whirling.
Your place is neither ahead nor behind,
Neither right nor left. The world is round.
Make the sound of your breathing. (109)

Knight wishes his daughter a life of fullness. The theme he presents, which is reflected in much of Knight's work, is that Tandiwe (we) must speak in harmony with the multifarious flow of the world so that her (our) single voice is in tune with this infinite and nonhierarchical, cosmic circle.

In another tributary poem, "For Malcolm, A Year After," Knight gives commentary to the art of poetry when in contrast to the politics of history. The words of Malcolm X may be constrained in the classic structures of poetic "foot and strict iamb" in order to compose a more "proper verse," suitable for high art and Anglo propriety, but such a verse will not endure time. It is the memory of this man that is everlasting, while the death of false words pass on, forgotten. "For Malcolm" (*The Essential Etheridge Knight*) presents motifs of each theme discussed: The prison theme is implicit in that both men were incarcerated, self-educated, and profoundly changed by their prison experience; and the toast and oral tradition is evident in Malcolm X as hero, whose memory "burst" through formal patterns of poetic verse, while Knight simultaneously reminds the reader/audience of the jazz great, John Coltrane, "Death might come singing sweet like C" (67). The poem is also testimony to Knight's double-voicedness, juxtaposing the lyrical with the vernacular, the warrior poet with the singer poet as he pays poetic homage to Malcolm X:

Evoke no image, stir no flame,
And spin no yarn across the air.
Make empty anglo tea lace words—
Make them dead white and dry bone bare.

Compose a verse for Malcolm man,
And make it rime and make it prime.
The verse will die—as all men do—
But not the memory of him! (67)

The poem is concerned with the questions of ideology and structure. It is also evidence of Knight's craftsmanship in fusing voice and form. Frank Allen (1986) has observed, "There is no sense that experience is being forced into an alien form or that an extraneous form is being forced into experience. It is not that he 'selects' a form, anymore than he selected the nature of experience" (77–78).

The themes reflect Knight's philosophy of the poet, the poem, and the people, and his artistic genius in showing us the logic and beauty of his thinking.

SURVEY OF CRITICISM

Although to date there is no book of criticism on the work of Etheridge Knight, there are numerous articles that provide insightful and probing analyses.

One of the most comprehensive examinations of Knight's work appears in the *Painted Bird Quarterly* (1988). Here several writers give commentary and analyses of Knight as a philosopher, performer, and poet. Knight's poetry is explored through his use of language and orality, experiential and political themes, and the issues of structure. Christopher Gilbert, in ''The Breathing / In / An Emancipatory Space,'' discusses the context and poetry, giving us a personal glimpse of his interaction with Knight.

Patricia Liggins Hill has analyzed the influence of oral traditions on Knight's work. In '' 'Blues for a Mississippi Black Boy': Etheridge Knight's Craft in the Black Oral Tradition'' (1982), Hill discusses elements in the poems that are not only part of the indigenous black oral tradition but are also adaptations of oral traditions by such writers as Langston Hughes and Sterling Brown that influenced Knight. Hill goes beyond theme and discusses these traditions in terms of their structural properties.

The Hollins Critic (1981) published ''Belly Songs: The Poetry of Etheridge Knight,'' which examined Knight's fourth volume, *Born of Woman*. Howard Nelson, who wrote the analysis, stated that his approach in examining Knight's poetry was to look at ''people, relationships between and among people'' since this, he believes, is the primary focus of Knight's work (3). Nelson has provided a sensitive and comprehensive analysis of this volume, giving detailed discussions on themes of selected poems as they relate to the life and culture of the poet.

BIBLIOGRAPHY

Works by Etheridge Knight

Poems from Prison. Detroit, Mich.: Broadside Press, 1968.
Black Voices from Prison. New York: Pathfinder Press, 1970.
Bellysongs and Other Poems. Detroit, Mich.: Broadside Press, 1973.
Born of a Woman: Selected and New Poems. Boston: Houghton Mifflin, 1980.
The Essential Etheridge Knight. Pittsburgh: University of Pittsburgh Press, 1986.

Interviews with Etheridge Knight

McCullough, Ken. ''Communication and Excommunication: An Interview with Etheridge Knight.'' *Callaloo: An Afro-American and African Journal of Arts and Letters* 5 (February–May 1982): 2–10.
Pinsker, Sanford. ''A Conversation with Etheridge Knight.'' *Black American Literature Forum* 18 (Spring 1984): 1–4.

Price, Ron. "The Physicality of Poetry: An Interview with Etheridge Knight." *Obsidian: Black Literature in Review* 52 (Spring 1986): 1–4.

Tracy, Steven C. "A MELUS Interview: Etheridge Knight." *MELUS: The Journal of the Society for the Study of Multi-Ethnic Literature of the United States* 13 (Summer 1985): 7–23.

Studies of Etheridge Knight

Allen, Frank. " 'We Free Singers Be': Poetry of Etheridge Knight." *Iowa Review* 16 (February 1986): 164–76.

Bremen, Paul. *You Better Believe It.* New York: Penguin Books, 1973.

Camp, Louis, Hoanna Di Paolo, and Louis McKee., eds. *The Painted Bride Quarterly* (Issue on Etheridge Knight), 32–33 (May 1988).

Crowder, Ashby Bland. "Etheridge Knight: Two Fields of Combat." *Concerning Poetry* 16 (Fall 1983): 23–25.

Franklin, H. Bruce. "The Literature of the American Prison." *Massachusetts Review* 18 (1977): 51–78.

Hill, Patricia Liggins. " 'Blues for a Mississippi Black Boy': Etheridge Knight's Craft in the Black Oral Tradition." *Mississippi Quarterly: The Journal of Southern Culture* 36 (Winter 1983): 21–33.

———. " 'The Violent Space': The Function of the New Black Aesthetic in Etheridge Knight's Prison Poetry." *The Black American Literary Forum* 14 (Fall 1980): 115–20.

Nelson, Howard. "Belly Songs: The Poetry of Etheridge Knight." *The Hollins Critic* 18 (December 1981): 2–11.

Pinckney, Darryl. "You're in the Army Now." *Parnassus: Poetry in Review* 9 (Spring–Summer 1981): 306–14.

Randall, Dudley. *Broadside Memories: Poets I Have Known.* Detroit: Broadside Press, 1975.

Werner, Craig. "The Poet, the Poem, the People: Etheridge Knight's Aesthetic." *Obsidian: Black Literature in Review* 7 (Summer 1981): 7–17.

ALAN T. BELSCHES

LeRoy Leatherman
(1922–1984)

LeRoy Leatherman can best be appreciated for his nonfiction and fictional explorations of the creative process. His nonfiction works clearly illustrate the description of creativity by depth psychology and myth criticism, and his fiction mirrors these qualities in his characters.

BIOGRAPHY

On February 10, 1922, LeRoy Leatherman was born into a middle-class family in Alexandria, Louisiana. His father, LeRoy Sessums Leatherman, was a salesman; and his mother, Mary Aline Dugger, was a housewife. After his high-school graduation, the younger LeRoy attended Vanderbilt University from 1939 to 1941 and then spent the next year at Kenyon College with a John Crowe Ransom Creative Writing Scholarship. During World War II, while in the intelligence division of the United States Army Air Force from 1942 to 1946, he attended the University of Illinois during the 1943 to 1944 academic year. In 1948 he completed a B.A. at Southern Methodist University in Dallas, Texas, and received an M.A. the next year.

After graduation he began work in 1949 with the Dallas Public Library, eventually becoming the director of its films and recordings department. In 1950 Leatherman published his first novel, *The Caged Birds,* a sensitive rendering of a young boy's struggle in the 1930s to choose among adults who pose conflicting demands of him. Set in the oil-boom times of the 1930s in what seems to be Louisiana, the novel presents from multiple viewpoints the eighth birthday of Jim Daigre as he struggles to determine the importance to his self-concept of his dead grandfather, his parents, the eccentric neighbor Mr. Aristo, and the adopted son Luke Aristo.

During 1949 Leatherman also began his lifelong association with Martha Graham when she and her dance company performed in Dallas. The next year he served as the company's manager for its first appearances in Europe. This relationship would become so successful that in 1953 he would leave his library job to become the director and personnel manager for the Martha Graham School and Dance Company in New York City until 1960.

During these years he published his second novel, *The Other Side of the Tree* (1954). This work continues with the life of Jim Daigre 8 years after the conclusion of *The Caged Birds*. In struggling to determine his self-concept this time, Jim feels pulled by positive and negative attitudes toward the restrictions of his community and his family's heritage.

Leatherman also received a *Sewanee Review* fellowship for 1957 to 1958 and left his position with Martha Graham in 1960. For two years he lived in southern France and in 1961 completed his third book, *The Springs of Creativity,* with Dr. Heinz Westman. This nonfiction text explores the explanation by depth psychology and myth criticism of how the creative urges spring from deep psychic urgings that have been constant in all cultures throughout the ages.

By 1962 Leatherman had returned to New York City to become a producer and writer of films for the International Film Foundation. Among his credits are films about Yugoslavia, Turkey, and dance. In 1966 he resumed his close ties with Martha Graham by becoming the Executive Director of the Martha Graham Center of Contemporary Dance and by publishing with photographer Martha Swope his fourth major work, *Martha Graham: Portrait of the Lady as an Artist.* Leatherman's biography shows how Martha Graham's creative process exemplifies the ideas he had explained in *The Springs of Creativity.*

In 1972 Leatherman continued to apply his administrative skills in the theatre by becoming the Assistant Dean of the School for the Arts of Boston University and the Executive Director of the Tanglewood Institute. From 1974 to 1976 he served as the Associate Vice-president for Government and University Relations for Boston University.

In 1979 Leatherman moved west to become a special assistant to the Dean of the University of Southern California's School of Performing Arts and then the public-information officer in 1982 in the university's School of Music. On April 9, 1984, Leatherman died in Daniel Freeman Hospital in Inglewood, California. He was 62 years old.

MAJOR THEMES

The common Southern themes of the importance of the past, the family, and the power of the community over the individual appear in Leatherman's fiction. But an even more central concern is coping with adversity, how to confront conflicts with evil, draw from inner resources, and channel the psychic turmoil into creative acts.

During the Depression of the 1930s, the small Southern town of *The Caged Birds* experiences a major economic disruption when oil is discovered inside its

limits, and this change mirrors the disruption occurring in the neighboring Daigre and Aristo households, with 8-year-old Jim Daigre at the center of each.
When Aline Daigre turns from her husband toward her son, James senses the
rejection of his wife and turns to Jim for evening games of catch. The aging
Mr. John Aristo, who realizes that he has no successful relationship with his
adopted son Luke, now seeks Jim as a substitute son through their Greek lessons,
and Luke would like to adopt Jim as a partner to share his new sports car and
his recently completed mansion in the swamps. By varying the narrative viewpoints among Jim, Aline, and Mr. Aristo, Leatherman exposes the struggle of
each to cope with problems. Jim must face all of these competing forces; he
retreats to memories of times with his grandfather in order to gain inner strength
for resolving these issues.

What ties these three perspectives together and what makes LeRoy Leatherman a special writer is the way in which he shows his characters struggling
with the good and evil elemental forces symbolized through their actions. Each
character must turn inward, struggle with the past, and face that evil or that
good by recognizing each for what it is. By the end of the novel, Mr. Aristo
can be glad that Luke has left their home in town for his new mansion in the
swamp. This loss has been an exorcism that has freed Mr. Aristo from Luke's
control and that allows him to see Jim as a symbol of his own good: "Like
other people, he had set his own evil out in broad daylight: he had set Lucius
out, evoked him out of a swamp night. . . . Jim was the good in him, his true
innocence, his vital self. Having projected it into the world and having recognized it, he could now draw it back into his own heart" (247).

From the very beginning of the novel, young Jim Daigre sees himself as a
hunter, a searcher, an Odysseus on a voyage that forces him to develop his own
identity. In the final scene of the novel, Jim is most like Odysseus as he, Mr.
Aristo, and Luke roar toward Luke's mansion through a changing landscape that
stresses the oil boom's effect on the town. Jim must decide which lifestyle to
adopt as his own—either Luke's modern gaudy splendor or the ancient calmness
of Mr. Aristo. He resembles Quentin Compson returning at night to Sutpen's
Hundred with Miss Rosa Coldfield in William Faulkner's *Absalom, Absalom!*

When Luke asks Jim if he would like to be adopted, Leatherman has Jim turn
"his sight directly down into himself" (270) and swoon at what he finds. Part
of his choice is made for him with Luke's death in a car wreck near the story's
end, but the novel's final image is of Jim in a hospital bed, imagining his sailing
with his grandfather and stating, " 'I am Jim Daigre, Sir' " (281). Jim has found
himself, not as Luke nor as Mr. Aristo, but as a self with ties to his grandfather.

Aline Daigre, too, had been fascinated with Mr. Aristo when she had been a
child, and now he provides a tangible link to her memory of her father Robert
Phillips, who had attended college with Mr. Aristo. Aline mourns her father's
death because her father had been central to her and to her son Jim. With her
father's recent death and her rejection of her husband, a man Robert Phillips
had not liked, no one seems present to care for Jim or for her. Leatherman

parallels Aline's life with that of the birds she gives Jim for his birthday. The female birds kill each other to be the partner of the one male, and then the new mother rejects the father for the male offspring she bears. Only the shock of Jim's near death at the novel's conclusion awakens Aline from her summer illness and causes her to seek inward for the will to face her situation as her grandmother had done when captured by an Indian.

By the novel's end Luke is dead, but Mr. Aristo, Aline, and Jim are "at home in [their] own mind[s]" (93) with a freedom each has achieved through confronting inner struggles.

The odyssey Jim Daigre began in *The Caged Birds* on his eighth birthday continues in Leatherman's second novel, *The Other Side of the Tree.* Now 16, Jim has returned to the small fishing and hunting village of Big Creek. His family has vacationed there since he was 9, the year after the events of *The Caged Birds.* This summer his main interest is courting Margaret Rainey to whom he had written throughout the year. Unlike *The Caged Birds,* the setting here focuses on Jim's Daigre ancestors rather than the Phillipses, and the opening imagery focuses on Jim as a knight: Jim takes Tennyson's *Idylls of the King* with him on his fishing trip, not Homer's *Odyssey.* But during this summer Jim must deal with his feelings not only toward Margaret but also toward his family's past and the community of Big Creek. Where does he fit into the scheme? In this novel Leatherman depicts Jim's inner struggle with good and evil, but Leatherman places this conflict within the context of an individual's struggle with the community, the past, and his Southern heritage.

In Big Creek life does not change. The community still discusses the story of Miss Ida Field, who allowed herself to be carried off by Joe Wainwright, the local Rough Rider hero of the Spanish-American War. Like the Snopeses of William Faulkner's novels, the Wainwrights have always been considered as lower class, as the thieves and gamblers in the community's history. But now a Wainwright is mayor, and his daughter's engagement party that Miss Ida is expected to attend provides Leatherman an opportunity to narrate the story of Miss Ida's life and seduction. Jim as chief listener must determine how the story is relevant to him.

In old Mr. Ed Hatheway's telling of this community saga to Jim, Leatherman continues his mastery in manipulating point of view. Through flashbacks the reader sees Leatherman interweave Jim's suspicions of Margaret's unfaithfulness with the conflicts between the Fields and the Wainwrights. But Leatherman has Mr. Ed imagine the events occurring through the perspectives of various major actors in the drama. As he had in *The Caged Birds,* Leatherman shifts from character to character, sometimes presenting differing interpretations of the same event and each time presenting additional facts to the reader. Miss Ida's father, her brother who manages the local newspaper, her sister who has seduced Jacob Sidney, Sidney who comes each day to watch Miss Ida from the other side of the tree, the preacher, and Ed Hatheway who has a crush on Miss Ida present various versions of Miss Ida's marriage to Joe Wainwright.

The problem for Jim Daigre is reminiscent of Quentin Compson (in William Faulkner's *Absalom, Absalom!*), who attempts to make sense of Miss Rosa Coldfield's tale of the evil Thomas Sutpen, and of Jim Burden (in Robert Penn Warren's *All the King's Men*), who attempts to face the truth of the Cass Mastern episode. As Jim listens to Mr. Ed's tale, he sees his emotional turmoil over Margaret mirroring the same feelings exhibited by many of the actors in Mr. Ed's story. Just as Fitz Blake in 1853 had committed suicide by diving into the vortex of the local swimming hole to prove to Victoria Daigre's father that it had a bottom, Jim whirls amidst present and past until he realizes that in Big Creek "whatever happened kept happening, never lay quiet, never died: blood was blood" (26). Finally he understands what Mr. Ed learned over 50 years ago, namely, that a balance between the lives of the past and his own can be achieved. If Jim did kill his friend Corley in a fit of rage over the accusation that Margaret has often been unfaithful to him, the murder would become just another story for the community to tell. And when Jim sees Margaret at the engagement party, he refrains from confronting her because he has realized the universality of his situation: "There was no desert where memories dried up; what had happened would go on happening in steady suspension, awhirl, like Blake's bones down in the channeled dark" (174).

The struggle with good and evil continues as Leatherman's major pattern in *Other Side of the Tree*. After Jim begins to suspect Margaret's unfaithfulness, he realizes that he is in a world "where things stood, like tree-to-tree, with their opposites" (35), where Daigre and Phillips blood flowed separately, where Wainwrights and Fields battled for women, and where Gawains and Launcelots could claim an equal hold on his soul. Like Jacob Sidney (Big Creek's revered saint and sinner), like Joe Wainwright (who tricks Miss Ida into marrying him and then actually falls in love with her), and like Mr. Ed (who struggles with leaving the community to see the world or remaining within its bounds), Jim feels torn both ways. Only through listening to Mr. Ed's story and drawing on the perspectives of these characters from history is Jim able finally to decide that he will make his own way, that he will endure the modern ordeal, and that he will not submit to the wiles of women, neither the whores in Polluck nor Margaret.

The Springs of Creativity, which Leatherman published in 1961 with the German psychologist Heinz Westman, provides a scientific explanation for many of the themes that Leatherman explored in his novels. Here Leatherman and Westman trace the development of the psyche through such poetic representations from ancient works of literature as the *Enuma Elish* of Babylon and the Genesis stories in the Old Testament. Leatherman and Westman's point is that up to the Middle Ages the Christian image of a whole man helped mankind maintain a psychic wholeness. With the Reformation's revolt against the authority of the Church this image of wholeness ended. Descartes' "I think, therefore I am" attempted to explain the psyche rationally and contributed to mankind's loss of wholeness. In worshipping the rational man, "we have ignored other essential aspects of reality, because we have neglected our other gifts and failed to respect those faculties by which we experience the inner world, make use of its potential and communicate its values, we fail in any relation with forces of the psyche'' (15). Thus, when modern science fails to provide rational explanations, we are thrust back on our fears, our own emptiness, because we have lost contact with those forces that rage in our inner worlds.

For Leatherman and Westman, mankind needs anxiety in order to grow. It is vital to the development of our psyches and our personalities. Archetypes in dreams and in literature become symbols of man's deep-seated urgings that create anxiety for us. In our reading of literature, we may achieve a moment of realization from the symbols of these anxieties in our psyches.

The biblical stories of creation and of God's developing relationship with the Israelites show the Hebrew poets' awareness of these urgings in our psyche. Leatherman and Westman believe that Christian stories provide better examples of wholeness than do other ancient religious stories. The main theme of these accounts in the Bible is "Man's growth toward wholeness—the ontogenesis of the psyche in the midst of, perhaps through the blessing of, all the dualities and oppositions of human existence" (82). Even though modern man has a Grecian view that destruction looms over us and we cannot control it, the Bible shows a different alternative. Modern man must first confront evil, "look at the 'agent of death,' " and "see the image of destruction" in order to thwart it. In this "encounter," "the psyche naturally and immediately acts to counteract it" (125). Thus, people have the innate power to overcome problems if they will first face them. They cannot destroy evil, but they will be able to cope with it if they just try.

The case study of a young artist at the conclusion of the book provides a tangible application of Leatherman and Westman's ideas. Sir Herbert Read's introduction to this section stresses that "a hasty judgment might conclude that a measure of psychosis is good for the artist. Certainly one cannot exclude conflict from the formative influences in art—art does not proceed from inertia" (170). The creative artist's imagination is energized by conflict and can be resolved by the "harmony" and "balance" (171) of the work produced, exactly what Leatherman illustrates in his study of Martha Graham.

Martha Graham: Portrait of the Lady as an Artist, with photographs by Martha Swope, is Leatherman's case study of how one creative artist composes her artwork from the recesses of her psyche. Not a personal biography but rather a creative biography, this work shows Martha Graham drawing from a variety of literary, artistic, and personal resources to develop her dramatic presentations. But Leatherman suggests that creativity comes chiefly from within, where the artist imposes order over the various urgings and emotions that rage within the mind—and, thus, is able to create a work of beauty. The process is, of course, difficult—if not terrifying; but facing the realities of the psyche is a must, and the truths one learns must be told. As Graham once learned after lying to her father, ''movement never lied'' (47). Thus, in her dances she sought to tell physically ''the truth, to reveal the individual and the state of his being on the instant'' (49) in a way that would not lie.

Leatherman's nonfiction buttresses the ideas first discussed imaginatively in his two novels. Only by directly confronting evil within himself or herself can the individual hope to overcome it or learn to live with it. This universal struggle is felt by all of Leatherman's characters, but history can be a source of strength. In *The Caged Birds* 8-year-old Jim Daigre draws on memories of his dead grandfather Phillips in order to decide which life to lead. In *The Other Side of the Tree,* Leatherman shows how Jim can learn from the cyclic effect of history, achieve that moment of realization, and confront the truth about himself and others around him.

SURVEY OF CRITICISM

Leatherman's critical reputation has been minimal. Outside of initial reviews of his works when they were published, almost nothing has been written about him. Robert Welker's article in *Southern Writers: A Biographical Dictionary* (1979) and an entry in *Contemporary Authors* (1977) provide basic biographical information.

Reviews of *The Caged Birds* were mixed. Charles Spielberger in the *New York Times* (1950) notes echoes of Faulkner and Carson McCullers in the novel but feels that the Southern environment plays too important a role in the development of *Caged Birds.* Jack E. Brown in *Library Journal* (1950) admires Leatherman's skill in creating suspense ''from this meagre fare'' but feels the novel lacks action and an appropriate ending. But Coleman Rosenberger in his article in the *New York Herald Tribune Book Review* (1950) shows that the few incidents in the novel gain an importance from their parallelism and through their telling, a style Rosenberger compares to the precision of an ''engraver's art'' (8).

Reviews of *The Other Side of the Tree* have been much more favorable. Charlotte Capers in the *New York Times* (1954) and Doris Grumbach in *Commonweal* (1954) both see Leatherman achieving something new in the Southern novel because of the masterful style he uses in telling the story. Capers puts him in ''the front ranks of contemporary Southern writers'' (18), and Grumbach sees Leatherman as standing ''different, unique, alone'' (420) among the Southern school of Welty, Capote, and Williams. Arthur Mizener, in the *Sewanee Review,* (1955) points to parallels with Quentin Compson and Jim Burden and praises Leatherman's skillful use of ''indirect and suspended narration'' (493).

Of Leatherman's two nonfiction works, only the second received reviews. Walter Terry in his review of *Martha Graham: The Lady as an Artist* in *Book Week* (1966) praises Leatherman's explanation of how Graham draws from within herself in creating her plays and calls Leatherman's work a ''brilliant revelation of a towering artist'' (29). Nancy Wilson Ross in the *New York Times*

Book Review (1966) also praises Leatherman's exploration of the "depths of the human psyche" (1), and Eudora Welty (1967) praises the "intense forms of human insight" (530), which Leatherman explains as the source for Graham's work.

BIBLIOGRAPHY

Works by LeRoy Leatherman

The Caged Birds. New York: Harcourt, Brace, 1950.
The Other Side of the Tree. New York: Harcourt, Brace, 1954.
The Springs of Creativity. With Heinz Westman. New York: Atheneum, 1961.
Martha Graham: Portrait of the Lady as an Artist. New York: Alfred A. Knopf, 1966.

Studies of LeRoy Leatherman

Brown, Jack E. "Review of *The Caged Birds.*" *Library Journal* 75 (August 1950): 1292.
Capers, Charlotte. "Big Creek Summer." *New York Times* (July 25, 1954): 18.
Grumbach, Doris. "South Wind." *Commonweal* 60 (July 1954): 420–421.
"Leatherman, LeRoy." In *Contemporary Authors: First Revision,* edited by Christine Nasso, vol. 21–24, 520–21. Detroit: Gale Research, 1977.
Mizener, Arthur. "Fiction Chronicle." *Sewanee Review* 63 (July–September 1955): 484–94.
Rosenberger, Coleman. "Review of *The Caged Birds.*" *New York Herald Tribune Book Review* (October 1, 1950): 8.
Ross, Nancy Wilson. "She and Her Work Are One." *New York Times Book Review* (October 23, 1966): 1, 52.
Spielberger, Charles. "Small Town South." *New York Times* (October 1, 1950): 35.
Terry, Walter. "The Poetry of Motion." *Book Week* (November 27, 1966): 29.
Welker, Robert L. "LeRoy Leatherman." In *Southern Writers: A Biographical Dictionary,* edited by Robert Bain, Joseph M. Flora, and Louis D. Rubin, Jr., 274–75 Baton Rouge: Louisiana State University Press, 1979.
Welty, Eudora. "Movement Never Lies." *Sewanee Review* 75 (July–September 1967): 529–33.

JUDY JO SMALL

Susan Ludvigson
(1942–   )

A South Carolina poet transplanted from the North and influenced by sojourns in Europe, Susan Ludvigson is not a regional writer. Rather, a Romantic quester in a postmodern era, she writes as a woman searching for wider, deeper experience of herself and her world. Her carefully crafted, informal lyrics are streaked with dark wit and quiet passion.

BIOGRAPHY

Susan Ludvigson was born in the small town of Rice Lake, Wisconsin, on February 13, 1942. The oldest of four children in a prosperous family, she felt privileged and somewhat pampered. Her father (Howard C. Ludvigson) owned two small restaurant-cafes and, when she was thirteen, bought forty acres of rolling land where they began raising and riding Arabian and appaloosa horses. Her mother (Mabel Helgeland) was of pure Norwegian stock, and her father's family was mostly Norwegian and Swedish. They were churchgoing though not devout Presbyterians, but Susan became intensely religious as a child. At one point she was so moved by stories told by two missionaries back from Africa that she gave them all her saved birthday money and allowances and resolved to become a missionary herself; there is a reference to that experience in the poem "Little Women" (*Northern Lights,* 1981).

The smooth comfort of her life was disrupted when, just before her nineteenth birthday, during her freshman year in college, she became pregnant. On February 19, 1961, she married her long-time "steady" boyfriend David Bartels, also a freshman, but her parents were angry and did not come to the wedding; she remembers it as a "pretty grim" occasion in "a marriage mill kind of Place, Pine City, Minnesota," with Dave's parents and his brother and one of her friends in attendance. The marriage was happy enough for a while, and their son Joel David was born in September; but it took many years for her to get over the shame of "having to get married." References to these events appear in "The Will to Believe" (*The Beautiful Noon of No Shadow,* 1986).

Ludvigson graduated from the University of Wisconsin at River Falls in 1965 with honors in English and Psychology. Her interest in psychology later became important to her poetry; she still believes, as she wrote me, that "poetry works best when it comes as straight from the unconscious as possible." She taught high school in River Falls and nearly finished work for a master's degree in psychology there before moving to Ann Arbor, where she taught junior high school while her husband earned a graduate degree at the University of Michigan. In 1971 Ludvigson and her husband moved to Charlotte, North Carolina; at the local branch of the university, she worked in the Institute for Urban Studies and Community Service and in 1973 completed her M.A. in English. During these years she began writing poetry seriously. She attributes much of her growth as a poet to the support of a group of women writers in Charlotte who met regularly and critiqued each other's work; the composition of the group, which is still active, has varied over the years, but Ludvigson has mentioned Harriet Doar, Judy Goldman, Dannye Romine, and Julie Suk as fellow writers who have been particularly important to her. After her poems had appeared in various magazines, she published a first collection, *Step Carefully in Night Grass,* which won the North Carolina Poetry Council Award for the best book of poems by a North Carolinian. She has subsequently come to regard this early work as inferior.

In 1974 she began graduate work at the University of South Carolina, separating from her husband and bringing her son with her to Columbia. She studied with James Dickey, whose poetic style has influenced hers. But the graduate program, reverently oriented toward the established canon of poets, ultimately seemed inhibiting; and in 1975 she took a position as instructor in the English Department at Winthrop College in Rock Hill, South Carolina, where she has remained ever since. Now professor and poet-in-residence, she teaches courses in poetry, American literature, and the creative process in the arts.

Ludvigson's marriage ended in divorce in February 1977. After she began living with another man, she acquiesced in her teenage son's decision to live with his father. She has called this one of the "few serious regrets of my life." The pain of his adolescent upheavals is reflected in the powerful poem "Point of Disappearance" (*The Beautiful Noon of No Shadow*). Now grown and happily settled, he lives in Colorado.

Among the numerous fellowships and awards that Ludvigson has received, four have been particularly important. Between 1979 and 1981 she had fellowships to the Virginia Center for the Creative Arts and to the MacDowell Colony. A Guggenheim grant in 1983 enabled her to travel to England and to spend nearly a year in France. A Fulbright award in 1984 sponsored a tour of Yugoslavia, where she met with writers' unions and gave readings in various cities; some of this experience appears in the chapbook *Defining the Holy* (1986). A

National Endowment for the Arts fellowship sponsored another year in Paris. It was here, in the Rodin Museum, that she saw the Claudel exhibit that inspired "The Gold She Finds." (Reine-Marie Paris's biography *Camille* supplied details.) The Munch exhibit in the Petit Palais also prompted a series of poems. On a trip to a conference in Toulouse, she visited the Romanian sculptor Nicolae Flessig, whose sculptures gave rise to the poem "To Enter" (*To Find the Gold,* 1990) and whose account of the death of his girlfriend became the substance of "Miracles," *(The Beautiful Noon of No Shadow)*. He showed her a sixteenth-century house in the village of Puivert, which she bought and arranged to have restored by a local *bricoleur*. She returned to the restored house in 1986 ("The Turning" *[The Beautiful Noon of No Shadow]*) and has arranged with Winthrop College to teach half of every year and to live the other half in Puivert.

On October 28, 1988 Ludvigson married Scott Ely, a novelist who had joined the Winthrop faculty the previous year. His teenage daughter Laura came to live with them, and the experience has seemed to the poet "a kind of redemption." In fall 1990 Laura entered the South Carolina Governor's School for Math and Science, and Ludvigson and her husband went to Bellagio, Italy, on a Rockefeller Foundation grant. Ludvigson has begun a series of poems about violence in America.

MAJOR THEMES

Susan Ludvigson's poems reflect the perspective of a Southerner aware of her citizenship in the world. She became a Southerner as an adult, and her early poems express the dislocation she felt when she first moved to the Carolinas, her uneasiness in a region of copperheads and spiders, kudzu and assembly-line houses. Images of a remembered North recur throughout her poetry, and European travel has added new subject matter to her recent work, where various landscapes intermingle. Yet the South and Southern writers have shaped Ludvigson's poetry, lending it a strong narrative element and an affinity for the grotesque.

Ludvigson produces two characteristic types of poems, openly autobiographical lyrics and dramatic renderings of other, often bizarre, personalities. Her personal poems, subdued but intimate, recount family memories, details of love affairs, private anxieties, deaths of friends—the joys and frustrations of a middle-class American woman. Other poems, however, focus on figures from history, alien cultures, or freaky situations in newspaper headlines. The foreignness of the subject is often so extreme that one is amazed at the believable narrative the poet invents and the coherent, even sympathetic, psychology she constructs to explain it. The stark photograph of a little girl in a coffin, from Michael Lesy's *Wisconsin Death Trip,* for example, becomes in her hands a vignette of the mother—who, after staying up two nights sewing the burial dress, feels benumbed relief both that her daughter is "perfect, serene" and that a pot of coffee is ready for the men who will return to work in the fields as soon as the child is underground. A whole bleak world comes alive here ("A Few of the Women," *Northern Lights*). Likewise, though most people have never considered what it felt like to be "The Man Who Brought the Gypsy Moth" (*The Swimmer,* 1984) to America, it is hard to forget this portrait of a sensitive romantic soul whose dreams of wrapping his beloved in beautiful blue silk turned to nightmare when "the town began to fill with black worms" and he became "the most hated sight in New England" (25, 26).

The same poetic vein becomes comic-macabre when it treats such subjects as a frustrated husband who hacks his mother-in-law with an ax, having convinced himself that she is a raccoon, or a farm woman who languorously exhibits herself to a neighborhood peeping Tom and then sends hate mail to his wife. The delight of these often grotesque poems arises from their disclosure that the primitives, aliens, and crazies they depict are people we can identify with. In juxtaposition, the personal poems and the character poems illuminate each other. For example, the personal poem "Motherhood" (*Northern Lights*), in which a woman regrets her failure to live up to her image of the perfect parent, acquires extra meaning when it resonates through the poem about a warped animal trainer who lovingly wishes he could spin his elephants' straw into gold but winds up beating them when "the youngest refuses / to eat" or "they cry all night / for nothing" ("Trainer's Temper Bars Him from His Beloved Elephants," *Northern Lights,* 18). Poems that at first seem to be escapes from the self, then, oddly enough, become ways of discovering the deeper recesses of the self in the Other.

The world of Ludvigson's poetry is a world without secure metaphysical foundations, where every seeming stability is perpetually threatened by forces of disintegration. The overarching theme of her work is that one can find ways to survive such reality, even gladly. In the fine poem "Lesson," which opens her first serious volume, *Northern Lights* (1981), the swamps of a remembered Wisconsin childhood provide a mythic image of a treacherous world. The father warns the child who is about to venture into the swamps that there are hidden pitfalls and dreadful quicksand, but the mother offers practical advice for safety: "Watch / for blackbirds . . . / Wherever they land is safe"; at last, triumphant, the child emerges with a treasure of cattails and blue blossoms. The opposition between these two parental attitudes—fear and confidence, skepticism and belief—persists as a tension in Ludvigson's poems. Terror is an everyday component of the experience they chart; not least among the "Things We Can't Prepare For" (*Northern Lights*), as one title puts it, are deaths of friends and relatives, relationships that do not work out, and worries that "life is narrowing" to commonplace dullness "where love / will be a small vacation, a month / at most, when you'll neglect the yard" (70). But the philosophical substance of these poems is the necessity of summoning courage to risk disappointment again and again. "Some Notes on Courage" (*The Swimmer*) offers as models the child heading out into a new neighborhood with his baseball glove, the "pregnant woman / whose first child died," anyone who decides to love again, like a tightrope artist climbing the ladder after "that last / bad fall when the net didn't hold" (5).

Consequently, beginnings are a crucial subject for Ludvigson. The titles of three of her poems refer to beginnings, and these three poems nicely illustrate the subtle religious quest that animates her work. The first poem, "In the Beginning" (*Northern Lights*), presents a scene from a day recollected: While her mother cries over some unmentioned sorrow and a sunlit patch on the floor lengthens and turns to dark, a child learns to print her name. The biblical echo in the title links the child's "imperfect word" with a faulty *Logos,* thus transforming the simple scene into a mythic initiation into knowledge and selfhood in a fallen world. In the second poem, "From the Beginning," Ludvigson observes that, although we know intuitively that "the end of every road is grief," we regularly decide to believe in love, which we sense "must be salvation / or its closest twin" (49). The poem, placed at the end of *The Beautiful Noon of No Shadow*, is an equivocal but deliberate *da capo.* The third, called "This Beginning" (*To Find the Gold*), looks at events in America and France during World War II and forty years later, when on both sides of the Atlantic the smoldering hatreds of war still burn in and around us; the epigraph, from a manifesto of the Groupes de Liaison Internationale, is an oblique call for conversion. What these three poems suggest is summed up directly by lines from "Waiting for Your Life" (*The Beautiful Noon of No Shadow*):

> You'll tell me that life
> is not literature,
> cannot begin *in medias res.*
> But I tell you, it can. (17)

The lines could stand as the poet's credo.

Ludvigson's is a peculiarly visual imagination. Memories and dreams, important elements of the subconscious experience in her poems, generally take the form of sharp visual images. Remorse, for example, is vivid as a flown lovebird with iridescent feathers ("The Dream of Birds" [*The Beautiful Noon of No Shadow*]). Art works—photographs, sculptures, and paintings—provide frequent starting points for Ludvigson's poetic meditations. An El Greco portrait of a "Nobleman with His Hand on His Chest" elicits a sly, knowing, wonderfully familiar apostrophe to the painted figure, whose splendid white ruff and lace belie his penitential pose: "Your sins glitter like your sword, / ornate and handsome. / You take them out in the dark / to admire" (*The Swimmer,* 37). A more elaborate version of the same approach is used in the sequence "Dreaming the Summer Nights" (*To Find the Gold*), for which eleven turn-of-the-century Scandinavian paintings, little known to most Americans, furnish the basis. Each poem describes a painting, transforming the image into an emotion-charged moment of an experience that extends beyond the painted surface. Evocative motifs of light and color link the disparate scenes, and epigraphs direct attention to symbolic hints of spiritual awakening that would otherwise be difficult to discern.

Allusions to poems by other authors are also important in Ludvigson's work. On a deep level, she connects with Rilke's struggle for transcendence: Quotations from his *Duino Elegies* provide the structural framework for *The Swimmer* (1984), and two poems in *The Beautiful Noon of No Shadow* mold personal thoughts around recollections of Rilke. Yeats, too, has been a significant influence, as in the comic "All I Ever Wanted Was a God" (*Northern Lights*), which wryly bewails the failure of dull modern men to match romantic dreams stirred by Yeats's feathered glory; Mona Van Duyn's poems responding to "Leda and the Swan" also play a role here. An oblique allusion to "Dover Beach" deepens the thematic sense of "Sunday in Normandy" (*The Beautiful Noon of No Shadow*): As Japanese filmmakers build a sand replica of a Spanish cathedral on a pleasant French beach while children play in old German bunkers nearby, there is a momentary, almost magical vision of harmony among conflicting cultures; but when the tide washes away the cathedral (the original of which, ironically, is only an unfinished shell), one hears a faint Arnoldian echo of eroding faith and clashing armies.

Love in its many forms is the central concern of Ludvigson's poems. Though occasionally Ludvigson views love from a male perspective, most of the time her poems express women's desires, vulnerabilities, and anxieties. Ludvigson's poems celebrate sensual abandon, refusing any definition of the holy that excludes the mysterious music of sex. Bodily love, perhaps even more than love of souls, achieves a kind of transcendence both in present ecstasy and in persistent memory. Realistically, though, images of imminent dark fringe the moments of fulfillment; and promising relationships are disrupted by quibbling disputes, insecurities, and betrayals. For all their latent romanticism, the poems strive to be honest. Little girls sense that marriage is a trap where they will be left to manage crying babies and domestic crises while their husbands drop in only occasionally "to sample the cookies" ("Little Women," *Northern Lights*). Ugly young women know that handsome fellows do not take them on picnics for the potato salad or their personalities ("Alice and Frances," *Northern Lights*). Older women, laughing, swap stories of preposterous men they have put up with ("Trying to Make Light of Our Loneliness," *Northern Lights*). And a woman whose lover has left her struggles to concede that his "perfection" may have been "the mere projection" of her desire ("When There Is No Surface," *The Beautiful Noon of No Shadow*). But never do these poems deny that it is love that transforms and vitalizes. Moreover, though these poems contain plenty of disappointment, they are surprisingly free of anger. Disappointment may just be the nature of things, as in the poem "New Physics" (*To Find the Gold*), where colliding subatomic particles and orbiting heavenly bodies provide metaphors to explain the mysterious flights and attractions that cause so much human hurt.

The most ambitious of Ludvigson's poetic efforts is "The Gold She Finds" (*To Find the Gold*), a sequence of lyrics on the life of the sculptor Camille Claudel. The simple, pellucid language of these nineteen poems reads like the distilled essence of Camille's experience. Beginning with a scene in her childhood, the poems move through the stages of her long affair with Auguste Rodin, her years of independent sculpting, and her 30-year confinement in an insane asylum. All except the first two poems are spoken in Camille's voice, and most of them take the form of letters to her brother Paul or to Rodin. Turbulent passions are conveyed in a spare but rich style that makes plainest facts resonate—like *The Gates of Hell* that Rodin is at work on when Camille enters his life. The joy of love and artistic creation is vividly realized:

> You discovered
> something quiet in me, and made it grow,
> just as you lift a breast in your hands,
> gently blowing, breathing
> more life into it. I am no longer
> that country girl with talent,
> but a woman whose joy has found
> its voice in marble. (7)

Yet, from the moment Camille naively assures her brother that she will be "helper, / student, apprentice" to the master and still "do [her] own work," a subtle dramatic irony plays over the affair (6). When she casually remarks that she has stopped remembering her dreams, it is ominous.

The pain of the slow break is recompensed by her discovery of her own identity: "I'm separate / just now, I'm Camille" (15). But the past that she carries within propels her to embody all that suffering in art, and drives her half-mad as well. At last though, too, her memories of Rodin and his sexual power enable her to let go of hate. In the first poem she looks up to clouds hoping to see a saint, but on her deathbed her "spirit is nourished / by raisins and milk" and by thoughts of her "hands wet in plaster" (26). It is a moving story, doubly powerful because the handling is so quiet and restrained. Two of the poems (VIII and XVIII) closely follow the language of Camille's actual letters, and the same fresh sense of felt truth is everywhere in the sequence. It seems effortless.

Most of Ludvigson's poems are brief, cadenced, free-verse poems with natural, unforced diction. Her poetic sequences expand the magnitude and effect of the compressed units that are her natural bent. For relief from free verse, she is fond of terza rima, which she manages unobtrusively, with subtle partial rhymes and attention to endings, where, instead of a concluding couplet, she frequently leaves an unrhymed line, with nice effect. One sestina, aptly, is addressed to artist friends. But a studied informality is her dominant mode. She never seems to be trying to dazzle us, though at her best she often does.

SURVEY OF CRITICISM

Ludvigson's works have not been extensively reviewed. The notice they have received, however, has been largely favorable. *Northern Lights* was recognized especially for its emotional complexity, its creation of psychologically convincing portraits. Stephen Corey (1982) commented that Ludvigson "imagines herself into [her] characters so intimately that she disappears from our thoughts, leaving us with only the voices she has become." R. T. Smith (1982) admired her sympathetic understanding, gothic humor—and, especially, her "sinewy," "evocative" language. Gilbert Allen (1983) chided her for writing too many catchy poems based on news clippings but praised the range of feeling that separates her work from most of that composed, like hers, in the clear, terse "period style" dominant in contemporary verse.

The Swimmer earned plaudits from P. B. Newman (1984) for its "skillful use of motifs" and its dramatic force; Ludvigson's dark humor, Newman noticed, "results from an interplay of laconic or prosaic language with an explosive situation" (76). Vernon Shetley (1985) delineated Ludvigson's stylistic traits—an avoidance of both rhetorical flight and sudden colloquialism, a "decorous minimalism," intense emotion presented through "sharply etched visual metaphor." Shetley also suggested that these virtues produce an austerity that occasionally verges upon blandness.

Of the poems in *The Beautiful Noon of No Shadow,* Alice Fulton (1988) preferred the most structured: two poems in terza rima, "Point of Disappearance" and "From the Beginning." Analyzing *Beautiful Noon* as a whole, Dorothy Barresi (1987) observed that, in facing the suffering imposed by family, death, and "love's betrayals," it is more "private and introspective" than Ludvigson's previous work. Barresi called the book "a meticulously crafted, elegant meditation on the movement toward accepting life's losses" (74).

The reviews of *To Find the Gold* are not yet in. In spite of a three-part structure that it shares with the three preceding volumes, this latest book lacks the clear thematic unity that in the others is so effective. It contains a number of strong poems, though, and they doubtless will be recognized. The Claudel poems alone should secure Ludvigson's reputation.

BIBLIOGRAPHY

Works by Susan Ludvigson

Step Carefully in Night Grass. (Under the name Susan L. Bartels) Winston-Salem, N.C.: John F. Blair, 1974.
The Wisconsin Women. Tempe, Ariz.: Porch Publications, 1980.
Northern Lights. Baton Rouge: Louisiana State University Press, 1981.
The Swimmer. Baton Rouge: Louisiana State University Press, 1984.
Defining the Holy. Emory, Va.: Iron Mountain Press, 1986.

The Beautiful Noon of No Shadow. Baton Rouge: Louisiana State University Press, 1986.
To Find the Gold. Baton Rouge: Louisiana State University Press, 1990.

Interviews with Susan Ludvigson

Romine, Dannye. "Winthrop Poet's Writing Flourishes in Foreign Land." *Charlotte Observer* (April 29, 1990): F1, F2.
Thesing, William B. "Susan Ludvigson." In *Conversations with South Carolina Poets,* edited by Gayle R. Swanson and William B. Thesing, 98–117. Winston-Salem, N.C.: 1986.

Studies of Susan Ludvigson

Allen, Gilbert. "Measuring the Mainstream—A Review Essay." *Southern Humanities Review* 17 (Spring 1983): 171–78.
Barresi, Dorothy. Review of *The Beautiful Noon of No Shadow. Southern Poetry Review* 27 (Fall 1987): 74–76.
Corey, Stephen. Review of *Northern Lights. Southern Poetry Review* 22 (Fall 1982): 69–72.
Feldman, Paula R. Review of *Northern Lights. South Carolina Review* 16 (Spring 1984): 141–43.
Fulton, Alice. "Main Things." *Poetry* 151 (January 1988): 360–77.
Green, William H. "Recent Academic Poetry in the Carolinas." *South Carolina Review* 22 (Spring 1990): 142–48.
Holden, Jonathan. "The Contemporary Conversation Poem." In *Style and Authenticity in Postmodern Poetry,* 33–44. Columbia: University of Missouri Press, 1986.
Newman, P. B. Review of *The Swimmer. Southern Poetry Review* 24 (Fall 1984): 75–77.
Shetley, Vernon. Review of *The Swimmer. Poetry* 146 (April 1985): 41–43.
Smith, R. T. "Pain Inflicted and Pain Shared." Review of *Northern Lights. Poet Lore* 77 (Summer 1982): 122–25.
Stitt, Peter. "The Objective Mode in Contemporary Lyric Poetry." *Georgia Review* 36 (Summer 1982): 438–48.

JEFFREY H. RICHARDS

David Madden
(1933–   )

A published writer since he was 18, David Madden has produced a large body of work that covers several genres: poetry, stage drama, radio plays, screenplays, reviews, personal essays, criticism, and short and long fiction. While Madden clings to an idea of the writer as one who can express himself through a variety of vehicles, he has established himself foremost as a fiction writer. Even so, he defies easy categorizing; a Southerner who foreswears Southern milieu fiction, he is also an experimental artist whose stories often have the flavor of Appalachian yarns.

BIOGRAPHY

Born in Knoxville, Tennessee, on July 25, 1933, Gerald David Madden (until the mid-1960s he was called Jerry, but now prefers David) grew up there in a struggling family. He describes his father, James Helvy Madden, as a ''lovable drunk,'' not unlike the ineffectual father of Lucius Hutchfield in Madden's novel *Bijou.* To his mother, Emile Merritt Madden, was left the task of supporting herself, David, and David's elder and younger brothers (another brother died in early childhood). At one point, Madden's mother even baked pies at home for restaurants, as did Mildred Pierce, a character from one of Madden's favorite authors, James M. Cain. By his accounts in interviews, growing up in Knoxville was both a miserable and wondrous experience, providing the sort of rich turmoil that Thomas Wolfe, an early Madden influence, found in Asheville.

A major figure in Madden's early life was his grandmother, a great storyteller in the Appalachian oral tradition. The young Madden listened carefully to her tales of family history, remembering not so much the content of the stories as the technique and love for the telling that she displayed. Very early, Madden began performing stories for other children, providing all the voices. Storytelling gave Madden—who was bright and imaginative, though poor and physically small—additional opportunities for popularity beyond his boyhood prowess at fighting, thieving, and playing. By age 10 or 11, he was writing his stories.

While in junior high school, Madden continued to write stories and make his own comic books. At age 12, he was diagnosed as having Friedreich's ataxia (clawfoot deformity), a condition that was medically corrected when he was 13. At this time also, he began to work as an usher at the Bijou movie theater in Knoxville, a job that allowed him to indulge a passion for films. The movies had already had an influence on his writing; a story written at age 11 was based on the film *Frenchman's Creek*. The combination, then, of the Appalachian oral tradition and Hollywood storytelling provided Madden with a dual idiom not only for his youthful efforts but also for his later work.

The adult Madden as critic would proclaim the power of imagination over experience; meanwhile, the young author as high-school graduate seems to have been a great seeker after adventures. Enrolled briefly in 1951 at the University of Tennessee, he left to travel about and sample the literary life of Greenwich Village—only to be disappointed. He then shipped out as a messmate with the merchant marines, sailing as far as Chile and unintentionally gathering experiences that would later provide material for his first novel. With the Korean War still in progress, Madden was drafted into the army in 1953, soon becoming a suspected security risk for refusing to sign a loyalty oath that was forced upon the army by Senator Joseph McCarthy (Madden did, however, take the army's own oath). Eventually cleared, he was sent to Alaska to finish his tour of duty. Despite the difficulties and frustrations of this period, he published his first story in 1952 and while in the army wrote the first version of *Cassandra Singing,* as a one-act play, in 1954.

In 1956 Madden returned to his undergraduate studies, first at Iowa State Teachers College (University of Northern Iowa) (where he married Roberta Margaret Young), then at the University of Tennessee (where he had been encouraged in his writing by C. P. Lee since high-school days). After graduation, he spent 1957 to 1958 at San Francisco State College; he found the Beat scene uninspiring but wrote prodigiously, feeling confirmed in his artistic direction—if not "influenced"—by Walter Van Tilburg Clark. There he wrote for his master's thesis the novel that would be published as *The Beautiful Greed.* The following academic year, he taught at Appalachian State Teachers College (now Appalachian State University) in Boone, North Carolina, a mountain town where he would spend the next four summers writing and revising play and fiction versions of *Cassandra Singing.* While he was in Boone, the religious drama *From Rome to Damascus,* which Madden had written in Alaska in 1955, won the Pearl Setzer Deal prize. From 1959 to 1960, he attended the Yale Drama School on a playwriting fellowship and worked there on *Cassandra.*

If the 1950s were a period of constant movement, immersion in experience, and experimentation, the 1960s eventually brought Madden his first real successes. While teaching at Centre College in Danville, Kentucky (1960–62), Madden saw the publication of his first novel, *The Beautiful Greed* (1961). With its title from Conrad's *Lord Jim* and its opening evocative of Melville's *Moby-Dick,* the book begs comparison to other sea literature. The protagonist, Alvin Henderlight, is a Southerner in New York; eager for adventure, he signs on a merchant ship, the *Polestar,* as a "wiper." Like Melville's Ishmael, Alvin learns he is to have an unusual bunk mate, "Franco," a middle-aged sailor and cipher who plays scapegoat for the crew's cruel humor. Put next to Conrad or Melville, Madden's story of shifting relations between two outsiders was treated roughly by the few critics who wrote on it. Even Madden himself, quoting two negative reviews (Williams 1962; Greenberg 1962) in his *Poetic Image,* shared in the attack, adding to the criticism of his talky style his own dismissal of the book as too "subject-dominated." Although the plot is oblique and the tone depressive, the novel moves forward on a discomforting subtext. Alvin, like Poe's Arthur Gordon Pym, encounters impenetrable texts of all sorts—in Alvin's case, the sea, the captain, the crew, the great sea novels he cannot finish, the weird messages on the mess chalkboard, and especially the multinamed Franco. Read as a story of an unsophisticated reader's problems with reading, *The Beautiful Greed* offers more than an un-Conradian sea adventure or an awkward style.

For the rest of the decade, Madden found new voices to use. After teaching 2 years at the University of Louisville, he moved to Kenyon College, where he wrote "The Singer" (1966), one of his best experimental stories, and conceived what would become his major novel, *Bijou.* The following 2 years were spent at Ohio University in Athens, though for five weeks he was a writer-in-residence at the University of North Carolina at Chapel Hill (1967). During this time, he published *Wright Morris* (1964), the first of several books of criticism. Madden's reading of Morris's fiction provided him with the example of a writer who took the aesthetics of fiction seriously; and though Morris was the more important influence, Madden's study of James M. Cain (about whom he has written two books) led him to see the art behind popular fiction and to become an early contributor to the then-new field of popular culture studies.

In 1968 Madden ended his institutional peripeteia by moving to Baton Rouge as a writer-in-residence at Louisiana State University. By agreeing to teach only one course every other semester with "proportional pay," he bought himself the time to write, finally completing his oldest project in 1969. The product of over a decade of revision (a writer's task he has written about extensively), *Cassandra Singing* probes the lives of a poor Kentucky coal-country family through the medium of a stark, intense, image-clashing diction that evokes, yet at the same time undermines the Appalachian subject matter. Wayne "Lone" McDaniel, alienated motorcyclist but naive, causeless rebel, shares a tumbledown house with his parents, the beleaguered Charlotte and the oft-exiled drunk, Coot, and a bedroom with his chronically ill sister, Cassie. Cassie begs Lone for stories about his adventures, and he obliges; over time, however, he seems to grow spiritually depleted as he feeds the fancy of his physically weak but imaginatively inexhaustible sister. He rides with the magnetic Boyd Weaver, a smoldering, vicious hood who both predates (in conception) and absorbs the kind of two-wheeled tough played by Lee Marvin in the film *The Wild One.* Disgusted by Lone's ambivalence and his companion's belief in purity, Boyd humiliates "Saint Lone" in an almost unbearably sadistic (but not gruesome) scene—an episode that leads, ironically, to the final liberation of Cassie from sickbed wraith to motorcycle moll. When Cassie and Lone strip down at story's end, some readers expect, as a reviewer for the *Virginia Quarterly Review* (1970) put it, "an incestuous romp"; but in fact, the resolution suggests that the implied incest has, in Cassie's new freedom, become moot.

In 1969 Madden received a Rockefeller grant that took him to Venice to begin work on his long autobiographical novel, *Bijou.* But before that book would be finished, two other books of fiction appeared: a story collection, *The Shadow Knows* (1970), and a short novel, *Brothers in Confidence* (1972). The latter was republished in slightly altered form in a longer novel, *Pleasure-Dome,* and will be discussed below. The stories, however, show one of Madden's great strengths: his tight management of short, compact, resonant narratives about characters who strain their limited resources of articulation in trying to make sense of inexplicable realities. Three stories—"The Shadow Knows" (featuring Alvin Henderlight, whom Madden will call Lucius Hutchfield, in *Bijou*), "The Pale Horse of Fear," and "Love Makes Nothing Happen" *(Shadow Knows)*— show children who encounter a menacing, often absurd world that adults cannot explain or for which the grownups take little responsibility, leaving the children to stumble into death. In two other stories, "The Day the Flowers Came" and "No Trace" *(Shadow Knows),* husbands and fathers face inadmissable losses. Both stories focus on ordinary people trying to read—through often dumb signs and their own reluctant imaginations—the awful truth behind puzzling messages.

Madden's big book, *Bijou* (1974), showed the author at his best and worst; and as a result, the reviews, though generally favorable, ran the gamut from praise for his main character to denunciation of his method. By tapping into his adolescent days as a theater usher, Madden realized he had hit a deep vein; producing a draft of 2,200 pages in six weeks, Madden called his writing process a "Wolfean outpouring" followed by a "Joycean paring." Even with the Apollonian cutting of his Dionysian text (to use his words for the Joyce-Wolfe polarity in his fiction), the book struck some reviewers as too immersed in nostalgic detail to sustain reader interest. But complaints about length, though they spoke to a genuine problem, ignored the creation of a singular adolescent protagonist, Lucius Hutchfield. The 13-year-old boy from Cherokee (Knoxville) lives for movies, writing, and love; as an usher, seeing life behind and beneath— as well as on—the screen, Lucius enters a world at once seedy and magical, all transformed through his consciousness by what Madden calls the "charged image" of the movie house. Lucius reads life by its surfaces but hopes for more. Only the clot of period detail prevents us from seeing the more universal elements in the boy's striving. Madden has recently revised *Bijou* to only about a third of its original length; as yet unpublished, the new version, he says, will keep the charged image "at the heart of it."

Four other books of fiction appeared between 1978 and 1982. *The Suicide's Wife* (1978), Madden's tautest novel and the one he considers his best, depicts a passive woman who slowly extricates herself from an enforced identity as her late husband's mate. Knowing little about Wayne, a college teacher, or herself, Ann Harrington makes inquiries that yield only small bits of light but that lead indirectly to her feeling free to lead her own life by novel's end. Made into a television movie, this book was widely and favorably reviewed.

Pleasure-Dome (1979) combines Madden's earlier short novel *Brothers in Confidence* with other material to show Lucius Hutchfield as an adult writer working to reconcile the demands of art with the lives of people to whom he tells stories or about whom he intends to write. By itself, *Brothers* is a jaunty little fiction about a writer who helps to get his check-forging younger brother out of jail. Recast as an episode in the Hutchfield saga, the new version deepens the storytelling theme; for behind the "stories" about Bucky that Lucius tells to the people whom his brother swindled is the usher–tale-teller's obsession with converting life into fictionlike narratives. The rest of the book—in which Lucius goes to a small mountain town to interview a woman who may have been a mistress of Jesse James—shows how stories, legends, rumors, gossip, history, and fantasies engage different people in competing ways and force a writer to choose carefully what sort of truth he will tell.

Another novel, *On the Big Wind* (1980), is a compilation of previously published stories recycled and reenvisioned as episodes in the life of a radio announcer. Each chapter shows Big Bob Travis in a new radio or television persona; but except for clues in chapter titles, the author makes no overt attempt to bridge the separate parts. The whole package makes an intriguing idea for a novel: a character who has no other life than his on-air ("big wind") voices, who has no continuity between selves except to keep pleasing audiences. Reviewers of the these last two novels have been either enthusiastic or unimpressed.

Published in 1982, *The New Orleans of Possibilities,* a second collection of stories, showed Madden still experimenting with subject and form. "A Part in Pirandello," about a college athlete dragooned into playing a female role in an absurdist drama, suggests the indeterminacy of life that many of Madden's characters face. Identities become unhinged, as in the title story, when a man discovers what appears to be a photo of himself in a box of pictures that a know-nothing girl sells by the handful, or "In the Bag," where a man is stuffed into a bag, then dumped onto a stage and into a play in process. What role does he play? The whole collection of theatically self-aware stories, Michael Kreyling has said (1983), is "about masks."

Since 1982 Madden has continued to write stories, poems, essays, introductions to edited works, and textbooks. Keenly interested in the Civil War, he has edited a collection of essays (1991) on "classics" of Civil War fiction. Although his book-length fiction on the war has not yet been published, stories that appear in it have. "Willis Carr at Bleak House" (1985)—about a boy in the Civil War who later has trouble sorting out public history, private tales, and his own clouded memory of the conflict—gives an overview of the projected novel. Madden also plans two other Lucius Hutchfield novels, one centered on his McCarthy-era army experience and another in which Lucius returns to the Bijou after 40 years, as in a recent story, "The Demon in My View" (1989). David Madden has no lack of material or energy, but his future reputation as a fiction writer may depend on his getting these new novels published.

MAJOR THEMES

His ideal reader, David Madden says, is someone who lets the author's sentences and stories work on consciousness without demanding that they yield up themes. He calls himself an "art-for-the-reader's-sake writer"—one who, though personally active in social causes, rejects the notion that fiction should be about subject matter or "real life" first. From that perspective, talking about Madden's "themes" seems like a contradiction in terms.

Nevertheless, Madden's work presents a reader with a varied and often contradictory discourse; and if we take seriously his urging in interviews that critics view his work aesthetically, one finds many recurring elements anyway. One major theme is storytelling itself. Many of his fictions either feature characters who are storytellers—Lucius, for example—or use narrative techniques that call into question the ways in which all experience is rendered as story. Often, narratives contain lists of story possibilities, as with Lucius's survey recollection of his own history in "Night Rituals" (*Bijou*) or the point-of-view character's attempt to identify the subjects of photographs in "The New Orleans of Possibilities," (*New Orleans*). In *Pleasure-Dome* stories become a kind of coinage; after con man Bucky has fed his marks the stories that land him in jail, storyteller Lucius tells the victims new stories to get them to drop charges. As Madden has suggested elsewhere, the writer is a kind of "benevolent con-man," trying to beguile people who want to be "taken."

A related theme is reading. In many stories, characters either have no stories to go on, or they try to read stories into fragmentary bits of information. The father in "No Trace" combs through his late son's dorm room, looking for any message that might yield up a coherent story of the young man's short life. In "James Agee Never Lived in This House" (1990), a woman who lives in the late Knoxville writer's home rebuffs a visitor, "David Madden," in a conflict between two different "readers" of Agee and his life. From *The Beautiful Greed* to the Willis Carr stories, individuals puzzle over the meaning of events—sometimes concluding that their imagined truth has more worth than unstoried experience.

A third theme centers on Madden's existential use of popular culture as a prevailing motif. Films play an obvious role in *Bijou* as a source of stories for

Lucius; but film, along with radio, television, and other forms—even commedia dell'arte—provides both a style of narrative discourse (as in Big Bob's big-wind patter) and a set of metaphors for detachment. Characters involve themselves with popular media in ways that cause them to lose contact with the self. In Madden's fiction, those characters most fully involved with pop culture are those either without any fixed identity or those who struggle against the limits of popular discourse for some statement of self. Lone McDaniel buys into the leather-and-cycle scene, but it offers an inadequate vocabulary with which to express not only his alienation but also his drive for purity in a houseful of palpably flawed people. Big Bob, on the other hand, has decided nothing matters but surface; as a result, radio and television provide the vehicles he needs to be what he wants at any moment.

Madden's life in his fiction is, in a sense, the theme that underlies all others. Through many short stories, including ''The Cartridge Belt'' and ''Lindbergh's Rival'' in *The New Orleans of Possibilities,* and many of the novels, Madden has recalled large chunks of his own experience. Sometimes transmission of his life into fiction seems unedited, as in *Bijou;* at other times, as in the second part of *Pleasure-Dome,* the whole story seems so whimsically far-fetched that it could only come from dreams. Whatever the case, Madden's career appears to be its own never-ending subject—but a ''subject'' that dissolves itself through the transforming power of the creative process (storytelling and reading) into the theme of imagination.

SURVEY OF CRITICISM

Little scholarly work has been done on Madden. Two reasons suggest themselves: He has yet to publish a masterwork, though *Cassandra Singing, Bijou,* and *The Suicide's Wife* are all original, engaging, and very different works; and he does not fit into a tidy critical box. Still, given his many interests, his popularity as a reader and storyteller on college campuses, and his theoretical bent, the lack of attention seems surprising. The Anna H. Perrault bibliography—the most complete to date, though not authoritative—lists many titles, as will the updated version being prepared by Peggy Bach; but most comments on Madden are restricted to short reviews, reference-text entries, or brief mentions in critical surveys. The best and most complete overview article is by Thomas E. Dasher (1980); William C. Bamberger's essay (1986) is also useful and has a good select bibliography. Deborah A. Straub (1981) cribs themes from Dasher but surveys reviews. The only journal article to date on a single Madden work is Sanford Pinsker's on *Cassandra Singing* (1973). The most insightful review of any Madden book is by James M. Davis, Jr. (1981), but Gelfant (1975), Kreyling (1983), Gaillard (1974), Walters (1977), Garrett (1977), Sale (1974), and May (1979, 1984) suggest fruitful lines of inquiry.

Though Madden's contribution to the *Contemporary Authors Autobiography Series* (1986) is a deliberate patchwork of poems and paragraphs from his fiction and nonfiction, he has commented extensively on his work. Madden's *Poetic Image in 6 Genres* (1969) is a good starting point, followed by the Pinsker (1973), Laney (1975), Prestridge (1977), Jones (1982), Parrill (1984), Folks (1987), and Crowder (1990) interviews. Madden's essay on the storyteller as con man (1974), his work on 1930s proletarian and tough-guy writers (1968), and his "conversation" with and writings on Wright Morris (1964, 1982) develop ideas about the art of fiction, as do his chapter on the aesthetics of fiction in *Cain's Craft* (1985) and his essay on "the 'real-life' fallacy" (1989). He has also been helpful in providing information for this chapter.

Many aspects of Madden's work need addressing: his frequent reuse and revision of texts (which sometimes leads to an unfair criticism that he is short of material), his relation to the South and Southern literature, and his aesthetics. A further issue is the place of criticism and other genres in Madden's work as a whole. His diversity has, in some ways, worked against his acceptance as a serious fiction writer, but he deserves attention for recent critical work—for example, such essays as his critique (1991) of a work by the long-neglected Joseph Stanley Pennell or such essays as "The Death of the Ominbus Review" (1987) and "On the Loose: A Memoir" (1990).

Madden's career would make a good subject for a doctoral dissertation; and certainly, articles are needed on single works and on his work in relation to his theories of fictional technique, especially his ideas about "impingement" and "implication."

BIBLIOGRAPHY

Works by David Madden

The Beautiful Greed. New York: Random House, 1961.

Wright Morris. New York: Twayne, 1964.

Cassandra Singing. New York: Crown, 1969.

The Poetic Image in 6 Genres. Carbondale: Southern Illinois University Press, 1969.

James M. Cain. New York: Twayne, 1970.

The Shadow Knows. Baton Rouge: Louisiana State University Press, 1970.

Brothers in Confidence. New York: Avon, 1972.

Bijou. New York: Crown, 1974.

"The Story Teller as Benevolent Con Man." *Appalachian Heritage* 2, no. 3 (1974): 70–77.

Creative Choices: A Spectrum of Quality and Technique in Fiction. Glenview, Ill.: Scott, Foresman, 1975.

Harlequin's Stick—Charlie's Cane: A Comparative Study of Commedia dell'Arte and Silent Comedy. Bowling Green, Ohio: Popular Press, 1975.

The Suicide's Wife. Indianapolis: Bobbs-Merrill, 1978.

Pleasure-Dome. Indianapolis: Bobbs-Merrill, 1979.

On the Big Wind. New York: Holt, Rinehart, and Winston, 1980.

A Primer of the Novel: For Readers & Writers. Metuchen, N.J.: Scarecrow, 1980.

"The American Land, Character, and Dream in the Novels of Wright Morris." In *American Writing Today,* vol. 1, edited by Richard Kostelantz, 155–68. Washington, D.C.: U. S. International Communication Agency, 1982.

The New Orleans of Possibilities. Baton Rouge: Louisiana State University Press, 1982.

"Barry Hannah's *Geronimo Rex* in Retrospect." *Southern Review* 19 (1983): 309–16.

" 'The Cruel Radiance of What Is.' " *Southern Quarterly* 22, no. 2 (1984): 5–43.

"The Dominance of the Speaking Voice in the 1930s in the United States." *Letterature d'America: Rivista Trime strale* 5 (1984): 24–25, 107–22.

Cain's Craft. Metuchen, N.J.: Scarecrow, 1985.

"Willis Carr at Bleak House." *Southern Review* 21 (1985): 522–33.

Revising Fiction: A Handbook for Writers. New York: New American Library, 1988.

"Continually Astonished by Everything: The Army Stories of George Garrett." In *To Come Up Grinning: A Tribute to George Garrett,* edited by Stuart Wright, 47–54. Houston: Texas Review Press, 1989.

"The Demon in My View." *Southern Review* 25 (1989): 421–32.

"A Personal View: The 'Real Life' Fallacy." In *The American Writer and the University,* edited by Ben Siegel, 179–89. Newark: University of Delaware Press, 1989.

"The Violent Meditations of Willis Carr, Sharpshooter (1848–1933)." *South Dakota Review* 28, no. 1 (1990): 111–27.

"James Agee Never Lived in This House." *Southern Review* 26 (1990): 422–36.

"On the Loose: A Memoir" [on Jesse Hill Ford]. *Southern Review* 26 (1990): 766–83.

"On Joseph Stanley Pennell's *The History of Rome Hanks and Kindred Matters.* In *Classics of Civil War Fiction,* edited by Madden and Peggy Bach, 181–203. Jackson: University Press of Mississippi, 1991.

"Photographs in the 1929 Version of *Sanctuary.*" In *Faulkner and Popular Culture,* edited by Doreen Fowler, 93–109. Jackson: University Press of Mississippi, 1990.

"The Test of a First-Rate Intelligence: Agee and the Cruel Radiance of What Is." In *James Agee: Reconsiderations.* Edited by Michael A. Lofaro. Knoxville: University of Tennessee Press, 1992.

Works Edited by David Madden

Proletarian Writers of the Thirties. Carbondale: Southern Illinois University Press, 1968.

Tough Guy Writers of the Thirties. Carbondale: Southern Illinois University Press, 1968.

American Dreams, American Nightmares. Carbondale: Southern Illinois University Press, 1970.

Rediscoveries: Informal Essays in Which Well-Known Novelists Rediscover Neglected Works of Fiction by One of Their Favorite Authors. New York: Crown, 1971.

The Popular Culture Explosion. With Ray B. Browne. Dubuque, Iowa: Brown, 1972.

Nathanael West: The Cheaters and the Cheated. Deland, Fla.: Everett/Edwards, 1973.

Remembering James Agee. Baton Rouge: Louisiana State University Press, 1974.

Writer's Revisions: An Annotated Bibliography of Articles and Books about Writers' Revisions and Their Comments on the Creative Process. With Richard Powers. Metuchen, N.J.: Scarecrow, 1981.

Studies in the Short Story. 6th ed. New York: Holt, Rinehart, and Winston: 1984.

Rediscoveries II: Important Writers Select Their Favorite Works of Neglected Fiction. With Peggy Bach. New York: Carroll and Graf, 1988.

Interviews with David Madden

Crowder, A. B. "David Madden." *Writing in the Southern Tradition: Interviews with Five Contemporary Authors,* 153–82. Amsterdam: Rodopi, 1990.

" 'The Dictates of Style': A Conversation between David Madden and Wright Morris." In *Conversations with Wright Morris,* edited by Robert E. Knoll, 101–19. Lincoln: University of Nebraska Press, 1977.

Folks, Jeffrey H. "Interview with David Madden: On Technique in Fiction." *Southern Quarterly* 25, no. 2 (1987): 24–38.

"If a Writer's Works Are His Life. . . " In *Contemporary Authors Autobiography Series,* vol. 3, edited by Adele Sarkissian, 185–206. Detroit: Gale Research, 1986.

Jones, Ray. "An Interview with David Madden." *New Orleans Review* 9 (1982): 29–35.

Laney, Ruth. "An Interview with David Madden." *Southern Review,* n.s., 11 (1975): 167–80.

Parrill, William. "The Art of the Novel: An Interview with David Madden." *Louisiana Literature* 1 (1984): 4–12.

Pinsker, Sanford. "A Conversation with David Madden." *Critique: Studies in Modern Fiction* 15, no. 2 (1973): 5–14.

Prestridge, Samuel. "An Interview with David Madden." *Mississippi Review* 6, no. 3 (1977): 99–112.

Studies of David Madden

Bach, Peggy. *"The Suicide's Wife." Magill's Literary Annual 1979,* edited by Frank N. Magill, 727–31. Englewood Cliffs, N.J.: Salem, 1979.

Bamberger, William C. "Madden, (Jerry) David." In *Contemporary Novelists,* 4th ed., edited by D. L. Kirkpatrick, 555–58. London: St. James, 1986.

Binding, Paul. *Separate Country: A Literary Journey through the American South.* Rev. ed., 38–40, 84. Jackson: University Press of Mississippi, 1988.

Callison, Helen V. Review of *The Shadow Knows. Studies in Short Fiction* 8 (1971): 651–53.

Cook, Martha E. "Old Ways and New Ways." *The History of Southern Literature,* edited by Louis Rubin, 527–34. Baton Rouge: Louisiana State University Press, 1985.

Dasher, Thomas E. "David Madden." In *American Novelists since World War II,* vol. 6 of *Dictionary of Literary Biography,* edited by James E. Kibler, Jr., 192–201. Detroit: Gale Research, 1980.

Davis, James M., Jr. Review of *On the Big Wind. Denver Quarterly* 16, no. 1 (1981): 117–19.

Gaillard, Dawson. "Perspective: 'Then What. . . ?' " Review of *The Shadow Knows. New Orleans Review* 4 (1974): 276–82.

Garrett, George. *"Cassandra Singing."* In *Magill,* edited by Frank N. Magill, 1104–6.

Gelfant, Blanche. "Chronicles and Chroniclers: Some Contemporary Fictions." Review of *Bijou. Massachusetts Review* 16 (1975): 127–43.

Greenberg, Martin. "Fiction Chronicle." Review of *The Beautiful Greed. Partisan Review* 29 (1962): 149–58.

Kreyling, Michael. Review of *The New Orleans of Possibilities. Studies in Short Fiction* 20 (1983): 61–62.

"Madden, David." In *Contemporary Authors,* vol. 1–4, edited by James M. Ethridge and Barbara Kopala, 618. Detroit: Gale Research, 1967.

"Madden, David." In *Contemporary Literary Criticism,* vol. 5, edited by Carolyn Riley and Phyllis Carmel Mendelson, 265–66. Detroit: Gale Research, 1976.

"Madden, David." In *Contemporary Literary Criticism,* vol. 15, edited by Sharon R. Gunton and Laurie Lanzen Harris, 350–51. Detroit: Gale Research, 1980.

Magill, Frank N., ed. *Survey of Contemporary Literature.* Rev. ed. Vol. 2. Englewood Cliffs, N.J.: Salem, 1977.

May, John R. "Louisiana Writers in Film." *Southern Quarterly* 23 (1984): 18–31.

———. Review of *The Suicide's Wife. New Orleans Review* 6 (1979): 401–2.

McManis, Jo. Review of *Bijou. New Orleans Review* 4 (1974): 283.

Perrault, Anna H. "A David Madden Bibliography, 1952–1981." *Bulletin of Bibliography* 39, no. 3 (1982): 104–16.

Pinsker, Sanford. "The Mixed Cords [sic] of David Madden's *Cassandra Singing.*" *Critique: Studies in Modern Fiction* 15, no. 2 (1973): 15–26.

Review of *Bijou. New Yorker* 50 (May 27, 1974): 105–6.

Review of *Cassandra Singing. Virginia Quarterly Review* 46 (Spring 1970): xliv.

Review of *The Suicide's Wife. New Yorker* 54 (December 4, 1978): 237.

Rubin, Louis D., Jr., et al. *The History of Southern Literature.* Baton Rouge: Louisiana State University Press, 1985.

Sale, Roger. Review of *Bijou. New York Review of Books* (June 27, 1974): 24–25.

Schott, Webster. Review of *Pleasure-Dome. Washington Post Book World* (January 6, 1980): 9.

Shapiro, Charles. Review of *Bijou. New Republic* (March 30, 1974): 29–30.

Straub, Deborah A. "Madden, (Jerry) David." In *Contemporary Authors.* New Revision Series. Vol. 4, edited by Ann Evory, 393–96. Detroit: Gale Research, 1981.

Swann, Roberta Metz. Review of *The New Orleans of Possibilities. North American Review* 267 (September 1982): 80.

Walters, Thomas N. *"Bijou."* In *Magill,* edited by Frank N. Magill, 705–8.

Wier, Allen. Review of *The Suicide's Wife. Hollins Critic* 16, no. 1 (February 1979): 19.

Williams, Thomas. "Ducks, Ships, Custard, and a King." Review of *The Beautiful Greed. Kenyon Review* 24, no. 1 (1962): 184–88.

Young, Thomas Daniel. *Tennessee Writers.* Knoxville: Tennessee Historical Commission and University of Tennessee Press, 1981.

LYNNE P. SHACKELFORD

Jeff Daniel Marion
(1940–   )

Air, earth, water—out of these natural elements Jeff Daniel Marion creates an elemental literature that explores what is fundamental and sustaining in life. Best known as a poet, though also a fiction writer and essayist, Marion has chosen as his subject the scenes and the people of eastern Tennessee.

BIOGRAPHY

In his essay ''The Poem Itself: A Map of the Heart's True Country'' (1980), Jeff Daniel Marion has observed that the predominant characteristic of his work is a sense of place, which he believes ''is linked, in a very vital way, to knowing who you are'' (1). Knowing who Danny Marion is has much to do with his heart's true country, the area around Rogersville, Tennessee, where he was born on July 7, 1940. His family roots grew deep in the region, for his mother, Eloise Gladson, and his father, J. D. Marion, were raised on nearby farms and knew each other from childhood. Indeed, the Gladsons and the Marions were linked not only by his parents' marriage but also by the betrothals of Eloise Gladson's two sisters to J. D. Marion's brothers. The three couples lived within a mile of one another and, as the only offspring of those three unions, Danny Marion benefited from an unusually close-knit family who nurtured his poetic sensibility.

From his father, an ink specialist for a commercial printing company, Danny gained a love of art. The boy, fascinated with his father's artistic touch in judging the tack of the ink, grew into the adult who lovingly prints broadsides and chapbooks on his father's proof press. A second gift that Marion's father bequeathed to his son was an attentiveness to nature. With his penetrating vision, Danny's father taught his son to notice a rabbit underneath a bush or to appreciate the fluttering of hummingbird wings. From his mother the boy learned to value books. At a time when the family had limited financial resources, Danny's mother purchased *Bedtime Stories for Children* for her son and spent countless hours reading to him—a cherished ritual that Danny Marion followed in raising his own children, Stephen and Rachel.

Other relatives played significant roles in Danny Marion's upbringing. Undoubtedly the most powerful influence was exerted by Danny's maternal grandmother, Lucy Gladson, whose 150-acre farm was a favorite playground. Blind from a cataract condition, Lucy Gladson encouraged her grandson to share his sight with her through precise, crystalline images. She also entertained him with a seemingly endless stock of stories. Two aunts fostered Danny's interest in nature. One aunt, her mind an encyclopedia of botanical information, taught Danny the names of plants, flowers, and trees. The other aunt, with whom Danny shared long walks and imaginative adventures, so revered nature's creatures that she could not bring herself to destroy the cobwebs in her home, because, she explained, ''Spiders have to live too.''

Like many Southern writers who grew up in small communities, Danny Marion has profited from a rich cultural legacy. One source of creative sustenance for him has been the wonderful talk he listened to during his childhood—at family gatherings, by the side of his grandmother's rocker, or at ''The 96,'' a combination general store and service station that he has described as ''the local gathering place for talking, swapping tales and whittling, whiling away the hours.'' Another important source has been his religious upbringing. He grew up in the Baptist Church, attending Sunday School, church picnics, tent revivals, and—usually with reluctance—choir practice. The sense of spiritual communion Marion first experienced in his family church has led him upon a continuing pilgrimage to seek enlightenment. Bothered by a narrow-minded denominationalism and aggressive proselytizing, he today draws upon various religious traditions, including Buddhism and the Quaker faith.

From 1958 to 1962 Marion studied at the University of Tennessee, earning a B.S. in Education, with a major in English and a minor in Speech and Sociology. Upon graduation he taught high school, first in Knoxville and then in his hometown of Rogersville. In 1965 he returned to the University of Tennessee; and the following year, after completing a thesis on William Faulkner, he was awarded an M.A. in English. He has done further graduate study at the University of Tennessee, the University of Southern Mississippi, and the University of Alabama.

While Marion was working on his master's thesis he became friends with a graduate of Carson-Newman College, a small Baptist school in Jefferson City, Tennessee. His friend frequently shared with him fond memories of his college days. Eager to teach students from a rural background, Marion decided that Carson-Newman would be an ideal place for him, and so in 1966 he sought and secured employment there. Thus began a long and satisfying teaching career at the school—a career interrupted only by a brief sojourn from 1968 to 1969 in Hattiesburg, Mississippi, where Marion taught at William Carey College and took graduate courses at the University of Southern Mississippi. While in Mississippi, he began writing poetry seriously, in part as a means of combating homesickness for East Tennessee. When the academic dean at Carson-Newman asked him to return to the school for the 1969–70 academic year, Marion needed little prodding, for he then knew that he wanted to spend the rest of his life in his native region.

Marion continues to teach at Carson-Newman. He offers courses in composition, creative writing, and contemporary poetry, carefully arranging his schedule to allow time for writing. He is an enthusiastic teacher who views teaching, he told me in 1989, as "an artistic process in which you are developing a relationship and then you are shaping another by that relationship." Because of his desire to help young writers shape their vision and to correct the distorted notion he himself had in his youth that all poets died sometime during the nineteenth century, he has participated in the Poet-in-the-Schools program in Virginia and Tennessee and has taught at the Tennessee Governor's School for the Humanities. He has lectured and conducted poetry workshops throughout the Appalachian region and was awarded a Literary Arts Fellowship by the Tennessee Arts Commission in 1978. In 1975 he founded *The Small Farm,* a little magazine committed to publishing works that convey a strong sense of place. *Small Farm* soon earned a distinguished reputation for the high quality of its poetry and criticism, including Marion's penetrating poetry reviews. He edited the magazine until 1980. Marion now edits a new regional literary review entitled the *Mossy Creek Reader.*

The year 1976 was particularly significant in Marion's career as a poet, for it was then that he published two chapbooks, *Almanac* and *Watering Places* and his first major poetry collection, *Out in the Country, Back Home.* As Dan Leidig (1983) has noted, "What is striking about the *Almanac* poems, ostensibly pastoral pieces, is the immediate prophecy of darkness, not merely of inevitable death, but of the dark woods of the living, the painful cost of knowing" (146). That dark quality also appears in the poems in *Watering Places,* which depict the poet's return to those special scenes from the past that renewed him. *Out in the Country, Back Home,* whose cover is illustrated with an eighteenth-century map of "Tennassee," maps the places, people, and experiences that have enabled Marion to find himself within the Tennessee landscape. With wry humor, he captures the meanderings, colorful phrases, and fable-making quality of rural Southern voices. According to Robert Morgan in his introduction to the volume, Marion, with the power of nomination of the Emersonian poet, "speaks as though for the first time of these people and places and things in the Tennessee foothills of the Smokies."

Among Marion's more recent work are his 1981 poetry collection *Tight Lines* (which is beautifully illustrated with linedrawings by George Chavatel), "By the Banks of the Holston: Memories of a River" (1984), (which is a paean to the river and combines epigraphs, prose, and poetry with illustrations by William Houston), *Vigils* (a volume of selected poems published in 1990), and *Hello, Crow* (a children's book published by Orchard Books in 1991). Currently Marion is concentrating upon fiction writing. He has written several short stories, which he says are the narratives behind the lyric poems in *Out in the Country, Back Home*. He is also at work on a juvenile novel in which, in the tradition of Mark Twain's *Adventures of Huckleberry Finn*, a boy meets a hermit who lives in a cave and then journeys with his newfound friend down a river.

Marion resides with his dog Gypsy on a small farm. The windows of his study afford him a spectacular view of the Holston River, his vital link with the past—his grandfathers once rode log rafts right by the spot where his house stands—and his present and, most likely, future inspiration.

MAJOR THEMES

There is a magical—indeed, spiritual—word in Jeff Daniel Marion's vocabulary. It appears in the title of his first major poetry collection, it shines forth in the lines of many of his poems, it resonates in his conversation. The word is *home*. Home for Marion is not merely a geographical locale, though having lived most of his life within fifty miles of where he was born, he is firmly grounded in a sense of place. Nor is it an absolute that he has already attained. Rather, Marion perceives home as a process, the goal of each person's pilgrimage of self-discovery. It is what sustains us in a dark and cold world. "Much of my writing," Marion told me, "has been a process of trying to seek out the elements of home. . . . It is a process, I think, that I am always looking for or trying to touch base with. And the moments when I feel best are the moments when I have touched that resonating spirit." Such a moment occurs in "Unnamed" (*Out in the Country, Back Home*), in which home becomes a metaphor for the goal of the poetic act itself:

> Dark, darker: waves coming,
> rising within to wash our lives.
> Outside, each snowflake locks in light
> laying down a whiteness.
>
> When the earth gives us these moments,
> We ride all the way back:
> twenty years and each chosen rock
> an animal, shaped by water toward
> our naming: a few horses, some cows,
> a mule or two, and always the unnamed
> ones, presences that moved strangely,
> awaiting the shape our words
> would give them. They lie there still
> in that field next to the woods,
> sheltered on the oldest ark we know:

its waves touch us still and our words
like snowflakes go out searching that home
so far and cold in this darkness we move through. (30)

The quintessential means of seeking home for Marion is through a strong sense of one's heritage preserved by memory, which he considers to be both a storehouse of sensory data and a shaper of experience. He is highly sensitive to the past as a legacy passed on from one generation to the next—not a tradition to be adopted mindlessly, but to be adapted to the present and one's particular circumstances. His is an autumnal, elegiac vision in which a return to a cherished site recalls the ephemerality of youth, the loss of loved ones, the inevitability of change. As he writes in "Heritage" (*Out in the Country, Back Home*), a poem recounting his return three years after his grandmother's death to a patch of ground she loved, there is "a sharpness / not unlike pain" to the "dark memories" of what is no more (32). Yet the connectedness with the past he finds ultimately sustaining. To cite a metaphor he uses in a number of his poems, it is a cool and refreshing drink from a well-spring that quenches a soul's thirst. As he reveals in "Ebbing and Flowing Spring" (*Out in the Country, Back Home*):

You reach for the dipper
that's gone, then
remember to use your hands
as a cup for the cold
that aches & lingers.
This is what you have come for.
Drink. (65)

Marion writes in the tradition of American Transcendentalism. Like Ralph Waldo Emerson, Henry David Thoreau, and Walt Whitman, Marion fervently believes that "Nature is the symbol of spirit." Therefore, as with Robert Frost's poems, Marion's nature lyrics, although satisfying on a literal level, attain their greatest power when the reader recognizes their philosophical or religious dimension. In his work, Marion constantly moves from physical reality to spiritual insight through metaphor—for example, from a wren's "twiggy nest" to his own "tangled nest / of words hopeful but wingless" ("Wren in the Window," *Vigils* 41), from a glimpse of a tree through windows to the revelation "Leaf by leaf I learn my life" (*Almanac* VIII), from a mesmerizing encounter with a groundhog to his own emergence from his burrow "to meet the world, / my shadow / not far behind" ("Groundhog Day Meditation: A Letter to Ginny Nash"). Marion affirms, "The basic thrust out of which I write is communal. I am trying to commune with some spirit that is much greater than I could ever be and that nourishes me, that feeds me, that gives me this great gift of the world" (Interview with author, 1989).

In his essay "The Poem Itself: A Map of the Heart's True Country," Marion provides a useful categorization of his poetry. He divides his work into poems of place, poems of objects within a place, and poems of people.

Marion's poetry of place grew out of a young child's desire to be an artist. After realizing his drawing talent did not live up to his standard of perfection, Marion discovered instead that he could paint in words. "Watercolor Of An East Tennessee Farm," "American Primitive: East Tennessee Style," "Landscapes" (*Out in the Country, Back Home*)—his very titles emphasize the painterly quality of his work. His verbal canvases or photographs freeze the moment: the motion of an old woman pitching water outside, the arched neck of a great blue heron framed in a window, the rust-colored spears of tobacco piled beside a barn, moonlight reflected in the water under the archway of a stone bridge. "You begin what you have come for, / set up the camera, choose an angle / of view, try to save a passing moment" (48), Marion writes in "At the Railway Station Back Home" (*Out in the Country, Back Home*). That, in essence, is the method of his poetry of place.

In his poetry of objects, Marion rekindles the imaginative wonder at the world that he possessed as a child. He takes the unusual and makes it miraculous, the ordinary and makes it extraordinary. With a wave of his poetic wand, the pragmatic becomes aesthetic, as in "Old Mason Jars" (*Out in the Country, Back Home*):

> blue skin of summer sky
> * * * * *
>
> bone's breath sealing
> garden marrow
> * * * * *
>
> cellar's zodiac planted
> in rows moon-capped
> * * * * *
>
> winter shell cache for
> blackberries, squash, pole beans
> * * * * *
>
> sand's blue ice (16)

In "Hoe" (*Out in the Country, Back Home*), the farmer's tool becomes transformed into a mysterious force that harnesses us "in its dark power" (22). His "Gourds" become repositories of timeless secrets. Marion's poems of objects have an Oriental sparseness. He strategically uses white space and avoids capitalization—and sometimes end punctuation—to capture the compelling fullness of his subjects, to unfold their essence.

As with Edgar Lee Masters' and Edwin Arlington Robinson's narrative poems, Marion's poetry of people acknowledges the pain, loss, loneliness, and suffering of the human condition. Many of his poems evolved from his haunting childhood memories of the "many strange wanderers" who came through Rogersville, wanderers such as Rambling Rose, an albino women who supposedly sold her children shortly after each was born in order to support herself and her husband. In other poems he recalls the lives of deprivation of his schoolmates, for instance, J. L., "second son of parents who farmed / their lives hoping for that good year" ("Going Back for J. L.," *Out in the Country, Back Home,* 34), or the "girl in the backrow / whose only gift for Christmas / is a pencil box" ("Hand-Me-Down Days," from unpublished manuscript entitled *Lost and Found*). As indicated by the title he chose for his volume of selected poems *Vigils,* Marion keeps tender watch over these people who have imprinted their spirits upon his memory. Through their portraits he celebrates the triumph of endurance across a range of humanity. There is a dignified beauty in his blind grandmother's sifting of flour, as she substitutes touch for sight; a heart-wrenching patience to Orpha's futile trek to "rusting mailboxes" to seek the "daily bread" of communication with kin ("Orpha," *Out in the Country, Back Home,* 28); a phenomenal faith in Barsha Buchanan's ritualistic dinner preparations for a faithless husband who long ago deserted her. Marion feels almost a religious calling to preserve the memory of these lives. He explains:

It's as though I have had the privilege of encountering these spirits on their journey, on their pilgrimage, and many of them are ordinary lives on the surface but extraordinary when you see what they've had to endure. These are primarily people who are not going to be remembered in any history book, and maybe part of why I feel they have to be remembered is there was something in that life that was significant. It was a human spirit struggling to survive and endure with some sense of dignity—or striving to. (Interview with author, 1989)

Marion is gifted with the power of seeing Christ in others; he does not merely describe his characters but, rather, elevates them.

Perhaps the most pervasive of Marion's themes—or at least the theme he has emphasized through his choice of initial and concluding poems in his chapbooks and collections—is the self-referential nature of poetry: Many of Marion's poems are about poetry. Through metaphors of fishing, harvesting, and land surveying and through spiritual identification with nature's creatures, Marion has proclaimed his goal of self-discovery through an awareness of place; he has elucidated for his readers the surfaces and depths of his art; he has defined his characteristics as a poet. "Boundaries," the concluding poem of *Out in the Country, Back Home,* provides his most explicit and impassioned statement of his objective as a writer:

Yoked in these lines
I mean to work this land

What comes up won't be wasted
& what's between the rows
is welcome, too.
Maybe occasionally a green heron
will visit my pond.
I'm always at home here
still believing
the reward of this labor
is vision
honed to the blue sharpness
of ridges. (66)

In "Tight Lines," the first poem in his volume of the same title, he tells his
readers how to fish for imaginative flashes of eternal truths, beguiled by the
flow of the current, then lured by the depths of dark reality. Many of Marion's
works describe himself as a poet. In the evocative "River Canticle" that opens
"By the Banks of the Holston: Memories of a River," Marion assumes various
roles. He is the dragonfly that "rises from and enters into the river," "the water
strider who skates on the faith of surfaces," the kingfisher hovering in the air,
then plunging into the depths of the river, driven by hunger "for what's beneath," the great blue heron whose "vision scales the curves of distance," the
deer who steps into the current to drink the sacramental water (3). He is linker
of light and darkness, surface and depth, past and present, observation and intuition. Like Emerson, Thoreau, and Whitman, Marion envisions the poet as
see-er and seer, but he assumes that role with a humility of spirit that is uniquely
his own. Marion best describes himself in "Crossing Clinch Mountain in February" (*Vigils*):

In this dusk
I am your single candle,
faint echo of starlight
on far mountain roads
singing the way
home. (22)

SURVEY OF CRITICISM

Because Marion's work is so deeply rooted in the culture of East Tennessee,
the critical attention to it has been largely regional. But many of the reviews
and essays have come from fellow Southern writers who recognize Marion as
one of the most significant voices of Appalachia.

In an influential review (1977) of Marion's first major collection of poetry,
Out in the Country, Back Home, Guy Owen identified Marion as a member of
"the group of young Southern contemporaries who are creating a new pastoral
poetry"—a poetry that eschews a sentimental prettification of natural scenes

and instead depicts the often harsh realities of rural life as well as the threats to folk culture that "progress" brings (64). Indeed, so enthusiastic was Owen over Marion's achievement that he predicted that if the young writer continued in his poetic development, he would attain the literary preeminence of Wendell Berry, Robert Morgan, and Fred Chappell.

Owen's article proved seminal in introducing the most widely discussed concern of Marion's critics: the poet's pastoralism. The year following the publication of Owen's article, Jim Wayne Miller, in reviewing Marion's *Out in the Country, Back Home* and Robert Henry Baber's *Assorted Life Savers and Poems from the Mountains,* contended that contemporary Appalachian poetry could be divided into two schools: the Political and the Pastoral, with Marion's book being a prime example of the latter category. Frank Steele (1979), Frank Einstein (1980), and George Ella Lyon (1981) have further examined Miller's thesis. Probably the most powerful response has been from Einstein, who was bothered by Miller's division. Einstein suggested that the pastoralists use nostalgia to serve political ends—as "a touchstone to judge the present" (38) and as "a progressive force in poetry" (39).

The two most perceptive discussions of Marion's work are Dan Leidig's article (1983) and Gerald C. Wood's essay (1985). Both survey Marion's career and offer detailed analyses of his poems. Leidig and Wood have agreed that there is a dark quality and a religious dimension to Marion's work. Marion, according to Leidig, takes his readers to the "rim of knowing" as they journey with him on a quest into "the heart's true country" (155). Similarly, Wood has observed that "the poet is like a priest who makes an endless quest toward meaning and order in a world rimmed by darkness" (42).

Leidig and Wood differ, however, in their assessments of the applicability and limitations of the label "pastoral" in considering Marion's work. Leidig emphasizes the writer's firm grounding in the pastoral tradition: "There, still stuck in the mud beside Spivey Creek, unconverted and unredeemed, recalcitrant and quaint as an unreconstructed, pre-revolutionary, antediluvian mule, stands Marion fishing in the same old stream!" (144) Of course, Leidig realizes that it is no Arcadia inhabited by frolicking nymphs and amorous shepherds that Marion portrays in his poetry. In fact, to his catalogue of familiar pastoral subjects found in Marion's poems—"the sense of local place, the creative force of memory, the presence of story in history, the abiding connections of family, the neighborly character of the small town, the intimacy of the small farm, the irreducible character of country things, the art in ordinary work, and 'just plain days gone by,' " (145) Leidig adds a virtually ignored poetic concern—what the writer himself terms the "darker ways of survival."

In contrast to Leidig, Wood believes the term *pastoral* to be inadequate and even misleading. He finds Marion decidedly contemporary in his use of poetry as an intensely personal way of creating meaning from his own experiences. Wood is particularly interested in the dynamism beneath the seemingly static Oriental surface of Marion's verse. He sees in Marion's work "a poetry of intense dramas—between poet and audience, a dynamic personality and his changing place, the present and the past, the shallow and the deep'' (40).

Recent criticism of Marion's work includes Rita Sims Quillen's examination (1989) of Marion's quest to understand nature's rituals, Tim Elledge's study (1990) of Marion's creative process, and Larry Richman's sensitive reading (1992) of selected poems from *Vigils*.

Having won the respect of such writers as Guy Owen, Robert Morgan, and Jim Wayne Miller, as well as the appreciation of Appalachian readers, Marion seems guaranteed of an enthusiastic response to his future publications.

BIBLIOGRAPHY

Works by Jeff Daniel Marion

Almanac. Jefferson City, Tenn.: Small Farm Press, 1976.

Watering Places. Knoxville, Tenn.: Puddingstone Press, 1976.

Out in the Country, Back Home. Winston-Salem, N.C.: Jackpine Press, 1976.

"Starting Places: Notes from the Ground." *Puddingstone* 3 (Spring 1977): 22–27.

"The Poem Itself: A Map of the Heart's True Country." *Carson-Newman Faculty Studies* 4 (Spring 1980): 1–14.

Tight Lines. Emory, Va.: Iron Mountain Press, 1981.

"By the Banks of the Holston: Memories of a River." *Iron Mountain Review* 1 (1984): 3–13.

Vigils: Selected Poems. Boone, N.C.: Appalachian Consortium Press, 1990.

"Wild Flower." *Now and Then: The Appalachian Magazine.* 7 (1990): 22–25.

"Wayside Diner." *Journal of Kentucky Studies* 8 (September 1991): 7–9.

Hello, Crow. New York: Orchard Books, 1992.

Studies of Jeff Daniel Marion

Coward, John. "Jeff Daniel Marion and His Poetry: Mapping the Heart's Place." In *An Encyclopedia of East Tennessee,* edited by Jim Stokely and Jeff D. Johnson, 312–13. Oak Ridge: Children's Museum of Oak Ridge, 1981.

Einstein, Frank. "The Politics of Nostalgia: Uses of the Past in Recent Appalachian Poetry." *Appalachian Journal* 8 (Autumn 1980): 32–40.

Elledge, Tim. "The Truth Behind the Fiction." *Tennessee Alumnus.* 70 (1990): 42–43.

Leidig, Dan. "On the Rim of Knowing: The Achievement of Jeff Daniel Marion." *Appalachian Journal* 10 (1983): 142–56.

Lyon, George Ella. "Contemporary Appalachian Poetry: Sources and Directions." *The Kentucky Review* 2 (1981): 3–22.

Owen, Guy. Review of *Out in the Country, Back Home. Southern Poetry Review* 17 (1977): 64–65.

Quillen, Rita Sims, "Jeff Daniel Marion." *Looking for Native Ground: Contemporary Appalachian Poetry.* Boone, N.C.: Appalachian Consortium Press, 1989.

Richman, Larry. Interview and review of *Vigils: Selected Poems. The Sow's Ear* 3 (February 1992): 12–15, 18–21.

Steele, Frank. "Two Kinds of Commitment: Some Directions in Current Appalachian Poetry." *Appalachian Journal* 6 (1979): 228–38.

Wood, Gerald C. "The Poetry of Jeff Daniel Marion." *Appalachian Heritage* 13 (1985): 39–45.

BES STARK SPANGLER

Heather Ross Miller
(1939–   )

Recognized initially for her "exquisite style," Heather Ross Miller has steadily produced highly crafted poetry and fiction since the publication of her first novel in 1964. Although her works have been identified as Southern Gothic, Miller's portrayals of psychological and physical violence in time-haunted existences result more from her interest in universal themes than from a desire to examine social influences. While writing is her true vocation, she has also taught creative writing for more than 25 years in homage to her teacher, friend, and mentor Randall Jarrell. Pursuing both writing and teaching careers with customary vigor, Miller approaches midlife with the publication of a newly collected volume of poetry entitled *Hard Evidence* (1990).

BIOGRAPHY

Heather Ross Miller was born on September 15, 1939, in Albemarle, North Carolina. The daughter of Fred E., a journalist, and Geneva Smith Ross revealed in early childhood that she would be another of the "writing Rosses." Although her aunts Eleanor Ross Taylor and Jean Ross Justice both wrote and were married to writers, these aunts did not attempt to influence Heather's writing. Instead, they frequently mailed books to her, encouraging her to read. Because the Rosses were a family of storytellers, Miller observed first hand the way in which family incidents become narratives and myths. Her competetive nature surfaced when she was 10 years old and discovered that her father had published a novel (his first and only) before she did.

Fulfilling her early sense of vocation, Heather Ross seriously pursued writing when she attended college. Not "keen" on going anywhere, she chose the Woman's College of the University of North Carolina, Greensboro, because her Ross aunts had gone there. She had, of course, heard Randall Jarrell's praises sung by her family; but with the diffidence of youth, she was determined to be "unimpressed." Miller overcame her indifference to both college and Jarrell. A Phi Beta Kappa student, she graduated magna cum laude in 1961 and was awarded a Woodrow Wilson Fellowship. In Randall Jarrell she found an inspirational teacher who taught her to recognize what was "cooked-up and phony" in her poetry. Although Jarrell was not interested in close analysis of students' poems (he always read them aloud), he indicated lines that should be removed and urged students to write truthfully. Miller continues to value Jarrell's instruction and his conviction that poems "are sort-of mystical creations," but she prefers teaching the workshop method that she learned in other classes at Women's College. In tribute to Jarrell, poet and teacher, Miller has commemorated him in poetry ("October 1965," "The Cremation of R. J.," and "Coyote Ghost: The Rising of Randall Jarrell"), in essay ("The Gift of True Pitch: Randall Jarrell"), and in a forthcoming critical book, *The White Snake.*

In 1960 Heather Ross married Clyde H. Miller, a state-park superintendent. Living for several years on a reserve in the eastern part of North Carolina with her husband and her two children, Melissa Martha and Kirk Alexander, Heather Miller experienced firsthand an isolation similar to that endured by early American settlers. This experience profoundly influenced Miller's art, leading her to examine the effects of isolation on the individual and the community. She has set stories and poems in state parks. The narrator of her first novel, *The Edge of the Woods,* is married to a park superintendent, and she plans to write a "state-park" novel that will include "murder and violence." These park settings, stripped of the civilizing effects of society, reveal the violence that lies beneath the surface of the ordinary.

While teaching at Pfeiffer College (1965–67), Heather Miller returned to Greensboro for an MFA, which she received in 1969. From 1969 to 1972, she chaired the Departmant of English at Southeastern Community College, Whiteville; and from 1972 through 1974, she participated in the "Poetry-in-the-Schools" program sponsored by the North Carolina State Department of Education. She returned in 1974 to her native Stanly County for a term as writer-in-residence at Stanly Technical Institute. In 1977 she accepted a position as chair of the Department of Speech and Writing at Pfeiffer College. A year as Visiting Professor of Creative Writing at the University of Arkansas (1983–84) turned into a permanent position when she assumed the directorship of the university's MFA program in writing. Since 1984, Miller has taught at the University of Arkansas, returning frequently to her home in Badin, North Carolina. In 1992 Miller moved from Arkansas to Washington and Lee University in Lexington, Virginia, where she teaches creative writing and serves as fiction editor for *Shenandoah.*

Although Heather Miller is a committed teacher, she is, first, a writer. The talent that Jarrell recognized and fostered bore immediate fruit with *The Edge of the Woods* (1964). Recognized as an impressive first work, the novel was awarded the National Association of Independent Schools Award for Best First

Novel in 1964. Her second novel, *Tenants of the House* (1966), received the Sir Walter Raleigh Prize for Fiction in 1966. The following year, Miller received a Creative Writing Fellowship from the National Endowment for the Arts; and her first book of poems, *The Wind Southerly* (1967), was awarded the Arnold Young Cup for Poetry in 1968. Her third novel, *Gone a Hundred Miles,* appeared in 1968.

During the 1970s, Miller continued the pace she had set in the 1960s. She received her second Creative Writing Fellowship from the National Endowment of the Arts in 1973 and was awarded the Alumni Award for Outstanding Achievement in Literature by the University of North Carolina at Greensboro in 1976. Red Clay Books published a second book of Miller's poetry in 1973, *Horse Horse Tyger Tyger;* and John F. Blair brought out a collection of Miller's short fiction, *A Spiritual Divorce and Other Stories,* in the following year. *Confessions of a Champeen Fire Baton Twirler,* a book that Miller has since rewritten and renamed *Champeen,* appeared in 1976. Twenty years of intensive writing and teaching closed with a Cultural Exchange Fellowship from the National Endowment for the Arts in 1979, enabling Miller to live and write in England.

Like many other Southern writers, Miller has enjoyed popularity in France. Gallimard has published *L'Ore Des Bois (The Edge of the Woods)* and *L'Autre Bout Du Monde (Gone a Hundred Miles).* Stories appearing in various editions of *La Nouvelle Revue Française* include "Tante Zina," "Delphee," and "La Jupe Espagnole." *Freaks of Nature* (novella) is currently being translated by Michael Gresset (University of Paris), who has translated several of her works.

Miller enters middle life with the same disciplined energy and vitality she has displayed throughout her career. Teaching in the afternoon, she writes every morning. As an artist who values craftsmanship, she revises as she writes. To achieve the "magic of scenes" and authentic voice in the pared-down style she prefers, Miller will rewrite an entire manuscript two or three times before submitting it to her agent. Her attitude toward point of view has shifted during the 25 years she has been publishing. She now regards first person point of view (except in the hands of a few masters such as Mark Twain) as "self-indulgent." For this reason, she has rewritten *Confessions of a Champeen Fire Baton Twirler* and contemplates rewriting *The Edge of the Woods,* deleting in both the confessional aspects. In the meantime, Miller has completed and handed over to her agent two new novels, *A Family Picture* and *Romance at Short Notice,* and a collection of short fiction, *Common Mistakes in English. Friends and Assassins,* a collection of poems, appeared in 1992.

In the 1980s Miller ventured into new territory as she collaborated with David Ott, musician friend and colleague from Pfeiffer College, to write libretti for several oratorios and operettas he composed. Three of their commissioned works have been performed, including an oratorio celebrating the birthday of Martin Luther King, Jr., commissioned by DePauw University Choir. Presently, she is revising a long poem, "Aluminum," which is being set to music by composer

Ed Johnson. Her achievement in writing and teaching earned her the North Carolina Award in Literature in 1983.

Still very much in the Southern tradition regarding voice, centrality of family, and concern with the past as a germinating force in the present, Miller transcends local or regional identities as she examines in fiction and in poetry the human desire to order and to understand the natural world and to reconcile infinite yearnings with finite existence.

MAJOR THEMES

Set in the Uwharrie hill country of North Carolina, *The Edge of the Woods,* is a first-person narrative alternating between present and past time. As an adult, the protagonist Anna Marie seeks through marriage and motherhood to reclaim the faith in the patterns of life she lost as a child in witnessing her grandfather murder his second wife and grandchild (Anna Marie's brother). Played out against the remnants of the Ocoee Mountains, "the oldest range in America," human action is both diminished and elevated in this novel: diminished by the passage of time signified by the mountains; elevated by the universality of the human drama.

In this novel as in most of Miller's works, innocence as an ambiguous and troubling aspect of existence is a major theme. As a child, Anna Marie is as much betrayed by parents whose innocence keeps them from suspecting the possibility of evil in the ordinary as she is by the grandfather who beats to death the grandchild he once played with by the fire. Later, Anna Marie marries a man who lives "in harmony with the earth," hoping through him to be reconciled with her haunted memories. She comes to believe that his acceptance of life results partly from the fact that "there was no perplexity in [his] childhood." She cannot, therefore, submerge herself in him. She must find her own way to live with her knowledge that innocence is betrayed. Anna Marie is the first of several protagonists in Miller's fiction and poetry who survive through such knowledge.

In her second novel, *Tenants of the House,* Miller traces the lives of several families in order to reveal the emptiness underlying the rituals of small-town life. Set in the same region of North Carolina, this narrative depicts the lives of various "tenants" of Jonesboro, an aluminum-company town of "identical apartments spread out around the narrow streets that were crisscrossed at corners by cement drainage ditches or graveled back alleys" (7). Miller's use of T.S. Eliot's "Gerontion" as both the source of the novel's title and epigraph, indicates the continued influence of his wasteland vision on her work. (In *The Edge of the Woods,* Anna Marie's husband is a Fisher King figure, promising new life.)

Thematically, the "dry season" alluded to in the Eliot reference is manifest in the loneliness brought about by failed connections among the townspeople. Occurring in the background, World War II is a muted reminder of chaos;

enmity between couples and indifference among neighbors suggest the loss of a center nearer home. Raymond Rundus has correctly asserted, however, that the novel affirms life by closing with "the cyclical pattern of nature . . . and [linking this pattern] with the cycle of human life and with the past, present, and future of Jonesboro" (125).

The appearance of Miller's first book of poetry, *The Winds Southerly* (in 1967), revealed patterns in her use of dreams, literary allusions, imagery, even character and situation familiar to readers of her fiction. Several poems, including "Waianae Mary," "Midwatch," and "Gunnery," recall the Pacific War where Gene Boyette of *Tenants of the House* serves on the battleship *West Virginia*. "Apion" anticipates her third novel, for the lovers in this poem are central characters in the fiction. The murder-suicide subject of "Gilead" resembles the memory that haunts Anna Marie in *The Edge of the Woods*. In the poem, Miller deals directly with the repressive effects of a religion practiced by "hollow women" and "their strange mates." In the novel she implies the influence of sterile religious practices through character and plot development. Irony, a dominant tone in many of Miller's poems, is achieved primarily through her juxtaposition of the violent crime with the promise that the tree in Gilead will "heal the sin-sick soul."

The poems in *The Wind Southerly* suggest Miller's control of language and her thematic interest in forms of separateness, the ultimate irony of existence. Two poems portray sterility through images of snow and whiteness. "Snow Prison" describes a place where "the window of winter is a tight tear-freeze." In "Queen Anne Street," the speaker associates the snow with the isolation of life in a city.

Like other Southern writers (notably Eudora Welty), Miller frequently uses myths directly or indirectly in her works. Often she recouches a myth in colloquial speech to reassert its original vigor in a contemporary setting, or she sets a mythic character in a modern setting to dramatize the distance between human and divine natures. In this collection, "Grandma Leda" is determined to show her granddaughters that hell is not a remote mythic place but a dark upstairs bedroom in the farm house where a framed swan "hoists his big wings."

Women as lovers, mothers, and presentient human beings recognize in Miller's poems that all alliances—whether between men and women, parents and children, or humans and the natural world—are but tentative at best. A comet "thrusting west" reminds the wife who watches the phenomenon that the unexpected always appears in the midst of the ordinary; life cannot be controlled.

Miller occasionally writes in her own voice, drawing on her personal experiences; but she is not a "confessional" poet. In "Poem for My Daughter," for instance, the speaker contrasts her summers of "simple blue" skies with her daughter's view of nature in the "deer park" they inhabit. Innocent eyes perceive both worlds, but the mother recognizes the implied differences between the "green-dark" afternoon her daughter knows and her own open-skied childhood.

Miller turns to history in her third novel, *Gone a Hundred Miles,* to examine the destructive effects of power on an individual. North Carolina novelist and journalist Sylvia Wilkinson observes that "the background of this book is the familiar South but the perspective is new as we watch a character from the outside who can bend and twist the land and people to suit his wishes" (552). Dr. Philip Tscharner brings his French wife to North Carolina in 1824, settles in Larkin County, and devotes his life to taming the wilderness and healing the "strange primitive people that occupy the land around his Apion Mountains" (Wilkinson 552). In developing the character of Dr. Tscharner, Miller draws on the diary and horticultural notes of Dr. Franz J. Kron housed in the Stanley County, North Carolina, Public Library. The final scenes of the novel show Dr. Tscharner's destruction by the natural forces he had struggled to contain.

Creating an "absorbing narrative experience" (Rundus 127), Miller explores themes common to fictional and nonfictional accounts of settlement in the New World. Isolation, even more than poverty, erodes civilizing graces and imposes an intense loneliness on the settlers. The lack of companionship, occupation, and purpose finally destroys the doctor's first wife, Kaethe. Born in Larkin County, Tscharner's second wife, Cassandra, draws knowledge and strength from the physical world. She serves the doctor faithfully as wife and medical assistant (she has firsthand knowledge of medicinal plants) but offers, also, a contrasting relationship to nature. She has the ability to lose her identity in nature; he must impose rational order.

The darker potential of both the natural and human worlds threatens to overwhelm the inhabitants of the remote settlement. A foreshadowing event in the first chapter in which an owl "unnaturally" attacks the doctor's horse as he rides through a misty forest climaxes in the unnatural severity of a storm that destroys the doctor's plantation and takes his life. Not versed in natural things, Tscharner does not possess the survivor's ability to accept the dark and "unnatural" as part of the larger cycle of existence. Miller's ironic perpective is clear. The truly unnatural element in the story is the imperial human will. The incestuous subplot reinforces this irony. A brother and sister denied love by their parent, turn to one another. Preoccupied with curing the sick and cultivating the land, Dr. Tscharner fails to nurture his children with love and thereby fosters destructive behavior.

Although his defiance and blindness to troubles in his family destroy the doctor in the end, Dr. Tscharner does possess the wisdom usually reserved for Miller's enduring characters. In a conversation with Cassandra regarding the bodily decay occurring after death, Dr. Tscharner claims that knowledge compensates for loss and decay when he tells her that "the fact that you and I can comprehend such thoughts is more significant than perhaps the sea, which has no mind and comprehends nothing" (211). Although the doctor represents pioneer arrogance in his efforts to subdue the wilderness on his own terms, he also represents those settlers who asserted the civilizing influence of reason on a chaotic new world.

Horse Horse Tyger Tyger, Miller's second volume of poems, includes poems with political overtones, poems about the environment, poems about Native Americans, and poems that update fairy tales and myths. As she revealed in her first collection, Miller is especially concerned with the patterns shaping women's lives.

Four poems linked together under the title "Mama" allow "Grandma Mary Virgin," "Ribmama," "Grandma Jocasta," and "Cinderellamama" to present their versions of their celebrated narratives or roles. Looked at from the long reach of time, the four women speak for all women bound to earth and home and childbearing and knowledgeable "about life, about men."

Miller believes that men and women are generally not successful at interchanging voices. Although she writes consistently in a female voice, she is not stridently feminist. Her women express their insights in melancholy, sardonic, or matter-of-fact voices, feeling a little superior to be "in" on the "joke" of life, but finding compensations and even rewards in their roles. Historically, women may have been denied heroic roles, but the power they realize through their knowledge brings them other kinds of victories. As Prioska reminds the wolf in the poem named for her, "I wear your teeth around my neck."

Using short lines and direct statements, most poems in this collection blend colloquial speech with strong visual imagery. The speaker in "Lumbee Children" informs the present moment by acknowledging the history of the Lumbees when the speaker identifies the children as "figurines" and "relics."

Several poems in the collection deal with the paradox of parenthood. As the child experiences each stage of growing up, the mother recognizes the distance between herself and her child widening; at the same time, she becomes acutely conscious of her own life's progression in the child's cyclical replay. Miller confronts this paradox directly in "Growing Old," where the mother regrets the inevitable "turning loose." In "Melissa Learning to Write," "The Chemistry Set," and "Taking Steps at Thirteen Months," the mothers express both the childrens' struggles to move forward and their own bittersweet awareness that each success widens the gap between parent and child. The final poem in the collection, "Happy Horse," from which the title of the book is derived, suggests the fierceness of a mother's love through animal imagery. Even though the mother's love leaps "like a tyger," it cannot prevent the approaching womanhood of her daughter who must "sing her own song."

Miller's first collection of short stories, *A Spiritual Divorce and Other Stories* (1974), is dedicated to Michel Gresset, who has translated into French several of her works, including three stories in this collection. The stories are psychological studies in which dreams figure prominently. Economically constructed, the stories end with implied rather than stated resolutions in the manner of much contemporary short fiction. Two of the stories, "Little Orlando" and "Don't

Cry,'' are set in state parks and draw on Miller's experiences as the wife of a forest ranger. Emma's husband in ''Little Orlando'' and Anne's husband in ''Don't Cry'' resemble Mark in *The Edge of the Woods*. They are men ''at one with the snow and the forest, the wild snarling dogs, the placid January sky'' (''Don't Cry'' 120). The wives have also married ''unperplexed'' men; and like Anna Marie in the novel, they hope to stabilize their own imaginative natures. Both women find themselves more lonely than they were when they lived ''ordinary'' fragmented community lives. They discover that isolation demands a kind of innocence they have either lost or never had. Contrary to Thoreau's gospel, living in the woods brings them too close to the edge, the boundary where savage and civilized pull them in conflicting directions. Their lives make them acutely conscious of the frailty of life and the possibility that it may be meaningless.

Several stories in *A Spiritual Divorce* present children, uncannily wise for their years, facing a crisis. In these and other stories, dreams reveal subconscious fears or foreshadow future events. The children's narratives balance the poems about parenthood by showing how terrifying growing up can be, especially when parents abnegate their roles. In the title story ''A Spiritual Divorce,'' 5-year-old Jason already knows that he cannot find safety in ''the big house . . . with all the modern conveniences'' (6). The people in his life who offer him stability are the black maid, Rosalind, and her ''spiritual'' husband, Monrow. When he is with them, Jason is not just a ''personae in a pretty drama''; he is a real human boy who can ''sinfully swing on tree limbs'' (7). Jason loses this security at the end of the story when confronted with circumstances suggesting a dark and frightening side of life he is not ready to face.

In ''Maria Is Hurt,'' Maria dreams she will be devoured by a lion during her feverish bout with polio. As she drifts in and out of consciousness, Maria is aware that her warring parents quarrel even as they hover over her bed. Knowing that her handsome father has ''betrayed'' her mother, Maria both fears her father and senses his attraction. The lion in her dream comes to resemble, with significant Freudian implications, her father.

Although the psychological patterns are clearly revealed in the behavior, thoughts, and dreams of her fictional children, Miller does not present merely case studies. She embues her children with a saving knowledge that arms all of her survivors. Facing their existential crises early, they are prepared for adulthood. The adolescent girl in ''Aunt Zena'' learns the secret of survival as she walks ''under the frozen trees'' one winter listening to her Swedish aunt-in-law relate stories of her life in Sweden. As the season and Zena's tale of being lost in the frozen mountains of her native land progress, the 15-year-old niece bears the cold of her own life more easily. The story culminates with a dream, almost identical to Zena's story, in which the narrator discovers a frozen river. Following the river, she understands that ''being cold [is] a way of life'' (22). When she awakens in the cold darkness of her room, she rises from her bed to see how ''sharp the [stars were] through the glass'' (22).

Miller also revitalizes myths with earthy dark humor. Such is the case with the story "Delphi." The "oracle" in this narrative is a strong-willed, worrisome (to her children) old woman who hears a voice coming up from the heat register by her "emerald green arm chair." Usually the voice tells her homely news— for example, that her son Donald is writing her a letter. But as the story climaxes, Mrs. Ricks hears the voice in the register become bolder and louder as it urges her to "Wean them. Shuck them off and trample on them in the dust, the husband and babes of your bosom! It's the Lord's Will" (76). The final lines of the story suggest that Mrs. Ricks might indeed "shuck them off" as she turns from the pier glass and its crazy reflections to attack. Although she does not always blend the ordinary and the mysterious in such grim or darkly foreboding ways, Miller consistently presents life as complex and paradoxical.

Confessions of a Champeen Baton Twirler offers a comic view of a spirited young girl's coming of age in Palestine, North Carolina (the aluminum-town setting of *Tenants of the House*). Titania Anne Gentry describes herself as "twelve going on eighteen" in the year she wants "a crimson sequined body-suit, a long silver baton aflame at either end, and the radiant crown of a champeen set firmly on [her] head" (6). She also wants, later in the year, when he returns home to recover from wounds received in the war, "Soldier Sebastian McSherry." The first person narration recounts Titania's efforts to become a champion fire-baton twirler and to win the love of Soldier Sebastian. Along the way, she must persuade her mother, who "believed . . . in more practical things like pianos, good looks, and a complete set of sterling silver, Brier Rose pattern," that baton twirling is a respectable achievement (7).

Like Miller's other child narrators, Titania adopts a maternal attitude toward her parents, whom she calls Joan and Franklin. She witnesses many arguments between them, generally caused by Franklin's drinking and infidelity. Once, Joan dramatically tries to commit suicide by jumping out of the second-story bedroom window. Her daughter's description of the incident is one of the funniest in the novel.

As an initiation story, this narrative traces a child's maturation through her loss of innocence. The ironic twist on the expected plot development is that Titania's innocence is blended with adult wisdom. Although she wisely recognizes her parents' frailties, Titania must learn to differentiate between her own unrealizable fantasies, such as her desire to marry the soldier next door, and attainable ambitions. Sebastian's friendly efforts to help her perfect her baton twirling and his practical assistance in attaching burning torches to her baton ease the disappointment the young girl feels at being denied her romantic dreams.

Confessions of a Champeen Fire Baton Twirler is not without the sobering themes characteristic of Miller's works. The action is set against the background of World War II. While the war's action seems as remote as it does in *Tenants of the House,* a bizaar accident occurring one afternoon when an airplane suddenly falls into the lake "as neatly as if the pilot had made it fall with his cunning champeen's tricks'' (59), reminds Titania that the ''world was a naked place,'' even in the beehive community of Palestine, North Carolina (58).

The child's efforts to win her own victories as the world's first fire-baton twirler merges with her spiritual quest to know her worth. The adult Titania, who recalls the year of the baton, remarks early on in the narrative that she has ''made choices which were in the last examination, compromises, clearly rainbow-colored Peaces with God'' (3).

Miller has rewritten this novel, eliminating the confessions by changing the point of view from first to third person. She has also added characters, changed the opening scene, and eliminated passages, but the novel is still, as its title indicates, about a *Champeen.*

The 1980s were productive years for Miller. She published poems in *Southern Poetry Review, North Carolina Folklore, Redbook, The Crescent Review, Ploughshares, Shenandoah,* and *Abatis.* Having published a number of her poems, *Kentucky Poetry Review* awarded her their Blaine Hall Award for ''I Dream I Drown Myself on Purpose, Not on Purpose,'' in 1988, and in 1990 published a Heather Ross Miller issue including contributions from ''friends and acquaintances.'' *The Laurel Review,* which has included Miller's poems in several issues, nominated her poem ''Playing Dress-Up'' for a Pushcart Prize in 1989.

Poems published in periodicals of the 1980s are collected with unpublished poems in *Hard Evidence* (1990), and in 1992, Miller published a poetry collection, *Friends and Assassins.* In newer poems, Miller continues to explore topics and themes familiar to her readers. Leda is a modern consumer in ''Leda Talks Back to Zeus.'' Through her complaints and boasts, the poet satirizes American consumerism, and, at the same time, questions the place of religion in contemporary life. A different perspective on divine/human interactions is expressed in ''A Girl with Many Moving Parts.'' The poem's speaker, a syrinx perfectly designed of ''mouthpieces and fingerholes,'' is angered by the paradox of her existence; she hurls epithets at her creator, claiming that his role as a shepherd is a hoax. As the poem climaxes, the physical/spiritual duality is resolved.

Miller's religious poems may also be read as poems about the role of the artist in the world. ''The Liberating'' presents the descent into hell and the resurrection of the god-figure in terms of a being trapped in a bleak winter landscape. As the god ascends from the river, he realizes his human/divine nature in both language and form; so, too, poets may rejuvenate frozen landscapes by infusing immanence with transcendence.

Entering her fourth decade as a writer of uncompromising integrity, Heather Miller continues to sing of ''dragons and horses'' and to create memorable female survivors armed for life with the knowledge that they may not run with the wolf, but they may wear his teeth 'round their necks.

SURVEY OF CRITICISM

Richard Walser (1986) called Miller's early fiction, ''Southern Gothic.'' His identifying tag represents the general consensus of reviewers who responded to

Miller's fiction in the 1960s. These reviewers called attention to Miller's stylistic achievements, hailing *The Edge of the Woods* as a remarkable first novel. W. Warren Wagar (1965) praised the book for "commanding attention by its uncompromising honesty, subtle indirections of style and technique, and its indescribably haunting overtones" (viii). Similarly, a reviewer for *New York Review of Books* (1966) described her style as "genuinely poetic . . . without a trace of the obfuscations of Spanish moss and other growth that frequently cloud the style of Southern writers" (23). Barbara Solomon (1964) remarked about Miller's "extraordinary sense of style, knowing just where to begin, what to put in, and what to leave out" (20).

When *Tenants of the House* appeared in 1965, reviewers, expecting another award-winning novel, were disappointed. Most found much to praise in the novel, regretting primarily its brevity. *The Virginia Quarterly Review* noted that in "slightly more than one hundred pages, Mrs. Miller writes of the inhabitants of a small Southern town and their lives during the Second World War. . . . There are too many events and too many characters for such a slow and brooding novel which is also so small: a symphony scored for string quartet." A critic for the *New York Review of Books* found the novel satisfying as a poem, "a symbolist poem at that. Much of its distinction comes from the way in which the centripetal movement typical of symbolist fiction is countered by the outward pull of history and the actual world" (23). Less inclined to appreciate the brooding quality or the symbolist style of the novel, Barbara Raskin (1966) attacked the novel as derivative and formulaic, an example of fiction being written by "educated writers for a 'trained audience' " (227).

In spite of its flaws, most critics admired *Tenants of the House* for its ambitious scope and stylistic strengths, and reviewers of her third novel, *Gone a Hundred Miles,* were impressed by Miller's control of her material. Sylvia Wilkinson (1968) applauded the novel's realization of the central character, Dr. Tscharner. Wilkinson noted that the "background . . . is the familiar South but the perspective is new" (552). Miller's short story collection, *A Spiritual Divorce and Other Stories* earned approval for its display of "extraordinary power."

Two longer pieces will assist scholars beginning work on Miller. For her M.A. thesis (1968), Doris Annette Wenger explored Miller's use of dreams and dream imagery to allow "several perspectives upon her characters" (4). Finding the major theme of the first two novels to be the isolated individual's search for identity and for a way to "build personal relationships," Wenger pointed out that Miller uses dreams both as psychological expressions of repressed instinctive urges and as a means for the character to deal with unresolved problems. Her study includes a discussion of the novel's "dream-like quality," manifest in the writer's use of "imagery, allusions, and symbolism" (48). Wenger's thesis is also valuable for its bibliography of reviews and background sources related to the dreams and to mythic, legendary, and literary allusions.

Raymond J. Rundus (1975) traces common themes in Miller's first three novels. Rundus notes first that Miller in 1968 was much more than a ''promising young writer, [for] her early writing already showed strong discipline in style, plotting, and characterization and a deep and assertive exploration of the human condition'' (123). Calling attention to the fact that the ''key motifs'' in all three novels are ''memory, dream, and forecast, motifs that also permeate the tragedies of Aeschylus and Sophocles,'' Rundus examines each novel in detail to illustrate Miller's ability to ''particularize'' universal experiences in ''individual experience'' (123).

Miller is an artist who confronts and relishes complexity. She is a Southern writer who explores the American experience and human struggles for identity so central in American experience. She provides a rich variety of female characters who are refreshing alternatives to conventional portrayals of women. As a Southern writer, Miller explores the prevalence of social aberrations among people too long exposed to poverty and repressive forms of Protestantism, but she also celebrates the beauty and mystery of the natural world and the dignity of enduring individuals. Her continued publication of award-winning poetry and impressive fiction forecasts long overdue critical attention.

BIBLIOGRAPHY

Works by Heather Ross Miller

Works of Poetry

The Wind Southerly. New York: Harcourt Brace Jovanovich, 1967.
Horse Horse Tyger Tyger. Charlotte, N.C.: Red Clay Books, 1974.
Adam's First Wife. Camden, S.C.: Chapbook Poetry, Briarpatch Press, 1983.
Hard Evidence. Columbia: University of Missouri Press, 1990.
Friends and Assassins. Columbia: University of Missouri Press, 1992. (First published Raleigh, N.C: North Carolina Review Press, 1976.)

Works of Prose

The Edge of the Woods. New York: Atheneum, 1964.
Tenants of the House. New York: Harcourt, Brace & World, 1966.
Gone a Hundred Miles. New York: Harcourt, Brace & World, 1968.
A Spiritual Divorce and Other Stories. Charlotte, N.C.: Blair, 1974.
Confessions of a Champeen Fire Baton Twirler. Raleigh: North Carolina Review Press, 1992. (First published Raleigh, N.C.: North Carolina Review Press, 1976.)

Essays and Reviews

''The Candlewalk: A Midwinter Fire Festival.'' *North Carolina Folklore Journal* 19 (1971): 53–56.
Introduction to *Down Zion's Alley,* by Emily Herring Wilson. Winston-Salem, N.C.: Drummer Press, 1972.
''Like the Bones of Dreams.'' *American Scholar* 45 (Autumn 1976): 688–92.
''Down a Dark Road.'' *American Scholar* 55 (Summer 1986): 423–29.

Translated Works

L'Orée des bois (The edge of the woods). Translated by Michel Gresset. Paris: Gallimard, 1967.

À l'autre bout du monde (Gone a hundred miles). Translated by Michel Gresset. Paris: Gallimard, 1970.

"Delphée" (Delphi). *La Nouvelle Revue Française* (February 1972).

"Tante Zina" (Aunt Zina). *La Nouvelle Revue Française* (February 1972).

"La Jupe Espagnole" (The Spanish Skirt). *La Nouvelle Revue Française* (November 1987).

Interviews with Heather Ross Miller

Jarrell, Randall Seminar. Heather Ross Miller, participant. University of South Carolina Institute for Southern Studies, September 30–October 3, 1988, Columbia, S.C. Audiotape of the seminar housed with the SC Institute for Southern Studies.

Miller, Heather Ross. Videotaped interview with Parks Lanier. Highlands Summer Conference, Radford University, June 1988. Housed in the Radford University Library, Radford, Va.

Studies of Heather Ross Miller

Corsini, Ray Pierre. "Everytown, U.S.A." *New York Times Book Review* (February 27, 1966): 42.

Dalmas, Victor. "The Exquisite Style of Heather Miller." *Pembroke Magazine* 8 (1977): 183.

"Heather Ross Miller." In *Contemporary Authors,* edited by Evory, Ann, 372–73. Vol. 5. Dctroit: Gale Research, 1982.

Hicks, Granville. "Window on an Inner Wilderness." *Saturday Review* 40 (August 15, 1966): 32–36.

Parker, Elaine. "Heather Ross Miller's *A Spiritual Divorce and Other Stories.*" In *A Critical Survey of Short Fiction: Current Writers with Index,* vol. 7, edited by Frank N. McGill. Englewood Cliffs, N.J.: Salem Press, 1981: 2722.

Pine, J. C. Review of *Tenants of the House. Library Journal* 91 (February 1, 1966): 715.

Prescott, Orville. "A Poetic Example of Southern Gothic." *New York Times* (August 17, 1964): 3.

Raskin, Barbara. "Taking No Risks." Review of *Tenants of the House. Nation* (September 12, 1966): 227–29.

Review of *Edge of the Woods. New York Review of Books* 4 (April 8, 1965): 8.

Review of *Tenants of the House. New York Review of Books* 6 (April 28, 1966): 23.

Review of *Gone a Hundred Miles. New York Review of Books.* 10 (April 11, 1968): 36.

Review of *A Spiritual Divorce and Other Stories. Virginia Quarterly Review* 51 (Summer 1975): 114.

Rundus, Raymond J. "The Fiction of Heather Ross Miller." *Pembroke Magazine* 6 (1975): 123–28.

Solomon, Barbara P. "The Nightmare of Anna Marie." *New York Times Book Review* (August 30, 1964): 20.

Wagar, W. Warren. Review of *Edge of the Woods*. *Virginia Quarterly Review* 41 (Winter 1965): 8.

Walser, Richard, and E. T. Malone, Jr. *Literary North Carolina*. Raleigh: Division of Archives and History, North Carolina Department of Cultural Resources, 1986.

Wenger, Doris Annette. ''Heather Ross Miller's Use of Dreams to Elucidate the Search for Identity.'' Master's thesis, University of North Carolina, Chapel Hill, 1967.

Wilkinson, Sylvia. Review of *Gone a Hundred Miles*. *American Scholar* 37 (Summer 1968): 552.

JOYCE DYER

Jim Wayne Miller
(1936–   )

With his watershed volume *Dialogue with a Dead Man* (1974), and especially with the introduction of his character the Brier in *The Mountains Have Come Closer* (1980), Jim Wayne Miller's position as a major Appalachian poet was secure. In addition, Miller is actively involved in the promotion of the Appalachian movement through his work as educator, speaker, and theorist.

BIOGRAPHY

Jim Wayne Miller was born to Edith Smith Miller and James Woodrow on October 21, 1936. He attended Leicester elementary and high schools in Buncombe County, North Carolina, the place of his birth. In his volumes of verse and fiction, Miller frequently incorporates essential moments from his Appalachian boyhood. We meet chairmakers from the neighborhood, hear his grandfather's story about a great squirrel migration, feel the pain of a whipping his mother received over a lost carpenter's tool, and watch his grandfather's Walker foxhound anguish in a trap that Miller as a boy was warned not to set.

Miller's Appalachian background has provided him with a unique and important sense of family and land and with a distinct aesthetic. In his highly autobiographical novel about boyhood titled *Newfound* (1989), Miller recalls the shame of difference he was made to feel when he entered a consolidated school in eighth grade. Teachers closely examined Newfound children for head lice, preached manners rather than shoeless pleasure, and worked in missionary fashion for uniformity. The young narrator writes, "I never grew accustomed to feeling shame. Each time, it flared up hotter than before, and raced from the center out, popping and cracking like a brush fire, leaving everything black and smoldering inside" (98).

But at Berea College, the school Miller entered in 1954 and graduated from in 1958 with a B.A. in English, his regional experience would be strongly validated. The rural world of his maternal and paternal grandparents, including the original way they spoke ("Did you come to borry fire?"), was praised at Berea rather than ridiculed. At Berea, Miller developed his interest in German language and culture, participating in the Experiment in International Living program in 1957, which took him to Germany. But even more important was the role Berea played in the development of Miller's lasting commitment to Appalachia and mountain ways.

Miller married Mary Ellen Yates, originally from Carter County, Kentucky, on August 17, 1958, shortly after his graduation from Berea. Mary Ellen is an associate professor of English at Western Kentucky University, where she has assisted with such special projects as the establishment of a Canadian Studies Program and the Robert Penn Warren Center. The Millers are parents of James Yates (b. 1962), Fred Smith (b. 1963), and Ruth Ratcliff (b. 1967). All three children are currently pursuing art careers.

After teaching high-school German for two years at Fort Knox dependent schools in Kentucky, Miller headed to Vanderbilt University on a National Defense Fellowship. There he studied both American and German literature, working closely with Donald Davidson and Hawthorne scholar Randall Stewart. He completed his Ph.D. in 1965.

Since 1963, Miller has been on the faculty of Western Kentucky University in Bowling Green, Kentucky, where he is Professor of German Language and Literature in the Department of Modern Languages and Intercultural Studies. His commitment to Western Kentucky and his profession has brought him frequent recognition from his university. In 1969 he won the Sigma Tau Delta Topaz Award for Distinguished Service to the University; in 1976 he received his institution's faculty award for research and creativity; in 1982 he was presented with the faculty award for public service. Berea College awarded Miller its highest honors—an honorary doctorate of letters in 1981 and the Distinguished Alumnus Award in 1983. In 1991 Miller received the Laurel Leaves Award from the Appalachian Consortium.

Miller earned the Alice Lloyd Memorial Prize for Appalachian Poetry in 1967 for poems in *Copperhead Cane,* the prestigious Thomas Wolfe Literary Award for *The Mountains Have Come Closer,* and the Appalachia Writers Association Award in 1984 for *Vein of Words.* He always receives honors with a humility born from both innate shyness and his hatred of pretension. He has eloquently announced his suspicion in the poem "I Share" from *The Mountains Have Come Closer:* "I am wary of commencements, ritual initiations, / the keynote address at three-day conferences, / programs where any honor is conferred" (10).

The title most commonly associated with Miller is "poet." He currently has published seven volumes of poetry—the first, *Copperhead Cane,* in 1964. In the 1960s, Miller published only a few poems beyond those in this volume. Like many young poets, he seemed to be learning his craft through short stories, publishing over a dozen in that decade.

Miller, who grew up in the midst of banjo and french-harp players and whose wife's great-uncle Lige Adams was a songwriter, published his second collection of poetry in 1971, a group of folk ballads about change and politics in Appalachia called *The More Things Change the More They Stay the Same.* But it would be 3 more years before his watershed volume *Dialogue with a Dead Man* would appear and vault him into prominence. In that volume's first section, Miller has included seventeen of the original twenty-one poems from *Copperhead Cane.* Although in this volume Miller has expressed the deep personal regret over the death of his grandfather and of the old ways, his writing in the last two sections exhibits significant artistic evolution and expansion. In these last two sections, Miller gradually moves away from individual grief toward a more comprehensive family grief, shifting simultaneously from the sonnet to free-verse forms.

In *The Mountains Have Come Closer,* Miller's next collection of poems, Miller introduced a new element into some of his poems that has since become his trademark—the figure of the Brier. In a 1988 interview with Loyal Jones at the Emory and Henry College literary festival, Miller called the Brier "an Appalachian Everyman," "a synecdoche." A key piece titled "Brier Sermon— 'You Must Be Born Again' " ends Miller's 1980 volume with remarkable intensity.

After *The Mountains Have Come Closer,* Miller published two volumes of poetry before returning to the Brier, though throughout the 1980s he was publishing Brier poems in independent journals and anthologies. *Vein of Words* (1984) gives advice to aspiring poets and writers. *Nostalgia for 70* (1986), in part a collection of many earlier pieces in periodicals, records the disillusionment of the suburban academic.

In *Brier, His Book* (1988), Miller continues to advance the story of the Brier, introduced in Part Two and Part Three of *The Mountains Have Come Closer.* The Brier truly has come back home now, has seen the problems and changes in his region and in himself, and has begun to be "reborn" to the sort of Appalachian consciousness outlined in "Brier Sermon."

Miller often writes in forms other than poetry. Whatever he writes, however, is informed by his innate lyrical sense as well as his insatiable interest in Appalachian matters. In his interview with Loyal Jones, Miller modestly assessed his ability as a writer of fiction: "I don't think I have the narrative power a novelist requires." And yet, Miller's long story *His First, Best Country* (1987) has enjoyed exceptional popularity and critical acclaim, encouraging him to transform the story into both a two-act play and a novel. In 1989 Orchard Press successfully marketed Miller's *Newfound* as a novel for young adults. Deeply connected to the people, episodes, and images in the poems that precede it,

Newfound was selected by *Learning Magazine* as Best Book of the year. And Miller's 1993 novel-length revision of his 1987 short story, also titled *His First, Best Country,* has been hailed as "a small miracle," "as beautiful and as absolutely mysterious as the 500 redbirds or the 500 black and orange butterflies we read about within its pages" (Dyer 1994, 206).

The satirical essay is one of Miller's favorite forms. In 1986 he published *Sideswipes,* a collection of essays that poke fun at American consumerism and the regional tendency to embellish and mythologize history. *The Wisdom of Folk Metaphor* (1988), a long poem, also belongs in the category of satire, cynically attacking both education and students of the 1980s. And in *Round and Round with Kahil Gibran* (1990), Miller bitingly and cleverly concludes that what Gibran composes are not poems, but "fuzzy-wuzzies—adorable pastel cuties that hang in the mind the way carnival prizes dangle from rearview mirrors."

Miller has also translated a major work by Austrian poet Emil Lerperger, *The Figure of Fulfillment* (1975), as well as individual poems by Christine Busta, Peter Henisch, and Wolfgang von Urgan-Sternberg.

Miller has promoted Appalachian awareness and appreciation as an educator as well as a writer. He is perhaps more responsible for Appalachian educational reform and curricular changes, at all levels, than anyone else in the region. He has written for educators, urging the importance of preserving Appalachian values while understanding their relationship to mainstream culture. His articles on Appalachian education have appeared with frequency in *Appalachian Journal* and *Appalachian Heritage.* A substantial essay on Appalachia's complicated history called "Southern Appalachia: American Borderland with a Triple History" is contained in the *Virginia English Bulletin.* An exceptional book-length manuscript entitled "Appalachian Values/American Values: The Role of Regional Colleges and Universities" was published in six consecutive issues of *Appalachian Heritage,* beginning in fall 1977.

In his role as critic, Miller has devoted abundant energy to the assessment and (re)discovery of Appalachian literature. He has defined the role of Appalachian critics in his *Appalachian Journal* review of Louis D. Rubin, Jr.'s *The History of Southern Literature.* He attacks the established literary notion that the South is essentially homogeneous, claiming that literary history has been defined by those who "desire to banish poor cousins to the outhouse and put out the best uncracked china for company" (64). In an interview with Thomas Rain Crowe (1989), he criticized the Fugitive/Agrarians for stressing the commonality of the lowland South rather than recognizing the uniqueness of the mountain South.

A prolific reviewer of books that have the mountains at their center, Miller is as comfortable discussing volumes of poetry by Robert Morgan and Wendell Berry as he is reviewing works about Kentucky history or Appalachia's place in the American South. His reviews have appeared regularly in the *Park City*

Daily News (Bowling Green, Kentucky), the *Courier-Journal* (Louisville, Kentucky), and numerous journals, such as *Magill's Literary Annual* (for which he reviewed primarily in the early 1980s), *Appalachian Mountain Books, Now and Then,* and *Appalachian Heritage.* He has edited and introduced volumes by both Jesse Stuart and James Still, as well as written numerous essays and entries about them.

Miller's most public role has been as spokesperson for the Appalachian South at innumerable conferences, seminars, gatherings and events. Every August since 1978 Miller has been on the staff of the Appalachian Writers Workshop at Hindman-Settlement School. The summers of 1986, 1987, and 1988 he ran NEH-sponsored Summer Institutes at Appalachian State University. An eighty-nine-page publication, *The Examined Life: Family, Community, and Work in American Literature* (1989), grew out of these three Institutes. Miller has been instrumental in the formation of the Appalachian Consortium, the Appalachian Studies Conference (chairing it in 1983), and Appalachian studies centers throughout the region.

From 1973 to 1980, Miller served as a visiting professor to the Appalachian Studies Workshop at Berea College and from 1984 to 1985 to the James R. Stokely Institute for Liberal Arts Education at the University of Tennessee. He was Poet-in-Residence in 1984 at Centre College of Kentucky, and was the artist honored on February 4 and 5, 1988, at the Literary Festival at Emory and Henry College in Virginia. Miller has been a consultant to poetry workshops in six states, and he has actively participated in the Poet-in-the-Schools program in the Virginia public-school system since 1977. Currently Miller is an advisory and contributing editor to *Appalachian Heritage,* and advisory editor for the *Kentucky Review.*

To his various roles, Miller has brought a remarkable sense of humor. Several of his essays appear in Loyal Jones and Billy Edd Wheeler's 1987 volume *Laughter in Appalachia,* and he has contributed humorous pieces to *Thalia: Studies in Literary Humor.* He spoke about this with Loyal Jones: "I think that some poets who wax doleful are affecting a poetic stance. . . . I'm not interested in that" (16). Although in the same interview he admired Fred Chappell's ability to see abstruse images in the clouds—"the stoning of Saint Stephen, the face of Mephistopholes"—he freely admitted the greater simplicity of his own vision. "When I looked up at the clouds back then I usually saw a ducky or a pony! Still do" (15).

MAJOR THEMES

In the poem "On Native Ground" from *Dialogue with a Dead Man,* Miller has included an image that he and his critics have returned to repeatedly. From his youth, Miller had observed the strange phenomenon of trees once nailed with barbed wire actually growing new layers of bark around the painful wounds. The memory moved into metaphor in these lines: "Life grows in rings around a hurt, / a tree with barbed wire running through its heart'' (58). In a 1979 interview with *Appalachian Journal,* Miller recited these lines when asked about his central themes. He explained, ''I think that that's the theme that runs through all the poetry, if there is one theme that will encompass it all, or one theme into which all the poems can flow like little tributaries into a larger stream. It's of growth and becoming. I would say they have to do with the dialectic involved in change'' (211).

Miller's first volume, *Copperhead Cane,* is a collection of elegaic sonnets that introduce the idea that the narrator's world can never be the same after overwhelming loss. In these poems Miller mourns the death of Fred Smith (''S.F.S''), Miller's beloved grandfather, who died in 1962. The narrator relates details from the funeral and burial and emphasizes how lonely it is without this man born in 1875 on Sandy Mush Creek in Buncombe County. The narrator has lost the person who taught him how to foxhunt and fish, build fences, and hang burley.

Often what appear to be themes in Miller's verse he has preferred to call ''occasions.'' For example, in 1979 Miller insisted that the idea of death that dominates *Copperhead Cane* and segments of his *Dialogue with a Dead Man* was not the theme but, rather, ''the occasion . . . the catalyst, the inciting experience'' (211). Other ''occasions'' of importance in Miller's verse are American greed and ecological irresponsibility (*The More Things Change the More They Stay the Same*), American frenzy (documented in Part One of *The Mountains Have Come Closer*), aesthetics (*Vein of Words*), domestic and professional disillusionment (*Nostalgia for 70*), and the displacement of rural Appalachians to the cities (recorded in ''Small Farms Disappearing in Tennessee'' from *Brier, His Book*). But these and other ''occasions'' function primarily to prompt growth and change—the subject that is unquestionably Miller's major theme.

Miller is not excessive in his nostalgia about the loss of the old ways. He told Ron Larson in a 1983 interview: ''Nobody who has lived a rural subsistence existence is going to find anything bucolic or pastoral about it'' (52). He believes in the absolute importance of growth, redefinition, and change. Even in a volume as full of sadness and loss as *Copperhead Cane,* Miller begins to look for ways to recover. In the innovative second and third parts of *Dialogue With a Dead Man,* the narrator realizes that the relationship of future generations to Fred Smith, and the era he represents, can be positive and permanent. In ''Family Reunion,'' the dead ''who pose / all year in oval picture frames'' are present: ''They are looking out of the eyes of children, / young sprouts / whose laughter blooms / fresh as the new flowers in the graveyard'' (78).

In poems published throughout the late 1970s—and, more dominantly, in *The Mountains Have Come Closer*—Miller introduced the Brier. This highly inventive decision allowed him to shift his theme dramatically from personal to collective change. He had shifted his emphasis from individual to family in ''Family Reunion'' and other poems, but with the Brier he was ready to embrace

Appalachians he had never met. The *Brier,* a term long used among Northerners for the representative Appalachian migrant, represents several million Appalachian Americans in Miller's verse. The Brier became Miller's highly original trademark, the perfect embodiment of his theme.

In *The Mountains Have Come Closer,* Miller began to define the problem of Appalachian identity through the Brier's confusion and growing awareness. Forced to leave his mountain home for better opportunities in the North, the Brier has been physically and psychologically displaced. Driven to Northern cities and suburbs, he begins to recognize the terrible distance he has put between himself and home. In "Down Home," Miller says of the Brier, "He had to admit it: he / didn't live here any longer. He was / settled in a suburb, north of himself" (28).

The North that receives the Brier does nothing to help him connect the two cultures that he has inherited. Up North, the Brier is "white trash," a "red neck." In "Brier Reviewing Novels," the Brier observes the perpetuation of this stereotype in mainstream literature. In "The Brier Losing Touch with His Traditions," the Brier feels its effects. In this poem, the Brier moves to Cincinnati to have a better market for his chairs, but finds that his orders drop off when it is discovered that he uses a power saw and sometimes wears flowered shirts—that he does not fit the image Northerners have of him. In "Restoring an Old Farmhouse" in Part Two, Miller suggests a remedy. A farmhouse is rebuilt by salvaging the good boards and cutting them into new lengths: "Two times mingled. Fresh sawdust / spumed yellow as sunlight from old timber" (29). Not every board can be saved, but some can. Those that are still sturdy must be recut by a modern saw and hand.

The last poem of *The Mountains Have Come Closer* is one of Miller's most original and important pieces, a poetic outline of how contemporary Appalachians can bridge the two worlds they've inherited—the world of country roads and concrete highways. The poem has given direction and inspiration to the Appalachian movement throughout the 1980s and into the 1990s. In "Brier Sermon—'You Must Be Born Again,' " the Brier preaches, lyrically and wisely, on a street corner right across from a Greenstamp Redemption Store. Appropriately, he faces the world of coupons and American consumerism that has so deeply intruded on Appalachian town and character. He urges the people to come home, for "the house our foreparents left had a song, had a story" (54). But the return is not a simple one, not an easy relinquishing of the new for the old. The Brier asks for thoughtful synthesis. In order to explain himself better, he practices through metaphor what he preaches, turning a cliché from mainstream culture into Appalachian emblem: "You've heard it said you can't put new wine in old bottles. / Well, I don't know. / But don't be too sure you're new wine. / Maybe we're all old wine in new bottles" (56). He concludes, "It's going back to what you were before / without losing what you've since become" (63).

In *Brier: His Book,* we watch the Brier living out the theory he has preached, showing himself and others how Appalachian character can be preserved in a contemporary form. The Brier returns home and faces the ruined farms, cisterns gone dry, ditches full of old cars, gates unhinged. But he is nonetheless buoyant, eager for recovery and signs. In ''A Turning,'' just ''One blade of birdsong'' makes the Brier's world green.

The Brier has taken the initiative to learn more about his region. He has become an historian of sorts and a more literary man. In ''How America Came to the Mountains'' the Brier tells only about modern ways coming to the hills, the asphalt and diesel transformation. But the Brier who appears in Miller's second Brier volume goes back to the beginning to understand. In ''The Brier's Pictorial History of the Mountains,'' we are given a correctly visual account of Appalachian history from the time of Indians on buffalo trails to strip mining and development.

In *Brier, His Book,* Miller urges Appalachians to become politically as well as historically aware, for growth necessarily involves political choice. In ''On Trammel Creek,'' a folksy version of ''The Country of Conscience,'' local custom and state law are both realities of the Brier's world, and he must learn their relationship. While fishing, the Brier recognizes that law and custom usually do not get in each other's way, ''the way the creek / swung away from the church house'' (14). He knows that both exist and must be recognized, but customs for him are always a little stronger than laws—an idea reinforced by the image of Trammel Creek very naturally crossing over state lines from Tennessee to Kentucky. Comically, the Brier never offers strangers ''in a dry country'' a drink from his whiskey flask (he obeys the laws most of the time), that is, ''unless the stranger looked / like he wanted one'' (14).

The same sort of blend is achieved in ''Brier Ambassador.'' The Brier admits and accepts his responsible duty to a larger land. As Ambassador, he flies to Washington, though wishing he could stay home and fish. But while he flies out of his land, he realizes that his only interest must be in the ''rivers, lakes, and ponds.'' Thus Brier knows that lifting himself above the mountains and acquiring a wider perspective are beneficial primarily in allowing home to be seen more clearly.

Developing a community conscience, born of political and historical awareness and perspective, is one of the most important components in Miller's concept of Appalachian growth. In his 1979 interview he talked about Appalachian isolation—partly a result of geography, partly of choice by original settlers. He compared the condition to the fragmentation of pre-1870 Germany, broken once into thirty-nine monarchies, and hinted that the role of the Brier might parallel the role of the Brothers Grimm. The stories of the Brothers Grimm helped make German unification possible, and perhaps the Brier stories might do the same for Appalachia.

The dialectic of change compels Miller's fiction as well as his verse. *His*

First, Best Country (1987) tells the story of Jennings Wells, an Appalachian academic who has chosen to spend his leave of absence writing books "back home," in the tenant house at the end of the pasture. But he meets Roma, the essence of country, and begins to discover what he has lost by moving away. On a trip down old North 23 to a Conway Twitty concert in Johnson City, Tennessee, Jennings realizes that his heart has grown less responsive and his speech has lost its natural poetry. Miller will not permit Jennings Wells easy answers for recovery, however. Home can never be the same after his father's death, nor after his recognition that there is no country pastoral. But Jennings will now begin working to connect his two lives.

In *Newfound,* dedicated to "My Newfound Family, Friends, and Neighbors," Miller has examined the same process of connecting when change occurs, but has here explored it through a youthful figure about to enter a broader, more mainstream America, rather than a more experienced character who has been there and returned. "Wells" is a family name (his Grandmother Miller was Matilda Irene Wells Miller), and Miller has indicated that he intends Robert as a somewhat autobiographical early phase of Jennings Wells. Robert Wells's small corner of Tennessee widens during the course of Miller's first novel: He attends a consolidated school (West Madison), rides with Kermit Worley up the creeks in Madison and Bunker counties in the "rolling store" trading food and supplies on Saturdays, helps George Hawkins haul watermelons from the deep South to Mountain City on summer vacations, and finally heads to Berea College, seeming to leave home behind entirely. But very much like Miller himself, Robert realizes that the stories and events he had grown up with had whittled him in profile and were his (and him) forever. He ends his roughly two-hundred page narrative this way, as a young man starting college in Kentucky: "Still, the more I learned about other places, the more interesting, even mysterious, my home in the mountains grew. I had lived on Newfound Creek, and now, I was discovering, Newfound Creek lived on in me, and would live in me, no matter how far away I might travel" (213).

Miller's thematic commitment to the dialectic of change has deeply affected his aesthetic. He tirelessly revises poems, seeing them—as he sees the Appalachian character—always in evolution. He told Jerry Williamson in 1979, "[M]any of my poems are revised *into* existence" (224). In "A Letter on Poetry from Jim Wayne Miller" that concludes the 1982–83 double issue of *Kentucky Poetry Review,* Miller talks about himself as a *bricoleur,* a person who transforms "materials lying around" into something new—for Miller, poems. He writes, "A good poem is always an unexpected amalgam of disparate things" (57). In this letter he also works to break down divisions between imagination and experience and between the private and public world.

It was this same aesthetic of change that deeply influenced Miller's decision to convert his story "His First, Best Country" into both a play and a novel. In the summer of 1992, Horse Cave Theater in Kentucky produced his two-act play about Jennings Wells and Roma. And in 1993 Gnomon Press issued his

216-page novel of the same title. We are presented with a more complicated Jennings in this version. In Chapters 17, 18, and 27, the incidents in the short story unfold. But not until Chapter 27 do we return to the storyline of the original telling. Throughout added segments, new characters and new events force Jennings Wells to think about home with all the complications and ambiguities it presents. This new Jennings Wells comes to realize the contradictions and ambivalence within his own character, as well as within the community of Newfound, as he reexamines his bloodthirsty youth hunting and fishing, as he makes plans to dismantle and reassemble a log cabin on his own property, as he moves toward the paradoxical conclusion that home is "Mean, and sweet" (211).

Transformation is also at the center of Miller's language and use of metaphor. He changes biblical rhetoric into Appalachian adage, as in "The Brier Plans a Mountain Vision Center": "People saw smokestacks in their neighbors' eyes— but / not the stripmines in their own" (56). In "Giving at the Office," he blends the old and the new in an image of a country academic who "pulse[s] with neon" (12). In "Land and Language," he weaves Appalachian expressions with formal prose, conscious that "in a swirling storm of new sensations/words melt—firedog, milkgap, singletree, sundad— / like snowflakes on the tips of children's tongues" (38). People relearning their relationship to the land fuse with it metaphorically: The Brier signs a letter "with a muddy paw" and catches "six redhorse" with his hands in "The Brier Grows Wild" (41); the narrator of "Bud Sizemore," thinking about the Appalachians living in Dayton and Flint, says, "I reckon we're the root and they're the stem" (39).

Miller, comfortable with the dialectic, has frequently expressed the opinion that there exists no clear division between the regional and universal aspects of his art and theme. He refuses to find regional themes and images "limiting," or to perpetuate in any way the idea that the regionalist must "transcend" the local in order to have something of lasting importance to say to all readers. He explained in his *Appalachian Journal* interview, "Everything is local some- where, as William Stafford has said. . . . The Bible is universal certainly, but when you think about what it's actually written about, it's written about a bunch of desert nomads, and it's more or less the history of their progress through the centuries" (213).

The Jim Wayne Miller who wrote "The Country of Conscience" in 1981 is "global" in his vision as well as "universal." Dedicated to Lithuanian poet and Nobel laureate Czeslaw Milosz, "The Country of Conscience" fully dem- onstrates the compatibility Miller sees in local and global perspectives. He un- derstands that the need to return home for regional nourishment is not just Appalachian, but truly global. The poem prophetically announces separatist movements throughout the world, uncannily even mentioning "Georgian cheese bread" (a reference to the Soviet Union, not the American South).

It is impossible to know exactly what Miller will do next. Currently, he is semi-retired from Western Kentucky University, allowing him to work even more vigorously on his poetry and fiction. Like his Brier, he is the embodiment of his theme, always eager for growth, invention, and change. In his poem "Poetry Workshop," Miller compares the reader to a troutfisherman who wades in a stream, "rounds a bend and comes on a piano / lodged high in the forks of a sycamore." When we turn a corner in Miller's career, we never know exactly what we'll find—a Brier, a piano in a tree, an Appalachian sermon thirteen pages long. But for that very reason, Miller's readers seldom can wait to round the next bend.

SURVEY OF CRITICISM

A few critics were looking seriously at Miller's work in the 1960s. In 1963 Maxine Kumin drew attention to Miller's work, ten elegaic sonnets submitted for consideration to *The Writer* (most later to appear in *Copperhead Cane*). Through her admiring article, many readers, especially outside the region, heard about Miller for the first time. *Copperhead Cane* attracted several reviewers. Some, like H. E. Francis (1965), qualified their general enthusiasm for Miller by their concern with his tendency to be technically indulgent and self-conscious.

Throughout the 1970s, reviews of Miller's work appeared in greater numbers. But it was *Dialogue with a Dead Man* that accelerated critical interest in Miller and began to secure his reputation. Numerous critics discussed this third volume, mentioning differences between poems in the first part, largely a reprint of *Copperhead Cane,* and the second and third parts. Most critics preferred the more vernacular and relaxed style of Miller's new poems.

Reviews of Miller's fourth collection of poems, *The Mountains Have Come Closer,* placed him in the ranks of the most prominent Appalachian poets. Nancy Joyner (1980) wrote that *"The Mountains Have Come Closer* demonstrates a clear development in Miller's art. . . . [T]he collection itself differs from the earlier volumes in its richness and control. It is, simply, a better book" (6). In a 1980 article for *Appalachian Journal,* Fred Chappell grouped Jim Wayne Miller with Robert Morgan and Hilda Downer; Chappell noticed the effectiveness of what he termed "double language" in *The Mountains Have Come Closer,* the easy mix of local idiom and literary discourse.

In the 1980s literary essays about Miller's work appeared with frequency. The proceedings of the annual Appalachian Studies Conference, published by the Appalachian Consortium Press, have often included major papers on Miller. Harold Branam (5th Annual Conference), John Mongle (6th Annual Conference), and Ricky Cox (10th Annual Conference) read essays on Miller that were later collected. Harold Branam wrote an elaborate review of *Brier, His Book,* with background, for *Appalachian Heritage* in the fall of 1988. Joyce Dyer discussed and assessed Miller's works between 1984 and 1988. In 1990 Sharyn McCrumb, Steve Mooney, and Susan Walker wrote favorable reviews of *Newfound,* as did Dyer of *His First Best Country* in 1994.

Special issues publications throughout the 1980s have also drawn attention to Miller's work. In 1983 the *Kentucky Poetry Review* dedicated a special double issue to him, including a brief profile, four of his poems, and a letter he wrote to explain his poetic theory. In the fall of the same year, *Grab-a-Nickel* featured his achievement. *Kentucky Writing* highlighted Miller's work in the spring 1989 issue.

In 1988 the Department of English at Emory and Henry College made a major contribution to the Miller Scholarship. After the college's Literary Festival, which honored Miller, the spring issue of *Iron Mountain Review* published manuscripts and various tributes from the celebration. It contains some of Miller's verse (old and new), an excellent interview between Miller and Loyal Jones, a reprint of Maxine Kumin's essay, lengthy articles by Grace Toney Edwards, Wade Hall, and Don Johnson, and the most complete bibliography of Miller's work to date, prepared by Jefferson D. Caskey.

Biographical and critical information on Miller is beginning to appear in standard references. His name is mentioned, for example, by James Justus in Louis D. Rubin, Jr.'s *History of Southern Literature* (1985); he is listed as one of several poets (the list includes James Applewhite, Fred Chappell, Van K. Brock, and Jeff Daniel Marion) whose work "recalls the life on the old lands in synecdochic images" (549). Critical and biographical information on Miller is also included in Frank Magill's *Critical Survey of Short Fiction: Current Writers* (1981), the 1987 New Revision Series of *Contemporary Authors,* William Ward's *A Literary History of Kentucky* (1988), and Adrienne Bond's *The Voice of the Poet: The Shape and Sound of Southern Poetry Today* (1989).

Masters' theses about, or including Miller, are also beginning to appear. Rita Quillen's revised thesis was published as a book in 1989, *Looking for Native Ground: Contemporary Appalachian Poetry.* Rhonda Catron of Radford University completed a thesis titled "Political Implications of Jim Wayne Miller's Poetry" in 1989.

In addition to the selective bibliography of Miller's writings prepared by Jefferson Caskey, Rita Quillen published a comprehensive bibliography of primary and secondary citations to mountain poetry in 1983, including numerous references to Miller.

Although Robert Morgan and Fred Chappell are now slightly better known outside the region than Miller, Miller is gaining rapidly in deserved reputation and respect. Chappell and Morgan themselves recently praised Miller exuberantly in prefatory comments to the *Iron Mountain Review* issue. Chappell said, "If it were not for Miller, the Appal lit movement might have foundered before it got started" (2). Morgan called Miller "both bard and prophet," applauding his ability to write "at once of Appalachia and the planet" (2). Miller's vigor, inventiveness, and wisdom have won him the respect of his critics and his fellow poets, and of a loyal and growing readership.

BIBLIOGRAPHY

Works by Jim Wayne Miller

Copperhead Cane. Nashville, Tenn.: Allen, 1964.

The More Things Change the More They Stay the Same. Frankfort, Ky.: Whippoorwill Press, 1971.

Dialogue with a Dead Man. Athens: University of Georgia Press, 1974. Reprint. University Center, Mich.: Green River Press, 1978.

"A Mirror for Appalachia." In *Voices from the Hills: Selected Readings of Southern Appalachia,* edited by Robert J. Higgs and Ambrose N. Manning, 447–59. New York: Ungar, 1975.

"Appalachian Values/American Values." *Appalachian Heritage* 5 (Fall 1977): 24–32; 6 (Winter 1978): 30–37; 6 (Spring 1978): 11–19; 6 (Summer 1978): 23–24; 7 (Fall 1978): 47–54; 7 (Winter 1979): 49–57.

The Mountains Have Come Closer. Boone, N.C.: Appalachian Consortium Press, 1980.

Grab-a-Nickel [special Jim Wayne Miller issue] 6, no. 6 (Fall 1983).

Kentucky Poetry Review [special Jim Wayne Miller double issue, including "A Letter on Poetry from Jim Wayne Miller"] 18, no. 2; 19, no. 1 (1983).

"Poetry: A Beginner's Guide." Media Resources Center, Western Kentucky University, Bowling Green, Kentucky. 1984. Videocassette.

Reading, Writing, Region: A Checklist, Purchase Guide and Directory for School and Community Libraries in Appalachia. Boone, N.C.: Appalachian Consortium Press, 1984.

Vein of Words. Big Timber, Mont.: Seven Buffaloes Press, 1984.

"I Have a Place: The Poetry of Jim Wayne Miller." Media Resources Center, Western Kentucky University, Bowling Green University, Kentucky. 1985. Videocassette.

" . . . And Ladies of the Club." *Appalachian Journal* 14, no. 1 (Fall 1986): 64–69.

Nostalgia for 70. Big Timber, Mont.: Seven Buffaloes Press, 1986.

Sideswipes. Big Timber, Mont.: Seven Buffaloes Press, 1986.

"Anytime the Ground Is Uneven: The Outlook for Regional Studies—and What To Look Out For." In *Geography and Literature: A Meeting of the Disciplines,* edited by William E. Mallory and Paul Simpson-Housley, 1–20. Syracuse: Syracuse University Press, 1987.

His First, Best Country. Frankfort, Ky.: Gnomon Press, 1987.

Brier: His Book. Frankfort, Ky.: Gnomon Press, 1988.

"Southern Appalachia: American Borderland with a Triple History." *Virginia English Bulletin* 8, no. 2 (Fall 1988): 2–14.

The Wisdom of Folk Metaphor. Big Timber, Mont.: Seven Buffaloes Press, 1988.

The Examined Life: Family, Community, and Work in American Literature. Boone, N.C.: Appalachian Consortium Press, 1989.

Kentucky Writing [special Jim Wayne Miller issue] 5, no. 1 (Spring 1989).

Newfound. New York: Orchard Books, 1989.

Round and Round with Kahlil Gibran. With an introduction by Sharyn McCrumb. Blacksburg, Va.: Rowan Mountain Press, 1990.

"A People Waking Up: Appalachian Literature since 1960." In *The Cratis Williams Symposium Proceedings: A Memorial and Examination of the State of Regional*

Studies in Appalachia, 47–76. Boone, N.C.: Appalachian Consortium Press, n.d.
His First, Best Country. Frankfort, Ky.: Gnomon, 1993.

Works Edited by Jim Wayne Miller

I Have a Place. Pippa Passes, Ky.: Appalachian Center, Alice Lloyd College, 1981.
Songs of a Mountain Plowman. With an introduction by Jim Wayne Miller. Ashland,
        Ky.: Jesse Stuart Foundation; Morehead, Ky.: Morehead State University's Ap-
        palachian Development Center, 1986.
The Wolfpen Poems. With an introduction by Jim Wayne Miller. Berea, Ky.: Berea
        College Press; Frankfort, Ky.: Gnomon Press, 1986.
*A Ride with Huey the Engineer: Fact and Fiction from a Colorful Era of America's
        Past.* Edited and introduced with James M. Gifford and Jerry A. Herndon. Ash-
        land, Ky.: The Jesse Stuart Foundation, 1988.

Works Translated by Jim Wayne Miller

Lerperger, Emil. *The Figure of Fulfillment.* University Center, Mich.: Green River Press,
        1975.

Interviews with Jim Wayne Miller

Crowe, Thomas Rain. "Rocks in the Stream: A Conversation with Jim Wayne Miller."
        Arts Journal 14, no. 11 (August 1989): 10–13.
"Jim Wayne Miller." In *Contemporary Authors Autobiography Series,* edited by Doyce
        Nakamura, 273–93. Detroit: Gale Research, 1992.
Jones, Loyal. "An Interview: In Quest of the Brier." *Iron Mountain Review* 4, no. 2
        (Spring 1988): 13–21.
Kelly, Patricia P. "An Interview with Jim Miller." *Journal of Reading* 34, no. 8 (May
        1991): 666–69.
Larson, Ron. "The Appalachian Personality: Interviews with Loyal Jones and Jim Wayne
        Miller." *Appalachian Heritage* 11, no. 3 (Summer 1983): 48–54.
Williamson, J. W. "An Interview with Jim Wayne Miller." *Appalachian Journal* 6, no.
        3 (Spring 1979): 207–25.
"*The Wolfpen Notebooks:* James Stills' Record of Appalachian Life." *Appalachian Her-
        itage* 19, no. 3 (Summer 1991): 20–24
"Reading, Writing, Region: Notes from Southern Appalachia, an American Periphery."
        Thinker Review 1, no. 1 (April 1993): 119–34.

Studies of Jim Wayne Miller

Arlett, Bob. "Poet Breaks Ground." Review of *Dialogue with a Dead Man. Mountain
        Review* 1, no. 2 (Winter 1975): 17–18.
Bond, Adrienne. *The Voice of the Poet.* Atlanta, Ga.: Humanities Council, 1989.
Branam, Harold. "Generations: The Theme of Jim Wayne Miller's *Dialogue With a*

Dead Man." In *Critical Essays in Appalachian Life and Culture,* edited by Rick Simon, 69–75. Boone, N.C.: Appalachian Consortium Press, 1982.

———. Review of *Brier, His Book. Appalachian Heritage* 16, no. 4 (Fall 1988): 63–65.

Caskey, Jefferson D. "The Writings of Jim Wayne Miller: A Selective Bibliography." *Iron Mountain Review* (Jim Wayne Miller issue) 4, no. 2 (Spring 1988): 37–40.

Catron, Rhonda K. "Political Implications of Jim Wayne Miller's Poetry." Master's thesis, Radford University, Virginia 1989.

———. Letter to the Editor. *Appalachian Journal* 17, no. 2 (Winter 1990): 108–12.

Chappell, Fred. "Double Language: Three Appalachian Poets." *Appalachian Journal* 8, no. 1 (Autumn 1980): 55–59.

Clark, Kenneth. Review of *The More Things Change the More They Stay the Same. Kentucky Folklore Record* 17 (October–December 1971): 87.

Claudel, Alice Moser. "The Past Alive in the Present" Review of *Dialogue with a Dead Man. Appalachian Journal* 2, no. 3 (Spring 1975): 232–33.

Cope, Steven R. "Jim Wayne Miller: Something About His Poetry." In *Kentucky Voices: A Bicentennial Celebration of Writing,* 25–38. Lexington: Kentucky Bicentennial Commission, 1992.

Cox, Ricky. "The 'Brier Sermon' Signpost in Appalachian Studies." In *Remembrance, Reunion and Revival: Celebrating a Decade of Appalachian Studies,* edited by Helen Roseberry, 21–28. Boone, N.C.: Appalachian Consortium Press, 1988.

Crooke, Jeff. "Sonnet Forms and Ballad Feelings." *Iron Mountain Review* (Jim Wayne Miller issue) 4, no. 2 (Spring 1988): 23.

Dyer, Joyce. "The Brier Goes to College." *Appalachian Journal* 16, no. 3 (Spring 1989): 226–241.

———. Letter to Rhonda K. Catron. *Appalachian Journal* 17, no. 2 (Winter 1990): 112–14.

———. Review of *His First, Best Country. Appalachian Journal* 21, no. 2 (Winter 1994): 202–6.

Edwards, Grace Toney. "Jim Wayne Miller: Holding the Mirror for Appalachia." *Iron Mountain Review* (Jim Wayne Miller issue) 4, no. 2 (Spring 1988): 24–28.

Eisiminger, Skip. Review of *Dialogue With A Dead Man. Green River Review* 7, no. 2 (1976): 111–15.

Francis, H. E. Review of *Copperhead Cane. South Atlantic Bulletin* (March 1965): 14–15.

Hall, Wade. Review of *The Mountains Have Come Closer. Louisville Courier-Journal* (September 7, 1980): D–5.

———. "Jim Wayne Miller's Brier Poems: The Appalachian in Exile." *Iron Mountain Review* (Jim Wayne Miller issue) 4, no. 2 (Spring 1988): 29–33.

Johnson, Don. "The Appalachian Homeplace as Oneiric House in Jim Wayne Miller's *The Mountains Have Come Closer." Iron Mountain Review* (Jim Wayne Miller Issue) 4, no. 2 (Spring 1988): 34–36.

Joyner, Nancy. "Jim Wayne Miller: A Bridge between Past and Present." *Arts Journal* 5, no. 12 (September 1980): 6–8.

Justus, James H. "Poets after Midcentury." In *The History of Southern Literature,* edited by Louis D. Rubin, Jr., 535–55. Baton Rouge: Louisiana State University Press, 1985.

Kuehn, Jim, and Jim Stokely, producers. *Appalachian Writers* [Thirty-minute film programs about Fred Chappell, Jeff Daniel Marion, Jim Wayne Miller, and James

Still]. Children's Museum of Oak Ridge and WSJK-TV, Tennessee Educational Television System, Knoxville, 1979.

Kumin, Maxine. "The Poetry Workshop." *The Writer* (July 1963): 22 ff. Reprint. *Iron Mountain Review* (Jim Wayne Miller issue) 4, no. 2 (Spring 1988): 22.

Lanier, Parks, Jr., ed. *The Poetics of Appalachian Space.* Knoxville: University of Tennessee Press, 1991.

Lewis, Leon. Review of *Nostalgia for 70. Cold Mountain Review* 14 (1986): 39–40.

McCrumb, Sharyn. Review of *Newfound. Appalachian Heritage* 18, no. 1 (Winter 1990): 59–60.

Magill, Frank N., ed. *Critical Survey of Short Fiction: Current Writers,* Index 7, 2723. Englewood Cliffs, N.J.: Salem Press, 1981.

Marion, Stephen. "Gleaning the Unsayable: The Terrain of Vision in Poems by Robert Morgan, Fred Chappell, and Jim Wayne Miller." *Mossy Creek Journal* 9 (1985): 25–33.

Mongle, John H. " 'Rings Around a Hurt': The Dialectic Structure of *The Mountains Have Come Closer.*" In *The Appalachian Experience.* edited by Barry Buxton, 45–53. Boone, N.C.: Appalachian Connsortium Press, 1983.

Mooney, Steve. Review of *Newfound. Appalachian Center Newsletter.* (April 1990): 8–9.

O'Dell, Susan. "Stepping Out Our Own Front Door." *Mossy Creek Journal* 7 (Spring 1983): 38–39.

Quillen, Rita S. "Modern and Contemporary Mountain Poetry: A Bibliography." *Appalachian Journal* 13, no. 1 (Fall 1985): 51–77.

———. *Looking For Native Ground: Contemporary Appalachian Poetry.* Boone, N.C.: Appalachian Consortium Press, 1989.

Verhulst, Pat. Review of *Brier, His Book* and *His First, Best Country. Now and Then* 5 (Fall 1988): 35–37.

Ward, William S. *A Literary History of Kentucky.* Knoxville: University of Tennessee Press, 1988.

Westermoreland, Thomas. Review of *The Mountains Have Come Closer. Green River Review* 12, no. 1 (1981): 115–19.

Winkler, Karen. "Students of Appalachia's Rich Literary Tradition Struggle against the Region's Hillbilly Stereotype." *Chronicle of Higher Education* March 31, 1980): 5.

Woodhull, Kenny. "Old Wine in New Bottles." *Mossy Creek Journal* 9 (1985): 13–19.

William Mills
(1935–   )

An accomplished poet, William Mills has also distinguished himself as a writer of fiction and nonfiction and as a nature photographer. His work is marked by a close and honest treatment of the relationship of the human being with his or her environment. Mills is a writer at home in the outdoors, with his focus on individual human perception.

BIOGRAPHY

Born on June 17, 1935, in Hattiesburg, Mississippi, William Mills is the oldest of five sons of William W. Mills and Frances Finney Mills. During the late 1930s the Mills family moved around a good deal in both the South and North, following the father's work as a welder, returning to Mississippi in 1939, and then settling in Baton Rouge, Louisiana.

Through personal correspondence with me, Mills graciously recounted the pertinent facts about his life and his feelings concerning those facts. Mills revealed a strong sense of family tradition and an obvious admiration for his parents, who, he says, "both worked hard, and never ran off to California to find themselves." He grew up listening to his parents' and grandparents' stories about their families, especially those told by his mother's father, "a great Irish story teller" who held him enthralled for hours at a time. These stories "were not invented by television companies in New York." His family was strongly religious, and Mills listened to Methodist sermons every Sunday as well as to biblical stories at home. He also spent considerable time outdoors—camping, hunting, and fishing—and began to develop the strong love and respect for nature that is reflected in his writing.

During the academic year of 1953–54, Mills attended Centenary College in Shreveport, Louisiana, developing a new interest: literature and philosophy. In

1955 he joined the United States Army and was sent to Kyoto, Japan, where he served for 3 years. While there, he lived with Werner Kohler, a Swiss theologian and philosopher who had been a student of Karl Barth. Conversations with Kohler whetted Mills's already keen interest in philosophy, which continues unabated today: "Philosophers that I find particularly congenial are Plato (above all), the Pre-Socratics, Meister Eckhard (some would not consider him a philosopher), Nietzsche, Kirkegaarde, Heidegger, and Berdyaev." Mills adds. "The love of philosophy has never left me though I have, unfortunately, no skill."

Following his military service, Mills went to Germany where he studied philosophy both formally and informally in Tubingen, Munich, and at the Goethe Institute in Blaubeuren. Upon his return to the United States, he enrolled at Louisiana State University where he received his B.A. in 1959 and his M.A. in 1961. He then worked in a variety of positions both academic and nonacademic before returning to Louisiana State University and earning his Ph.D. in 1972. In 1961 Mills married Sylvia Richard; the marriage ended in 1973.

William Mills has had an extremely varied career. Among other occupations, he has been a Methodist preacher, has worked in oil refineries in Nicaragua and Louisiana, has written for NBC's "Texas," and has raised cattle in Louisiana and Missouri. He has taught at a number of colleges and universities, including Louisiana State University, East Carolina University, Oklahoma State University, the University of Arkansas, and the University of Missouri. Meanwhile he has traveled, photographed, published nine books, written an introduction to another, and has recently completed a book of short stories. His poetry, stories, and essays have appeared in numerous journals, magazines, and anthologies.

During the 1977–78 academic year, Mills served as coeditor of an exhibition titled "The Contemporary American South," sponsored by the United States Information Agency. He has traveled extensively through Europe, the Near and Far East. During the spring of 1978, he read and lectured on Southern poetry in Hungary, Russia, Latvia, Finland, Turkey, and Italy.

In 1979 Mills married Beverly Jarrett who, he told me in a letter, has been his "principal sustainer since 1973" and who shares his love of the outdoors, particularly of fishing. William and Beverly met when Beverly copyedited William's first book for the Louisiana State University Press. They live on a farm in Howard County, Missouri, with "lots of deer, turkey, and quail" and where he has recently been hard at work stringing barbed-wire fences. Mills is now a visiting writer at the University of Missouri, Columbia; his wife is editor-in-chief at the University of Missouri Press.

Mills's last two nonfiction books—*Bears and Men: A Gathering* (1986) and *The Arkansas: An American River* (1988)—clearly indicate his growing concern about the environment. These works testify to his belief that "anyone who is opposed to unrestricted economic growth is anti-American. Yet nature is there to teach us limits as well as 'wildness and power.' " Such statements certainly place him in the Southern agrarian tradition in his distrust of the almost unlimited power held by those in the service of science and technology. He adds, "In the modern way, there is no longer a vision of nature as an emerging, self-gathering power that comes forth from darkness and gathers itself into a particular form or visible radiance which achieves power through limit. The whole idea of limits (by custom or common sense) is perceived as conservative ideology or being anti-technology.'' Mills's religious sense of nature and its ability to teach us limits contrasts sharply with what he views as the predominant, ''modern way,'' one which leads to a misunderstanding of the ''natural way'' as one of unlimited power.

MAJOR THEMES

''You see better in the dark after you've been in it for a while.'' These words begin William Mills's novel *Those Who Blink* (1986), whose title is taken from Chaucer: ''And as for those who blink when they should look, / God blot them from his everlasting Book.'' The quotations reflect a metaphoric treatment of vision—seeing and not seeing, understanding and not understanding—that runs through much of Mills's work and that is often connected to a knowledge gained from nature.

Mill's portrayal of human perception through metaphors of perspective comes partly from his love of the natural world and partly from his study of philosophy and literature. After finishing his doctoral dissertation on the poetry of Howard Nemerov, he published *The Stillness in Moving Things: The World of Howard Nemerov* (1975). Although it suffers somewhat from academic prose style (as do most books based on dissertations), this work helped fill a void. In analyzing Nemerov's poetic method of reflecting the beauty of reality through such devices as mirror images of running water, Mills has also indicated some of his own ideas about human perception and how to treat these ideas poetically.

Mills's first book, *Watch for the Fox* (1974), is an impressive if somewhat uneven and widely varied collection of poems written over a period of several years. Most of the poems are brief, direct, and focus on the plain folk of the Mississippi and Louisiana countryside, on love and lust, hunting and fishing, on moments of pleasure torn from humdrum lives. Mill's poetry here clearly illustrates his strong belief in ''the principle of economy of language,'' and many of these poems are stripped to the bare bones. Mills is sharpest in this volume with his depiction of working men and women seizing a few moments of joy in jukebox joints. In ''I Know a Spot Just over the Hill,'' he writes about his perception of the Saturday-night women met in just such places:

> I thought they stood
> For good times.
> Women on any Monday
> My mother
> Were Saturday night Circes,
> Their sagging milksacks

    Adjusted to goddess shapes
    By a factory in New Jersey. (4)

Throughout many of these poems runs a sardonic and playful humor and an authentic echoing of the sights and sounds of the Southern countryside; but there is a downside too—disease, death, unfaithfulness—that Mills also treats, usually in an ironic fashion. He both celebrates and points out lessons inherent in everyday experiences. People do and should enjoy their simple pleasures, but they should ''watch for the fox'' and be cautious even in moments of ecstasy.

Mill's second volume of poetry, *Stained Glass* (1979), is less rooted in the particulars of the Deep South landscape, containing works set in places as varied as Russia, Finland, Oklahoma, and Arkansas. A number of poems treat love and lost lovers as the poet finds himself traveling by train or plane and musing on these subjects. The title of one poem, ''On Being Asked to Write More Humorous Poetry,'' accurately shows Mills's awareness of the tone of this book.

Two very different longer poems in *Stained Glass,* however, are among Mills's finest. The first, ''Wedington Woods,'' is a lustily humorous description of a noontime tryst in Wedington Woods, away from shopping centers:

    This beats the parking lot of the Dairy Queen.
    You are my dairy queen. I am your Ferdinand.
    I am your Raleigh, too. Lie down my love
    Here on the Sears' T-shirt, these Penney's pants. (29)

The poem concludes as the couple bury the woman's ''Dior panties'' in an armadillo hole and imagine puzzled people in the future seeing ''an armadillo dressed strangely human'' (30). The elegiac ''Our Fathers at Corinth'' has the poet visiting the grave of his great-grandfather, killed in June 1862 at the battle of Corinth, Mississippi. As he thinks of his young ancestor going to war in the spring, he identifies his own experience as a soldier with him:

    We have been mostly the infantrymen
    Of the country's armies. . .
    . . . .
    We feel the earth as we walk to the world's wars,
    And remembering, we return to care again. (57)

After visiting, the poet can conclude:

    Your home is large now, your wraith has a name.
    You rest in your sons
    Who must keep you to themselves. (57)

This is Mills's most traditionally Southern poem, remindful of Allen Tate's "Ode to the Confederate Dead" and concerned with the Southerner's understanding of himself through the past.

In *The Meaning of Coyotes* (1984) the poems are again set in various worldwide locales with topics ranging from love's transience to an attempt to understand death. Some of the works in both this and *Stained Glass* are more expansive than those in *Watch for the Fox:* the language is less terse, sardonic, and metaphoric; the lines are longer: the images are more fully developed; and the meanings are clearer. In "Rituals Along the Arkansas" (*The Meaning of Coyotes*), Mills describes a fishing trip as a ritual uniting man and nature. The conclusion pictures a flight of white pelicans high above their boat:

> There in the high summer sun
> Their great helix of white
> Drew fish and man with them.
> We are wedded to what we use,
> What we love, what we find beautiful. (7)

The final poem in *The Meaning of Coyotes* is Mills's most powerful. "Lords," based upon his photographic expedition to the Arctic, conveys the awe felt on seeing a giant polar bear "Moving as if the whole white world / Were his, a majesty of generations" (51). Although the poet is content to watch the "lord," the scientists of his group have come "to measure, / To send reports to that place / Where all numbers are gathered" (51). After the bear is tranquilized with a shot from a helicopter, the men move in for a closer look, with guns in their hands. Mills then shifts to the "thoughts" of the helpless bear, emphasizing the origin of the strangely religious feeling of humans throughout the ages on beholding, hunting, killing, and eating bears:

> As long as you have known yourself as man
> You have tried to put on my power,
> My head on your head
> In skull-lined caves across the world. (52)

Mills makes it clear that the scientific method will never explain the awe-inspiring majesty of the bear, who thinks: "Without me you walk in deserts. / Imprison me, you cage yourselves" (53). Mills's method here is similar to James Dickey's technique of "exchange," as the narrator not only reports the thoughts of the bear but somehow moves back in time through racial memory to his prehistoric ancestors. It is an act of discovery for him.

Mills's earlier short stories, like many of his earlier poems, concern apparently everyday happenings in small-town and rural Louisiana. In *I Know a Place* (1976) the three stories are told in a straightforward yet subtle manner, leading the reader, in each case, to an act of discovery or perception. "To Pass Him

Out'' recounts the visit of a young boy and his aunt to the musty home of an older woman, Mrs. Fanny, who specializes in nursing wealthy old men. Mills's Faulknerian descriptions of the sights, sounds, and smells of the house and its inhabitants—including the old man being nursed—combine with his image of the boy leaving the house with a vase of lilies to create an understanding in the reader, not shared by the boy, of what the locals mean when they say that Mrs. Fanny is ''passing him out.'' This tale of socially tolerated murder is followed by similarly rendered stories of masochism and suicide. In all three cases, Mills prepares the reader carefully for his discovery.

In *Those Who Blink,* a very tightly structured and hard-hitting novel, Mills has the latitude to develop characters and explore theme more fully. Farley Stokes, a Korean War veteran working in a chemical plant near Baton Rouge, Louisiana, narrates this story of the 1950s. While in the army, Stokes had ''learned to keep a low profile, to perfect the art of bugging out'' (3), and he continues his art in his civilian job.

Through Stoke's ambition to live on the land and raise cattle on his family's now-deserted farm, Mills tells the story of a changing South caught between an agrarian past and an increasingly industrialized present. Stokes is no hero, and he believes he has no illusions about himself; but he does have a genuine love for the land and thinks that, with some financial help, he can make a go of it. When he meets Bo Simmons, a union organizer with mysterious connections and plenty of money, he ignores his misgivings and persuades himself to act on his dream. Simmons, an amoral charmer with no feeling for tradition or (Mills would say) limits, has little trouble nudging Strokes into a period of moral blindness.

It takes Stokes's discovery of his betrayal at the hands of his love, Ruth, and the death of Simmons himself to bring him out of his moral wasteland. Mills ends the book on an affirmative note, however. The spring rains have finally come, new clover is abundant, and Stokes is thinking of ways to stay on the farm. There are echoes of the conclusion to *The Waste Land* in the final scene as Stokes sits on his pond bank fishing with a friend, Jo Anne, who is ''not real bright, . . . but she stood by me'' (176). Stokes says. ''I sat on the bank waiting for a bite while a kingfisher was biding his time, watching the reflecting surface and trying to see beyond it'' (177). The kingfisher suggests Eliot's fisher king, and both the bird and Stokes would seem to be trying to see beyond the surface.

Mills is totally honest in his depiction of character and setting in this novel. He duplicates without exaggeration the speech of the country people, white and black, and he presents Stokes's inborn love of land without sentimentality. Stokes is a working man ''who blinks,'' but he survives to try again. After all, to him life on the land has to be preferable to a job in a caustic chemical plant.

Two of Mills's most recent books have been photographic essays with a special emphasis on ecology. In 1977 he had written the introduction to a book of photographs by Turner Browne entitled *Louisiana Cajuns,* in which he expressed his admiration for the traditions of the Cajuns and their special relationship with the land and waters on which they lived, hunted, and fished. *In Bears and Men: A Gathering* and *The Arkansas: An American River,* Mills records with camera and words his feelings and thoughts about the wilderness and civilization. His photographs in both works are striking; they complement his sometimes poetic or philosophic, sometimes factual prose.

Bears and Men tells of the photographic expedition made by ten men to the western shore of Hudson Bay where polar bears gather each fall, waiting for the water to freeze. Although Mills's main interest is in the bears, he also focuses on the reactions of men. Mills is fascinated with the special appeal of bears: "For nearly everyone bears are magical animals" (11), ranging as they do through our lives from teddy bears of childhood to Goldilocks and her bears to "Smoky the Bear, my bear leader" (12), to "the bear of our greatest novelist, Faulkner" (12). Mills tells of man's special reverence for the bear through the ages in all lands as an "object of worship and as a source of nourishment" (137). And, he says, "paradoxically, trying to possess the animal by making a picture of it recalls the Paleolithic cave artist who tried to do the same" (120). He clearly explains the special value of seeing animals in their natural environment, the vanishing wilderness: "In the face of the terrifying fragmentedness of so much contempory existence, returning to the world of the animal . . . is a way, our intuition tells us, to feel some sense of wholeness" (150).

In *The Arkansas,* Mills tells of his journey on and beside the Arkansas River from its origin in the Rocky Mountains in Colorado to its mouth in the Mississippi River in Arkansas. Again, his camera records objectively while his prose tells the story of the history of the regions he passes through and the precarious balance of nature that exists in places today. As in *Bears and Men,* he works with the ideas of perspective and understanding and with the theme of limits. He begins with "how easy it is to take a river for granted" (5) and procceds to show how much is lost by taking the wilderness for granted.

Mills has recently completed a collection of short stories entitled *Properties of Blood* (1992). Among the eight stories in this collection is one called "Belle Slough," a finely crafted account of a memorable duck hunt told through the consciousness of an attorney named Adam, clearly Mills's persona. Adam expresses both "dread" and "disgust" when he thinks of the contemporary disdain and disregard for any forms of limits, including the limit on ducks. "Ritual, even etiquette, seemed to have disappeared in Adam's lifetime. What was left was naked appetite, unbound to any necessity" (28). Adam, who has begun to feel like "a dinosaur" in the modern world, is further burdened by news of the death of a good friend. But he is brought out of his despondency by the "forest epiphany" of the hunt wherein "in a great coalescence, the bird and Adam became one" (26) and by the sheer pleasure of the evening meal consisting of birds, bread, and burgundy, wherein the bird and Adam do indeed become one. As the story ends, Adam recalls "how beautiful the duck's flight had been and how beautiful it was now. How important it was to eat when one is eating" (30). In a letter to me, Mills explained that Adam is reminded, through the ritual of the hunt and the death of his friend, of limits and of the "futility of unre-strained futurism." Mills added, "the old Adam was given limits." Adam has to get away from his daily existence of "urban puritanism" to regain this knowl-edge of limits and of the importance of eating when one is eating "rather than being preoccupied with some rootless idea or non-existent future."

Mills's increasing concern for the environment has coincided with the evo-lution of his writing style. His recent fiction and nonfiction are marked by a less detached and less ironic vision of life, as is his more recent poetry. Mills, how-ever, still practices the strong "economy of language" that he says he developed in the 1960s with the special help of Miller Williams; and Mills credits the example of James Dickey during that time for showing that "poetry did not have to be effete and precious." In fiction, Mills mentions Hemingway and Faulkner as early favorites: "Hemingway's commitment to writing has always been a source of support. Faulkner, for a Mississippian, is a gigantic presence "who taught him to look at his region" in a new way, which is what "writers should do."

SURVEY OF CRITICISM

Although Mills's books have been warmly reviewed, they have received nei-ther the detailed criticism nor the national attention they deserve. All of his works have been published in the South—all but two by Southern university presses, which has limited their availability to a wider audience of readers and critics. This survey will include only those sources generally available to readers and will exclude most newspaper reviews.

From the beginning, Mills's books have been reviewed before publication and have been highly praised by such distinguished writers as Walker Percy, William Stafford, John Ciardi, Miller Williams, and James Dickey. Criticism, although not extensive, has been almost overwhelmingly favorable. In her essay-review of *The Stillness of Moving Things* (1976), Anne B. Dobie speaks of Mills's "acute critical insight" (891) and calls his analysis "a significant contribution to the critical study of modern poetry" (894). Mills's three volumes of poems have, more often than not, been treated in cursory fashion. Richard Lattimore's comments in the *Hudson Review* are fairly typical: "William Mills, though neither simple nor easy, is direct and immediate, as well as being personal and cross" (451). In her review of *The Meaning of Coyotes* (1985), Betty Adcock has analyzed several poems in some detail and concludes that "this poet's eye is sure. He is a master of the details of places, the world's *differences*" (71). And James H. Justus (1985) has intelligently and succinctly analyzed Mills's poetic style, commenting on Mills's disciplined "severity of form" (541) in his early poems and his subsequent movement toward a closer perspective on his subjects so that "the warmer tones finally make the later verse more accessible" (542).

Mills's prose works deserve more attention. The most thorough review of his novel is by Colin Walters (1986). Walters praises "the tightness of Mr. Mills's demonic, very outdoors-American-masculine plot and the overall elegance of his design" (8M). In a review of *Bears and Men* (1987) David Miller has mentioned Mills's "quest of an essential animal self" (675) on the Arctic ice fields. And James Kilgo (1989), in reviewing *The Arkansas,* calls attention to Mills's extensive knowledge of "ecosystems, geology, anthropology, and history" (cxx).

BIBLIOGRAPHY

Works by William Mills

Watch for the Fox. Baton Rouge: Louisiana State University Press, 1974.
The Stillness in Moving Things: The World of Howard Nemerov. Memphis: Memphis State University Press, 1975.
I Know a Place. Baton Rouge: Press of the Nightowl, 1976.
Introduction to *Louisiana Cajuns,* by Turner Browne. Baton Rouge: Louisiana State Press, 1977.
Stained Glass. Baton Rouge: Louisiana State University Press. 1979.
The Meaning of Coyotes. Baton Rouge: Louisiana State University Press, 1984.
Bears and Men: A Gathering. Chapel Hill, N.C.: Algonquin Press, 1986.
Those Who Blink. Baton Rouge: Louisiana State University Press, 1986.
The Arkansas: An American River. Little Rock: University of Arkansas Press, 1988.
"Risking the Bait: John William Corrington, 1932–1988." *Southern Review* 25 (Summer 1989): 586–88.
Properties of Blood. Fayetteville: University of Arkansas Press, 1992.

Studies of William Mills

Adcock, Betty. Review of *The Meaning of Coyotes. Southern Poetry Review* 25 (Fall 1985): 71–73.
Dobie, Ann B. "The Poet as Critic: *The Stillness of Moving Things." Southern Review* 12 (Autumn 1976): 891–94.
Jarrett, Beverly. "William Mills." In *Southern Writers: A Biographical Dictionary,* edited by Robert Bain, Joseph M. Flora, and Louis D. Rubin, Jr., 309–10. Baton Rouge: Louisiana State University Press, 1979.
Justus, James H. "Poets after Midcentury." In *The History of Southern Literature,* edited by Louis D. Rubin, Jr., Blyden Jackson, Rayburn S. Moore, Lewis P. Simpson, and Thomas Daniel Young, 535–55. Baton Rouge: Louisiana State University Press. 1985.
Kilgo, James. "Instructed in Self-Restraint." *Sewanee Review* 97 (Fall 1989): cxviii–cxx.
Lattimore, Richard. "Poetry Chronicle." *Hudson Review* 32 (Autumn 1979): 451–52.
Miller, David. "Exploring the End of the Earth." *Sewanee Review* 95 (Fall 1987): 675–78.

Penaskovic, Richard. Review of *The Meaning of Coyotes. Southern Humanities Review* 20 (Winter 1986): 93.

Walters, Collin. ''The Cowman's Comeuppance.'' Review of *Those Who Blink. Washington Times Magazine* (March 24, 1986): 8M.

WILLIAM HARMON

Robert Morgan
(1944–   )

Since 1969, when his first book was published, Robert Morgan has enjoyed a high and growing reputation as a distinguished writer of occasional fiction and criticism but most of all as a poet of what Wordsworth called those ''little nameless unremembered'' objects, actions, and persons. Much of Morgan's work has to do with his birthplace in the mountains of southwestern North Carolina, marked by a particular landscape, climate, language, history, and personality; but Morgan has also written substantially about upstate New York, where he has spent most of his adult life—along with a few poems about places as distant and diverse as Hawaii and Scotland. Since 1975, Morgan has been celebrated as one of the boldest and most engaging experimenters with verse form.

BIOGRAPHY

Robert (Ray) Morgan was born on October 3, 1944, in Hendersonville, North Carolina, which is in Henderson County, near the southwestern corner of the state, on the border with South Carolina. The area was settled in the eighteenth century by the customary mixture of English, Scottish, and Welsh colonists and became a popular summer resort during the nineteenth century, offering a more comfortable climate than the lower ground of Charlotte, Columbia, and Charleston. The area contains many mansions built during the nineteenth century, one of which became the final home of Carl Sandburg, who lived in Flat Rock, just outside Hendersonville, from the middle 1940s until his death in 1967.

For about a hundred years now, the region has also been known for mining, and Morgan's family—mostly farmers and builders—live in the Green River community near the slightly larger community called Zirconia, named for the zircons and zirconium mined there.

At 16, Morgan went off to Emory University, intending at first to study science and mathematics. He transferred to North Carolina State University in Raleigh, where he had a creative-writing class with the celebrated writer and teacher Guy Owen; and he transferred again, this time to the University of North Carolina at Chapel Hill, where, after study with Jesse Rehder, he graduated with honors in writing in 1965. After a year of graduate study at Chapel Hill, he switched to the M.F.A. program at the University of North Carolina at Greensboro. His most influential teacher there was Fred Chappell, who, like Morgan, was from the mountains of western North Carolina and wrote both fiction and poetry with a strong sense of place and character. After being awarded an endowed master's degree at Greensboro, Morgan taught at Salem College (1968–69) and then lived for 2 years back in his native area, supported by a fellowship from the National Endowment for the Arts and by his work as a house painter. "Suddenly in 1971 Cornell offered me a job teaching creative writing," he has said (*Small Farm*, 40). He has been at Cornell ever since, rising through the ranks to a full professorship and serving a term as acting chairman of the English Department.

Morgan married Nancy Bullock in 1965, and they have one son and two daughters. They live in rural Freeville, just outside Ithaca.

Morgan's first book, *Zirconia Poems*, was published in 1969 by Lillabulero Press, which was run by two friends whom Morgan had met during his time in Chapel Hill: William Matthews and Russell Banks, both of whom later achieved celebrity in literature. His next six publications were books or chapbooks published by different publishers in different states (New York, Louisiana, Colorado, Kentucky, and Virginia); but from 1987 on, he settled down with Wesleyan University Press, which has published his two most recent volumes of poetry and a "new and selected" volume in 1991. Morgan's fiction—in the form of stories and novellas—has appeared in a volume published by Peachtree Publishers of Atlanta, which published a second volume in 1992. *The Hinterlands: A Mountain Tale in Three Parts* came out in 1994.

Morgan has received fellowships from the National Endowment for the Arts and the Guggenheim Foundation. Some of his critical essays have been published, and a number of his poems are appearing in anthologies. A special issue of Jeff Daniel Marion's *The Small Farm* (March 1976) was devoted to Morgan's work, as was the Eighth Annual Literary Festival of Emory and Henry College in Emory, Virginia (March 29–30, 1990), accompanied by a special issue of *Iron Mountain Review* (Spring 1990). Morgan travels a good deal, taking part in workshops and giving readings.

Although he is still young, Morgan has the distinction of having long been an inheritor and custodian of all that is good and wise in American literature—from the naturalists of the eighteenth century and the visionaries of the nineteenth century through the great exemplars of the modern age.

MAJOR THEMES

Morgan specializes in carefully wrought meditative lyrics; and although he cannot be called a didactic poet, he is thoroughly aware of the implications of what his poetry does. In whatever form, style, or idiom—and Morgan's are extraordinarily varied—Morgan's writings *concentrate*. Morgan targets some precise particular subject or object; maybe a character, maybe a gadget, maybe a bird or flower in a natural setting (he has very few urban scenes); he renders the object with uncommon attention to detail. He may let the thing speak for itself, or he may draw the moral explicitly. From early to late, the titles alone suggest the scope and level of Morgan's look: foxfire, watertanks, swamp, cellar, woodpile, bass, whippoorwill, stove, faucet, stump, hubcaps, flood, hogpen, rice, copse, plankroad, slop bucket, blackberries, earache, shovel, feather bed, manure pile, nail bag, odometer, rearview mirror, spirit level, uranium, overalls. Morgan can be lofty and even transcendental now and again; but an attentive reader has to notice that, more often than not, the focus or emphasis is on the small things of the world. Morgan's eye, like God's, is on the sparrow; but his eye is not all that's on it (his ear and heart are, too), and the sparrow is not all that his eye is on.

Morgan's indulgent sympathy for all creatures great and small has reminded some critics that the original name of the heresiarch Pelagius was Morgan. *Morgan* in Welsh means ''by the sea,'' of which *Pelagius* is the Greek equivalent. Although Morgan-Pelagius was attacked by Augustine and excommunicated by Pope Zozimus I in 420, the Pelagian heresy remains the most appealing. The denial of original sin tallies with much of our actual experience, and many may regard as rather exaggerated a universal punishment of the entire species because of a flaw in the prototype. In ''Mockingbird'' in *Trunk and Thicket* (1978), Morgan suggests that ''the statute of / limitations has run out on original / sin'' (40–41); one critic has called Morgan's earth-poems ''Pelagian georgics.''

Alongside the concentration on the modest, Morgan has attempted some more ambitious long poems that combine science, art, philosophy, and religion, in much the same way in which those enterprises were tested and mixed by Morgan's nineteenth-century precursors, among whom Poe, Thoreau, and Melville are preëminent. The best of these is the aforementioned ''Mockingbird.'' This long poem—supposedly part of one even longer—concentrates on the meaning of the sounds of the world, as they are centered in a nocturnal birdsong enchantingly registered:

> While the bee sleeps in the southern night
> and weeds weigh under dowries of dew,
> above the distant honky tonk of falls in
> the July dark, before the katydids, when
> the only frost is lunar, a voice that
> raises the hackles on mountains and chills

the barometric spine, that radios through
many channels in the crab orchard and from
maples above the road. What madrigalist
watering the night with polyphony. (35)

One recollects here that ''georgics'' means ''earthworks,'' and this devout attention to the sounds of the world is the stamp of the serious maker. More than
any overtly stated sentiment, Morgan's technique itself says, ''Concentrate . . .
pay attention.'' The bird itself says as much:

Play with matches,
correspondences. Keep the covenant
with bottomlands and shovel down into
the atom's masonry. (37)

In its climactic section, ''Mockingbird'' distills from the bird's mimetic song a
series of messages that display Morgan's lyric skills as well as his background
in science:

I will be what I will be. It is the
dead speaking now from every petal
of the compass, every atom in
the dark traffic. The voice ascends at the
wavelength of mountains out of swamp musk
into the crypt of sky, builds loglog concision
in the night of Babylonian weight,
a table whose bulbed legs whirl gyroscopically
vertical, with grain distinct as the
thumbprint of a file or the ingots of
a snake's belly . . . (40)

A look at a birdwatcher's guide will confirm that the wavelength of the song
of *Mimus polyglottos* (mockingbird), expressed in meters, would be about the
size of a mountain; ''loglog'' recalls the now-defunct lexicon of the slide-rule
with a function that could express logarithms and logarithms *of* logarithms (on
a ''loglog'' scale) with notable concision, as well as building with log on log—
and maybe even not so far from the science that Kenneth Burke calls Logol-
ogy.

''Mockingbird'' ends with ''anonymity,'' and Morgan, in keeping with his
mountain manners, seems to prefer an introvert's reticence and modesty, especially in his writing. He is as far as could be from the confessional and autobiographical idioms that have come to seem all but inescapable in much
post-modern writing. Morgan, however, has enough confidence in his own
mind and voice, so that he does not need to advance the cause of his own ego.
He presents himself, at most, as a Morgan, a member of a large, interesting

family—one member, illiterate and bold, won the battle of Cowpens in the Revolution; another (the uncle for whom Robert is named) died in World War II; another (his extravert father) has spoken in tongues. In one uncharacteristically personal pun, Morgan ends the volume *At the Edge of the Orchard Country* (1987) with *morgenland,* which in German means "morningland," or "Orient."

Morgan has reversed the pattern of growth that can be seen in a number of American poets born during the 1920s, about a generation older than he is. With Louis Simpson, W. S. Merwin, James Wright, and Robert Bly, for example, the earliest poems are examples of conventional rhymed verse that gives way, in later poems, to varieties of free (or at least freer) verse, touched with symbolist and surrealist gestures. Morgan, on the other hand, began with poems like "Waking Late in the Afternoon" *(Zirconia Poems)*:

> An oak burns in the cold wind, sky of stained glass.
> In the dream it was my death singing,
> a blue sphinx lighting the sand reefs, the flowing
> savannahs.
>
> I lay at the bottom of a lagoon,
> my body a clock's hand turned by the current. (6)

Eventually, through the 1970s and 1980s, Morgan came to add the pleasures of convention to the pleasures of invention. He experimented with many difficult and demanding forms, such as the triolet and the pantoum. His "Earache" *(Bronze Age)* is a terza rima sonnet, a form so rare that only a few poets have tried it (they include Shelley, Hardy, Frost, John Frederick Nims, Michael McFee, and Philip Larkin). Morgan is the only poet in English who has used the form called chant royal for a serious poem. Morgan's "Chant Royal" *(At the Edge of the Orchard Country)* is sixty lines long: five eleven-line stanzas plus a five-line envoy, all the parts using the same rhyme-sounds but not the same rhyme-words, so that sixty lines have to be written with just five rhyming sounds. It is significant that Morgan's "Chant Royal" appeared in the *place d'honneur* at the beginning of the first issue of *Poetry* magazine edited by John Frederick Nims. Just as Morgan has attended to humble subjects, he has also attempted serious poetry in manners usually reserved for play. The end of "Chant Royal" invokes a spirit to "inhere herein," and "Mountain Graveyard" consists of nothing but six anagrams:

> stone notes
>
> slate tales
>
> sacred cedars
>
> heart earth

asleep please

hated death

SURVEY OF CRITICISM

To date there has been little criticism of Robert Morgan's poetry and practically no criticism of his fiction. Most of the studies listed at the end of this
essay concentrate on placing Morgan in a context—either spatial, as an Appalachian writer, or temporal-historical, as a member of the distinguished generation of American poets born in the 1940s, including James Tate, William
Matthews, Alan Williamson, Dave Smith, Louise Glück, Everette Maddox, Norman Dukes, and Albert Goldbarth.

As yet, there is no book-length study, but two periodicals have devoted special
issues to Robert Morgan. *Small Farm* (March 1976) contains the interview listed
above and material by Louis M. Bourne, Fred Chappell, J. B. Merod, and William Matthews. *Iron Mountain Review* (Spring 1990) contains the proceedings
of the Emory and Henry College Eighth Annual Literary Festival, which honored Morgan. It contains the interview listed above and materials by Michael
McFee, Stephen Marion, Mary C. Williams, and John Lang. The following list
of studies is adapted from Lang's valuable "Robert Morgan Bibliography" in
Iron Mountain Review.

BIBLIOGRAPHY

Works by Robert Morgan

Zirconia Poems. Northwood Narrows, N.H.: Lillabulero Press, 1969.
The Voice in the Crosshairs. Ithaca, N.Y.: Angelfish Press, 1971.
Red Owl: Poems. New York: Norton, 1972.
Land Diving: New Poems. Baton Rouge: Louisiana State University Press, 1976.
Trunk and Thicket. Fort Collins, Colo.: L'Epervier Press, 1978.
Groundwork. Frankfort, Ky.: Gnomon Press, 1979.
Bronze Age: Poems. Emory, Va.: Iron Mountain Press, 1981.
At the Edge of the Orchard Country. Middletown, Conn.: Wesleyan University Press,
     1987.
The Blue Valleys: A Collection of Stories. Atlanta: Peachtree Publishers, 1989.
Sigodlin. Middletown, Conn.: Wesleyan University Press, 1990.
Green River: New and Selected Poems. Middletown, Conn.: Wesleyan University Press,
     1991.
Watershed. Atlanta: Peachtree Publishers, 1991.
The Mountains Won't Remember Us and Other Stories. Atlanta: Peachtree Publishers,
     1992.
Good Measure: Essays, Interviews, and Notes on Poetry. Baton Rouge: Louisiana State
     University, 1993.

The Hinterlands: A Mountain Tale in Three Parts. Chapel Hill, N.C.: Algonquin Books, 1994.

Interviews with Robert Morgan

"Biographical Note." *Small Farm,* no. 3 (March 1976).
Booker, Suzanne. "A Conversation with Robert Morgan." *Carolina Quarterly* 37 (Spring 1985). Reprinted in *Good Measure,* 131–43.
Harmon, William. "Imagination, Memory, and Region: A Conversation." *Iron Mountain Review* 6 (Spring 1990). Reprinted in *Good Measure,* 158–70.
Rubin, Stan Sanvel, and William Heyen, eds. "The Rush of Language: A Conversation with Robert Morgan." In *The Post-Confessionals: Conversations with American Poets of the Eighties.* Rutherford, N.J.: Fairleigh Dickinson University Press, 1989.

Studies of Robert Morgan

Chappell, Fred. "Double Language: Three Appalachian Poets." *Appalachian Journal* 8 (Autumn 1980): 49–53.
Einstein, Frank. "The Politics of Nostalgia: Uses of the Past in Recent Appalachian Poetry." *Appalachian Journal* 8 (Autumn 1980): 32–40.
Harmon, William. "Robert Morgan's Pelagian Georgics: Twelve Essays." *Parnassus* 9 (Fall–Winter 1981): 5–30.
James, Roger D. "Robert Morgan." In *Contemporary American Poets, Dictionary of Literary Biography,* edited by R. S. Gwynn. In press.
Liotta, P. H. "Pieces of the Morgenland: The Recent Achievement in Robert Morgan's Poetry." *Southern Literary Journal* 22 (Fall 1989): 32–40.
Marion, Stephen. "Gleaning the Unsayable: The Terrain of Vision in Poems by Robert Morgan, Fred Chappell, and Jim Wayne Miller." *Mossy Creek Journal* 9 (1985): 25–33.
Quillen, Rita. *Looking for Native Ground: Contemporary Appalachian Poetry.* Appalachian Consortium Press, 1989.
Schultz, Robert. "Recovering Pieces of the Morgenland." *Virginia Quarterly Review* 64 (Winter 1988): 176–88.
Williams, Mary C. "Place in Poetry: Preserving and Deconstructing Southern Mythology." *Pembroke Magazine* 20 (1988): 124–31.
Wright, Stuart. "Robert Morgan: A Bibliographic Chronicle, 1963–81." *Bulletin of Bibliography* 39 (September 1982): 121–31.

Willie Morris
(1934–   )

Willie Morris of Mississippi has earned national recognition as a journalist, novelist, storyteller, autobiographer, and especially as editor and essayist. His major contribution has been to make available to contemporary American journalism the considerable resources of the Southern "literature of memory"— themes and techniques developed by early Modernist novelists Thomas Wolfe and William Faulkner and later Modernist novelists Ralph Ellison and William Styron.

BIOGRAPHY

The standard source of information on Morris's early life is *North Toward Home,* the Wolfe-like autobiography he published, in 1967, when he was 33. There he describes his ancestors (including a distant relationship on his mother's side to a Mississippi governor), his father's job delivering Cities Service gasoline, and the family's move when he was 6 months old from Jackson, Mississippi, where he was born on November 29, 1934, to Yazoo City, Mississippi, a town that sits "on the edge of the delta, straddling that memorable divide where the hills end and the flat land begins" (4). In Yazoo City, he grew up, in J. S. Carroll's words, as "a bright but otherwise conventional middle-class small-town white Southern Protestant boy."

In 1952, when he was 17, taking his father's advice "to get the hell out of Mississippi" (*North Toward Home,* 140) he began his studies at the University of Texas. There he was transformed from an intelligent but prank-loving boy without many books or important ideas into the muckraking editor of the university's *Daily Texan,* ready to support desegregation at the school and courageous in his attacks on the university's board of regents as well as the oil and gas interests that ran the state. His work at Texas brought him a Rhodes Scholarship (1956–1960) to New College, Oxford, where he earned a B.A. and M.A. As he reveals in a later essay, "The Other Oxford," reprinted in *Terrains of the Heart* (1981), Oxford taught him to recognize nonsense when he saw it, "especially in himself"; and Oxford not only showed him what it meant to be "a participant—not . . . an outsider or an interloper—in the process of learning," but also made him realize that he bore the responsibility of becoming one of the writers of history, not a mere observer or passive reporter. During the Oxford years, he married Celia Buchan in 1958, in Houston, Texas. In 1959, Willie and Celia's son David Rae Morris was born in Oxford, England.

From Oxford, Morris came back to Texas in 1961, to edit the liberal *Texas Observer* in Austin. Covering the state's political and literary activities from his new base, Morris witnessed the increasing Dixie-fication of the nation as Texas-and-South-connected Senator Barry Goldwater of Arizona forged the far-right wing of the Republican party in a political setting heated by the secretive John Birch Society.

Morris's contributions to the *Texas Observer* made possible his move in 1963 to an editorship at *Harper's* magazine and to New York. Before ascending to editor-in-chief in 1967, he edited a special supplement, *The South Today* (1965), in which he put his own Southern spin on interpretations of national changes by including essays by C. Vann Woodward, William Styron, Walker Percy, Edwin Yoder, Whitney Young, Arna Bontemps, Jonathan Daniels, James Kilpatrick, and others. Because opinions varying from those of Whitney Young to James Kilpatrick's cover a wide range, Morris's collection spoke for a more inclusive and enlightened South than that represented by Goldwater's Southern connections and for a less grandiose South than that of the Texan who was then president, Lyndon B. Johnson. The region that Morris's supplement identified anticipated the South that Jimmy Carter would embody as he commanded national attention a decade later. Morris continued to represent the liberal and moderate South on the national scene with *North Toward Home,* which appeared (as a Houghton Mifflin Literary Fellowship Book) in the same year in which he became editor-in-chief at *Harper's,* a conjunction that caused the reviewer for *America* magazine to proclaim that *"Harper's* is indeed in good hands."

As the youngest editor-in-chief in *Harper's* history (1967–71), Morris put together a group of productive and reasonably well-paid contributing editors— David Halberstam, Larry L. King, John Corry, and Marshall Frady, with Midge Decter as executive editor—and well-known contributors, including Norman Mailer, William Styron, and Morris himself. This group made *Harper's,* in William Moss's words (1989), "probably the most significant magazine in America during a time of fundamental change" (1967), a journal that published, according to Stuart Little (1971), "some of the most provocative and . . . longest pieces in magazine journalism" (45), including 45,000 words from Styron's *The Confessions of Nat Turner.* The prices Morris paid for important work, however, (combined perhaps with Mailer's frank opinions and language in a controversial contribution, "The Prisoner of Sex") led his publisher William S. Blair to persuade the owner, a Minneapolis newspaper executive, to pressure Morris to resign. Seven of his editors also resigned, in one of the most dramatic protests in recent times of "the literary men," in Morris's words, against "the money men." Morris's fate foreshadowed that of many editors and writers in the following two decades as larger and larger business conglomerates took over once esteemed publications and publishers.

On leaving *Harper's,* Morris, whose marriage to Celia Buchan had ended in 1969, wrote from his home in Bridgehampton, Long Island. There novelist James Jones, author of *From Here to Eternity* (1951) and other important novels of World War II, was his good friend. During the 1970s Morris published *Yazoo: Integration in a Deep-Southern Town* (1971), *Good Old Boy: A Delta Boyhood* (1971) (filmed in 1988 by Walt Disney Studios, shown on television in 1989), *The Last of the Southern Girls* (1973) (his first novel), *A Southern Album* (1975), and *James Jones: A Friendship* (1978). Morris also completed *Whistle* (1977)— the novel that Jones was working on when he died—by constructing the final twelve pages (of 452) from notes and instructions left by Jones.

Of these books from the 1970s, *Yazoo* must stand with *North Towards Home* as one of the finest works that Morris has yet published. The style is more restrained, freer from echoes of Wolfean rhetoric, and sharpened by fresh observations of the vital moment in Southern history when small towns in the Deep South picked up the weight of 350 years of Southern history and, by integrating their public schools, regained a pride in the strength of true community. Like many of Faulkner's works, it is a moving record of the Southern heart in conflict with itself. But in Morris's book the balance of forces is weighed in favor of racial progress. For Morris's pride in the relative success of his own town in starting the transition and his reasoned defense of integration, in a decade when radical voices were espousing separatism, sets the dominant tone of the short study of Yazoo. The personality sketches of individuals involved in integration—including the then-unknown Alice Walker—are among the sharpest elements in the volume.

The integration of Yazoo may have triggered a mirroring process within Morris himself. For having concluded his autobiography over a decade before with the observation that leaving the South felt as though "someone had taken some terrible weight off my shoulders" as he "turned north toward home" (437–38), Morris decided, during a Mississippi football weekend in 1979, to return to Mississippi to live. In 1980 he became writer-in-residence at the University of Mississippi at Oxford. In his first year he offered a course on the modern American novel and was able to bring to the campus William Styron, John Knowles, and James Jones's widow, Gloria Jones, to discuss *Sophie's Choice, A Separate Peace,* and *From Here to Eternity.* Members of the English department reportedly did not know what to do with the Morris phenomenon. While the chairman considered the publicity he brought to the university invaluable, Morris's approach sometimes strained the established course format of the department.

Of the books that Morris published during the 1980s, the titles of the first and fourth convey the direction of his psychological movement. The books are *Terrains of the Heart and Other Essays on Home* (1981); *The Courting of Marcus Dupree* (1983); *Always Stand in against the Curve and Other Sports Stories* (1983), including seven stories by Morris and sixteen pages of photographs from his school days; and *Homecomings* (1989), including six essays by Morris, fourteen pages of color plates by Mississippi-born "hypothetical realist" painter William Dunlap, and a dialogue between the painter and the essayist; and *Good Old Boy and The Witch of Yazoo* (1989). Of these books, *The Courting of Marcus Dupree* has attracted most attention. Here Morris reports on the way in which universities showered scholarship offers on Marcus Dupree, a talented black football player from an integrated high school in Philadelphia, Mississippi. Because Philadelphia was also the scene of the 1964 murders of the three civil-rights workers, James Earl Chaney, Andrew Goodman, and Michael H. Schwerner, Morris was able to use sections of his book as a retrospective contrasting attitudes in the town in 1964—the year of Dupree's birth and of the civil-rights murders—with the generally sympathetic interest that the youthful star's fellow citizens took in his football future.

In 1990 Morris continued in Oxford, Mississippi. There he was closely connected with the Yoknapatawpha Press and its publishers, Dean Faulkner Wells, whose uncle was William Faulkner, and Larry Wells, who raised the money from Mississippi businessmen that permitted the university's English faculty to hire Morris as a writer-in-residence. On September 14, 1990, Morris married JoAnne Prichard of Jackson, Mississippi.

A spiteful *Washington Post* reporter has pictured Morris, "broad of beam," sitting by the fire in the Wellses' house, drinking his bourbon, his black Labrador Pete at hand. Morris himself reports that he spends his time traveling "the roads of Mississippi, Louisiana, Arkansas, Alabama, Georgia, Texas, and Tennessee selling Yok Press books," which now include a number of his own titles. With five or more books out in each of the two decades since he left *Harper's,* in addition to teaching duties (now chiefly in the journalism department), Morris remains busy. He has recently seen the publication of *Faulkner's Mississippi* (1990) and the sequel to *North Toward Home* titled *New York Days* (1993); and he has completed final revisions of a novel, underway since 1981, called *Taps,* about a small town during the Korean war. As such essays as "Anybody's Children" and "Capote Remembered" in *Homecomings* demonstrate, Morris's prose has never been stronger or more lucid.

MAJOR THEMES

Although Morris has written two novels, an autobiography, a memoir of James Jones, and two studies of contemporary social phenomena, integration and sports exploitation, his primary literary form has been the personal essay of ten to thirty pages in which he combines memory with contemporary observation. The essays vary greatly in length and theme. Some like "The Phantom of

Yazoo'' develop humorous anecdotes from a childhood obsessed with baseball and sports in general. Others like his brief ''The Lending Library of Love'' and the book-length *Yazoo* examine the important social changes of the age.

His works frequently draw on techniques and themes developed by major Southern novelists of the twentieth century. From Wolfe and Styron come respect for writing from the personal point of view, an inclusive and flexible style that is both powerful and accessible, and an American myth that views the South as a web that both draws and repels the talented young, while seeing the North as the Rock, or dark Cave, that both challenges the neophyte and tempts him or her with fame and fortune. With Faulkner and especially with Ellison, Morris shares the soul-wrenching conviction that both the South and America must find a way to reconcile racial diversity with brotherhood. Like these masters, Morris knows that the best Southern writing dramatizes the individual heart in conflict with itself, a struggle often centered on the conflict between the challenge of change and the demands of memory—between the present and the past.

Frequently, Morris's memories go back to the small towns of Mississippi—to Yazoo City, Philadelphia, Oxford—that are the repositories of the personal and community associations most important to him and, in many cases, to his contemporaries. For it was in such small towns that his ancestors thrived, that his parents shaped his character, that he and other young men participated in pranks and sports, that the esteemed William Faulkner lived. These were the settings that the supreme social transformation of his generation—racial integration—chose for its crucible.

His researches into present and past often lead to what endures of the Southern respect for the natural aristocrat hidden in men and women. In his past he discovers (*Homecomings*) the great-grandfather who during the debate on the Compromise of 1850 protested against the ''fanaticism and folly—ultraism and sectionalism . . . dogmas at which every patriot breast must stand appalled'' (7). In the present he finds reasons for pride in the progress his hometown has made toward integration; pride in the courage of a young black man, a football superstar, who brings blacks and whites together in a town infamous for its racial crime; pride in the work of friends and fellow writers Jones, Styron, Ellison, Capote, Richard Wright. Because he possesses this ''generosity of spirit'' that has enabled him always to keep one eye on the courage in his subjects, he has seldom seemed strident when he has attacked what is false and pernicious in the John Birch Society, Southern segregationists, callous city dwellers, shallow and insecure critics and intellectuals. If on occasion he has grown emotional about the comforts of returning home, he has generally managed to prick the bubble of his own sentiment with a comic memory or sardonic touch—like tires flattening roses left on the asphalt of a parking lot where the house of one's grandparents stood. Because in his essays Morris has combined a deftness of tone and observation with a remarkable intelligence and a sureness of style, those essays are always a delight to the ear and good food for the mind—entertainments worth the time.

SURVEY OF CRITICISM

Thus far attention to Morris's works has been largely limited to reviews in magazines and newspapers. He himself, however, has been the subject of much attention in the national press, in part because his past is often the subject of his work and because his career has furnished several dramatic incidents.

Investigation of Morris's life begins with essays by Thomas J. Richardson, in *Lives of Mississippi Authors, 1817–1967* (1981), and by William Moss, in *Encyclopedia of Southern Culture* (1989). These short pieces should be supplemented with Stuart Little's article (1971), "What Happened at *Harper's*," describing matters relevant to Morris's resignation from the magazine, in addition to Norman Mailer's reply to Stuart and a competing account in *Publisher's Weekly* titled "Morris Quits at Harper's; Cites 'Severe Disagreements.' " The author's essays and books add other, intriguing details. But in evaluating the autobiographical materials one should bear in mind that Morris is on record as agreeing with Mark Twain that " 'sometimes you've got to lie to tell the truth,' " and that, in his own words, "invention is the highest form of reality."

Reviewers, in general, were kinder to Morris when he was a power at *Harper's* than they have been since he became an independent writer living in Mississippi. *North Toward Home,* for example, attracted positive reactions. E. P. J. Corbett in *America* (1967) called it "one of the best books of the year in any category. . . . It's a remarkable, memorable book" (720). J. S. Carroll in *New Republic* (1967), found the way Morris related his "slow initiation into the intellectual life" of America "superb" (32). Madison Jones in the *New York Times Book Review* (1967) believed the book lacked a "really solid center" or "meaningful unity," but applauded the "fine sketches" of the "abrasiveness, loneliness and violence" of life in New York City and "the many vivid sketches of persons and places." Jones found the prose "extraordinarily clean, flexible and incisive" (5). In contrast, Alfred Kazin in *Vogue* (1967) found the sections on New York "full of standard Southern responses," "echoes of other Southerners," but liked the earliest parts that "radiate an old-fashioned normalcy and manliness" and that are "redolent of all the sensuous and lovely experiences that have made Southern writing valuable" (173). Peter Schrag in *Reporter* (1967) compared the book to *The Education of Henry Adams* and judged that Morris was "a very funny man who has produced a magnificent book" (44). Finally, Granville Hicks in *Saturday Review* (1968) called the autobiography a "contribution to the intellectual history of the United States in the Fifties and Sixties" because Morris brought to his New York City job "a familiarity with other parts of the country" (77, 81).

Reviews of *Yazoo* were equally favorable. Robert Clayton in *Library Journal* (1971) spoke of the book's "appealing sensitivity" and "superb understanding of contemporary Mississippi and the South." "This forceful book," he suggested, "must be given wide circulation so that it may speak to all of us" (1958). Dan Wakefield, in the *New York Times Book Review* (1971) discovered the "great gentleness" and "deep sense of decency" underlying Morris's story of the pain and anger of his hometown (42). Geoffrey Wolff in *Newsweek* (1971) applauded the way in which Morris "faces down the contraries at war within him" and "comes to terms with" school desegregation by supporting the "potential community of Southern blacks and whites" based on "many, many shared values and instincts" (110). R. Z. Sheppard in *Time* (1971) approved of the way the blend of journalism and autobiography put "graceful reins on [Morris's] prose, which sometimes seems about to run wild like Thomas Wolfe's or feed royally on itself like Norman Mailer's" (93).

Reviewers treated *Good Old Boy* as a book for boys. A reviewer for *Library Journal* (1972) called it "a shortened and somewhat simplified version of the 'Mississippi' section" of *North Towards Home* (290). T. H. Stahel in *America* (1972) found it "good reading, especially for boys" and for "anyone who appreciates reminiscences vividly remembered and lovingly recounted" (324). Stahel's views found support from J. F. Smith in *Christian Science Monitor* (1972) and Brooke Anson in *Library Journal* (1972).

Response to Morris's first novel, *The Last of the Southern Girls,* was more critical than the reception of the earlier books. Jonathan Yardley in *New Republic* (1973), for example, found Morris's story of Carol Hollywell and her meteoric rise from Arkansas debutante to belle of Capitol Hill in the late 1950s and 1960s to be "witty, intelligent and engaging"—a "roman à clef" to "set the tongues to wagging" at Washington cocktail parties. But Yardley also recognized that Morris as novelist had "difficulty weaving expository material into his story" and felt that, at times, Morris's usually skillful prose lapsed "into mush" (28). The *New Yorker*'s reviewer (1973) thought Morris "too complex a writer to . . . write a semifactual popular novel"—that is "mostly slick and . . . shallow" (122). A reviewer for the *New York Times Book Review* (1973) found the novel "serviceably written" but unastonishing, unoffending, unenthralling; the result is a book no more significant than its "beautiful, witty, competent," self-centered protagonist (7).

Morris's *James Jones* fared little better with the critics who noticed it. R. J. Kelly in *Library Journal* (1978) thought it a "refreshing tribute" to Jones, a "skillfully rendered" account, "an engaging portrait: anecdotal and affectionate, witty and wise" (2114). Mitchell Ross in *New Republic* (1978) found Morris too worshipful of Jones, but recommended the portrait as a serviceable source of "details of Jones's life . . . until a full biography comes along" (37). Seymour Krim in *Nation* (1978) faulted Morris, however, for neglecting "the complex element of buddyship among American men" that was "basic to all of Jones's writing" and for avoiding "the seductive bisexual charm that Jones exercised without losing his gruff authority" (447).

The notices that *The Courting of Marcus Dupree* drew were respectable, but not as enthusiastic as one would desire for a major work of 450 pages. Phoebe-Lou Adams in *Atlantic* (1983) called the author "an intelligent observer, a fine reporter, and a southerner," but finished the book with "the suspicion that in

Philadelphia he encountered an invisible and impenetrable wall'' (116). Josephine A. DeLapo in *Library Journal* (1983) found it "an exceptional book," "certainly not for the average fan looking for a simple football story"—'this is for a special audience'' (2095). Susan Lardner in the *New Yorker* (1984) wrote that "Morris labors to see something of himself in Dupree, but the effort fails, and he is driven to rumination and rhetorical questions'' (136). Beth Brown in *Journal of Black Studies* (1987) noted that Morris's successful treatment of the Dupree story "culminated in a tremendous piece of reporting, historical analysis, and biography in an exciting, although cumbersome, combination'' (513). David Bradley in the *New York Times Book Review* (1983) took a more positive position than most. For Bradley, the book was "not just a piece of history but a work of prophecy''—"a well-conceived and well-crafted book that has topical impact, a luckily timed piece of publishing that is also a document of significance and undeniable truth'' (11).

Morris's other works, all of them published in the South rather than New York, have attracted few national reviews but have drawn favorable notices. *Homecomings,* for example, caused Michael Pearson in the Atlanta *Journal-Constitution* (1990) to ask if there is "another essayist writing today who can describe the South with such honesty and affection'' (sec. N 9). Of the same collection, Kerry Luft in the *Chicago Tribune* (1989) wrote: "Five of the six essays sparkle, and the sixth, which is about Morris's great-grandfather, is better still'' (3). Gail Caldwell in the *Boston Globe* (1990) described the essays in *Homecoming* as ranging "from the poignant to the peripheral to the searingly acute'' and concluded that "there's damn fine life left in this man's prose'' (69).

In addition, the scholarly literary journals have begun to pay attention to Morris's works. For example, Paul Mitchell in *Notes on Mississippi Writers* (1970) has taken up Madison Jones's charge that *North Towards Home* lacks a unifying center. According to Mitchell's analysis, "the quest motif . . . serves as the artistic center'' and gives the autobiography its unity (105). Finally, William L. Andrews in *Southern Review* (1988) has compared four Mississippi autobiographies—by William Alexander Percy, Richard Wright, Anne Moody, and Willie Morris. Andrews stresses Morris's desire to confirm "a core of southern experience and a fundamental southern view of life'' "beneath and beyond the racial differences.'' Andrews cites this need in suggesting why Morris was troubled, when he first met Richard Wright in Paris in 1957, by Wright's difference from Morris "in temperament and loyalty and experience.'' Andrews sees Morris's encounter with Wright as a warning to "white readers about . . . the totalizing tendencies'' of the ideals held by all white integrationists who identify "as truly southern only those aspects of black experience that buttress, rather than destabilize'' their ideal of oneness (56–57). After Andrews's essay appeared, Morris published a second version of his first meeting with Wright, in "Dialogue: The Author and Artist,'' the preface to *Homecomings*. In his account of tracing Wright's Mississippi roots with Wright's daughter Julia, Morris stresses the black novelist's "warm, friendly, humorous'' (xxi) side in addition to the bellicose quality, the difference that Morris had expected. This interplay of texts, along with the work of Mitchell and Andrews, suggests that the deep critical assessment of Morris's work has only begun.

BIBLIOGRAPHY

Works by Willie Morris

North Toward Home. Boston: Houghton Mifflin, 1967.

Good Old Boy: A Delta Boyhood. New York: Harper, 1971.

Yazoo: Integration in a Deep-Southern Town. New York: Harper, 1971.

The Last of the Southern Girls. New York: Knopf, 1973.

A Southern Album: Recollections of Some People and Places and Times Gone By, edited by Irwin Glusker, narrative by Willie Morris. Birmingham, Ala.: Oxmoor House, 1975.

James Jones: A Friendship. Garden City, N.Y.: Doubleday, 1978.

Terrains of the Heart and Other Essays on Home. Oxford, Miss.: Yoknapatawpha, 1981.

The Courting of Marcus Dupree. Garden City, N.Y.: Doubleday, 1983. Reprint. Jackson: University Press of Mississippi, 1992.

Always Stand in against the Curve and Other Sports Stories. Oxford, Miss.: Yoknapatawpha, 1983.

Good Old Boy and The Witch of Yazoo. Oxford, Miss.: Yoknapatawpha, 1989.

Homecomings. With the Art of William Dunlap. Jackson: University Press of Mississippi, 1989.

Faulkner's Mississippi. With Photographs by William Eggleston. Birmingham, Ala.: Oxmoor House, 1990.

After All, It's Only a Game. With illustrations by Lynn Green Root. Jackson: University Press of Mississippi, 1992.

New York Days. Boston: Little, Brown, 1993.

Interviews with Willie Morris

Frost, David. "The South Is a Split Infinitive Trying To Get Together: Willie Morris Interview." *The Americans,* 100–107. New York: Stein and Day, 1970.

Jones, John Griffin. Interview. In *Mississippi Writers Talking.* Oxford: University Press of Mississippi, 1983.

Studies of Willie Morris

Adams, Phoebe-Lou. Review of *The Courting of Marcus Dupree. Atlantic* 252 (December 1983): 116.

Andrews, William L. "In Search of a Common Identity: The Self and the South in Four Mississippi Autobiographies." *Southern Review* 24 (1988): 47–64.

Anson, Brooke. Review of *Good Old Boy. Library Journal* 97 (January 15, 1972): 290.

Bradley, David. Review of *The Courting of Marcus Dupree. New York Times Book Review* 88 (December 18, 1983): 11.

Brown, Beth. Review of *The Courting of Marcus Dupree*. *Journal of Black Studies* 17 (June 1987): 511–13.

Caldwell, Gail. Review of *Homecomings*. *Boston Globe* (January 10, 1990): 69.

Carroll, J. S. Review of *North Toward Home*. *New Republic* 157 (November 18, 1967): 32.

Clayton, Robert. Review of *Yazoo: Integration in a Deep Southern Town*. *Library Journal* 96 (June 1, 1971): 1958.

Corbett, E. P. Review of *North Toward Home*. *America* 117 (December 9, 1967): 720.

DeLapo, Josephine A. Review of *The Courting of Marcus Dupree*. *Library Journal* 108 (November 1, 1983): 2095.

Griffith, Thomas. "Cutting Down to Size." *Time* (January 17, 1983): 45.

Hicks, Granville. "How to Succeed at an Early Age." Review of *North Toward Home*. *Saturday Review* 51 (January 13, 1968): 77–78, 81.

Jones, Madison. Review of *North Toward Home*. *New York Times Book Review* (October 22, 1967): 5.

Kazin, Alfred. Review of *North Toward Home*. *Vogue* 150 (1967): 173.

Kelly, R. J. Review of *James Jones: A Friendship*. *Library Journal* 103 (October 15, 1978): 2114.

Krim, Seymour. Review of *James Jones: A Friendship*. *Nation* 227 (October 28, 1978): 447.

Lardner, Susan. Review of *The Courting of Marcus Dupree*. *New Yorker* 60 (March 5, 1984): 136.

Little, Stuart. "What Happened at *Harper's*." *Saturday Review* 54 (April 10, 1971): 43–47, 56.

Luft, Kerry. Review of *Homecomings*. *Chicago Tribune* (December 25, 1989): sec. 5: 3.

Mitchell, Paul. "North Toward Home: The Quest for an Intellectual Home." *Notes on Mississippi Writers* 2 (1970): 105–09.

"Morris Quits at Harper's; Cites 'Severe Disagreements.' " *Publisher's Weekly* 199 (March 15, 1971): 51.

Moss, William. "Morris, Willie." In *Encyclopedia of Southern Culture,* edited by Charles Reagan Wilson and William Ferris. Chapel Hill: University of North Carolina Press, 1989.

"Norman Mailer's Side on 'Harper's.' " Letter. *Saturday Review* 54 (June 12, 1971): 56.

Pearson, Michael. Review of *Homecomings*. Atlanta *Journal-Constitution* (February 11, 1990).

Review of *The Last of the Southern Girls*. *New Yorker* 49 (June 2, 1973): 122.

Review of *The Last of the Southern Girls*. *New York Times Book Review* 78 (May 20, 1973): 7.

Richardson, Thomas J. "Morris, Willie." In *Lives of Mississippi Authors, 1817–1967,* edited by James B. Lloyd, 344–46. Jackson: University Press of Mississippi, 1981.

Ross, Mitchell. Review of *James Jones: A Friendship*. *New Republic* 179 (November 25, 1978): 37.

Schrag, Peter. Review of *North Toward Home*. *Reporter* 37 (November 30, 1967): 44.

Sheppard, R. Z. Review of *Yazoo: Integration in a Deep Southern Town*. *Time* 97 (May 10, 1971): 93.

Smith, J. F. Review of *Good Old Boy*. *Christian Science Monitor* (February 24, 1972): 7.

Stahel, T. H. Review of *Good Old Boy*. *America* 126 (March 25, 1972): 324.

Wakefield, Dan. Review of *Yazoo: Integration in a Deep Southern Town*. *New York Times Book Review* 76 (May 16, 1971): 42.

Wolff, Geoffrey. Review of *Yazoo: Integration in a Deep Southern Town*. *Newsweek* 77 (May 10, 1971): 110.

Yardley, Jonathan. Review of *The Last of the Southern Girls*. *New Republic* 168 (May 19, 1973): 28.

BILLY J. HARBIN AND JILL STAPLETON BERGERON

Marsha Norman
(1947–   )

Marsha Norman gained international recognition as an important American play-wright in 1983 when her fifth play, *'night, Mother,* was awarded the Pulitzer Prize. Her first play, *Getting Out,* written only six years earlier, came out of her experiences as a teacher of disturbed children at Kentucky's Central State Hos-pital. The extraordinary success of *Getting Out* brought Norman critical attention as a new Southern writer; and, like Beth Henley, she became identified with the world of the "walking wounded," the folks, as Norman herself put it, "you wouldn't even notice in life" (quoted in Guerrini 1982, 361). Her second play, *Third and Oak* (consisting of two parts, *The Laundromat* and *The Pool Hall*), further reveals Norman's passion for depicting the suffering and grace that hu-manizes and dignifies the ordinary. In *'night, Mother* Norman explores the pri-vate terrain of individual anguish—a young woman's spiritual struggles to free herself from the hold of others so that she may direct her own destiny. The familial bonds that repress rather than nurture, that imprison rather than liberate, and the Ibsenesque imperative that the greatest individual freedom is that which comes from within—these are ideas that pervade the play and that, indeed, have a place in virtually all of Norman's work. Religious questions, too, emerge significantly; in her first play the unseen character of the chaplain represents a positive force that Arlene carries tentatively into her new life; and in later plays, especially *Traveler in the Dark,* struggles of faith become dominant concerns.

BIOGRAPHY

Marsha Norman, born Marsha Williams, on September 21, 1947, the first of four children, grew up in the suburbs of Louisville in the strict fundamentalist home of her parents, Bertha and Billie Williams. Mrs. Williams kept a tight rein on her daughter's activities, discouraging her association with neighborhood children. In interviews Marsha Norman has spoken of her loneliness as a child; denied the companionship of other children, she found interests in reading, music, and her imaginary friend, Bettering.

Marsha Williams began writing while attending Durrett High School in her native Louisville. Her essay on Job (''Why Do Good Men Suffer?'') won first prize in a local contest and subsequently appeared in the *Kentucky English Bulletin* (Spring 1964). Although she felt a passion for writing, it did not occur to her that it might lead to a career. She has said that ''as a girl growing up in Kentucky, I had no models, I had no one like I am today. One of the great joys to me about my success is that no girl who grows up in Kentucky ever has to wonder about that again'' (quoted in Stone 1983, 59).

She considered studying music at Julliard, but instead accepted a scholarship in philosophy at Agnes Scott College, a Presbyterian school for women in Decatur, Georgia. While there she volunteered time at the pediatric burn unit at Grady Hospital in neighboring Atlanta. She earned a B.A. in 1968 and married Michael Norman, her former English teacher from Louisville, whose name she has kept (they divorced in 1974). Marsha Norman later taught at Kentucky's Central State Hospital. This experience became a valuable source for her first play: ''What we had there were children who never talked at all, as well as ones who would just as soon stab you in the back . . . one girl in particular, a 13 year old . . . was absolutely terrifying . . . she was so vicious. She is now in the Federal prison for murder and always was headed that way'' (quoted in Klemesrud 1979, 673).

From 1970 to 1972 Norman taught gifted students in the Jefferson County (Kentucky) school system, receiving her master's in Education from the University of Louisville in 1971. In 1972 she conducted film classes for two years for the Kentucky Arts Commission, which gave her the opportunity to spend two summers at the Center for Understanding Media in New York City, where she earned nearly enough credits for a second master's degree. Soon thereafter she began writing full-time.

Norman's early professional writing includes reviewing books for the *Louisville Times* and creating for the newspaper a Saturday children's supplement entitled *The Jellybean Journal.* She also wrote for Kentucky Educational Television's remedial reading program. In 1977 Jon Jory of the Actors Theatre of Louisville offered to commission a play by Norman, suggesting that she write about some urgent social issue, possibly school integration. Norman rejected the suggested topic and offered instead to write *Getting Out,* which Jory accepted. The play premiered at the Actors Theatre in November 1977, receiving unreserved praise from the local critics; word of its brilliant success spread quickly to regional theatres throughout the country. Norman became playwright in residence for Jory's 1978–79 season. At this time, she met Dann Byck (whom she married in 1978 and divorced a few years later), a prominent Louisville businessman who had been one of the founders and first president of the Actors Theatre. *Getting Out* gained several awards and much attention for Norman.

After its opening, it was presented in the next year at the Mark Taper Forum in Los Angeles, the Phoenix Theatre in New York, and then reopened at the famed off-Broadway house, the Theatre De Lys, on May 15, 1979 for a long run of 237 performances. *Getting Out* was voted the best new regional play by the American Theatre Critics Association, and Norman received the John Gassner New Playwrights Award from the Outer Critics Circle. She also was the recipient of the first George Oppenheimer-Newsday Playwriting Award and a grant from the Rockefeller Foundation, which supported her playwright-in-residence post for the 1979–80 season at the Mark Taper Forum.

Norman continued to premiere most of her new works in the familiar surroundings of the Actors Theatre. *Third and Oak* opened in March 1978 to good notices, but *Circus Valentine,* a play about a traveling circus on a small-town circuit, opened in February 1979 to a harshly negative reception, and Jory closed the production after eleven performances. Norman says that the failure "was devastating. It took me about two years to recover from it and regain my confidence" (quoted in Miller 1984, 311). In the summer of 1980 the Actors Theatre company staged a workshop production of *The Holdup,* which subsequently had runs at the Circle Repertory Company and the American Conservatory Theatre. The play, set in New Mexico in 1914, looks at a time when the Old West was fading into the stuff of myth and legends, when the horse was being replaced by the motorcar, and when, no less than now, unstable family relationships crippled human potential. Norman's fifth play, *'night, Mother,* in a rural Kentucky setting, explores a mother-daughter relationship and the daughter's choice to deliberately end her life. The Pulitzer Prize–winning play had a staged reading at the Circle Repertory Theatre in 1981 and premiered at the American Repertory Theatre in Cambridge before moving on to Broadway's John Golden Theatre, where it opened on March 31, 1983. The play received the Hull-Warriner Award, the Susan Smith Blackburn Prize, and was adapted for the screen (in a motion picture starring Sissy Spacek and Anne Bancroft) by the playwright.

In 1984 Norman wrote *Traveler in the Dark,* which develops the subtle religious motifs of earlier plays into a major dramatic crisis. Sam, a brilliant, world-famous surgeon, despairingly reexamines his moral values after his devoted friend and long-time nurse, Mavis, dies under his hands on the operating table. The central dramatic conflict emerges between the cynical, spiritually adrift surgeon and his father, whose earlier fundamentalist religious fervency has in his older years matured into a confident and articulate expression of faith. The play's resolution has the son shifting into a more compassionate understanding of his father and his beliefs, and discovering, too, that the wife whom he had rejected he now needs and loves.

In recent years, Norman has written her first novel, *The Fortune Teller* (1987), completed "Sarah and Abraham" (1988, unpublished), a play commissioned by Jon Jory for his theatre's Humana Festival of New Plays. Set in a regional theatre, the drama concerns the company's production of the biblical story of

Sarah and Abraham. In 1991 Norman adapted the book (and created lyrics) for a musical version of Frances Hodgson Burnett's popular children's novel *The Secret Garden.* It opened on Broadway in the spring, and in June 1992 Norman received a Tony award for the best book of a musical for 1991. After her divorce from Dann Byck, Norman married Tim Dykman, with whom she has a son, Angus.

MAJOR THEMES

Family relationships, the major concern in virtually all of Marsha Norman's plays, has been a dominant theme for American dramatists since O'Neill. In the wake of the feminist movement of the 1960s, women writers emerged during the next two decades to provide their own explorations of family fragmentation, parental instability, and sibling rivalries. Plays by Tina Howe, Beth Henley, and others trace connections between dysfunctional parents (crippled by marital separation or divorce, disease, ignorance, or death) and their confused children, who stumble forward in life, unmoored, isolated, and lonely. Sometimes the consequences are self-destruction; sometimes an eventually discovered inner resourcefulness gives one the strength to endure, forgive the past, and take charge of the future. Variations upon this theme have become commonplace in American drama as the rootlessness of family, confusion about moral and religious values, and loss of emotional and spiritual nurturing have come to characterize the anguish of our age. The dilemma is human—not merely feminine—and it is from this perspective that Norman has explored the issues in her plays.

Norman's first play, *Getting Out,* has for its protagonist an adolescent murderer who, after serving time for the crime, is returned to society. During her imprisonment, the angry and vicious Arlie becomes aware of another self within her—innocent, resourceful, and likeable—yearning to be realized. This self she calls Arlene; and as the play progresses through the first two days of her freedom, the "reformed" Arlene wrestles hopefully with the destructive influences of her past, vanquishes (although never entirely) the tortured Arlie, and tentatively asserts control of herself and her future.

Although it may seem that Norman resolves too happily Arlie/Arlene's struggle to find redemption within herself, the playwright's emphasis throughout the play is upon the significance of the struggle rather than its resolution—which, in any case, is ambiguous, not absolute. The play demonstrates belief in an inherent human goodness that gives battle to the destructive, antispiritual forces that invade or overwhelm us; and Norman continues to explore this theme in successive plays.

Norman's *'night, Mother* examines the mutually dependent relationship of a mother (Thelma) and daughter (Jessie). The passive Jessie has drifted through a loveless marriage, suffered the loss of her delinquent child's respect, and, having fled to the womblike sanctuary of her mother's home, finds herself re-peating her childhood role of "belonging" to Thelma. She becomes enslaved to the will of another, vulnerable to her mother's indulgent needs and to some profound need of her own to demonstrate her love for Thelma through dutiful service. When the play begins, Jessie has decided to take control of her life by ending it. The dramatic tension of the play has to do with whether Thelma can prevent Jessie from carrying out her threat. She cannot, and the play ends with Jessie's suicide. Clearly, Jessie views her self-execution as a positive—even triumphant—act, which redeems a lifetime of subjugation to the will of others. She grasps control of herself at last and dramatically directs her own destiny. She sees it as a rational and responsible act that brings dignity, authority, and even grace to her last hours. Norman does not seem to suggest any ambiguity or irony in Jessie's choices, thus diminishing the subtlety and complexity of the play. Are we to accept Jessie (or Norman's) view of the suicide as a noble act of self-realization? Or is Jessie self-deluded? Is the suicide an expedient escape, representing defeat rather than victory? Certainly, such questions have been debated by critics of the play, especially women. Karen Malpede believes that "the play's theme pander[s] to those who believe that women, left to their own devices, are merely self-destructive and neurotic" (quoted in Bigsby 1985, 3: 438).

Traveler in the Dark (1984), a play that concerns loss of faith and spiritual quest, followed *'night, Mother*. Perhaps the exterior, pastoral setting, the mul-tiple characters, and the shift away from lack of parental guidance to excessive (or dominant) parental influence all signal Norman's deliberate attempt to free herself of the claustrophobic worlds of *Getting Out* and *'night, Mother*. Perhaps she sought to translate her own struggles of faith into a drama that reflects to some extent the spiritual despair of her time. *Traveler in the Dark* not only signifies Norman's concern about matters of faith, but, like previous plays, it also depicts a passionate inquiry into the relationship of parents and children. Here the struggle is between father and son. Everett, a "country preacher," has reared his son Sam (now a renowned surgeon) in an environment of evangelical sermons, revival meetings, and a judgmental God whose oppressive, vengeful presence pervaded Sam's childhood. Sam's exceptional intelligence and talents, early recognized by his father, led to an exploitation of his gifts, and he became a child evangelist in the service of his father and God. But in young adulthood, he rebelled, perceiving other pathways for his talents. He rejected the religious teachings as fraudulent fiction, and rejected his father, too, whose paternal role Sam could not distinguish from that of moral oppressor. Thus, when Sam lost his faith, he also lost his father. *Traveler in the Dark* depicts Sam's quest to recover both—a pursuit arising more out of some profound longing for spiritual and parental comfort than from intellectual choice. The play's resolution permits Sam, ultimately, to reach out to those whom he had rejected (his father and his wife); and in doing so, he takes a leap of faith, which commits him to hope rather than despair.

SURVEY OF CRITICISM

Lisa McDonnell, in an article for *Southern Quarterly* (1987), groups Marsha Norman with other contemporary Southern writers, such as Beth Henley, identifying as common characteristics "their remarkable gift for story telling, their use of family drama as framework, their sensitive delineation of character and relationships, their employment of bizarre Gothic humor and their use of the southern vernacular to demonstrate the poetic lyricism of the commonplace" (95). It has become a convention to lump Southern writers together in this way, which can be helpful but if overstressed can also diminish a writer's uniqueness. Norman's plays, above all, do not reflect the extravagant, antic humor usually associated with the Southern tradition. Her dramas do share with that tradition (as well as with a tradition as old as drama) a faith in the potential of human spirituality to ennoble and redeem individual suffering.

Critical response to Norman's work (except for numerous reviews of productions) came largely in the wake of her Pulitzer Prize (1983) and has been primarily from women who sought either to account for her significance as a Southern dramatist or to assess her achievement as a woman writer in the context of the feminist movement of the last two decades. Lisa McDonnell (1987) has pushed too hard to make Norman's plays share the characteristics of other Southern writers, without identifying the playwright's significant differences. Lynda Hart (1987) has assessed the playwright's emphasis upon self-control and self-realization, which is also the focus of Jenny S. Spencer's review (1987). Laura Morrow (1988) has examined gratification through food as a metaphor for familial and spiritual deprivation. In contemporary drama, the pervasive use of food, liquor, or narcotics as indulgent substitutes for familial or moral nurturing has become by now almost a cliché; Norman emphasizes this theme only in *'night Mother*. Judith Ann Dillon (1985) has rightly recognized the religious/ spiritual impulse that pervades all of the playwright's works.

Karen Malpede, as noted above, has thought that Norman's depiction of Jessie in *'night Mother* presents a traditional concept of the female as loser. The playwright Elizabeth Wray has "deplored Marsha Norman's co-option by Broadway," whereas writer and director Roberta Sklar has viewed *'night, Mother* "as being accommodated to a male tradition of playwriting," a tradition which centered creative human action in the male, and reinforced the idea of the female as isolated from "communal action and creativity" (quoted in Bigsby 1985 3: 438).

Except for the musical version of *The Secret Garden* and the unpublished "Sarah and Abraham," Norman has created no new plays since *Traveler in the Dark,* a play ignored by critics in favor of her most successful pieces *Getting Out* and *'night Mother*. Whereas critics have insisted upon viewing her work in the context of either a Southern or feminist tradition, future assessments of her work might profitably take fresh direction. Needed is an analysis of her art in the context of her entire canon, which means that her so-called lesser works,

Circus Valentine, The Holdup, Third and Oak, Traveler in the Dark, and ''Sarah and Abraham'' need to be assessed alongside her celebrated plays if we are to reach a more reliable judgment of her individual artistry and her place in contemporary American drama.

BIBLIOGRAPHY

Works by Marsha Norman

Getting Out. New York: Dramatists Play Service, 1979.
Third and Oak—The Laundromat. New York: Dramatists Play Service, 1980.
'night, Mother. New York: Dramatists Play Service, 1983.
''Winter Shakers.'' Unpublished lyrics, music by Norman L. Excerpt, performed as workshop production at the Kentucky Center for the Arts, November 1983.
Third and Oak—The Pool Hall. New York: Dramatists Play Service, 1987.
The Holdup. New York: Dramatists Play Service, 1987.
''Sarah and Abraham.'' Unpublished. Produced at Actors Theatre, Louisville, 1988.
The Fortune Teller. New York: Random House, 1987; London: Collins, 1988.
Four Plays By Marsha Norman [*Getting Out, Third and Oak, The Holdup, Traveler in the Dark*]. New York: Theatre Communications Group, 1988.
The Secret Garden. New York: Theatre Communications Group, 1992.

Studies of Marsha Norman

Bigsby, C. W. E. *A Critical Introduction to Twentieth-Century American Drama: Beyond Broadway,* vol. 3. Cambridge: Cambridge University Press, 1985.
Carlson, Susan L. ''Women in Comedy: Problem, Promise, Paradox.'' *Themes in Drama* 7 (1985): 159–72.
Chinoy, Helen Krich, and Linda Walsh Jenkins. *Women in American Theatre: Careers, Images, Movements.* New York: Crown, 1981.
Dillon, Judith Ann. ''Dramas of Faith: Marsha Norman's Portrayals of Spiritual Achievement.'' Master's thesis, Pennsylvania State University, 1985.
Dolan, Jill. *The Feminist Spectator as Critic.* Ann Arbor: University of Michigan Press, 1988.
Guerrini, Anne M. ''Marsha Norman.'' In *Contemporary Authors,* vol. 105, edited by Frances C. Locker, Martha G. Conway, B. Hal May, and David Versical, 361–62. Detroit: Gale Research, 1982.
Gussow, Mel. ''Women Playwrights: New Voices in the Theater.'' *New York Times Magazine* (May 1, 1983): 22, 25–29, 38, 40.
Hart, Lynda. ''Doing Time: Hunger for Power in Marsha Norman's Plays.'' *Southern Quarterly* 25 (Spring 1987): 67–79.
Herman, William. ''Marsha Norman.'' *Understanding Contemporary American Drama.* Columbia: University of South Carolina Press, 1987.
Keyssar, Helene. ''Success and Its Limits: Mary O'Malley, Wendy Wasserstein, Nell Dunn, Beth Henley, Catherine Hayes, Marsha Norman.'' In *Feminist Theatre: An*

Introduction to Plays of Contemporary British and American Women, 148, 161–66. New York: Grove, 1985.

Kintz, Linda. *The Subject's Tragedy: Political Poetics, Feminist Theory and Drama.* Ann Arbor: University of Michigan Press, 1992.

Klemesrud, Judy. "Playwright Marsha Norman." *New York Times Biographical Service* (May 1979): 673–75.

McDonnell, Lisa J. "Diverse Similitude: Beth Henley and Marsha Norman." *Southern Quarterly* 25 (Spring 1987): 95–104.

Miller, Mary Ellen. "Marsha Norman." In *Dictionary of Literary Biography Yearbook,* edited by Jean W. Ross, 308–12. Detroit: Gale Research, 1984.

Miner, Madonne. " 'What's These Bars Doin' Here?'—The Impossibility of *Getting Out.*" *Theatre Annual* 40 (1985): 115–34.

Morrow, Laura. "Orality and Identity in *'night, Mother* and *Crimes of the Heart.*" *Studies in American Drama, 1945–Present* 3 (1988): 23–29.

Murray, Timothy. "Patriarchal Panopticism, or The Seduction of a Bad Joke: *Getting Out* in Theory." *Theatre Journal* 35 (October 1983): 376–88.

Natalle, Elizabeth. *Feminist Theatre: A Study in Persuasion.* Metuchen, N.J.: Scarecrow, 1985.

Pevitts, Beverly Byers. "Feminist Thematic Trends in Plays Written by Women for the American Theatre, 1970–1979." Ph. D. diss., Southern Illinois University, 1980.

Ramay, Steven J. "Marsha Norman's *Getting Out:* A Production Thesis in Directing." Master's thesis, Louisiana State University, 1981.

Schreiber, Loren P. "*Getting Out* by Marsha Norman: A Production Thesis in Scene Design." Master's thesis, Louisiana State University, 1981.

Spencer, Jenny S. "Norman's *'night, Mother:* Psycho-drama of Female Identity." *Modern Drama* 30 (1987): 364–75.

Steadman, Susan M. "Marsha Norman." In *Notable Women in the American Theatre,* edited by Vera Mowry Roberts, Milly S. Barranger, and Alice M. Robinson, 491–95. Westport, Conn.: Greenwood Press, 1989.

Stone, Elizabeth. "Playwright Marsha Norman: An Optimist Writes about Suicide, Confinement and Despair." *Ms.* 12 (July 1983): 56–59.

Stout, Kate. "Marsha Norman: Writing for the 'Least of Our Brethern.' " *Saturday Review* 9 (September–October 1983): 28–33.

MARY C. WILLIAMS

Guy Owen
(1925–1981)

As editor, poet, novelist, and essayist, Guy Owen always spoke for the South. His subject in fiction was Cape Fear County, North Carolina—a mythical place, in the sense that it does not literally exist. The Flim-Flam Man never actually traversed its narrow roads offering to recharge lightning rods. Yet Guy Owen located all his fiction in the tobacco culture, the folklore, and the communal life of Bladen County, North Carolina, communities, attempting to preserve and recreate them.

BIOGRAPHY

> I was born in Clarkton, North Carolina. Five hundred people—five hundred citizens, counting the doctor's cow. Somebody said our population remained the same because any time a young lady had a baby, a young man had to slip out of town. Gone to Texas.
>
> (quoted in John Carr 1972, 240–41)

So begins the mythologized version. The reality was less humorous. Guy Owen was born in Clarkton, North Carolina, on February 24, 1925, the son of Guy and Margaret Ethel Elkins Owen and eldest of four boys. His birth marked the onset of his mother's mental illness—or so he believed; it was an illness that recurred throughout his mother's life. For this he always carried a burden of partial responsibility, as well as the fear of inherited illness.

For a while Owen's family lived in South Carolina and then in Florida. Because of his mother's ill health and his father's drinking, the family was broken up for a time, during which period 6-year-old Guy and one of his brothers lived with a family in St. Augustine. In the hard times of the Depression,

Owen's father lost his job selling insurance. Without resources, the family moved back to the home of Mrs. Owen's parents in Elkton where Guy, Jr. entered a period that he later looked back on as idyllic—a period of stability and nurturing, thanks to his loving grandparents and doting aunts. Thanks also to the gift from Mr. Elkins of a farm, the Owen family remained in Elkton, where on his grandfather's and father's farms Guy Owen acquired an authentic knowledge of farm chores and tobacco barns, fields, and warehouses.

Books were scarce, but Owen knew well *The Adventures of Tom Sawyer, Huckleberry Finn, Captain Blood,* and *The Swiss Family Robinson.* A sympathetic high-school English teacher encouraged Owen to write and helped him to place poems in the Raleigh *News and Observer* and the Beta Club magazine. The English teacher started a high-school newspaper that Owen edited. In his senior year in high school, Owen was president of the twenty-nine–member class, class salutatorian, and a rather small member of the football team.

Following graduation in 1941, Owen went to Wilmington, North Carolina to become a welder in a shipyard. After 3 months, however, he was hurt in an industrial accident and returned home to learn that his mother had already sent in his application for admission to the University of North Carolina at Chapel Hill. He had one year there, earning his way as a waiter, before joining the army in 1943. Sent overseas, he served in France and Germany as one of General Patton's soldiers. He came home troubled in mind and instilled with a profound hatred for war. At the time of the Vietnam conflict, he joined the line of silent protestors that formed every Wednesday noon in front of the courthouse in downtown Raleigh.

After two more years at the University of North Carolina, he was graduated in 1947. During his college years he stretched his GI Bill allowance to help his younger brothers with their educations. For one semester he did graduate work at the University of Chicago, but found the wind blowing across Lake Michigan far too cold and returned to the University of North Carolina to take his M.A. in 1949 and his Ph.D. in 1955, specializing in Elizabethan and Jacobean drama. He was an instructor at Davidson College for two years after receiving his M.A. and taught at Elon College for one year while he was finishing his dissertation. On receiving his Ph.D., he took a position as assistant professor of English at Stetson University. By this time he had a family; he had married Dorothy Jennings in 1952, and they later had two children, William James and John Leslie.

At Stetson, Owen and others formed a group who not only were writers and lovers of literature but also were interested in all sorts of literary endeavors, including publishing and printing. Under this influence and with his dissertation behind him, Owen was overwhelmed by a powerful urge to write a novel. Over the next 5 years he wrote and rewrote *Season of Fear,* published by Random House in 1960.

While at Stetson, Owen wrote and published a number of poems and founded—and subsidized—the magazine *Impetus* as a showcase for the work of his students in creative-writing classes. By the third issue it had so far outgrown its student aspect that it announced itself as "The Work of British and American Poets" and included poems by James Dickey, Marion Montgomery, and James Whitehead. This periodical took the title *Southern Poetry Review* in 1964 after it was moved to North Carolina State University. Though there was no intent that *Southern Poetry Review* should be—or should be seen as—a regional journal, the title indicates Owen's fierce impulse to witness to the excellence and significance of Southern poetry. Another attempt at witnessing grew out of a conversation with William Taylor, coeditor of *Impetus: Southern Poetry Today,* which was published in 1962 and which was the first anthology of Southern poetry since *The Lyric South* in 1938. Owen also brought out a volume of his poetry, *Cape Fear Country and Other Poetry* (1958).

In 1961 Guy Owen took a big risk: He asked for a year's leave of absence and went with his family to the North Carolina mountains near Moravian Falls to write. Every morning he milked his mother-in-law's cow, then shut himself in a small abandoned post office where he worked on the first draft of *The Ballad of the Flim-Flam Man.* The prospects for marketing a novel in Southern dialect to New York publishers seemed dim—and, in fact, the book did not sell for 2 years. Fortunately, however, it not only found a publisher but was later made into a successful film with George C. Scott as the Flim-Flam Man.

Instead of returning to Stetson, Owen accepted a position as associate professor at North Carolina State University (becoming full professor in 1964). He thought he should be in Raleigh since his mother was so often confined in the mental hospital there. At North Carolina State University, with equal intensity, he taught (American literature, modern poetry, and creative writing), lectured, edited, and wrote—chiefly novels, short stories, and essays, both scholarly and journalistic. During a semester as writer-in-residence at Appalachian State University, he wrote and revised poems that appeared in *The White Stallion* in 1969.

Until the end of 1977 he successfully edited *Southern Poetry Review* with the goals of publishing good poetry and also of helping worthy new poets to find an audience. A 1974 anthology of poems from *Southern Poetry Review* (from University of North Carolina Press) includes A. R. Ammons, Wendell Berry, Fred Chappell, James Dickey, Josephine Jacobsen, Donald Justice, Vassar Miller, Linda Pastan, Dave Smith, and other well-known poets. The journal garnered a modest but respectable readership, a good deal of praise, and enough grants to keep it going, including an NEA grant for editing in 1969. The editors published several chapbooks as special issues; in addition, the editors brought out anthologies of North Carolina poetry (published by John Blair) and of contemporary Southern poetry (from Louisiana State University Press). This last anthology, considerably more comprehensive than *Southern Poetry Today,* was one of the very few devoted to Southern poetry and was intended to call attention to the South's excellent poets, so much overshadowed by its writers of fiction. Owen also edited or coedited volumes of essays on American literature and served as coeditor of *North Carolina Folklore* from 1966 to 1972.

A number of awards came his way: He was a Danforth fellow; he had a Bread

Loaf grant (1960) and a Yaddo grant (1968); and he received the Sir Walter award for fiction for *Joedel* in 1970, the North Carolina Award for literature in 1972, and the Henry Bellamann Foundation Literary Award in 1964, among others.

Winter and summer he spent nearly every day and nearly every evening in the office, behind a huge sheaf of scattered papers, with overflowing drawers and file cabinets on either side. He took refuge in the persona of the absent-minded professor with no money in his pocket and apparently no practical sense, and ruthlessly pared down his family and mundane responsibilities, generally leaving them up to his patient wife. But when it came to his literary life, he was very much in control and had a superb grasp of detail.

A popular teacher, who was recognized with a distinguished teaching award, Owen also did readings and lecturing around the state, some under the auspices of an extension program. Someone informally dubbed him "ambassador for literature" in recognition of his forays into small communities all over North Carolina—and as such he was a rousing success. Nobody could be warmer or funnier or more interesting, and nobody had a louder, more contagious laugh.

This jovial persona, which increased in Southernness the farther north he went, was basically authentic, but it was also something of a cover. His disappointment grew when his autobiographical novel found no publisher, when in the fall of 1977 he had had to pass *Southern Poetry Review* on to another editor (mostly owing to lack of secretarial resources), and when he did not have the enthusiasm to finish the academic novel that he was working on. He drove himself harder than ever, in considerable bitterness of spirit. He churned out journalistic pieces, essays on Erskine Caldwell, and some tall tales (the Uncle Corny stories). Then in late November 1980 he found himself worn out, with a severe pain that he at first took to be gallbladder trouble. Despite two operations for cancer, in 8 months he was dead, dying on July 23, 1981, at the age of 56.

MAJOR THEMES

Guy Owen was convinced that the South maintained a regional identity that shaped its sons and daughters—and, in particular, its writers—that went unappreciated by New York publishers. He was affronted at the idea of labeling as a Southern writer someone who had not grown up in the rural Southland. He had a mission: to publish this region to the world through his own fiction and his editing, reviewing, and lecturing. Important in Owen's work are the cluster of characteristics that he identified as Southern: the sense of place; the focus on family life, on the past, and on racial tensions; and the influence of religion. Owen's fiction and poetry were old-fashioned—and deliberately so—following the traditions of a form rather than trying to be experimental. Particularly Southern also in his own view of his work were the sharp fixing of idiosyncratic character or physical appearance and the concern for language. Owen saw Southerners in a traditional way as natural storytellers whose yarns were often the only entertainment and whose dialect, humor, folk traditions, and particular aptitude for pungent simile he wanted to represent.

In his fiction Owen endeavored to record the look of a field of corn in the early morning or of a tobacco barn stark against the sky. He conveys the sight and sound of the mockingbird, thrush, and martin; Queen Anne's lace, fennel, and broom sedge; the brown river; the pecan, persimmon, and chinaberry trees. He provides an exact portrayal of Ellers Bend with its rundown store, its fertilizer plant, the sawmill, the scattering of houses, and the ferry as it is rowed back and forth across the river by a deaf mute. He also gives a sense of the rhythms of farm and small-town life and of the processes of cotton picking or tobacco curing.

Tobacco is really the focus of Owen's two serious novels, *Season of Fear* (1960) and *Journey for Joedel* (1970); it is important in his two *Flim-Flam Man* novels as well as his short stories. These works reflect his ambivalent feelings toward a crop that seemed to have a kind of moral worth, in that so much grueling labor went into producing it, and that did have monetary worth because it was the mainstay of a farm family's economy—but which was a poison and a cause of disease to those who used it. It was produced only to be burned up. Clearly, in Owen's work tobacco becomes a metaphor for his ambivalence about the South: admiration for the sturdy, hard-working character of its people; compassion for the harshness of their lives; contempt for the meanness, narrowness, and gradual rotting away of Southern small-town existence; regret for the displacement of its work and culture by machine technology and by the homogenizing influence of the media.

In *Season of Fear* tobacco and tobacco culture are important both as process and as symbol. In this dry season in which many crops die, the protagonist, Clay Hampton (''Hamp''), sees both the blistered land and the lightness of the golden leaf as a judgment of God on the moral lightness of a sinful people. Clay prays and struggles, obsessed equally by sexual desire for whatever girl lives in the house across the way and by his painful love for the Christ in agony in the poster on his wall. Everything about the growing of tobacco—which is his life—takes on significance. The horny-headed tobacco-spitting worms crawling on tobacco leaves seem to him like the devil crawling everywhere, and the hot intensity of the fire in the tobacco barn gives a glimpse of hellfire. The process of tending tobacco, suckering it, poisoning it (to kill destructive insects), and curing it offers an equivalent to Hamp of a process of destroying and curing the sin of his world. As a first step he manages to use the local Ku Klux Klan members, headed by the preacher, to drive out the family of lewd Naomi Powell (across the way) who sleeps with her stepfather. And when Laura Dell Dune (the adorable blond teenager whose family replaces the Powells) marries the vicious Kurt Wiles, Clay responds to what he thinks is a sign from God and uses dynamite to kill Kurt. Then he expects rain for the crops, but no rain falls.

Except for Hamp and Laura Dell, almost everyone in the novel uses tobacco and smells of it: They smoke, they dip snuff, they chew. Clay's elderly mother and aunt dip snuff and spit all day. The efforts of a tobacco speculator to cheat Hamp and the low price paid for his best tobacco show Hamp the futility of the long days of sweaty labor, the hot nights under the barn to keep the fire up.

Yet, paradoxically, in the novel the golden color of the dried tobacco leaves, so beautiful a gold, is the color that symbolizes all that is wonderful and promising—for example, the yellow dress that Laura Dell wears and the golden oranges hanging on the trees in Florida, the paradisical place where Hamp hopes to start a new life.

The same ambiguity appears in *The Ballad of the Flim-Flam Man* (1965). The tobacco market is portrayed as the scene of such careless excitement and sudden prosperity that Mordecai Jones, the Flim-Flam Man, can steal in, like a hornworm, and profit by pinhooking (that is, speculating in tobacco), once selling the same basket three times over in one day. The grand birthday party for the warehouse owner, with high-spirited dancing, reflects the elation of a whole community at having brought in the crop and having cash in the pocket after so many months of doing without. Yet the festive evening culminates in drunkenness, fighting, and the burning down of the warehouse.

In *Journey for Joedel* the tobacco market is the focus of the whole novel, which recounts one day in the life of a 13-year-old half-Lumbee boy. The success or failure of the sale will determine the lives of a family for the next year. Economically, tobacco is the family's lifeblood. The sale goes well, and father and son return with presents for all; yet the events of the day leave Joedel less innocent, depressed by the compromises and accommodations that he must make to the cruelties, imperfections, and contaminations of his world. A basket of damaged tobacco, given Joedel by the kindly Captain Eller, represents the ambiguity of the view of tobacco in the novel. The basket is sold for a fairly good price. But Joedel's pride in having his own basket to sell is lessened by his knowledge that he is cheating the buyer and is lessened even more by his father's pretense that it sold for a smaller amount so that the father can mask a gambling loss.

In his novels Owen has described the process of growing and selling tobacco with such a density of detail that his description is one of the best contributions to the realistic portrayal of Southern life. (One of his disappointments with the film *The Ballad of the Flim-Flam Man* came with the decision to shoot the movie in Kentucky. What viewers see is—ye gods!—*burley* tobacco.) The realism of these novels of the 1930s (*Season* and *Joedel*) and 1950s (*Flim-Flam Man*) is aided by Owen's accuracy of eye, ear, and memory and his research in old newspapers, visits to the locale, and such experiences as once again sleeping under a tobacco barn to remember how it was.

The pronounced realism of this portrayal of Southern life is particularly successful in *Season of Fear* because of the characterization of Hamp, the protagonist. Owen said that this book began with a newspaper story and an image of a man at a window, and he gives the reader a character who is unable to participate in communal life but instead looks out at the world from so far within himself that the very intensity of his thinking and his beliefs drives him to see it unrealistically—and, thus, act wrongly. Owen has given a compassionate and compelling picture of the ache of Hamp's terrible loneliness, of his confined life on the farm—dominated by two old women, especially his possessive, nosy, angry mother—and of the nature of his poverty-stricken, work-filled existence and the narrowness of his religious faith. Hamp has almost no control over his life. He is always on the edge, always spying at the window to watch and overhear, but never participating. The only time that he is ever alone with Laura Dell and has a chance to declare his love, he is being tricked. Even at a revival, when he stands to testify, he is silent. Only when he denominates himself the agent of God, acting for God to rid the land of sin (the land is only Eller's Bend), does he begin to live his life actively and influence others'—and then his actions are both mean and violent. Yet he is fundamentally so kind, so honest, so generous to the black family nearby, whose members are equally generous to him, that he remains sympathetic even as his life erupts into murder and hostility.

The realism of such characterization often gains acceptance and compassion for the harsh, hostile, or mean. No wonder this sense of reality prevails, for the place and quite a few of the characters of Owen's work have their origins in his own neighborhood or his own life. One of his techniques was to give his characters the names of real persons, then change them just before the final typing. A number of his short stories and his final, unpublished novel were autobiographical, at least in part. Joedel Shaw, the protagonist of *Journey for Joedel,* and Joedel's trip to the auction to sell his basket of tobacco were based on Owen's brother James (not long dead of cancer at the time of writing) and a similar experience that James had. The 4-mile journey of the novel accurately follows the route of the school bus that Owen drove during his high-school days.

Yet there was always a transformation of the autobiographical into fiction and a broadening of focus in order to say more about the South. In *Joedel,* for instance, the central character is half-Lumbee, and the novel illustrates a number of the painful effects of racial prejudice. Prejudice against blacks is important both in plot and characterization in *Season of Fear;* and the kindness of Doll Boney and his family, who are the only friends of the isolated Hamp, is especially poignant. These portrayals are examples of an effort to set things right on the part of a man who as a rural Southerner experienced personally and intensely tangled feelings and conflicts with regard to race.

Very consciously and even self-consciously intermingled with the realistic aspects of the novels are the symbolic, the mythic, and the allusive. In Owen's fiction, the mythic characteristics of Mordecai Jones, the tall tales included here and there, the symbolism of tobacco, the initiation motifs in the stories of Curley Treadaway and Joedel Shaw, and the pastoral and communal nature of Cape Fear country take the reader beyond simple realism. There are numerous motifs from folklore—for instance, the rising of a white bird into the sky after someone dies. Also, apart from a few extremely well-realized characters, such as Hamp in *Season of Fear* or the father in *Journey for Joedel,* characters are often stereotypical or lightly sketched and are familiar from other literary contexts. Owen's young women, for example, fuss and primp and switch and flounce until one wants to beg them to hold still for a minute. The braggart in the loud shirt; the sly schemer; the red-faced, jug-butted deputy sheriff—these are all recognizable and are brought off well but sketchily.

Among the literary influences on Owen's work that have been commented on are the works of T. S. Eliot (the effect of *Waste Land* on *Season of Fear*) and of such Southern writers as Faulkner and Wolfe. Owen himself spoke of the importance of Erskine Caldwell to his writing. The pervasiveness of Mark Twain's cynicism and irreverence in *The Ballad of the Flim-Flam Man* is easily remarked. Owen had deliberately included numerous allusions to *Huckleberry Finn* in this novel, to make evident the parallel between the wanderings and maturing of Curley Treadaway and Huck Finn, but he cut most of them out, at the last minute, from the proofs. Although Owen read a number of books on con men and their tricks (and also got ideas for his characters' scams from the daily paper), he was drawing on literature as well—in particular, the works of Thomas Dekker and Thomas Middleton, subjects of his master's and doctoral theses. The hilarious caricature world of clever tricksters and ignorant, greedy marks owes much to the coney-catching pamphlets of Dekker and the plays of these progenitors. Owen has managed to catch both Dekker's friendliness toward his characters and Middleton's outrageousness. One of Owen's favorite characters was Captain Jim Eller, who appears in several novels and stories. He was a favorite because he was modeled on Owen's beloved grandfather, Jim Elkins. This vital little fellow, loved for fair dealing, always preaching the values of hard work and devotion to duty—and living by those values himself—is essentially a serious character; yet in his feistiness and his ability to energize everyone around him, Captain Jim has something of Dekker's Simon Eyre in *The Shoemaker's Holiday.* Captain Jim begins the novel as a kind of sprite and presiding genius in *Journey for Joedel.*

Mordecai Jones, the Flim-Flam Man, is also a character with a number of literary ancestors, including Chaucer's Pardoner, some of whose methods he emulates, as has been noted. He remains always a character both elusive and greater than life because of distancing through the narrator, Curley Treadaway, who mediates between Mordecai Jones and the reader. Uneducated Curley, who dropped out of school after repeating the eighth grade, has no idea why Jones uses such pseudonyms as Titus Oates or Increase Mather. Nor does he understand his mentor, though he appreciates his kindness and is grateful for "the enhancing" of his life by Jones. He doesn't comprehend Mordecai's love of freedom and individualism or appreciate how the Flim-Flam Man's way of life comments on an acquisitive society and its debased code. Mordecai is one "who puts his trust in the taint of corruption in the human heart" (*The Ballad of the Flim-Flam Man,* 8). Jones, much more than Curley, enjoys his mastery of the ignorant and greedy. Immensely knowledgeable, Jones always has a new dodge, and his bottomless suitcase never runs out of fake money, false diamonds, punch boards, calling cards, and other essentials for preying on the marks. The law can catch up with Mordecai Jones but never keep him. Always mysterious, Jones is a preacher's son and despises greed—yet is not totally invulnerable to it. Although for Curley the story of *The Flim-Flam Man and the Apprentice Grifter* has a happy, conventional, pastoral ending, the Flim-Flam Man, one may be sure, continues his mythic travels from town to town, following the skin trade. As he explained to Curley on first acquaintance, "Greed's my line, lad. And fourteen-carat ignorance" (*The Ballad of the Flim-Flam Man,* 8).

There is a dark side to Mordecai Jones, as Owen's novels acknowledge through Curley's troubled conscience and desire to get away from his mentor and to pay back all those persons who were deceived. Mordecai knows too much and cares too little; there is a hardness and loneliness about him that contrasts with the comfortableness of guitar-playing Curley. The result is a mixture of tones that may signal a certain uneasiness in the author. When Curley reforms and assumes a conventional social role, Jones must be exiled from the ending.

Owen's four novels and his numerous fine short stories, some of which are still to be collected, are highly crafted and polished works. Although his usual method of composition was to write paragraphs, using pen and yellow pads to compose a section here and another there, he revised and revised successive triple-spaced typewritten drafts. He wanted to get the dialogue right—and he did—to make the descriptions accurate, and above all to achieve the flavor of Southern talk. Curley feels "lower than a snake's belly," is so scared that he has a "tail string puckered tighter than Dick's hatband," and rides on a road as crooked as a fishhook and bumpy as a durn squash. He and Mordecai "balled the jack through the village like there was hornets in our drawers" (*Ballad* 59) and make someone so mad that the water on his kneecaps came to a boil. In its realism, this vivid language savors of Southern dialect; in its exaggeration (e.g., "so far back in the sticks the folks had cordwood on their breath and ticks in their navels" [*Ballad* 99]) it mimics the tall tale.

Unsurprisingly, Owen's poetry is equally careful both in form and diction; he liked rhyme (and loved slant rhyme) and especially enjoyed writing brief and clever imitations of Greek epitaphs. *The White Stallion* presents a great variety of subjects in a small book: female students, meditations on works of art, his children, Jonathan Edwards, a white stallion, a mule; but the most powerful poem is the tightly controlled "My Father's Curse." His father's "anvil boots," "iron fingers," and "fiery plow" wound the earth he cursed but are answered by God's sexual force as God "fleshed Himself in fruit" (2). Owen loved and taught poetry, but thought he did not grow enough as a poet; fiction worked better for him in representing the humor, the warmth, the fortitude, the pathos, the racial cruelty, and the narrowness and deprivation of the South and Southernness as he had known them.

SURVEY OF CRITICISM

Criticism of Owen's works is sparse. Most reviewers wrote sympathetically of the honesty, fresh humor, unsentimental warmth, and technical skill of the novels; but the reviews are brief. And after Owen's death his work disappeared from critical view too soon for him to be included in the compilations of contemporary criticism, which are now preserving many writers and encouraging young critics to consider their works. *Pembroke Magazine* (1981), edited by Shelby Stephenson, is very useful for its interview with Owen and tributes to him as teacher, editor, and writer, along with a bibliography by Dorothy Owen and some critical essays. Included also are comments by Owen on his use of place; his comments here, in the interview with Stephenson, and in another interview with John Carr in *Kite-Flying* offer the best insight into Owen's fiction. An essay by Charles Frazier (1980) affords a thorough treatment of the poetry, as does Richard Vela's essay (1973).

BIBLIOGRAPHY

Works by Guy Owen

Cape Fear Country and Other Poetry. Lake Como, Fla.: New Athenaeum Press, 1958.
Season of Fear. New York: Random House, 1960; London: Gollancz, 1961. Reprint. London: Pan American, 1965.
The Guilty and Other Poems. Lanham, Md.: Goosetree Press, 1964.
The Ballad of the Flim-Flam Man. New York: Macmillan, 1965; Reprint, new and rev. New York: Pocket Books, 1967.
The White Stallion and Other Poems. Winston-Salem, N.C.: Blair, 1969.
Journey for Joedel: A Novel. New York: Crown, 1970; Reprint. New York: Avon, 1970.
The Flim-Flam Man and the Apprentice Grifter. New York: Crown, 1972.
The Flim-Flam Man and Other Stories. Durham, N.C.: Moore, 1980.
Papers, University of North Carolina Library, Chapel Hill.

Interviews with Guy Owen

Carr, John. "The Lumbees, the Klan, and . . . Hollywood." In *Kite-Flying and Other Irrational Acts: Conversations with Twelve Southern Writers,* edited by John Carr, 236–62. Baton Rouge: Louisiana State University Press, 1972.
Stephenson, Shelby. Interview. *Pembroke Magazine* 13 (1981): 101–12.

Studies of Guy Owen

Dalmas, Victor. "Guy Owen and the World of Cape Fear County." *St. Andrews Review* 3, no. 2 (Spring and Summer 1975): 43–50.
Euliss, Daphne. "Folk Motifs in Guy Owen's *Journey for Joedel.*" *North Carolina Folklore Journal* 24 (1976): 111–14.

Frazier, Charles. "Guy Owen." In *American Poets Since World War II,* vol. 5, Pt. 2, of *Dictionary of Literary Biography,* ed. Donald J. Greiner. Detroit: Gale Research, 1980. 145–49.

French, Warren. "Owen, Guy (Jr.)." In *Contemporary Novelists,* 3d ed., edited by James Vinson, 508–9. New York: St. Martin's Press, 1982.

Rundus, R. J. "American Pastoral: The Novels of Guy Owen." *Pembroke Magazine* 4 (1972): 15–20.

Shinn, Michael A. "Guy Owen's Flim-Flam Novels and *Journey for Joedel:* Odysseys into Maturity." *Pembroke Magazine* 19 (1987): 135–39.

Stephenson, Shelby, ed. *Pembroke Magazine* (Guy Owen special issue) 13 (1981).

———. "The Place of Poetry in Guy Owen's *The Ballad of the Flim-Flam Man.*" *Pembroke Magazine* 16 (1984): 125–27.

Vela, Richard R. "This Naked Pond, That Naked Tree: The Realities of Guy Owen." *South and West* 11, no. 3 (Winter 1973): 14–20.

White, R. B. "The Image of Sexual Repression in *Season of Fear.*" *North Carolina Folklore* 19 (March 1971): 80–84.

Ishmael Reed
(1938–   )

Whether they praise or condemn his work, readers and critics must acknowledge that Ishmael Reed is one of the most innovative Southern writers of his generation. A perceptive observer of humanity and the social scene, Reed has consistently used American, African-American, and other cultural traditions to create a body of literature that not only illustrates what might be gained from expanding the boundaries of genres but also reveals the possibilities and limitations of life in a multicultural society. Reed's novels, essays, and poetry are distinguished for their wry humor, experimental form, and imaginative challenging of ideas. They are informed by Reed's adversarial postures and by his penchant for iconoclasm. He uses language to stand against concepts and attitudes that are inflexible; he blends traditional literary forms and topples the idols of American thought in order to show that tolerance for difference and change is necessary in order to achieve cultural plurality. Although Reed's indebtedness to his Southern roots emerges in several of his works—and particularly in his use of folk culture (the basis for his neohoodoo aesthetic)—what is quintessentially Southern about his work is to be located in the rage to explain.

BIOGRAPHY

Ishmael Scott Reed was born on February 22, 1938, in Chattanooga, Tennessee, the son of Henry Lenoir, a YMCA fund-raiser, and Thelma Coleman, a salesperson. The date of Reed's birth and his mother's choice of his first name are fated markers, because twenty-two is considered to be powerful in hoodoo numerology; and Genesis 16:11–12 seems an apt commentary not only on the circumstances of Reed's birth but also on the public and literary stances that he would cultivate as a writer. There was certainly affliction in his being born outside the prevailing social norms, and the reception of his ideas and writing provides a gloss for the statement "His hand will be against every man, and every man's hand against him." Reed's life and work, to some degree, seems to manifest the prophecy about his biblical namesake.

Reed's mother married Bennie Stephen Reed, an autoworker, and moved to Buffalo, New York, in 1940 in search of better employment opportunities; Reed, who had been left in the care of relatives, joined his mother and stepfather in 1942.

During his early childhood, Reed showed promise as a musician and writer, and as a teenager he wrote a jazz column for the *Empire State Weekly,* a black newspaper in Buffalo. He graduated from East High School in 1956 and began attending the University of Buffalo. He dropped out of the university in 1960 and married Priscilla Rose. Shortly after the marriage, Ishmael and Priscilla's daughter Timothy Brett was born. Reed worked briefly for the *Empire State Weekly* as a staff reporter and lived for a time in Buffalo's Talbert Mall Project. He described this period in his life as a time of political activism followed by a time of cynicism. The traumatic experiences of living in the project are reflected in Reed's first novel, *The Free-Lance Pallbearers* (1967). Reed and his wife separated in 1963 and were subsequently divorced.

In 1962 Reed moved to New York City and became associated with the now legendary Umbra Workshop, which included such members as Calvin Hernton, Tom Dent, Lorenzo Thomas, and David Henderson. Reed was interested primarily in writing poetry; and two of his earliest poems, "Patrice" and "Time and the Eagle," appeared in *Umbra* magazine (1963). According to Reed, he worked at various jobs to support himself and other members of the collective. He was a reporter for the Newark, New Jersey, newspaper *Advance,* of which he became editor in 1965. In that year he also became a cofounder of the prototypical underground newspaper *East Village Other* and began writing his first novel. Reed remained in New York until 1967, but he had grown weary of the parochialism of the East Coast literary establishment and had discovered the more favorable climate for literature in California. He moved to Berkeley and began teaching at the University of California. Still a faculty member there, he has also taught and lectured at the University of Washington, Seattle (1969), the State University of New York at Buffalo (1975 and 1979), Yale (1979), Dartmouth (1980), Columbia (1983), Harvard (1987), and the University of California, Santa Barbara (1988).

Reed has been an exceptionally productive writer and cultural activist from 1967 to the present, and his work is representative of his growth as an artist and thinker. In 1969 his second novel, *Yellow Back Radio Broke-Down,* was published. In 1970, the year in which he married the choreographer Carla Blank, Reed published his first collection of poems, *catechism of d neoamerican hoodoo church,* and the anthology *19 Necromancers from Now.* These works seemed to put into practice ideas that Reed had synthesized in "Neo-Hoodoo Manifesto," published in the *Los Angeles Free Press* (1970). In that blueprint for art and writing, Reed revised Richard Wright's concept of "the forms of things unknown," recognizing the untapped energies of a literary use of black folklore and of popular culture. As he has argued in his introduction to *19 Necromancers,* Reed was attuned also to the urgency of rethinking how "American" literature is constituted. The anthology is a prototype for those that seek to revise the canon. Reed was not content to talk about what American literature should be; in 1971, he cofounded Yardbird Publishing Company; and in 1973 he, Steve Cannon, and Joe Johnson founded Reed, Cannon & Johnson Communications. In 1976 Reed and other California writers founded Before Columbus Foundation, an enterprise to publish and distribute the work of ethnic writers.

Reed's commitment to the neohoodoo tradition is quite evident in the works published in 1972: *Conjure,* his second book of poems, and the novel *Mumbo Jumbo,* a seminal text in the development of the black novel. This novel, which received great critical acclaim, was a watershed in Reed's career. He followed it with a substantial output: *Chattanooga* (1973), poems that honor his Tennessee origins; *The Last Days of Louisiana Red* (1974), a probing treatment of intraracial conflicts, which won the Richard and Hinda Rosenthal Foundation Award in 1975; *Flight to Canada* (1976), a clever appropriation and revision of the genre of slave narrative; *A Secretary to the Spirits* (1978), a book of poetry and mixed-media illustration on which he collaborated with Betye Saar; and *Shrovetide in Old New Orleans* (1978), essays that Reed claimed were the beginning of his intellectual autobiography. The decade of the 1970s was a peak period for Reed, marked not only by his own output, but also by his service from 1975 to 1979 on the Coordinating Council of Literary Magazines and his editing of *Yardbird/Y'Bird* magazine.

In the 1980s, Reed published three novels—*The Terrible Twos* (1982), *Reckless Eyeballing* (1986), and *The Terrible Threes* (1989)—and two collections of essays, *God Made Alaska for the Indians* (1982) and *Writin' Is Fightin'* (1988). "Being a black man in America," Reed complained in the Spring 1988 special issue of *Life,* "is like being a spectator at your own lynching." The complaint is understandable given that the alleged sexism of *Reckless Eyeballing* made Reed the target of much criticism. On the other hand, it is reassuring to hear Reed say in *Writin' Is Fightin'* that regardless of criticisms he deems it "important to maintain a prolific writing jab," because there are "issues worth fighting about" (6).

MAJOR THEMES

The surface of Reed's post-Modern fiction, poetry, and nonfiction—sometimes surreal, sometimes offensive, always challenging—is a mask for a powerful and brilliant intelligence that resists preordained categories. To understand the primal themes in his work—time, oppression and freedom, conflict, devisiveness, resistance to Western hegemony—it is essential to consider the interdependence of theme, form, and Reed's artistic vision, his will to explore the "power of blackness." In the body of work that Reed has produced up to 1990, especially in his fiction, themes are related to choices of narrative genre; themes in his poetry and nonfiction (which are not examined here) complement, extend, or serve as interpretive keys for the fiction. Thus, his use of themes might be conceptualized as stages in a literary project in which the dominant mode is satire and the main targets are Western ideas about religion, history, art, and ways of knowing. Read chronologically, his novels reveal that Reed has been obsessed with the ambiguous and problematic relations that can exist in any time and place between those who have power and those who are controlled.

Reed's themes represent various ways of dealing with the problem of modernity, the intense awareness of being situated within the specific temporal and spatial dimensions of a present. What is time? What is space? What is the significance of time and space for the person who experiences them? Is man the subject or the object of time and space? For Reed, such questions are to be dealt with through imaginative writing or discourses that prevent one's being locked into a single conception of how reality is constructed.

For example, history as time, one major theme in Reed's work, is rooted in his sense of place and displacement in the world of people who, in a broad sense, have been the suffering outcasts—those outside the dominant community. Reed thematizes outsideness or difference in his work because the "freedom" of the outsider to confront the status quo is assumed to be essential. In his first novel, *The Free-Lance Pallbearers,* however, the possibility of such freedom for those who accept the American Dream without qualification is challenged. The form of the novel is akin to the genres of slave narrative and progress autobiography. Moreover, it fits into the tradition of muckraking novels that address the spiritual malaise of the United States and provides an interesting twist: the novel steps outside realism just enough to provide the illusion that its subject matter can be verified affectively, if not cognitively. Bukka Doopeyduk, the novel's antihero, evolves from model citizen to unwitting revolutionary in the world of HARRY SAM (America or the fallen world of excremental vision); although his progress is based on a series of integrationist choices so typical in black novels involving search for identity, his ultimate reward is death. In this satiric novel, Reed portrays the very condition of outsideness as problematic. The oppressed—as Reed shows here and in *The Last Days of Louisiana Red, Reckless Eyeballing,* and the *Terrible* novels—can be as lacking in virture as the corrupt oppressors.

Written before Reed had worked out a theory of neohoodoo writing, *The Free-Lance Pallbearers* undermines belief in the viability of social organizations and the promise of pragmatic behavior. The American Dream as colored by Horatio Alger is a nightmare. In such later novels as *Mumbo Jumbo, Flight to Canada, The Terrible Twos,* and *The Terrible Threes,* Reed makes it obvious that America's official myths and civic religion are basically destructive and racist. The oppressed who survive the destruction of their own dreams of freedom do so with the ineffable aid of hoodoo.

Whereas hoodoo as an alternative source of knowledge and power is hinted at in *The Free-Lance Pallbearers,* it is more fully developed in *Yellow Back Radio Broke-Down.* Loop Garoo, the ostensible hero derived from the voodoo pantheon, survives in the time-warped world of the American West or in history as an infinitude of experiences. His survival, however, depends upon his ability to conjure—to defy the logical or "scientific" explanations of nature and human existence. In short, survival, like the composition of the novel itself, depends upon using the possibilities of syncretism, the adaptation and transformation of elements from many sources into a positive whole. In a novel that is a parody of the yellow-back westerns of the late nineteenth century and that juxtaposes Thomas Jefferson, Lewis and Clark, contemporary Native Americans, the loa of voodoo, and the Pope—Reed attacks the linear conception of history and replaces it with the synchronicity that is a feature of the African sense of time. Ultimately, it is Euro-American ideas about epistemology and history that the novel calls into question. Reed also attacks the Western conception of Christianity as it finds itself in competition with so-called outlaw religions, a forecast of things to come in *Mumbo Jumbo.* As Reed suggested in a 1973 interview, synthesizing and synchronizing are very important in his work. His creative method has involved combining elements as one would in making a gumbo and "putting disparate elements into the same time, making them run in the same time, together. Like using a contemporary photograph to illuminate a text which has something to do with the past and at the same time making them exist in the same space (Gaga).

Reed's creative methods and dominant themes are fully and richly displayed in *Mumbo Jumbo.* In this story, the voodoo detectives Papa LaBas and Black Herman seek to discover the mystery of the text of Jes Grew, the hoodoo aesthetic that originated in ancient Egypt. A revision of the myth of conflict between Osiris and Set, the novel foregrounds the conflict between the Atonists or Christians who would stamp out the plague that threatens their control and civilization and those who understand Jes Grew to be a positive life force. The setting is the Harlem Renaissance of the 1920s, but Reed bends time in the narrative to achieve a synchronicity of events in Egyptian, European, and African-American history. Of course, Harlem Renaissance is as much a state of mind as an event; as a series of practices, it consisted in detecting black self-images that were alternatives to those proffered by a racist nation.

Conflict over what is imaged as a germ, epidemic, or plague in *Mumbo Jumbo* is reworked in *The Last Days of Louisiana Red* as disruption within the African-American community attributable to the cancer of Louisiana Red, the evil that keeps blacks divided against one another. Papa LaBas resurfaces in this novel, intent on discovering why Ed Yellings, who has discovered a cure for Louisiana Red, is murdered. Given that much of the satire in the novel exposes the divisions among black nationalists in the 1960s and 1970s, Reed has suggested that no ethnic group has a monopoly on the desire for power. And to give the theme of conflict classic dimensions, Reed incorporates the story of Antigone and uses the Chorus as the voice of black Americans.

The themes of freedom, oppression, and resistance emerge quite naturally in

Flight to Canada, where Reed subverts *Uncle Tom's Cabin,* restoring the voice of the slave in the character of Raven Quicksill. As a runaway slave poet, Quicksill writes himself out of slavery with the poem ''Flight to Canada.'' But Canada, as a region of freedom and as the dream of being free, is discovered to be other than what it seems. Like Loop Garoo in *Yellow Back Radio Broke-Down,* Quicksill learns that flight from the clutches of oppression is dependent upon one's inventiveness.

In his most recent political novels, *The Terrible Twos, Reckless Eyeballing,* and *The Terrible Threes,* Reed has emphasized the theme of conflict. As books that destroy the possibility of making a generic distinction between the essay and the novel, they stress ideas about conflict as they have been dealt with in Reed's three collections of essays, *Shrovetide in Old New Orleans, God Made Alaska for the Indians,* and *Writin' Is Fightin'. Reckless Eyeballing* focuses on the division between black male and black female writers occasioned by feminist ideology and by the whims of the literary marketplace. Using the legend of Santa Claus (St. Nicholas) and his partner Black Peter, Reed provides bristling satires on capitalism, the evils of selfishness championed by the Reagan administration, and the discontent between the haves and the have-nots in America.

The primal themes in Reed's novels suggest that humanity can cope with the spatio-temporal dimensions of being only by recognizing patterns of behavior and decoding the myths that sustain them. Unlike Richard Wright, who sought to locate value in recognizing the meaning of suffering, Reed uses themes that situate value in alternative ways of creating meaning and negotiating reality. His fictions are both theoretical text and praxis. They are never pure fictions, for they involve multiple referents to verifiable historical events. Nevertheless, the referents are knowable in many ways and always remain open. For Reed, who is concerned with awakening us from ignorance and complacency, the past truly commits the future.

SURVEY OF CRITICISM

The critical reception of Reed's first two novels was decidedly mixed, ranging from dismissals of his experimental satires as nonsense to insightful estimations of Reed as one of the most promising new voices in American fiction. Commenting on *The Free-Lance Pallbearers,* Keneth Kinnamon (1967) linked Reed with such writers as William Burroughs and John Barth and has noted that Reed's technique ''disperses rather than concentrates his satiric energy'' (18). On the other hand, Toni Cade (1969) has found this novel refreshing because of Reed's facility in using language.

The widespread critical attention given to Reed's third novel, *Mumbo Jumbo,* secured Reed's place in American and African-American literature, because critics acknowledged that he was a writer of major talent. He received very positive reviews in such important publications as *Nation, New York Times Book Review, Saturday Review,* and *Virginia Quarterly Review.* Houston Baker (1972) proclaimed the novel to be groundbreaking: "*Mumbo Jumbo* is perhaps the first Black American novel of the last ten years that gives one a sense of the broader vision and the . . . brainwork that [is] needed if we are to define the eternal dilemma of the Black Arts and work fruitfully toward its melioration" (64). Reed's fellow novelist Clarence Major (1972) thought the book was "more clearly conceived and more total" than the earlier ones and that it was a fine challenge to "the terms on which America's most popular mores and myths exist" (61).

In the 1970s and 1980s Reed's mastery of the satiric tradition and his importance as a literary innovator were clearly recognized, and it was commonplace to find serious, academic critics attending to his work. Neil Schmitz drew (1974) attention to Reed's restoration of oral tradition to a place of honor in American literature, and Robert Scholes (1974) noted that *The Last Days of Louisiana Red* made Reed as important a satirist as Juvenal. Addison Gayle (1975) discussed Reed's importance in the development of black writing, and Jerome Klinkowitz (1975) speculated on Reed as "a modern American conjure man" and as a major creator of new fiction.

The Edenic period was marked, however, by rather hellish moments as critics who had given Reed high praise began to make reassessments. Houston Baker found *The Last Days* to be sophomoric; Neil Schmitz (1975) found the same book to be ultimately evasive; Addison Gayle (1976) condemned Reed's *Flight to Canada* for not being responsible enough in portraying the truth about racism in America. The barbs were offset a little by the favorable attention that Chester Fontenont (1978), Henry Louis Gates (1987), and Charles Nichols (1978) gave to Reed's aesthetics, intelligent use of history, development of the comic mode, and power as a social critic. When Reed's *Reckless Eyeballing* offended many feminists, the novel was deemed vicious, and there were personal attacks on Reed for his paranoia.

In the late 1980s, preludes to book-length studies of Reed and his work began to appear and to set new directions for criticism. Articulating a position congenial to some feminists and womanists, Michele Wallace noted in "Ishmael Reed's Female Troubles" (first published in *Village Voice Literary Supplements* in December 1986) that Reed's books had a tendency "to blame women characters for every evil that comes into the world" (153). If Reed's texts reinforce oppressive ideas as they seek to liberate readers from those ideas, it is probable that critics will draw more attention to Reed's limitations as an artist. On the other hand, Bernard Bell (1987) identified Reed as "the leading promoter of black postmodernist writing" (329). Although Reginald Martin (1987) provided useful insights about Reed's work up to *Reckless Eyeballing,* Martin's focus is on the essential tension between Reed's ideas about the neohoodoo aesthetic and the thinking of such pioneering black aesthetic critics as Addison Gayle, Houston A. Baker, and Amiri Baraka. Martin's study is significant for the value placed on Reed's work in African-American intellectual and literary history. A third of Robert Eliot Fox's *Conscientious Sorcerers* (1987) is devoted to showing how Reed's writing "involves countering the hegemonic code inscribed by the master culture with alternatives of discourse and desire (transformational longings)," (1). In his essay "On 'The Blackness of Blackness': Ishmael Reed and a Critique of the Sign," in *The Signifying Monkey* (1988), Henry Louis Gates demonstrated how rewarding it can be to read closely the language, intertextuality, and rhetoric in Reed's fiction. From quite different angles, Martin, Fox, and Gates suggested that Darryl Pinckney was wrong, in his essay "Trickster Tales" (1989), to conclude that Reed's "literary separatism is doomed to obsolescence because Afro-American writing only comes to life as a junction of traditions" (24). For these critics, and those who will follow their lead, the Reed canon is an exceptionally rich junction of traditions.

BIBLIOGRAPHY

Works by Ishmael Reed

The Free-Lance Pallbearers. Garden City, N.Y.: Doubleday, 1967.
Yellow Back Radio Broke-Down. New York: Doubleday, 1969.
catechism of d neoamerican hoodoo church. London: Paul Breman, 1970.
Conjure: Selected Poems, 1963–1970. Amherst: University of Massachusetts Press, 1972.
Mumbo Jumbo. Garden City, N.Y.: Doubleday, 1972.
Chattanooga: Poems. New York: Random House, 1973.
The Last Days of Louisiana Red. New York: Random House, 1974.
Flight to Canada. New York: Random House, 1976.
A Secretary to the Spirits. New York: NOK, 1978.
Shrovetide in Old New Orleans. New York: Doubleday, 1978.
God Made Alaska for the Indians: Selected Essays. New York: Garland, 1982.
The Terrible Twos. New York: St. Martin's Press/Marek, 1982.
Reckless Eyeballing. New York: St. Martin's Press, 1986.
New and Collected Poems. New York: Atheneum, 1988.
Writin' Is Fightin'. New York: Atheneum, 1988.
The Terrible Threes. New York: Atheneum, 1989.
Airing Dirty Laundry. New York: Addison-Wesley, 1993.
Japanese by Spring. New York: Atheneum, 1993.

Works Edited by Ishmael Reed

19 Necromancers from Now. With an introduction by Ishmael Reed. Garden City, N.Y.: Doubleday.
Calafia: The California Poetry. Berkeley, Calif.: Y'Bird Books, 1979.
The Before Columbus Fiction Anthology. Edited with Kathryn Trueblood and Shawn Wong. New York: Norton, 1992.
The Before Columbus Poetry Anthology. Edited with J. J. Phillips, Gundars Strads and Shawn Wong. New York: Norton, 1992.

Interviews with Ishmael Reed

Abbott, Ruth, and Ira Simmons. "An Interview with Ishmael Reed." *San Francisco Review of Books* 1 (November 1975): 13–20.

Gaga. "Interview with Ishmael Reed." *Mwendo,* no. 4 (Fall 1973).

George, Nelson. "A Conversation with Ishmael Reed." *Essence* 17 (July 1986): 38.

Helm, Michael. "Ishmael Reed: An Interview." *City Miner,* no. 11 (1978): 7–9, 37–42.

Henry, Joseph. "A MELUS Interview: Ishmael Reed." *MELUS* 11 (Spring 1984): 81–93.

Martin, Reginald. "An Interview with Ishmael Reed." *Review of Contemporary Fiction* 4 (Summer 1984): 176–87.

Northouse, Cameron. "Ishmael Reed." In *Conversations with Writers II,* edited by Matthew J. Bruccoli, 213–54. Detroit: Gale Research, 1978.

O'Brien, John. "Ishmael Reed." In *The New Fiction: Interviews with Innovative American Writers,* edited by Joe David Bellamy, 130–41. Urbana: University of Illinois Press, 1974.

―――. "Ishmael Reed: An Interview." In *Interviews with Black Writers,* edited by John O'Brien, 165–83. New York: Liveright, 1973.

Shepard, Walt. "When State Magicians Fail: An Interview with Ishmael Reed." *Nickle Review* (August 28–September 10, 1968): 72–75.

Studies of Ishmael Reed

Baker, Houston A., Jr. "Books Noted." *Black World* 22 (December 1972): 63–64.

Bell, Bernard W. *The Afro-American Novel and Its Tradition.* Amherst: University of Massachusetts Press, 1987.

Berben, Jacqueline. "HooDoo and Who Don't: Authorial Tone of Approval and Disapproval Towards Black Magic." *Cycnos* 3 (Winter 1986–1987): 75–82.

Byerman, Keith E. "Voodoo Aesthetics: History and Parody in the Novels of Ishmael Reed." In *Fingering the Jagged Grain: Tradition and Form in Recent Black Fiction,* 217–37. Athens: University of Georgia Press, 1985.

Cade, Toni. *"The Free-Lance Pallbearers." Liberator* 9 (June 1969): 20.

Duff, Gerald. "Reed, Ishmael." In *Postmodern Fiction: A Bio-Bibliographical Guide,* edited by Larry McCaffery, 493–96. New York: Greenwood, 1988.

Fontenot, Chester J. "Ishmael Reed and the Politics of Aesthetics; or, Shake Hands and Come Out Conjuring." *Black American Literature Forum* 12 (Spring 1978): 20–23.

Fox, Robert Elliot. *Conscientious Sorcerers: The Black Postmodernist Fiction of LeRoi Jones/Amiri Baraka, Ishmael Reed, and Samuel R. Delany.* Westport, Conn.: Greenwood, 1987.

Gates, Henry Louis, Jr. "The Blackness of Blackness: A Critique on the Sign and the Signifying Monkey." In *Figures in Black: Words, Signs, and the "Racial" Self,* 235–76. New York: Oxford University Press, 1987.

―――. *The Signifying Monkey: A Theory of Afro-American Literary Criticism.* New York: Oxford University Press, 1988.

Gayle, Addison. *The Way of the New World: The Black Novel in America.* Garden City, NY: Anchor Press/Doubleday, 1975.

———. "Black Women and Black Men: The Literature of Cartharsis." *Black Books Bulletin* 4 (Winter 1976): 48–52.

Harris, Norman. "Politics as an Innovative Aspect of Literary Folklore: A Study of Ishmael Reed." *OBSIDIAN* 5 (Spring–Summer 1979): 41–50.

———. "The Gods Must Be Angry: *Flight to Canada* as Political History." *Modern Fiction Studies* 34 (Spring 1988): 111–23.

Kinnamon, Keneth. "The Free-Lance Pallbearers." *Negro American Literature Forum* 1 (Winter 1967): 18.

Klinkowitz, Jerome. *Literary Disruptions: The Making of a Post-Contemporary American Fiction.* Urbana: University of Illinois Press, 1975.

Lindroth, James R. "From Krazy Kat to Hoodoo: Aesthetic Discourse in the Fiction of Ishmael Reed." *Review of Contemporary Fiction* 4 (Summer 1984): 227–33.

McConnell, Frank. "Ishmael Reed's Fiction: Da Hoodoo is Put on America." In *Black Fiction: New Studies in the Afro-American Novel Since 1945,* edited by A. Robert Lee, 136–48. London: Vision, 1980.

Mackey, Nathaniel. "Ishmael Reed and the Black Aesthetic." *CLA Journal* 21 (March 1978): 355–66.

Major, Clarence. "*Mumbo Jumbo* by Ishmael Reed." *Black Creation* 4 (Fall 1972): 59–61.

Martin, Reginald. *Ishmael Reed and the New Black Aesthetic Critics.* London: Macmillan, 1987.

Mason, Theodore O., Jr. "Performance, History, and Myth: The Problem of Ishmael Reed's *Mumbo Jumbo.*" *Modern Fiction Studies* 34 (Spring 1988): 97–109.

Nazareth, Peter. "Heading Them Off at the Pass: The Fiction of Ishmael Reed." *Review of Contemporary Fiction* 4 (Summer 1984): 208–26.

Nichols, Charles. "Comic Modes in Black America." In *Comic Relief Humor in Contemporary Humor.* Edited Sarah Blacker Cohen, 105–26. Urbana: University of Illinois Press, 1978.

Oren, Michel. "The Umbra Poets Workshop, 1962–1965: Some Socio-Literary Puzzles." In *Belief vs. Theory in Black American Literary Criticism,* edited by Joe Weixlmann and Chester J. Fontenot, 177–223. Greenwood, Fla.: Penskevill, 1986.

Pinckney, Darryl. "Trickster Tales." *New York Review of Books* xxxvi (October 12, 1989): 20, 22–24.

Schmitz, Neil. "Neo-HooDoo: The Experimental Fiction of Ishmael Reed." *Twentieth-Century Literature* 20 (April 1974): 126–40.

———. "The Gumbo That Jes Grew." *Partisan Review* 42 (1975): 311–16.

Scholes, Robert. "The Last Days of Louisiana Red." *New York Times Book Review* (November 10, 1974): 2.

Settle, Elizabeth A., and Thomas A. *Ishmael Reed: A Primary and Secondary Bibliography.* Boston: Hall, 1982.

Spillers, Hortense J. "Changing the Letter: The Yokes, the Jokes of Discourse; or, Mrs. Stowe, Mr. Reed." In *Slavery and the Literary Imagination,* edited by Deborah E. McDowell and Arnold Rampersad, 25–61. Baltimore: Johns Hopkins University Press, 1989.

Wallace, Michele. "Ishmael Reed's Female Troubles." In *Invisibility Blues: From Pop to Theory,* 146–54. London: Verso, 1990.

Weixlmann, Joe, Robert Fikes, and Ishmael Reed. "Mapping Out the Gumbo Works: An Ishmael Reed Bibliography." *Black American Literature Forum* 12 (Spring 1978): 24–29.

ROBERT L. PHILLIPS

George Addison Scarbrough
(1915–   )

George Scarbrough has been a journalist, a high-school teacher, a college professor, and a novelist; but his primary interest is poetry. With his recently published *Invitation to Kim (1989),* once again he has a major collection of poems in print, one that was nominated for the Pulitzer.

BIOGRAPHY

George Addison Scarbrough was born on October 20, 1915, at Patty Station, about nine miles from Benton, Tennessee, in Polk County. The third child of William Oscar and Louise Anabel McDowell Scarbrough, George had an older brother, Robert Lee, an older sister, Edith Emmeline, and four younger brothers, Charles Spencer, William Athol, Blaine Pleasant, and Joseph Kenneth. These family members appear often in Scarbrough's poems. *A Summer Ago* (1986) is an autobiographical novel in which Lee has a major role; the youngest brother is the Kim of the latest collection of poems, *Invitation to Kim.*

William Oscar Scarbrough, who farmed the thin, rocky, worn-out soil of East Tennessee on shares, had Indians among his forebears. George's maternal grandfather was for several years the county physician of Polk County, but Dr. McDowell devoted little time to the education of his children. Farm life for a family of sharecroppers in East Tennessee was a life of hard work and few opportunities. Scarbrough remembers moving twelve times during his childhood. Whether the family farmed on two-thirds shares or one-third depended upon whether William Oscar could furnish a team for wagon and plows. George's mother, Anabel (or "Belle"), entertained her children with tales, and she sang the mountain ballads. His father had little learning and little interest in it, but his mother encouraged George in his studies. With various interruptions he finished high school in Benton in 1935, 3 years behind his first-grade class.

In 1935 Scarbrough began studies at the University of Tennessee. Twelve men in Benton contributed ten dollars each to send Scarbrough to Knoxville. This money saw Scarbrough through the first quarter; loans from the university enabled him to finish the year. For the next few years, until 1941, Scarbrough farmed and wrote for the local newspapers in East Tennessee. Gilbert Govan of the *Chattanooga Times* took an interest in Scarbrough's poetry and helped him to earn a literary fellowship to the University of the South at Sewanee. For two years Scarbrough studied under Mr. Tudor Long, Dr. George Baker, and Andrew Lytle, who was then the editor of the *Sewanee Review*. Finally in 1947 Scarbrough received his B.A. from Lincoln Memorial University in Harrogate, Tennessee, and an M.A. in 1954 from the University of Tennessee, to which he returned briefly for further study in 1966. He participated in the Writers' Workshop at the State University of Iowa in 1957.

During those years when Scarbrough was not actively a student, he continued to write for the Tennessee newspapers and to teach. From 1965 to 1967 he was an English instructor at Hiwassee College in Madisonville, Tennessee, and in 1968 he spent a year as a professor at Chattanooga College. His primary interest, however, during these years was poetry. His first collection, *Tellico Blue*, was published in 1949 and was reviewed widely in the national press. Two years later Dutton published *The Course Is Upward* (1951) and in 1956, *Summer So-Called.* For the next 20 years Scarbrough published no collections; but he was, nevertheless, busily engaged in his writing. He was publishing in literary magazines and winning prizes for his work. In 1961 came the Borestone Mountain Award and in 1964 the prestigious Mary Rugeley Fergueson Poetry Award from the *Sewanee Review*. His poetry has appeared in over fifty periodicals including, the *Sewanee Review, Spirit* (which in 1978 awarded him its Sheena Albanese Memorial Prize), *Atlantic, Harper's, New Republic, Saturday Review,* and *Poetry.* His work has been included in over twenty anthologies of poetry.

New and Selected Poems, Scarbrough's fourth collection, appeared in 1977. His only novel, *A Summer Ago,* was issued in 1986; *Invitation to Kim* was published in 1989. The publication of *New and Selected Poems* led to Scarbrough's receiving the Governor's Outstanding Tennessean Award in 1978.

Scarbrough now lives in Oak Ridge, Tennessee, where he continues his writing.

MAJOR THEMES

Scarbrough's overriding theme is the cultivation and preservation of the self. Often in his poems he speaks in the first person; and Alan, the principal figure in Scarbrough's novel *A Summer Ago,* shares a great deal with the persona of Scarbrough's poems. This self is a persona formed in a starkly romantic sensibility that gathers most of its images and metaphors from rural East Tennessee and that values deeply its agrarian antecedents.

The echoes of the poetry that helped shape Scarbrough's imagination are unmistakable—Robert Frost, Dylan Thomas, John Crowe Ransom, and Donald Davidson. Scarbrough mentions Seamus Heaney and Denise Levertov, and he dedicates poems to Heaney, Jorge Luis Borges, and William Carlos Williams. Like the narrator of "Old Thomas" in *Invitation to Kim,* Scarbrough has read widely in those poets whom he is "so addicted to."

In "The House Where Rivers Join: Confluence of Ocoee and Hiwassee" (*New and Selected Poems*), Scarbrough declares himself to be a lover of houses. The figure of the house with its rooms appears repeatedly in Scarbrough's poetry as a metaphor for those experiences, dreams, and memories that make up the self. Moments of intense awareness of self refract often into the narrator's memories of the houses with which he identifies particular moments or events. But, as in "The House Where Rivers Join," the associations expand so that the enclosure, the imaginative territory, becomes more than room and house. It becomes East Tennessee, the land of the Ocoee and the Hiwassee Rivers. The fine house on the hill above the confluence has a round window in its attic, but the house where the speaker lived as a child was not as fine. It had "shoddy glass," so that when he peered through it familiar shapes in the yard appeared wavy or narrow or wide or elongated. It was through such a vision, though, that he became a romantic, so that in his imagination he could claim to "have lived in all houses," having given up the expectation "of owning time"—and, by owning it, reducing it to fit into a single house.

Scarbrough's broad romantic vision has its origins in particular concrete images of East Tennessee and in his experience there. Often it involves the memories of an older speaker remembering particular events. Again "The House Where Rivers Join" is typical in that Scarbrough draws on events of childhood. The poem develops from two particular events depicted as memories. The first occurred when the narrator was 6 and stole a skiff that he rode down the river past the house and the confluence of the rivers. The older narrator, looking back, observes that he was seeking "being" or "the indestructible I"—believing, perhaps naively, that he could find some "definition" of self as concrete as a "room" in a house. He remembers visiting the house 3 years later while selling berries he had picked. This time he had a glimpse of the house's dark interior, in which the bright certitude of his earlier visit seemed to be lost. Such reflections upon memories of childhood experiences occur in many of Scarbrough's poems and particularly in the prose sketches published at the beginning of *New and Selected Poems*.

Looking through the "shoddy glass," the boy believes that "trolls live behind the chimney / in the cellar under the house" (96). Several of Scarbrough's verses feature these imaginary creatures and the interior world of dreams and fantasies they represent. In "Dreams" (*New and Selected Poems*) the narrator focuses on his hands, which are "the mind's best observer" (198). Passing into sleep and dreams these hands "dance brokenly / all night to the mind's music" (199). The poet's conscious work is driven by the insights that well up in his dreams. In a poem titled "Dream" he imagines himself passing into a forest where the stark horizontal trees became a zebra, living and breathing with a sound shaped into music. Passing through this forest and the daisy field beyond, he dreams he reaches home to find six "beautiful" 7-year-old sons waiting. Knowing these as his offspring and loving them, he feels "the consuming pride of God." But then the sons begin to whisper apart and an ominous figure of "incommensurable shape," a woman, summons both the speaker and the sons. The music of the forest reasserts itself. These sons whom his dream has shaped—such offspring as a single man may have—are, on the one hand, his siblings and, on the other, his poems. He apparently has fears for what they may become in our interpretative hands.

Even though the sons whom Scarbrough has are those that his imagination creates, his real family—father, mother, five brothers and one sister—plays a prominent role in almost all of his writing. *A Summer Ago* is an autobiographical episodic novel, more a series of sketches than a narrative. It features, in addition to his parents, his older brother Lee; Scarbrough himself appears in the book as Alan. Time—the passing of summer and the growth of the calf that will be sold in the fall for school books—provides the narrative framework. Typical activities of the children of farmers include berry picking, milling, syrup making, going to church and revivals, swimming in the creek. But these are the acts that tie the narrator—an agrarian—to the living, reproducing earth. He, time, and the physical world make a harmonious whole.

"Invitation to Kim," the title poem of his latest collection, invites Scarbrough's youngest brother to enter "the house / That George built" (3). It is an invitation to his world of imagination shaped into text. "George" tells his brother that he has all of his life tried to shape a single message that has two parts: "How to let a / Brother live as he will / And die his own way" (9). "George's" way of living "as he will" has been through language; and yet at the end of the poems and the book there remains a nagging sense of unfulfilled possibility. "I am an unfinished house," "George" declares (in "My Brothers"), "fallen into ruin" (134).

SURVEY OF CRITICISM

Criticism of Scarbrough's work to date has appeared principally in reviews of individual books. There are brief mentions of Scarbrough in *Who's Who in America, Who's Who in the South and Southwest,* and a more substantive biographical sketch in *Contemporary Authors* that contains Scarbrough's comment on his agrarian interests.

Reviewers have praised Scarbrough's craftmanship, focusing on his sense of form. In his early verse particularly he used traditional form and rhyme. Most of the later poetry is in blank verse, but lines and stanza forms are carefully measured by accent and syllable. Critics have noticed appreciatively the rural imagery, the emphasis on memory and childhood, and the mythic presence of family, especially of the father figure. In doing so they have credited Scarbrough for his ties to the earlier Tennessee Agrarians.

In his review of *A Summer Ago* Dan Leidig (1987) has evaluated the novel in the context of theme and metaphor in Scarbrough's published poetry. It is the most comprehensive study of Scarbrough to date.

Most reviewers have thought well of Scarbrough's accomplishment. The only complaint raised with any consistency is that the erudition of the language seems not to fit with the rural imagery and the emphasis on family. Scarbrough apparently recognizes this, but for him language is what enables the poet to find or achieve order.

BIBLIOGRAPHY

Works by George Scarbrough

Tellico Blue. New York: Dutton, 1949.
The Course Is Upward. New York: Dutton, 1951.
Summer So-Called. New York: Dutton, 1956.
New and Selected Poems, edited by Patricia Wilcox. Binghamton, N.Y.: Iris, 1977.
A Summer Ago. Memphis, Tenn.: St. Luke's, 1986.
Invitation to Kim. Memphis, Tenn.: Iris, 1989.

Studies of George Scarbrough

Davis, Lloyd. "The Southern Renascence and the Writers of Tennessee." In *The Literature of Tennessee,* edited by Ray Willbanks, 21–36. Macon, Ga.: Mercer University Press, 1984.
Eaton, Charles Edward. "A Dominion in Tennessee." Review of *New and Selected Poems. Sewanee Review* 86 (January 1978): xviii–xx.
Francisco, Edward. "Familiarity and Honest Remembrance." *Southern Review* 26 (Autumn 1990): 920–23.
Hay, Sara Henderson. "Double Meanings and Emotion." Review of *Tellico Blue. Saturday Review* 32 (July 9, 1949): 38.
Justus, James H. "On Reading Scarbrough." Introduction to *Invitation to Kim.* Memphis, Tenn: Iris, 1989.
———. "Poets after Midcentury." In *The History of Southern Literature*, edited by Louis D. Rubin, Jr., Louis P. Simson, Thomas Daniel Young, Rayburn S. Moore, Blyden Jackson, Mary Ann Wimsatt, and Robert L. Phillips, Jr., 535–55. Baton Rouge: Louisiana State University Press, 1985.
Leidig, Dan. Review of *A Summer Ago. Appalachian Journal* 14 (Summer 1987): 384–88.
"Notes on Current Books." Review of *New and Selected Poems. Virginia Quarterly Review* 54 (Winter 1978): 10.
"Scarbrough, George (Addison) 1915-." In *Contemporary Authors New Revision Series,* vol. 38, edited by James G. Lesniak and Susan M. Trosky, 375. Detroit: Gale Research Inc., 1993.

WILLIAM AARNES

James Seay
(1939–)

Perhaps because 16 years passed between the publications of James Seay's second collection and his third, he has not received the recognition of such contemporaries as Robert Morgan, Dave Smith, and Henry Taylor or of such younger, more prolific writers as David Bottoms. Nonetheless, Seay has received the respect of fellow poets for writing accessible, resonant poems about searching for happiness in our troubled lives. He has written many memorable poems, among them "Grabbling in Yokna Bottom," "The Hand That Becomes You," "The Motion of Bodies," "Time Open-Faced Yet Secret Before Us," and "Mountains by Moonlight."

BIOGRAPHY

Born on January 1, 1939, James Seay grew up in Panola County, Mississippi. His early poems often focus on life in the small-town rural South, dwelling, for example, on the difficulties of catching fish in a bottom ("Grabbling on Yokna Bottom"), on the misconceptions that kids pass on to impressionable playmates ("The Pomegranate"), or on the disturbing thrill of learning to hunt ("The Dove"). A few of Seay's poems allude to the loss of his right eye, which was hit by a stone thrown by a rotary mower when he was 12.

Seay attended Mercer University for two years but worked at various jobs before finishing his B.A. at the University of Mississippi in 1964. In his senior year he took a creative-writing course, during which, despite the emphasis on fiction, he began focusing on poetry. After graduating, Seay worked the next year as a claims adjustor and, as he has told interviewer John Carr (1972), gave himself the "valuable training" of "writing all that time, doing exercises in sonnets and various stanza forms" (48). In 1965 he entered the graduate program in English at the University of Virginia, where he took a writing course with George Garrett and was stimulated by the visits of other writers. Seay's reading of such poets as Richard Wilbur and James Dickey improved his sense of poetic form and energy. By the time he received his M.A. in 1966, Seay thought he was well on his way toward a collection of poems and decided to teach rather than pursue a doctorate.

From 1966 to 1974, Seay taught at the Virginia Military Institute, the University of Alabama, and Vanderbilt University. In 1967 he married the novelist Lee Smith (they have two sons and were divorced in 1981). Seay established himself as an accomplished, well-respected poet by publishing *Let Not Your Hart* in 1970 and *Water Tables* in 1974.

In 1974 Seay moved to Chapel Hill to begin teaching creative writing at the University of North Carolina. In 1978 he published *Where Our Voices Broke Off,* a limited edition containing two poems. In the late 1970s Seay also tried his hand at freelancing (reading "The Wicked Witch of North Carolina," one of two engaging articles that appeared in *Esquire,* though not necessary for understanding "Clouds over Islands" and "Mountains by Moonlight," increases a reader's appreciation of those poems). In order to devote more time to poetry, Seay took 1985 off from teaching. During that year he published *Said There Was Somebody Talking to Him through the Air Conditioner.* In 1987 Seay became director of the creative-writing program at Chapel Hill and in 1988 received an award in literature from the American Academy and Institute of Arts and Letters. Both a film documentary he coscripted, *In the Blood,* and his third collection of poems appeared in 1990. This collection, *The Light as They Found It,* reflects, among other things, Seay's visits to England and Russia and his fondness for fishing trips. In 1991 he married Caroline Szymeczek.

MAJOR THEMES

The poems in *Let Not Your Hart* depict a world that is often troubling and at times life threatening. Well water that tastes sweet can be contaminated with flat worms, a reborn Christian can put people's lives in peril by passing on a blind curve, and a man can injure (if not kill) himself and his fellow coon hunters by deciding to catch fish by firing his double-barreled shotgun into the water. In the world of *Let Not Your Hart,* where cannons are the final reasoning of kings, a former schoolmate can die in a "small war."

In this troubling, threatening world, many live and die "sundered from the normal." In his 1973 review of James Wright's *Collected Poems,* Seay noted that Wright has often focused on "social outcasts" (76), on "despairing humanity" (78). A number of Seay's poems in *Let Not Your Hart* share this focus, perhaps in part because Seay feels camaraderie with "the Lame, the Halt, the Half-Blind." Admittedly, Seay does not limit his focus to the unfortunate. For example, the speaker in "Kelly Dug a Hole" praises a worker for digging a "true" foundation hole that "will hold / When things begin / To slide and fall" (83). Nonetheless, a number of poems consider people who lived or live marginal lives. In "Touring the Indian Dead," the speaker finds himself drawn to the graveyard of the ostracized: a malformed baby, a misshapen arthritic, two men whom the speaker takes to have been homosexuals, and a woman who, for an unknown reason, had been scalped and disowned. In "The Feather," the speaker has a Wordsworthian conversation with a girl who, to help feed her family, collects "good" dead fish from the seashore (34). "The Day Speedo Stole the Meat Wagon" recounts the doings of an unsavory character who has lived on the streets and who hated and cursed those better off than he. And in "Does Anybody Wanna Buy My Little Brother?" the speaker finds himself forced to attend to the compulsive talking and weeping of a man who, as a child, stood on a corner while his brother tried to sell him.

Such subject matter could make for grim reading. But *Let Not Your Hart* is not a despairing book. As one section title puts it, some of the poems are "Light-Hearted," most notably "My Secret Iago Heart or Renal Calculus," in which Iago secretly attends a panel discussion of his motivation, and "The Majorette on the Self-Rising Flour Sign," in which Seay's penchant for verbal play is seen in the many *double entendres*. But even those poems acknowledging the plight of troubled people are carefully shaped works that are bemused, playful, and even affirmative in tone. The collection reads as if Seay has seen "the troubled hart" but can reassure himself that he need not take "the hunt / Into a deeper wood" ("Let Not Your Hart Be Trouble" 23). Instead, he makes trouble the basis of resilient, sometimes cheering art.

"The Bluebottle Tree" both exemplifies and suggests worries about such blending of troubling subject matter with cheering response. The poem's protagonist may wish, as does the husband in Eudora Welty's "Livvie," that his bottle tree will keep worries away, but whatever his motivation he creates a positive response to his difficult life. The first eleven-line (or fourteen-line?) verse paragraph describes his crafting of a bottle tree:

> Through years of fear and midnight wrath you've wrestled
> Bat-winged things, fled
> The fast white spiders and tried to outshout
> The loud gods; mornings
>   come uneasy.
> The bottle pile beside your shotgun house
> Grows bigger—empty bottles: the beers are brown,
> The whiskeys clear, and milk of magnesia
>   comes in bottles of translucent blue.
> But on this summer day you've cut a green bay tree,
> Sheared the leaves away, stubbed the branches,
> Stuck it upright in your yard, yard that it is,
> And slipped bottles over the stubs,
>   many blue bottles. (81)

This man's troubles give rise to an affirmative flourish, the kind of gesture made by other characters in *Let Not Your Hart*. In "The Feather" the girl who gathers dead fish also plants a feather in the seashore. Speedo's curse in "The Day Speedo Stole the Meat Wagon" is so disgusting (he hopes that those whom he dislikes will pass through a dragon's digestive track) that it is joyous. In other poems the speakers rather than the characters invent playful, fanciful affirmations. In "No Man's Good Bull" the speaker imagines that the gaseous bull, rather than being cured or dying, becomes a mythical creature that returns "Each night" with "his flame, blue and soft" (13). The speaker in "One Last Cheer for Punk Kincaid" imagines that Kincaid, though drowned, is nonetheless still returning "a punt / From deep inside his own territory" (37). And in "The Lame, the Halt, the Half-Blind" the speaker imagines a festival in which "We shall be making half-blind love, / King and court and countryside" (36).

The second verse paragraph of "The Bluebottle Tree" ends by telling us that the maker of the tree sees it as an affirmation. And his affirmation elicits from the poet an octave and sestet:

> Blueblazing in three o'clock sun
> Above the raw rusted gulley,
> It blares in elemental glory,
> Your bluebottle tree, a hard-won
> Stay against confusion,
> Bought with gnawed-out bellies
> Like those of Giacometti's
> Models, mere cinders of the sun.
> Must these always be the terms?
> Do ulcers, worms, or utter fear
> Have to be the roots of your blue word?
> And yet you grin and in grinning affirm,
> Through haze of magnesia, whiskey, or beer,
> That you have a tree fit for a golden bird. (81)

Admittedly, this verse paragraph, one of two sonnets in *Let Not Your Hart,* is more formal than most of the poems in the volume, many of which are in free verse. But this notable shift to a traditional rhyme scheme suggests the importance form has in this volume. Although Seay wrote these poems when many prominent poets were writing almost entirely in free verse, his lines are often iambic, and he frequently employs stanzas and rhymes. A few poems rely on refrains for their effects, particularly "The Feather" and "The Gars." And sometimes, as in "Toward Other Waters" and "The Big Money Comes to My Hometown," Seay deftly rewords phrases to give a poem both point and shape. Whatever the subject matter and whether his poem is more or less formal, in *Let Not Your Hart* Seay usually creates a "Stay against confusion" that leaves the reader pleased, if not with life, at least with the poet's art.

But clearly in "The Bluebottle Tree" the poet does more than recreate in different form the tree maker's affirmation; he also worries about how such an affirmation relates to life. He worries that it is the man's troubles that provoke as well as provide material for the gesture. "Must these always be the terms?" the poet asks, thus questioning whether art such as the tree maker's (and his own) need to be rooted in the difficulties of life. In addition, the poet's attention to the manhandling of the bay tree, which is "cut," "Sheared," stubbed," and "stuck" in the ground, suggests an uneasiness about affirmations achieved through reshaping life into art.

And, what is more, the poet leaves us concerned about his own role as an artist. In the sonnet, he makes clear his distance from the impoverished, "grinning" tree maker by making allusions to Frost's "The Figure a Poem Makes," to Giacometti's sculptures, and to Yeats's "Sailing to Byzantium." Does the poet expect the tree maker to understand these allusions? Does the poet expect him to understand that part of the apostrophe is shaped as a sonnet? One might say that the tree maker is only ostensibly the audience in a poem meant to be read by others. Nonetheless, by making the tree maker his putative audience and by being as literary as he is, the poet creates an obvious distance between himself and his subject. And that distance makes it hard not to read the sonnet as the musings of a poet who has appropriated a poor man's affirmation into his own while using "terms" the tree maker will barely comprehend. The poet so dramatizes himself that he allows the reader to think that the tree maker would probably sense, perhaps more than any sympathy, the poet's superiority.

This disconcerting distancing of the poet from his subject is an indirect expression of a quality in Seay's poetry that Vereen M. Bell noted in a 1975 review: "Aestheticism and humanism in Seay's poetry are mutually dependent, and the two guard each other from excess" (934). Seay explored this play of art and compassion more directly in two other poems in *Let Not Your Hart*. In "Moonwing" the speaker ostensibly addresses his fear of flying but also worries about the need, at the expense of others, to be above things, a need that can become the basis of, among other things, literary invention. In " 'Does Anybody Wanna Buy My Little Brother?' " the speaker is a photographer who rides a bus in order to be able to "shoot" a pigeon "At rest where converging lines / Begin to suggest, come near / Final things" (77). The speaker fails to take the photograph he wants because he sits next to a man so disturbed by the memory of his youth that he weeps and jerks the speaker the moment the shutter snaps. The unstated comment seems to be that the photographer's focus is wrong, that his arty concerns have led him to establish a mistaken distance from the man who shares a seat with him on the bus. What Seay addresses implicitly in "The Bluebottle Tree" and more explicitly in these two poems is a worry about the writing of untroubled poems about troubles. On the whole Seay succeeds in converting troubles into art that is a "Stay against confusion." Still, *Let Not Your Hart* contains suggestions that the making of such stays can leave the poet troubled.

In all but nine of the forty-five poems in his first collection, Seay capitalizes the initial letter of each line. In his second volume (and in later poems), however, he capitalizes only the initial letters of sentences. This change, though superficial, is nonetheless representative. For if *Let Not Your Hart* contains poems demonstrating that Seay shares with other Southern poets of his generation what James H. Justus has called "a residual fondness for conservative forms and techniques" (535). Then the poems in *Water Tables* show Seay preferring free verse. Although two of the twenty-five poems consist mainly of what might loosely be termed quatrains, no sonnets appear, and end-rhyme rarely occurs. Most of the poems consist of one or more verse paragraphs of varying length, made up of lines of varying length. In *Water Tables* Seay, like many of his contemporaries, shows little interest in working with traditional forms.

But Seay still enjoys wordplay. In "Another Sentimental Journey," *time* refers to both the lapse of events and the newsmagazine (25). In "The Quintessential Pencil," which opens with a pun on a *shaft* ("On theme day they give me the shaft"), the speaker seems to employ as many synonyms for *essential* as he can (40). In "Natural Growth" the speaker notes that "Poppies support their habits." He also asks the reader to take literally the notion of *planting one's eyes* and further asks that a "solid bank of trees" be seen as having "no money" (51). And in "Naming the Moon," which deals in part with how the speaker's son can give any number of names to the moon, the speaker concludes the poem with his being reminded that *moon* can refer to his son's "small butt" (13).

Seay's delight in wordplay is most engaging in "The Motion of Bodies." For each of the five sections of this poem Seay provides an epigraph from Newton's *The Motion of Bodies*. The first epigraph from Newton's work reads, "Two bodies attracting each other mutually describe similar figures about their common centre of gravity, and about each other mutually." That such a dry proposition has unintended suggestiveness is what Seay elaborates on in "The Motion of Bodies." Reworking this epigraph, Seay describes the movements of lovers. In the second section Seay quotes a problem about determining "the resistance of a globe moving uniformly forwards in this medium" and then imagines a lover's breasts moving through his vision; he concludes "that our findings are close at hand: / the perfect resistances, the solid proof" (44). And so the poem continues for three more sections.

As enjoyable as "The Motion of Bodies" is, the poem addresses a serious concern of *Water Tables*: the desire to achieve or recover well-being. In this poem it seems a person can, through lovemaking, achieve a fulfillment that seemingly transcends everyday experience. The speaker finds it "Hard to resist the notion / that these figures have infinite possibilities, / the way we defy the gravity of this place" (43). And he says of his lover's body that its "curves / confer with space, for instance, / in terms so elliptical / they've taken on the dimensions of mystery" (45).

A few other poems in *Water Tables* entertain the possibility of well-being. In "Natural Growth" the speaker explores the prospect of having one's eyes take root in a "bank of trees." If one is successful, the speaker suggests, "every cheer that reaches you is one / you know by heart'' (51). Another suggestion of possible well-being occurs at the end of ''The Hand That Becomes You,'' in which the speaker imagines ''you'' being transformed into a sailor who hears shipmates say:

> There is a New World out there,
> you lucky bastard you, a New World,
> islands of spice and fruit and friendly natives
> ever willing to give a helping hand. (39)

These poems suggest that Seay is able to record or imagine a blissful wholeness of the self along with a satisfying communion with the world.

Central as such poems are to *Water Tables,* the dominant mood of the collection is dissatisfaction. The delight expressed in ''The Motion of Bodies'' is more than offset by the book's sixth section, four studies of men who find that being attracted to women involves not pleasurable motion but unpleasant complications. In ''One of the Big Differences,'' the speaker recounts an affair and counterbalances any thought that lovers might find delight in each other by complaining, ''Cut yourself to ribbons / getting out of that girl's hair'' (59). The well-being imagined in ''Natural Growth'' is similarly negated. Seay's concern for the environment is mostly an undercurrent in *Water Tables,* but in the opening poem the speaker imagines his son focusing on the greenery while the speaker has to accept that people not only are marked for death but also are destroying the green earth. ''A Question of Elements'' suggest that the human being is not the only obstacle to communion with nature. The speaker in this poem turns to the four elements and receives replies that (reminiscent of Stephen Crane's universe) suggest a lack of concern for humanity. And in ''The Green World,'' the closing invitation, ''Make yourself at home,'' reminds one that the guest being invited into this world is, after all, not at home (54). Also qualified is the positive conclusion of ''The Hand That Becomes You,'' in this case by the poem itself. Besides opening with the ghastly image of a severed, gloved hand lying on a beach, the poem seems less about the well-being imagined at the end than about the thorough transformation needed to gain such happiness. Indeed, ''The Hand That Becomes You,'' despite its upbeat ending, seems more properly to be grouped with those poems exploring the main focus of the book: the lack of—and need for—well-being.

As in *Let Not Your Hart,* in *Water Tables* Seay has concerned himself with troubled people in a troubling world, but there is an important shift in focus. In *Let Not Your Hart* the speakers often focus on the troubles of others, these speakers keeping the troubles at bay with formal skill and imaginative flourish. In the third poem in *Water Tables,* ''On the Way,'' the speaker seems to have this ability when he writes that he and his sons ''saw the dangers long ago / and found a song or a saying / to keep us free'' (14). But typically in *Water*

Tables the speaker (or the "you" whom the speaker imagines as protagonist) is not free from trouble because trouble has already created unhappiness.

In "It All Comes Together Outside the Restroom in Hogansville," the speaker expresses a desire present in many poems in *Water Tables* when he states, "I wanted a different life" (37). This want—this need—prompts the speakers and their protagonists to try to change their lives. In "On the Island" the protagonist tries to change things by traveling:

> Things had not been right
> and you thought another place
> would bring you back around to your old self. (19)

The trip remedies nothing. Though "Things ought to go smooth" (19), the island is a place of uneasiness, where "you" finally sense that the crabs "will be moving / all over your body, / burning you down / like the things of the earth / you could not live with" (21). If getting away fails to improve one's life, then being remade can be tried, as in "The Hand That Becomes You" or "Drilling for Fire." In "Drilling for Fire," the speaker imagines a student having his transformation imposed on him by a girl who sneaks into his room and takes some of his belongings. She also leaves a tape with such advice as "study your life / as though it were on fire" (34).

Another possibility for remaking one's life is to try, as part of the title of the book's closing poem puts it, "Patching Up the Past." But employing this method of recovery seems to lead to failure. To try to touch the past is to "find again that something / has come between your hand / and the flimsy curtain / you want to pull away" ("Another Sentimental Journey," 25). To taste the past is to "taste fossils, clouds, failure" (71). If the past is a water table, what we find in it is "a water that offers nothing / from the private past, / a water that down to its last / and smallest particle resists our will" ("Patching Up the Past with Water," 71). With the past we will never obtain "that dreamed absence of succession / in which to reassemble the whole being" (71). Looking into the past, we do find ourselves confronting poignant moments: A memory of the speaker's father after the man has been caught stealing frogs and a photograph of a mother at 17 are the most memorable moments in "Patching Up the Past with Water." But even such moments fail us: The son never discovers "what was said and done" (68), and it seems impossible to be true to the past by "waiting out here in the future" (71). Like other means of trying to discover well-being, looking to the past, seems to be a little more than futile "straining." In *Water Tables* the protagonists struggle to obtain or regain well-being, but they hold on to happiness no better than a sieve holds water.

Published in a limited edition in 1985, *Said There Was Somebody Talking to Him through the Air Conditioner* seems a more mature, fuller (eight-part, fourteen-page) version of "The Bluebottle Tree." Again Seay's poem is occasioned by someone else's handling of troubles, this time an appeal for help by a man who makes up and seems to believe, despite inconsistencies, a story that three blacks with an abducted white woman have broken into his mobile home to kill him. Again Seay's response is artful, but in *Said There Was Somebody Talking* literariness does not distance the poet from the troubled man. Instead, in lines that often stretch more than twenty words across the page, Seay creates a wise, thoughtful voice that weaves together stories, trusts to leaps of association, and worries about the relation of his troubling life to the man's troubled fiction. *Said There Was Somebody Talking* also resembles "On the Way," the poem in *Water Tables* depicting Seay and his sons as developing sayings to keep themselves safe. By the end of *Said There Was Somebody Talking,* it is clear that, besides the troubled man's story, another occasion for the poem is Seay's worry about what kind of story he should live and tell as the divorced father of his sons.

In working toward a concluding hope that he is providing his sons with the right story, Seay considers the different kinds of stories that we tell ourselves. He wants to avoid delusional, sometimes pathological stories, an example of which is the story of the man who imagines he is about to be murdered. He also worries about a story his father told about killing a Japanese pilot during World War II. What Seay finds problematic about this factual story is that, even if not necessarily expressing hatred, it does not lessen that feeling. A third kind of story, the kind that Seay wants to endorse, is the socially useful one that people should be treated as humans. In the poem's final section, Seay meditates somewhat defensively (worrying about his approval of hunting) on the life he has shared with his sons when he has been with them. This life involves a blend of hunting, stargazing, and storytelling that Seay hopes will give his sons fictions that are adequate alternatives to sickness and hate.

Seay's third collection, *The Light as They Found It,* is a work of relaxed seriousness. The poems are often occasioned by Seay's experiences as a vacationer, a sightseer, a stargazer, a rock-and-roll fan. Whatever skilled revision they may have required, the poems are seemingly effortless and fittingly casual. Four of the nineteen poems are blocked off into stanzas, and a few intermittent rhymes occur; but even the apparently more controlled poems share with those written in lengthy verse paragraphs (with shorter lines than those in *Said Somebody Was Talking*) a leisurely combination of narration or description with meditation. In these poems Seay seems at ease, working with a form that allows him to ruminate, to digress from one narrative to an echoing anecdote, to pause over details, and to qualify his thoughts.

Easygoing as *The Light as They Found It* is in its manner, it is not the work of a poet who is completely comfortable with life. The book opens with a poem dealing with a lost friendship and closes with a pair of poems dwelling on his failed marriage. And several poems consider the concern that life is not what we imagine it to be.

Seay emphasizes this concern with his title *The Light as They Found It,* a phrase implying that how one finds an experience is not necessarily the experience. He illustrates this idea in "Mountains by Moonlight," the poem from which he took the book's title. In this poem he focuses on a postcard his grandparents once sent while on vacation. He concludes by remembering that his family thought of his grandparents as never having questioned the sights they saw as being anything other than what they saw. But Seay, worrying over such innocence, questions the motives for sending postcards (the poem includes an account of how F. Scott Fitzgerald sent a postcard to himself), mentioning what postcards do not picture, and making clear that the postcard the grandparents sent had a retouched moon rather than the actual one. At times Seay entertains the idea that perception and event can in some ways correspond; in "An Ideal of Itself," he suggests that the happiness of his failed marriage expressed itself in a shared sensibility that seemed to match experience. Usually, however, he accepts the disparity between mind and event, either settling for less than he would have liked to imagine (as in "Easter Sunrise, The Constant Moon We Settled For") or, more often, insisting on the value of what the imagination adds to experience. One impulse behind Seay's interest in this concern has been his own desire to add to his experiences something more—something "otherworldly," something glamorous in the sense of magical. This desire informs Seay's striking meditation on a ruined Jamaican plantation in the third section of "Time Open-Faced Yet Secret Before Us." In this leisurely-paced passage, he masterfully evokes someone other—a woman from colonial times—with whom to share a view that is at once part of and beyond experience.

SURVEY OF CRITICISM

To date, criticism of Seay's poetry consists of book reviews, a brief minor article by David Bottoms (1977), and a one-page discussion of Seay's work in James H. Justus's overview (1985) of southern contemporary poetry.

The reviews have been largely favorable (with the notable exception of a review of *Water Tables* in *Shenanodoah,* the reviewer grudgingly admitting that some of Seay's poems are "quite frustratingly engaging.") Besides Vereen M. Bell's comment (1975) about the play of "aestheticism and humanism" in Seay's poetry, a comment by Josephine Jacobsen (1971) also merits remarking. Jacobsen has found that *Let Not Your Hart* has "peculiarly southern humor, with a sort of subterranean dark reach under its casual surface." She stresses Seay's "reliable gift" for creating poems with an "eerie resonance" of "ambiguous danger, human vulnerability, and somber forces."

In his survey of "Poetry after Midcentury," Justus has made a similar point by suggesting that Seay's poems acknowledge "the totems and detritus of village life" and "invest such phenomena with mysterious potentiality that transforms them into the stuff of legend." Both Jacobsen and Justus are right to suggest that the reach of Seay's poems often extends hauntingly beyond the experiences that occasion the poems.

BIBLIOGRAPHY

Works by James Seay

Let Not Your Hart. Middletown, Conn.: Wesleyan University Press, 1970.

"A World Immeasurably Alive and Good: A Look at James Wright's *Collected Poems.*" *Georgia Review* 27 (Spring 1973): 71–81.

Water Tables. Middletown, Conn.: Wesleyan University Press, 1974.

"The Wicked Witch of North Carolina." *Esquire* 86 (October 1976): 116–17, 161–65.

Where Our Voices Broke Off. Deerfield, Mass.: Deerfield Press, 1978.

Said There Was Somebody Talking to Him through the Air Conditioner. Winston-Salem, N.C.: Paleamon Press, 1985.

The Light as They Found It. New York: Morrow, 1990.

Interviews with James Seay

Carr, John. "An Interview with James Seay." *Notes on Mississippi Writers* 5 (Fall 1972): 35–55, 57.

Studies of James Seay

Bell, Vereen M. "The Purchase Lost: The Poems of James Seay." *Southern Review,* n.s., 11 (Autumn 1975): 933–36.

Bottoms, David. "Notes on the Structure of James Seay's 'It All Comes Together Outside the Restroom in Hogansville.' " *Notes on Contemporary Literature* 7 (September 1977): 6–7.

Collins, Floyd. "Ideology and Diversity in Recent Poetry." *Gettysburg Review* 5 (Winter 1992): 146–51.

Gall, Sally M. "Seven from Wesleyan." *Shenandoah* 26 (Fall 1974): 54–70.

Jacobsen, Josephine. "Three Poets." *Poetry* 118 (June 1971): 166–69.

Justus, James H. "Poets after Midcentury." In *The History of Southern Literature,* edited by Louis D. Rubin, Jr., Blyden Jackson, Rayburn S. Moore, Lewis P. Simpson, Thomas Daniel Young, Mary Ann Wimsatt, and Robert L. Phillips, 535–55. Baton Rouge: Louisiana State University Press, 1985.

ELSA NETTELS

Eve Shelnutt
(1941–)

Eve Shelnutt is best known as a writer of finely wrought short stories of family relationships, many of them set in her native South Carolina. She is also a widely published poet and the author of three books on the art and teaching of writing.

BIOGRAPHY

Eve Shelnutt was born on August 29, 1941 in Spartanburg, South Carolina, the second of three daughters of James Marion Waldrop and Evelyn Brock Waldrop. Her father, now retired, was a news broadcaster. Her mother, formerly a violinist and teacher of music, owns an advertising agency.

Shelnutt considers her Southern background a defining influence upon her work, but she has expressed little sense of attachment to any one place. During her childhood and adolescence, her family moved often, sometimes more than once a year, living in California and New York as well as in the South. In an essay titled "Morning Tales," in *The Confidence Woman: 26 Women Writers* (1991), a collection she edited, she recalls the early formative experiences that shaped her fiction and poetry: compulsive reading; sojourns in rented houses with her mother and her sisters, Cynthia and Anne, while her father was away; travels of the whole family back and forth across the continent in two cars and trailers—"the 'stable' home"—filled with their books and musical instruments, Wedgewood china and silver—migrations so frequent that "my sisters and I are unable to list the places where we lived, so numerous are they." Her father's desire for motion, colliding with her mother's longing for stability, resulted in a "war of visions" between parents twice married and twice divorced. Until she left home at 17, she was absorbed by the unfolding drama of the five family members, "each a changing scene in a mysterious play."

During the next decade came her first marriage, in 1961, to James William

Shelnutt, an engineer on the faculty of the University of North Carolina at Charlotte. Their son, Gregory William Shelnutt, born in 1963, is a sculptor and head of the sculpture program at the University of Mississippi in Oxford. In 1972 Eve Shelnutt received her B.A. from the University of Cincinnati, having also studied at the University of Michigan at Flint, Carson-Newman College, and Wright State University. She received her M.F.A. in 1973 from the University of North Carolina at Greensboro, where she held the Randall Jarrell Fellowship and studied with novelist and poet Fred Chappell. During the next year she worked as a journalist and taught at the Mt. Adams School for the Performing and Creative Arts, in Cincinnati. Since 1974, she has held university appointments with tenure in the English departments of Western Michigan University (1974–80), the University of Pittsburgh (1980–88), and since 1988 at Ohio University, where she is currently a professor of English. She lives in Athens, Ohio, with her husband, Mark Logan Shelton, a writer of nonfiction and senior editor of *Ohio Magazine.*

In "The Benefits of Tension," an address given at Ohio University in 1990, Shelnutt has traced her development as a writer of fiction. She described her first published story, "Affectionately, Harold," which won the *Mademoiselle* Magazine Fiction Award in 1967, as an example of traditional realism depicting "recognizable characters acting within recognizable situations." During the next 5 years, she served her "writing apprenticeship to the 'traditional' story" but felt increasingly hampered by its constraints. Her reading of Pynchon, Barthelme, and Hawkes moved her to question the premises of conventional realism, but she chose not to follow the path of the post-modernists. "I was not interested in giving up wholly the traditional story, with plot, characters, tension, action, resolution, a sense of closure." Instead, she chose to experiment within tradition, to invite a reader "into a traditional, mimetic story, which, while the reader was under its sway, I would then subvert." In an essay on V. S. Naipaul in *Genre* (1989), she describes herself as "a fiction writer whose work admits both the realist tradition and its strictures."

Her repeated choice of epigraphs for her stories from the works of Wallace Stevens and Elizabeth Bishop identifies two of the writers most important to her. In her essay "Driving to the Interior: Elizabeth Bishop, Guide" in *Agni* (1988), Shelnutt identifies Bishop as "my mentor" and describes "the profound effect [her] poetry would have on my fiction" (94). In Bishop's poetry, more than anywhere else, she found the language to inspire fiction: "Certain images as epigraphs seemed to suggest ways into stories I had wanted to tell without knowing they were lodged in memory" (96).

In the past 20 years Shelnutt has published more than fifty stories and seventy poems in scores of literary magazines, including the *Virginia Quarterly Review, American Review, Epoch, Prairie Schooner, Nimrod,* and *Ploughshares.* Her mature fiction is well represented in the three collections of stories published by the Black Sparrow Press. The first, *The Love Child* (1979), received the Great Lakes College Association Fiction Award, and the story "Angel" was reprinted in *O. Henry Prize Stories* (1975) and *Stories of the Modern South* (1977). The second collection, *The Formal Voice* (1982), received the South Carolina Press Association Fiction Award. "Andantino" in the third collection, *The Musician* (1987), received the Pushcart Prize. "Voice" in the same collection was included in *New Stories from the South* (1988). She has recently completed a fourth story collection titled *Distance*.

Three collections of Shelnutt's poetry, *Air and Salt* (1983), *Recital in a Private Home* (1988), and *First a Long Hesitation* (1992) have been published by Carnegie-Mellon University Press. Her book *Josephine Jacobsen: A Study of Forms* is forthcoming from the Ohio University Press. She frequently publishes essays on contemporary literature and creative writing pedagogy in such journals as *Genre, Confrontation, Cream City Review, Manoa, Southern Quarterly,* and *College Teaching.* She continues to be a regular book reviewer for the *Atlanta Constitution, Columbus Dispatch, Plain Dealer* (Cleveland), and *Milwaukee Journal.*

From the beginning of her career, Shelnutt has successfully combined the writing of fiction and poetry with the teaching of writing. She has conducted scores of workshops for students and teachers in colleges, high schools, and elementary schools; she has given readings at many colleges and universities in the East, Midwest, and South; has presented papers and participated in panels on pedagogy; and has served as a judge for many literary competitions. Her commitment to the teaching of writing is also evidenced in three books: *The Magic Pencil: A Workbook for Parents and Teachers* (1988) includes exercises to engage children in the writing of descriptions, stories, diaries, letters, poems, and plays; *The Writing Room* (1989) and *Writing: The Translation of Memory* (1990), the latter containing work twenty-two of Shelnutt's former students at the University of Pittsburgh, are designed for college writing courses. She is also the author of "Notes from a Cell: Creative Writing Programs in Isolation" (published in *Creative Writing in America: Theory and Pedagogy* by NCTE Press in 1989 and reprinted in the AWP *Chronicle* in February 1990), a major essay on the place of the MFA program in the university curriculum.

Shelnutt has held fellowships at the Yaddo Colony, the MacDowell Colony, and the Virginia Center for the Creative Arts. Her work has also been supported by the Michigan, Pennsylvania and Ohio councils on the arts. Her achievements in fiction, poetry, and the essay and her teaching of these arts have established her as one of the most versatile and accomplished writers of her generation.

MAJOR THEMES

A number of Shelnutt's short stories portray a family similar to her own: father, mother, two or three daughters, sometimes a grandparent, a sister's child, a lover of one of the parents or the daughters. Although the collections lack the novelistic unity of such integrated works as *The Country of the Pointed Firs* and *Winesburg, Ohio,* recurrent elements link the stories, like variations on a theme. The dominant subject is the effect upon the mother and her daughters of the departure of the father, whose absence makes him a haunting presence in the minds of his family. The absent father, usually named James or Jim, may die in war (as in "Feet") but usually he simply leaves without explanation and returns without warning, sometimes bearing inappropriate gifts for his wife and daughters. Occasionally identified as a film producer or radio announcer, he is lured to California, Florida, or New York by the mirage of the perfect job. In "Andantino," he is a disembodied voice reading the poetry of Elizabeth Barrett Browning and Emily Dickinson on a radio program, which his daughter and a neighbor listen to until the series ends and he goes off the air. Too proud to take mundane jobs like reporting the weather even when his family is in need, he carefully preserves his handsome appearance and buys his wife Evan-Picone suits; but for ready cash, he will pawn her violin, not his gold cuff links with ruby eyes. He fills one daughter with anger and bitterness, another daughter with longing for his love and attention. Said to have many wives and many children, he becomes an almost legendary figure, joining a long line of male characters in American literature who escape home and family to seek self-fulfillment in some undisclosed destination.

The mother, usually named Pauline—sometimes Elizabeth, Juanita or simply "Momma"—remains with her daughters in rented houses where she combats loneliness, sexual hunger, and depression. In several stories she teaches music at the local school. Occasionally she is the focal character; but most of the stories, whether narrated in the first or third person, register the observations and memories of the second daughter—Annie, Lucy, Rosette—who in childhood observes the signs of adult passion without comprehending them and in later years loves and is loved by good men who, unlike her glamorous father, are steadfast and faithful to the women they choose. A younger sister, Josie, efficient and practical, marries into money and ease, unlike the elder sister, Claire, recalled by the narrator in many lights: as a beautiful child, as a talented pianist, as a woman grown fat and mentally disturbed. The stories that show the same people at different ages from different perspectives have been compared to photographs in a family album. The several names for each family member, "standing in ablaut relationship to one another," as Shirley Scott (1988) has observed, suggest emphasis on different aspects of the character, from one story to another.

Mother and daughters are usually left to sustain themselves in towns in North or South Carolina—Henderson, Asheville, Greenville, Landrum, Spartanburg. In the contemporary world of K-Marts, Television, and Tupperware, traditional activities of an earlier time—church suppers, choir rehearsals, and family picnics and reunions—still take place; but far from creating a sense of community, they highlight the isolation of Shelnutt's fragmented families, sealed off from the life of the town, visited in times of crisis by curious neighbors and church ladies bearing casseroles, to whom the mother and daughters remain strangers.

Events in the outside world rarely obtrude; only the Korean War profoundly affects the characters. The victims include a mother, appropriately named Irene (peace), who slowly goes insane in anxiety for her son in battle ("Disconsolate"); a crippled soldier who lives out his last months, paralyzed, in a wheel chair ("Setting"); a woman bereft by her husband's death, who turns for love and solace to her widowed landlord ("Feet"). In these and other stories, the act of waiting for the absent man's return consumes the energies of the characters, converting seemingly trivial acts into telling signs of mental states. The perfectly made tablecloth with rickrack in "Questions of Travel" signifies the mother's will to sustain order for herself and her daughter. Pauline's look that frightens Jehovah's Witnesses away from her door tells of her collapse in "Fable without End."

Traumatic events occur, always portrayed from the perspective of onlookers: A daughter runs away; a cuckolded husband bursts into his rival's house; a man saws off his thumb and bids his daughter look for it. Death, provoking conflict and stirring memory, touches nearly all the characters: sometimes the death of the mother; more often the death, in disease or old age, of the father, lover, or grandfather, whose dissolution fixes in the mind of the narrator images of shaking hands, bleached skin, and a body that barely lifts the sheet covering it. No weddings are portrayed and few are remembered; but the act of love, which concludes a number of the stories, allows characters (and readers) the sense of fulfillment—complete, if temporary.

Shelnutt's fiction deals with the universal themes of love and conflict, isolation and death, and with the primary feelings—desire, joy, guilt, fear. Her fiction maintains the illusion created by realism that imagined characters live in the "real world." But the stories are not traditional in form and style, often thrusting the reader into a world of mysterious conjunctions where even familiar signposts of conventional syntax and punctuation may be gone. All three volumes of stories reflect Shelnutt's decision to subvert the conventions of realism and, thus, confound the reader's expectations of chronological sequence, climax, and resolution. Her own life experiences, "radical, upsetting of unity," were best reflected, she believed, by "the tension between the traditions of the story form and my arguments against them reflected in form." Convinced that plots "ordered so logically as to produce resolution" are deceptive, encouraging in the reader falsely sentimental illusions about life, she wished to compel from readers a "nonhabitual response," to dispel "definitions of stability, order, right and wrong," reinforced by the traditional story.

In several essays Shelnutt has said that her stories originate not in a plot or an idea but in a word, a phrase from a poem, or a title that produces the words that construct the story. The generative impulse of such stories as "Disconsolate" and "Questions of Travel" produces continuous progression forward through linear time, but more of the stories move without transitions backward and forward in time, yoking events and memories associated by a logic often buried deep in the narrator's mind. Defined by one critic as "calculated estrangements that take on their own reality," the stories often create surreal effects, rendering in dreamlike image and sequence events pregnant with a meaning that resides within the accumulation of detail and accentuation of the stories' rhythms.

Shelnutt's rejection of the conventions of traditional realism reflects her need to use language to free herself from traditional kinds of discourse and to sustain her own identity. She has traced her attachment to Bishop's poetry to "an uneasy relationship to language, a result, possibly of a Southern background." Her Southern heritage confronted her with forces to be resisted: an oral tradition that "absorbed personality or subtle idiosyncracy"; a language of deception and evasion created to conceal "histories of defeat" and promote the ruling ideology. "If I was to claim any language as my own," she says in her essay on Bishop, "it would have to be a language no institution I knew had won" (97).

In her essay "Benefits of Tension," Shelnutt has noted that her refusal to participate in the traditions of Southern storytelling infused language with an extraordinary power when she began to write fiction. "I felt, simply, that, with words, I could make *myself*." Language became animate, "dynamic almost in and of itself." Her fictional characters likewise feel the explosive or corroding power of words. In "Angelus" the narrator would instruct her mother: "Words, Momma, eat like sulphur, come out rolled around the motorized tongue, and your children didn't know what to do with the power." In "Disconsolate," Irene, refusing to mouth the official euphemisms about war, strives vainly to express her feelings to her husband, as if "her lips were a pea pod unzipping to reveal pellets of words lined up separate, with a life of their own."

The economy that preserves the life of words requires that the narrative voice be terse, clipped, unemotional, chary of adjectives, save those that describe the visible—size, color, age, shape. Narrators, third person and first person, for whom "observation is sustenance," do not analyze feelings or even denominate them but convey them in metaphor and simile and intonations of the narrative voice. For Shelnutt, fiction, no less than poetry, to which her prose is often compared, derives power from what is unsaid. "What is not written into a story can act upon a reader as much as what is included even though the reader's primary focus will seem to be on the words themselves."

Shelnutt has described her fiction as a "literature of silence," reflective in its "absence of explanation," of the "early absences" experienced in childhood, particularly the absence of mechanical purveyors of others' words—telephones, radios, television. In *Writing: The Translation of Memory,* she argues for what Willa Cather has called the *novel démeublé,* the novel unencumbered by catalogues of material objects and physical sensations. Shelnutt's objection to the "plethora of objects in contemporary American fiction" is both esthetic and social criticism of a "self-conscious clutter" that announces one message: "We have been overwhelmed by the material world." In her fiction, she would make "a political statement about noise," would seek to show "what happens between people in the absence of noise that clutter accumulates around itself and the informing substantiality of objects when they are few."

These purposes likewise inform Shelnutt's poems, in which many of the themes and images of the short stories appear. Her first collection, *Air and Salt,* presents familiar figures: the mother, her three daughters, and their absent father (identified by his French cuff links, his Nash-Ambassador, and his many wives). Again the figure of the father evokes powerful and ambivalent feelings. In "Father, Counting," he gives life and the names Eve and Cynthia to his daughters. In "Family Getting Back to God," after the death of the father, whose "moving sound is sin," the daughters unite in a sacramental meal to exalt the mother: "they lift the mother up."

The dying of the narrator's lover, Carlos, remembered in the story "Ligature," is memorialized in two poems, "Carlos, 1937–1979" and "Language, for Carlos." Rosette appears in "Prodigals" in a golden pastoral landscape warmed by afternoon light at harvest time. The speakers of the poems share with the narrators of the stories memories of Easter bread with the single egg inside, the father reading Max Brand Westerns, the ritual of meals at tables formally set with silver and crystal—order amidst upheaval. The collection might have been titled *Transformations,* for most of the poems define or prophesy change: children growing out of innocence, the bones of women "untied" by their lovers, the body translated by death into the primal elements, "air and salt."

The title of Shelnutt's second collection, *Recital in a Private Home,* suggests the intimacy of a family setting, but many of the poems move beyond the circle of family members and private loves to more impersonal subjects and public arenas. Instead of the slow natural processes of growth and dying, the speaker in *Recital* creates images of latent energy compressed, portending explosive violence in an undisclosed future: The world is a woman whose house contains the fuel that will destroy it; girls in a convent library yearn to rise as their bodies fill with the weight, like water, of unwanted facts; a little square in an Italian town becomes the stage where a blacksmith and a baker's wife are potential actors in a drama of adultery and murder.

Regarding the blacksmith and baker's wife, the title of their scene, "A Cuneiform in Italy," suggests how Shelnutt's images are to be read—as signs in a language, often mysterious, to be interpreted by speaker and reader. Among the most provocative of signs are paintings that inspire the speaker of the poem to meditate on the relation of living subject and pictorial image, on the canvas that can be owned and the reality that cannot. The paintings identified—Van Gogh's "Fishing in Springtime," Breughel's "Two Monkeys," Matisse's "Luxe, Calme and Volupte"—are natural choices for a writer who seeks to evoke the mystery inhering in the "substantiality of objects" and whose fiction and poetry often dissolve the boundaries between human and animal, person and object, dream and waking, real and imagined.

The art most pervasive in Shelnutt's work is music, as indicated by story titles: "Obbligato," "Allegro ma non Troppo," "Undersong," "Descant,"

"The Musician," "Andantino," and "The Black Fugatos." Music fills the lives of her characters—listeners as well as the violinists and pianists who play Bach and Chopin and Mendelssohn. For the narrator, who rarely performs, family members are like musical instruments producing harmony and discord; time has its passages of rubato and syncopation; and a concluding event is "the last variation finding its theme." Shelnutt's reading of Thomas Mann, a novelist of special importance to her, may have suggested the use of the leitmotif, as the music historian Margaret W. Freeman has noted. That characters of different names are associated with the same motifs—example, the twin brother dead at birth, the father's gold cuff links with the ruby eyes—reveals their shared identity as possessors of their creator's memory, the deepest source of her fiction and poetry.

SURVEY OF CRITICISM

Detailed analysis of Shelnutt's work appears in several reviews of her short stories. Although the body of criticism is relatively small, a number of critics have identified Shelnutt's as a writer of unusual power, subtlety, and originality. They have stressed her innovative use of language and the poetic compression of her prose, which produce fiction of "extraordinary intensity" that demands sustained engagement on the part of the reader. In Fred Chappell's words (1978), the reader must "concentrate upon the story almost as hard as if he were composing it in order to comprehend." Reviewers have compared Eve Shelnutt to Eudora Welty, Louise Erdrich, James Purdy, and John Hawkes, among others; but reviewers have stressed the distinctive character of Shelnutt's work, which makes it impossible to place her in any one tradition. Shirley Clay Scott (1988) distinguishes the poetic intensity and dreamlike effects of Shelnutt's stories from the realism of such writers as Jayne Anne Phillips, Ray Carver, and Bobbie Ann Mason. Patrick Samway (1985) places Shelnutt outside the "oral tradition" that Barry Hannah, Grace Paley, and Alice Walker exemplify. Fred Chappell, in his review of *The Love Child,* describes the world of her fiction as a "universe new-minted"; the stories are "like no other stories being written."

Because Shelnutt's fiction resists classification in traditional categories, reviewers have devoted much of their space to analyzing the methods of her fiction and describing its effects, usually beginning with the idiosyncratic properties of the narrative voice, described by John Baskin as "muted, but perfectly modulated," and by Samway as "excessively private, deeply feminine, constantly backlooping, highly elliptical . . . one of the most distinctive of today's literary scene." To illustrate the poetic rhythms of Shelnutt's prose, Robert Early (1988) has set the opening sentences of the story "Angelus" in verse form. He notes, that, like a poem, "Angelus" is impelled forward as if by a "tiny grain" to be "mined" for the energy that transmits itself from sentence to sentence. What results is neither poetic prose nor prose poetry but narration opening up "new dimensions'' for the use of techniques of which Shelnutt is the ''inventor/protector.''

Among the most illuminating studies of Shelnutt's work are her own essays in which she defines her methods and artistic aims. In *The Writing Room,* she reconstructs the writing of the story ''Feet'' and explains the purposes of her experiments *''within* tradition.'' In ''The Sources of 'Questions of Travel' '' (*Writing*) Shelnutt not only explicates the title story but also explores the complex interplay of her life experiences, reading, and artistic purpose that are fused in literary form. These essays, notable for their objectivity and self-knowledge, guide the reader through the private worlds of stories described by their author as ''deeply autobiographical'' in their method and forms.

BIBLIOGRAPHY

Works by Eve Shelnutt

Sparrow 62. Santa Barbara, Calif.: Black Sparrow Press, 1977.
The Love Child. Santa Barbara, Calif.: Black Sparrow Press, 1979.
Descant. Raleigh, N.C.: Palaemon Press, 1982.
The Formal Voice. Santa Barbara, Calif.: Black Sparrow Press, 1982.
Air and Salt. Pittsburgh, Pa.: Carnegie-Mellon University Press, 1983.
The Musician. Santa Rosa, Calif.: Black Sparrow Press, 1987.
The Magic Pencil: Teaching Children Creative Writing. Atlanta: Peachtree Publishers, 1988.
Recital in a Private Home. Pittsburgh, Pa.: Carnegie-Mellon University Press, 1988.
The Writing Room: Keys to the Craft of Fiction and Poetry. Marietta, Ga.: Longstreet Press, 1989.
Writing: The Translation of Memory. New York: Macmillan, 1990.
First a Long Hesitation. Pittsburgh, Pa.: Carnegie-Mellon University Press, 1992.

Works Edited by Eve Shelnutt

The Confidence Woman: 26 Women Writers at Work. Atlanta: Longstreet Press, 1991.

Studies of Eve Shelnutt

Barrett, Lynne. *''The Formal Voice.''* *Quarterly West,* no. 16 (1983): 187–90.
Baskin, John. *''The Formal Voice.''* *Yale Review* 72 (1982): xvii.
Chappell, Fred. ''Eve Shelnutt's *The Love Child.''* *Ploughshares* 4 (1978): 169–74.
Coppula, Katherine. *''The Musician.''* *Crazy Horse* 35 (1988): 124–32.
Davis, Alan. *''The Musician.''* *Small Press* 5 (1987): 42–43.
DeWitt, Henry. ''Literary Magazines and the Writing Workshop.'' In *Creative Writing in America: Theory and Pedagogy.* Urbana, Ill.: NCTE Press, 1989.
Early, Robert. *''The Musician.''* *Mid-American Review* 8 (1988): 217–20.

Greene, Melissa Fay. *"The Love Child." Georgia Review* 33 (1979): 951–54.

Martin, David. *"The Musician." Cream City Review* 13 (1989): 314–16.

Samway, Patrick. "Crafter of Stories," *America* (December 14, 1985): 427.

Scott, Shirley Clay. "The Recovery of Story: *The Musician* by Eve Shelnutt." *Nimrod* 32 (1988): 133–39.

Dave Smith
(1942–)

At midcareer, Dave Smith's contributions to American poetry and literature are already extraordinary. He is not only a distinguished poet, but also a fine fiction writer and essayist, a devoted and influential teacher, a respected literary scholar, critic, and editor. As a poet, he began by writing what appeared to be Southern regional poems; but his poetry soon resisted categorization as he pushed at the boundaries of form, perception, place, and time in his search for a more powerful, more accurate, more inclusive poetry. He writes disturbing, passionate poems, immense in scope and precise in detail. Smith is one of the most widely read and admired poets of his generation.

BIOGRAPHY

Born on December 19, 1942, in Portsmouth, Virginia, to Ralph ("Jeddie") Smith and Catherine Mary ("Kitty") Cornwell, David Jeddie Smith grew up in the working-class suburbs of Portsmouth. His father was a naval engineer who loved sports and fast cars, and his mother worked as a telephone operator and later as a civil-service secretary. Like many American families, Smith's family had spent generations pulling up roots to move to where there might be work— or better work than they had—hungry for the promised American dream of the middle class. In his essay "In Search of the Real Thing," he describes his early ancestors as "grim-faced pragmatic issues of English wanderers who settled the coal ridges of Maryland and West Virginia" (155), and in "Hunting Men" (1989) Smith describes his maternal grandfather as a stern, silent man who "came alone to Virginia when the depression cracked." The family had lost what land they had, and "people without land need jobs" (545). From this man, who took his grandson on quiet Saturday hunting trips in the Virginia woods,

Smith came to understand the significance of physical displacement and the need of human beings to belong somewhere.

For the Smiths, as for most of post–World War II America, this longing for permanence and place translated into the pursuit of home ownership. The Smith's began in an apartment in one suburb, graduated to a small box house in another suburb, then moved to a house in still another suburb, and finally built their own house in a new suburb called Sterling Point. Even when the family seemed to have achieved its dream of a stable middle-class existence, there was a significant transitory atmosphere. Smith's father had designed his son's bedroom as a future den (looking forward to when the boy would grow up and move out) at the center of the house with doors passing through it and furnished it with a pull-out sofa rather than a real bed. The irony of all this upheaval in the pursuit of stability, and the conflicts contained in American social mobility, are topics confronted again and again in Smith's poetry.

The dream of flight, or at least of speed, is as American as the dream of home; and as Smith grew up he fell naturally into his father's obsession with cars. Cars represented freedom, he writes in "In Search," "a means to discover manhood, time, and distance" (158), and he and his father spent much of their time dreaming of and working on cars. It was *Hot Rod Magazine* (one of the two magazines his father subscribed to; the other was *Sports Illustrated*) rather than literature classes that first taught him what language could do. He became aware of the energy and passion possible in writing, and the consistent American message he got from *Hot Rod Magazine* was "life was out there somewhere and down the road" (159).

Portsmouth was a working town filled with shipyard laborers and sailors, and Smith grew up well aware of the rough side of American life, but his sensibility seems to have been shaped as much as anything by the time he spent as a child in the company of his generous and loving grandmother in the tidewater area of Chesapeake Bay with its romantic historical implications and overwhelming sensory impressions: "many small tidal rivers and creeks, all sweet and salty at once, with black bottom steaming in the sun and scuttling fiddler crabs and the tangy smell of swamps," described in his essay "In Search" (156). His approach to the world was also influenced by the hunting he did with his grandfather (and later with friends), by his passion for cars, and by sports. He was, by his own account, "a modest athlete," playing football, basketball, and golf in high school. In some ways, he had an extremely typical American boyhood. In 1960, however, when Dave Smith was 17 years old, any illusion of permanence or stability that the family had fostered was shattered when Smith's father died tragically in a car accident that seriously injured his mother as well.

After his father died, Smith finished his remaining year of high school and went directly into the University of Virginia, intending to go out and find his place in the world. Although this would seem to be a giant step toward the center of tradition (and, therefore, cultural identity) for a working-class boy, Smith always felt a little out of place: "Coming from a family with no college experience," he writes in "In Search," "I had no idea what this culture represented. But I loved the green English lawns, the stiff class-engendered formality, the unforgiving honor system" (161). He even joined a college fraternity. "We thought we were gentlemen because we wore coats and ties, drank bourbon prodigiously, were faithful to our ugliest prejudices. Because I wanted so badly to belong," he says, "I embraced the worst and the best" (161). Although he was always slightly on the outskirts of the genteel life at Charlottesville, Smith nevertheless developed his passion for literature there and a deep appreciation for intellectual life.

After graduation, Smith took a job teaching high-school French and English (as well as coaching football, baseball, and basketball) at Poquoson High School in Poquoson, Virginia. Living and working in this obscure fishing town, called Bull Island by its residents (also the title of Smith's first small collection of poems), was crucial to Smith's understanding of self and to the inherent American conflicts he had been living with, and would go on living with, all his life. "Even now I but dimly understand how the opposition of Poquoson and Charlottesville forecast the long, unresolvable struggle of the physical and the intellectual in my poems. It is reflected in choice of speaker, and subject, and each poem or story dramatizes a case for ultimate belonging" (162).

He admired the citizens of Poquoson and learned from them. They had "always been watermen, American renegades with hard hands, bowed backs, salty tongues, a tribal capacity for loyalty, courage, and admiration for the work a man or a woman could do" (162). Smith says he felt more at home there than he has anywhere. These people seemed to have the sense of identity and purpose he'd been looking for: "If you live on what the sea allows you, it is a lonely severe life. But often enough it is heroic, human, firsthand life" (162). While he was living in Poquoson, he met and married his wife, Dee, and it was there also that he began to write.

During the next few years, Smith made his serious commitment to teaching and writing, earning an M.A. at Southern Illinois University, where he edited *Sou'wester* and wrote a master's thesis on the poetry of James Dickey, followed by four years in the United States Air Force (fortunately stationed at Langley Air Force Base, very near the town of Poquoson, Virginia), working days on the base, teaching English at local colleges in the evenings, and writing poems until 3:00 or 4:00 in the morning. Smith's work gradually began to appear in various little magazines and, while still in the Air Force, he edited and published *Back Door,* a little magazine and small press (Back Door Press published ten chapbooks during this period). These crowded years illustrate clearly the sheer will and energy characteristic of Smith's career and evident in the power of his teaching and his writing.

In 1973, on his discharge from the Air Force, Smith went to Ohio University to pursue a Ph.D. He was publishing regularly by this time: *Mean Rufus Throw Down* had come out in 1973 and Ohio University Press published *The Fisherman's Whore* in 1974. Smith interrupted his doctoral studies to take a temporary teaching position at Western Michigan University and another the next year at Cottey College in Missouri. Somehow, he managed to keep writing continually through all the moves and interruptions; and by the time he completed the Ph.D. at Ohio in 1976, Smith had a growing literary reputation. *Cumberland Station* (1976) was due out in the fall from Illinois Press, and he had accepted an appointment at the University of Utah as director of its creative-writing program.

With the publication of *Cumberland Station* Dave Smith began to be recognized as one of the nation's finest young poets. While he was at Utah, he also emerged as a respected critic, writing essays and reviews for many different magazines, and he proved himself to be an extremely devoted and energetic teacher as well. By this time he and Dee had three children (Jeddie, Lael, and Mary Catherine), he was traveling frequently to do readings and conferences, and he had been elected to the board of directors of the Associated Writing Programs. During this period, when he was in his mid-30s and his career was clearly taking off, Smith learned that he would be an insulin-dependent diabetic for the rest of his life. During this period he also wrote most of the essays included in *Local Assays: On Contemporary Poetry* (1985) all of the poems collected in *Goshawk Antelope* (1979), most or all of *Dream Flights* (1981) and *Homage to Edgar Allan Poe* (1981), and much of the work on his novel *Onliness* (1981).

At the urging of the novelist John Gardner, in 1980 Smith left Utah to take a job at SUNY-Binghamton. He left there a year later to teach at the University of Florida; and the next year he moved his family to Richmond, Virginia, where he taught at Virginia Comonwealth University for a number of years, spending most summers teaching workshops at Bennington College's Summer Writers' Conference. In 1990 Smith began teaching at Louisiana State University where he is coeditor of the *Southern Review.*

All this moving around might be seen simply as the transient life of a contemporary academic, but Smith seems to have been literally repeating the circling search of his family in childhood, still trying to find that home place. The circles are ever widening, encompassing whole regions, but he is still looking in from the edge, trying to find the right perspective, never quite centered in the urban intellectual life, and never quite at home anywhere else. Much of Smith's strongest writing grapples with the tension between the urge to belong and the urge to take flight, to find that life "out there somewhere and down the road." Smith says in "In Search of the Real Thing" that his son, now grown, had lived in ten different houses in seven states by the time he was 18. If regular uprooting of family to move around the country represents a searching for something, a restlessness in Smith, then it manifests itself in the work as a kind of mythic journey or flight. There are "dream flights" away from and back to the personal and historical past in the poems, and there is the circling geographical and imagistic pattern that occurs again and again in individual poems as well as in the structure of entire books.

One of the country's most prolific writers, Dave Smith has already written an impressive body of work that includes twelve full-length collections of poems, several chapbooks and broadsides, a novel, a collection of short stories, and a collection of essays. He has edited major studies of Edgar Allan Poe and James Wright, an anthology (with David Bottoms) of contemporary poetry, several literary journals (for various lengths of time), and has served for many years as poetry editor for the University of Utah Press. He has twice been runner-up for the Pulitzer Prize in poetry (for *Goshawk, Antelope,* which was also a finalist for the National Book Critics Circle Award, and for *Dream Flights*), has won a Guggenheim Fellowship (1982), two NEA Fellowships (1976, 1982), an American Academy and Institute of Arts and Letters Award (1979), and a Lyndhurst Fellowship (1987), among other awards. Individual poems and essays are widely anthologized and appear regularly in magazines and literary journals.

MAJOR THEMES

Dave Smith's poetry is often referred to as regional, and it frequently depends on direct engagement with the details of a physical place and a particular landscape. His early work, especially, is almost always tightly focused on the specific landscape and people of coastal Virginia; but his later work moves inland to Cumberland, Maryland, west to the stark geography of Wyoming and Utah, east again to the wooded hills and villages of upstate New York and Pennsylvania, and back to Virginia. The idea and fact of geographical setting itself (more than a single, specific place) is what functions so powerfully in the poems. Smith is also known for his reliance on narrative structure, and one of his main structural paradigms is a kind of mythic journey—a journey of the self—back to, through, and even away from the literal and symbolic geographies that flesh out the poems. In this respect, the work can certainly be seen as "regional," not in the sense that its vision is limited in any way to a specific time and place, but in the more complicated sense that one of its main subjects of exploration is the concept of regionalism itself, with all of its familiar implications and inherent contradictions.

In order to avoid lapsing into mere provincialism, any poem written from an American regional perspective must expand significantly beyond itself to contain its own roots and future. It must contain the longing for permanence and conservation as well as the equally powerful drive to "light out for the territory"— flight, progress, freedom. The honest poet won't be satisfied with the simple either/or argument of tradition versus progress; he or she must take a more complicated stance—a perspective somewhere between stasis and change—accepting the tension itself as a valid (if uncomfortable) circumstance that includes an imagined past *and* an imagined future, exile and citizen. This writing will not face one way or the other, but must attempt the impossible task of looking both ways at once. Smith's writing accepts that challenge and continually employs the specific material of his personal and regional past to explore what he sees as the contemporary American condition of loss, of change, of perpetual homelessness, of restlessness.

The speaker of "Cumberland Station," for instance, goes back to his family's hometown for a funeral and visits the train station where his grandfather and uncle worked when he was a child. "This time there's no fun coming back," he says. The place he ought to connect to—a place of family origin—has become the physical reflection of death: "old stories cracked like wallets," "dirt poured down," "malignant headlamps"—everything reeks of poverty and decay. But rather than respond with nostalgia, as one might expect, Smith's speaker remembers pain and hardship associated with this place, as in "what you said a long time ago welts my face / and won't go away"—or "a child / diced on a cowcatcher," a grandfather who has "escaped the ticket seller's cage," and Cumberland Station is certainly the same emotional place it was in his youth. This man is trying to make a comforting connection with his past, but he cannot do it. He doesn't go see the grandfather addressed in the poem. He leaves again, saying: "This is a place I hope / I never have to go through again" (25–27).

Smith has deliberately confused place and emotional state in those last two lines, pushing us to see that the ideas of "home" and "familiar" may be no more than a longing for something we imagine we once had. In *Local Assays,* he has written about the common religious belief in an ultimate state of bliss where "all is fused, flowing, emphatically joined." This belief, he says, is "based on the implicit recognition that the fundamental fact of *this* existence is our division from one another, our utter isolation." Smith takes this point further: "We bond ourselves sometimes for life and we even speak of how in our love we can become part of another. This is wishful thinking and poor metaphor." According to Smith, humans are "always and essentially apart, alone" (19).

None of this certainty about the impossibility of connection denies the paradoxical existence of the longing for it, or the ability to imagine it. The sometimes desperate need to belong somewhere, with someone, is very clearly dramatized in Smith's poems. He has many poems about the idea of home, of land, of family, of generation; and as many about moving, leaving, traveling, or dying. In Smith's work, this human issue has a peculiarly American slant. He once told another poet that he "would never write about suburban life because it seemed as boring as Eisenhower." But after *The Fisherman's Whore,* he has admitted, "I have hardly done anything else" (168).

In Smith's poems, the problem of postwar suburban life comes to signify the fundamental American problem of cultural definition by negation. Most of us define ourselves by what we believe we have left behind, or what we are *not* a part of. Our ancestors in Europe, or Africa or Asia—or even New England, Virginia, or California—are not us, and we are not them; but we continue to pursue those connections passionately. We would like to recover that family home, that specific plot of land, that sense of continuous identity. But we have lost what our ancestors had, or it was taken from us long ago—if, in fact, it ever existed. We are a nation of outsiders, transients, suburbanites; and Smith is willing to accept that stance, that marginal perspective: a lone figure, both comforted and haunted by his ability to imagine (or remember) a community, a connection with a past, a continuous tradition, a satisfying context for the future of the self.

In "To Isle of Wight," the striking first poem in *Cuba Night* (1990), Smith follows a white man in Virginia on a short, but terrifying journey to see his brother. Much of the poem contains a very literal, detailed description of a road trip; and at the same time it is a dreamlike journey through a historical, social, and emotional landscape. This is what Smith does best. The speaker in the poem is at once native and alien to the region he drives through, as well as to the home he's trying to get to. As he drives, he's very much aware of the features of the landscape, its people, and its history; and as he gets close to his destination, he begins to feel "home." "I'm near / home when I see stoops with setting faces," he says as he speeds past shacks on the sides of the road:

> Even the blacks are my kin at some point
> I don't know. Their stories mine in a speech
> I once understood. Go past their doors.

But he never gets home. This is the speaker's native region. He knows the people, the history, every detail along the road. But the poem ends with a car accident, and the speaker is dying alone in a place that "could be / anywhere on earth. Nothing looks the same." And to the people he'd been feeling such kinship with, he might as well be from "some cosmic zone/of otherness" (17–25). In an interview with Calvin Bedient (1991) Smith talks about the harshness of this poem. He discusses the irony of the speaker's never reaching his brother to whom "he's bound by blood and experience" but somehow estranged from as well; and he explains that "the same thing becomes more true of the community of people around him. . . . I mean, he's bound to them by language and experience and not by blood, and yet he never arrives home, there's ultimately no home for him" (150).

In many of his poems, Smith seems to circle the perimeter of what we usually think of as American life, both geographically and historically. The perspective is often from a traveler's point of view or involves some kind of journey. The central perceiving self, in any case, is almost always somehow displaced. Even in domestic family poems, the speaker is usually a husband or father, awake alone while his family sleeps without him. It is from this outsider perspective that Smith in his poems makes a courageous attempt to discover what, if any, communal connections are possible in a society virtually devoid of any coherent urban or village or even agrarian community in the traditional sense. Smith, like

Melville, has seen ours as an orphaned culture and, also like Melville, has refused to settle for anything less than an inclusive vision of that circumstance.

In an early interview, Smith talked about reading Robert Penn Warren's *Or/
Else.* "One poem says it's this way, the next says it's that way. Sooner or later
you come upon a poem that tries to circumscribe the whole thing and say that
this way and that way are both in the circle and you have to take the circle and
not either one" (Maxson 1982). Smith has clearly shown his preference for the
poem that attempts the whole picture. In the same interview, he states that he
believes the poem to be a "moral act." . . . "One of the things a poem can do
is try to get at the truth." And truth has always been an obsession in Smith's
poems. He refuses to simplify or exclude complications. Instead, he constantly
circles the issue—like one of his hawks, observing and including everything
that adds truth to the perception, and constantly expanding his range of vision.

In many of the poems in *Goshawk, Antelope,* for instance, he has pushed
narrative completely out of shape in an effort to see more accurately than sequence allows. In "The True Sound of the Goshawk," a man is watching a
goshawk in flight, and when it dives

> Through memory I follow its falling
> and become what I was, a child playing in dirt,
> my face up and frozen enough to see a hawkish
> face in that second story window,
> the brightness of flesh. (25)

The face turns out to be the speaker's mother and the hawk has merged with
his memory, past with present. Smith's circle of perception has dilated to include
more than we normally think of as possible, and the poem shows us that the
linear passage of time is no more real, or true, in its ordering of events than the
deconstruction of time by memory or imagination. He has also allowed himself
to risk blurring the focus, juggling too many times and places and even topics.
Unsatisfied with the limited picture of the world we get from the narrowly
focused linear approach and preoccupied with the notions of time and loss and
memory, Smith has pushed language to reconnect time in a new order, allowing
the reader to comprehend subjectively, as if the reader were looking at the world
through the lenses of our specific memories and imaginations.

In the title poem of *Goshawk, Antelope,* as the name suggests, the predator
and prey become one, and the observing speaker's past life merges into the
present natural violence. This poem lays the perfectly domestic image of a gallery of "framed family faces" like a transparency over the terrifyingly primal
attack of the goshawk, which is seen through the windshield of a car. Smith's
layering of events and images creates a spatial rather than sequential story, a
technique especially effective for poems dealing directly with memory and landscape. In this way, he has been able to telescope the narrative, to look through

small precise objects or incidents vividly described, to see the larger complexities of human existence.

In *Cuba Night,* his newest book, in the title poem Smith actually has the speaker looking in a mirror, shaving; and when the speaker glances out a window to the yard, his past losses—innocence, youth, parents, wife—come at him more clearly and honestly than any objective attempt could manage. One of the most devastating details here is "the fly on its back, feet up in dead air / between the storm-doubled panes" (77). The fly is absolutely marginalized, caught between worlds, and the speaker has to look past it—through it—to glance outside.

No matter how close he has gotten, Smith has never written from the center of things, but always from a little distance (not a Modernist "objective irony" kind of distance, but the more subjective distance of a window—a car, a train, an airplane) forcing the reader to question the validity or even the existence of these various repositories of communal identity. Did the past of our forefathers—or even the past of our own memories—really ever exist at all? And even if it did, can we ever truly know it? The wife in "Southern Crescent" says: "*I don't know where home is now. A place / is just a sound where people / stay alive.*" Home, like time, is just another intellectual and linguistic construct, lovely but undependable. Smith leads his readers to the inevitable conclusion that our central cultural characteristic is the contradiction embodied by our ability to conceive of that which we can never attain and the longing to recover that which may never have been ours.

SURVEY OF CRITICISM

Still in his early 50s, Dave Smith has already written a sizable body of work and has received much careful and positive critical attention. There have been two book-length studies of Smith's poetry: Bruce Weigl's *The Giver of Morning* (1982), which includes essays by Weigl, Robert DeMott, Helen Vendler, T. R. Hummer, as well as an interview and a selected bibliography; and Julia West's "No Home But the Heart's Hut: Thematic Development in the Poetry of Dave Smith" (1985), an M.A. thesis at East Tennessee State University. There have also been several excellent comprehensive essays covering four or more collections of poems, many in-depth studies of single volumes, several interviews, and dozens of reviews. His work is also an obvious and integral part of most current discussions of contemporary poetry and is anthologized regularly.

One of the earliest important critical responses to Smith's work was Helen Vendler's essay "Oh I Admire and Sorrow" (1977), which appeared shortly after the publication in 1976 of *Cumberland Station.* Vendler traces Smith's development from his early *Bull Island* poems through *Cumberland Station,* describing him as a "poet of the utmost ambition and the utmost care." She praises his descriptive power and his command of language and structure. She admires "his characteristic speed-up of mass," the "wonderfully constructed momentum'' of his poems, and his attention to sound, particularly the use of an Anglo-Saxon four-beat line.

But it is the sheer scope and ambition of Smith's work that Vendler finds most remarkable. She points out Smith's variety of approaches and subjects from the early geographic and social portraits of Virginia coastal towns, to the inclusion of more personal family and domestic poems in *The Fisherman's Whore* (1974), to a deepening and broadening of both strains in the best poems of *Cumberland Station*. Smith's insistence on inclusion—on including the whole experience of lives—is what attracts Vendler most to the poems.

The most thorough look at Smith's early work is Robert DeMott's extensive essay ''A Poem is a Kind of Country: Sacrament and Geography in Dave Smith's Poetry,'' first published in 1980 and covering all five collections of poems through *Goshawk, Antelope* (1979). His assessment is as positive as Vendler's and places Smith even more squarely in the American Romantic tradition. DeMott sees Smith's poetry as both experiential and visionary, characterized by passionate but rigorously shaped language in the Emersonian tradition of ''artful thunder.'' ''At its most charged,'' DeMott says, ''Smith's poetry embodies the rythmical cadence of testimony, the full and imaginative awareness of human vulnerability witnessed and transfigured'' (9).

DeMott points out Smith's preference for narrative structure and his uses of the architectural dimensions of story, calling attention to Smith's ''passionate attraction to the myriad possiblities of ways poems can be written,'' and ''the large thematic formal, and conceptual demands'' Smith makes of himself as a poet. DeMott's is a comprehensive and responsible study, giving credit to influences (Hopkins, Hardy, Dickey, Warren, Wright, Lowell, Faulkner, Anglo-Saxon poetry, and the Bible), and carefully examining each book as the work evolves toward what DeMott sees as the ''consequential development of Smith's consolidation of persona and landscape'' in *Goshawk, Antelope* (16).

Cumberland Station received a fair number of reviews and notices—Smith's poems were appearing regularly by that time in *The New Yorker* and other very visible magazines—and was highly praised; but it wasn't until *Goshawk, Antelope* that Smith's work attracted wide critical attention. This book, with its dramatic departure from the Southern regional landscape and life that Smith's readers had come to expect, and its shocking, almost surreal imagery, caused some real excitement. Stephen Yenser (1982) correctly predicted that *Goshawk, Antelope* would ''at first surprise and perplex'' admirers of Smith's previous work. He writes that even though Smith had sometimes shown a ''flamboyant, bardic, eloquent side,'' and one could find poems in *Cumberland Station* that were ''crowded with adjectives, powered by a seemingly self-generating consonantal music, their heavily enjambed lines [giving] the illusion of a headlong rush of thought,'' Smith had been writing for the most part ''a more straightforward, earthy poetry, colorful and energetic, but cinched up and reined in'' (32).

Yenser sees this as a breakthrough book, where Smith, the ''master of the plain style" moves toward a poem that begins to rely on a wilder, dream-like imagery—an intense subjectivity. There is a blurring in this book of rational and irrational methods of perception. Clear shifts in time are abandoned for a kind of dream-time, Yenser observes; and Smith is no longer letting the things of the world "translate feelings for him," but here he "lets his feelings translate the things" (33). The "arrogance of dream" imposes itself onto reality, and pushes the world into its own shape.

This was clearly Smith's most ambitious book so far, and it was met with excitement and interest even when the critical responses weren't completely positive. Although Peter Stitt (1980) calls Smith a "pure natural poet" who, with respect to "pure verbal energy, has to be among the most talented poets we have" (207), he objects to the obscurity he finds in the poems of *Goshawk, Antelope*. He worries that this book "embodies a lack of correlation between style and content, resulting in a strange hybrid, Western life and landscape rendered in a lush Southern style" (208). Smith, according to Stitt, is a "poet in the midst of change;" and he makes it clear that he'd rather see Smith continue to "render the texture of his native area into verse" (209). Vendler, on the other hand, responded to *Goshawk, Antelope* with a glowing review in the *New Yorker* (1980), in which she says that Smith has "emerged as a distinguished allegorist of human experience." She describes the writing as "torrential, impatient, exasperated," and respects Smith's refusal to allow language to subdue or soften reality. She addresses the obscurity that Stitt and others object to by suggesting that its origins are at least partially in Smith's "ethical strictness"—his refusal to simplify (and so falsify) the complexity of the human experience he has attempted to understand (419). Gary Waller (1983) went even further, praising this new complexity of language for its post-Modern implications. The poems in *Goshawk, Antelope,* he says, "are caught between an eloquent confidence and an anxiety about language that at once dishevels and enriches the poetry and points beyond stylistic conflict to interesting ideological contradictions" (127).

With the publication of *Dream Flights,* a more comfortable but less complex book, followed quickly by *Homage to Edgar Allan Poe* (both appeared in 1981), critics had plenty to work with and began to make comprehensive assessments about the direction, merit, and literary significance of this poet's work. Stephen Sandy, in *Poetry,* wrote that Smith's gift is a "largeness of conception" (294); echoing several earlier critics, Sandy compares Smith to Whitman in language, in energy, and in his "poetics of total encirclement" (295). In a review of *Dream Flights* (1983), Charles Molesworth calls Smith one of several contemporary poets (including Galway Kinnell and others) returning to a poetry that "offers music and pleasure along with a full awareness of painful, modern reality." He admires Smith's ability to combine "a full, lush music" with an "honest, relentless search for truth" (157). On the other hand, Peter Stitt, also writing about *Dream Flights,* (1982) objects to the way Smith characteristically "weaves concrete and abstract elements together in such a way that they become less and less distinct, less and less clear; the reader ends up tangled in a dense, perhaps impenetrable web'' (681).

The risk that complexity will collapse into obscurity and that the frustration of the speaker will become too frustrating for the reader has provided a major point of discussion for the critics of these middle books. And at the same time, Smith's persistent thematic examination of family relationships—especially of fathers and sons—has begun to be seen as an ongoing poetic discussion; and the subjects of personal family and regional history have started to be seen as an outwardly expanding circle, an examination of the larger domestic relationships of region and nation. Several writers have pointed out the continuity between the books, how they together seem to make a psychological and geographical journey of importance.

The appearance of Smith's novel *Onliness* (1981) and *In the House of the Judge* (1983), a new book of poems, provoked several comprehensive critical studies. Thomas Swiss (1983) and Paul Christensen (1984) each published lengthy discussions of the work in the four books from *Dream Flights* to *In the House of the Judge*. Christensen focuses on the theme of youth and age in Smith's poems and makes an interesting argument for the presence of the archetypal *puer eternus* in what he calls ''the poetry of reminiscence'' in American literature. With its core in Southern fiction and modern poetry, Christensen says that this archetype pervades Smith's immediate tradition (Dickey, Roethke, Wright); and Christensen gives a convincing psychological/mythological reading of Smith's newest work, in which the poet attempts to ''merge the voice of the elder with his other self—as if the poem at work were a seance between the severed halves of the poet.'' Christensen describes Smith's poems as ''coaxing the soul to stretch from one end to the other, and in those heightened moments of perfect merger, if there are such moments, the western dream of self-unity climaxes in lyric revelation'' (159).

Swiss's essay is a more methodical study, looking carefully at each collection and providing particularly insightful examinations of *Homage to Edgar Allan Poe* and *In the House of the Judge*. He points out the more noticeable presence of the feminine in this newer work. A poet well known for his focus on men, fathers, fishing, and hunting, Smith had now widened the domestic scene to include more poems about parenting, daughters, mothers, wives. *In the House of the Judge,* a book that explores Smith's own metaphor of home, seemed somehow to get lost in the critical shuffle of all the books that came so closely before it. Sidney Burris, however, in an excellent article (1984), declares that *In the House of the Judge* is a pivotal book in Smith's career and that the title poem redefines and provides clarification for his previous work. It embraces, he says, all of Smith's predominant themes: love, history, family, loss, home, social connection. For Smith, Burris explains, ''memory is always a process, a busy shuttle service where the events of the poet's past impinge on the present moment, and are revived, creating the historical and emotional continuity that is proclaimed lost by most generations of poets'' (102). Burris predicts that we will return to this poem "on those pale, ordinary days when we find ourselves wanting to read the most accomplished verse of the period" (105).

Publisher's Weekly declared that the publication of *The Roundhouse Voices: Selected and New Poems* in 1985 established Smith "as a very young eminence." But the reception of this relatively slim volume of selected poems met with more critical resistance than previous books, perhaps at least partly because of the growing perception that Smith had simply published too much too soon. "Why is it necessary," asks Peter Stitt in his third essay on Smith's poetry (1985) "to publish so much, spinning out eleven major volumes (including poetry, fiction, and criticism) in just eleven years?" (859). But Stitt continues to be attracted to Smith's "remarkable facility with words" and he sees much to admire in this volume. He thinks that the three books published closest together (between 1979 and 1981) are the weakest, and he most admires *The Fisherman's Whore, Cumberland Station,* and *In the House of the Judge,* which he says are much tighter and more consistent in quality than the others.

Anthony Libby wrote a positive (with a few quibbles) review (1986) in which he chose *Dream Flights* as his favorite collection. *The Roundhouse Voices* seemed to provoke this pick-your-favorite reaction among many of the critics who had been following Smith's work. Libby generally liked the book and observed that although Smith is usually described as a narrative poet, "his most characteristic successes meditate on action more than they describe it." A domestic incident or a natural scene is evoked, according to Libby, "only to be expanded to allegorical proportions, or an event is turned through different perspectives, the meditation often circling one moment in time" (17).

Calvin Bedient was more wholeheartedly excited about this book. He begins his essay (1986), a review of several new books of poetry, with a call for a big Whitman-like, communal poetry. Smith's work, he believes, is what he had been looking for: that rare American poetry that "repeatedly swells humane involvement to the great plural." He notices in Smith's poems "the kind of empathy that flourishes in regional memory" (657), and he particularly points out Smith's anger against time: "His ambivalence toward the past is staggering, a whirlpool that has the reader both coming and going, torn, exposed, and reluctant" (663). There is one extremely negative review by Bruce Bawer (1985) that is worth mentioning only because it so obviously uses the occasion to strike out against creative-writing programs in universities.

The biggest serious objection to this book is its very selectiveness. Phoebe Pettingell (1986) has complained that Smith's individual collections have each shown a new and interesting direction, but those distinctions have been unfortunately blurred in this volume because of the poems chosen for exclusion and by the rewriting of some of those included. She say that this book has a "homogenized" feel to it, that it should have been a third longer and should have provided a more representative grouping of Smith's work. Helen Vendler seems to agree. In a recent *New Yorker* (1990) review of Smith's latest book *Cuba Night* (1990), she mentions *The Roundhouse Voices* as "a book too austerely

thinned to give an adequate overview of his twenty years of poetic production'' (113).

With the publication of *Cuba Night*, it looks as though Smith's career has taken another large stride. The initial response has been extremely positive. Vendler (1990) calls *Cuba Night* ''both representative and rebellious'' in relation to Smith's previous work. She points to poems in which Smith ''bursts out in the midst of poems with questions that polite company has long since disallowed.'' The familiar Smith themes are still present, but his vision has deepened and darkened: the hope of ''historical intelligibility or philosophical consolation is becoming ever more precarious.'' These new poems, she says, have the ''grimness and tenacity of someone shaking life by the throat and commanding it to speak'' (113–16). Sidney Burris (1990) also sees this as an exciting and very powerful book: ''Here is a poetry of personal force, regional intuition, and without indulging the Whitmanesque excesses, a poetry of national importance.'' ''*Cuba Night*,'' he writes, ''is easily Smith's most ambitions collection of verse, and because its ambitions are roundly fulfilled, it is his most distinguished collection'' (465).

BIBLIOGRAPHY

Works by Dave Smith

Poetry

Bull Island. Poquoson, Va.: Back Door Press, 1970.
Mean Rufus Throw Down. Fredonia, N.Y.: Basilisk Press, 1973.
The Fisherman's Whore. Athens: Ohio University Press, 1974. Reprint. Pittsburgh: Carnegie-Mellon University Press, 1989.
Drunks. Edwardsville, Ill.: *Sou'wester,* 1975.
Cumberland Station. Urbana: University of Illinois Press, 1976.
In Dark, Sudden with Light. Athens, Ohio: Croissant, 1976.
Goshawk, Antelope. Urbana: University of Illinois Press, 1979.
Apparitions. Northridge, Calif.: Lord John, 1981.
Blue Spruce. Syracuse, N.Y.: Tamarack Editions, 1981.
Dream Flights. Urbana: University of Illinois Press, 1981.
Homage to Edgar Allan Poe. Baton Rouge: Louisiana State University Press, 1981.
Gray Soldiers. Winston-Salem, N.C.: Wright, 1983.
In the House of the Judge. New York: Harper, 1983.
The Roundhouse Voices: Selected and New Poems. New York: Harper, 1985.
Cuba Night. New York: Morrow/Quill, 1990.
Selected Poems. London: Bloodaxe Books, 1990.

Fiction

Onliness. Baton Rouge: Louisiana State University Press, 1981.
Southern Delights: Poems and Stories. Athens, Ohio: Croissant, 1984.

Nonfiction

"The Strength of James Dickey." *Poetry* 136 (March 1981): 349–58.
Local Assays: On Contemporary American Poetry. Urbana: University of Illinois Press,
    1985.
"Robert Penn Warren: The Use of a Word Like Honor." *Yale Review* 74 (Summer 1985):
    574–80.
"Introduction: On Regionalism." *New Virginia Review* 4 (Fall 1986): 11–14.
"A Secret You Can't Break Free." *Washington Post Magazine* (July 6, 1986): 4–12.
    Reprinted in *A World Unsuspected,* edited by Alex Harris, Duke University Press,
    1987.
"In Search of the Real Thing." In *Contemporary Autobiography,* edited by Mark Zad-
    rozny, 155–69. Gale Research, 1988.
"Hunting Men." *Sewanee Review* 97 (Fall 1989): 543–55.

Works Edited by Dave Smith

The Pure Clear Word: Essays on the Poetry of James Wright. Urbana: University of
    Illinois Press, 1982.
The Morrow Anthology of Younger American Poets. edited with David Bottoms. New
    York: Quill, 1985.
New Virginia Anthology Four. Richmond, Va.: *New Virginia Review,* 1986.
New Virginia Anthology Eight. Richmond, Va.: *New Virginia Review,* 1990.
The Essential Poe. New York: Ecco, 1991.

Interviews with Dave Smith

Balakian, Peter. "Heroes of the Spirit: An Interview with Smith." *Graham House Review*
    6 (Spring 1982). Reprinted in *Local Assays,* by Dave Smith, 233–52. Urbana:
    University of Illinois Press, 1985.
Bedient, Calvin. Interview with Dave Smith on *Cuba Night. New England Review* 14
    (Fall 1991): 149–61.
Maxson, H. A. "The Poem as a Moral Act: An Interview With Smith." In *The Giver
    of Morning: On the Poetry of Dave Smith,* edited by Bruce Weigl, 52–60. Bir-
    mingham, Ala.: Thunder City, 1982.

Studies of Dave Smith

Bawer, Bruce. "Dave Smith's 'Creative Writing.' " *New Criterion* 4 (December 1985):
    27–33.
Bedient, Calvin. "New Confessions." *Sewanee Review* 88 (Summer 1980): 474–88.
———. "Burning Alone." *Sewanee Review* 94 (Fall 1986): 657–68.
Bold, A. Review of *Onliness. Times Literary Supplement* (November 27, 1981).
Brown, Laurie. Review of *Southern Delights. Library Journal* 109 (March 15, 1984):
    598
Burris, Sidney. "Where I Live, It Rounds, Whistles, and Holds Me." *Prairie Schooner*
    58 (Summer 1984): 100–104.

————. "Four American Poets." Review of *Cuba Night. Southern Review* 25 (Spring 1990): 456–65.

Christensen, Paul. "Malignant Innocence." *Parnassus* 12 (Fall–Winter 1984): 154–82.

DeMott, Robert. "A Poem Is a Kind of Country: Sacrament and Geography in Dave Smith's Poetry." In *The Giver of Morning: On the Poetry of Dave Smith,* edited by Bruce Weigl, 7–17. Birmingham, Ala.: Thunder City, 1982. Originally published in the *Dictionary of Literary Biographies.* Detroit: Gale Research, 1980.

Flint, R. W. "Debut and Continuity." Review of *In the House of the Judge. New York Times Book Review* (February 13, 1983): 15–38.

Gardner, John. "On Dave Smith." *Three Rivers Poetry Journal* 10 (1977): 6–9.

Grosholz, Emily. "Poetry Chronicle." *Hudson Review* 33 (Summer 1980): 293–308.

————. "Master-Workers and Others." *Hudson Review* 36 (Autumn 1983): 582–92.

Haislip, John. "Flood, Salt Debris, Relief: The Poetry of Dave Smith." *Sou'wester,* n. s., 2 (Spring–Summer 1974): 56–64.

Holden, Jonathan. Review of *Local Assays. Choice* (January 1986): 745.

Hummer, T. R. "Dave Smith's *Homage to Edgar Allan Poe:* 'Pushed' Time and the Obsession of Memory." In *The Giver of Morning: On the Poetry of Dave Smith,* edited by Bruce Weigl, 75–87. Birmingham, Ala.: Thunder City, 1982.

————. "The Heroics of Clarity." *Kenyon Review,* n.s. 8 (Spring 1986): 113–22.

Jarman, Mark. "Singers and Storytellers." *Hudson Review* 39 (Summer 1986): 334–47.

Johnson, Dillon. "Looking Through Three Poets." *Shenandoah* 26 (1975): 96–101.

Jones, Roger. "Wreckage, Redemption." *Southern Poetry Review* (Spring 1985): 73–76.

Kent, Robert. "Between Wild Dreams and Tame Realities, and Elsewhere." *Parnassus* (Fall–Winter 1975): 195–205.

Libby, Anthony. Review of *Roundhouse Voices. New York Times Book Review* (January 12, 1986): 17.

McFee, Michael. "Into the Big Leagues." *Parnassus* (Fall–Winter 1980): 63–110.

Mesic, Penelope. Review of *In the House of the Judge. Poetry* 143 (February 1984): 304–5.

Molesworth, Charles. "An Almost Unshakable Hold." Review of *Dream Flights. Commonweal* 110 (March 11, 1983): 157–59.

————. "Poetic Relations." Review of *Roundhouse Voices. Nation* 241 (October 5, 1985): 320–22.

Parini, Jay. "A Volume of Poetry to Treasure." *Boston Globe* 10 (November 3, 1985): B32.

Pettingell, Phoebe. "On Poetry: Fathers and Children." *New Leader* 64 (December 14, 1981): 16–17.

————. "Comment: Dave Smith's Voice." *Poetry* 147 (March 1986): 346–50.

Phillips, Robert. "Poetry Chronicle: Some Versions of the Pastoral." *Hudson Review* 34 (August 1981): 420–34.

Plumly, Stanley. "Chapter and Verse." *American Poetry Review* 7 (January–February 1978): 15–19.

Sandy, Stephen. "Experienced Bards." *Poetry* 140 (August 1982): 293–301.

Stitt, Peter. "The Sincere, The Mythic, The Playful: Forms of Voice in Current Poetry." *Georgia Review* 34 (Spring 1980): 202–12.

————. "Poems in Open Forms." *Georgia Review* 36 (Fall 1982): 675–85.

————. "Contemporary American Poems: Exclusive and Inclusive." *Georgia Review* 39 (Winter 1985): 849–63.

Swiss, Thomas. " 'Unfold the Fullness': Dave Smith's Poetry and Fiction." *Sewanee Review* (Summer 1983):483–90.

Vendler, Helen. "Oh, I Admire and Sorrow." *Parnassus* (Spring–Summer 1977). Reprinted in *Part of Nature, Part of Us: Modern American Poets,* 289–302. Cambridge: Harvard University Press, 1980.

———. "The Mind's Assertive Flow." Review of *Goshawk, Antelope. New Yorker* 56 (June 30, 1980): 96–. Reprinted in *The Music of What Happens: Poems, Poets, Critics,* 413–23. Cambridge: Harvard University Press, 1988.

———. "Looking for Poetry in America." Review of *Local Assays. New York Review of Books* 32 (November 7, 1985): 53–60.

———. "Southern Weather." Review of *Cuba Night. New Yorker* 66 (April 2, 1990): 113–16.

Waller, Gary. "I and Ideology: Demystifying the Self of Contemporary Poetry." *Denver Quarterly* 18 (Autumn 1983): 123–38.

Weigl, Bruce. "The Deep Well of Celebration: Dave Smith's *Goshawk, Antelope.*" In *The Giver of Morning: On the Poetry of Dave Smith,* edited by Bruce Weigl, 69–74. Birmingham, Ala.: Thunder City, 1982.

Weigl, Bruce, ed. *The Giver of Morning: On the Poetry of Dave Smith.* Birmingham, Ala.: Thunder City, 1982.

West, Julia C. "No Home But the Heart's Hut: Thematic Development in the Poetry of Dave Smith." Master's thesis, East Tennessee State University, 1985.

Williamson, Alon. "Three Poets: The Rhythm of Rhetoric." *Washington Post Book World* (October 4, 1981): 4.

Yenser, Stephen. "Sea Changes: On Dave Smith." *American Poetry Review* 11 (January–February 1982): 32–35.

Young, Vernon. Review of *The Fisherman's Whore. Hudson Review* 27 (Winter 1974–75): 6, 11–14.

LINDA WELDEN

R. T. Smith
(1947–   )

Auburn University Alumni Writer-in-Residence R. T. Smith is a college professor, a journal editor, a fiction and criticism writer, and a polished and seasoned performer; but he is primarily a poet. With ardent humanity and honesty, his poetry explores the mysterious paths of the spirit. Critics have hailed him as a major contemporary poet rising out of the South.

BIOGRAPHY

R. T. Smith teaches at Auburn University, Alabama, but prefers to live in Opelika, a mill village between the university and the Chattahoochee River that provides the border between Alabama and Georgia. Smith has roots deep in Georgia clay. His parents were native to Griffin in Spalding County, and much of his upbringing took place there, his time divided between both sets of grandparents. His father, Roland McCall Smith, was a World War II veteran who married his high-school sweetheart, Mary Helen Thaxton. Following the war the couple settled in Washington, D.C., where Roland pursued his boyhood dream of working as a special agent for the Federal Bureau of Investigation. His son was born in the nation's capital on April 13, 1947, on the birthday of fellow writers Seamus Heaney, Eudora Welty, and Samuel Beckett. Because Rodney Theodore Smith was born in the District of Columbia, his extended family labeled him a Yankee and made him distrust his pedigree. He developed a lasting enthusiasm for the study of history in his attempt to learn all that he could about the South in order to ''out-Southern the Southerners'' (the words of R. T. Smith quoted in this essay are taken from an unpublished interview with the poet in Opelika, Alabama, on June 24, 1992).

A writer schooled in the new critical tradition, Smith has cautioned against biographical analysis of his work. Values that he developed in childhood, however, are intrinsic to his poetry. He spent summers and other extended vacations in Georgia until age 11. Rod recalls having to employ intelligence and story-telling as a substitute for physical superiority over the older country boys who were his playmates. "There's a kind of rose quartz that could be found under the clay in my grandmother's back yard," Smith recalls. "I had these guys convinced they were rubies and I had them out there with picks and shovels digging." On these Georgia visits he was introduced to the rituals of rural life. The fascination with ritual carried over into his spiritual life, leading him to choose Catholicism over the Baptist and Methodist versions of Protestantism that his grandparents practiced. Smith claims to have been a somewhat mystical child who "talked to God a lot."

His maternal grandfather, John Thaxton, was a carpenter who built their house along with numerous other buildings on East McIntosh Road. Like other indus-trious rural Georgians of the time, the Thaxtons raised corn and hogs, gardened, and lived off the land. John Thaxton, along with his wife, also worked at the Dundee Towel Mill until his death from cancer in 1953. Smith treasures not only the legacy of well-honed pocketknives that his grandfather used in carpen-try but also the memories of the warm affection that both grandparents bestowed on their only grandchild. Lizzie Thaxton, who had married at 15, continued to work at the mill as a seamer after her husband's death. The visiting child spent weekends with her and weekdays with the Smiths, hitching rides across town with "the Jewel Tea man," a traveling salesman who sold tea and spices out of his brown truck.

Grandmother Margie House Smith was a stern disciplinarian who tried ex-treme measures to harness the spirit of her grandson, whose memories of switch-ings and of being locked in the cellar mingle with recollections of pecan orchards, a branch, and woods for a young boy to run freely. John James Wil-liam Smith was an insurance salesman with an office over the Rexall drugstore. He was an officer in the Masons, which in Spalding County at the time seems to have had connections with the Klan. Rod has spoken wryly of "a great line I was never able to use: 'My father played the fiddle in the Ku Klux Klan dance band.'" If the story is factual, it did not prevent Roland from becoming an F.B.I. agent.

In 1953 Roland Smith's family, now with the addition of a daughter, Sharon, moved to Charlotte, North Carolina. Rod remembers being "a good, dutiful student who mostly made B's" in Ashley Road Elementary School, Berry Hill School, and Wilson Junior High, until his sixth-grade teacher, Mrs. Isley, al-lowed him to develop his interest in history by reading whatever he desired. He chose the *Iliad,* the *Odyssey,* and the *Aeneid,* and he credits Homer as the first and most influential poet in his life.

Adults in his family were readers. J. J. W. Smith had a home library stocked with self-improvement and condensed books; Lizzie Thaxton read the Bible "over and over," while Rod's parents had tastes for detective stories, westerns, and romance novels. Rod developed a curiosity about books and taught himself to read. He remembers reading the newspaper aloud for company as a pre-schooler. Reading, he says, "was the most natural thing in the world." His favorite boyhood book was Douglas Southall Freeman's four-volume *R. E. Lee: A Biography*. Rod's grandparents subscribed to the periodical *Grit,* and he would embellish versions of its stories for his neighborhood friends. He also remembers standing on metal yard chairs and making up stories for the pictures on the drive-in movie screen across the road from his grandparents' house.

Although poems such as "Sally Soapsud" imply a heritage of family stories, his tales are predominantly R. T. Smith's own creations. His father stimulated his interest in storytelling. Roland became an arson investigator for the National Board of Fire Underwriters, traveling the western half of North Carolina during the week. On weekends he would tell his son detailed, factual accounts of his work. Although his father did not have "a whole lot of tolerance for exaggeration as a legitimate, radiating and illuminating facet of storytelling," Rod says, "I was interested." Roland's storytelling style was the inverse of his son's, who freely admits: "The meadow of my imagination has always been something that I wouldn't want to have to pay property taxes on."

Following graduation from Charlotte's Harding High School, where he had played football, wrestled, run track, and belonged to the chess club, he entered Georgia Tech but soon transferred to the University of North Carolina, first at Charlotte and then at Chapel Hill. Floundering without real focus, and knowing that he would soon be drafted, he quit college and joined the U. S. Marine Corps, serving in Vietnam until field surgery and an ensuing infection led to his early release from military duty. He returned to the University of North Carolina at Charlotte; he credits an introductory philosophy class under professor Bob Byerly with awakening his hitherto dormant intellect. Through a course in modern British fiction with Dr. Seth Ellis, he developed a continuing interest in the writing of James Joyce. Smith graduated with a B. A. in Philosophy in 1969, began a brief marriage, and started his teaching career as a language arts teacher, basketball and football coach in a junior high school at Sherrills Ford, North Carolina. To receive his teaching certificate, he returned to college in the summer, working at night as a security guard. For the next 2 years he taught college-preparatory English at East Mecklenburg High School in Charlotte. In 1973, determined to become a writer, he entered the graduate program in English at Appalachian State University in Boone, North Carolina. A natural feeling of belonging in the mountains as well as a determination to avoid a university with a large sports program guided his choice of a graduate school.

In 1974 he attended a summer-long writing workshop in Santa Fe, New Mexico. His poetry teacher, Bill Taylor, suggested the necessity of a poet's reading a hundred poems for every one he writes, a notion that Smith finds "a modest estimate." During that summer, Rod read all the books on modern poetry in the Santa Fe library. He credits Taylor with guiding him to a method of revision, "tightening and testing and working for internal consistency."

The Appalachian graduate program did not include a creative-writing course;

but Smith, with the assistance of advisor and mentor John Trimpey, designed his own degree, concentrating on poetry. In the absence of formal instruction, Smith and fellow graduate writers Donald Secreast, Vic Moose, and Jo Ann Eskridge served as poetry teachers for one another. Smith declared: "I loved my last couple of years in college and graduate school so much that still after sixteen years at Auburn I cannot understand the mind of a person who is here for some reason other than to drain the well." This thirst led to the founding of the *Cold Mountain Review,* Smith's brainchild and Appalachian State's respected literary magazine. Established writers, including founding editor Smith, continue to submit work to the publication, now nearing its twentieth anniversary. As a graduate student, R. T. Smith published his first collection of poems, *Waking under Snow,* in 1975; he also received poetry prizes from noted literary magazines, including *Miscellany, Sanskrit,* and *Crucible.* Upon graduation in 1975 with an M.A. in English, Smith accepted his teaching position in the English Department at Auburn University. He was appointed Alumni Writer-in-Residence in 1983 upon the retirement of Madison Jones.

R. T. Smith has continued to receive awards for poetry at both the regional and national levels. These awards include: the first annual Tamarack Award in 1979 for "Grandfather's Razor"; the 1980 Sam Ragan Prize for "In the Hawk's Eye"; the 1981 John Masefield Award for Narrative Poetry from the Poetry Society of America for "Suppose a Man"; the 1986 Eugene W. Field Poetry Prize, judged by William Stafford, for "Harpwing"; and the 1989 Emily Dickinson Award from the Poetry Society of America for "Susan Gilbert Dickinson." *From the High Dive* was the Water Mark Poets Book Award winner for 1982. *The Hollow Log Lounge* won the 1985 Texas Review Poetry Award. In 1986 A. R. Ammons chose the collection *Birch-Light* as winner of the Brockman Award from the North Carolina Poetry Society. In 1988 the Alabama Arts Association awarded Smith the Alabama Governor's Award for Achievement by an Artist. Smith's poems are frequently selected for inclusion in the *Anthology of Magazine Verse and Yearbook of American Poetry* as well as in *Annual Survey of American Poetry.*

Both the Alabama and North Carolina Arts Councils have awarded Smith grants; and artist colonies including Wurlitzer, Ossabaw, and Millay have given him fellowships. In 1991 he received a Fellowship in Literature from the National Endowment for the Arts, allowing him to spend several months in Galway, Ireland, where he expanded his knowledge of and interest in that country's art and culture. Drawn by an enthusiasm for Irish music, and "very much under the spell of Seamus Heaney," he had made his first pilgrimage to Ireland in 1988. Acquaintances and observations made during that trip and subsequent others have widened the scope of his poetry. His poems have been published in *Irish Times, Poetry Ireland Review, Connaught Tribune's Writing in the West,* and other periodicals. A professional writer with deep interest in the community of artists and in the distribution and recognition of their work, Smith has held many editorial positions, including a contributing editor of *International Poetry*

Review, associate editor of *Southern Humanities Review,* and poetry editor of *National Forum.*

The author of twelve books of poetry to date, R. T. Smith has published hundreds of poems along with short stories and criticism in both the United States and Europe. A talented performer, he is in frequent demand for poetry readings. Rehearsals for his performances often lead to revisions of his poetry. He follows his own advice to "write it, then say it out loud to your own best audience, which is your own better self." Smith writes continually, deserving and achieving recognition as a sensitive and gifted artist among the best of his generation.

MAJOR THEMES

R. T. Smith is a Southerner who has set many poems in the South, but anyone who would categorize Smith's art in the "good ol' boy school" of Southern poetry is misreading. His poems transcend place and time, sharing a poetic kinship with the multistratified creations of Robert Frost and Emily Dickinson, whom Smith holds to be the greatest American poets. His personae bring the universe to themselves through insight and observation and are at home wherever they reside. Amherst, New Bedford, Greece, the American West, Ireland, Ossabaw Island, the Blue Ridge Mountains and an implied Alabama residence provide the settings in a representative volume, *The Cardinal Heart* (1991). Smith's poetry is thematically, as well as geographically, disparate. He observed: "There's a whole community inside of me, and I don't organize that community in any coherent governance." As a result, his poems tend to be self-contained works of art rather than segments of a whole. Smith's books are either chapbooks or collections of poems that were written over a span of time to cohere in retrospect. Constantly maturing as an artist, Smith revises and transforms even his published work. Consequently, some poems appear in multiple versions throughout his collections.

Although he has employed a multiplicity of themes, in all of his work the poet poses philosophical questions of existence but affirms a sacred life force. Through his poems, Smith explores, discovers, and expresses possibilities for abundant living. Smith's personae demonstrate the full life through profound engagements: in ritual and worship, in observation and prophesy, in witness and testimony. The personified fish in "Self as Trout" (*The Cardinal Heart,* 1991) establishes intent for poet and persona: "I will be a story, a prayer / for the Angel of Forgetting . . . Who will climb me / in the leached instant of transformation / to the body of light?" (39). In the award-winning narrative "Suppose a Man" included in *From the High Dive* (1983), the speaker challenges the reader through a credo of life and art:

> Will you know that to live by other than bread
> you must surpass your own breath, let the barb of belief snag you

and the line cut across your life,
know that just receiving the story cannot purify
unless you share the solitude
and feel the pain ignite in your step
like the moon seen burning in the lake
by one man wildly wounded and fighting to survive?
And will you testify? (12)

In original and unorthodox ways, Smith's poetry is deeply religious, investigating the nature of truth. He considers poetry "a lie that tells the truth." The poet explains through recalling: "A long time ago I figured out in arguments about the literalness of the Bible that it's a much more powerful document if it is metaphorical than if it is literal." Metaphorical power is abundant in his poetry. In "Curing Shed" found in *Rural Route* (1981), for example, the persona stands in an abandoned tobacco shed, the central symbol of the poem, and meditates on the past as an intermingling of fact and fiction. The persona confesses, "I remember what I can't invent, what endures" (88). The speaker embraces his past as he turns from it, asking: "Yet who could still be ill at ease here where . . . darkness lacquers the heart to preserve. . . what lies we told that grew to be the truth?" (88).

Smith's poems celebrate human learning and the life of the mind. At the same time, they recognize the power and mystery of natural aptitude and understanding. The tensive pulls between intellect and instinct frequently provide vitality for his lyric personae. Smith evokes the intellectual, creative life through references to visual artists, writers, musicians, and philosophers; he characterizes the instinctive life in narrative poems in which the speakers are unlearned seers. The life of the richly engaged spirit, Smith seems to say, is sustained and nourished and fueled from the paired perspectives of fully developed intellect and instinctive knowing. In "Birch-Light, Abandoning Wittgenstein" published in *Birch-Light* (1986), the cultured, articulate speaker, aware of his "thirst for clarity," climbs a hill as he ruminates on the nature of symbolism. He comes upon two animals he readily classifies as "spike bucks." Unaware of the persona and of his name for them, the bucks stand "oblivious to 'wanting,' though probably watching / the birch-light with satisfaction / unavailable in the meditative act." Caught between human capability and the mystery of nature, the speaker is left in silence, "somehow revealed and truly dismayed" (41).

The speaker in the poem "The Cardinal Heart" (*Cardinal Heart* 1991) personifies the same unquenchable thirst for understanding. He establishes his own artistic and religious sensitivity when the color of a dead cardinal reminds him of "the pantaloons on one of Goya's infant princes" as well as of "the Beatitudes in print" (2). In an elemental ritual of curiosity, the speaker dissects and extracts the heart of the fallen bird to enrich the soil of his garden. Symbolic and mythic, the heart remains a mystery beyond knowledge and explanation and is "a wet tearose / more miracle than / flight, art / history / or religion" (3).

The symbol reappears in "Cardinal Directions" (*Cardinal Heart* 1991), a title exemplary of the word games Smith's poems often provide through meticulous language choices. In this poem Smith employs one of his favored structural devices; a pair of stanzas. In the first stanza the poet establishes the temporal, ravenous nature of the bird—a mirror for the central figure in the second stanza, who concludes: "The one bird / heavy in my chest, the cardinal / heart, still has ambitions to forage, sing the litany beyond language, and fly" (8). In all of his work Smith explores the vast and isolated landscape of the human heart, juxtaposing art and nature to embody the extremes of intellectual literacy and animal curiosity.

Smith has admiration and affection for people and things natural and close to the earth. Speakers in his dramatic poems as well as in his lyric work are often solitary souls deep in thought and activity within some isolated, wild environment that the speaker has momentarily civilized. Smith's poetry is literally and figuratively elemental, referencing and celebrating the symbolic power and nobility of earth, air, fire, and water. In the foreword to *From the High Dive,* Charles Fishman has summarized this theme: "Although they are quirky and stubborn, the men and women in Smith's poems are only occasionally *grotesques;* above all else, they are individuals who have touched the bristling back of the living beast—wild nature—before which they stand damaged, mystified, but waiting to be saved."

Characters abound in Smith's poetry. The poet has traced Native American ancestry through his maternal grandmother and Irish lineage through both sides of his family, and many of his created characters reflect and extend his personal history. These dramatic speakers are frequently rustics who live his philosophy of simplicity as a crucial aspect of sophistication. One such speaker is Roosevelt (*Roosevelt Unbound* 1985), based on an elderly black neighbor of Smith's in Opelika, "full of simple wisdom and very little embellishing foolishness," very like Smith's own much-admired grandfather. Smith said that "Roosevelt knew what the main road was and never confused it with the tributaries. And I don't just admire that, I envy it."

Another series of poems published in *Poetry* features the character of Gristle, an inventive alter ego of the poet. Begun during Smith's first sojourn in Ireland, the Gristle poems present a rugged, bitter character, filled with hatred but seeking reconciliation, who defies nature to roam the Irish countryside, committing barbaric acts. Gristle's language is at once wild, gnarled, and elevated, mingling English and Latin with French and Gaelic. The poems resonate with the tones of his poetic ancestors, but they are unique to R. T. Smith's voice and vision and are among his most complex and original creations.

Whether his speakers are alone or engaged in communal acts, Smith's poems are vehicles for reaching an audience. As Shelby Stephenson (1982) has pointed out, "Smith goes out from the scrap of feeling, circling and settling in his nature the ragged disorder of order, forming finally in any given poem a story of the heart's desire to communicate" (3). Smith demonstrates his commitment to communication through categorization, attention to detail, precise naming, and a fascination with words and the possibilities of their meanings. In the poems, the communication theme is also manifest in the reverence for the human voice. The critic Jo D. Bell (1986) has noted: "Smith's lyrical, highly alliterative lines beg to be spoken aloud, in the oral traditions of the Southern Appalachian region he lovingly draws on in much of his work" (118). R. T. Smith explained: "The vocal machinery is an important part of what I'm after. I compose poems for how they feel in my throat and on my tongue." Maturity has led Smith away from his youthful act of talking to God. Smith has reflected: "Maybe making a poem—because there's so much of the process of making a poem that is not willed or rational or intellectual—maybe it's a way of listening to God. And maybe it's about time."

SURVEY OF CRITICISM

In an article in *Crazy Horse* (Winter 1992, no. 45: 122), Scott Ward has called his Auburn University colleague "a poet with vision," asserting that "the genuine poetic vision never fails to surprise, involve, and satisfy." Essays on Smith's work, appearing in the review sections of journals, literary magazines, and newspapers, trace the development of his visionary poetry. Grace Gibson had detected Smith's visionary aspect when she reviewed *Walking under Snow* (1975), Smith's first book of poems. Writing in *Pembroke Magazine,* Gibson notes that Smith's "vivid vision often speaks through paradox" and praises Smith's "strong narrative gift" and "lively metaphorical sense" (345).

Good Water (1979), Smith's second volume, is a chapbook published as the Tamarack Award Book of 1979. P. B. Newman (1980) admired "the complex weaving of images of disaster and rebirth through which the narrator comes to a stronger recognition of selfhood" (73). Philip Shirley (1979) noted "the richness of Smith's diction and his fine, attentive eye for detail" and called Smith "a poet to be reckoned with" (27). Tamarack also published Smith's first major volume of poetry, *Rural Route,* in 1981. The collection showed Smith's increasing maturity as an artist, and it received widespread critical attention. Shelby Stephenson (1982) wrote from North Carolina that Smith "writes with an energy contagious and inspiring" (5). Stephenson further observes: "Smith desires to make his lines true as the woods and wildlife he loves" (5). Jerry Bradley (1981) wrote from New Mexico: "Though considerably rustic, Smith's poems refuse to be needlessly nostalgic or sentimental. He is more entranced by the world as it is than as it used to be" (82). Fellow poet Jim Wayne Miller (1982) wrote of Smith: "Many of his most successful poems have the qualities of a still life, a scene or object rendered with the sharpness of detail ... many readers will associate with the work of Robert Morgan" (327). Miller detected an occasional slackness of line but praised the "use of folk speech" as "generally convincing and effective" (326). William Paulk (1983) wrote from Montana that Smith had "recreated the countryside and its people with vivid, fresh imagery" and with "intimations of something beyond mortality" (9).

Lois V. Walker (1984) summarized the critical response to Smith's 1983 collection, *From the High Dive:* "The presence of R. T. Smith is fiercely human and brings with it a consciousness of physical pain, ritual violence, carrion, and the primitive equations for survival" (10). She asserted that the book derives its universality from "the relentless honesty of its search for a language and imagination that come together exactly where the living must touch the dead or dying" (11).

Ralph Hammond reviewing *Birch-Light* (1986) called Smith "a major voice rising out of the South" (172). He concluded: "R. T. Smith's weaponry of poetic engagement should serve as a challenge to all poets that indeed the English language is a crafted work of art when used to its maximum possibilities" (172). Jo D. Bell (1986) praised *Birch-Light* for its "range of eloquent voices" (118) and asserted: "For all its diversity, this collection doesn't have a bad side. It reads well from any angle, a double-woven tapestry full of rich colors, finely drawn threads, and splendid patterns" (118). In a letter awarding *Birch-Light* the Brockman Award in 1986, A. R. Ammons wrote:

The poetry allows us access to what is possible to a solitary life finding its engagement chiefly with natural surroundings.... The states of mind represented in his poems are not exhausted myths, projected onto otherness, but subtle and responsive weavings, questioning and doubtful, as much as penetrating and rejoicing. These are NOT nature poems in the accepted sense, but states of mind, skeptical of their own formings, and so, unusually informing for us.... There is sizable multiplicity and profound searching, the searching and the finding equally convincing.

The Cardinal Heart (1991) was widely reviewed and highly acclaimed. Fellow poets gave it glowing praise. Rodney Jones sent Livingston Press a quotation for the book jacket and called it "a wonderful book," noting that Smith, "in poem after poem, arrives at the rare, difficult ending with that momentary ease, which seems both lucky and right and is the signature of the most exacting craft." Don Johnson (1992) said: "More than any book I've read in the past decade, this collection lifts my spirits and renews my faith in the value of poetry" (36). Shelby Stephenson (1992) called Smith "one of North Carolina's and contemporary poetry's major narrative poets" (3).

In 1983 Brendan Galvin designated Smith "the kind of young poet I've been waiting for: a muscular line, a clear eye, a believable voice speaking in fresh air" (53). Galvin's review (1992) of *The Cardinal Heart* provides a fitting summary of current regard for the poetry of R. T. Smith: "Increasingly he's showing up in the best magazines here and abroad. This handsomely printed collection ... should bring him the audience these fine poems deserve" (55).

BIBLIOGRAPHY

Works by R. T. Smith

Waking under Snow. Boone, N.C.: Cold Mountain Press, 1975.
Good Water. Syracuse, N.Y.: Tamarack Press, 1979.
Rural Route. Syracuse, N.Y.: Tamarack Press, 1981.
Beasts Did Leap. Syracuse, N.Y.: Tamarack Editions, 1982.
Finding the Path. Hartesville, Pa.: Black Willow Press, 1983.
From the High Dive. Huntington Bay, N.Y.: Water Mark Press, 1983.
Roosevelt Unbound. Syracuse, N.Y.: Tamarack Editions, 1984.
Birch-Light. Ithaca, N.Y.: Tamarack Editions, 1986.
The Hollow Log Lounge. Huntsville, Tex.: *Texas Review* Press, 1986.
Banish Misfortune. Livingston, Ala.: Livingston University Press, 1988.
The Cardinal Heart. Livingston, Ala.: Livingston University Press, 1991.
The Names of Trees. Troy, Maine: Nightshade Press, 1991.

Studies of R. T. Smith

Allworthy, A. W. *"The Hollow Log Lounge* and *Roosevelt Unbound." Fessenden Review* 11, no. 2 (1987): 76–78.
Bathanti, Joseph. "Poet's Knack for Naming Shines." *Charlotte Observer* (February 2, 1992): D–I.
Bell, Jo D. *"Birch-Light,* by R. T. Smith." *Texas Review* (Spring 1986): 117–18.
Bradley, Jerry. *"Rural Route.* R. T. Smith." *New Mexico Humanities Review* IV, no. 2 (1981): 82.
Galvin, Brendan. "R. T. Smith. *The Cardinal Heart." Poet Lore* 87, no. 1 (Spring 1992): 52–55.
Gibson, Grace. *Pembroke Magazine* 7 (Spring 1976): 345.
Hammond, Ralph. "R. T. Smith, *Birch-Light." Negative Capability* 6, nos. 3–4 (1986): 172.
Johnson, Don. "R. T. Smith, *The Cardinal Heart." Poet and Critic* 23, no. 2 (Winter 1992): 35–37.
Lynskey, Edward C. *"The Cardinal Heart:* A Review." *Chattahoochee Review* 12, no. 3 (1992) 56.
———. *"Rural Route,* by R. T. Smith." *Hollins Critic* 20, no. 3 (June 1983): 17–18.
Miller, Jim Wayne. "Reviews: *Rural Route,* by R. T. Smith." *Appalachian Journal* 9, no. 4 (Summer 1982): 326–28.
Newman, P. B. "Reviews: *Good Water.* R. T. Smith." *Southern Poetry Review* 20, no. 2 (Spring 1980): 72–73.
Oliver, Julia. "This New Poetry Pulses with Energy." *Birmingham News* (April 19, 1992): 10.
Paulk, William. *"Rural Route,* by R. T. Smith." In *Hard Row to Hoe,* edited by Art Cuelho, 9–10. Big Timber, Mont.: Seven Buffaloes Press, 1983.
Stephenson, Shelby. "Smith a 'Good Celebrant' of Nature in His Poetry." *The Pilot* (Southern Pines, N.C.) (June 12, 1982): 5.

————. "Book to Keep and Remember. *The Pilot* (Southern Pines, N.C.) (February 20, 1992): 3.

Suk, Julie. "*The Cardinal Heart:* R. T. Smith." *Southern Poetry Review* 32, no. 1 (Spring 1992): 74–75.

Walker, Lois V. "Capsules: *From the High Dive,* by R. T. Smith." Newsletter. Huntington, N.Y.: Long Island Poetry Collective, 1984.

Dabney Stuart
(1937–   )

Although Dabney Stuart has written prose fiction, book reviews, and a volume of literary criticism, his major achievement is as a poet. Since 1966 he has published nine volumes of verse, and his work has been included in dozens of anthologies, such as *The New Yorker Book of Poems* (1969), *The New York Times Book of Verse* (1970), *Contemporary Southern Poetry* (1979), and *Strong Measures* (1986). An eclectic writer, he has made poems that might be classified as formalist, confessional, elegiac, mythic, surrealistic, or satiric. He has excelled in the lyric mode but has often experimented with narrative and dramatic verse as well.

BIOGRAPHY

Dabney Stuart was born on November 4, 1937, in Richmond, Virginia. He grew up in that "squat and stolid city," as he characterizes it in one of his early poems, in a two-story brick house in Ginter Park. His father, Walker Dabney Stuart, Jr. (1901–1971), ran the Richmond Hardware Company at the corner of Fourteenth and Cary Streets near the James River. The building still stands, though deserted. The future poet would often visit his father's warehouse on Saturday mornings and slide down a metal chute leading from the top level to the shipping dock. The first poem in *The Diving Bell* (1966), "The Warehouse Chute," presents this setting as exhilarating at the time, but in retrospect it seemed like a kind of commercial hell, void of any guiding presence such as Dante's Virgil or Beatrice.

The poet also vividly remembers being pressed "into a neat, ironed, well-mannered puppet" at family dinners at his paternal grandparents' house. Stuart's paternal grandfather, Walker Dabney Stuart (1880–1963), appears as the embodiment of a hypocritical, insensitive business world in early poems such as "Elegy for My Grandfather" (*The Diving Bell*).

More happily, the young Stuart spent a great deal of time—"nearly six months of the year"—at his maternal grandfather's home in Hampton, Virginia. Even though he was also a successful businessman, in emotional terms this grandfather was the antithesis of the other. In addition to founding The Merchants National Bank, Leopold Marshall von Schilling (1874–1954) enjoyed sailing, talking with bootleggers, and operating a small amusement park. A first-generation German immigrant, he was accused of subversion during World War I—an injustice that helped to inspire the poet's lifelong suspicion of simple-minded patriotic zeal.

At the age of 5, Stuart was saved from drowning by von Schilling. Stuart has reconstructed the event in his essay "Knots into Webs: Some Autobiographical Sources":

All the stories I've heard since then present the incident as accidental. I remember sitting on a dock of weathered gray boards at my maternal grandparents' place.... My grandfather is in the bowels of the boat curing the engine of some ailment. I push the bow of the boat away from the dock with my toes. It eases away from me, reaches the end of the line, groans, swings back.... I push again, but this time the momentum carries my little body off the edge of the dock into the water. I can't swim....

I never try to surface.

My grandfather pulled me out, though I don't recall that part at all.

"A Garland for Marshall" in *The Diving Bell* and "Taking the Wheel" in *Don't Look Back* (1987) deal explicitly with the incident. In both poems the child's physical danger is juxtaposed with the grandfather's slow, agonizing death 11 years later, after a stroke that left him paralyzed. Robbed of his memory, the old man shouted "God damn it to hell" over and over again from his bed. The five words imprinted themselves indelibly upon the poet's mind.

Stuart began writing verse at 14, while he was at a summer camp in the Virginia mountains. Edgar Allan Poe's incantatory rhythms and romantic isolation seemed especially attractive to him. When even younger, "when nothing else worked," Stuart would go to sleep while his mother recited "The Raven."

After attending public school in Richmond, Dabney Stuart entered Davidson College, where he became a member of Phi Beta Kappa before his graduation in 1960. While still an undergraduate, he published verse in *Epos* and *Impetus,* two nationally circulated literary journals. In 1962, as a Woodrow Wilson Scholar, he earned his M.A. from Harvard. The most vivid evocation of his Harvard years is found in "The Charles River," a long meditative poem from Stuart's second volume, *A Particular Place* (1969).

Stuart returned to his native Virginia to become an instructor of English at the College of William and Mary. While there, he received the Howard Willett Research Prize from the college and the Dylan Thomas Award from the Poetry

Society of America. Showing the mark of these years is "For Dear Life" (*The Diving Bell*), an early narrative poem about an old aristocratic lady reduced to dressing up in eighteenth-century costume for tourists. "Comic Relief" (*The Diving Bell*), also has a setting in colonial Williamsburg. "Tourist trap, opulent buzzard" the town seems to force a young teacher and a black janitor to assume supporting roles within an idealized historical drama.

Since 1965 Stuart has taught at Washington and Lee University, where he is currently a professor of English and editor of *Shenandoah,* one of America's best-known literary journals. He has served as a visiting professor or as a poet-in-residence at Middlebury College (1968–69), Ohio University (1975), Trinity College (1979), and the University of Virginia (1981, 1982–83). During the 1970s he also worked extensively with the Poets in the Schools Program in Virginia. Over the years he has received many grants and awards: nineteen John M. Glenn grants from Washington and Lee, a summer stipend from the National Endowment for the Humanities (1968), literary fellowships from the National Endowment for the Arts (1974, 1982), and a Guggenheim Fellowship in Poetry (1987–88) that allowed him to spend a year in New Zealand.

Stuart has been married four times, first in 1960 to Suzanne Bailey, the mother of his daughter Martha. The couple were divorced in 1962. A brief marriage to Betty Kantor also ended in divorce. On August 14, 1965, he married Martha Varney. They had two sons, Nathan von Schilling and Darren Wynne, before their divorce in 1977. In 1983 Stuart married Sandra Westcott of Chattanooga, Tennessee. Throughout his career, many of Stuart's poems have reflected his love for his children and his complex, deeply ambivalent feelings toward courtship, marriage, and separation.

MAJOR THEMES

Although Dabney Stuart's first collection of poems is written in the formalist tradition that dominated American verse in the late 1950s and early 1960s, many of the themes of this collection continue to appear in later works. *The Diving Bell* is a book preoccupied with family ties and tensions: its three-part structure ("Paternal," "Maternal," and "Others, Up to Now") reflects this preoccupation. The first section concentrates upon the poet's father and paternal grandfather. Stuart consistently questions the materialism that he sees dominating the lives of both men. In "Kissing Kin," the grandfather appears as a malevolent Daddy Warbucks, whose smelly cigar and "soggy affection" radiate hypocrisy at family gatherings. In "Elegy for My Grandfather," the poet is even more critical. After enumerating the injustices that the grandfather has heaped upon his own son—withholding business secrets, forcing him to become a salesman upon graduation from college, and refusing to grant him authority within the family—the poet states simply, "I'm glad you're dead." In other poems such as "The Warehouse Chute" and "Taking Sides," Stuart and his father seem separated by the commercial world that has treated the father shabbily but that he has not joined his son in renouncing.

The second section of *The Diving Bell* is more celebratory in tone, even if much of that celebration is sombered by the maternal grandfather's painful death in 1954. In contrast with the poet's other grandfather, who was "stunted" both physically and morally, Marshall von Schilling rejected materialism to keep "[b]alanced and afloat" in life. Stuart also praises his maternal grandmother in "The Widow," where she loyally visits her husband's grave 10 years after his death, even though she can no longer remember the incidents that are preserved in the photograph album waiting for her at home.

The third section, "Others, Up to Now," often continues the family motif with poems about a young sister, a dissolving marriage, and an infant daughter. Some poems, however, are not in the dominant autobiographical mode. "Flatfish," a brief dialogue between a flounder and the sea that recalls the method of Emerson's "Fable," anticipates the terse, stylized myths of Stuart's future books. "Rifle Range" is a short narrative poem about a soldier's "real world of sleep" in which the man dreams of shooting a person instead of a mere target. The implied social criticism will resurface in Stuart's later work, although it will become more oblique, often surrealistic. In "Dogged," the poet compares chasing a dog to trying to capture thoughts. An elusive certainty becomes "a mongrel bitch" whose pursuit never seems to lead to self-discovery. Although this suspicion of rationality is at odds with the traditional forms and the narrative clarity of most of *The Diving Bell,* it is an impulse that will strongly influence the poet's future exploration of open forms and of feelings that lie beneath or beyond the level of everyday thought.

This quest begins in *A Particular Place,* the poet's second volume. Its first section, "Sources," is totally new for Stuart: thirteen poems whose short, often unpunctuated lines create a vatic breathlessness. If the models for *The Diving Bell* were the formal confessions of Robert Lowell's *Life Studies* and W. D. Snodgrass's *Heart's Needle,* then the models for "Sources" appear in the incantatory fragments of W. S. Merwin's *The Moving Target* and *The Lice.*

A Particular Place is a transitional volume. Although it contains some poems with the everyday voice of *The Diving Bell,* even these works seem less narrowly personal and more generous in spirit. The book's concluding poem, "To His Father, Dying," was praised by John Unterecker (1969) as a "major poem by any standard." Here, Stuart combines his earlier autobiographical subjects with his new mythic language. Written primarily in free verse with short rhymed lyric interludes, the poem resembles T. S. Eliot's *Four Quartets* in structure. Indeed, the poem's refrain, "*See, they depart, and we go with them,* alludes to the end of the fourth quartet, "Little Gidding." Stuart's imagined interaction with his dying father, like Eliot's imagined interaction with the "familiar compound ghost," enables the poet to see that the contemplation of a particular person or a particular place can lead to its transcendence. Whereas the redemptive force in Eliot's poem is the dove of Christianity, the redemptive force in

Stuart's poem is the new awareness that the poet is also a parent; and in mourning his father, he is mourning himself.

The Other Hand (1974), Stuart's third volume, abandons the personal for the archetypal, although as Joseph Parisi (1975) has noted, the poet is still concerned with the process of self-discovery. Terse pronouncements are made in general terms—such as *wind, flight, darkness, light, stone, shadow, bones,* and *breath*—in the attempt to evoke the deepest levels of human consciousness. Despite the title of the book's last section, "The Real World," most of these poems have few and tenuous relationships with everyday objects and events. "Poetry: A Lecture on the Discrete" is perhaps the best gloss on Stuart's method here. The poem suggests that multiple masks, through their apparent evasiveness, enable the wearer to consider parts of himself that he might otherwise ignore. Such "singular fictions" allow the poet to move toward a fuller understanding of his total being.

Round and Round (1977) is subtitled "A Triptych," emphasizing both stylistic differences and thematic unity. Stuart has summarized that unity as follows: "I think that the primary concern . . . is the continual pressure exerted on *anyone* in our culture to disappear, if that person asserts energy in unfamiliar forms." The book's first "panel," "Ground Speed," is a collection of ballads and songs in the tradition of W. B. Yeats and Edwin Muir. The primary characters are the Fool, the Slut, and the Poet, who appear individually or together in thirteen of the twenty-eight poems. The Fool seems to embody nonconformity, which often appears to the uninitiated as madness; the Poet and the Slut represent art and sexuality, respectively. As in Yeats's Crazy Jane poems, the Slut usually has the last word, suggesting that the bed is the bedrock of human experience.

The second panel, "Fair," takes place in a carnivalesque world that Stuart researched by spending a summer visiting small amusement parks on the East Coast. "The Ferris Wheel" provides a metaphor for the power of conformity in the world at large, a "unison" held to be "ruthless." "Mirrors," on the other hand, implies that a fragmented self, however disturbing, is preferable to the poet's gazing backward over his shoulder—presumably to behold, as Lot would have, a ruined city and a single image turned to salt.

The book's final panel, "Data Processing," is less archetypal and more contemporary in its references. It uses surrealism and satire to imply that America is governed by commerce and television. It is a world with Green Stamp catalogues in lieu of real grass, mechanical phrases such as "Do sit down" and "Help yourself" in lieu of real feelings. Many of the poems end with short, cynical statements by a male antagonist who seems intent upon bullying the main speaker.

In *Common Ground* (1982) there is a movement back toward the autobiographical concerns so clearly apparent in *The Diving Bell* and *A Particular Place.* These new poems, however, are much more open in feeling and form than the earlier work. The poet's divided self and his own psychic distress are often in the foreground. "Two Elegies for Walker Dabney Stuart, Jr.," for example, contains a brief narrative section reconstructed from a newspaper account of the father's football heroics in 1920. But it also contains allusions to nursery rhymes, Western movies, Shakespeare, and Dame Juliana of Norwich, as well as general meditations upon death. The overall effect is in keeping with the polyvocal self established in *Round and Round.* In "Finding One of the Ghosts," a bleak narrative poem about divorce, the husband (an amalgam of his father and Charlie Chaplin) seems as fragmented as the marriage that he is leaving. Such dark whimsy abounds in *Common Ground,* although there are a few moments of tender, lyric clarity in poems such as "Mining in Killdeer Alley" and "Turntables."

Despite its title, *Don't Look Back* (1987) is the most personal book that Dabney Stuart has written since the 1960s. Perhaps his strongest volume to date, it is full of paradoxes and qualifications. In "Talking to the Small Voice," the book's prefatory poem, the speaker must accept his earlier self, sheltering it as if it were a child in the rain. Only thus can the speaker stop the anguish, the "burning" that has consumed his life. That burning includes childhood jealously of a younger brother, sexual longings, divorce, and the relentless approach of death.

Stuart returns again to the inspiration of his maternal grandparents. He gives them both a pair of lyric names. "Lady" and "Heartbeat" identify the grandmother, whose gentility is admired but whose "laced aloofness" in sexual matters is chided. Like her husband before her, she died a slow, painful death. She has bequeathed the poet a sense of generosity even in the face of pain, to complement the legacy suggested by the grandfather's lyric names, "Duststroke" and "Curseworld."

Other family poems have whimsical, surrealistic imagery. "Finding My Face," another poem about the search for identity, has the speaker asking his mother for her nipples so his tears can be "milk for the hungry children of the world"; later on the father mistakes his child's nose for a raisin, then hands it to him. At the end of the poem, it is laughter, not certainty, that helps the speaker to make his best way in the world.

On other occasions, family life seems hauntingly sinister. In "The Perfect Headache," for example, the speaker's ancestors become a sovereign nation inside his head; they insist that the only way he will ever become a citizen is by being a "*perfect image*" rather than his real self. The book's title poem has a setting that recalls Stuart's family dinners at his maternal grandfather's house. There are both "bubbling glasses and happy people" present. Yet there is also an uncle who sits on a child while the rest of the family drops ice cubes into his crotch. The past is not altogether pleasant—we may want to tell ourselves not to look back—but the "yesterday of forever" is both inescapable and lost, gone from the world but alive in the mind that must reinvent it.

Narcissus Dreaming (1990), Dabney Stuart's newest collection of poems, contains more attempts to blend autobiography, myth, and surrealism. "The

Hospital of Lies'' is perhaps the most compelling example. It combines three visions: a man carrying his grandfather's shrunken body from the hospital, his boyhood self jealously running out of the hospital with his newborn brother, and his future self entering the hospital for a horrific operation. At the end of the poem, the speaker wakes to the "greasy mudtumble" of both life and memory.

SURVEY OF CRITICISM

Critical responses to Dabney Stuart's work have been mixed. Writing in an age in which everything is possible and nothing is certain, Stuart is at times a bewilderingly eclectic poet. Some reviewers have enjoyed his experiments in style and subject, coupled with his careful arrangements of poems within volumes to suggest an overarching unity. Other critics have found the poems derivative, vague, or overly ingenuous.

X. J. Kennedy wrote the first substantial essay on Stuart's work in 1966, and it is still one of the most incisive commentaries available. Kennedy praised the "remarkable unity" of *The Diving Bell,* seeing in both the poet's photograph and the poems themselves "a hungry man, ready to devour experience and make it part of him" (97). Although Kennedy found fault with the neatness of Stuart's metaphors in "Air Raid U.S.A." and considered "Two for My Daughter" unduly influenced by W. D. Snodgrass, he praised the entire book as original, direct, and clear. A formalist poet himself, Kennedy found many of the qualities in Stuart's early work that he had been striving to achieve in his own verse.

Both John Unterecker (1969) and Dannie Abse (1971) have praised Stuart's willingness in *A Particular Place* to experiment with open form and nonautobiographical subjects. Unterecker found the terse, mythic poems in the book's first section especially impressive. He considered the more formal, autobiographical poems "uneven . . . sometimes marred by an excess of wit" (72–73). Abse's enthusiasm for the new Stuart is in keeping with an entire culture's fascination with mysticism around 1970: "Dabney Stuart's restlessness of style has led him to write poems since 1969 that are even more abstracted from prose reality, that are even more rarefied than the poems in the first section of *A Particular Place.* Such obfuscations are no longer modest: indeed, his pretensions are now grand and reach toward mystery" (139–40).

The Other Hand, possibly Stuart's weakest book, has unfortunately received the most critical attention. D. E. Richardson, in an omnibus review of books by Southern poets (1976), singled out Stuart as a "modernist of the now, alas, old-fashioned sort" (885). According to Richardson, "one must think and feel deeply" (887) to enjoy the book's "spareness and silence" (886). Joseph Parisi (1975) was less enthusiastic, calling the poems "carefully made . . . but . . . rather complacent" (229). David Bromwich (1975), in what is probably the most eloquent adverse review of Stuart's work, found *The Other Hand* far too influenced by the example of W. S. Merwin: "The method here partakes of a constitutional vagueness of motive which virtually forbids that the poet should ever find his emotive ground" (736). Although this criticism of *The Other Hand* is a telling one, it has little relevance either to Stuart's earlier work or to his more recent work.

J. D. McClatchy (1978) found *Round and Round* "a pleasant experience, but rarely ever more than that" (294). He has objected to the book's three-part structure; in particular, he considered the third section to be a miscellany in which the poet's satire is too predictable.

Stuart's most recent volumes have received a fair number of short notices but almost no extended reviews. Stephen Dobyns (1982) has discovered a kinship between the stylistic flourishes in *Common Ground* and those in jazz solos. He admires the poet's virtuosity but feels at times "bullied by surprise." A fine short commentary upon *Don't Look Back* has appeared in the Autumn 1987 issue of the *Virginia Quarterly Review*. The unnamed author has shown familiarity with Stuart's career, noticing his "return to the concerns of his earlier books, with fervent elegies for grandparents, parents, brothers, sons, and daughters" (136). He also believes that Stuart "seems more relaxed and comfortably at home with a variety of approaches than he has been in his previous collections" (137).

The spring 1991 issue of the *Kentucky Poetry Review* focuses on Dabney Stuart. It contains six new poems by Stuart as well as poems dedicated to him by Daniel Hoffman, Conrad Hilberry, Heather Ross Miller, Kelly Cherry, Fred Chappell, Deborah Keenan, and Jeanne Murray Walker. The issue contains two essays: Fred Chappell's impressive analysis of Stuart's allusions to film and Gilbert Allen's review of *Narcissus Dreaming*.

BIBLIOGRAPHY

Works by Dabney Stuart

The Diving Bell. New York: Knopf, 1966.
A Particular Place. New York: Knopf, 1969.
Autobiographical note. In *Corgi Modern Poets in Focus,* vol. 3, edited by Dannie Abse, 140–42. London: Corgi Books, 1971.
Friends of Yours, Friends of Mine. Richmond: Rainmaker Press, 1974.
The Other Hand. Baton Rouge: Louisiana State University Press, 1974.
Round and Round. Baton Rouge: Louisiana State University Press, 1977.
Nabokov: The Dimensions of Parody. Baton Rouge: Louisiana State University Press, 1978.
"Knots into Webs: Some Autobiographical Sources." *Poets in the South* 2, no. 2 (1980–84): 5–7.
Rockbridge Poems. Emory, Va: Iron Mountain Press, 1981.
Common Ground. Baton Rouge: Louisiana State University Press, 1982.

Don't Look Back. Baton Rouge: Louisiana State University Press, 1987.
Narcissus Dreaming. Baton Rouge: Louisiana State University Press, 1990.

Studies of Dabney Stuart

Abse, Dannie, ed. *Corgi Modern Poets in Focus.* London: Corgi Books, 1971.
Allen, Gilbert. "A Dream Not of Wholeness, but of Endless Dreaming." *Kentucky Poetry Review* 27 (1991): 81–84.
Bromwich, David. Review of *The Other Hand. Georgia Review* 29 (1975): 736–37.
Chappell, Fred. "The Long Mirror: Dabney Stuart's Film Allusion." *Kentucky Poetry Review* 27 (1991): 85–92.
Dobyns, Stephen. "Three Poets of the Potomac." *Washington Post Book World* 12 (November 7, 1982): 4–5.
Kennedy, X. J. "A Face to Meet the Faces." *Shenandoah* 17 (1966): 96–100.
McClatchy, J. D. "Grace and Rude Will." *Poetry* 132 (1978): 294–95.
Parisi, Joseph. "Personae, Personalities." *Poetry* 126 (1975): 229–231.
Richardson, D. E. "Southern Poetry Today." *The Southern Review* 12 (1976): 885–87.
Tillinghast, Richard. "Seven Poets." *Poetry* 110 (1967): 260–61.
Unterecker, John. "The Validity of the World." *Shenandoah* 21 (1969): 70–76.

ELIZABETH MCGEACHY MILLS

Henry [Splawn] Taylor
(1942–   )

During the 1987 commencement at Shenandoah College and Conservatory of Music where he was awarded an honorary degree, Henry Taylor wished the graduating class "purity of language, and strength of recollection," as recorded in "Strength of Words" (602). Both are qualities that Taylor possesses. In addition, however, he is a maker of poems, a crafter of imaginative recollection in language that he has formally ordered into art. His poems demonstrate his careful attention to details of person, place, and thing and his ability to capture nuances of speech, event, and meaning; they disclose subtle shifts of time and space in the external and internal landscapes that real people inhabit; and they show disciplined concern for the way in which form and meaning meld in effective poems.

BIOGRAPHY

Henry Taylor's roots go deep in Loudoun Country, Virginia, where he was born on June 21, 1942. His Quaker forebears first inhabited that rolling farmland in northern Virginia, about 50 miles west of Washington, D.C., in the 1780s. The house where his grandparents and parents lived on Coolbrook Farm was built by Taylor's great, great grandfather in 1828. Although he only returned to live in the immediate area in 1977, Taylor, in an autobiographical essay (1988), insists that this landscape "seems to . . . have colored almost everything [he has] done" (173).

Tom Taylor, Henry's father, married Mary Splawn, who had moved from Texas to the Washington area with her father W. M. W. Splawn, an economist who later became chairman of the Interstate Commerce Commission. Tom Taylor was a dairy farmer, and between 1942 and 1949 the Taylors had four children—Henry, Mary Jay, Carolyn, and Julie. The parents were literate people who read to their children frequently. Tom Taylor was famous throughout the area for reading and reciting narrative poetry (such as "The Highwayman" or the works of Edward Arlington Robinson), a talent his son cultivated early. The family was also part of a larger community that, although rural, included what Taylor recalls (in his autobiography) as "a remarkable amount of fairly ambitious cultural activity" (174). In his autobiographical sketch, Taylor states that he "had the amazing good fortune to encounter the idea of the artist through encounters with people whose pretensions, if any, were surpassed by their stature as artists" (174). The painter Arshile Gorkey and guitarist Carlos Montoya were among the visitors that the Taylors entertained.

Through the ninth grade, Taylor attended local schools. He has described himself as a daydreamer, a lover of literature, often asked to recite poems, but known to be weak in math. His greatest interest during those years appears to have been horseback riding. The horse he rode for over fifteen years was named "Silver Streak" by its original owners, and Taylor called him "Silver," until he entered him in competitions using the name "Small Change." Both names appear later in Taylor's poems. Despite leaving Lincoln to attend George School, a Quaker institution in Bucks County that many members of his father's family attended, Taylor maintained his relationship with Silver and gained a reputation as an excellent rider. After his freshman year in college, he tried out for the Olympics; but because Silver was ill, Taylor rode another, less familiar, horse. Although his performance in that competition was adequate, Taylor determined to pursue his studies at the University of Virginia rather than the Olympic dream.

The years at George School had given Taylor contact with several great teachers and competition with other strong students. In response to the excellent instruction and influence of John T. Carson, his science teacher, Taylor graduated from high school intending to major in biology and become a physician; however, documents kept by his religion teacher reveal that even at this time Taylor had a keen interest in becoming a writer. Certain developments at the University of Virginia fostered that interest.

During Taylor's first year there, he belonged to a poetry writing workshop led by English instructor Fred Bornhauser. James Dickey, at Bornhauser's request, met with the group and encouraged Taylor by thoroughly critiquing several of his poems. Contact with Dickey led to Taylor's sending poems, while still an undergraduate, to Robert Bly for publication in his journal *Sixties*. During Taylor's second year at Virginia, his English professor Robert Scholes encouraged the reluctant student to submit some poems to Stephen Spender, who was spending a few weeks at the university as a writer-in-residence and conducting several individual conferences with students. That interview led Taylor to submit his poem "Toad" to *Encounter,* the journal for which Spender served as poetry editor. As Taylor has recounted in his autobiography: "He took the poem, paid me five pounds for it, and published it in an issue containing work by three other poets: John Berryman, Donald Hall, and Theodore Roethke" (180). Taylor was still only a third-year student at the university. That same year, George

Garrett, whom Taylor has called both mentor and friend, joined the University of Virginia faculty, where he taught the first regular course in creative writing. One project that Garrett's class pursued developed into *The Girl in the Black Raincoat,* a collection of poems and stories to which Taylor contributed a story. That story, in turn, led to Taylor's correspondence with May Sarton, who remains a favorite critic and friend, as well as a poet about whom Taylor himself has written. Garrett also instigated a connection between Taylor and Louisiana State University Press, which led to the publication of the younger poet's first book. Miller Williams originally asked Taylor to submit some poems to an anthology entitled *Southern Writing in the Sixties: Poetry;* after reading those poems, Williams asked Taylor to send a book of the poems. *The Horse Show at Midnight* was thus accepted for publication while Taylor was still an undergraduate.

In 1965 Taylor graduated from the University of Virginia, married, and won a fellowship in creative writing at Hollins College near Roanoke, Virginia. Although Taylor's marriage did not last, his work prospered. He studied with Louis Rubin, who was in charge of the program, William Jay Smith, Julia Randall, and John Alexander Allen. Friendships begun during his days at the University of Virginia with writers Richard Dillard and Kelly Cherry continued. In the spring of 1966, *The Horse Show at Midnight* was published, and Taylor graduated from Hollins with an M.A. in Creative Writing.

Remaining in the Roanoke Valley, Taylor began teaching at Roanoke College in Salem, Virginia, a position he held through 1968, when he and his new wife, Frannie Carney, moved to Salt Lake City. Taylor taught in the English department of the University of Utah from 1968 to 1971. Although far from the familiar green landscape of Virginia, Taylor and his wife found close ties in that desert. Brewster Ghiselin, a poet and colleague for whom Taylor later organized a Festschrift called *The Water of Light: A Miscellany in Honor of Brewster Ghiselin* (1976), turned out to be Frannie's cousin. The Taylors' son Thomas was born in Salt Lake City in 1970.

Nevertheless, when Larry McMurtry suggested that Taylor might apply for the former's soon-to-be-vacant position at American University, in Washington, D.C., Taylor sought and won the job. In 1971 he began teaching there as an associate professor; he was promoted to professor in 1976, served as director of the American Studies Program from 1983 through 1985, and continues as co-director of the M.F.A. in Creative Writing Program. After 2 years in McLean, Virginia, where their son Richard was born in 1975, the Taylors moved to a home that they built on the corner of Ferris Hill farm outside Lincoln.

Taylor continued to write poetry while teaching at the University of Utah and later at American University. In 1971 Solo Press published almost five hundred copies of *Breakings,* a volume of seven poems by Taylor. Those poems found a wider audience when combined with 36 others in *An Afternoon of Pocket Billiards,* published in 1975 by the University of Utah Press. In 1979 the Unicorn Press from Greensboro, North Carolina, published *Desperado,* a broadside of three poems from a work in progress portraying the experiences and opinions of a Southern redneck character named Desperado. Taylor's Pulitzer Prize winning book *The Flying Change* was published by Louisiana State University Press in 1985. Individual poems appeared in journals such as *Georgia Review, Hollins Critic, Nation, Ploughshares, Poetry, Southern Review,* and *Virginia Quarterly Review.* Others appeared in such anthologies as *Contemporary Southern Poetry,* edited by Guy Owen and Mary C. Williams; *An Introduction to Poetry,* by X. J. Kennedy; and *The Morrow Anthology of Younger American Poets,* edited by Dave Smith and Dave Bottoms.

Taylor also continued other scholarly activities, publishing the textbook *Poetry: Points of Departure* (1974), editing *The Water of Light* (1976), and collaborating with Robert A. Brooks on a translation of Euripides' *Children of Herakles* (1981). He wrote numerous reviews for such journals as *Western Humanities Review, Nation, Masterplots,* and *Magill's Literary Annual,* for which he served as editor in 1972, 1973, and 1975. In 1981 he completed *A Map of the Loudoun Valley in Virginia, Showing Principal Roads, Towns, and Separately Taxed Parcels of Land, Spring 1980.*

Taylor's major awards include creative-writing fellowships from the National Endowment of the Arts in 1978 and 1986, a research grant from the National Endowment for the Humanities in 1980, and the Witter Bynner Prize for poetry administered by the American Academy and Institute of Arts and Letters in 1984, as well as the Pulitzer Prize in 1986.

Among the courses that Taylor currently teaches at American University are the poetry writing workshop for graduate students, an introduction to poetry for honors undergraduates, and graduate courses in literary journalism and literary translation. He frequently gives poetry readings; in 1985 the Watershed Foundation published *Landscape With Tractor,* a tape of Taylor reading 23 poems.

MAJOR THEMES

For over 30 years Taylor has been patiently and meticulously creating poems. Although he has sometimes written in free verse, Taylor has more often used technically demanding fixed forms, such as the sonnet and the sestina. His method brings immediate experiences—common actions such as mowing grass, driving a child to school, or riding a horse—to life through ordinary words arranged in extraordinary ways. Such a combination of freedom of subject and restraint of expression is not easy. As he has said in a personal interview (1990), "A good, fast hot streak for me is six poems a year." Each of his three major books of poems was completed about ten years apart and published at the center of its decade. Given such a span of time, one would expect to see major shifts in themes, especially as the poet emerged from callow youth to middle age. Certain themes persist, however, the first of which is the interplay between emotional expression and rational control, an essential ingredient of the poet's craft.

Without doubt Taylor's years of disciplined riding led him to use horseman-ship as one vehicle for showing the roles that feeling and thinking play in creation and performance. *The Horse Show at Midnight* opens with an epigraph by William Steinkraus, which speaks of the relationship between a horse and its rider, claiming that "if you ride confidently and well, and ask confidently and soundly for the horse's best level of performance, his response will be to the ride you give him, and not to your secret thoughts." Although the quotation obviously refers to a real horse and rider, in the context of Taylor's book, the instruction and proclamation imply that writing a successful poem is not so different from riding a horse successfully. The task of the poet is like that of the horseman since both demand confidence and control. Effusion of emotion, "secret thoughts," will not move the horse or the poem. The poet, like the rider, must govern. Technical skill matters.

The metaphor of horseback riding appears in "The Circus Rider's Depar-ture," a poem from the first section of *Horse Show*. Here the speaker is a crowd pleaser; moving before an audience whose members "have not seen through to hours that must / Be spent imagining true form," he is adept at "tricks to seem to know what no one knows" (18). The goal of his show is "an act of mind: / *Reveal some evidence of strain, / Conceal that which cannot be learned*" (19). But the deception becomes unbearable in its Sisyphean psychic demand, and the speaker abandons public performance for private activity: "Beneath no lights I take the reins, / And I place my foot in a stirrup. / Slowly, astride, I ride away" (21). The actual situation remains unspecified although the speaker's determination to change arenas is clear. Within the context of this first volume, the poem may describe professional choices that the poet has made, for this book includes several poems in which Taylor plays verbal tricks by cleverly imitating famous contemporary poets such as James Dickey, J. V. Cunningham, Howard Nemerov, Denise Levertov, and Robert Bly. Like the rider in his poem, the poet can perform tricks with the best, but perhaps he seeks something more self-directed, a greater challenge.

The last and title poem of Taylor's first book also recounts the relationship between the rider and the horse, with particular emphasis on the communication between the two. The poem, divided into two sections, begins with the speech of the rider, who moves "alone" in the empty ring and functions as both "judge" and rider (51). The speaker is able to bring forth horses with his "thought-out call"; they emerge "noiselessly, weightlessly / Their hoofs beating only within me" (51–52). After they perform, the horses depart, leaving only "one horse that I love" (52). This horse the rider mounts and mysteriously rides once but cannot force to remain. As in many other of Taylor's poems, the speaker is a survivor, left alone to describe an experience.

The second section of the poem presents the same experience but with the horse as speaker. Here the horse reveals the rider's means of communicating: "Still I move to the beat of a heart / That brought me out of the stable . . . I march / From the ring to the sound of the heart" (54). The deep rhythmic connection between horse and rider, a connection dependent upon emotion ("heart") and intellectual control ("my thought-out call"), mirrors in its non-rational privacy the connection between the poem and its maker. In *Poetry: Points of Departure* Taylor says that for the reader as well, "the best poems reward examination with more lasting reverberations at the nonrational level"; Yeats's "fascination of what's difficult applies to reading poems as well as to writing them, as it applies to learning an athletic skill or a complicated dance step" (2). But with its elegaic subject and tone, "Horseshow at Midnight" also appears to speak about the poet's choice of poetry over riding. The horse speaks last, accepting the change while noting the rider's "heart singing deeply within / A shape that moves with new life. / I believe in the singing, and sleep" (54).

"An Afternoon of Pocket Billiards," the title poem of Taylor's second volume, uses the medium of the poem and the metaphor of the pool game, rather than riding, to portray the relationship between ordered control and disordered emotion. The speaker of the poem admits: "I try to beat a game, half chance, half cold / and steady practice, struggling for the skill / that might kill chance" (13). A "half-remembered love," "a chain of treacheries," a "gradual disease" plague the speaker, so that his "knocking heart / shatters skill and chance, and takes the game apart" (13–14). Although for a time, "words will not connect," finally the speaker follows sound "down below green felt toward solid stone," which enables him to say, "Now, / within the strictness of my touch, I feel / a surge of steadiness," and to assert, "I'll be right someday: / though one song of old love has died away, / an older song is falling into place" (15–16). The game continues, but the speaker understands now "that all days in this cavern are the same: / endless struggles to know / how cold skill and a force like love can flow / together in my veins, and be at peace" (16).

While expressing his own experience, the speaker also voices the complex task of the poet who must skillfully evoke and control emotion. "An Afternoon of Pocket Billiards" stands as evidence of Taylor's own skill as a poet. Emerging, as he has admitted, from the failure of his first marriage, the poem becomes during the nine years of its crafting far more than an autobiographical lament. The poet's technical control of personal tragedy is both beautiful and astonishingly skillful. Here is a poem that initially sounds like the sad confession of one who tries to escape personal woe through a pool game, but with closer examination the poem becomes a complicated creation of eleven stanzas each of which maintains the rhyme scheme *aabcdcdeeb*. In addition, the opening line of each of the first ten stanzas becomes part of a coherent statement in the eleventh stanza.

Some of the poems in the section of *An Afternoon of Pocket Billiards* titled "From Porlock" present other statements, often more explicit, about poetry, its creation and its effect. In "The Writer-in-Residence Discusses His Working Habits," for instance, Taylor mocks the pretensions of the superficially successful poet. But "To Hear My Head Roar," the final poem in this section, demonstrates the fine combination of sound, form, and meaning that makes successful poems. In this poem the speaker recalls his earliest experiences with poetry; and as the speaker names his father Tom Taylor, the autobiographical connection is more pronounced. The personal and emotional recollection—the speaker says, ''My heart cracks''—is conveyed through an intricately bound form (50). The poem contains twenty-one stanzas of three lines, the end rhyme of each stanza intertwining with the next in a progression: *aba, bcb, cdc, ded,* and so forth through the final stanza where the central line's rhyme is an exact repetition of the first line in the poem. Thus the rhyme, as well as the overall discourse, reiterates the subject through the repetition of the word *poetry* itself.

The title poem of Taylor's third volume, *The Flying Change,* returns to the metaphor of horseback riding, this time extending the art of poise between opposites more ostensibly from poetry to life. The poem itself is a formal contrast, opening with a ten-line prose description and explanation of a canter and concluding with three stanzas of poetry describing and meditating upon a moment of observation in the speaker's daily life. The prosaic and poetic passages, though seemingly at odds, enrich each other through the interplay of images. In the first section the speaker tells how, when free, the horse can ''change leads without effort during the moment of suspension''; the rider's presence, however, ''makes this more difficult'' (50). The speaker concludes: ''The aim of / teaching a horse to move beneath you is to remind / him how he moved when he was free'' (50). In the second part of the poem the speaker describes how the turn of a leaf moves him to a former time and place, when he ''studied on that barbered stretch of ground,'' schooling himself as well as the horse (50). He acknowledges the fear, especially of aging, that change can ''sometimes'' arouse in him; but at this moment free, like the cantering horse, he says: ''I hold myself immobile in bright air, / sustained in time astride the flying change'' (50). Like Keats's figures captured on the Grecian urn, the speaker lives forever the feeling of this moment within the controlled space of the poem. An interesting continuity exists between a speaker in Taylor's first book and this one. Whereas the speaker in ''The Circus Rider's Departure'' concluded, ''Slowly, astride, I ride away'' on a horse (21), this speaker holds himself ''astride'' the moment itself (50). It is as if the voice from the first book, who feared ''the trick I do not dare perform'' (20), has grown into the wiser, braver, and more accomplished rider of the ''The Flying Change,'' one who attempts and succeeds at the seemingly impossible.

Always concerned with the artistic shaping of that tension between internal feeling and external expression, Taylor presents other themes as well in his poems. Almost all of his poems portray people who are part of some narrative. Sometimes he presents teachers and students interacting. At times he lays bare the teacher's inadequacies, as in ''Shapes, Vanishings'' (*Flying Change*). At other times he shows the gift of the inspiring teacher, as in his poem ''In Medias Res'' (Horseshow) where J. B. Laramore instructs his students about '' 'the tears at the heart / Of things' '' and about how '' 'all things change' '' (3–4). That note of sadness in the world and that concern with change are themes that Taylor also displays in his second and third books. In "Riding a One-Eyed Horse" (*Afternoon*), for instance, Taylor uses the matter-of-fact reality of a half-blind horse to portray the deep sadness of an incomplete life, one that will always carry "the heavy dark" even as it will "see you safely through diminished fields" (53). The inevitability of change permeates all of the poems in *The Flying Change,* but grows especially poignant in "Heartburn," where the speaker confesses:

> If you need a change, just stand here,
>
>> by God, and you'll get it.
>> So turn once again, back up
> the driveway, thinking, as lately you've come to
>> that you can still make a wrong step
>> on rough ground, in the dark, and not
> quite cripple yourself. (20)

Sometimes Taylor's poems display family members. Poems such as "Over the River and Though the Woods," "For Mary Jay, Practicing Archery," and "A Story for My Mother," all from *Horseshow,* use family relationships to speak about the difficulty of a young person's deciphering life. "Things Not Solved Though Tomorrow Came" (*Horseshow*) presents those difficulties from the point of view of a father who, returning from leaving his daughter at school, experiences "one instant / Of the coldest dread, one moment so short / It could contain but one impression, to be thought / About forever after it" (44). "Breakings" and "Harvest," both from *Afternoon,* point out the joy and sorrow of returning home, while "My Grandfather Works in His Garden" and "Bernhard and Sarah" (*Afternoon*) illustrate the deeply positive influence of ancestors whose eyes, the speaker says, "light up the closet of my brain / to draw me toward the place I started from, / and when I have come home, they take me in" (78).

The love and grace of family, a support in the midst of change, resonates through "At the Swings," the last poem in *Flying Change.* Here the multigenerational pull on the middle-aged speaker produces within him an elegiac sense of perfection lost, the memory of what once was "a day of thorough and forgetful happiness . . . gone for good," combined with a longing for "holy permanence" that gives way to wonder and appreciation for "that dappled moment at the swings" (55). Pain and joy, permanence and loss mingle in the speaker's experience of family.

Although "At the Swings" creates "a state / still and remote as an old photograph" (54), not all of Taylor's pictures are so poignant. Powerful in a different, less melancholy, way are those poems called "snapshots," which capture people and speech in a flash of verbal clarity. Such poems appear in all three books. The thematic message common to them all is that individuals display their inimitable uniqueness through their choice of words, as when the huge Mr.

Shipman (*Afternoon*) confronts the boy hired to unbutton his fly and help him urinate after the boy has claimed, "'Mr. Shipman, I can't find it.' 'Well, / God damn it, boy, you the last man had it'" (23). Or again, when the New York cabbie tells the speaker of "The View From a Cab" (*Afternoon*), who complains of the sour weather, that the astronauts are the cause: "'Fuck with the moon, the sun don't like it'" (32).

Most, although not all, of Taylor's poems are set in a country landscape. The poems in *Afternoon* display a love and hate relationship between the speaker and the country he calls home. The sestina "Goodbye to the Old Friends," for example, conveys the power of the Quakers to inspire the reluctantly returning speaker. On that Easter morning the speaker says he does not see Christ there, but "with the tongue of man he speaks to me / and to his Friends: there are no angels here" (4). The holiness that the speaker experiences is grounded in a real place, among human beings. "I have risen," he says, "I am thinking, as I break away from here" (5). Poems such as "The Hughesville Scythe" and "Pastoral" (*Afternoon*) emphasize that the place is not without its own horrors. "Landscape With Tractor," and "Barbed Wire" from *Flying Change* likewise show the frightening violence that the pastoral landscape can contain. Other poems in *Flying Change* such as "Hawk," "Not Yet," and "Projectile Point, Circa 2500 B.C." also make manifest the splendid continuity of place in the face of human mutability. The speaker of "Projectile Point" conveys an unsentimental sympathy when, finding an arrowhead, he speaks of that "one hot afternoon when I stood sole-deep / in soft ground, wondering at the four thousand years / between the two men who had touched this stone" (51). The land is before and after the man, for he knows there will come a time "when the rocks and the water are alone here again" (51). Such a realistic yet mysterious rural place forms the permanent home of Taylor's best poems.

SURVEY OF CRITICISM

No critical investigation, neither essay nor book, examines Henry Taylor's work. Stuart Wright's essay (1988) provides an excellent nine paragraph summary of the poet's career and selected critical responses to it, as well as a year by year listing of Taylor's own work. But, whereas Wright has claimed that Taylor "is absolute master of a thing well-wrought, a poem perfect on the page and to the ear" and "the best poet of his generation," Wright's bibliographic task does not permit analysis of the poems in support of his high praise (79, 80). Reviewers of Taylor's three major books have also produced general comments about the poet's work, but have devoted little space to specific evidence.

Dorothy Curley judged *Horseshow at Midnight* "a pleasant but rather slight collection of poems by a young Virginian who has studied under May Sarton and William Jay Smith among others" (2851). Calling the poems "generally direct and loose-jointed" she suggests that the collection should "be bought more as an encouragement to youthful talent and to marginal publishing ventures than for the work itself.'' In contrast, the anonymous reviewer of ''Notes on Current Books'' in the *Virginia Quarterly Review* (1966) saw Taylor as ''a new young poet of distinctive voice and sure craftsmanship,'' adding that Taylor's ''first volume of poems is not the promise but the arrival of an accomplished poet'' (xcvi).

In reviewing Taylor's second book, *Afternoon of Pocket Billiards,* the anonymous reviewer of the *Virginia Quarterly Review* noted the poet's interest in form and praised his forthrightness: ''While he has many notable attributes— ear, eye, humor, a strong sense of irony—his great strength is his disciplined honesty. No coyness, no evasive games with his audience, no gushy emotions. Every word is authentic and controlled'' (80). Paul Ramsey (1976) included Taylor's *Afternoon* in his analysis entitled ''Image and Essence: Some American Poetry of 1975.'' Ramsey declared: ''The author has shown real development since his earlier, rich, Dickey-haunted work'' (539). Ramsey commented on Taylor's poems ''Amazing but True'' and ''The Hughesville Scythe,'' which, he said, use ''an old and sound method: the presentation of an object or narrative followed by a meditation on the meanings'' (539). Although asserting that ''Burning a Horse'' does not convince him, Ramsey found ''Riding a One-Eyed Horse'' able ''through the entirely actual, to convey a deep sense of the wholly strange. It is an example, almost a parable, of the relation of knowledge to poetry'' (540). D. E. Richardson (1976), examining works by A. R. Ammons, James Applewhite, Wendell Berry, Fred Chappell, James Seay, and Dabney Stuart, saw *Afternoon* as an indication ''that verse recognizably southern, and particularly Virginian, is still possible'' (885). He also thought the work an improvement over Taylor's first book and claimed that ''An Afternoon of Pocket Billiards'' is ''the most beautiful poem in the book and one of the best poems written by a southern poet in recent years'' (885). Richardson believes that ''intentionally or not, Taylor represents continuity in southern poetry; he writes as a man who has a father and therefore a history; who has been taught, as he knows, both well and ill, and is not self-created; and who has an unsentimental affection for the land'' (885). Claiming that ''the chief restraining forces are form in poetry and manners in society'' John Vernon declared that:

one of Henry's implicit insights is that these two things are one. The seemingly spontaneous language in very tight forms is the measure of a southern gentleman conscious of his family and roots in the soil, perhaps an almost extinct species these days, but none the less a gentleman, a gentle man, for that. Restraint that holds a fulness in check, and comes to be expressed with ease, grace, and wit; also the *severity* of restraint, of knowing when to stop before one has said too much. (266)

Although he praised Taylor's mastery of form, calling it ''sure, intelligent, almost flawless,'' Vernon thought that sometimes form overpowers the poems' emotional content, as it does in the book's title poem (267). He called ''To Hear My Head Roar'' ''the best [poem] in the book'' because in it, ''the emotion is completely embodied by the words and the form, not avoided or left unexplored, and not—since this is a danger of a formal poem—fabricated'' (267).

Reviews of *Flying Change* were more expansive, but smaller publications continued to present the fullest analyses. In the *New York Times Book Review* Peter Stitt (1985) said that *Flying Change* has ''been given the Pulitzer Prize for poetry'' (notice the verb) and that Taylor ''writes the poems of a country squire,'' sometimes poems about ''preppy picnicking'' and at other times poems that evoke a ''sense of nostalgia for his home country [that] is a traditional American feeling and one of the strengths of this solidly written, hauntingly conceived volume'' (22). The review is laconic, contradictory, and condescending. It cites only five poems from the book and analyzes none.

R. H. W. Dillard (1986) and David Shapiro (1987) have plumbed Taylor's work more deeply. Dillard described Taylor's concern with ''questions of time and mutability''; he saw the poems as manifesting the tension between a desire for freedom from time and an awareness of its restraint. He said that the poems themselves display that tension, casting ''plain talk and individual identity . . . in traditional forms, rigorously controlled'' (15). He also noted the ''violence of language and of fact'' that permeates the book. Dillard called Taylor ''an American Hardy, intensely aware of the darkness that moves around us and in us'' (15). Shapiro also saw Taylor's dark, ironic cast, warning that ''Taylor has to beware his own facility in scorching us with irony'' (349). Shapiro's main concern, however, was to show the ''house'' that Taylor's poems create, claiming that ''in all Taylor's most richly felt poems, lived place and time are the beginning of the poem's 'site specificity' '' (349).

That no more detailed examination of Taylor's poetry exists than several brief reviews probably says more about the number of excellent contemporary poets publishing today than it does about lack of interest in Taylor's work. Taylor's three major books certainly contain many poems worthy of analysis. Much more remains to be said, many more connections need to be drawn, before the complexity of Taylor's poems will be thoroughly mined. As Taylor has observed in *Poetry: Points of Departure,* ''A good poem can withstand the most brutally minute examination'' (3). Taylor's best poems deserve such close reading.

BIBLIOGRAPHY

Works by Henry Taylor

''And Bid a Fond Farewell to Tennessee.'' In *The Girl in the Black Raincoat,* edited by George Garrett, 36–52. New York: Duell, Sloan, and Pearce, 1966.
The Horseshow at Midnight. Baton Rouge: Louisiana State University Press, 1966.
Breakings. San Luis Obispo, Calif.: Solo Press, 1971.
''Vantage and Vexation of Spirit.'' *Georgia Review* 25 (1971): 17–26.
''Home to a Place beyond Exile: The Collected Poems of May Sarton.'' *Hollins Critic* 11 (1974): 1–16.

Poetry: Points of Departure. Cambridge, Mass.: Winthrop Publishers, 1974.
An Afternoon of Pocket Billiards. Salt Lake City: University of Utah Press, 1975.
"On Reading Poems." In *From Three Sides: Readings for Writers,* edited by Joseph
    Malolo, 10–14. Englewood Cliffs, N.J.: Prentice-Hall, 1976.
The Water of Light: A Miscellany in Honor of Brewster Ghiselin. Salt Lake City: Uni-
    versity of Utah Press, 1976.
"Artichoke." Winston-Salem, N.C.: Palaemon Press, 1979.
Desperado. Greensboro, N.C.: Unicorn Press, 1979.
*A Map of the Loudoun Valley in Virginia, Showing Principal Roads, Towns, and Sep-
    arately Taxed Parcels of Land, Spring 1980.* Privately printed, 1981.
"The Singing Wound: Intensifying Paradoxes in May Sarton's 'A Divorce of Lovers.' "
    In *May Sarton: Woman and Poet,* edited by Constance Hunting, 193–200. Orono,
    Maine: National Poetry Foundation, 1982.
Landscape with Tractor. Washington, D.C.: Watershed Tapes, 1985.
The Flying Change. Baton Rouge: Louisiana State University Press, 1985.
"The Strength of Words: The Grip of Time." *Vital Speeches* 53 (1987): 600–602.
"Henry Taylor." *Contemporary Authors Autobiography Series* 7 (1988): 171–89.
Compulsory Figures: Essays on Recent American Poets. Baton Rouge: Louisiana State
    University Press, 1992.
The Horseshow at Midnight and An Afternoon of Pocket Billiards. Baton Rouge: Loui-
    siana State University Press, 1992.

Studies of Henry Taylor

Curley, Dorothy. Review of *The Horseshow at Midnight. Library Journal* 91 (1966):
    2851.
Dillard, R. H. W. Review of *The Flying Change. Hollins Critic* 23 (1986): 15.
"Henry (Splawn) Taylor: *The Flying Change.*" *Contemporary Literary Criticism* 44
    (1987): 300–303.
"Henry Taylor." In *The Writer's Voice: Conversations With Contemporary Writers,*
    edited by George Garrett, 120–40. New York: Morrow, 1973.
Ramsey, Paul. "Image and Essence: Some American Poetry of 1975." *Sewanee Review*
    84 (1976): 533–41.
Review of *An Afternoon of Pocket Billiards. Virginia Quarterly Review* 52 (1976): 80.
Review of *The Horseshow at Midnight. Virginia Quarterly Review* 42 (1966): xcv–xcvi.
Richardson, D. E. "Southern Poetry Today." *Southern Review* 12 (1976): 879–90.
Shapiro, David. Review of *The Flying Change. Poetry* 149 (1987): 348–50.
Stitt, Peter. "Landscapes and Still Lives." Review of *The Flying Change. New York
    Times Book Review* (May 4, 1986): 22–23.
Vernon, John. "A Gathering of Poets." *Western Humanities Review* 30 (1976): 265–76.
Whittemore, Reed. "Pastoral Poet's Jolts for Lazy Days." Review of *The Flying Change.
    Washington Times* (March 24, 1986).
Wright, Stuart. "Henry Taylor: A Bibliographic Chronicle, 1961–1987." *Bulletin of Bib-
    liography* 45 (1988): 79–91.
Young, Diane. "Virginia's Pulitzer-Winning Poet." *Southern Living* 22 (1987): 133–34.

ED INGEBRETSEN

Richard [Williford] Tillinghast
(1940–   )

Richard Tillinghast's first collection of poetry, *Sleep Watch,* was published in 1969, when he was 29. Like other Americans of his generation, Tillinghast has been committed to justifying private experience in light of its connections to a larger, public world. In his verse he shows the influence both of Robert Lowell's intense inwardness while displaying, as one critic notes, the fugitive's "carefulness" and emphasis on craft.

BIOGRAPHY

Richard Tillinghast was born on November 25, 1940 in Memphis, Tennessee, the son of Raymond Charles Tillinghast and Martha Williford. He finished his B.A. at the University of the South, in Sewanee, then completed an M.A. (1963) and Ph.D. (1970) at Harvard. While finishing the Ph.D. and immediately afterward, he taught at the University of California at Berkeley (1968–73). From 1976 to 1979 he was associated with the College of Marin and taught in the college program at San Quentin State Prison. In 1979 he returned to the University of the South as a visiting assistant professor. Subsequently he accepted the position of Briggs-Copeland Lecturer at Harvard (1980–83). Tillinghast left Harvard to accept a position at the University of Michigan, Ann Arbor, where he presently teaches. Tillinghast is married, with three sons and one daughter. He has received numerous awards, including a Woodrow Wilson Fellowship (1962), a grant from the National Endowment for the Humanities (1980), a Bread Loaf Fellowship (1982), and a grant from the Michigan Arts Council (1985). He has been a resident at the Millay Colony (1985) and at the Yaddow Writer's Retreat (1986). He received a grant from the American Research Institute in Turkey in 1990, a year when he also accepted an Amy Lowell Travel Grant for travel in Ireland (1990–91).

MAJOR THEMES

The title *Sleep Watch* defines Tillinghast's themes while outlining the nature of his poetic inquiry. In *Sleep Watch* he catalogues the various nuances of consciousness, the waking that is a kind of sleep, the sleep that is a kind of waking—the "dreams of other nights" that "are something from another life" (53). Like Roethke, he chooses as his poetic program the exploration—the exfoliation, better—of the inner life. His verse offers a measured look at the fluidity and Byzantine complexity of preconsciousness as it wrestles itself into the rhythms and shapes of formally defined experience. He follows the confluence of the streams and eddies of consciousness. A mystical sensibility informs Tillinghast's verse, though it is epistemological rather than religious or Romanticist: the perplexities and ecstacies of the self coming upon evidence of its operations.

Tillinghast's associative method, even in his highly formal verse, focuses on the problematics of the poetic project itself. In his verse Tillinghast asks, can a poet ever escape the tyranny of viewpoint, the narcissism of memory? How does one escape epistemological uncertainty to reach public and shareable meaning? "The Old Mill" in *Sleep Watch* (*SW*), is a long, loosely structured series of reflections and memories; it explores the relation between the poet's inner and outer worlds and the organizing consciousness that attempts to relate them. Tillinghast placed the poem directly in the center of the volume as if to underscore his intentions: that this journey "straight through the dark" (42) through the subterranean lands beneath the old mill provides an analogue to the collection's other forty-nine poems. The labyrinthian tunnels in the depths of the mill describe as well the labyrinths of the self that Tillinghast explores in these poems. The journey downward and through the old mill reflects the journey inward into the poet's organizing consciousness. By the poem's end, however, the journey results in an increasing sense of epistemological confusion that in no way is limited to "The Old Mill" itself.

"The Old Mill" concludes with a series of questions that reflect Tillinghast's poetic inquiry and his inquiring poetics: "What is expected of us?" (43); "What would you have seen   or remembered?"; "And on the way back, what does one wish for?"; "Did you dream it   or did someone actually say?—/ 'You can wake up now   it's over' " (44–45). Neither memories of person or place, neither symbolic forms or formal operations ("numbers") nor moral or aesthetic imperatives ("What is expected of us?") help direct or organize the latent content of the sleep/waking dream of life.

"The Old Mill" is probably the best example of Tillinghast's Roethkean world, his attempt to grasp the individuation and precise otherness at the heart of things. Like Roethke, he has articulated a world of implication that lingers around the edges and presumptions of sight, a world that remains unseen because too close. Tillinghast, however, differs from Roethke in never forcing a unity or oneness upon what he sees and experiences. His is an oddly calm vision of the discreteness and stasis that lie just beyond "tricks of vision" (39), illustrated in these lines from "The Old Mill":

> This is how a leaf falls:
> from as high as it has been
> to as low as it goes
> without choice   not knowing
> Who are these people?   the spots of clouds
> changing to different brightnesses
> Fireflies swarming in the olive trees
> What do these numbers mean   why do they go in a circle? (43)

As the speaker rides along through the dark underside of the mill, he recalls how familiar the tunnels were to him when he was a boy, though he wonders still about their power to fascinate him: "Why did we cherish those tunnels   those empty drainage pipes / my brother and I?" He confesses that what was once a "refuge" (42) is now an unknowable world, perhaps because unimaginable and unseeable by his adult, daylight vision. As a consequence, its memory proves to be unmanageable as well: "But the Old Mill was odd beyond our knowledge" (42), a world that appears the more strange because of its haunting familiarity. It is a place where there lived, according to legend, "blind fish born white," "dragonflies that could swim like crabs," "nails with eyes," "whole cats that glowed in the dark," "bats that curled themselves like mopheads" (42). Reflecting upon his experience, the speaker imagines: "In a long hall I stood / at the first doorway of the lost life" (42–43). Tillinghast, like Jung, has sensed how heavily the unlived life weighs upon the present moment. We can only seek freedom in our history; we cannot be free from it. And the life below conscious reflection—unowned, unclaimed, unordered—always claims its price.

Nonetheless, Tillinghast's affirmations, finally, are less certain than Roethke's—more tentative and perhaps more fearful. They depend more upon the ability of the ordering consciousness to escape its traps and to discipline itself. If Roethke could write, "In a dark time, the eye begins to see," Tillinghast, in "Old Mill," has only acknowledged, minimally, being "used to the dark—

but seeing nothing" (41). Whereas Roethke's interior journeys took him to a point of affirming the mystical integrity of all things, Tillinghast has remained more suspicious of the imperialism and aggression of consciousness as it paws over the remains of the past: "The mind of a man in a warm room / A lion / pawing the memories," he says in "Old Mill" (57). Besides, confesses the poet in "Old Mill," "It is never as I had remembered" (52).

In "Dozing on the Porch with an Oriental Lap-rug" (*SW*), Tillinghast wryly admits "I am in love with my own thinking" (58). Yet Tillinghast would concur with Wallace Stevens's conviction that "it is the human that is the alien," the human that "demands his speech / From beasts or from the incommunicable mass'' (Wallace Stevens, *Collected Poems* [New York: Knopf, 1955], 328). The "mirrored eye," in Tillinghast's phrase, is always evident, making, remaking—and, inevitably, estranging. Tillinghast shows (*SW*) the pressure of consciousness reflecting upon itself: "When morning pumps into my veins / I feel the strangeness of it" (34). In "Enter Your Garden" (*SW*) he physically falls asleep only to "waken," and "feel / you dreaming all the colors of our life" (31). In a poem about the confluence of love and sleep (*SW*) he reflects on the way "daylight and its forms imposed / themselves on us" (23).

Consciousness is obtrusive; it goes by habit the way it goes, trapped within its own angles of vision and forms. In "Sea Cycle" (*SW*), for instance, the intricately varied repetitions of phrases, lines and rhythms draw attention to the mechanical repetitiveness of the unchanging refrain: "Alone, I awake" (12). Of all rhythms, the perceiving self alone maintains an "unnatural" rigidity of pattern. Nonetheless, whatever the shaping eye shapes—whatever *is*—is not complicit with human designs upon it. In "Winter Insomnia" (*SW*) Tillinghast invokes, by denying, Yeats: "The world refuses / to bless / or to be blessed" (67).

The habit of consciousness—like love, it is a conscious act, Tillinghast has made clear—is not, however, always negative; escape from the repetitions of the self can be possible, when as in moments of poetic articulation, the self reaches for the world of form—the world of rhythm, line, and the conventions of meaning that define the world of common experience. This is a world of moral and aesthetic necessity, a world of beauty and loss. Tillinghast treats the idea implicitly in "The Creation of the Animals" (*SW*) his Dickeyan fable of a fall from grace—or perhaps, a fall into a different kind of grace: "We were angels before the sky lost us" (49). The poem ends poignantly as the former angel runs "on the grass" and feels "the rain in my fur," remembering dimly the satisfactions of a former life: "I begin to forget   I flew once   and knew the order / of a beauty / I no longer have the mind for" (49).

Tillinghast never completely succumbs to the habit of self-elucidation, so it is not quite accurate to call him an autobiographical or a confessional poet. He is at his best when his verse centers and places the poet in a shareable, but finely particular, world. At such times there is a spareness and quiet, a dignity and understatedness about Tillinghast's verse. In " 'Come Home and Be Happy' " (*SW*) memory's potential for nostalgia is disciplined by irony:

> At last you enter.
> Knowing your shape the walls contract around you.
> This is home, she is here.
> Wherever you step you inflict a comfortable pain.
> Love is real—and you have done the work yourselves,
> haven't you— (77)

The world of person and events has its own rhythms, its own patterns of lights and darks that accrue metaphoric—and sometimes symbolic—weight.

Consequently Tillinghast often writes a psychologically intense poetry bordering on the surreal. His attentiveness to detail—especially in his poems about the complications of domesticity or in his carefully sketched country scenes—and his attention to the rhythms of perception help the reader feel the quiet singularity of event that lies behind and that informs a life: waking from a nap; reading alone by winter; the quiet of a kitchen morning—waking, strangely enough, on the kitchen floor; even the intimacy of anticipating aloneness (*SW*): "I try to imagine the absence of you" (59). Tillinghast renders the common uncommon and marvelous—and thus keeps it ever before the reader's eye.

In general the poems of *Sleep Watch*—characterized as "juvenalia" by one critic—recall Robert Frost's comment that a young poet begins as a cloud of all the other poets he has read. The presence of other poets—Frost, Lowell, Williams, Dickey, Roethke, to name a few, in formal imitation, allusion, theme—mutes Tillinghast's precise and distinctive voice. In these early poems one senses a kind of poetic indecision. The sometimes frenetic allusiveness and the distracting array of styles offer imitation without, also, indicating direction. In addition, Tillinghast's poetic reflections on the past reveal his need to remember without, as yet, offering any organizing reason or purpose for memory.

Tillinghast is at his clearest when he reflects on the past without becoming lost either in nostalgia or in the self-indulgence of exclusively private meanings—as, for example, happens in "To My Grandfather, Dead Before I Was Born" (*SW*) and "The Old Mill." In other poems, however—one thinks of "If You Love the Body," "The Beauty of the World (*SW*)"—Tillinghast's clear, spare diction allows the reader to participate in detailed observations of a world that maintains its strangeness no matter how closely the poet's eye captures it in perception. At his best he offers reflections that do not fragment or dissociate, as in the lovely, closely observed miniature, "The End of Summer in the North" (*SW*), or "In the Country You Breathe Right" (*SW*). In this last-named poem, the poet puts to rest his troubles with sleeping and waking—"and sleep / in a single breath / the length of the darkness. Here, also, "Things are / as you remember them" (75).

In *The Knife and Other Poems* (1980) Tillinghast moves with a greater assuredness and control in two diverging directions: On the one hand, he continues his explorations inward, deeper and backward into the cruxes of consciousness. In such poems as "Return," "The Knife," and "Summer Rain," he shows the pressure of past memories and desires as they shape and shadow the present. On the other hand, he moves outward into the shareable, if equally mysterious, world of public memory and consequence. In many of the poems—especially the three poems of the second section ("Sovereigns," "Views of the Indies," and "Today in the Cafe Trieste")—Tillinghast's associative method attends to the fragmentations and fissures of culture as well as those of the individual consciousness. He moves in a transpersonal world of symbolic and political forms, a reticulated pattern of social consciousness, awareness of history, ecological and international themes.

Tillinghast's method in these eighteen poems—"The Thief," and "My Ghost," for instance—resembles the method of *Sleep Watch*. He is understated, cautious, occasionally "psychological," sometimes surreal and dreamlike— even symbolistic ("My Ghost," significantly, is subtitled "After Baudelaire"). Tillinghast's finest poems demonstrate poetry's power to peel inner experiences away from strictly private contexts and to assume symbolic depth and dimension. Thus, just as in *Sleep Watch,* the strange wonderfulness of experience becomes as much a part of poetic method as poetic theme. The quality of perception is still important in these poems, and Tillinghast has taken care to see well. In "Return" he writes, "Sunburst cabbage in grey light / summer squash bright as lemons / five kinds of chilis burning in cool darkness, / sunflower's lion's heads / in the blue Chevy pickup" (11).

Tillinghast's second collection focuses most directly upon the question implicitly posed by "The Knife," the title poem: "What was it I wonder?" "What was it / like a living hand / that spun me off the freeway / and stopped me" (23). "The Knife" opens with the kind of inquiry that characterizes his early poems—notably "The Old Mill." The poet senses connections with the past and explores motivations, but now in addition he seeks to understand the familial, historical, public consequences of his private experiences. Tillinghast's pervasive use of hunting metaphors becomes appropriate to this poem as well, since he parallels his brother's dive after a lost knife with his memory's restive quest for meaning. Both knife and poem, "shaped now, for as long as these words last," are "like all things saved from time" (24). The knife, a weapon, becomes a memorial, as does the poem, each "filling more space than the space it fills" (24). The pervasive tensions of fraternal competition that lend interest to "The Knife" highlight Tillinghast's growing concern for the enigmatic nature of relationships. The poet implicitly addresses family, culture and history—and, ultimately, language—and he makes his political context evident by placing "Hearing of the End of the War" immediately after "The Knife."

In "The Knife" public consequence and private memories—the real and symbolic violence between perspectives, brothers, and cultures that we know as history—contrast and parallel each other. The speaker's memory of his brother's dive makes him realize his complicity in the event—first as brother, then as poet. The underlying hint of violence—the knife "carries a shape like the strife of brothers / —old as blood" (24)—nonetheless makes possible the "worn gold on my father's hand" (25); and the speaker comes to accept the violence as purposeful, even graceful—and, finally, reconciling. This acceptance prepared Tillinghast for a similar exploration of culture, violence, and memory in "Sewanee in Ruins."

Most recently Tillinghast has moved from the fragmented world of the poeticizing self—"however you wish to imagine it," he says in *Sleep Watch* (45)— to the more profound ambiguities that inscribe the self in language, the self in history, the self in myth. For the self, too, the poet now realizes, resembles the knife and poem, the instruments of human violence and human art. The self, too, must be "saved from time." *Our Flag Was Still There* (1984) consists of a description of the politics of the imagination, an intention signaled by the title, a phrase taken from Francis Scott Key's triumphant but jingoistic "Star-Spangled Banner." In the title poem of the collection Tillinghast emphasizes the phrase's irony by contrasting the vacuous public rhetoric of the wartime United States against the cultural poverty that such rhetoric represents. He links the private emptiness of words with the illiteracy of culture—for which both the war and its rhetoric must share responsibility.

Tillinghast's most recent collection, suggests that a people's language is its fate. This marks the difference between the hesitancy of his initial self-studies in *Sleep Watch* and the purposeful political energy of *Our Flag Was Still There* (*OFWST*). Tillinghast's political engagement has become his poetical program, as he enlists himself in a war for consciousness, a war for symbolic forms through which to explain the past and to make possible a present. Abandoning the political "gestures" of his early poetry, he has acknowledged the more imperative political battle over words and their fate. More generally, he addresses the fate of any past—memory or history—enscribed or hallowed in words. The speaker of "Sewanee in Ruins," an alumnus of the University of the South who returns as an instructor, muses about his relationship to his students. He reflects on their past and on the Civil War–ravished culture and school he shares with them. The poem—a Williamsian pastiche of primary texts, reconstructive history, and personal reflection—is a meditation on the history of Sewanee University since its troubled beginnings during the War Between the States. But the speaker's own motivations and anxieties—his understanding of his personal history and future—emerge as important. He questions his motivation for writing, for teaching, and, by implication, he wonders why he reflects or bothers to remember anything at all.

Implicit in Tillinghast's surreal, self-exploratory and self-questioning verse has been the question of the value of memory and individual experiences. It must be said, however, that Tillinghast has moved to a final point of qualified affirmation. In the young teacher's reflections on the history of Sewanee, Tillinghast finds himself implicated—as, also, in the frantic command of the Confederate colonel and teacher at Sewanee (*OFWST*), who brought to war and education alike a "capacity for furious moral tantrums": "My God, gentlemen, *do* something" (27). In the concluding lines of "Sewanee in Ruins" (*OFWST*), one senses that Tillinghast has reached a place of peace. The speaker realizes the impossibility of his task as an educator. He sees that literacy—the public face of culture—is as fractured and fissured as any private experience could be, and its future is as unclear. Yet somehow through the violence of time and war a perspective has been reached through which emerges a community of memory, a source, a sacrament: "This was a place / where the sacraments were kept, / and people were kind" (47). Here "the old names / for flowers / were remembered" (47). In a simple gesture the poet realizes the power of memory. He sees more clearly the necessary politics of the imagination:

> Literate people lived here,
> whose sense of themselves as a nation drew breath
> long after their armies disbanded;
> whose pride was made homely by ruin;
> who gave more than they got.
>
> In their community the gifted and the gracious led;
> but everyone had a place,
> and no two people were the same. (47)

Finally, in its calm assessment of the unknowable, yet unescapable, burden of the past, "Sewanee in Ruins" captures the complexity of the mind as it engages a history it could not know—but must, nonetheless, tell. The speaker knows that his research has not necessarily brought him closer to fact or truth, since what he learns is, at least in part, "an old story but not a true one, / we learn, after these years of telling it." (39). But is the truth of the matter justification for writing? No, says the poet. We tell the necessary stories: "What flesh and blood, / what whispers, what glances, what twists of fate, / are wrapped in words!" (41).

Tillinghast's debt to Robert Frost is pervasive and strong. Consequently, it is not surprising that "Sewanee" opens and closes with echoes of "Directive," Frost's poem of historical reconstruction. In "Directive," Frost has linked the efficacy of truth to the fertility of the imagination. He has sought to validate and to understand the moral claim that poetry makes upon the imagination. Like Frost, Tillinghast has concluded that poetry is the necessary human act—a sacramental, transcendent, life-creating act. In memory you find yourself, in poetry you make yourself and construct a human place saved from time. Poetry is not life recollected in tranquility—as Tillinghast wisely asks in one of his poems, "Were things as I remembered them?" Rather it is the mind, "filling more space than the space it fills," as stated in *The Knife and Other Poems* (24). And these things—human things—will mean more than they mean.

SURVEY OF CRITICISM

Until Alan Williamson's *Introspection and Contemporary Poetry* (1984), response to Richard Tillinghast had been limited to short notices in journals and a handful of longer review essays. Williamson himself originally reviewed Tillinghast in 1970, drawn to him, he said, first as a "confessional poet." At the time, Williamson credited the poet for "repossessing areas of feeling, the exotic and the nostalgic" and for encouraging "intensity without rhetoric" (91–92).

Eleven years later (1981), Williamson reviewed Tillinghast's *The Knife and Other Poems,* observing that the "spiritual journeys and renewals," the concrete memories and fantasies" of *Sleep Watch* have been placed in a context emphasizing "what politics . . . remain available to the poet" (249). In *Introspection and Contemporary Poetry* Williamson comments about the trend in contemporary confessional poetry. In his words, "What had begun as a method of in-

vestigating sensibilities became, itself, a sensibility'' (150). He studies
Tillinghast in a chapter (''The Future of Personal Poetry'') whose concerns
include ''the tactics of autobiography'' (148). He sees Tillinghast as being
shaped by Southern fugitive ''carefulness,'' though modified by ''popular music
of the 1960s; the mystical and revolutionary West Coast Counterculture'' (155).
Speaking of Tillinghast's ''surrealism,'' Williamson suggests that what sets him
apart from his contemporaries is the ''yearned-for, exotic lavishness of the inner
world invoked'' (155).

A number of critics have drawn attention to Tillinghast's historical and, in
some cases, archetypal sensibilities. James Atlas, whose anthology *Ten American Poets* (1973) includes Tillinghast, elsewhere has commented on the poet's
ability to connect a moment's experience with a broader range of human concerns: ''Then every instant becomes a history, a past, forging from the eye's
experience an impression of what it means to be alive.'' Wyatt Prunty (1984),
similarly, has observed that the early Tillinghast ''seems to have looked at history from the perspective of one whose myth has failed'' (966). In attempting
to make up for what he found lacking, according to Prunty, Tillinghast has
moved in his more recent poetry from ''a question born of history'' to one that
has ''expanded to mythical dimensions'' (967). Tillinghast's long poem on the
history and future of the University of the South (''Sewanee in Ruins'') confirms
the observations of these critics.

Stephen Behrendt (1982), noting that James Dickey has called Tillinghast
''the best poet of the younger generation'' (89), suggests it is too early for ''accolades'' (90). Nonetheless, there seems a growing number of critics who see in
Tillinghast's work a quality particularly—and importantly—American. Mark
Jarman (1985) calls Tillinghast a ''narrative poet,'' who is ''in touch with the
American moment'' (334–35). Jonathan Holden, also reviewing *Our Flag Was
Still There,* (1985) concludes that it is ''an important book. Its attempt to re-
construct some sense of quotidian American historicity is daring.'' (158). Thomas Swiss (1985) calls this volume of six poems ''one of the best books of
poetry published in 1984'' (lxxx). His reasoning echoes other critics and seems
an appropriate summation of Tillinghast's strengths: ''Tillinghast's method of
attribution and allusion always enlarges the vision of the poem [''Sewanee in
Ruins''], giving it a psychological and sociological depth that is particularly appealing in a time when so much of our poetry seems limited by self-
consciousness and generalized introspection. . . . Tillinghast's poem blends . . .
public events and private utterance'' (lxxxi).

BIBLIOGRAPHY

Works by Richard Tillinghast

The Keeper. Cambridge, Mass.: Pym-Randall Press, 1967.
Sleep Watch. Middletown, Conn.: Wesleyan University Press, 1969.
The Knife and Other Poems. Middletown, Conn.: Wesleyan University Press, 1980.

Sewanee in Ruins. Sewanee, Tenn.: Sewanee University Press, 1983.

Our Flag Was Still There. Middletown, Conn. Wesleyan University Press, 1984.

Twos. Ann Arbor: Otherwind Press, 1987.

A Quiet Print in Kinvara. Galway, Ireland: Salmon, 1991.

"An Elegist's New England, Duddhist's Dante." *New York Times Book Review* (February 24, 1991): 18–19.

"Poems That Get Their Hands Dirty." *New York Times Book Review* (December 8, 1991): 7.

"A Hornpipe, a Reel and a Pint." *New York Times* (December 29, 1991): sec. 5, 8.

"Across Ireland, Leisurely." *New York Times* (October 18, 1992): sec. 5, 8.

"James Dickey: The Whole Motion." *Southern Review* 28 (October 1992): 971–80.

"Letter from Galway." *Hudson Review* 44 (Winter 1992): 534–41.

"Memphis Barbecue: Hold the Frills." *New York Times* (January 17, 1993): sec. 5, 8.

The Stonecutter's Hand. Boston: Godine, 1994.

Interviews with Richard Tillinghast

"An Interview with Shelby Foote." *Ploughshares* 9 (1983): 118–31.

Studies of Richard Tillinghast

Atlas, James. "At the First Doorway of the Lost Life." *Chicago Review* 22, no. 1 (Autumn 1970): 131–37.

Behrendt, Stephen. "The Sharp and the Dull." *Prairie Schooner* 56, no.1 (Spring 1982): 89–90.

Bennett, Bruce. "Ghosts and Crises." *New York Times Book Review* (May 10, 1981): 12, 27–28.

Breslin, Paul. "Points West and South." *New York Times Book Review* (July 22, 1984): 15.

Cotter, James Finn. "Outer and Inner Poetry." *Hudson Review* 34, no. 2 (Summer 1981): 277–89.

Cox, C. B. Editorial. *Critical Quarterly* 23, no. 3 (Autumn 1981): 2–4.

Doreski, William. "The Mind Afoot." *Ploughshares* 7, no. 1 (1981): 157–63.

Grosholz, Emily. "Arms and the Muse: Four Poets." *New England Review and Bread Loaf Quarterly* 5, no. 4 (Summer 1983): 634–46.

Holden, Jonathan. "Recent Poetry." *Western Humanities Review* 39 (1985): 155–64.

Jarman, Mark. "Generations and Contemporaries." *Hudson Review* 38, no. 2 (Summer 1985): 334–36.

Morris, Harry. "The Passions of Poets." *Sewanee Review* 79 (Spring 1971): 301–9.

Prunty, Wyatt. "Myth, History, and Myth Again." *Southern Review,* n.s. 20 (October 1984): 958–68.

Stanford, Donald E. "Adventures among the Absolutes: Four Contemporary Volumes of Poetry." *Michigan Quarterly Review* 25, no. 3 (Summer 1986): 607–15.

Swiss, Thomas. "Speaking for the Past." *Sewanee Review* 93, no. 4 (Fall 1985): lxxix–lxxxii.

Taylor, Henry. "Boom, Recent Poetry from University Presses." *Georgia Review* 24, no. 3 (Fall 1970): 349–55.

Watson, Robert. "Five Sleepers." *Poetry* 97, no. 3 (December 1970): 204–10.
Williamson, Alan. "At Borders, Think." *Parnassus: Poetry in Review* 9, no. 2 (Fall–Winter 1981): 247–54.
———. "The Future of Confession." *Shenandoah* 21, no.4 (Summer 1970): 89–93.
———. *Introspection and Contemporary Poetry.* Harvard University Press: Cambridge, 1984.

Margaret Walker
(1915–   )

Margaret Walker's place as poet and novelist is already firmly established. Her first collection of poems, *For My People,* earned her the Yale Award for Younger Poets in 1942. Twenty-four years later Houghton Mifflin published Walker's *Jubilee* (1966), an historical novel that has since been translated into many languages and gone through scores of printings. Twenty-five years after *Jubilee,* in addition to two books of poems, she saw the publication of her biography of Richard Wright (1988), her collection of new and previously published poems (1989), and her essay collection (1990). All of her titles remain in print.

BIOGRAPHY

Margaret Abigail Walker was born in Birmingham, Alabama, on July 7, 1915. In spite of being black in the rigidly segregated South, she grew up with a strong sense of self-worth and an awareness that the oppression of her people was cruel and unjust. This confidence must partially be traced to her parents, Reverend Sigismund Walker and Marion Dozier Walker.

Both parents were well-educated and never questioned that Margaret, her two younger sisters, and younger brother would be also. Sigismund Walker had come from Jamaica to the United States to complete his education. Dissatisfied with the applied programs at Tuskegee, he went to Gammon Theological Seminary in Atlanta for a divinity degree. He met Margaret's mother when he took his first Methodist pastorship in Pensacola, Florida. Later he received an M. A. in biblical literature from Northwestern University. Margaret Walker has always identified with her father's love for ideas and his broad humanism, a humanism reflected in his proficiency in several ancient and modern languages. Margaret's mother played the piano for the church and taught music. She read poetry to

Margaret as a child and was the first to have confidence in Margaret as a poet. Although both parents were deeply religious, Marion Walker's upbringing had been Baptist and more traditional. She admired Booker T. Washington, a man for whom Margaret's father had little patience. He had friends among the Garveyites and embraced the ideas of W. E. B. Du Bois.

The Walkers moved several times during Margaret's early childhood. After first grade in Meridian, Mississippi, at age 5, Margaret returned to Birmingham for 2 or 3 years. When Margaret was 10, the Walkers moved to New Orleans, where the family still has the home that her father bought that year. Margaret's maternal grandmother, Elvira Ware Dozier, was with them always. The stories that Elvira Dozier told Margaret about slave life in Georgia and Elvira's own mother, Margaret Duggans Ware Brown, provided the impetus for Walker's novel *Jubilee,* with the main character Vyry modeled after Margaret's great-grandmother. Margaret completed high school and her first 2 years of college in New Orleans, all by the age of 16.

Throughout her childhood Margaret was exposed to famous black people. She spent much of her youth on black college campuses where both parents taught. Margaret heard James Weldon Johnson read from *God's Trombones* and heard Marian Anderson and Roland Hayes sing. When she was 16, Langston Hughes read at New Orleans University (now Dillard) where both her parents were teaching. Hughes read some of Margaret's poems and encouraged her to pursue formal training, which he thought only possible outside the South.

Less than a year later, Walker enrolled as a junior at Northwestern University. During her first year at Northwestern, she heard and met W.E.B. Du Bois, whom she counts with Langston Hughes and Richard Wright as one of the three black writers who influenced her thinking. Walker graduated with a B.A. in English in 1935, shortly after her 20th birthday. In spite of excellent professors at Northwestern, her favorite being Edward Buell Hungerford, the Chicago years following were the most vital to her creative development. She told Nikki Giovanni (1974), "I found my voice in the thirties" (48): 1936 to 1939 seem to be the pivotal years. During those pivotal years Walker published some of the powerful poems that she is still best known for—those, for example, published in the journal *Poetry:* "For My People" (1937), "We Have Been Believers" (1938), and "The Struggle Staggers Us" (1939). To the same years belongs her involvement in the Federal Writers' Project, which provided not only a living wage but also a chance to write and be among a host of talented people, such as Nelson Algren, Arna Bontemps, Fenton Johnson, Frank Yerby, Katherine Dunham, and—most important for Walker—Richard Wright.

When Walker met Wright in February 1936 at a gathering of what became the South Side Writer's Group, Wright had already been in Chicago for 9 years. That spring Walker joined the Federal Writers' Project and saw Wright again. The two Southerners became good friends. Addison Gayle, Jr., literary critic and a Wright biographer, in his work *Richard Wright: Ordeal of a Native Son* (Garden City: Doubleday, 1980), judges Walker's friendship as contributing im-

portantly to Wright's work. According to Gayle, Wright could lower his pro-
tective shield somewhat, "discuss his own writing and other writers, and offer
philosophical reflections upon the world" with a woman whose "intellect [was]
equal to his own, a woman who disdained condescension" (91). They read each
other's work in progress and revised together. Walker typed *Lawd Today* and
guided the self-educated man in grammar. After Wright moved to New York in
1937, at his request for newspaper clippings regarding Robert Nixon's confessions to multiple murders and rapes, Walker sent him clippings from five Chicago papers for a solid year, knowing how uncannily applicable the Nixon
material was to Wright's own work on *Native Son* (1940).

Wright's and Walker's differences must have been stimulating and corrective
also. Whereas Wright wrote out of anger, Walker never has. With her basic
idealism and grounding in Christianity, she could not accept the dialectical materialism of Wright's fellow communists. Still, Wright contributed to Walker's
thinking about race and class. In her interview with Jerry Ward (1988), Walker
said that "ever since Chicago days I have been committed to a life of the artist
for the people. I think that's the one thing I got out of my association with
Wright" (526). It was a severe blow when in June 1939, a few days into the
League of American Writers Congress in New York, Wright abruptly refused
to have anything to do with Walker. His biographers, including Walker, have
attempted to account for this sudden and permanent rupture. Whatever the explanation, their few years as friends had been mutually beneficial.

The year 1939 marked another transition for Walker. An act of Congress
placing 18-month limits for participation in the Writers' Project meant that
Walker's term was up. Through Arna Bontemps's indirect recommendation,
Walker went to Iowa to pursue a master's in creative writing. There she roomed
with Elizabeth Catlett, whose 1987 portrait *For My People—With Love, For
Margaret, My Friend* is the frontispiece for *This Is My Century*. Although Walker clashed with Paul Engle, with whom she studied, she has credited him with
prompting her to use folk traditions and the ballad form in her poetry. Walker's
thesis at Iowa became her first collection of poetry, *For My People*. Several
poems, such as the title one, appeared in print in the 1930s, but most were new.
Two years later, in 1942, she won the prestigious Yale award, and the book
was published with a foreword by Stephen Vincent Benét.

Walker has supported herself and her family most of her life by teaching: 2
years at Livingstone College in North Carolina, where she met and married
Firnist Alexander in 1943; an intervening year at West Virginia State College;
and from 1949 until early retirement in 1979, at Jackson State in Jackson, Mississippi, which remains her home and, as she told Ward, the "epicenter of her
life" (515). During her teaching years she researched *Jubilee* when she could;
but without funded leave time, writing was impossible. Walker continually dealt
with the demands of teaching while receiving salaries that were low at best—
and blatantly lower for women. Her health was poor and her husband disabled,
and by the 1950s four children depended upon her. In "On Being Female, Black,

and Free,'' in *The Writer on Her Work,* edited by Janet Sternberg (New York: Norton, 1980), Walker stated that ''keeping the wolf from the door has been my full-time job for more than forty years'' (101).

Fortunately, there have been intervals off for funded research. In 1953 she had a Ford Fellowship, which allowed time for travel, and research and writing at Yale. She began concentrated work in the Ph.D. program at Iowa in 1962. After two years of course work and exams, Walker finally could write full-time the Civil War novel about her great-grandmother, the story she had determined to tell from the time she was a child listening to her grandmother. Her long essay *How I Wrote "Jubilee"* chronicles the intense but fragmented time she had spent with the material since, at age 19, she first typed three hundred pages for Professor Hungerford's class at Northwestern. Walker completed the novel, which was her dissertation, and received her Ph.D. in 1966.

While Walker was at Iowa, Jackson had become a center for some of the impassioned and violent confrontations of the civil-rights era. Walker was shaken by both public and personal events. At her own segregated institution, Jackson State, the administration warned students and faculty against questioning the system. Medgar Evers, the black civil-rights leader who was fatally shot in front of his house in 1963, was her neighbor. In 1970, two students at Jackson State were killed. That same year one of her sons returned from serving as a marine in Viet Nam. A calculated act of violence nearly killed her other son, a law student at the time. Disturbing, too, was her 1977 lawsuit against Alex Haley and his publisher for Haley's alleged plagiarizing from *Jubilee* for his *Roots.* In September 1978, a New York federal-court judge dismissed the charge of copyright infringement, finding that the similarities were based on folk custom, standard scenes, or typical expressions, none of which were protected by the copyright laws.

During those turbulent years Walker published two volumes of poetry, *Prophets for a New Day* (1970) and *October Journey* (1973), and a book of conversations with Nikki Giovanni, *A Poetic Equation* (1974). She initiated a Black Studies program for Jackson State; and in the early 1970s, she became the director of the Institute for the Study of History, Life, and Culture of Black People at Jackson State. This directorship allowed her to put such exceptional programs together as the Phillis Wheatley Poetry Festival in 1973. In 1972 she conducted research under NEH for the Wright biography continuing, as she had for years, to lecture and give readings, participate in conferences, and serve on national boards. She was a visiting professor at Northwestern University in the spring of 1969, and since that time has received an honorary doctorate from there as well as from several other universities. She received the 1989 Feminist Press literary award for her achievements. She has served on the advisory committee of the ambitious Black Women Oral History Project at Radcliffe's Schlesinger Library and has also been one of the sixty-six black women whose significant contributions to black life prompted their being chosen as subjects of the tapes and ten-volume printed collection issued in 1991.

Since she entered her 70s, three important books have been added to her oeuvre: *Richard Wright: Daemonic Genius* (1988), *This Is My Century: New and Collected Poems* (1989), and *How I Wrote "Jubilee" and Other Essays on Life and Literature* (1990). In 1991 the biography brought Walker before the courts a second time, this time against charges of copyright violations made by Wright's widow. In a ruling heralded by free speech advocates, a Manhattan federal appeals court supported Walker's right as biographer to use segments from his unpublished letters and journal entries. Walker is now writing her autobiography and has plans for turning her unfinished novel *Goose Island* (from the 1930s) into a short-story collection. She stated in 1986 that she had "four novels left," among them *Minna and Jim,* a sequel to *Jubilee*. Still, Walker sees herself first and always as a poet—and the poetry continues.

MAJOR THEMES

In her first published poem, "I Want to Write," the 19-year-old Margaret Walker expressed her wish to be both transcriber of her people's experience— "I want to write the songs of my people"—and the visionary interpreter whose words will provide "a mirrored pool of brilliance in the dawn." Most of her writings in the ensuing fifty-six years reveal that she has remained true to those objectives. As Maryemma Graham points out regarding Walker's essay "The Humanistic Tradition of Afro-American Literature," in *How I Wrote "Jubilee" and Other Essays on Life and Literature,* Walker has ascribed a revolutionary role to art. Her poetry and novel restore and reaffirm for black Americans what has been denied or negated and provide hope of a new day. The opening of the last stanza of "For My People" (1937) is now famous: "Let a new earth rise." The penultimate line in the last poem of *This Is My Century,* "The Labyrinth of Love" (1986), looks to "the glory of the morning of all life" before concluding, "AMEN."

Walker's commitment to her people has been deep and thorough. Even though she was educated according to a traditional British and American canon, she has neither alluded to these works nor adhered to any purely Western style. Instead, her writing is consistent with her claim in "The Humanistic Tradition" that African-American literature is not Anglo-Saxon or Anglo-American "in content, in tone, or in philosophy; and always it is permeated with ideas of revolt against artifice, sterility, self-consciousness, [and] contrived morality" (122). Her style is always natural and the material easily accessible. Walker has drawn on such African-American traditions as folk legends, spirituals and blues, the Bible, African-American history as she has witnessed and researched it, and both Africa and the American South as homeland to be reclaimed.

The South is subject and theme in some of Walker's most moving poems, such as "Southern Song," "Sorrow Home," "Delta," and "October Journey." Each evokes specific images of a beautiful and nurturing natural world, which contrasts ironically and disturbingly with the pain and violence issuing from that land. Such tensions and piling on of contradictory images and emotions in order to encompass the complexity of black life in America are typical of many other poems as well, including the seven-poem group called *Farish Street* that concludes *This Is My Century.* The oppression and suffering of black Americans are there, but so are stoicism, mystery, and vitality.

A number of her poems, especially in *Prophets for a New Day,* arise out of the shocking events and heroic acts of the civil-rights movement. She has couched eight of those poems in Old Testament imagery, linking Old Testament prophets with six black leaders of the period: for example, Amos, a pastor "in the depths of Alabama"; Jeremiah, now an Atlanta man named Benjamin; Isaiah, sitting in court in New York. By this method individual heroism transcends time and place and certainly race. These poems point to another important theme of Margaret Walker's work—that is, the humanity and power of black Americans to redeem us all. She has discussed this potential in "Humanistic Tradition" and best illustrates it with the heroic Vyry of *Jubilee.* In the course of the long novel, Vyry endures outrage after outrage that went hand-in-hand with slavery and its aftermath. She forgives her slave mistress and finally even elicits some white neighbors' goodwill in the racist and violence-prone post-Civil War community where she and Innis Brown manage to settle. As her husband Innis Brown learns, Vyry is "touched with a spiritual fire and permeated with a spiritual wholeness that had been forged in a crucible of suffering." Walker suggests that it takes one who has suffered so to resurrect what is good and true in the human spirit.

SURVEY OF CRITICISM

With her reputation established in the 1940s, Walker is still viewed primarily in the light of her early accomplishments and as a bridge between writers of the Harlem Renaissance and black writers since the 1960s. Although most scholars think of Walker first as a poet, *Jubilee* currently receives as much critical attention as her poetry, perhaps because novels by black women have emerged with such authority and power in the last decades. *Jubilee* and Walker's first volume of poetry, *For My People,* remain her best known and most respected works. But Walker also has a strong presence as a personality—from the young poet who spoke for her people in the 1930s to a *grand dame* of black women writers—a woman who, as Sonia Sanchez has written in a poem inspired by Walker's presence at a Black Feminist Conference in 1977, is "a strong gust of a / woman" who makes "our names be- / come known to us."

Jubilee is read, translated, sold, and included in course syllabi far out of proportion to the critical attention it has received. The initial reviews tended to be very positive, though reservations voiced then have persisted. As a historical novel, it has been criticized both for the imperfect blend of historical data and fiction and for Walker's reliance on Southern stereotypes of nineteenth-century blacks and whites (see, e.g., Chapman (1966), Christian (1980), and Davis

(1974)). Troublesome to some critics has been Vyry's message of forgiveness after her lifetime of outrages at the hands of whites.

Nevertheless, Walker is praised for being the first to render faithfully and extensively Southern black experience of the Civil War and for the wealth of folk tradition illuminating the text. And some thoughtful studies assert that in crucially effective and realistic ways Walker's portrayal of her central characters has revised stereotypes. Bell (1987) calls Vyry "one of the most memorable women in contemporary Afro-American fiction" (287), and Gabbin (1990) claims that Vyry "breaks the mold" (254) of stereotypes. Klotman (1977) treats *Jubilee* within the slave narrative tradition. Traylor (1987), Pettis (1990), and Gwin (1985) see *Jubilee* as a singular achievement. Gwin considers *Jubilee* the culmination of a century-long literary tradition of "profoundly ambivalent relationships between black and white southern women," with Vyry's character, her gestures of forgiveness, demonstrating that "racial reconciliation is possible" and "love is redemptive and regenerative" (153). Pettis calls Walker a "primary forger" in a new tradition of black historical novels with female protagonists: for novelists who represent atypical women under slavery, according to Pettis, Walker's thorough portrayal of Vyry's slave culture is the "necessary prerequisite."

Both Traylor and Spillers (1987) have analyzed aspects of Walker's narrative method and its relation to the novel's meaning. Traylor argues that *Jubilee* reflects the "blues mode," a mode arising from West African religion and black experience in America. Walker's songs throughout the text serve as an analogue of Vyry's—and a people's—repeated but progressive movements from dissolution toward wholeness. Spillers makes a good case for Walker's having imaginatively extended her hero Vyry and Vyry's story into metaphor, with Vyry an heroic representative, a "corporate ideal," of a people responding to the divine will of God.

Just as some critics have seen Vyry's story as the story of her people, almost every critic has found Walker's poems, particularly those in *For My People,* truly what the title proclaims. The poems communicate directly and powerfully in cadences that recall the sermons Walker grew up hearing. Most written about and praised has been the title poem. The editor of *Poetic Equation* (1974) calls "For My People" "not only [Walker's] signature poem, but the signature poem of a people" (xi). Collier (1984) says, "We knew the poem. It was ours," and singles out *For My People* as Walker's "most vital contribution to our [black] culture." On the basis of these poems, Hull (1975) names Walker the major black poet from 1930 to 1945. In his 1942 foreword, Benét declares, "Out of deep feeling, Miss Walker has made living and passionate speech." Barksdale (1986) analyzes the sources of the rhetorical power, paying special attention to "For My People," which, he says, by itself is a singular literary achievement. Barksdale and others find that Walker has managed to fuse with the verbal power the pain, joy, collective memory, and "down-home" religion—that is, the complexity, richness, and contradictions of the black experience in America.

Although *Prophets for a New Day* has never received the attention of the first volume, Barksdale names it "the premier poetic statement of the death-riddled decade of the 1960s," and Miller (1986) judges many poems in *Prophets* superior to the second and third sections of *For My People.* For Miller, the volume's grounding in biblical myth has helped to restore the cadence and tighten the images. The influential anthology *The Forerunners: Black Poets in America* takes two of its three Walker poems from *Prophets.*

October Journey, which is shorter and less unified, has prompted less attention, and there has been little time for critical response to the nearly forty new poems in Walker's *This Is My Century: New and Collected Poems.* Traylor's long discussion, which preceded publication of *This Is My Century* by two years, is not very useful since she does not approach the volume critically and quotes extensively without providing the final pagination. Although very positive, Howe's review (1990) is more attentive to the earlier poems.

Both of Walker's two recent books in prose, *How I Wrote "Jubilee" and Other Essays* and *Richard Wright: Daemonic Genius,* have been welcomed by most reviewers, but the biography has generated more interest and some mixed responses. Nearly all readers of the biography have agreed that Walker's accounts of Wright at a critical period in both of those writers' lives have contributed substantially to our understanding of Richard Wright. A number of these readers have voiced some reservations about her style, degree of objectivity, or psychological approach. Wright biographer Michel Fabré (1989) has been the most outspoken critic, going through passage after passage in order to refute information given as fact, to question Walker's sources or authority, and to point out what he considers irresponsible innuendo. Whatever their response to the biography, most readers would heartily disagree with Fabré's conclusion that the biography "raises serious questions about Margaret Walker as writer and critic." And the 1990 collection of Walker's essays and speeches reaffirms in yet another genre her great importance as a spokesperson for her time and place and all her people.

BIBLIOGRAPHY

Works by Margaret Walker

For My People. New Haven: Yale University Press, 1942.
Jubilee. Boston: Houghton Mifflin, 1966.
Prophets for a New Day. Detroit: Broadside, 1970.
How I Wrote "Jubilee." Chicago: Third World, 1972.
October Journey. Detroit: Broadside, 1973.
Richard Wright: Daemonic Genius. New York: Warner Books, 1988.
This Is My Century: New and Collected Poems. Athens: University of Georgia Press, 1989.
How I Wrote "Jubilee" and Other Essays on Life and Literature. Edited by Maryemma Graham. New York: Feminist Press, 1990.

Interviews with Margaret Walker

Egejuru, Phanuel, and Robert Elliot Fox. "An Interview with Margaret Walker." *Callaloo* 2 (May 1979): 29–35.

Freibert, Lucy M. "Southern Song: An Interview with Margaret Walker." *Frontiers: A Journal of Women Studies* 9 (1987): 50–56.

Greenlee, Marcia. "Margaret Walker Alexander." In *The Black Women Oral History Project* vol.2, edited by Ruth Edmonds Hill, 1–65. Westport, Conn.: Meckler, 1991.

Jones, John Griffin. "Margaret Walker Alexander." In *Mississippi Writers Talking,* vol. 2, edited by John Griffin Jones, 120–46. Jackson: University Press of Mississippi, 1983.

A Poetic Equation: Conversations between Nikki Giovanni and Margaret Walker. Washington, D.C.: Howard University Press, 1974.

Rowell, Charles H. "Poetry, History and Humanism: An Interview with Margaret Walker." *Black World* 25 (December 1975): 4–17.

Tate, Claudia. "Margaret Walker." In *Black Women Writers at Work,* edited by Claudia Tate, 188–204. New York: Continuum, 1983.

Ward, Jerry W., Jr. "A Writer for Her People: An Interview with Dr. Margaret Walker Alexander." *Mississippi Quarterly* 41 (1988): 515–27.

Studies of Margaret Walker

Barksdale, Richard K. "Margaret Walker: Folk Orature and Historical Prophecy." In *Black American Poets between Worlds, 1940–1960,* edited by R. Baxter Miller, 104–17. Knoxville: University of Tennessee Press, 1986.

Bell, Bernard W. *The Afro-American Novel and Its Tradition.* Amherst: University of Massachusetts Press, 1987.

Chapman, Abraham. Review of *Jubilee. Saturday Review* 49 (September 24, 1966); 43–44.

Christian, Barbara. *Black Women Novelists.* Westport, Conn.: Greenwood, 1980.

———. " 'Somebody Forgot to Tell Somebody Something': African-American Women's Historical Novels." In *Wild Women in the Whirlwind: Afra-American Culture and the Contemporary Literary Renaissance,* edited by Joanne M. Braxton and Andree Nicola McLaughlin, 326–41. New Brunswick, N.J.: Rutgers University Press, 1990.

Collier, Eugenia. "Fields Watered with Blood: Myth and Ritual in the Poetry of Margaret Walker." In *Black Women Writers (1950–1980): A Critical Evaluation,* edited by Mari Evans, 499–510. Garden City, N.Y.: Anchor-Doubleday, 1984.

Davis, Arthur P. *From the Dark Tower: Afro-American Writers, 1900–1960.* Washington, D.C.: Howard University Press, 1974.

Fabré, Michel. "Margaret Walker's Richard Wright: A Wrong Righted or Wright Wronged?" *Mississippi Quarterly* 42 (1989): 429–50.

Gabbin, Joanne V. "A Laying On of Hands: Black Women Writers Exploring the Roots of Their Folk and Cultural Tradition." In *Wild Women in the Whirlwind: Afra-American Culture and the Contemporary Literary Renaissance,* edited by Joanne M. Braxton and Andree Nichola McLaughlin, 246–63. New Brunswick, N.J.: Rutgers University Press, 1990.

Garner, Linda Mebane. ''Twentieth-Century Marble Goddesses: Victorian and Modernist Portrayals of the Antebellum Southern Lady in Stark Young's *So Red the Rose,* William Faulkner's *The Unvanquished* and *Absalom, Absalom!,* and Margaret Walker's *Jubilee.''* Ph.D. diss., University of Missouri, 1987.

Giddings, Paula. ''Some Themes in the Poetry of Margaret Walker.'' *Black World* 21, no.2 (1971): 20–25.

Goodman, Charlotte. ''From Uncle Tom's Cabin to Vyry's Kitchen: The Black Female Folk Tradition in Margaret Walker's *Jubilee.''* In *Tradition and the Talents of Women,* edited by Florence Howe, 328–37. Urbana: University of Illinois Press, 1991.

Graham, Maryemma. Preface and introduction to *How I Wrote ''Jubilee'' and Other Essays on Life and Literature,* by Margaret Walker. Edited by Maryemma Graham. New York: Feminist Press, 1990.

Gwin, Minrose C. *Black and White Women of the Old South,* 151–70. Knoxville: University of Tennessee Press, 1985.

Harris, Trudier. ''Black Writers in a Changed Landscape, Since 1950.'' In *The History of Southern Literature,* edited by Louis D. Rubin, Jr., Blyden Jackson, Rayburn S. Moore, Lewis P. Simpson, and Thomas Daniel Young, 66–77. Baton Rouge: Louisiana State University Press, 1985.

Howe, Florence. ''Poet of History, Poet of Vision.'' Review of *This Is My Century. The Women's Review of Books* 7 (July 1990): 41–42.

Hull, Gloria. ''Black Women Poets from Wheatley to Walker.'' *Negro American Literature Forum* 9, no. 3 (1975): 91–96.

Jackson, Blyden. ''Margaret Walker.'' In *Lives of Mississippi Authors, 1817–1967,* edited by James B. Lloyd, 444–46. Jackson: University Press of Mississippi, 1981.

Johnson, Charles R. ''Richard Wright Loved, Lost, Hated, Missed.'' Review of *Richard Wright: Daemonic Genius. Los Angeles Times Book Review* (February 19, 1989): 9.

Keizs, Marcia Veronica. ''The Development of a Dialectic: Private and Public Patterns in the Work of Margaret Walker and Gwendolyn Brooks.'' Ph.D. diss., Columbia University Teachers College, 1984.

Klotman, Phyllis Rauch. '''Oh Freedom'—Women and History in Margaret Walker's *Jubilee.''* *Black American Literature Forum* 11, no. 4 (1977): 139–45.

Lee, Ulysses. ''Two Poets in Wartime.'' Review of *For My People. Opportunity* 20 (December 1942): 379–80.

Martin, Waldo E., Jr. ''The Troubled Journey of Richard Wright.'' Review of *Richard Wright: Daemonic Genius. Washington Post Book World* (April 16, 1989); 6.

Miller, R. Baxter. ''The 'Intricate Design' of Margaret Walker: Literary and Biblical Re-Creation in Southern History.'' In *Black American Poets Between Worlds, 1940–1960,* edited by R. Baxter Miller, 118–35. Knoxville: University of Tennessee Press, 1986.

Pettis, Joyce. ''Margaret Walker: Black Woman Writer of the South.'' In *Southern Women Writers: The New Generation,* edited by Tonette Bond Inge, 9–19. Tuscaloosa: University of Alabama Press, 1990.

Spillers, Hortense J. ''A Hateful Passion, A Lost Love.'' In *Feminist Issues in Literary Scholarship,* edited by Shari Benstock. Bloomington: Indiana University Press, 1987.

Thomas, Keith L. ''Margaret Walker Gives Voice to Literary Legacy of Richard

Wright.'' Review of *Richard Wright: Daemonic Genius. Atlanta Constitution* (December 21, 1988); C1.

Traylor, Eleanor. '''Bolder Measures Crashing Through': Margaret Walker's Poem of the Century.'' *Callaloo* 10 (Fall 1987): 570–95.

———. ''Music as Theme: The Blues Mode in the Works of Margaret Walker.'' In *Black Women Writers (1950–1980): A Critical Evaluation,* edited by Mari Evans, 511–25. Garden City, N.Y.: Anchor-Doubleday, 1984.

Williams, Delores S. ''Black Women's Literature and the Task of Feminist Theology.'' In *Immaculate and Powerful: The Female in Sacred Image and Social Reality,* edited by Constance H. Buchanan and Margaret R. Miles, 88–110. Boston: Beacon, 1985.

THOMAS E. DASHER

James Whitehead
(1936–   )

James Whitehead's great-great-grandfather served as a Confederate surgeon in the Civil War and later wrote a prose romance about the conflict between the life of practical activity and the life of the spirit. In many ways, Whitehead's poetry, fiction, and life could fill such a romance. Perhaps best known as director of the Creative Writing Programs at the University of Arkansas, among the top programs in the country, he is also the author of two well-received volumes of poems and of the novel *Joiner* (1973), which has been called one of the fourteen major Southern fictions after Faulkner. Teacher, poet, and novelist, Whitehead has combined these often disparate roles with remarkable success during his 25-year career.

BIOGRAPHY

James Whitehead was born in St. Louis on March 15, 1936, the son of Dick Bruun Whitehead, a bacteriologist, and Ruth Ann Tillotson Whitehead, a social worker. After several moves and his father's service in the military, the family settled in Mississippi when Whitehead was in the fifth grade. In Hattiesburg, "all hell broke loose. It was the wound; it was the absolute trauma" (Carr 1972, 265). Like Royal Boykin in *Joiner,* Whitehead was tied to a tree and stoned because he was considered an outsider. Repeatedly humiliated, he discovered football. "I put on my equipment and ran out on the field and began to leap on people and drag 'em to the ground and everybody began screaming and yelling and here were all the bastards that had been beating the hell out of me, and under the legalized ritual of the game I was tromping the hell out of them. And they left me alone" (Carr 1972, 265–66). An uneven student, he worked in the local lumber mills from the time he was 15. He also became a dedicated athlete who graduated from Jackson Central High School in 1954 after playing on several winning football teams.

On a football scholarship, Whitehead entered Vanderbilt University but was hurt in his freshman year and was red-shirted in his sophomore year. He never played much because of his injured arm, which had to be held in place with a chain when he played. Earlier he had written stories, but he had mainly written devotional material for the Presbyterian Church. In fact, he planned to be a minister and wrote sermons to preach—one of the last in iambic pentameter, but he left the church while at Vanderbilt, unable to accept the theology associated with Christology and special revelation. At Vanderbilt he majored in philosophy even though he initially hated the school, having lost his high-school sweetheart, his religion, and his ability to play football during his freshman year.

During his last 3 years (he stayed to work on his M.A. in English, which he received in 1960), he discovered, as he has said, "where I was to be, to a certain extent, in the world" (Jones 1983, 159). He studied under Donald Davidson and Walter Sullivan, made several important friends, and began to write poetry and fiction, which were published in the Vanderbilt literary magazine, *The Vagabond.* During his junior year, after he had written and published his first story, he went on a pilgrimage to see William Faulkner. For several hours, he talked with his fellow Mississippian, who asked the young man to cut hay with him. Because of the weather, they never cut the hay; but Faulkner remained an influence on Whitehead's work. As Whitehead has said, "Faulkner is like the humidity in Mississippi. You don't avoid Mr. Faulkner, you grow up with him" (Jones 1983, 155). Whitehead insists, however, that Faulkner's influence was mostly indirect and that other writers, for example, Joyce Cary—for his "sensuality"—and Henry Miller—" for the descriptions of nature"—more clearly remained with him over the years.

A major turning point in his life during this period was meeting his future wife, Guendaline ("Gen") Graeber—according to Whitehead, "the good luck of my life"—who attended the Mississippi University for Women and summer school at Millsaps College, where she met Whitehead in 1957; Gen and James were married in 1959. Having written a novel as his thesis, Whitehead returned with his wife to Jackson to teach at Millsaps for 3 years, from 1960 to 1963. There he taught fifteen hours per semester and studied with a fellow instructor, Bob Padgett, to whom he would later dedicate his novel *Joiner.* Together they prepared their lessons and talked about literature. Padgett was particularly helpful in the early stages of *Joiner* when he read parts of the first two drafts of the four or five that the novel eventually went through.

Also at Millsaps, Whitehead wrote his first real poems. At first, he despaired as he sat at the table that his father had made from a door and that would appear later in *Joiner.* He has said that he was initially "influenced by stream of consciousness, impressionistic, surrealistic poets like Dylan Thomas and the early Robert Lowell. I thought that I could write that kind of poetry, but, in fact, I couldn't because what I did was essentially write bad imitations of Dylan Thomas which was standard operation and procedure of the late 1950's'' (Burton 1973, 72). But he turned to Robert Frost and others, such as Robert Penn Warren and, especially, R. L. Thomas, from whom he learned his trade, to ''objectify'' his work. He also began to read and teach Browning, whose dramatic monologues opened up new possibilities for Whitehead's own poetry. He wrote ''Delta Farmer in a Wet Summer,'' later published as the third poem in *Domains* (1966), which made a great difference in his poetry and gave him confidence; he had found ''a voice, strategy, technique.'' Whitehead later declared that it was ''the first poem I ever wrote that was mine, and I knew it'' (Jones 1983, 167). Whitehead also realized he had to go back to school. He needed more time to write and knew he would continue to be a college teacher. Since he did not want a Ph.D., he decided to pursue an M.F.A. in Creative Writing (both fiction and poetry) at the University of Iowa. There he worked with Donald Justice and R. V. Cassill and completed most of the poems he would publish in *Domains.*

The summer before he left for Iowa, on June 12, 1963, Medgar Evers was killed. Whitehead had met Evers at a social-science forum at Tougaloo and found him to be ''one of the few absolutely confident men I've ever met, as well as being beautiful.'' Evers spoke of his own inevitable death, and Whitehead became even more committed to the civil rights movement. It was a rough period in his life. ''I was so harried by being a husband who didn't know how to be a husband and a father who didn't know how to be a father and a teacher who didn't know how to be a teacher and a writer who didn't know how to be a writer'' (Jones 1983, 170–72). The violence and struggle in Mississippi and the turmoil in his own personal life thus provided the context for the journey west to Iowa as he sought knowledge of how to live successfully the roles he had chosen. The domains of his poems would be both love and politics. He has said that his first published collection ''is essentially a dramatic, objective, narrative collection in which scene, character, action, grammar—everything—is highly logical and highly moral. The poems dramatized my aversion to racism. As they appeared, they tended to be thematic although they were not intended to be'' (Burton 1973, 72).

At Iowa, the Whiteheads and their three young children settled in. Whitehead's best poems were often not well received in workshop because they ''were thought to be too blunt, they were too rough in meter and texture, and often called obscure.'' His fellow poets, from other parts of the country, preferred poems with ''a sense of flash'' like that found in the poem ''Domains,'' which Whitehead has seen as containing too much ''exercising.'' He himself developed his belief in the importance of rhyme and meter. ''The tension between the bare material line and the prose expression focuses and amplifies everything that goes on in a poem. That's the main thing that separates a poem from prose'' (Jones 1983, 176–78). He also began *Joiner.* In the spring of 1964, he wrote a 75-page short story, ''What Went Wrong,'' for R. V. Cassill's workshop. The story focused on Sonny Joiner's divorce from his wife. It was not a good story; but

Whitehead began almost immediately to develop it into a novel. By the time he finished his degree in 1965 and was interviewed for positions at Emory and Arkansas, he had completed 150 pages. Yet before the novel was published in 1971, it would go through at least four drafts. It had been bought by Knopf on the basis of the early fragment; but over a 2-year period, he would work with his editor Bob Gottlieb, whose support proved vital, now that he was teaching at Arkansas and had a family of seven children.

During the 2 years after signing a contract, Whitehead worked on *Joiner*—developing the voice, at the center of which is pain, and shaping the events of Joiner's life. A long and demanding manuscript, nearly 6,000 pages, the novel, so Whitehead thought, should be 25 pages shorter (the published text has 463 pages). Bob Padgett, who wanted the novel to be much shorter, convinced Whitehead to cut only thirteen pages. Whitehead added the last 3 pages of the novel on the floor of an office at Knopf. Originally he had ended with a letter recounting the events he now told "straight out." It was a shift that confirmed the strengths of the novel; it is most successful when Joiner tells his story "straight out." Published to fairly glowing reviews in 1971, *Joiner* was proclaimed "a splendid novel" by a reviewer for *Newsweek,* a "huge, scrambled, loud, ambitious, lively, entertaining, basically unserious novel" by a critic for *The New Yorker,* and a "splendid first novel" by R. V. Cassill in *The New York Times Book Review.* In fact, two positive reviews of *Joiner* were published in the *New York Times* within a two-week period.

Whitehead won the Robert Frost Fellowship in Poetry of the Bread Loaf Writers' Conference in 1967 for *Domains,* an award for a distinguished first book of poems; he was also awarded a Guggenheim Fellowship in Fiction in 1972, the year after *Joiner* appeared. Having taught at the University of Arkansas since 1965, where he cofounded with William Harrison the Programs in Creative Writing in 1966, he was promoted to associate professor in 1969 and to professor in 1973. However, promotion came easier than his sequel to *Joiner.* Originally, he had planned a *Joiner* trilogy, intending the second volume to focus on Royal Carle Boykin and the third on Coldstream McTaggart. The Boykin novel was to be about Jackson lawyers and crop dusters and to take place 7 years after *Joiner.* Whitehead wanted to write "in a different style, more objective, more tightly plotted" (Burton 1973, 78). But in 1972 he did not know if it would work and didn't know where it was going. In an interview, he reported that he had a draft of the new novel written, entitled *Boykin Flying,* and that "Sonny wanders through it here and there." Already he realized that he "might not write into the third one. But I think that I will at this point, and I think I will because I may have to think I will" (Graham, 1973, 198). The Boykin novel has never appeared.

Ten years later, Whitehead admitted that he could not write the novel—that, in fact, the novel had become *Local Men* (1979), his second volume of poetry. He had spent over 2 years writing, doing research, and attending chancery court. According to Whitehead, "the lawyers and sheriffs and all the people I listened

to while I was—thought I was—writing a novel turned into that book of poems.'' Whitehead had once been plagued with the problem of being a writer
who did not know how to be a writer; now he was a writer who did not know
how to write his second novel. As a result, he literally ran off with a country-
music band while on his Guggenheim fellowship and traveled off and on for a
year with Tom T. Hall, with whom he has had a troubled friendship. He carried
the band's musical instruments, and the experience managed to ''shake the tree.
. . . It probably had as much to do with my finishing *Local Men* as anything.''
In fact, some of the poems are about that time; he dedicated the volume to
Glenn Ray, Hall's steel man.

After that year, Whitehead returned to Arkansas, his family, and his teaching.
He is often asked if his teaching has interfered with his writing, and he bluntly
responds that of course it has—perhaps even more than the 5 years he once
admitted to an interviewer. For him, teaching school is also an art that he practices; and he believes firmly that writers can be taught to write better through
hard-nosed editing. Yet his commitment is to more than teaching and writing.
''I suppose I will always wonder what I would have done had I not stayed
married and committed myself to trying to be a father of some kind or another
to seven children. But that is what I do and I love it.'' As he has recognized,
many believe that the artist must eschew domesticity; but for him, marriage and
family remain, along with teaching and writing, the defining elements of his
life. ''I am the advocate of marriage and the family. Brunn, Kathleen, Eric,
Joan, Philip, Edward, Ruth! I'm hostile to divorce, and I don't believe we are
supposed to thin ourselves out and give up breeding. In that way I'm a rank
conservative, I suppose. To hell with it'' (Jones 1983, 204).

Since *Local Men,* Whitehead had published in 1985 a small chapbook of
poems entitled *Actual Size,* dedicated to Tom T. Hall, which commemorates
Whitehead's reading in the Rare Books Room of the North Texas University
Library. Whitehead's new volume of poems *Near at Hand,* dedicated to Miller
Williams, John DuVal, and Tom T. Hall, appeared in 1993; and Whitehead
continues to work on several novels, including *Coldstream,* which fills many
legal pads.

MAJOR THEMES

In discussing the danger of writers' becoming too concerned with social issues, Whitehead told an interviewer:

The problem with causes very often will be the fact that people who get caught up in
causes somehow believe that the cause will remove them from the responsibility of their
mortality. The fact is we are finite, mortal creatures, and all of our efforts for order and
reason and decency will not go as far as we wish they would because we don't live long
enough. In the human race each generation dies off and the next generation learns only
a very little bit from the previous generation. History teaches us relatively little; although

what it does teach us is terribly important. Science *seems* to go forward, while art—and faith—are always starting over. Thank God. (Jones 1983, 169–70)

In his poems and fiction, Whitehead has repeatedly explored characters who must learn to live with their mortality. If each of us must start over developing our modus operandi for our relatively brief lives, then what, Whitehead has asked, connects us to another and yet separates us into unique beings? His answers are not especially complex, for in starting over we must learn anew what older generations have struggled with: love, politics, family, friendship, community, vocation, balance—and, finally, death.

Much of Whitehead's work begins with a voice, a central consciousness trying to make sense of his life or trying to communicate that struggle to us. In *Domains,* as Whitehead has said, love and politics dominate the collection. The forty-three poems move from a boy's recollections of "Floaters," dead bodies in the river, to a mature man's ruminations about his inability "to serve at once / Two dying bodies with equal wit" (117). Some of the author's favorites in the collection reveal well the range of that voice and the demands of both the communal and personal life. In "Delta Farmer in a Wet Summer," a farmer laments the fickleness of the weather that smells like "wasted borrowed money." The weather is no problem in California, he understands; it doesn't have to be counted "when going to the bank." Such predictability, such safety, is not for this man. He needs "the element of chance" in the fecundity and woods of the Delta. But this farmer's faith in the natural world is not contained in "McComb City, August, 1958." At night only the dogs patrol the streets, but "I watch them pad toward dawn where rage is." During the day a different animal inhabits the streets, and his patrol is not controlled by the weather. Contained within the hours of the day are those who are trapped like the animals in "The Zoo, Jackson, Mississippi, 1960." Out of place with unnatural, artificial barriers between them, the animals strain for some dignity—"at the edge of rage and sense / The eagle strains in truss" (84). The human being is also protected by the pretense of civility and decency, but that facade can crumble when rage and chaos tumble out. In "The Lawyer" this reality is recognized when the lawyer tries to convince an old Negro to be a witness to a crime. But, even the lawyer's talk about "the law / And *how the hell was justice done*" cannot overcome the fact that "there wasn't profit in it." Someone else has bribed the Negro earlier, and the lawyer must now leave feeling "more out of place than his machine" (87). Truth and justice can be as relative as money and fear. The men on the run in "Eden's Threat" also know "the gunfire / along the bayous was not so bright / as this day is" (91). What knowledge have they gained and how does Eden threaten them? In "Just North of Sikeston" that knowledge involves the realization that "some mean to die—/ Some, too much aware / Of spring and how the earth / Begins to hate them less" (95). These are the men who will intentionally swerve across the median into the path of the oncoming car. The driver in the poem can only offer a prayer that such men will die elsewhere, will not destroy him and his family. Thus, "It's love that dims / Our lights. It's praise that we take care to ease / Ourselves from every curve" (96). Yet love alone cannot protect family and sanity. Humans live in a world of chance that may delight a Delta farmer but that terrifies the father who knows the burden of memory and dream or nightmare in "For a Neighbor Child." He knows "the awful order of the past must be / the necessary lie." Nevertheless, such an order sends one child crashing through the branches of a tree that was climbed up too far and saves another who later weeps "against us great tears." Such a necessary lie cannot finally save the friend in "First Lecture" who goes mad because "he wanted to know why any man / Felt wise enough to speak / At all. This led to his fall" (107). In *Domains,* love can bring a kind of grace, and politics a kind of damnation. Whitehead himself has never seen the world in such stark, easily divided contrasts. Love can also destroy while politics can save. The human being, in this early collection, must struggle between the domains of his life in order to assert a necessary balance and control.

Joiner must also find that balance and control. In a big, grab-bag, comic, and violent novel, Joiner—all six feet and seven inches of him—strides through his early life protected by his size and his football ability. Bryan, Mississippi, grooms him carefully—taking care of his basic needs and shaping him with the values reflected in the small town. It is clear from the beginning, that Joiner's protected, carefully structured world is not as the community would have it. Other people and experiences also shape the young athlete as he matures into a man.

The fractured, fragmented structure of the novel itself reflects the pieces that Joiner cannot unite. In the opening pages his wife April is preparing to marry his childhood friend Royal Boykin—and, clearly, Joiner's life has collapsed. From the first, he struggles between acceptance and violent confrontation. Such a struggle is there in his earlier life, for his only sister dies as a result of a tragic accident, and Joiner kills an essentially innocent man with one blow to the head. His parents, never confortable with Joiner's public life, flee to Memphis to establish a separate, new existence—still very much loving their son but unable to stay in the small town, thus leaving their son alone.

In some ways, though, Joiner has always been alone, for the internal values and sharp intellect are masked by his bruising exterior. Winning his wife and the opportunity to play professional football contend with his intellectual growth as a college student and, especially, his refusal to accept the prejudice and bigotry of much of his region. Joiner must thus confront not only a different future based upon his intellectual, not physical, strength but also a past filled with violence, hatred, and warped tradition. He must study history and find there a context for his own personal rebellion and the much larger civil-rights struggle.

The historical past, though, provides only a context; and Joiner's future turns dark and bleak. His professional football career is quickly cut short by his badly broken arm, his marriage begins to crumble, and his return home is over-whelmed by his self-pity, his drinking, and his failure to find an effective al-ternative to football. One of the epigraphs to the novel, taken from a letter of Van Gogh's, talks of finding a vocation that one can embrace "with confidence, with a certain assurance that one is doing the reasonable thing." Joiner can find no such assurance. Thus, he thrashes around like a man drowning, kills another ex-football player in a violent racial confrontation, and is forced to leave town and family to find a future once again in the West. Slowly, Joiner does indeed discover a new vocation—teaching—and finds a new woman; and Whitehead would have us believe that at the end of the novel Joiner's return home will be far different and much more successful this time. Joiner has come to terms with his past, his responsibility for his actions, and the options still open for a mul-tidimensional ex-jock who has finally succeeded in resisting the one-dimensional.

Joiner is a demanding novel revealing Whitehead's love for his central char-acter, his region, and football. He never condescends to any of these three. The novel, though, struggles much like its hero. The repeated allusions to artists, the extensive quotes from historians and philosophers reveal much about Whitehead as well as Joiner. To join the world and the fragments of one's own existence at times seems easier than joining the pieces of the novel. But *Joiner* is a major novel that stands on its own, whether or not Whitehead's promised trilogy ever appears. In a world that he has depicted as dangerous and often cruel, he has finally selected the "comic ending," as he has called it. Joiner's life is an affirmation of the hope for and realization of grace in the modern world.

Local Men, Whitehead's second published collection of poems, grew out of his failed efforts to write a sequel to *Joiner* about Royal Carle Boykin, former football teammate, now successful lawyer and husband of Joiner's ex-wife April. The poems reflect the research for the novel, Whitehead's years of frustration to create the sequel, and a growing maturity in his poetic forms. As he says, "The way I write a poem, most of it will have ten syllables, ten to twelve syllables per line, it will rhyme more often than not, and it will be somewhere between fourteen and one hundred fifty lines long. This is a great relief. You are simply bound to one obligation, which is to make no mistakes" (Jones 1983, 198). There are few, if any, mistakes in *Local Men.*

In these fifty poems, the local men range from the lawyers and judges studied for the Boykin novel to the singers and musicians traveled with for a year soon after *Joiner.* Whitehead himself is one of these men who has recognized the vital necessity of accepting responsibility and a certain kind of peace. In "For Gen," he praises the love between him and his wife made manifest in his children, "Including three at once," and in "For our Fifteenth Anniversary," he prays that God will "shower sensuality upon / Our children as they come of age—/ Teach us to live with what they know—/ Point out right times for perfect rage" (49). Such a rage is contained in "For Berryman," Whitehead's fellow poet, who "builds his room / And voices natural enough to fit / The insane time

he does, then takes a dive'' (32). Neither the poet's art nor the judge's justice can create a saving world or a fixed order where no one spends time "Trying to Explain a Bad Man to a Good Man at the Neshoba County Fair in 1971." Such a bad man "might just listen for where you come from"; but then, he may "assault your body and break your face" (56). Throughout these vivid, tough poems, Whitehead's men are often better than they planned to be—and sometimes, through love and care, provide at least a momentary reconciliation between the ideals we set and the lives we are forced to live.

Whitehead's new collection, *Near at Hand* (1993), contains forty poems that continue to develop the themes that have pervaded his work from the beginning. He is a man of hope tempered with a steady realism that refuses to blink at man's ignorance or his fears. In spite of man's failures, he believes in the individual's ability not only to become and finally *be* an adult, but also to celebrate the moments of pleasure and joy that make mortality bearable.

SURVEY OF CRITICISM

Reviews of all three of Whitehead's published volumes have ranged from very positive to glowing. *Joiner* was especially well received in such national publications as *The New York Times Book Review, Life, Newsweek,* and *The New Yorker.* For example, Jonathan Yardley in *Life* (1971) has claimed that Whitehead's novel "takes southern fiction in new and potentially exciting directions"; and Walter Clemmons in *Newsweek* (1971) has said that "Joiner is a terrific creation."

Except for reviews, however, there has been little criticism written about Whitehead's work. James A. Grimshaw, Jr., provides a brief introduction to Whitehead in *Southern Writers: A Biographical Dictionary* (1979); and Michael Adams (1982) provides an initial critical assessment of Whitehead's career in the *Dictionary of Literary Biography Yearbook, 1981.* Adams says that Whitehead "is far from being simply a regional writer, for his work focuses on the alienation and despair of twentieth-century man, on the social, political, historical, and sexual forces, which can sometimes be understood but rarely controlled" (278). David L. Vanderwerken (1979) explores the idea of vocation in the novel, concluding that eventually Joiner's "teaching fulfills his demand that a proper vocation be life-giving, freeing and humane" (41).

BIBLIOGRAPHY

Works by James Whitehead

Domains. Baton Rouge: Louisiana Press, 1966. Reprint. 1973.
Joiner. New York: Knopf, 1971. Reprint. New York: Avon, 1973. Reprint. New York: Avon Bard Series, 1979. Reprint. New York: Ballantine, 1986. Reprint. Fayetteville: University of Arkansas Press, 1991.

Local Men. Urbana: University of Illinois Press, 1979.

Actual Size. Denton, Tex.: Trilobite Press, 1985.

Local Men and Domains: Two Books of Poetry. Urbana: University of Illinois Press, 1987.

Near at Hand. Columbia: University of Missouri Press, 1993.

Interviews with James Whitehead

Burton, Marda. "An Interview with James Whitehead." *Notes on Mississippi Writers* 6 (1973): 71–79.

Carr, John, and John Little. "Waiting for Joiner: James Whitehead." In *Kite-Flying and Other Irrational Acts: Conversations with Twelve Southern Writers,* edited by John Carr, 263–85. Baton Rouge: Louisiana State University Press, 1972.

Graham, John. "James Whitehead." In *The Writer's Voice: Conversations with Contemporary Writers,* edited by George Garrett, 183–99. New York: Morrow, 1973.

Jones, John Griffin. "James Whitehead." *Mississippi Writers Talking,* vol. 2, 149–204. Jackson: University Press of Mississippi, 1983.

Wilson, Austin. "What It Means to be a Southern Writer in the 80s: A Panel Discussion with Beverly Lowry, Reynolds Price, Elizabeth Spencer and James Whitehead." *Southern Quarterly* 26 (Summer 1988): 80–93.

Studies of James Whitehead

Adams, Michael. "James Whitehead." In *Dictionary of Literary Biography Yearbook, 1981,* edited by Karen L. Rood, Jean W. Ross, and Richard Ziegfield, 278–83. Detroit: Gale Research, 1982.

Cassill, R. V. Review of *Joiner. New York Times Book Review* 121 (November 7, 1971): 6–7.

Clemmons, Walter. Review of *Joiner. Newsweek* 78 (November 22, 1971): 132, 134.

Grimshaw, James A., Jr. "James Whitehead." In *Southern Writers: A Biographical Dictionary,* edited R. Bain, J. M. Flora, and L. D. Rubin, Jr., 485–86. Baton Rouge: Louisiana State University Press, 1979.

Review of *Joiner. The New Yorker* 47 (November 13, 1971): 198–99.

Smith, R. T. Review of *Local Men. Southern Humanities Review* 15 (Fall 1981): 371–74.

Vanderwerken, David. "From Tackle to Teacher: James Whitehead's *Joiner.*" *North Dakota Quarterly* 47 (Autumn 1979): 35–42.

Yardley, Jonathan. Review of *Joiner. Life* 17 (November 5, 1971): 15.

JOHN E. BASSETT

Jonathan Williams
(1929–   )

Jonathan Williams is a lyrical and satirical poet whose strengths are tied to his keen sense of voice, precise observations, wit, imaginative fusion of visual and verbal arts, and sheer delight in language. He developed as a poet within the environment of Black Mountain College, where he worked with Charles Olson and others in the 1950s. Since then, he has experimented with poetic techniques in ways that combine the visual and verbal, and he has served the world of poetry and art by publishing through the Jargon Society the works of underrated writers and artists.

BIOGRAPHY

Williams was born on March 8, 1929, in Asheville, North Carolina, coincidentally the year of the publication of *Look Homeward, Angel,* which made Asheville's Thomas Wolfe famous nationally and infamous locally. As Williams himself has observed, he and Wolfe have little in common except the "Buncombe County Virus," which, according to Williams, makes one want to eat, drink, read, and know everything. Wolfe the romantic writer of gargantuan novels, Williams the writer of pithy, precise lyrics, both do bear an uncertain relation to any "Southern" tradition and, as Appalachian residents often assert, may better fit the rubric "mountain writer" than "Southern writer." The family of Williams's father, Ben Williams, has been in the North Carolina hills for 150 years. Jonathan's mother, Georgia Chamberlain, however, came from Georgia.

In the early 1930s the family moved from North Carolina to Washington, D. C., where Ben Williams found work during the Depression. Jonathan graduated from what Ronald Johnson has called "that most British and Episcopalian of schools, St. Albans." He spent 2 years at Princeton before undertaking formal training in the visual arts—in Washington with Karl Knaths, in New York with

William Hayter, and briefly in Chicago at the Institute of Design. In his youth music and art were actually of more interest to Williams than was poetry. Although not an academic writer as measured by university positions or participation at critical conferences, he has taken education seriously—radically, Thoreau might say—and there is more learning beneath his written work than beneath that of most of his contemporaries. He has even said that his dissatisfaction at Princeton stemmed in part from the ''minimal quality of everybody's intensity'' there, the tendency of professors and students to try to do as little as possible to get by.

A conscientious objector, Williams served in the U. S. Army Medical Corps for 2 years (1952–54), but otherwise spent much of the early 1950s at Black Mountain, starting his own poetic career in earnest. He first went to Black Mountain to study photography but came under the influence there of Olson and other strong poets. He later moved beyond the Black Mountain influence and once said that of the group only Robert Duncan still remained an especially important poet for him. Williams also spent several months, in 1951 and again in 1954 and 1955, in San Francisco. During the active period of the Beat poets he associated with James Broughton, Kenneth Patchen, Robert Duncan, and Lawrence Ferlinghetti. He returned to Black Mountain in 1955 and stayed until it closed the following year. During the early 1950s he also established the Jargon Society and began to publish the works of others. Writing and publishing have continued to be the center of his life. He lived for a while in New York City, and he has spent a few semesters as a writer-in-residence at such colleges as Wake Forest, Kansas, Winston-Salem State, and the Maryland Institute College of Art. For the last two decades he has tended to spend half of each year in Highlands, North Carolina, in his family home on a mountain, and half in Yorkshire, where he lives in a stone farmhouse in Corn Close, Lower Dentdale, Cumbria. He lives and travels with his friend Thomas Meyer.

In the early 1950s Jargon began to put out books recognized for their visual quality and for their service in circulating writers undeservedly forgotten or ignored. From his youth Williams had been a book collector and treasured fine editions of, for example, the Oz books and *The Wind in the Willows*. He has said that he tried to bring to Jargon publications the same kind of care and quality he valued in such classic works for children. Establishing the press with a small legacy from a friend, Williams has tried to publish about four books a year—not in competition with commercial presses and never at any profit, for, like his neighboring farmers, he has said that he has to depend on ''a market that often does not exist.'' The name of the press was chosen with irony and as a word including such anagrammatic suggestions as ''agon,'' ''argo,'' and ''argon''; and, Williams adds, he also ''wanted to give those professional persons who refer to any current work as 'jargon' their satisfaction.''

Jargon brought the poetry of Mina Loy back from obscurity; gave Lorine Niedecker, the reclusive Wisconsin protegee of Louis Zukofsky, her only outlet after the war; helped the reputations of Edward Dahlberg, Stevie Smith, and

Basil Bunting; published important work by Black Mountain colleagues Olson, Creeley, Duncan, and Levertov; and brought out work by Kenneth Patchen, Ronald Johnson, Joel Oppenheimer, James Broughton, Paul Metcalf, and many others. It has brought more attention to the work of such photographers as Lyle Bonge, Doris Ulmann, Frederick Sommer, and Guy Mendes. Williams has also been a promoter, not one to make any money off performers but one to travel thousands of miles in old Pontiacs and Volkswagens to raise funds from public and private sources for the sake of poetry and the arts and to carry books of small presses to writers' conferences and bookshops in remote areas of the country. Buckminster Fuller once called his friend Williams the "Johnny Appleseed" of American poetry for his peripatetic poetic activities. Williams himself has called up the tradition of Parson Weems, "getting the books out in the provinces, the hinterlands." Robert Kelly in 1970 said that to read around in *An Ear in Bartram's Tree* (1969) "is to wander in america's largest openair museum, filled with real footnotes & splitting walkie-talkie lecturenotes as we pass, yes indeed, from exhibit to exhibit." Williams has also paid tribute to James Laughlin, who at New Directions set the model for alternative publishing. Once, in describing Jargon, Laughlin wrote that the "purpose of a writers' press like *Jargon* is restless and doomed. It is to make coherence in the avant-garde community." Another time Laughlin said Jargon was "one of the few presses that makes America worth fighting for—but it suggests giving the whole bloody country back to the Cherokees."

MAJOR THEMES

Jonathan Williams is one of the wittiest and most lyrical of post–World War II American poets but also one of relatively few explicitly political Southern poets of his generation. Often associated with the writers at Black Mountain College and influenced by the radical primitivism of Olson's "Projective Verse," Williams does not write as Olson did but has been more in line with an objectivist tradition from William Carlos Williams and Louis Zukofsky that emphasizes poems as linguistic, graphic objects, not merely referential signs. In a preface to *Untinears & Antennae for Maurice Ravel* (1977), for example, Williams has written that for him "each poem is both elegy and celebration. A poem is a linguistic, phonetic, graphic object." Like Olson throwing off parts of his Western tradition, he is not himself so much an antitraditionalist as one who like the older Williams has tried to redefine and re-create his own traditions, back to Martial and Catullus. In some ways a descendant of Whitman and his radical poetics without transcendentalism, of Dickinson and her conciseness without her secular Calvinism, he shows the imprint of several Modernist predecessors yet has a voice and mode personal, identifiable, unique. There are traces of Pound's erudition and juxtapositions without the pedantry, of Cummings' satire and sensuality, of Sitwell's imitation of musical patterns in verse, of William Carlos Williams's free verse without the urban and epic dimensions.

Jonathan Williams's varied interests are an index to the varied topics and themes of his poetry. He is a committed hiker and climber and has traversed most of the Appalachian Trail as well as many trails and paths in England. Although not a Wordsworthian poet of nature, he is a self-defined spiritual grandchild of William Bartram. The precision of his observations and listenings on the road comes across in poems such as "Five Trail-Shelters From the Big Pigeon to the Little Tennessee" and in essays such as "From St. Bees Head to Robin Hood's Bay." Williams is also a baseball fan, and his poems on Stan Musial's 3000th hit, Chuck Stobbs and Truman Clevenger toiling in the Washington Senators' bullpen, and Shotgun Shuba's memories of his Dodger days remind one of Marianne Moore, although with his general distaste for cities Williams would never have lived so many years in a Brooklyn apartment.

Among the deepest of his interests are art and music, and there are few contemporary poets who have Williams's solid understanding and appreciation of music and the visual arts. *Mahler* (1964) consists of poems drafted to the movements of Gustav Mahler's symphonies, "forty spontaneous poems" according to Williams, written after listening "to the forty movements." "Strung Out with Elgar on a Hill" (1970), with plates by Peter Bodner, is an erotic serial poem with parts designated by dates in March, rites of spring, as it were. The poem was, however, as much influenced by Vaughan Williams's music as Elgar's. "A Celestial Centennial Reverie for Charles Edward Ives, The Man Who Found Our Music in The Ground" connects Ives and American music with their roots in American folk culture, with New England writers (Emerson, Hawthorne, Thoreau, the Abbotts), and with European music. Robert Peters (1982) has said that this poem "reveals more of Williams's origins than anything else he has written." Other writings of Williams pay tribute to or use musical ideas of Ravel, Bruckner, and Delius; but a list of his favorites would also include greats of modern jazz such as Theolonius Monk, Miles Davis, and "Jelly Roll" Morton.

Williams's own training was in the visual arts, and if he has written poems about fewer artists than composers, the visual arts play a large role in his work in other ways. Some of his best essays are about photography and such photographers as Doris Ulmann, Frank Meadow Sutcliffe, Clarence John Loughlin, and Aaron Siskind; and he has published work of and about photographers. When a moving autobiographical memoir of the Rabelaisian Georgian, healer-painter-sculptor Eddie Owens Martin was published by Jargon in 1987, it was accompanied by fifty pages of Williams's own photographs. A 1988 publication of Jargon brought to wider attention the work of Vernon Burwell, a cement sculptor from Rocky Mount. Among Williams's best early poems is "Two Pastorals for Samuel Palmer at Shoreham, Kent," and the visionary graphic work of Palmer and William Blake was very important to him. The visual arts, however, may be best embodied in the sheer physical layout and production of Williams's books, some with graphics that preclude easy separation of verbal and visual.

Williams is also one of the wittiest of poets and has been a sharp satirist, particularly during the 1950s and 1960s. His patron saint of satire is Catullus; but his method is reminiscent of Cummings's, whether in political verse, such as "Everybody Twist" ("LAWLESS WALLACE UBER ALLES. . . '') or in the verbal/visual wordplay of "The Inevitable Form of an Early Flying Machine." "An Air-Express Collect, Fifty-Pound Watermelon for Senator James O. Eastland" includes a drawing ostensibly of Eastland's wide-open mouth. "Faubus Meets Mingus During the Latter's Dynasty" combines political commentary with reference to Charles Mingus' *Dynasty* album and wordplay. "Dear Reverend Carl C. McIntire" reflects Williams's delight in listening to broadcast preachers as he drives around the country. Humor in his poetry often appears in the wordplay of acrostics, puns, and anagrams. Sometimes it depends on capturing Appalachian voices, as in the monologue of "Old Man Sam Ward's History of the Gee-Haw Whimmy Diddle" or on pungent one-liners or the shock of recognition in a "found poem." Sometimes it is frankly sexual, marked by either straight or gay humor.

Williams's early verse, often printed first in broadside or folio fashion, was collected in *The Empire Finals at Verona* (1959), *Amen/Huzza/Selah* (1960), *Elegies and Celebrations* (1962), and a planned but unprinted "Jammin' the Greek Scene." *Empire,* verses enriched by collages, photographs, and drawings, was intended, according to Williams, "to use the 'junk' of the Eyes & Ears of the World—and lift it," a comment like William Carlos Williams's suggestion that poetry should "lift the world of the senses to the level of the imagination." The collection includes the strong lyrics "A Vulnerary" (for Robert Duncan), which revolves around language and human tenderness, and "The Grounds" (for Edward Dahlberg), which refers to Marvell, Poe, and Shelley in a poem of gardens, human love, and regeneration. *Amen/Huzza/Selah*, which Williams has tied directly to his Black Mountain experience, was advertised as "Southern-Fried Dada" and is full of witty wordplay, as in "Three Tavern Songs in the Late Southern T'ang Manner" and "A Little Tumescence," and several strong lyrics like "The Anchorite." *Elegies and Celebrations,* for which Duncan wrote a brief but sensitive preface, includes tributes to earlier writers such as Thoreau, Whitman, and Anderson, which in a way define Williams's poetic tradition through Whitman's device of using the most telling epithets for the occasion. Poems such as "The Tag Match" and "Some Southpaw Pitching" reflect his developing strength in capturing speech rhythms for both serious and witty purposes. "Jammin'," if published, would have been the most frankly erotic of the books, with poems such as "Stag or Drag (Come as You Are)," "The Honey Lamb," and "The Priapupation of Queen Pasiphae," expressing delight and humor in sexuality. It also derives its idiom in part, as the title implies, from Art Blakey, Miles Davis, and other jazz musicians.

Evident from all of these early books is the close connection in Williams's work between form and content, or format and content. One might point first to the book itself. More than other contemporaries, Williams has tended to print his work in separate texts—not in journals and magazines, but in its own wrappers. The separate publication is often a package where visual appearance becomes part of message. Shorn of accompanying graphics, poems in an omnibus collection may well have a different impact and meaning. The earliest Jargon printings, such as *Red/Gray* (1951) and *Four Stoppages* (1953), have drawings by Paul Ellsworth and Charles Oscar. In *The Empire Finals at Verona,* poems have been arranged in conjunction with photographs, collages, and drawings by Fielding Dawson, whose work Williams came to appreciate while living in New York. As reprinted in *An Ear in Bartram's Tree,* the individual poems lack some of their original punch. Most of Williams's later publications have continued to include drawings, lithographs, photos, or plates; and when read in that format his books—almost always planned, designed, and printed with distinction—give contemporary readers a fusion of form and sense. He has also created "postcard" poems; and, not surprisingly, he is a writer who revels in "found poems" and "found art"—though pieces when put between covers do not mean or look quite as they did on a back road in north Alabama.

In England's Green, actually written before Williams visited England, appeared in 1962, the same year as *Elegies,* but is a slightly more mature volume and marks a second phase in Williams's career. Such very different poems as "Two Pastorals for Samuel Palmer," "Cobwebbery," and "The Familiars" (a poem revolving around a "rattlesnake-master"), show new lyrical strength and a sharper sense of speech. A note he later appended to "The Familiars" suggests both the literary antecedents for these poems and their derivation from a 1,457-mile hike on the Appalachian Trail. Emerson's lesson to young American scholars to be influenced in order by nature, reading, and action is nowhere better in evidence. "Cobwebbery," as Eric Mottram (1982) has said, "concerns the wreckage of American nature by American human nature, the cold replacement of the local with petunias and the Chevrolet." Williams is an ecologist in his concern with the biology and the aesthetics of the environment, but also in his sense of the balance needed among forces operating in our world. *Mahler* comes from the same general period as *In England's Green* and was Williams's first published attempt to orchestrate a longer work out of parts. Three years later, R. B. Kitaj was inspired by the work to do a set of related silk-screen prints, and then Williams expanded the poem to include Mahler's tenth symphony. Thus, the symbiosis of the sister arts. Meanwhile, much of Williams's attention in the mid-1960s was on very short pieces—the social satire of *Lullabies Twisters Gibbers Drags* (1963) and miniatures of several kinds that he titled *Epiphytes* or *Lucidities* or *San-Aunt-Sank Shows.* Throughout his career he has also written many pieces in which the title is a good bit longer than the two- or three-word poem it prefaces, and more accurately might itself be called the poem.

As Williams reached the end of that second creative decade, he also brought out his first widely distributed collections: *An Ear in Bartram's Tree* (1969), which includes poems from the earlier books through 1967; *Blues & Roots/Rue & Bluets* (1971), which established him as the best writer of Appalachian dialect poetry and through its title alluded to Mingus; and *The Loco Logodaedalist in Situ: Selected Poems 1968–70* (1972), which includes not only recent shorter poems but some of his best longer lyrics from the 1960s, most notable "Strung Out with Elgar on a Hill" and a collection of minimalist pieces called "Excavations from the Case-Histories of Havelock Ellis, with a Final Funerary Ode for Charles Olson," in some ways his darkest poems.

In the 1970s Williams's work continued along both lines—short pieces printed as broadsides, postcards, and verbal games, on the one hand, and longer orchestrations such as "A Celestial Centennial Reverie for Charles Edward Ives" (1975), on the other. Some of that decade's work appeared in *Elite/Elate: Selected Poems, 1971–75* (1979), and then in 1982 *Get Hot or Get Out* gave the public a more general collection of a quarter century of his poetry. In 1985 a totally new edition of *Blues & Roots/Rue & Bluets* provided new examples of his Appalachian tang. The 1980s may have seen some slowdown in Williams's lyrical output, but not in his activity. He has been as experimental as ever, for example in the four lyrics of *The Delian Seasons* (1982) and in *Dementations on Shank's Mare* (1988), the latter being "Meta-Fours in Plus Fours"—that is, poems with four words to a line and no punctuation. He has delighted in publishing "clerihews" (of "Clara Hughes"), jargonelles, limericks, and several sets of memorable quotations. The recent collection *Aposiopeses: Odds & Ends* (1988), however, includes elegies and lyrics—suggesting that in quality, if not quantity, he is as strong a poet as ever. His essays, moreover, are appearing in collections, most notably *The Magpie's Bagpipe* (1982); and he continues to develop his writing and publishing careers in new directions not limited to the verbal.

SURVEY OF CRITICISM

Williams has never received the critical attention that his contribution to American poetry warrants, and he has almost always operated outside of mainstream literary and academic establishments. Surveys and topical studies of post–World War II verse may mention him in passing as one of several writers influenced by the Black Mountain experience; there is detailed discussion of the works of Duncan, Creeley, or Olson. The two best brief introductions to Williams's poetry are one by his friend Ronald Johnson, a sympathetic and insightful essay for the *Dictionary of Literary Biography* (1980), and Guy Davenport's 1969 introduction to *An Ear in Bartram's Tree*. Davenport traced a set of influences not only through a tradition of Whitman, Pound, Williams, Zukofsky, and Olson, but also to the satire of Catullus, the "eccentric" of Blake, and the wandering American, for example, William Bartram. Reviews of that book provided the first national and international notice of Williams's talent. Herbert Leibowitz (1969) called him "our best poet of serious tomfoolery," a "brilliant compositor and almanac of wisdom." Two years later in a review of *Blues and Roots,* Leibowitz said that Williams was trying "to find and sort out the crooked

genealogy of the common man, the lilt and flavor of his demotic speech'';
meanwhile literary journals were bringing out reviews of *Bartram*. Robert Kelly
(1970) was grateful that the ''revered postRomantic & razmatazz at last has a
big & necessary book for us to read together many of the fragmentary blitzed
perceptions His Speed has given us over the years.'' Ralph Mills attended to
Williams's remarkable ear for voice and sound. Anselm Hallo—more critically
but not without sympathy—considered the nervous quirkiness that can exasper-
ate some readers even amid the lyric and satiric strengths of the verse.

In 1973 Barry Alpert published a special issue of *Vort* on Williams and Fielding Dawson. Alpert's interview in that issue is still a good source of information
on Williams, and Eric Mottram (1973) has provided an excellent assessment of
Williams's poetry. After that early attention, however, there has been only limited commentary on Williams's verse, generally in *Parnassus*. Kenneth Irby's
1980 review of *Elite/Elate* was especially sensitive to the visual, aural, and
formal dimensions of Williams's creative work and cautioned against overem-
phasis on it as ''light verse,'' for as Irby has said, ''Williams is one of the most
considerable poets of our time, one whose work may be returned to again and
again, with ever renewing delight in the fineness of its workmanship.'' X. J.
Kennedy in a 1984 review attended to the kind of faithful observation, art of
listening, and sheer ''infectious glee'' that have made Williams ''so rare, so
appealing, so probably indispensable.'' Surprisingly *Get Hot or Get Out* received few reviews in major quarterlies. There have been several interviews and
articles on the Jargon Society, and there is a collection of often insightful tributes
in the volume celebrating Williams' fiftieth birthday. But there is no book-length
study of Williams.

BIBLIOGRAPHY

Works by Jonathan Williams

Red/Gray. Black Mountain, N.C.: Jargon, 1952.
Four Stoppages. Stuttgart: Jargon, 1953.
The Empire Finals at Verona. Highlands, N.C.: Jargon, 1959.
Amen/Huzzah/Selah. Highlands, N.C.: Jargon, 1960.
Elegies and Celebrations. Highlands, N.C.: Jargon, 1962.
Emblems for the Little Dells, and Nooks, and Corners or Paradise. Highlands, N.C.:
     Jargon, 1962.
In England's Green & A Garland & Clyster. San Francisco: Auerhahn Press, 1962.
Lullabies Twisters Gibbers Drags. Highlands, N.C.: Jargon, 1963.
Lines About Hills Above Lakes. Fort Lauderdale: Roman Books, 1964.
Affilati Attrezze Per I Giardini de Catullo. Milan: Perici Editore, 1966. Published as
     Sharp Tools for Catullan Gardens. Bloomington: Fine Arts Department, Indiana
     University, 1968.
Jonathan Williams' Fifty Epiphytes. London: Poet & Printer, 1967.
The Lucidities. London: Turret Books, 1967.

Polycotyledonous Poems. Stuttgart: Edition Hansjorg Mayer, 1967.

Descant on Rawthey's Madrigal: Conversations with Basil Bunting. Lexington, Ky.: Gnomon Press, 1968.

An Ear in Bartram's Tree. Chapel Hill: University of North Carolina Press, 1969.

Mahler. New York: Grossman, 1969.

Strung out with Elgar on a Hill. Urbana, Ill.: Finial Press, 1970.

Blues & Roots/Rue & Bluets. New York: Grossman, 1971.

The Loco Logodaedalist in Situ. London: Cape Goliard, 1972.

The Family Album of Lucybelle Crater. Highlands, N.C.: Jargon, 1974.

The Personal Eye. New York: Aperture Monograph, 1974.

Hot What? Dublin, Ga.: J. W. Mole Press, 1975.

Madeira & Toasts for Basil Bunting's 75th birthday. Dentdale, England: Jargon, 1977.

An Omen for Stevie Smith. New Haven: Sterling Library, Yale University, 1977.

"I Shall Save One Land Unvisited": Eleven Southern Photographers. Frankfort, Ky.: Gnomon Press, 1978.

Elite/Elate Poems: Selected Poems, 1971–75. Highlands, N.C.: Jargon, 1979.

Portrait Photographs. Frankfort, Ky.: Gnomon Press, 1979.

The Delian Seasons: Four Poems. London: Coracle Press, 1982.

In the Azure Over the Squalor: Ransackings and Shorings. n.p.: Jordan Davies, 1983.

Letter in a Klein Bottle: Photographs. Highlands, N.C.: Jargon, 1984.

St. EOM in the Land of Pasaquan: The Life and Times and Art of Eddie Owens Martin. Winston-Salem: Jargon, 1987.

Aposiopeses: Odds & Ends. Minneapolis: Granary Books, 1988.

Dementations on Shank's Mare. New Haven: Truck Press, 1988.

Le garage ravi de Rocky Mount: An essay on Vernon Burwell. Rocky Mount: North Carolina Wesleyan College Press, 1988.

Quote, Unquote. Berkeley: Ten Speed Press, 1989.

Uncle Gus Flaubert rates the Jargon Society. Chapel Hill: Hanes Foundation, University of North Carolina Library, 1989.

Interviews with Jonathan Williams

Alpert, Barry. "Jonathan Williams: An Interview." *Vort* 4 (Fall 1973): 54–75.

"Cloches à travers les feuilles." In *Contemporary Authors,* Autobiography Series, 12. Edited by Joyce Nakamura, 339–60. Detroit: Gale Research, 1990.

Corbett, William. "A Quarter Century of the Jargon Society: An Interview with Jonathan Williams." In *The Art of Literary Publishing: Editors on Their Craft,* edited by Bill Henderson, 116–33. Yonkers, N.Y.: Pushcart Press, 1980.

Studies of Jonathan Williams

Brown, Millicent. "The Jargon Idea." *Books at Brown* 19 (March 1963): 1–19.

Davenport, Guy. Introduction to *An Ear in Bartram's Tree: Selected Poems, 1957–1967.* Chapel Hill, N.C.: University of North Carolina Press, 1969.

———. Introduction to *Elite/Elate.* Highlands, N.C.: Jargon, 1979.

A 50th Birthday Celebration for Jonathan Williams. Frankfort: Gnomon Press, 1979.

Hallo, Anselm. "The Pleasures of Exasperation." *Parnassus* 1 (Fall–Winter 1972): 188–94.

Helms, Alan. "Over the Edge." *Partisan Review* 41 (1974): 151–57.

Irby, Kenneth. "'America's Largest Openair Museum.'" *Parnassus* 8 (1980): 307–28.

Jaffe, James S., comp. *Jonathan Williams: A Bibliographical Checklist of His Writings, 1950–1988.* Haverford, Pa.: Jaffe, 1989.

Johnson, Ronald. "Jonathan Williams." In *Dictionary of Literary Biography,* vol. 5, edited by Donald J. Greiner. 406–9: 1980.

Kelly, Robert. Review. *Caterpillar* 10 (January 1970): 231–32.

Kennedy, X. J. "Piping down the Valleys Wild." *Parnassus* 12 (Fall–Winter 1984): 183–89.

Leibowitz, Herbert. Review. *Hudson Review* 22 (Autumn 1969): 506–7.

———. Review of *Blues & Roots/Rue & Bluets. New York Times Book Review.* (November 21, 1971): Sec. 7, 54, 56–58.

———. Introduction to *Blues & Roots/Rue & Bluets: A Garland for the Southern Appalachians.* Durham, N.C.: Duke University Press, 1985.

McFee, Michael. "'Reckless and Doomed': Jonathan Williams and Jargon." *Small Press* 3 (September–October 1985): 101–6.

Meyer, Thomas. Introduction to *The Magpie's Bagpipe.* San Francisco: North Point Press, 1982.

Morgan, Robert. "The Sound of Our Speaking." *Nation* 213 (September 6, 1971): 188–90.

Mottram, Eric. "Jonathan Williams." *Vort* 4 (Fall 1973): 102–11.

Peters, Robert. Introduction to *Get Hot or Get Out.* Metuchen, N.J.: Scarecrow Press, 1982.

Russell, John. "Jonathan Williams." *New York Times Book Review* (February 13, 1983): 43.

Tamulevich, Susan. "Black Mountain Bard." *Mid-Atlantic Country* 11 (July 1990): 36–39.

TIMOTHY DOW ADAMS

Miller Williams
(1930–   )

Miller Williams is a multitalented man of letters, best known for his nine books of poetry, which have won numerous national and international prizes. In addition, he has translated poetry, directed the Program in Creative Writing and in Translation at the University of Arkansas. Williams founded and directed the University of Arkansas Press, which has in recent years been well regarded for its literary publications, including novels and short stories, poetry, memoirs, essays, and anthologies.

BIOGRAPHY

Miller Williams was born on April 8, 1930, the son of a Methodist minister, in Hoxie, Arkansas. Moving frequently as his father's duties required, Miller Williams grew up as a Southerner in a state sometimes thought of as being more Southwestern than Southern. After completing his undergraduate degree in biology from Arkansas State University, Williams earned an M.A. in zoology from the University of Arkansas in 1952. Following such jobs as movie projectionist, stock-car driver, and popsicle assembler, he began a 12 year career as a college science teacher. Following a brief stint as a tire salesman for Montgomery Ward, almost miraculously he turned himself into a poet, despite a complete lack of formal schooling in literature. Encouraged by John Ciardi, Williams attended the Bread Loaf Writers' Conference on a fellowship; and soon after, in 1964, he published the first of his nine books of poetry, *A Circle of Stone* (1964).

Although he has no academic degrees in English, Williams joined the English Department at Louisiana State University in 1962 and taught there and at Loyola University in New Orleans, where he established the *New Orleans Review* and with John W. Corrington edited two anthologies published by Louisiana State

University Press: *Southern Writing in the Sixties: Poetry* and *Southern Writing in the Sixties: Fiction.* Even at this early point in his career, Williams was attracted to international travel, receiving the Amy Lowell Traveling Scholarship in Poetry, teaching at the University of Chile and as a Fulbright Professor at the National University of Mexico, all the while publishing in such outlets as *Southern Poetry Review, Saturday Review, Prairie Schooner, Shenandoah,* and the *Chicago Review.* As a result of his stay in Chile, he edited an anthology of contemporary Chilean writing and translated two collections of poetry by Nicanor Parra.

In 1971 he joined the English Department at the University of Arkansas, later becoming not only Director of the Program in Creative Writing and in Translation, but also Chairman of the Department of Comparative Literature, University Professor of English and Foreign Languages, and Director of the University of Arkansas Press. Having won the Prix de Rome in literature in 1976, he spent the next year as a fellow at the American Academy in Rome, as a result of which he published a translation of the sonnets of Giuseppe Belli and edited an anthology of short pieces, stories, and poems by writing residents of the American Academy in Rome, including William Styron, Robert Penn Warren, Allen Tate, and others.

In addition to his creative and editorial endeavors, Miller Williams has also found time for scholarly work, having published academic studies of John Ciardi and John Crowe Ransom. From his first marriage, to Lucille Day, Williams has three children, Lucinda, Robert, and Karyn, well known from their cameo appearances in his poetry. Lucinda Williams is a well-respected country/folk singer. Miller Williams resides, never resting on his laurels, with his second wife, Jordon Hall Williams, in Fayetteville, Arkansas.

MAJOR THEMES

From his first book of poetry in 1964 until his most recent, in 1989, Williams has followed a steady pattern of publishing a book of poems every 2 or 3 years. Starting with *Halfway from Hoxie* in 1973, his books have sometimes been made up of his newest poetry in addition to his personal selection from previous books. By the time of *Living on the Surface* in 1989, his body of work had thus been refined until only his personal favorites from a lifetime of work have survived this personal winnowing process.

Throughout his career there have been certain recurring themes: science, doubt, form, order, religion, and chance. These ideas have been played out in a style characterized as both highly sophisticated and down-home, a combination of a hard philosophical debate about both practical and metaphysical worries— refined by a thinker who has been at home in both the scientific and the humanistic worlds—and an unmistakable personal voice that sounds like a real person speaking with a Southern accent.

Williams's poems are often apparently simple, nothing disturbing their surface tension on the first reading, but complex and sophisticated beneath the surface. What makes his poetry seem uncomplicated is its tone and subject matter. While many of his primary concerns are universal, they are often expressed in a style that might be described as resembling the country music of Tom T. Hall, whose epigram graces Williams's 1981 collection *Distractions* and whose book *The Acts of Life* was published by the University of Arkansas Press. Although many of Williams's poems are about such disturbing ideas as loneliness, fear, neglect, doubt, forgetfulness, and life at the edge, they are often darkly comic, as evidenced by the following titles: "In Your Own Words without Lying Tell Something of Your Background with Particular Attention to Anything Relating to the Position for which You Are Applying. Press Down" or "On a Trailways Bus a Man Who Holds His Head Strangely Speaks to the Seat beside Him."

In his first collection, *A Circle of Stone*, Williams established a dialogue between science and poetry that has recurred throughout his career. For instance, in "Level IV," his brief poem on poetry, he explains that essential to making a poem work is an understanding of work in its scientific sense: "a change in / temperature" (*A Circle of Stone*, 42). The collection's final poem "The Associate Professor Delivers an Exhortation to His Failing Students" features not a poetry professor but a scientist who rails at his students for not seeing the poetry behind the science on the syllabus: "The day I talked about the conduction of currents / I meant to say / be careful about getting hung up in the brain's things / that send you screaming like madmen through the town"(1).

In *So Long at the Fair* (1968), his second collection, he continued to make use of his scientific background, as in the short poem "Euglena," in which— like the contemporary dance company Pilobolus—he used both the form and the function of biology to make art. In "Euglena" he has turned a genus of a family of infusorians with brilliant green endoplasm into a "microscopic monster / germ father, founder of the middle way," of which he notes: "Swimming, you go to what meal is. / Green, you make what isn't" (*Halfway from Hoxie*, 34).

Despite his scientific background and lack of formal training in literature, Williams's poems are filled with allusions to literary ideas—for example, his poem "Done to His Mistress," a parody of Donne's poem, which also plays on scientific thought: "How will we know / when we are cubed and taken to our roots / alphas in some obscure calculus" (*So Long at the Fair* in *Halfway from Hoxie*, 43).

In his third collection, *The Only World There Is* (1971), his first book of poems published by a commercial rather than an academic press, Williams continued his series of scientific professor poems with "The Assoc. Professor (Mad Scientist) to (His Love) His Student in Physics 1200 Lab," a poem that uses such terms as *force, matter,* and *mass* in discussing the physical lines of force between a professor and his student. The tension between the scientific world of fact and the poetic world of fiction is essential to ''Let Me Tell You,'' a poem about how to write poetry, which argues that ''you cannot twist the fact you do not know'' (*Living on the Surface,* 16).

The new poems in *Halfway from Hoxie* seem darker, indicating that Williams had come not only halfway from the place of his physical birth, but back to Arkansas from halfway around the world where he had witnessed the political upheavals of Allende's Chile. He continued to work with scientific ideas, as in ''Thinking Friday Night with a Gothic Storm Going about Final Causes and Logos and Mitzi Mayfair,'' which includes these lines: ''The earth that seems / rocks and water is only force / moving through a shape'' (*Living on the Surface,* 32). But here the central answer to his doubt seems to lie, not in facts but in the mysterious power within words, as in ''Think of Judas That He Did Love Jesus'': ''Look quickly / behind the words you have heard and uncover creatures / looking the other way with words in their hands'' (*Halfway from Hoxie,* 124).

All of the poems in *Why God Permits Evil* (1977) are new, including the title poem—expanded into ''Why God Permits Evil: For Answer to This Question of Interest to Many Write Bible Answers Dept. E–7''—which, playing off of a matchbook promise, creates an imaginary world where actual characters exist, working in various bureaucratic departments designed to handle the volume of mail generated by the promise of the answer. A number of these poems are short and intriguingly enigmatic; the relation between the titles and the poems is often not at first clear. Questions of scientific skepticism have, in this collection, often become questions about the space-time continuum, such as the wonderful idea in ''Reading the Arkansas Gazette on Microfilm'' of literally going back to repeat the past, fast forwarding through a year in minutes, imagining ''a mind that saw it all go by / as fast as that in the first place.'' ''Notes from the Agent on Earth: How to Be Human'' is a long poem that repeats several times the line: ''What matters most is survival'' (*Living on the Surface,* 37, 52).

However, many of the people in *Distractions,* Williams's sixth collection, are not survivors; the poems are filled with accidents and near accidents, alienated people living on the edge of existence, staring blankly at the narrator, caught in a world where numbing distractions have become more important than achieving a sense of order, where survival consists, as the narrator of ''The Well-Ordered Life'' notes, of ''a constant laying of sandbags on the levee'' (*Living on the Surface,* 56). The final five poems of this book, what Williams has titled ''Parallel Lines,'' are his translations from German, French, Spanish, and Italian.

This international emphasis returned in his 1983 collection *The Boys on Their Bony Mules,* which begins with poems set in Paris, Ladispoli, Delhi, Rome, Calcutta, and Normandy Beach. The darkness of the previous collection has now given way to a sense of loss; a number of poems deal with the deaths of students, friends, lovers, political allies, and moral values. The characteristic Williams genre in which a college professor laments his inability to get the important things across to his class is represented in this collection for the first time by a professor, not of science, but of literature: "Paying Some Slight Attention to His Birthday, the Associate Professor Goes about His Business Considering What He Sees and a Kind of Praise." The literature professor is more bemused than angry, able to feel "sad and contented" rather than bewildered and terrified.

Imperfect Love (1986) has a different tone from the earlier books. Here the mood is bemused, ironic, fantastic, sometimes sounding like a cross between Stephen Crane and Rusell Edson. A number of the poems in this collection are dramatic monologues, featuring the devastatingly personal voices of a local politician, a lawyer, a businessman, and a field-worker in the Delta.

For his most recent book, *Living on the Surface,* Williams has selected poems from all of his past works, sometimes reprinted here with slight variations from the original. Among the new poems in this book are several that focus on such important contemporary worries as AIDS, nuclear disarmament, and the last days of Allende. In addition, there are more dramatic monologues, including "Rituals" (on the surface about making moonshine), as well as "The Ghost of His Wife Comes to Tell Him How It Is," "The Journalist Buys a Pig Farm," and "He Speaks to His Arguing Friends and to Himself." Throughout his work, a central concern has been an attempt to find a secure hold in a world caught in madness and the grip of chance, a world where neither science nor religion gives satisfying answers to personal doubts, a world where the purchase of order is bought with the price of ardor.

SURVEY OF CRITICISM

A collection of essays, *Miller Williams and the Poetry of the Particular,* edited by Michael Burns, was published by the University of Missouri Press in 1991. This collection contains Howard Nemerov's introduction to Williams's first book and essays by a number of poets, including Fred Chappell, Maxine Kumin, William Stafford, X. J. Kennedy, John Frederick Nims, Lewis Turco, and others. The collection concludes with "The Sanctioned Babel," an interview with Richard Jackson that originally appeared in *Poetry Miscellany.*

Central to many of the essays is a focus on form. As his authoring of *Patterns of Poetry: An Encyclopedia of Forms* suggests, however, Williams's poetry is characterized by attention to formal patterns, though the formality is not always obvious. Although he has written in such strict patterns as the villanelle, the sestina, and even a sort of ballad written in the Rubaiyat stanza—"Rubaiyat for Sue Ellen Tucker"—much of his poetry is disarmingly plain. Only by looking a second and a third time can we see that actually he is a master of the measured line and the scattered rhyme. His strongly conversational poetic voice, which strikes some readers as sounding like a country preacher, is actually a highly wrought sound, made up of complicated slant and off rhymes occurring at odd intervals, coupled with highly original metaphors.

Book reviews, which have appeared in all of the major periodicals have been nearly always praiseworthy, often pointing out the careful craftmanship of Williams's poems. Well-known poets such as Donald Justice, Dabney Stuart, John Ciardi, Dave Smith, Richard Hugo, Richard Wilbur, Sydney Lea, David Slavitt, William Meredith, and Alan Broughton have each praised the poetry. X. J. Kennedy, for instance, has praised Williams's prosody stating that "Williams at his best does not bend rhymes to his thought, but thinks in rhyme" (Burns 1991, 3); Maxine Kumin has noted her attraction to the cadence of his poems, the country rhythm of his diction, the seemingly direct frontal approach he takes to an often slithery subject, the way the language disarms the reader and then sneaks metaphysically behind him/her" (Burns 1991, 1). In his essay in appreciation, Fred Chappell has nicely summarized Williams's central concerns: "If neither philosophic introspection nor scientific investigation can provide absolutely certain data, if final metaphysical choices ought to be evaded or chosen for the sake of human convenience and spiritual comfort, then not much is left objectively to believe in, except for that one organ or faculty or talent which enables us to believe—that is, the mind itself" (8).

BIBLIOGRAPHY

Works by Miller Williams

Circle of Stone. Baton Rouge: Louisiana State University Press, 1964.
So Long at the Fair. New York: Dutton, 1968.
The Achievement of John Ciardi. New York: Scott, Foresman, 1968.
The Only World There Is. New York: Dutton, 1971.
The Poetry of John Crowe Ransom. New Brunswick, N.J.: Rutgers University Press, 1971.
Halfway from Hoxie: New and Selected Poems. Baton Rouge: Louisiana State University Press, 1973.
Why God Permits Evil. Baton Rouge: Louisiana State University Press, 1977.
Distractions. Baton Rouge: Louisiana State University Press, 1981.
The Boys on Their Bony Mules. Baton Rouge: Louisiana State University Press, 1983.
Imperfect Love. Baton Rouge: Louisiana State University Press, 1986.
Patterns of Poetry: An Encyclopedia of Forms. Baton Rouge: Louisiana State University Press, 1986.
Living on the Surface. Baton Rouge: Louisiana State University Press, 1989.

Works Edited and Translated by Miller Williams

Emergency Poems, by Nicanor Parra. Translated by Miller Williams. New York: New Directions, 1966.
19 poetas de hoy en los Estados Unidos. Edited by Miller Williams. USIS/Chile, 1966.
Southern Writing in the Sixties: Poetry. Edited by Miller Williams and John W. Corrington. Baton Rouge: Louisiana State University Press, 1966.

Southern Writing in the Sixties: Fiction. Edited by Miller Williams and John W. Corrington. Baton Rouge: Louisiana State University Press, 1966.

Poems and Antipoems of Nicanor Parra. Translated by Miller Williams. New York: New Directions, 1967.

Chile: An Anthology of New Writing. Edited by Miller Williams. Kent, Ohio: Kent State University Press, 1968.

Contemporary Poetry in America. Edited by Miller Williams. New York: Random House, 1973.

How Does a Poem Mean? Rev. ed. Edited by John Ciardi and Miller Williams. Boston: Houghton Mifflin, 1974.

Railroad. Edited by Miller Williams and James Alan McPherson. New York: Random House, 1976.

A Roman Collection. Edited by Miller Williams. Columbia: University of Missouri Press, 1980.

Sonnets of Giuseppe Belli. Translated by Miller Williams. Baton Rouge: Louisiana State University Press, 1981.

Ozark, Ozark: A Hillside Reader. Edited by Miller Williams. Columbia: University of Missouri Press, 1981.

Interviews with Miller Williams

"An Interview with Miller Williams." *Sam Houston Literary Review* 1 (1976): 55–61.

Jackson, Richard. "The Sanctioned Babel: An Interview with Miller Williams." In *Acts of Mind,* 7–12. Tuscaloosa: University of Alabama Press, 1983.

Studies of Miller Williams

Baker, David. "'To Advantage Dressed': Miller Williams among the Naked Poets." *Southern Review* 26 (1990): 814–31.

Burns, Michael. *Miller Williams and the Poetry of the Particular.* Columbia: University of Missouri Press, 1991.

Chappell, Fred. "Out of the Hills of Certainty: Miller Williams' Skeptical Science." *Cotton Boll/Atlanta Review* 4 (1989): 3–13.

Hagen, Lyman B. "Miller Williams: A Bibliography." *Bulletin of Bibliography* 44 (1987): 232–52.

Jarrett, Beverly. "Miller Williams." In *Southern Writers: A Biographical Dictionary,* edited by Joseph M. Flora, Robert Bain, and Louis D. Rubin, 495–96. Baton Rouge: Louisiana State University Press, 1979.

Morrow, Mark. Foreword by Erskine Caldwell. "Miller Williams." *Images of the Southern Writer: Photographs by Mark Morrow,* 94–95. Athens: University of Georgia Press, 1985.

Whitehead, James. "About Miller Williams." *Dickinson Review* 3 (1973): 26–40.

DAPHNE H. O'BRIEN

Tom Wolfe
(1931–   )

Tom Wolfe is a Virginia writer who has lived and written in New York for most of his career. An essayist and novelist, he is credited with founding the New Journalism, a genre that revolutionized the world of newspaper and magazine writing by applying techniques of fiction writing to factual reporting. He is counted among the country's most astute cultural observers, though his studies go far beyond the realm of facile observation. He brings to bear upon the metropolis—and, indeed, the nation—a Southern sensibility to class and mobility, and he writes from a traditionalist ethic. Wolfe is best known for two nonfiction works and a novel: *The Electric Kool-Aid Acid Test* (1968), *The Right Stuff* (1979), and *The Bonfire of the Vanities* (1987).

BIOGRAPHY

Tom Wolfe was born Thomas Kennerly Wolfe, Jr., in Richmond, Virginia, on March 2, 1931, 4 years after his parents moved to the city from a farm in the Shenandoah Valley. His father, with a Ph.D. in agronomy from Cornell, was a professor at the Virginia Polytechnic Institute and an agricultural leader, who moved to Richmond to edit the *Southern Planter,* a conservative farm magazine. His mother, intelligent and well educated, had been accepted into medical school as a young woman, although she chose not to pursue a medical career.

Growing up in the Sherwood Park neighborhood of Richmond, Wolfe was educated in the public schools until the seventh grade, when he began attending St. Christopher's, an Episcopal prep school. There he was an active honor student, coediting the school newspaper and writing a column called "The Bullpen." Wolfe had decided "at five or six" that he wanted to be a writer in emulation of his father; and he remembers being perplexed by the fact that he and Thomas Wolfe, whose books were on his father's desk, were not related.

Wolfe took a B.A. in English in 1951 from Washington and Lee, graduating cum laude. There he developed his interest in fiction writing, publishing two of his stories in the campus literary magazine, *The Shenandoah.* He also discovered the American Studies Curriculum, in which he took a Ph.D. at Yale in 1957, describing this period of his life as "tedium of an exquisite sort." At Yale, he began to doubt the validity of fiction as an art form because of its obsessively introspective orientation and turned his attention to journalism, drawn by the possibility of realism.

After leaving Yale, Wolfe embarked on a newspaper career, although he did not leave behind his literary aspirations. He saw himself as preparing for the time when, as he has explained in *The New Journalism,* he would "quit cold, say goodbye to journalism, move into a shack somewhere, work night and day for six months, and light up the sky with the final triumph . . . known as The Novel" (5). He began working for the Springfield (Massachusetts) *Union,* then in 1959 moved to the *Washington Post,* where he won the Washington Newspaper Guild awards for foreign news reporting and for humor in 1961. In 1962 he moved again, this time to the *New York Herald Tribune,* where competition among the feature writers fostered innovation. The following year Wolfe attempted his first magazine piece, convincing *Esquire* to send him to a custom-car show in California. The writer, overwhelmed by what he saw, found the language and conventions of the traditional feature story inadequate. In a scene that has become the set piece of New Journalism history, Wolfe describes himself wrangling with his experience but unable to write the story, despite pressure from his impatient client. Finally conceding defeat to the material, Wolfe agreed to send the magazine his notes so that someone else could do the story, working all night to shape his notes and thoughts in the form of a memorandum to his editor. Upon reading the forty-nine pages, the editor deleted the "Dear Byron" at the top, made a few minor changes, and ran the piece. The New Journalism was born. With the publication of "There Goes (Varoom! Varoom!) That Kandy-Kolored (Thphhhhhh!) Tangerine-Flake Streamline Baby (Rahghhh) Around the Bend (Brummmmmmmmmmmmmmm)," Wolfe became credited with inventing a new form for writers, a form that fused the techniques of fiction with the facts of reportage, creating a hybrid that was much more exciting to read and offered much more in-depth coverage of a subject. This essay gave its title in modified form to Wolfe's first book, a collection of essays published in 1965, which immediately became a best-seller.

Following this coup was a hectic productive period for Wolfe. He worked two days a week as general assignment editor for the *Herald Tribune*'s city desk, three days as a feature writer for the paper's Sunday supplement, *New York,* and spent the other two producing articles for *Esquire.* The supplement, because it was neither as serious as the regular newspaper nor as permanent as the magazine, gave Wolfe the perfect medium for experimentation in spelling, punctuation, and reader attention-getting techniques associated with his early style and gave him the license to experiment with point of view and narrative voices as well. In 1968 Wolfe published another essay collection, *The Pump House Gang,* and his first book-length study, *The Electric Kool-Aid Acid Test,* since considered the definitive work on the counterculture of the 1960s. Having gained fame as a journalist, main practitioner of an innovative genre, and a social critic, Wolfe published in 1970 *Radical Chic and Mau-Mauing the Flak Catchers,* two essays satirizing the upper-class pastime of embracing radical causes and examining the game of minority group intimidation of officials. He also produced an anthology (along with Edward Johnson) of New Journalistic writing, *The New Journalism* (1973). In 1975 he created a furor in the art world with *The Painted Word,* a short book suggesting that modern art is a great farce that would not exist without the critics whose rhetoric really created it. In 1976 he published *Mauve Gloves and Madmen, Clutter and Vine,* another essay collection. During this period, Wolfe was writing a longer work about the astronauts. Published in 1979, *The Right Stuff* won for Wolfe both the American Book Award and the National Book Critics Circle Award in 1980.

Yet despite his success, Wolfe still sought to master the form of the novel, which he envisioned as a great realistic urban social picture in the tradition of Dickens, Balzac, and Zola. As he struggled with his own work about New York, he continued publishing shorter works and collections: *In Our Time,* a collection of his drawings, with short illustrative essays (1980); *From Bauhaus to Our House,* a denunciation of modern architecture that infuriated many critics (1981); and *The Purple Decades: A Reader* (1982), collected essays. Frustrated by his inability to finish his novel, he contracted to run a first draft serially in *Rolling Stone,* to pressure himself into completing the work. *The Bonfire of the Vanities* then underwent extensive revision before its release in 1987 to a critical storm and fifty-six weeks on the hardcover best-seller list. Wolfe lives in New York with his wife, Sheila, and their two children and is currently at work on another novel.

MAJOR THEMES

Throughout Wolfe's career his name has been synonymous with the term New Journalism, although he chafes at the limitation that classification puts upon him. He has defined this form in his preface to *The New Journalism* and elsewhere as a nonfiction account enriched by four characteristics: scene-by-scene construction that uses as little historical narrative as possible; realistic dialogue to establish and define character and to engage the reader; third-person point of view to make the reader feel he or she is inside the character's mind; and, most important, the recording of details that are symbolic of people's status in life, meaning "the entire pattern of behavior and possessions through which people express their position in the world or what they think it is or what they hope it to be" (32). This critical recording of detail, Wolfe has said, "lies as close to the center of the power of realism as any other device in literature" (32). Wolfe's use of such detail makes him a powerful satirist and hallmarks his style.

Yet he is a more complex figure than his ubiquitous characterization as innovative stylist or clever pop-culture commentator would indicate, a writer whose underlying fascination with status has driven him to explore conflicts between the individual and the group. Studying the interplay between insiders and outsiders throughout his essays, short stories, and novels, Wolfe believes that "the task of a writer is to show how the social context influences the personal psychology" and that it is impossible to "understand the individual without understanding the society." Perhaps, as Toby Thompson (1987) and Joseph Epstein (1988) have suggested, Wolfe's Southern background has heightened his sensitivity to caste systems and the pursuit of status and has given him respect for traditional values, evident in his choice of such heroes as Chuck Yeager and Junior Johnson. Consequently, Wolfe's explorations take place in the context of his idea that the prosperity of the post–World War II era has brought America to indulgences in greed, vanity, and freedom that are ridiculous and ultimately destructive. Thus, his examination of the individual and the group to which the individual does or does not belong is rarely flattering and often cruel, *The Right Stuff* being a notable exception. Underlying much of his work, however, no matter how funny or cutting, is a note of pathos created by depictions of "statuspheres" in which people seek self-definition and to which they always want to belong.

Although Wolfe's depth comes from his sensitivity to the quest for belonging, his range as a social satirist comes from his willingness to confront status groups at all levels of society. He approaches those who enclose art and architecture as easily as those who control a spot on the California beach or the custom car circuit, dissecting his subjects with a mixture of humor, fascination, and repugnance.

In Wolfe's first essay collection, his interest in the relationship between the group and the individual and between groups themselves began to emerge. What so intrigued him about the custom-car-show circuit in "That Kandy-Kolored Tangerine-Flake Streamline Baby" was its existence as a "statusphere" in which the hero was the most talented car designer, who nevertheless remained outside the mainstream of Detroit. Wolfe also saw it as the manifestation of an underclass (teenagers) having the money to "build monuments to their own styles," styles that "have started having an influence on the life of the whole country" (xiii). In another essay in the volume, "The Last American Hero," Wolfe's examination of the world of stock-car racing in rural North Carolina, with Junior Johnson at its center, yielded more observations about the heroics of individuality and about social change. Commenting on the displacement of baseball as the South's most popular sport, Wolfe observes that the "shift from a fixed land sport, modeled on cricket, to this wild car sport . . . symbolizes a radical change in the people as a whole" (xiv). And as the "classes of people whose styles of life had been practically invisible" gain the means to express themselves without the approval or consent of the aristocracy, the aristocracy loses its own vitality, simply reflecting the identities of other groups.

Distinct from other more eclectic works, three short books—*Radical Chic and Mau-Mauing the Flak Catchers, The Painted Word* and *From Bauhaus to Our House*—expose the fallacies of the resulting fashionable aristocratic pretensions. In these works Wolfe sends up the culturati for allowing themselves to be railroaded into accepting a country full of ugly architecture because of a cowardly deference to the cast-off tastes of Europe, paralyzing any individual vision with the demand for conformity. He effectively humiliates the Leonard Bernsteins by describing a party at their apartment to raise money for the Black Panthers and puts an end to the relationship between radical groups and the chic new left, suggesting at the same time that a desire to fit in and conform to the new fashion of ''elegant slumming'' has eradicated individual consideration of issues and submerged the individuality of those in both groups in meaningless game playing. In *The Painted Word,* Wolfe infuriated the modern art intellectuals with an explanation of how art has consumed itself, becoming nothing more than illustration of theory, the ironic incarnation of ''the word,'' which it had shunned as passé. The demand for illustration of theory thus destroyed the individual vision of artists and drove them instead to seek to be accepted by the theorists, rather than to create art. Behind these challenges to the smug and insular New York elite—the suggestion that they are cowards and fools—is Wolfe's dismay at the trading of individual conscience and vision for status.

Wolfe's second essay collection and his first nonfiction novel have focused more pointedly on the issues of individual status and group behavior. In ''The Pump House Gang,'' from which the collection takes its title, Wolfe examines the conflict between youth and age, outwardly the conflict between a group of cool young surfers and an old couple who are unwittingly invading their territory by lying on a certain part of the beach. Yet the outward conflict is reflective only of the crisis of absorbing identity in a group requiring youth as a condition of membership. The outward confrontations dramatize and presage for each member the time when he will be cast off into a world he cannot define in any positive terms, only that of the black panther—an old unhip person. Thus, all commit a form of suicide, either literally, like a 19-year-old and his 21-year-old girlfriend, or figuratively, by lopping themselves from a group that provides their whole definition of selfhood. Other blackly comic essays in the volume examine the struggle of a London society girl to gain status within her group, the loneliness of San Francisco's most notorious topless dancer, the futile attempt by an English businessman to escape the English caste system by Americanizing himself, and the inability of a wealthy respectable couple with a fabulous art collection to be accepted by the old guard at New York's Museum of Modern Art. Underlying the comedy and satire in these essays is an unmistakeable poignancy, a sensitivity to the casualties of caste.

The Electric Kool-Aid Acid Test, an analysis of the birth of the California drug culture in the 1960s, under the leadership of novelist Ken Kesey, is less an examination of how individuals fail to fit in but of how a single individual, despite his personal charisma, ultimately fails to lead his followers through the

LSD experience to a higher existence where the need for the drug is transcended. Revealing the underside of the group's devotion to the ethic of individual freedom is the inescapability of the ethic of conformity. "You're either on the bus or off the bus," as Kesey said—in other words, part of the group (and identified with its ideals) or an outsider (i.e., not one of the elect). The tension between individual freedom and Kesey's need to exercise control and ensure a kind of cohesion sustains the thematic unity of the book.

The most intense examination of the group dynamic, however, is in *The Right Stuff,* where Wolfe has done "a brilliant dissection of the status pyramid in the modern officer corps" (Thompson 1987, 162). Ten years after examining a group of subcultural outcasts, Wolfe focused on the astronauts, national mainstream heroes, bred in military rigidity and the demand for comformity. Resulting is a look at a status system built almost entirely on individual rebellion, on ego that defies the limitations of the human being, nature, and the machine. The fighter pilots seem for Wolfe to be the ultimate elite group, judging one another's right to belong by the capacity to avoid death in the most dangerous of situations. Here, suspending for the most part his role as social satirist, Wolfe has explored the "psychological mystery" of men who want to take the great risk of military piloting—and, ultimately, space exploration—in a time characterized as "the age of the anti-hero." Personalizing the drama of the development of the astronauts, Wolfe has examined the private caste system and found it essentially like the religious exclusivity of Kesey's Pranksters: One was on the bus or off; one had the right stuff or didn't.

Despite the success of *The Right Stuff,* the culmination of Wolfe's career has come with the publication of his first novel, *The Bonfire of the Vanities.* In it he explores not only how conformity to the group shapes an individual but also what happens to the individual when he or she is cast out of the group and confronts other groups without the protection of his or her own. Because of his immersion in pursuing and maintaining status, the main character, Sherman McCoy, is the incarnation of empty group identity, doing all the right things, wearing all the right clothes, with the right kind of wife and a child in the right school. Yet there is pathos, too, as he must figuratively die as a member of his group before he can develop an identity belonging only to himself, though the nature of this new identity remains ambiguous. Because of his victimization as a convenient political football after a hit-and-run accident, Sherman is exposed to the power of groups unlike his own and among them must find his own self-definition. Sherman's fall, whether fortunate or not, takes place in a novel that, as the title suggests, is a morality play in which everyone's vanities at all levels of society are exposed.

SURVEY OF CRITICISM

The critical response to Wolfe from the beginning of his career has been immediate and heated. His flamboyant personal appearance, his cutting social criticism (which has spared few of the causes of modern intellectualism), his unorthodox writing style, and his hybridization of two time-honored and separate forms—journalism and fiction—have made him and his work subjects on which few are neutral. The furor created, for example, by his 1989 essay entitled "Stalking the Billion-Footed Beast: A Literary Manifesto for the New Social Novel" in *Harper's* led the magazine to publish pages of responses to Wolfe's assertion that the only valid form for the novel is realism of the kind he practices. This latest offense by Wolfe and its subsequent uproar typifies what has happened when any work by Wolfe has been published. Along with the shouts that have gone up when Wolfe has run roughshod over a particular political, moral, or artistic sensibility, have come more tenacious and prevailing concerns. Two primary issues have haunted critics and analysts, both stemming in some way from Wolfe's signature New Journalism approach—the author's ambiguous attitude toward his subject and the problematic ethics of presenting fiction as fact.

Wolfe has always been at the center of the controversy about the new form, even when it was no longer new. The late Dwight Macdonald, reviewing *The Kandy-Kolored Tangerine-Flake Streamline Baby* in the *New York Review of Books* (1965) has articulated concerns still relevant to Wolfe criticism. In "Parajournalism, or Tom Wolfe and his Magic Writing Machine," Macdonald attacks Wolfe's New Journalism as a "bastard form . . . exploiting the factual authority of journalism and the atmospheric license of fiction" for the purpose of entertaining rather than informing (3). He charges further that the prose, written "hastily and loosely" and characterized by "elaboration rather than development," will not endure. Macdonald also objects to the disturbing authorial ambiguity that Wolfe's shifting points of view have created. Although other responses, such as those from Kurt Vonnegut and Stanley Reynolds, have been favorable, even enthusiastic, the issues in Macdonald's piece have remained viable as Wolfe has moved from the realm of the book review to that of the scholarly journal and the doctoral dissertation.

When *The Electric Kool-Aid Acid Test* was published, C. D. B. Bryan (1968) compared it to Norman Mailer's *Armies of the Night* and Neil Compton (1969) placed it in the "literature of American self-exploration—a little below *On the Road*" (78). Yet the same critics who praised it were often troubled by its chameleonic narration. Examining Wolfe's achievements for the *Journal of Popular Culture* in 1974, Ronald Weber articulated this generally qualified character of enthusiasm for Wolfe, concluding, however, that Wolfe's attitude toward his material and the charge that "his medium is more important than his message, his manner more important than his matter" is less relevant than the fact that "whether he means it or not, he has consistently dramatized a cultural situation in which the received culture appears on its last legs, about to give way under a popular assault based on the new styles and attitudes of widespread affluence" (78).

Yet Morris Dickstein (1976) and Barbara Rose (1981), responding to *The Painted Word* and *Radical Chic,* have focused more relentlessly on the question of ethics and represent a less tolerant view of Wolfe's accomplishments. Calling *The Painted Word* "a book of no merit," Rose, returning to the issue of fact and fiction, characterizes Wolfe as a ruthless and ignorant popular figure who panders to the ignorant public's desire for apparent sophistication and who uses the alchemy of his own invented prose form to eschew the requirements for factuality by which any legitimate writer or critic is bound (28). Dickstein characterizes Wolfe as a failure in the new form because he is too shallow to examine "the kind of social forces that impel both manners and morals and politics," hiding behind ambiguous narrative voices (869).

The Right Stuff, Wolfe's counterpoint to *The Electric Kool-Aid Acid Test,* drew the expected conflict regarding truth and fiction. Although Ken Kesey is unlikely to end up in any history books, the astronauts are heroes in the mainstream community, already made larger than life by press coverage and magazine mythology. Therefore, critics were concerned about the fictionalizing of the astronauts' experiences and about the mixture of make-believe and science. For example, the presentation of hyperbolic figures was readily detectable as a literary device in a comic social satire but not so easily distinguished from real figures in a book such as this one. Yet, the point seemed to be less important as Wolfe evolved from journalist to literary figure. Suspending broad social satire for his exploration into the private world of the astronaut, Wolfe gained status as a serious writer. Thomas Powers in a *Commonweal* review (1979) calls for the book to be evaluated as literature, allowed "to stand or fall as a coherent text" (552). In 1981 Charles Ross studied the book's rhetoric in an article for the *Journal of General Education,* and in 1983 Ronald Weber wrote in the *Virginia Quarterly Review* that Wolfe should be classed with Philip Roth and John Updike. Weber distinguishes Wolfe as literary on the basis of the points that had given the critics of New Journalism so much difficulty—the subjectification of detail and the manipulation of point of view, asserting that it is "not finally the details that matter, but the mind, imagination, and unfettered rhetoric imposed upon them, turning them into a Wolfian world as recognizable as the fictional world of a good novelist, . . . fact turned toward literature, reporting aimed at art" (550).

The reaction to Wolfe's latest production, his first long work of fiction, reveals that he has moved beyond his characterization as New Journalism personified, if not beyond the echoing critical concern about his ethics and his attitudes toward his subject. The responses to *The Bonfire of the Vanities* have been polarized politically, as Wolfe has, characteristically, held no cows sacred and no subjects, even the volatile ones of race and ethnicity, taboo. Therefore, much of the negative response to the novel has come from those who charge Wolfe with snobbery or various forms of racism. Thus charged, however, Wolfe has challenged his critics to go where he has been and do their own reporting and see how different what they see is from what he saw. Although he is still taken to task for failing to transcend the level of clever craftsmanship or for simply playing a game of spreading malice, such evaluations are made in the context of discussion of such writers as Thackeray, Dickens, Dreiser, and Fitzgerald, reflecting the new company Tom Wolfe is keeping.

BIBLIOGRAPHY

Works by Tom Wolfe

The Kandy-Kolored Tangerine-Flake Streamline Baby. New York: Farrar, Straus, and Giroux, 1965.
The Electric Kool-Aid Acid Test. New York: Farrar, Straus, and Giroux, 1968.
The Pump House Gang. New York: Farrar, Straus, and Giroux, 1968.
Radical Chic and Mau-Mauing the Flak Catchers. New York: Farrar, Straus, and Giroux, 1970.
The New Journalism. New York: Harper and Row, 1973.
The Painted Word. New York: Farrar, Straus, and Giroux, 1975.
Mauve Gloves and Madmen, Clutter and Vine. New York: Farrar, Straus, and Giroux, 1976.
The Right Stuff. New York: Farrar, Straus, and Giroux, 1979.
From Bauhaus to Our House. New York: Farrar, Straus, and Giroux, 1981.
In Our Time. New York: Farrar, Straus, and Giroux, 1981.
The Purple Decades: A Reader. New York: Farrar, Straus, and Giroux, 1982.
The Bonfire of the Vanities. New York: Farrar, Straus, and Giroux, 1987.
"Stalking the Billion-Footed Beast: A Literary Manifesto for the New Social Novel." *Harper's* 270 (November 1989): 45–56.

Interviews with Tom Wolfe

Angelo, Bonnie. "Master of His Universe." *Time* 133 (February 13, 1989): 90–92.
Bellamy, David. Interview with Tom Wolfe. In *The New Fiction: Interviews with Innovative American Writers.* Urbana: University of Illinois Press, 1974.
———. "Sitting Up with Tom Wolfe." *Writer's Digest* 54 (November 1974): 22–29.
Dundy, Elaine. "Tom Wolfe . . . But Exactly, Yes!" *Vogue* 56 (April 1966).
Flippo, Chet. "Tom Wolfe." *Rolling Stone* (August 21, 1980): 31–37.
Gilder, Joshua. "Tom Wolfe." *Saturday Review* 8 (April 1981): 40–44.
Marchese, William J. "The Wolfe Man." *Writer's Digest* 60 (April 1980): 18–19.
Mewborn, Brant. "Tom Wolfe." *Rolling Stone* (November 5, 1987): 214–21.
Sanoff, Alvin P. "Tom Wolfe's Walk on the Wild Side." *U.S. News and World Report* 103 (November 23, 1987): 57–58.
Scura, Dorothy. *Conversations with Tom Wolfe.* Jackson: University Press of Mississippi, 1990.
"Tom Wolfe: The Years of Living Prosperously." *U.S. News and World Report* 107 (December 25, 1989): 117.
Zelenko, Lori Simmons. "What Are the Pressures Affecting the Art World Today?" *American Artist* 40 (April 1982): 12–17.

Studies of Tom Wolfe

Anderson, Chris. "Pushing the Outside of the Envelope." In *Style as Argument: Contemporary American Nonfiction,* 8–47. Carbondale: Southern Illinois University Press, 1987.

Atwill, William Dorsey. "Fire and Power: Narratives of the Space Age." Ph.D. diss., Duke University, 1990.

Beard, John. "Inside the Whale: A Critical Study of New Journalism and the Nonfiction Form." Ph.D. diss., Florida State University, 1985.

Booker, Christopher. "Inside the Bubble: Re-reading Tom Wolfe." *Encounter* 49 (September 1977): 72–77.

Bredahl, A. Carl. "An Exploration of Power: Tom Wolfe's Acid Test." *Critique* 23 (Winter 1981–82): 67–84.

Bryan, C. D. B. "The Same Day: Heeeeewack!!!" *New York Times Book Review* 73 (August 18, 1968): 1–2.

Cardinal, Esther K. "Journalistic Fiction: A Development from Early American Realism." Ph.D. diss., Kent State University, Ohio, 1981.

Compton, Neil. "Hijinks Journalism." *Commentary* 47 (February 1969): 76–78.

Crawford, Sheri F. "Tom Wolfe: Outlaw Gentleman." *Journal of American Culture* 13, no. 2 (Summer 1990): 39–50.

Dickstein, Morris. "The Working Press, the Literary Culture, and the New Journalism." *Georgia Review* 30 (Winter 1976): 855–77.

Eason, David L. "New Journalism, Metaphor, and Culture." *Journal of Popular Culture* xv (Spring 1982): 142–49.

Epstein, Joseph. "Tom Wolfe's Vanities." *New Criterion* 6 (February 1988): 5–16.

Hartshorne, Thomas L. "Tom Wolfe on the 1960's." *Midwest Quarterly* 23 (Winter 1982): 144–63.

Heilman, Patricia Kluss. "The Journalism-Fiction Connection in American Literature as Seen in Selected Works of Stephen Crane, Ernest Hemingway, and Tom Wolfe." Ph.D. diss., Indiana University of Pennsylvania, 1987.

Hellmann, John. "Reporting the Fabulous: Representation and Response in the Work of Tom Wolfe." In *Fables of Fact: The New Journalism as New Fiction,* 101–25. Urbana: University of Illinois Press, 1981.

Hersey, John. "The Legend on the License." *Yale Review* 75 (Winter 1986): 144–63.

Hurd, Myles Raymond. " 'The Masque of the Red Death' in Wolfe's *The Bonfire of the Vanities.*" *Notes on Contemporary Literature* 20 (May 1990): 4–5.

Jones, Dan Richard. "The Fiction of Fact: Toward a Journalistic Aesthetic." Ph.D. diss., University of Iowa, 1984.

Journal of American Culture. Special issue on Tom Wolfe. Edited by Marshall W. Fishwick. 14, no. 3 (Fall 1991): 1–51.

Kallan, Richard A. "The New Nonfiction: A Rhetorical Case Study of Tom Wolfe." Ph.D. diss., Northwestern University, 1976.

———. "Style and the New Journalism: A Rhetorical Analysis of Tom Wolfe." *Communication Monographs* 46 (March 1979): 52–62.

Lounsberry, Barbara. *The Art of Fact: Contemporary Artists of Nonfiction.* Westport, Conn.: Greenwood, 1990.

————. "Tom Wolfe's Negative Vision." *South Dakota Review* 20 (Summer 1982): 15–31.

Macdonald, Dwight. "Parajournalism; or, Tom Wolfe and His Magic Writing Machine." *New York Review of Books* 5 (August 26, 1965): 3–5.

Meyers, Paul Thomas. "The New Journalist as Culture Critic: Wolfe, Thompson, Talese." Ph.D. diss., Washington State University, 1976.

Nordquist, Richard F. "Voices of the Modern Essay." Ph.D. diss., University of Georgia, 1991.

Porsdam, Helle. "In the Age of Lawspeak: Tom Wolfe's *The Bonfire of the Vanities* and American Litigiousness." *Journal of American Studies* 25 (April 1991): 39–57.

Powers, Thomas. "Wolfe in Orbit." *Commonweal* 106 (October 12, 1979): 551–52.

Rafferty, Terrence. "The Man Who Knew Too Much." *New Yorker* 63 (February 1, 1988): 88–92.

Rice, Rodney P. "Wallace Stegner and Tom Wolfe: Cowboys, Pilots, and The Right Stuff." *Notes on Contemporary Literature* 21, no. 2 (March 1991): 5–7.

Rich, Frank. "The Right-Wing Stuff." *New Republic* (November 23, 1987): 42–46.

Rose, Barbara. "Wolfeburg." *New York Review of Books* 22 (June 26, 1975): 26–28.

Ross, Charles S. "The Rhetoric of *The Right Stuff.*" *Journal of General Education* 33 (Summer 1981): 113–22.

Smith, Kathy Anne. "Writing the Borderline: Journalism's Literary Contract." Ph.D. diss., University of Massachusetts, 1988.

Stokes, Lisa Oldham. "Tom Wolfe's Narratives as Stories of Growth." Ph.D. diss., University of Florida, 1989.

Stull, James N. "Presentation of Self in Contemporary American Literary Journalism, 1965–1980." Ph.D. diss., University of Iowa, 1991.

Tanrisal, Meldan. "New Journalism and the Nonfiction Novel: Creating Art through Facts." Ph.D. diss., Hacettepe Universitesi, Turkey, 1988.

Thompson, Toby. "The Evolution of Dandy Tom." *Vanity Fair* 50 (October 1987): 119–27, 160–64.

Vigilante, Richard. "The Truth about Tom Wolfe." Review of *The Bonfire of the Vanities. Time* 9 (November 1987): 101–104.

Weber, Ronald. "Tom Wolfe's Happiness Explosion." *Journal of Popular Culture* 7 (Summer 1974): 71–79.

————. "Staying Power." *Virginia Quarterly Review* 59 (Summer 1983): 548–52.

Whelan, Brent. " 'Further': Reflections on Counter-Culture and the Post-Modern." *Cultural Critique* 11 (Winter 1988–89): 63–86.

Wolcott, James. "Tom Wolfe's Greatest Hits." *New York Review of Books* 29 (November 4, 82): 21–23.

MARGARET MILLS HARPER

Charles Wright
(1935–   )

Wright's mature poems reach with unusual intensity for visionary insight, often figured as absence or disappearance, while they also insist on immediate and tangible reality. His stance is usually meditative; his favorite settings are rural or semirural landscapes; and his rhythms are more painterly than musical. However, the quiet of the verse is often tense with spiritual restlessness (a quality Wright has in common with mystics or religious poets such as Dante or Emily Dickinson). A dynamic interiority is rendered through the lines that are Wright's primary unit of composition and the particular vehicles for his formal skill. His poetry is dense and image-laden, in the manner of his poetic mentors Ezra Pound and Eugenio Montale, but his images do not sit still. They slip from concrete to abstract to transcendent, forced into motion by the poet's questioning, in lines of ''freed verse'' that move, at their best, with great power.

BIOGRAPHY

Today there is still more river than people where Pickwick Landing Dam, in Hardin County, Tennessee, widens the Tennessee River into Pickwick Lake. From there the river flows south again, away from the battlefield at Shiloh and toward Alabama and Mississippi a few miles farther downstream. Here, where he remembers being able to see three states from his front porch, Charles Penzel Wright, Jr., was born on August 25, 1935, to Charles Penzel (1904–1972) and Mary Castelman (Winter) Wright (1910–1964).

The family moved to the new planned town of Oak Ridge during Wright's early childhood, then after World War II to Kingsport in the mountainous eastern part of the state. Wright has traced his love of structure and order to his father, who was an engineer for the Tennessee Valley Authority; his mother passed down to her son an early interest in literature.

In Kingsport it would have been hard to avoid the impress of Appalachian music. Wright has acknowledged especially the importance to him of the Carter family, one of the most popular and influential groups in country music who, as it happened, lived just eight miles away. But music did not come only from the radio: almost every member of the maternal side of the family played an instrument (some very well indeed, notably the rock musicians Johnny and Edgar Winter, Wright's first cousins).

Evangelical Christianity encircled Wright as solidly as the granite mountains and had a large part in shaping his imagination even though he eventually rejected Christian faith. He was active in the Episcopalian church that his family attended, imbibing "English Catholicism" as altar boy, in Sunday School, and at summer Bible camp. His high-school years were spent at private schools: tenth grade at Sky Valley, a boarding school outside Hendersonville, North Carolina (with only seven other students); junior and senior years at an Episcopal boarding school, Christ School, in Arden, North Carolina.

Wright downplays his college years at Davidson College, from which he graduated in 1957 with a major in history. His education in poetry began in 1959, while he was stationed in Verona, Italy, at the beginning of a 4-year stint in the Army Intelligence Service. According to Wright, he read poetry seriously for the first time after a friend gave him a copy of Pound's *Selected Poems* and told him to go to Sirmione, a peninsula overlooking Lake Garda outside Verona where the Roman poet Catullus is said to have had a villa, and read Pound's "Blandula, Tenulla, Vagula," which was set there. Wright has said that his "life was changed forever" by this experience, which seems to have converted him almost immediately to his vocation. For the rest of his tenure in the army he read Pound intensely and alone, "with absolutely no preconceptions, no way of knowing what was acceptable and what wasn't, and I happened to pick up the most ambitious poet in the English language in the twentieth century to start with."

Pound was the first of several poetic mentors with whom Wright has had an almost religious communion. He has spoken with equal intensity of the time he spent in Rome and then in California reading Dante, canto by canto, in Italian. "It was the most glorious three months of reading I've ever done," he remembers. "I didn't write a line of my own during that entire time I was so completely filled and fulfilled. Nothing like it had ever affected me so before and I doubt anything ever will again." Wright also feels a particular kinship with Dickinson, "The only poet who, when I read her, I feel as though I understand, I know, and have heard before, somewhere, what she is trying to tell me." In other words, according to Wright, "Her disquietudes are my disquietudes."

A deciding step toward academic American poetry was taken in 1961 when Wright was accepted into the prestigious Writing Workshop at the University of Iowa—which happened "on a fluke," he claims, "as no one read the manuscript I sent in during the summer, and when the graduate school independently admitted me, I just assumed I could go into the Workshop. So I did. I registered for courses and went to them and kept my mouth shut for two years, as I knew after two minutes of the first Workshop class that I had stepped into deep stuff.'' Wright's maturation as a poet and a translator occurred during two periods of study there, among such poets and friends as Donald Justice and Mark Strand, and in an intervening year of postgraduate work at the University of Rome as a Fulbright scholar studying Dante and translating Montale and Cesare Pavese. Montale has been an enduring influence, and in general the experience of translating poetry has contributed greatly to the precision of Wright's language, his awareness of sound, and his interest in the inescapable failure of meaning. ''All poems are translations,'' he believes.

Upon graduation in 1966 Wright accepted a faculty position at the University of California at Irvine and stayed there until 1983, when he joined the faculty at the University of Virginia. Visiting lectureships have taken him to Iowa, Columbia, and Princeton, and he returned to Italy via another Fulbright Fellowship to the University of Padua in 1968–69. He is married to Holly McIntire, a photographer, and they have one son.

Wright's first book, *The Grave of the Right Hand,* was published in 1970. His reputation has steadily risen with eight subsequent volumes of poetry, three translations, and, recently, a collection of interviews and miscellaneous pieces. In addition to two Fulbright Fellowships, he has won numerous awards, beginning with the Eunice Tietjens Memorial Prize (*Poetry* magazine) in 1969. *Hard Freight* (1973), his second volume, was nominated for the National Book Award. In 1975 he received the Melville Cane Award from the Poetry Society of America for *Bloodlines,* and in 1976 he was granted the Edgar Allan Poe Award administered by the Academy of American Poets for the same volume. He was given an Academy-Institute Grant from the American Academy and Institute of Arts and Letters in 1977. Both the John Simon Guggenheim Foundation and the National Endowment for the Arts contributed to the writing of *China Trace* (1977). In 1979 *The Storm and Other Poems* won the Pen Prize for best translation of any book. Wright was made a Fellow by the Ingram Merrill Foundation for *The Southern Cross* (1981), a book that was also a runner-up for the Pulitzer Prize in poetry in 1982. In 1983 the American Book Award for Poetry was shared by Wright (for *Country Music*) and Galway Kinnell. The following year, *The Other Side of the River* was nominated for the National Book Critics Circle award in poetry.

MAJOR THEMES

In his poetry Wright is preoccupied with an essentially religious, even mystical, search. He writes in ''A Journal of English Days,'' in *Zone Journals* (1988):

I keep coming back, like a tongue to a broken tooth. . .
There is no sickness of spirit like homesickness

When what you are sick for
                                has never been seen or heard
    In this world, or even remembered . . . (14–15)

His poems are at the same time obsessively concrete, insisting upon material
details in landscape, memory, or travelogue, and stubbornly unwilling to subordinate these details to any transcendent abstraction. The mystery at the heart
of Wright's verse is that it may be possible to unite these two seemingly opposite
impulses through the agency of the poetic voice, inserted into the world by
speaking and making forms. It may heal rifts within a single psyche, between
people, and between the human and nonhuman worlds.

Paradoxically, of course, the poetic voice neither exists as physical reality nor
alters reality. It misnames and displaces, cannot genuinely represent, but can
nonetheless reconcile elements of a wayward truth. Wright's poetry is more
Modernist than postmodern in its devotion to meaning; but its light touch and
surreal quality, resulting from forced conjunctions of precise observation and
mystic vision, ally it to postmodernism. Half seriously, he has called his writing
"eschatological naturalism: a school of one," a phrase that captures the tendency of his verse to radiate outward and inward simultaneously.

The faith toward which Wright's work tends does not deny that obscuring is
part of illumination but holds that the use of language is salvific even as it is
fictive. As the title poem of *The Other Side of the River* puts it, "It's all a matter
of how / you narrow the surfaces. / It's all a matter of how you fit in the sky"
(24). The fit, we should notice, is both personal and impersonal, as is the pro-
noun *you* in these lines. "You" move into the ineffable by the imaginative act
of narrowing or creating "matter."

The danger, or perhaps the temptation, is that one may simply lose oneself—
fit into the sky and be gone. In his poems Wright often denies a unified self,
preferring to break it down into constituent parts. The speaker of the poem
"Reunion" (*China Trace*) is characteristic in asserting, "I write poems to untie
myself, to do penance and disappear / Through the upper right-hand corner of
things, to say grace" (49). But speaking remains, as perhaps does grace, in this
disappearing act.

So does the palpable world, which is often the setting for Wright's sleight of
hand. In keeping with Wright's interest in what can be found beyond the "upper
right-hand corner of things," his visible world is often seen in close-up, as if
close inspection of plants, insects, birds, or objects might yield vision unavailable to a long view. Likewise, although Wright's poetry is often autobiographical we are typically left without a sense of the unified person with which
autobiography is usually concerned. The poet eludes us through the very recitals
of data that should let us place him. In "Lonesome Pine Special" (*The Other
Side of the River*) the poet asks. "What is it about a known landscape / that
tends to undo us. / That shuffles and picks us out / For terminal demarcation[?]"
(13). In his poems Wright almost inevitably focuses on a remembered or re-

corded fact in order to pinpoint how it "undid" the speaker, separated him from his surroundings, and pushed him toward the abstract or the void. Thus, one of his self-portraits is "Self-Portrait in 2035" (*Southern Cross*), by which future date the poet—and perhaps the words of the poem as well—will be long erased. Thus, also, in his poems about family Wright tends to stress the fragmentation of death and the passage of time, presenting isolated memories, familiar objects, imprints that loved ones have made upon the living rather than continuous stories or whole portraits.

Given Wright's conviction of the role of language in composing truth, it is not surprising that he is preeminently a formalist even though he almost always works in structures of his own making. His evolution as a poet has paralleled the evolution of the forms in which he has cast his work. In general, Wright's developing skill has manifested itself in the handling of increasingly larger units as his career has progressed.

In his first book, *The Grave of the Right Hand,* the weight of individual words sometimes impedes the longer units. The poems are often memorable, but the images are given such power that they sometimes strain the wholes of which they are part. In *Hard Freight* homage and recognition are extended to poets, family, and land that have burdened and formed the poet. In this volume, the images and the usually implicit connections between them work in concert, causing the lines to move with musical and seemingly inevitable movement. This distinctive singing and pronouncing by the poetic line is possibly the greatest of Wright's achievements, and he has varied and refined it (and applied it to gradually longer lines) throughout subsequent books.

The tracks upon which the poems of *Hard Freight* run become a more complex and intertwined network in *Bloodlines.* Two sequences dominate this concentrically-organized volume, "Tattoos" and "Skins," series of meditations in free verse with stylistic affinities to sonnets. Elegies for Wright's father and mother separate the sequences from each other in the dead center of the book. The twenty "Tattoos" are improvisations upon events in the poet's past indelibly imprinted upon, or ceaselessly beat into, his consciousness (each poem is dated by the experience that provoked it, and each experience is listed factually in notes following the sequence). "Skins" are highly abstract renderings and sheddings of successive layers of feeling or conviction, none quite satisfactory, that envelop the living self, a notice attempt to "try for the get-away by the light of yourself" (59).

Wright once explained to an interviewer that " 'Tatoos' was me in relation to the past. 'Skins' is me in relation to the present. *China Trace* is me in relation to the future, "but" it is even more involved: *Bloodlines* is the center of the three books *Hard Freight, Bloodlines,* and *China Trace.* 'Tatoos' hooks up with *Hard Freight* and the past, and 'Skins' hooks up with *China Trace* and the future." *China Trace,* Wright's next volume, is a structure built of short poems that cohere by virtue of an almost invisible force joining image to image and poem to poem. In this volume, spiritual worries and possibilities are represented by concretions that draw attention to what is missing by the uncanny distances between the concretions and what they might be presumed to signify, and among the images themselves. Wright's skill in sound and metrics dominates this volume, making lines and stanzas memorable as few contemporary poems are and giving a sense of felt organization to highly original structures.

Southern Cross, the volume following the trilogy of *Hard Freight, Bloodlines,* and *China Trace,* marks a change: In longer, daringly daubed lines of uneasily surreal emblems, Wright explores the possibility of an objective self in a world of living and dead. The verse is more relaxed, more openly discursive, and more confident, showing the nod to Hart Crane that the title implies, while keeping the startling skill with image and sound that are Wright's trademarks. The volume opens and closes with long poems, ''Homage to Cézanne'' and ''The Southern Cross,'' that are especially acute in picturing what the dead and one's own entrapment in time can say.

In *The Other Side of the River* it is clear that Wright had entered new territory, although the poems are in familiar locations: the South, Italy, the interior world (one poem is set inside the human eye). But the search is for the infinite in the depth of the finite. Wright's continuing burden has been undertaken with less implicit trust in ''poetic'' language. In addition to the luminous image and the almost physical love of the word and the line, in *The Other Side of the Wright River*, is willing to use bald statement, abstraction, and rhetoric to propel his poems. The result is a volume of clarity and greater warmth than readers of Wright's earlier verse may have been used to, a more accessible and powerful volume.

Wright's most recent book of new poems, *Zone Journals,* joins *Southern Cross* and *The Other Side of the River* to form a second loose trilogy (or perhaps triptych, given Wright's medieval and painterly inclinations). The well-wrought poem has yielded to the ''journal,'' a deceptively direct, narrative, and evanescent form to contain Wright's passionate reach to connect word and world. It is risky to bring poetry as close to self-absorption, even self-indulgence, as Wright has done in these lengthy meditations, in which poetic mastery is not so much displayed as taken for granted. The long, luxuriating lines that are often broken to fill the page almost completely are reminiscent of Whitman; the unapologetically bardic stance recalls no poet so much as the late Yeats, although Wright's bard wears his position lightly, with humility and humor. The poems are difficult to excerpt and impossible to outline, an interesting development for a poet who has remarked that ''in poems, all considerations are considerations of form.''

In 1990 the Windhover Press published a small book entitled *Xionia* (the name of Wright's home in Virginia where the poems were written) containing fifteen journal-poems, the last of which is called ''Last Journal.'' *Xionia,* like Zion, is the place where a journey has come to rest, and Wright obviously intends us to read it as such: It appears, coda-like, at the end of a collection that includes *The Southern Cross, The Other Side of the River,* and *Zone Jour-*

nals (The World of the Ten Thousand Things). According to Wright, the journal form will now be replaced by another, surely something to contain his long line with its jazzlike movement and to allow for his love of the backlit image, remarked upon in "December Journal" (*Ten Thousand Things*): "I keep coming back to the visible. / I keep coming back / To what it leads me into" (209).

SURVEY OF CRITICISM

No books and relatively few full-length essays have yet been devoted to Wright's work, although his books are regularly reviewed. A turning point in the level of critical attention paid to Wright occurred in 1979, when Helen Vendler's admiration for the first trilogy appeared in the *New Yorker* and then in a collection of her essays.

In keeping with Vendler's formal interests and Wright's own academic background and experience, many opinions about his poetry register approval or disapproval with his formalism. He is most often praised for his linguistic and structural precision, the music of his line, and his metaphysical concerns (which lend themselves to comparison with Eastern philosophy and poststructuralist criticism). Critics who have found fault with him have tended to stress the difficulty of his image-laden lines and larger patterns, rhythms that are overly lush or "slick" rather than sincere. The same critics have found his poetry to be meditations verging on solipsism. Recent criticism has also registered either satisfaction or disgruntlement with his free use of high and openly declarative rhetoric.

Wright has been brilliant and generous in interviews (so it is perhaps not surprising that his most interesting interviewers, David St. John and David Young, are also his most perceptive critics). A number of the best interviews have been collected, along with short essays and utterances that Wright calls "improvisations," in the book *Halflife* (1988).

BIBLIOGRAPHY

Works by Charles Wright

"Correspondences." M.F.A. thesis, University of Iowa, 1963.
The Voyage. Iowa City: Patrician Press, 1963.
Six Poems. London: Freed, 1965.
The Dream Animal. Toronto: House of Anansi, 1968.
Private Madrigals. Madison, Wis.: Abraxas Press, 1969.
The Grave of the Right Hand. Middletown, Conn.: Wesleyan University Press, 1970.
The Venice Notebook. Boston: Barn Dream Press, 1971.
Backwater. Cosa Mesa, Calif.: Golem Press, 1973.
Hard Freight. Middletown, Conn.: Wesleyan University Press, 1973.
Bloodlines. Middletown, Conn.: Wesleyan University Press, 1975.

China Trace. Middletown, Conn.: Wesleyan University Press, 1977.
Colophons. Iowa City, Iowa: Windhover Press, 1977.
Wright: A Profile. With David St. John. Iowa City, Iowa: Grilled Flowers Press, 1979.
Dead Color. Salem, Oreg.: Seluzicki Fine Books, 1980.
The Southern Cross. New York: Random House, 1981.
Country Music: Selected Early Poems. Middletown, Conn.: Wesleyan University Press, 1982.
Four Poems of Departure. Portland, Oreg.: Trace Editions, 1983.
The Other Side of the River. New York: Random House, 1984.
Five Journals. New York: Red Ozier Press, 1986.
Halflife: Improvisations and Interviews. Ann Arbor: University of Michigan Press, 1988.
A Journal of the Year of the Ox. Iowa City, Iowa Windhover Press, 1988.
Zone Journals. New York: Farrar, Straus, and Giroux, 1988.
Xionia. Iowa City, Iowa: Windhover Press, 1990.
The World of the Ten Thousand Things: Poems, 1980–1990. New York: Farrar Straus, and Giroux, 1990.

Works Translated by Charles Wright

The Selected Poems of Eugenio Montale. New York: New Directions, 1965. (Nineteen poems translated by Wright.)
The Storm and Other Poems, by Eugenio Montale. Oberlin, Ohio: Oberlin College Press, 1978.
Motets, by Eugenio Montales. Iowa City, Iowa: Windhover Press, 1981.
Orphic Songs, by Dino Campana. Oberlin, Ohio: Oberlin College Press, 1984.

Interviews with Charles Wright

Friebert, Stuart, and David Young. ''Charles Wright at Oberlin.'' In *A Field Guide to Contemporary Poetry and Poetics,* edited by Stuart Friebert and David Young, 241–71. New York: Longman, 1980.
Remnick, David. ''An Interview with Charles Wright.'' *Partisan Review* 50 (1983): 567–75.
Wright, Charles. *Improvisations and Interviews.* Ann Arbor: University of Michigan Press, 1988.

Studies of Charles Wright

Agena, Kathleen. ''The Mad Sense of Language.'' *Partisan Review* 43 (Fall 1976): 625–30.
Bedient, Calvin. ''Tracing Charles Wright.'' *Parnassus* 10, no. 1 (Spring 1982): 55–74.
Bunch, Debbie. '' 'In All Beauty There Lies Something Inhuman.' '' *Daily Iowan* (Iowa City) (October 26, 1976):1, 5.
Costello, Bonnie. ''The Soil and Man's Intelligence: Three Contemporary Landscape Poets.'' *Contemporary Literature* 30 (1989): 412–33.
Francini, Antonella. ''In the Longfellow Line: Some Contemporary American Poets as

Translators of Eugenio Montale: A Study in Theory and Practice." Ph. D. diss., Drew University, Madison, New Jersey, 1985.

Hix, H. L. "Charles Wright and a Case of Foreshortened Influence." *Notes on Contemporary Literature* 18 (1988): 4–6.

Kinsie, Mary. "Haunting." *American Poetry Review* 11, no. 5 (September–October 1982): 37–46.

Jackson, Richard. "Worlds Created, Worlds Perceived." *Michigan Quarterly Review* 17 (1978): 543–62.

Jarman, Mark. "The Pragmatic Imagination and the Secret of Poetry." *The Gettysburg Review* 1 (1988): 647–60.

Kalstone, David. "Lives in a Rearview Mirror." *New York Times Book Review* 133 (July 1, 1984): 14.

Kennedy, X.J. "Lovers of Greece, Women and Tennessee." *New York Times Book Review* 123 (February 17, 1974): 6.

Lake, Paul. "Return to Metaphor: From Deep Imagist to New Formalist." *Southwest Review* 74 (1989): 515–29.

Logan, William. "Season to Season, Day to Day." *New York Times Book Review* 137 (September 4, 1988): 9–10.

McClatchy, J.D. "Recent Poetry: New Designs on Life." *Yale Review* 65 (1975): 93–105.

McCorkle, James Donald Bruland. "Gaze, Memory, and Discourse: Self-Reflexivity in Recent American Poetry." Ph.D. diss., University of Iowa, 1984.

————. *The Still Performance: Writing, Self, and Interconnection in Five Postmodern American Poets.* Charlottesville: University Press of Virginia, 1989.

Muske, Carol. "Ourselves as History." *Parnassus* 4, no. 2 (Spring–Summer 1976): 111–121.

Pankey, Eric. "The Form of Concentration." *Iowa Review* 19 (1989): 175–87.

Parmi, Jay. "From Scene to Fiery Scene." *Times Literary Supplement* (March 1, 1985): 239.

Pettingell, Phoebe. "Through Memory and Miniatures." *New Leader* 67 (August 20, 1984): 17–18.

Rosenthal, M.L. "Sensibilities, Ltd." *Parnassus* 7, no. 2 (Spring–Summer 1979): 119–23.

St. John, David. "The Poetry of Charles Wright." In *Wright: A Profile,* by Charles Wright and David St. John, 53–65. Iowa City, Iowa: Grilled Flowers Press, 1979.

Stewart, Pamela. "In All Places at Once." *Ironwood* 19 (1982): 162–66.

Stitt, Peter. Essay on Charles Wright. *Georgia Review* 32 (1978): 474–80.

————. "Words, Book Words, What Are You?" *Georgia Review* 37 (1983): 428–38.

————. "The Circle of the Meditative Moment." *Georgia Review* 38 (1984): 402–14.

————. "To Enlighten, To Embody." *Georgia Review* 41 (1987):800–813.

Van Winckel, Nance. "Charles Wright and the Landscape of the Lyric." *New England Review and Bread Loaf Quarterly* 12 (1990): 308–12.

Vendler, Helen. "The Transcendent 'I'." *New Yorker* 55, no. 37 (October 29, 1979). Reprinted in *Part of Nature, Part of Us: Modern American Poets,* 277–88. Cambridge: Harvard University Press, 1980.

Wright, Stuart. "Charles Wright: A Bibliographic Chronicle, 1963–1985." *Bulletin of Bibliography* 43 (1986): 3–12.

Young, David. "The Blood Bees of Paradise." *Field* 44 (Spring 1991): 77–90.

Supplementary Material on Three Contemporary Writers Included in *Fifty Southern Writers after 1900*

Appendix A updates the selected bibliographies of three authors who are subjects of essays in *Fifty Southern Writers after 1900,* edited by Joseph M. Flora and Robert Bain and published by Greenwood Press in 1987. Bibliographies in the *Mississippi Quarterly* remain the primary bibliography for Southern literary studies; those wishing full and current bibliographies of Southern writers should continue to consult this indispensable work.

A. R. AMMONS (1926–   )

Works by A. R. Ammons

Easter Morning. Winston-Salem, N.C.: Shadowy Waters Press, 1986.

The Selected Poems. New York: Norton, 1986.

Papers, 1944–1987. Manuscripts Department of the Southern Historical Collection of the University of North Carolina at Chapel Hill.

Sumerian Vistas: Poems. New York: Norton, 1987.

The Really Short Poems of A. R. Ammons. New York: Norton, 1990.

Poets in Person. Chicago: Modern Poetry Association, 1991. Sound Cassette.

Studies of A. R. Ammons

Cushman, Stephen B. "Stanzas, Organic Myth, and the Metaformalism of A. R. Ammons." *American Literature* 59 (December 1987): 513–27.

Grabher, Gudrun. *Das lyrische Du: Du-Vergessenheit und Möglichkeiten der Du-Bestimmung in der amerikanischen Dichtung.* Heidelburg, 1989.

McFee, Michael. "Form in the Long Poems of A. R. Ammons." Master's thesis, University of North Carolina, Chapel Hill, 1978.

Mills, Elizabeth M. "Wording the Unspeakable: Emily Dickson and A. R. Ammons."
    Ph.D. diss., University of North Carolina, Chapel Hill, 1985.
Reiman, Donald H. "A. R. Ammons: Ecological Naturalism and the Romantic Tradi-
    tion." *Twentieth Century Literature* 31 (Spring 1985): 22–54.
Vendler, Helen. "A. R. Ammons and Home: Dwelling in the Flow of Shapes." *South-
    west Review* 72 (Spring 1987): 150–67.
Wright, Stuart T. *A. R. Ammons: A Bibliography, 1954–1979.* Winston-Salem, N.C.:
    Wake Forest University, 1980.

JAMES DICKEY (1923–)

Works by James Dickey

In Pursuit of the Gray Soul. Columbia, S.C.: Clark, 1978.
Head-Deep in Strange Sounds: Free-Flight Improvisations from the Un-English. Win-
    ston-Salem, N.C.: Palaemon Press, 1979.
Falling, May Day Sermon, and Other Poems. Middletown, Conn.: Wesleyan University
    Press, 1981.
Helmets, 1981. Middletown, Conn.: Wesleyan University Press, 1981.
The Central Motion: Poems, 1968–1979. Middletown, Conn.: Wesleyan University Press,
    1983.
False Youth—Four Seasons. Dallas, Tex.: Prinworks, 1983.
For Reynolds Price. 1 February 1983. Printed privately, 1983.
Intervisions: Poems and Photographs. Penland, N.C.: Visualternatives, 1983.
Night Hurdling: Poems, Essays, Conversations, Commencements, and Afterwords. Co-
    lumbia, S.C.: Clark, 1983.
Alnilam. Garden City, N.Y.: Doubleday, 1987.
From the Green Horseshoe: Poems. Columbia: University of Missouri Press, 1987.
Wayfarer: A Voice from the Southern Mountains. Birmingham, Ala.: Oxmoor House,
    1988.
The Eagle's Mile. Middletown, Conn.: Wesleyan University Press; Hanover, N.H.: Uni-
    versity Press of New England, 1990.
The Whole Motion: Collected Poems, 1945–1992. New Hanover, N.H.: University Press
    of New England, 1992.

Interviews with James Dickey

The Voiced Connections of James Dickey: Interviews and Conversations. Columbia, S.C.:
    University of South Carolina Press, 1989.

Studies of James Dickey

Baker, Pamela M. "The Shadow Archetype in James Dickey's *Deliverance.*" *Journal
    of Popular Literature* 2 (Spring–Summer 1986): 67–75.
Baughman, Ronald. *Understanding James Dickey.* Columbia: University of South Car-
    olina Press, 1985.

Bloom, Harold. "James Dickey: From 'The Other' through *The Early Motion.*" *Southern Review* 21 (Winter 1985): 63–78.

Bloom, Harold, ed. *James Dickey.* New York: Chelsea, 1987.

Bowers, Neal. *James Dickey: The Poet as Pitchman.* Columbia: University of Missouri Press, 1985.

Bruccoli, Matthew Joseph. *James Dickey: A Bibliography.* Pittsburgh, Pa.: University of Pittsburgh Press, 1990.

Christensen, Paul. "Toward the Abyss: James Dickey at Middle Age." *Parnassus* 13 (Spring–Summer 1986): 203–19.

Gilman, Owen W., Jr. "Vietnam in the South: *Deliverance.*" In *Vietnam and the Southern Imagination,* 169–86. Jackson: University Press of Mississippi, 1992.

Griffith, James J. "Damned If You Do, and Damned If You Don't: James Dickey's *Deliverance.*" *PostS* 5 (Spring–Summer 1986): 47–59.

James Dickey Newsletter. 1984.

Kirschten, Robert. *James Dickey and the Gentle Ecstasy of Earth.* Baton Rouge: Louisiana State University Press, 1988.

Spears, Monroe K. "James Dickey as Southern Visionary." *Virginia Quarterly Review* 63 (Winter 1987): 110–23.

Van Ness, Gordon. *Outbelieving Existence: The Measured Motion of James Dickey.* Columbia, S.C.: Camden House, 1992.

Wright, Stuart T. *James Dickey: A Bibliography of His Books, Pamphlets, and Broadsides.* Dallas, Tex.: Pressworks, 1982.

SHELBY FOOTE (1916–   )

Works by Shelby Foote

Papers, 1935–1981. Manuscripts Department of the Southern Historical Collection at the University of North Carolina at Chapel Hill.

Memorial Tributes to Walker Percy. New York: Farrar Straus Giroux, 1991.

Interviews with Shelby Foote

Carter, William C. "Speaking the Truth in Narrative: An Interview with Shelby Foote." *Georgia Review* 41 (Spring 1987): 144–72.

Carter, William C., ed. *Conversations with Shelby Foote.* Jackson: University Press of Mississippi, 1989.

Studies of Shelby Foote

Cox, James M. "Shelby Foote's Civil War." *Southern Review* 21 (Spring 1985): 329–50.

Phillips, Robert L., Jr. *Shelby Foote: Novelist and Historian.* Jackson: University Press of Mississippi, 1992.

White, Helen. "Shelby Foote." In *The Literature of Tennessee,* edited by Ray Willbanks, 163–81. Macon, Ga.: Mercer University Press, 1984.

Contents of *Contemporary Fiction Writers of the South: A Bio-Bibliographical Sourcebook*

Preface

Introduction

Alice Adams (1926–   )
Barbara A. Herman

Lisa Alther (1944–   )
Mary Anne Ferguson

Toni Cade Bambara (1939–   )
Nancy D. Hargrove

Madison Smartt Bell (1957–   )
R. Reed Sanderlin

Larry Brown (1951–   )
Thomas J. Richardson

Rita Mae Brown (1944–   )
Barbara Ladd

Pat Conroy (1945–   )
Lamar York

John William Corrington (1932–1988)
Terry Roberts

Ellen Douglas [Josephine Ayres Haxton] (1921–   )
Carol S. Manning

Andre Dubus (1936–   )
Anne E. Rowe

Clyde Edgerton (1944–   )
R. Sterling Hennis, Jr.

John [Marsden] Ehle, Jr. (1925–　)
Leslie Banner

Jesse Hill Ford (1928–　)
Charmaine Allmon Mosby

Richard Ford (1944–　)
Frank W. Shelton

Kaye Gibbons (1960–　)
Julian Mason

Ellen Gilchrist (1935–　)
Robert Bain

Marianne Gingher (1947–　)
Lucinda H. MacKethan

Gail Godwin (1937–　)
Mary Ann Wimsatt

Alex [Murray Palmer] Haley (1921–1992)
Mary Kemp Davis

Barry Hannah (1942–　)
Owen W. Gilman, Jr.

[Henry] William Hoffman (1925–　)
Jeanne R. Nostrandt

William Humphrey (1924–　)
Stephen Cooper

Josephine Humphreys (1945–　)
Joseph Millichap

Gayl Jones (1949–　)
Barbara Patrick

Madison [Percy] Jones (1925–　)
David K. Jeffrey

Beverly Lowry (1938–　)
Merrill Maguire Skaggs

Bobbie Ann Mason (1940–　)
Joseph M. Flora

Cormac McCarthy (1933–　)
Jerry Leath Mills

Jill McCorkle (1958–　)
Lynn Z. Bloom

Tim McLaurin (1953–　)
Jerry Leath Mills

James Alan McPherson (1943–　)
Joseph T. Cox

Berry Morgan (1919–　)
Christina Albers

Helen Norris (1916–   )
Susan Snell

T[homas] R[eid] Pearson (1956–   )
John N. Somerville, Jr.

Jayne Anne Phillips (1952–   )
Dorothy Combs Hill

Charles [McColl] Portis (1933–   )
John L. Idol, Jr.

Padgett Powell (1952–   )
Thomas M. Carlson

Ferrol Sams (1922–   )
Linda Welden

Mary Lee Settle (1918–   )
Nancy Carol Joyner

Bob [Robert G.] Shacochis (1951–   )
Bert Hitchcock

Susan Richards Shreve (1939–   )
Katherine C. Hodgin

Lee Smith (1944–   )
Elizabeth Pell Broadwell

John Kennedy Toole (1937–1969)
Beverly Jarrett

Anne Tyler (1941–   )
Anne R. Zahlan

Alice [Malsenior] Walker (1944–   )
Laura J. Bloxham

James Wilcox (1949–   )
John M. Allison, Jr.

Sylvia Wilkinson (1940–   )
Joyce M. Pair

Calder [Baynard] Willingham, Jr. (1922–   )
Donald R. Noble

John Yount (1935–   )
Robert Bain

APPENDIX C

Studies of Southern Literature

This selected bibliography of books on Southern literature excludes anthologies, studies of individual authors, and studies of writing from a single state. Most books listed here were published after William Faulkner's death in 1962 and focus upon general studies of Southern writing.

Andrews, William L. *To Tell a Free Story: The First Century of Afro-American Autobiography, 1760–1865.* Urbana: University of Illinois Press, 1986.

Ayers, H. Brandt, and Thomas H. Naylor, eds. *You Can't Eat Magnolias.* New York: McGraw-Hill, 1972.

——. *Why the South Will Survive, by Fifteen Southerners.* Athens: University of Georgia Press, 1981.

Bain, Robert, and Joseph M. Flora, eds. *Fifty Southern Writers before 1900.* Westport, Conn.: Greenwood Press, 1987.

Bain, Robert, Joseph M. Flora, and Louis D. Rubin, Jr., eds. *Southern Writers: A Biographical Dictionary.* Baton Rouge: Louisiana State University Press, 1979.

Berry, J. Bill, ed. *Home Ground: Southern Autobiography.* Columbia: University of Missouri Press, 1991.

Bradbury, John M. *Renaissance in the South: A Critical History of the Literature of the American South.* Chapel Hill: University of North Carolina Press, 1963.

Brinkmeyer, Robert H. *Three Catholic Writers of the Modern South.* Jackson: University Press of Mississippi, 1985.

Callahan, John F. *In The African-American Grain: The Pursuit of Voice in Twentieth-Century Black Fiction.* Urbana: University of Illinois Press, 1988.

Carr, John, ed. *Kite-Flying and Other Irrational Acts: Conversations with Twelve Southern Writers.* Baton Rouge: Louisiana State University Press, 1972.

Clendinen, Dudley, ed. *The Prevailing South: Life and Politics in a Changing Culture.* Atlanta: Longstreet Press, 1988.

Cook, Sylvia Jenkins. *From Tobacco Road to Route 66: The Southern Poor White in Fiction.* Chapel Hill: University of North Carolina Press, 1976.

Core, George, ed. *Southern Fiction: Renascence and Beyond.* Athens: University of Georgia Press, 1969.

Dameron, J. Lasley, and James W. Mathews. *No Fairer Land: Studies in Southern Literature before 1900.* Troy, N.Y.: Whitson, 1986.

Dunn, Joe P., and Howard L. Preston, eds. *The Future South: A Historical Perspective for the Twenty-first Century.* Urbana: University of Illinois Press, 1991.

Evans, Mari, ed. *Black Women Writers: Arguments and Interviews.* London: Pluto Press, 1985.

Flora, Joseph M., and Robert Bain, eds. *Fifty Southern Writers after 1900.* Westport, Conn., Greenwood Press, 1987.

———. *Contemporary Fiction Writers of the South.* Westport, Conn.: Greenwood Press, 1993.

Gilman, Owen W., Jr. *Vietnam and the Southern Imagination.* Jackson: University Press of Mississippi, 1992.

Glikin, Rhonda. *Black American Women in Literature: A Bibliography, 1976–1987.* Jefferson, N.C.: McFarland, 1989.

Gossett, Louise Y. *Violence in Recent Southern Fiction.* Durham, N.C.: Duke University Press, 1965.

Gray, Richard J. *The Literature of Memory: Modern Writers of the American South.* Baltimore: Johns Hopkins University Press, 1976.

———. *Writing the South: Ideas of an American Region.* New York: Cambridge University Press, 1986.

Gwin, Minrose. *Black and White Women of the Old South: The Peculiar Sisterhood in American Literature.* Knoxville: University of Tennessee Press, 1985.

Harris, Alex, ed. *A World Unsuspected: Portraits of Southern Childhood.* Chapel Hill: University of North Carolina Press, 1987.

Havard, William C., and Walter Sullivan, eds. *A Band of Prophets: The Vanderbilt Agrarians after Fifty Years.* Baton Rouge: Louisiana State University Press, 1982.

Hobson, Fred. *The Southern Writer in the Postmodern World.* Athens: University of Georgia Press, 1991.

———. *Tell about the South: The Southern Rage to Explain.* Baton Rouge: Louisiana State University Press, 1983.

Hoffman, Frederick J. *The Art of Southern Fiction.* Carbondale: Southern Illinois University Press, 1967.

Holman, C. Hugh. *Three Modes of Southern Fiction.* Athens: University of Georgia Press, 1966.

———. *The Immoderate Past: The Southern Writer and History.* Athens: University of Georgia Press, 1977.

———. *The Roots of Southern Writing; Essays on the Literature of the American South.* Athens: University of Georgia Press, 1972.

———. *Windows on the World: American Social Fiction.* Knoxville: University of Tennessee Press, 1979.

Humphries, Jefferson, ed. *Southern Literature and Literary Theory.* Athens: University of Georgia Press, 1990.

Jones, Anne Goodwyn. *Tomorrow Is Another Day: The Woman Writer in the South, 1859–1936.* Baton Rouge: Louisiana State University Press, 1981.

Kennedy, J. Gerald, and Daniel Mark Fogel, eds. *American Letters and the Historical*

Consciousness: Essays in Honor of Lewis P. Simpson. Baton Rouge: Louisiana State University Press, 1987.

King, Richard J. *A Southern Renaissance: The Cultural Awakening of the American South, 1930–1955.* New York: Oxford University Press, 1980.

Kreyling, Michael. *Figures of the Hero in Southern Narrative.* Baton Rouge: Louisiana State University Press, 1987.

Kubitschek. Missy Dean. *Claiming the Heritage: African-American Women Novelists and History.* Jackson: University Press of Mississippi, 1991.

Lawson, Lewis A. *Another Generation: Southern Fiction since World War II.* Jackson: University Press of Mississippi, 1984.

Leary, Lewis. *Southern Excursions: Essays on Mark Twain and Others.* Baton Rouge: Louisiana State University Press, 1971.

MacKethan, Lucinda H. *Daughters of Time: Creating Woman's Voice in Southern Story.* Athens: University of Georgia Press, 1991.

———. *The Dream of Arcady: Place and Time in Southern Literature.* Baton Rouge: Louisiana State University Press, 1983.

Manning, Carol S. *The Female Tradition in Southern Literature.* Urbana: University of Illinois Press, 1993.

Moss, Elizabeth. *Domestic Novelists in the Old South: Defenders of Southern Culture.* Baton Rouge: Louisiana State University Press, 1992.

O'Brien, Michael, *The Idea of the American South, 1930–1955.* Baltimore: Johns Hopkins University Press, 1979.

Prenshaw, Peggy. *Contemporary Women Writers of the American South.* Jackson: University Press of Mississippi, 1984.

Rowe, Anne E. *The Enchanted Country: Northern Writers in the South, 1865–1910.* Baton Rouge: Louisiana State University Press, 1978.

Rubin, Louis D., Jr., Blyden Jackson, Rayburn Moore, Lewis P. Simpson, and Thomas Daniel Young, eds. *The History of Southern Literature.* Baton Rouge: Louisiana State University Press, 1985.

Rubin, Louis D., Jr., and Robert D. Jacobs, eds. *Southern Renascence: The Literature of the Modern South.* Baltimore: Johns Hopkins University Press, 1953.

———. *South: Modern Southern Literature in Its Cultural Setting.* Garden City, N.Y.: Doubleday, 1961.

Rubin, Louis D., Jr., and C. Hugh Holman, eds. *Southern Literary Study: Problems and Possibilities.* Chapel Hill: University of North Carolina Press, 1975.

Rubin, Louis D., Jr. *The Faraway Country: Writers of the Modern South.* Seattle: University of Washington Press, 1963.

———, ed. *A Bibliographical Guide to the Study of Southern Literature.* Baton Rouge, Louisiana State University Press, 1969.

———. *The Writer in the South: Studies in Literary Community.* Athens: University of Georgia Press. 1972.

———. *William Elliott Shoots a Bear: Essays on the Southern Literary Imagination.* Baton Rouge: Louisiana State University Press, 1975.

———. *The Wary Fugitives: Four Poets and the South.* Baton Rouge: Louisiana State University Press, 1978.

———, ed. *The American South: Portrait of a Culture.* Baton Rouge: Louisiana State University Press, 1979.

———. *A Gallery of Southerners.* Baton Rouge: Louisiana State University Press, 1982.

————. *The Edge of the Swamp: A Study in the Literature and Society of the Old South.* Baton Rouge: Louisiana State University Press, 1989.

————. *The Mockingbird in the Gum Tree: A Literary Gallimaufry.* Baton Rouge: Louisiana State University Press, 1991.

Simpson, Lewis. *Poetry of Community; Essays on the Southern Sensibility of History and Literature.* Atlanta: Georgia State University Press, 1972.

————. *The Dispossessed Garden: Pastoral and History in Southern Literature.* Athens: University of Georgia Press, 1975.

————. *The Man of Letters in New England and the South.* Baton Rouge: Louisiana State University Press, 1973.

————. *Mind and the American Civil War.* Baton Rouge: Louisiana State University Press, 1989.

————. *The Fable of the Southern Writer.* Baton Rouge: Louisiana State University Press, 1994.

Sullivan, Walter. *Death by Melancholy: Essays on Modern Southern Fiction.* Baton Rouge: Louisiana State University Press, 1972.

————. *A Requiem for the Renascence: The State of Fiction in the Modern South.* Athens: University of Georgia Press, 1976.

Watkins, Floyd. *The Death of Art: Black and White in the Recent Southern Novel.* Athens: University of Georgia Press, 1970.

————. *In Time and Place: Some Origins of American Fiction.* Athens: University of Georgia Press, 1977.

Watson, Ritchie D. *The Cavalier in Virginia Fiction.* Baton Rouge: Louisiana State University Press, 1985.

————. *Yeoman vs. Cavalier: The Old Southwest's Fictional Road to Rebellion.* Baton Rouge: Louisiana State University Press, 1993.

Wilson, Charles Reagan, and William Ferris, eds. *Encyclopedia of Southern Culture.* Chapel Hill: University of North Carolina Press, 1989.

Young, Thomas Daniel. *The Past in the Present: A Thematic Study of Modern Southern Fiction.* Baton Rouge: Louisiana State University Press, 1981.

Index

Compiled by Mark Canada; page numbers in **bold** refer to main entries.

Contributors

WILLIAM AARNES teaches at Furman University. He has written essays on Walt Whitman and Arthur Miller, and his poems have appeared in magazines such as the *Southern Review* and *Poet & Critic*. His collection *Learning to Dance* was published in 1991 by Ninety-Six Press.

TIMOTHY DOW ADAMS teaches at West Virginia University and serves as associate editor of *A/b: Auto/biography Studies*. He has published numerous essays on autobiography, biography, and other subjects in *Studies in the Novel, Critique, ESQ, Clio, Style, Southern Quarterly, Mosaic, Biography,* and *Prose Studies* and is author of *Telling Lies in Modern American Autobiography* (1990).

GILBERT ALLEN has taught at Furman University since 1977. He has published two collections of poetry: *In Everything* (1982) and *Second Chances* (1991). His work received the Amon Liner Award from the *Greensboro Review,* the Rainmaker Award from *Zone 3,* and the South Carolina Fiction Project Prize.

ROBERT BAIN has retired to part-time teaching at the University of North Carolina at Chapel Hill. With Joseph M. Flora, he has coedited *Fifty Southern Writers before 1900* (1987), *Fifty Southern Writers after 1900* (1987), and *Contemporary Fiction Writers of the South* (1993). He won a Tanner Award for Excellence in Undergraduate Teaching (1976) and from 1987 to 1990 held a Bowman and Gordon Gray Professorship of Undergraduate Teaching. He received a Distinguished Alumnus Award from Eastern Illinois University in 1989.

JOHN E. BASSETT, formerly head of the Department of English at North Carolina State University, is dean to the College of Arts and Sciences at Case Western Reserve. He is author of *Vision and Revision: Essays on Faulkner;*

Harlem in Review: Critical Reactions to Black American Writers, 1919-1939; and studies of Mark Twain, William Dean Howells, and other American writers.

ALAN T. BELSCHES is an associate professor of English and chair of the English and Humanities Department at Troy State University at Dothan, Alabama. He teaches courses in American literature and has published articles on Walker Percy, Eudora Welty, and Thomas Wolfe.

JILL STAPLETON BERGERON completed her Ph.D. in Theatre at Louisiana State University in 1992. She joined the faculty at Maryville College (Tennessee) in 1991.

GLENN B. BLALOCK is author and editor of *Background Readings for Instructors Using the Bedford Handbook* (1991; 2d ed., 1993). He has presented papers on colonial newspapers at the Southern Humanities Conference, on nineteenth-century literary annuals at the Philological Association of the Carolinas, and on writing at the Writing Across the Curriculum Conference and the Conference on College Composition and Communication.

MARY HUGHES BROOKHART teaches at North Carolina Central University in Durham. She has published essays on Eudora Welty, Ellease Southerland, and ''Spiritual Daughters of Black American South.''

HARRIETTE CUTTINO BUCHANAN is an associate professor of Interdisciplinary Studies, attached to the Learning Assistance Program, at Appalachian State University. She has published articles on Faulkner and Lee Smith. She frequently gives public lectures on contemporary American writers and has presented conference papers on Southern writers, on instructional technologies, and on teaching freshman writing.

WILLIAM GRIMES CHERRY III teaches at East Carolina University in Greenville, North Carolina. He has written and spoken on Southern writers. He edited *Thomas Wolfe's Notes on ''Macbeth''* (1992).

THOMAS E. DASHER is a professor of English and head of the Department of English at Valdosta State College in Valdosta, Georgia. He is author of *William Faulkner's Characters: An Index to the Published and Unpublished Fiction.* He has written articles on Faulkner, William Goyen, and David Madden.

R. H. W. DILLARD is a professor of English at Hollins College, where he chairs the Creative Writing Program. A novelist and poet as well as a critic, his most recent books are *The Greeting: New and Selected Poems, The First Man on the Sun,* and *Understanding George Garrett.* He is editor-in-chief of the scholarly journal *Children's Literature.*

SUSAN V. DONALDSON, an associate professor of English at the College of William and Mary, has published essays on William Faulkner, Eudora Welty, Walker Percy, Robert Penn Warren, and Nathaniel Hawthorne. She is currently at work on two book-length studies: one on alternative traditions among modern Southern writers and painters and one on Eudora Welty and the subversive imagination.

JOYCE DYER is Director of Writing at Hiram College in Hiram, Ohio. Her essays have appeared in the *Southern Literary Journal, Western American Literature, Appalachian Journal,* and *American Literary Realism, 1870–1910.* She won the 1990 NEH/*Reader's Digest* Teacher-Scholar Award from Ohio.

JOSEPH M. FLORA is a professor of English at the University of North Carolina at Chapel Hill. He is author of *Vardis Fisher* (1965), *William Ernest Henley* (1970), *Frederick Manfred* (1974), *Hemingway's Nick Adams* (1982), and *Ernest Hemingway: The Art of the Short Fiction* (1989). With Robert Bain and Louis D. Rubin, Jr., he edited *Southern Writers: A Biographical Dictionary* (1979). With Bain, he edited *Fifty Southern Writers before 1900* (1987), *Fifty Southern Writers after 1900* (1987), and *Contemporary Fiction Writers of the South* (1993).

PATRICIA M. GANTT is Language Arts Specialist for the public schools of Buncombe County, North Carolina. She has published articles on Southern literature, history, and folklore.

SUSAN GILBERT is a professor of English at Meredith College in Raleigh, North Carolina, where she teaches twentieth-century prose and American women writers. She is author of articles on Joan Didion and Anne Tyler and is currently at work on critical responses to American artists in the 1980s.

JAMES A. GRIMSHAW, JR., teaches at East Texas State University. His poetry has appeared in the *Southern Review, Southwestern American Literature,* the *Poet,* and *Texas College English.* Among his book-length publications is *Robert Penn Warren: A Descriptive Bibliography, 1922–1979.*

CORRINNE HALES teaches American literature and creative writing at California State University at Fresno. *Underground,* her collection of poems, was published in 1986 by Ahsahta Press.

BILLY J. HARBIN, Director of Graduate Studies in Theatre at Louisiana State University, coedited *Inside the Royal Court Theatre, 1956–81* (1990).

WILLIAM HARMON, a professor of English at the University of North Carolina at Chapel Hill, is author of five books of poetry and a study of Ezra

Pound's work. He has edited *The Oxford Book of American Light Verse* and has prepared the fifth and sixth editions of the Thrall-Hibbard-Holman *Handbook to Literature*. His work has appeared in *PMLA, Poetry, American Anthropologist, Antioch Review, Kenyon Review, Partisan Review,* and other journals. He is an unindicted coconspirator in *L'Affaire Uneeda Review,* now merged with the *Lonestar Cavalier Gazette* and the *Everlasting Cooglerite.*

MARGARET MILLS HARPER, an associate professor of English at Georgia State University, is author of *The Aristocracy of Art: Joyce and Wolfe* (1990); coeditor, with George Mills Harper, of volume 3 of *Yeats's "Vision" Papers* (1991); and author of articles on Robert Penn Warren, Thomas Wolfe, James Joyce, W. B. Yeats, and other topics. She is currently editing volume 4 of *Yeats's "Vision" Papers* and writing a critical and theoretical study of George (Mrs. W. B.) Yeats.

LUCY K. HAYDEN, a professor of English at Eastern Michigan University in Ypsilanti, Michigan, has done postgraduate work at Oxford University, the University of London, and the Bunting Institute at Radcliffe College. Formerly chair of the English Department at Central State University, Wilberforce, Ohio, and at Winston-Salem State University, North Carolina, she has published articles on African and African-American writers in the *CLA Journal, Journal of Caribbean Studies,* and *The Dictionary of Literary Biography.*

HILARY HOLLADAY has published poems in a number of journals. In addition to her study of Southern literature, her research interests include African-American literature and modern American poetry. She has published articles on Richard Wright's *Native Son* and Ann Petry's *The Street.*

ED INGEBRETSEN, S.J., teaches English at Georgetown University. He is currently studying the intersection of the Gothic, American religion, and American culture and is completing a book entitled *Religious Terror in American Culture.*

LA VINIA DELOIS JENNINGS teaches American literature at the University of Tennessee at Knoxville. She has published biographical entries on Chancellor Williams, Louise Thompson, Dorothy Peterson, and others. Her special interest is African-American female writers.

SARA ANDREWS JOHNSTON, an independent scholar, wrote her dissertation on the poets Matthew Arnold, T. S. Eliot, Wallace Stevens, Robert Frost, and A. R. Ammons. She is currently working on articles on Wallace Stevens.

CHIP JONES wrote his master's thesis at the University of North Carolina at Chapel Hill on Wilma Dykeman's progressive themes. He lives with his family in surburban Atlanta, where he is a technical writer and editor.

KIMBALL KING, a professor of English at the University of North Carolina at Chapel Hill, is coeditor of the *Southern Literary Journal.* He served for 10 years as the bibliographer of *American Literature.* His publications include four books on contemporary theatre, an edition of Thomas Nelson Page's *In Ole Virginia,* and a biography of Augustus Baldwin Longstreet.

GEORGE S. LENSING, a professor of English at the University of North Carolina at Chapel Hill, has written articles on William Faulkner, Flannery O'Connor, Randall Jarrell, and James Dickey. With Ronald Moran, he is coauthor of *Four Poets and the Emotive Imagination* (1976). He is author of *Wallace Stevens: A Poet's Growth* (1986).

LUCINDA H. MACKETHAN is a professor of English at North Carolina State University in Raleigh. There she directed the Freshman Composition Program and currently teaches Southern and American literature. She is author of *The Dream of Arcady: Place and Time in Southern Literature* (1980), numerous essays on Southern writing, and the editor of John Pendleton Kennedy's *Swallow Barn* (1986).

D. SOYINI MADISON teaches in the Department of Speech Communication at the University of North Carolina at Chapel Hill. Her research interests are centered on performance and criticism of literature by women of color.

ELIZABETH MCGEACHY MILLS is an assistant professor of English at Davidson College, where she has taught since 1985. Her scholarly interests include contemporary poetry and literature by women.

MERRITT W. MOSELEY, JR., is a professor of English at the University of North Carolina at Asheville. His work on American humor has appeared in the *Encyclopedia of American Humorists* and *Fifty Southern Writers before 1900.* Borgo Press published his *David Lodge* in 1991, and a book on Kingsley Amis is forthcoming from the University of South Carolina Press.

ELSA NETTELS, Nicholson Professor of Humanities at the College of William and Mary, won the 1975 SAMLA Studies Award for her *James and Conrad* (1977). In addition to her book *Language, Race, and Social Class in Howells's America* (1988), she has written numerous articles and essays.

DAPHNE H. O'BRIEN is completing her Ph.D. in American literature on the colonial poetry of Virginia at the University of North Carolina at Chapel Hill.

Her area of study is Southern American literature; she has published on Thomas Wolfe.

PATSY B. PERRY, a professor and coordinator of graduate English at North Carolina Central University in Durham, is author of critical studies of several African-American writers; she is writing a book on Alain Locke.

ROBERT L. PHILLIPS, a professor of English at Mississippi State University, is editor of the *Mississippi Quarterly* and author of *Shelby Foote: Novelist and Historian.*

DAVID PAUL RAGAN, English Department chair at Hammond School in Columbia, South Carolina, also teaches classes in American literature and fiction at the University of South Carolina. Author of *William Faulkner's 'Absalom, Absalom!': A Critical Study* (1987), he has written articles on Chappell, Faulkner, and other Southern authors.

JULIUS ROWAN RAPER, a professor of English at the University of North Carolina at Chapel Hill, is the author of *From the Sunken Garden: The Fiction of Ellen Glasgow, 1916–1945; Without Shelter: The Early Career of Ellen Glasgow;* editor of *Ellen Glasgow's Reasonable Doubts: A Collection of Her Writings. Narcissus from Rubble: Competing Models of Character in Contemporary British and American Fiction* (1992) is his most recent book.

JEFFREY H. RICHARDS teaches American literature at Old Dominion University. He is author of *Theater Enough: American Culture and the Metaphor of the World Stage: 1607–1789* (1991) and has written over two hundred reviews of contemporary fiction.

JOHN SEKORA, a professor of English and dean of the Graduate School at North Carolina Central University, is author of *Black Message/White Envelope* (1993).

LYNNE P. SHACKELFORD, an associate professor of English at Furman University, specializes in nineteenth- and twentieth-century fiction; she has published articles in *Studies in Short Fiction,* the *Henry James Review,* and *American Notes and Queries,* and has contributed to the *Dictionary of Literary Biography, Research Guide to Biography and Criticism, Popular Fiction,* and *Fifty Southern Writers before 1900.*

JUDY JO SMALL, an assistant professor of English at North Carolina State University, is author of *Positive as Sound: Emily Dickinson's Rhyme* and a contributor to *The Encyclopedia of Southern Culture.*

EDWARD B. SMITH has taught in the Communications Department at More-head State University in Kentucky. He wrote his thesis on the performative dimensions of Wendell Berry's sense of place and is doing research on the performance of contemporary Southern literature and the rhetoric of perform-ance in stand-up comedy.

BES STARK SPANGLER is a professor of English at Peace College in Raleigh, North Carolina. She has written and lectured on Southern writers ranging from Thomas Wolfe to contemporary Southern women authors.

PETER STITT is the author of *The World's Hieroglyphic Beauty: Five Amer-ican Poets* (1986) and the editor (with Frank Graziano) of *The Heart of the Light: James Wright* (1990). Now working on the authorized biography of James Wright, he is a professor of English and editor of the *Gettysburg Review* at Gettysburg College in Pennsylvania.

KATHRYN VANSPANCKEREN is a professor of English at the University of Tampa. She has published *Margaret Atwood: Vision and Forms* (1988) and *John Gardner: The Critical Perspective* (1982). She is at work on the forthcoming *History of U.S. Literature* and essays on contemporary multicultural North American literature and oral tradition. She thanks Donna Long and the Univer-sity of Tampa Honors Program for research leading to her essay on Florence King.

JERRY W. WARD, JR., a professor of English at Tougaloo College, has pri-mary interests in African-American literature and literary theory. He has pub-lished critical essays, reviews, and poems in many professional and literary journals. He is editor of *Black Southern Voices: An Anthology of Fiction, Poetry, Drama, Non-fiction, and Critical Essays* (1992).

LINDA WELDEN is a professor of Theatre at Appalachian State University, where she teaches and directs the performance of literature. Her research interest is in the performance of texts, particularly of Southern writers. She is currently at work on a dramatic adaptation of stories by Ferrol Sams.

MARY C. WILLIAMS is a professor emeritus of English at North Carolina State University. Although she has published a book on Ben Jonson and articles on Renaissance drama, her interest in contemporary poetry was fostered by her years as managing editor of *Southern Poetry Review*. With Guy Owen she co-edited several anthologies, including *New Southern Poets: Selected Poems from Southern Poetry Review, Contemporary Poetry of North Carolina,* and *Contem-porary Southern Poetry.*

RANDAL WOODLAND directs the Writing Center at the University of Michigan at Dearborn. He has published essays on Oscar Micheau, and on Ellen Gilchrist, Sheila Bosworth, and Nancy Lemann. He is completing a study of the idea of New Orleans in the Southern literary imagination.

MARLENE YOUMANS has taught American literature and creative writing at the State University of New York at Potsdam and is currently writing and publishing short stories and poems. In addition to her scholarship on Herman Melville and other American writers, she has published her poetry in *Southern Poetry Review,* the *South Carolina Review, Ploughshares,* the *Laurel Review,* and the *Carolina Quarterly.*

ISBN 0-313-28765-1

EAN

9 780313 287657

HARDCOVER BAR CODE